THE ENVIRONMENT OF MARKETING MANAGEMENT

The Wiley Marketing Series

THE ENVIORNMENT
OF MARKETING
MANAGEMENT

Selections from the Literature

THIRD EDITION

Robert J. Holloway

Professor of Marketing
University of Minnesota

Robert S. Hancock

Professor of Marketing
The University of Arizona

John Wiley & Sons, Inc., New York · London · Sydney · Toronto

Copyright © 1964, 1969, 1974, by John Wiley & Sons, Inc.

Library of Congress Cataloging in Publication Data:

Holloway, Robert J   ed.
    The environment of marketing management.

    (The Wiley marketing series)
    Previous editions published in 1964 and 1969 under title: The environment of marketing behavior.
        1. Marketing—Addresses, essays, lectures.
    2. Consumers—Addresses, essays, lectures. I. Hancock, Robert Spencer, joint ed. II. Title.
    HF5415.H742   1974   658.8′008   73-18322
    ISBN 0-471-40716-X

Printed in the United States of America

10-9 8 7 6 5 4 3 2 1

Preface

Since the original publication of this book in 1964, and the second edition in 1969, the continually changing social and economic factors affecting marketing indicate a need for a third edition. While a number of the original readings are retained, new and equally provocative points of view are included in this edition.

Academicians and students at several colleges and universities have been most constructive in their comments concerning the strengths and weaknesses of the earlier readings. Especially helpful with this edition were Richard Cardozo, Gary Ford, David Fulcher, Robert Hoel, Roger Kerin, James Nelson, Richard Sauter, Donald Shawver, Jerry Stiles, M. Venkatesan, and Orville Walker. In analyzing their suggestions, we have reorganized some of the material (with a separate section on buyer behavior), added new topics (consumerism, environmental issues, and humanism in marketing), and strengthened existing sections (buyer behavior, management, social challenges, and futurism). Several unique articles that show the breadth of marketing have also been included (for example, marketing among prisoners of war and marketing by the Post Office). Our goal was to improve each section and, therefore, some articles were dropped and new ones were added. We believe that the 65 selections from the marketing literature will provide many points for discussion and a good deal of perspective for the student.

We again found that our original criteria for the selections were sound and very helpful in compiling this edition. It is still our contention that basic concepts are the foundation of the learning process. Hence, our criteria for selecting a particular reading remain the same as before: (1) that it contributes to the basic framework and knowledge of marketing, (2) that it is more or less timeless regarding the concepts that are expressed, and (3) that it is a topic around which discussion or controversy can evolve in the classroom setting.

In reproducing the selections, it was necessary to take editorial license. Several readings are not reprinted in their entirety; some footnotes and other reference materials were deleted, and minor editorial adjustments were necessary to fit them more appropriately to the size and style limitations of the book. For these liberties, and the permission to reprint the articles, we thank the authors and their publishers. We also appreciate very much the many helpful suggestions from students and the suggested improvements from our colleagues.

R. J. Holloway
R. S. Hancock

Contents

IV. MARKETING MANAGEMENT IN A DYNAMIC ENVIRONMENT, 262

Contributors of Selections from the Literature

DAVID A. AAKER

ALVIN A. ACHENBAUM

WALTER ADAMS

WROE ANDERSON

JULES BACKMAN

MARTIN L. BELL

WILLIAM BERENBACH

CONRAD BERENSON

LEONARD L. BERRY

NEIL H. BORDEN

STEUART HENDERSON BRITT

LOUIS P. BUCKLIN

ROBERT D. BUZZELL

MURRAY CAYLEY

JOHN MAURICE CLARK

ROBERT L. CLEWETT

C. W. COOK

A. GRAEME CRANCH

JOSEPH F. DASH

GEORGE S. DAY

JOEL DEAN

STAHRL W. EDMUNDS

C. WILLIAM EMORY

GEORGE FISK

JOHN KENNETH GALBRAITH

CHARLES S. GOODMAN

E. T. GRETHER

STEPHEN A. GREYSER

KJELL M. HALVORSEN

BRUCE M. HANNON

EDWARD R. HAWKINS

JAMES L. HESKETT

HAROLD H. KASSARJIAN

GEORGE KATONA

JOHN G. KEANE

ROBERT J. KEITH

JOHN F. KENNEDY

PHILIP KOTLER

THEODORE LEVITT

PIERRE MARTINEAU

E. PATRICK MCGUIRE

WILLARD F. MUELLER

A. C. NEILSEN, JR.

LYMAN E. OSTLUND

JAMES PARK

R. A. RADFORD

BONNIE B. REECE

YVES RENOUX

W. B. REYNOLDS

BARRY M. RICHMAN

GEORGE W. ROBBINS

THOMAS S. ROBERTSON

PATRICK J. ROBINSON

FRANKLIN R. ROOT

FRANK K. SCHELLENBERGER

ARCH W. SHAW

JOHN E. SMALLWOOD

THADDEUS H. SPRATLEN

JAMES E. STAFFORD

WILLIAM J. STANTON

FREDERICK D. STURDIVANT

ARNOLD TOYNBEE

YOSHI TSURUMI

DONALD F. TURNER

ROLAND S. VAILE

ANDRÉ VAN DAM

PHILIP WAGNER

KELVIN A. WALL

FREDERICK E. WEBSTER, JR.

WILLIAM D. WELLS

JOHN H. WESTING

WALTER T. WILHELM

YORAM WIND

DANIEL YANKELOVICH

WILLIAM A. YOELL

WILLIAM G. ZIKMUND

Chapters in Marketing Texts Corresponding to Holloway and Hancock, *The Environment of Marketing Management.*

Section in H. H. Readings, 3rd Ed.	Holloway Hancock	McCarthy	Cundiff Still	Stanton	Buskirk	Fisk	Kotler
A	1, 2	1	1, 6	1	1	1, 2	1
B	3	2	2, 3	2	4, 5	3	2, 6
C	4					24	
D	5	3			2		3
E	6	3			2, 22	20	3
F	7	3	10		2, 25	21	3
G	8					20	3
H	9	6, 7	7	4	6	4	4
I	10, 11, 12	8	8, 9	5, 6	7, 8	5	4
J	13	9		7	6	6	5
K	14	28, 29	6, 11	27, 28	2, 27	14, 15	8, 12
L	15, 16	4, 5	13, 14	3	3	16	7
M	17	10, 14	16	8, 9	10	17	13
N	18, 19	15–19	4, 5, 17	11–16	12–16	7, 12, 19	15, 16
O	20, 21	23–27	18	17–20	17, 18	10	14
P	22, 23	20–22	19–21	21–23	19–21	9, 18	10, 17
Q	24	7		26	26		23
R	25				24	22, 23	22
S	26, 27				8	22	22
T	28						
	29	30		29			24
	30			29	27		

THE ENVIRONMENT OF MARKETING MANAGEMENT

A Comment on the Study of Marketing

Marketing as an academic discipline and as a major function of business enterprises has increased its dimensions during the last several decades. Both the academic and business communities have come to recognize the study of marketing as fundamental to the understanding of the business process and to the conceptual framework of our social and economic system. Where someone might be successfully involved with a segment of marketing without formal training, it is doubtful that he would understand all its complexities, its subtleties, and its relationships to other economic functions. And, without exposure and study of marketing as an orderly body of knowledge, one would probably not have an aggregative concept of the abundant research possibilities' posed by the marketing system.

As a person studies marketing, he will be struck by the difficulty of developing a precise definition of marketing and perhaps have even more difficulty in comprehending its dimensions. An explanation for breadth and complexity of marketing is needed. Perhaps an explanation may reconcile this potential dilemma.

Marketing is a social and economic phenomenon that exists by virtue of the nature of man. As any society evolves beyond the subsistence level of existence, marketing (or trade) comes into being. As a society moves through progressively more advanced stages of development, man responds by building institutions, devising social, economic, and political systems and engaging in the activities essential to economic progress and well-being. The precise character and dimensions of marketing differ from one society to another, and this is explained, at least partly, by the degree of specialization practiced. If the possessions and abilities of all people were the same, there would be no exchange and, hence, no need for a marketing structure and its attendant activities. Fortunately, this is not the case since most societies are characterized by people possessing different abilities and different goods—thus, exchange ensues and a marketing structure of some dimension develops. Similarly, marketing activities anchored in the marketing structure are carried on. Marketing, then, involves markets, marketing institutions, marketing systems, and marketing activities—all of which have been

1

devised to carry on the task of meeting society's material and service needs through its marketing structure.

Marketing as an integral part of our social and economic processes is not a narrow, precisely defined discipline. Instead, marketing is an eclectic discipline. That is, it is a discipline that recognizes and synthesizes those doctrines, methods, and principles that contribute to an understanding of marketing phenomena. Scholars from many fields have made significant contributions to marketing thought. For example, economics, sociology, psychology, anthropology, law, philosophy, history, and ecology all represent disciplines from which important segments of marketing knowledge have been drawn. Marketing scholars have been adaptive in their application of selected doctrines to improve and formulate marketing thought.

By the very nature of marketing, by the way marketing decisions are made, and by the way marketing operates, it will be influenced by the environment in which it is carried on. The environment of marketing comprises a number of forces that generate change in the marketing system, and, furthermore, the environment more often than not influences the character of marketing activities. If then, as the editors believe the environment of marketing explains its existence, character, and dimensions, it is perhaps most desirable to introduce students to the study of marketing within such a framework.

As the title of this book suggests, major emphasis is given to the environment of marketing and the way in which the environment influences the behavior of marketing and the attendant function of marketing management. Just what is the environment of marketing? What are the forces that generate change in marketing? In answer to these questions a schema, or model, for introducing marketing and its environment might be like the one shown on the next page.

The model depicts marketing as functioning within the interrelationships of the natural and human environments. A very large number of marketing decisions have had and continue to have an impact on the natural environment. Similarly, the human environment in our model conditions and influences marketplaces, marketing activities, our culture, our attitudes, restraints, and a host of marketing factors.

The design of this book incorporates the many environmental influences with the dynamics of marketing management. In many respects marketing management has emerged as an important factor in creating what we now recognize as a state of crisis for our natural environment. Only recently have we come to realize that marketing decisions about products must also consider the fact that consumers have biological as well as material needs.

In addition to the physical character and impact on the natural environment, marketing itself is strongly influenced by the economic, social, legal, ethical, and technological segments of the human environment.

The economic aspects of marketing are of twofold importance. First, the economic condition of consumers contributes to their behavior and makes it possible for other influences acting on them to be realized. When the economic status of consumers is combined with the social aspects of society, the impact of their behavior in the marketplace becomes a reality of major significance to marketers. Second, firms operating in the market and firms moving goods into

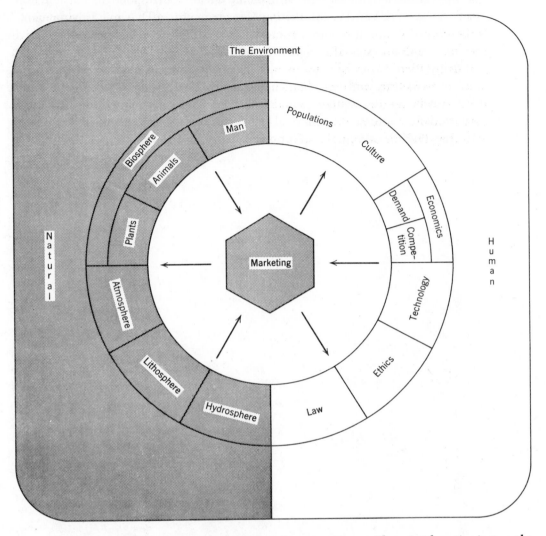

the market do so in an atmosphere of competition with price functioning as the core to exchange transactions. In this way the economic dimension is broadened, and the economic environment of the firm becomes a market force worthy of consideration.

All social and economic activities are carried on in a legal and an ethical framework. These segments of our model are concerned with the probabilities and permissive aspects of market behavior. The legal environment influences the character of pricing, competitive activities, market control, and promotional strategies. The ethical behavior (or lack of it) in the marketplace is a more nebulous subject. From one society to another, this aspect may be expected to vary by virtue of traditions, the mores of society, and the vaues of a society.

Technology is another force influencing marketplace behavior. Technology puts pressures on a marketing system to which it must adjust, and, similarly, technology has much to do with the products distributed and their eventual acceptance.

When marketing is cast in the framework of a comprehensive environment, the marketing activities of the firm should ideally correspond to that environment. As a result, Part IV, "Marketing Management in a Dynamic Environment," is developed within a research context followed by the major marketing activities that can be designed to adjust to and meet an ever-changing environment.

Finally, Part V provides the reader an opportunity to evaluate the performance of marketing and face challenging issues. The issues raised present problems of wide interest, without simple solutions. These are some of the challenges that students reading this material will face as they embark on their careers. May they find the acceptable solutions.

The Emergence and Nature of Marketing

In its several approaches to the study of marketing, this book gives emphasis to the environment of marketing. The major parts of this book are presented in order to provide the reader with an organized body of marketing thought. In dealing with the emergence and nature of marketing, the readings explore the environmental forces affecting marketing behavior, household and industrial buyer behavior, the environment in which marketing management makes decisions and executes marketing actions and, finally, an evaluative and futuristic grouping of thoughts that permit the reader to assess the performance of marketing in modern society.

It is important to establish the origin of marketing and to give emphasis to its emerging nature. The reading by George W. Robbins establishes the precepts and basic hypotheses that have been used in establishing the origin or conditions of trade. Robbins, in accord with the views long held by the editors, explains trade (marketing) as a function of "man and his adaptation to his environment through the institutions he builds."

Robbins' classical statement is complemented by the following two readings dealing with the origin of marketing. The basis of exchange, so essential to any marketing system, and how it is organized to serve society is explained by both Wagner and Radford. While Wagner discusses the organization of exchange for a peasant society, he carries his analysis to more complex societies as he recognizes exchange as a "general economic bond extending throughout . . . the economic life." This article simply and yet accurately describes the kind of institutional reliance and spatial character that is likely to develop as society engages in trade and thus exchange. The Radford reading deals with the economic phenomena of a P.O.W. camp. Have you ever thought that, in a somewhat different way, there can be a market organization in a camp of war prisoners? Yes—with products, prices, communication, and a money system. All these elements are essential to and characteristic of any marketing system.

Markets and market institutions are identified next. The reader is exposed to some of the brilliant minds of marketing and their discussions of markets, the marketing concept, segmentation of markets, and a series of basic concepts and problems relate to markets and marketing. Levitt's much used and quoted article, "Marketing Myopia," is paired with another view that emphasizes the great meaning of sound management, sound marketing, and sound technology. The marketing concept is strongly embraced by many marketing academicians. But, really, as we study the views of Reynolds, has the marketing concept been oversold? Or, should it be viewed with a different perspective?

The other readings in this section are selective. Each of them contributes to marketing thought and the planning of marketing activities. Perhaps of cardinal value is the understanding of Yankelovich's criteria for market segmentation. Here we get ideas on better ways of looking at and analyzing markets.

Up to this point the reader has been exposed to the origin of marketing, the essentials of markets, and their institutions. We now discuss the domestic marketing systems of Russia and China. This is known as *comparative marketing*. We recognize marketing as an important economic function in our own country, but we may seldom appreciate the marketing function in other economies. We can increase our understanding of other countries by learning about their marketing system and by recognizing that environmental influences contribute to the shaping of all marketing—wherever they may occur. While we often give emphasis to the differences that we recognize in comparing other marketing systems, what about the functions, marketing institutions, and marketing activities that are similar? The reader will be able to isolate these things for Russia and China. Here the reader may want to refer to the Tsurumi reading, appearing in Part IV dealing with international marketing. His reading refers to the Japanese marketing system and may be of dual value by using it with the concepts discussed for Russia and China. How best do we explain these differences and similarities?

A. The Origin and Emergence

1. Notions About the Origins of Trading

GEORGE W. ROBBINS

The origins of trade have been the concern of economists and anthropologists in the past in order to trace or to relate the present functions of trade to their primeval beginnings and to discover the basic character of this economic usage. While this preoccupation with origins is disappearing from the scientific literature, it is not uncommon to find its implications and assumptions in the more popular literature of business, and particularly on the subject of salesmanship.

References are often made to premises concerning the origin of trading as a means of explaining or analyzing the ethical position of modern selling, imputing to present practices in the market place the circumstances and virtues of an assumed primeval genesis. It is, for example, not uncommon to hear trading spoken of as universal and natural. On the other hand, anthropological evidence reveals primitive cultures with a complete lack of competitive trading and with insignificant exchange practices.

In the face of these opposing positions, it is desirable to examine the various notions concerning the origins of trading and to appraise them in the light of their usefulness in the analysis of trading in our own society. It is possible to do this without a true chronological history of trading, or without attempting to formulate an organic-evolutionary concept of trading which takes the form of extracting from succeeding cultures certain common characteristics, with the conclusion

that these have been passed down the lingering trail of institutional patterns.

Indeed, it should be evident that the accurate establishment of the origins of any human activity must await sufficient evidence from archaeological diggings.[1] The dearth of this evidence precludes a chronology that starts at the beginning. It is more profitable to avoid an historical recital in favor of an attempt to penetrate the internal logic of trading.

Our concern here is with the efficacy of employing, as either inarticulate or expressed premises, notions about the origins of trading in the evaluation of present-day trading practices from a functional or an ethical viewpoint. Is an understanding of the origins of trade an essential matter in the study of the ethics of selling and buying? Will it help to answer the problems of honesty and efficiency in selling? Does it throw light on the problems of the contests and conflicts of trading today in the economic institution?

It should be clearly understood that this inquiry differs from,, and is not in conflict with, the study of trade history as it can be established, through adequate records.[2] It

◆ SOURCE: Reprinted by permission from the *Journal of Marketing* (National Quarterly Publication of the American Marketing Association), Vol. 11, No. 3, January 1947, pp. 228–236.

---

[1] See Melville J. Herkskovits, *The Economic Life of Primitive Peoples* (New York: Alfred A. Knopf, 1940), Pt. I, for detailed comment on methodology in economics and anthropology.

[2] As for example: Clive Day, *A History of Commerce* (New York: Longmans, Green, 1938); George Burton Hotchkiss, *Milestones of Marketing* (New York: Macmillan, 1938); N. S. B. Gras, *An Introduction to Economic History* (New York: Harper, 1922).

relates to those histories only insofar as their authors employ reference to origins; and it is, of course, possible to treat a matter historically without assuming an organic evolution based on obscure beginnings.

It is well to keep in mind that we are concerned with trading—buying and selling—as a matter of social behavior rather than as a technical process in marketing. It is essential to assume that trading is not a fortuitous or whimsical phenomenon, but rather an observable datum governed by laws of behavior that are subject to discovery. Moreover, it is no part of assumption here that trading is good or bad, strong or weak, or favorable to any given environment. These matters must emerge only as conclusions based on adequate observation of group activity in a definable situation.

THE MEANING OF TRADING

The term "trading" may mean many things to say that a trade is an act of effecting an exchange, barter, transfer of title, persuasion, or even deception. It is not an oversimplification to say that a trade is an act of effecting an exchange of goods or services between a seller and a buyer; indeed, such a statement involves complexities of subtle premises. What lies both before and after the trade is of interest to this inquiry. The mere fact of communication between two individuals is a relatively superficial datum.

It may be helpful to clarify the thing we are discussing by examining definitions. Confusion will be avoided if it is remembered that a trade is a two-sided shield—it is both a purchase and a sale. While it is a popular misconception that the initiative in trading is largely with the seller, it is irrelevant to our purposes which side we take for reference. For the sake of brevity, only the selling side will be defined; and even the uninitiated may fill in a parallel definition of buying.

There are at least three types of definitions of *sale* which serve to illustrate the usual approaches to selling:

1. The legal: "Sale is an agreement by which one of the two contracting parties, called the 'seller,' gives a thing and passes title to it, in exchange for a certain price in current money, to the other party, who is called the 'buyer' or 'purchaser,' who on his part, agrees to pay such a price."[3]

2. The vocational: A sale is the exchange of goods or services resulting from the exercise of the art of salesmanship.

3. The professional: A sale is an exchange of goods or services resulting from rivalry in the productive effort of creating demand and of rendering service in the satisfaction thereof.

The legal definition leads to a concept of trading that is narrow and restricted mainly to the technical fact of title transfer in a society characterized by a highly refined property concept. It fails to provide for the student of the economic or sociological aspects of trading adequate attention to the circumstances precedent or subsequent to that transfer.[4]

The vocational approach to selling, on the other hand, emphasizes the importance of the arts of persuasion rather than their functional position. By contrast, what may be called the professional approach calls attention to the fundamental circumstance of human wants and of the existence of rivalry in the performance of the services that create and satisfy those wants.[5] It is not concerned with the contractual character of the sale; for contract is a usage of convenience, and the vast majority of sales are completed without the parties being aware that a legal contract is involved. Likewise, it does not deny that there is an

---

[3] Walter A. Shumaker and George Foster Longsdorf, *The Cyclopedic Law Dictionary* (3rd ed.; Chicago: Callahan, 1940), p. 992.

[4] This is not to say that the law has little influence on selling, but rather to emphasize that a legal definition is necessarily a cautious one and is more likely to represent a careful attempt to classify a concept rather than to penetrate it. It should be recognized, of course, that the law does place the intention of the parties to a contract in an important position as distinct from the transfer to title. See Nathan Isaacs, "Sales," *Encyclopedia of the Social Sciences* (New York: Macmillan, 1931), VIII, pp. 511–516.

[5] By calling this approach "professional," it is not necessarily implied that selling is a profession. However the social responsibility of the seller today certainly suggests a professional attitude, and it is clear that the acceptance of business as a profession will only follow, not precede, the adoption of such an attitude on the part of sellers. Cf. Louis Dembritz Brandeis, *Business—a Profession* (Boston: Small, Maryland, 1914), pp. 1–12.

important body of arts practiced by both sellers and buyers, which are effective in lubricating the process; but these arts are chiefly vocational techniques (however difficult to master). The professional approach places emphasis on the fundamental creative functions of selling in a highly competitive society.

While varying in approach, these three familiar concepts of selling have in common the functional position of selling in a society whose economic institution is characterized by a high degree of competitive effort—in short, a society like our own. In juxtaposition to these definitions, another, more fundamental, approach may be more suggestive of the real character of trading. A trade must always be a human relationship involving the behavior patterns of at least two persons.[6]

Hence, it is basically a *communication* and should be viewed as a part of the sociological field of communication.[7] It is subject to all the status barriers which define and separate individuals and groups. Again, any trade must be *cooperative* in the sense that two or more persons are acting together to achieve a new relationship which manifestly could not be achieved by each acting alone. Furthermore, every trade is an *organization* because it is a system, formal or otherwise, of consciously coordinated activities of at least two persons.[8] And lastly, the term is confined to situations where the ends are economic in order to exclude the multitude of other human relations which, without this modification, would fall unwanted into the area of our present concern.

Thus, we may define trading as a cooperative organization in communication to achieve economic ends. This definition carries no connotations with respect to the characteristics which may surround trading as the result of differing practices, usages, instruments, and mores to be found in the economic institution either at different times or in different locations. Like all other organizations in communication, trading belongs to a social institutional pattern, and becomes a part of the usages of that pattern. Specifically, it is part and parcel of the system of regulating economic contest and conflict, and is itself subject to contests and conflicts with usages of the other social institutions, marital, familial, educational, recreational, religious, scientific, and governmental.[9]

From the historical viewpoint, any inquiry into the nature of trading, to be significant, must be one that takes cognizance of the particular institutional fabric of which it is a part. To say that trading in our society today has its roots in the behavior of our primeval ancestors, or to say that this notion is confirmed by the habits of our "contemporary ancestors,"[10] the non-literate primitives now living, is to stretch the latitudes of scientific inquiry to the point of incredulity.

Yet it is true that many practitioners of selling base an important part of their philosophy on premises concerning the origins of trading that comprise the substance of these ideas. It is precisely this basic mistake of many writers on salesmanship that led them to attitudes which provoked the well-known, pointed, and inescapable criticism of salesmanship by Clarence Darrow.[11]

THE MAJOR HYPOTHESES

No one disputes the antiquity of trading; but the exact point and conditions of its origins provide the subject of consideration by many writers whose attempts may be classified in seven main hypotheses. Not a few students of anthropology and economics alike have supported one or more of these assumptions without even the benefit of tacit recognition of the implications.

(1) Trading Is Instinctive

It is perhaps most widely held that "to trade, or 'swap' is an inborn trait in the hu-

---

[6] This is the case even where impersonal or even mechanical implements are employed, (e.g., corporations, agents, or vending machines).

[7] Communication is "the process of exchanging commonly understood ideas, facts, or usages by means of language, visual presentation, imitation, suggestion." Constantine Panunzio, *Major Social Institutions* (New York: Macmillan, 1939), p. 529.

[8] This concept has been used effectively by Chester I. Barnard in his interesting analysis of business organization. See, "Comments on the job of the Executive," *Harvard Business Review*, XVIII, Spring 1940, pp. 295–308. See also his *The Functions of the Executive* (Cambridge: Harvard University Press, 1938).

[9] Constantine Panunzio, *op. cit.*, p. 7.

[10] Melville J. Herskovits, *op. cit.*, p. 35.

[11] "Salesmanship," *The American Mercury*, V, August 1925, pp. 385–392.

man being."[12] A variation of this view was expressed by Sombart, who believed that some have an inherent capacity to become traders (undertakers) while others do not. "Either you are born a bourgeois or you are not. It must be in the blood, it is a natural inclination."[13]

This palpable view is undoubtedly a sufficient explanation to many salesmen; it is certainly a comfortable refuge from the penetrating criticism of some of the ancient and modern practices of the market place. If it is "natural" to sell, then the criticism of traders is comment out of hand. But the evidence of scientific anthropology gives little support to this notion.

Not a few evidences exist to show that primitive peoples have existed for long periods without competitive trading.[14] The industrial civilization of the Incas is a striking case in point.[15] Polish peasants for centuries did not know the meaning of buying and selling between members of the same community. Their knowledge of trading came entirely from contacts with outsiders; and their resistance to selling has survived, since even today, peasants dislike to trade with neighbors."[16]

While it is a rare culture that does not produce some exchanges of commodities on occasion, it is rather common to find that among primitives trading, insofar as it possessed any formal existence, arises mainly to facilitate exchange between members of different groups rather than between individual members of the same group.[17] In a culture where the institutions support a strict control of production and allocation of wealth, trading between individuals in the society becomes unnecessary, as in the case of the Incas, or vastly restricted, as in the case of Soviet Russia in the early

years at least, where other stimuli than private profit were dominant.[18]

One would expect few psychologists to rank so complex a phenomenon as trading with fundamental instincts of self-preservation and sex as a basic drive. Unlike these fundamental urges, trading is not universal, intensive, or repetitive. And while it is true that trading appeared early in many different places and independently under different circumstances, these facts serve no more to demonstrate instinctiveness of trading than does the simultaneous scattered growth of the family institution prove that marriage is instinctive. Not only is this hypothesis too simple and superficial, but adherence to it may even retard the ability of present-day sales management to cope with its functional responsibilities.

(2) Trading Grew Out of Warfare

This "hostility" hypothesis has trading growing out of war between clans or tribes. It pictures primitive man as essentially war-like because of the pressure of population on the means of subsistence. It assumes that warfare has economic roots, and that it is inevitable when man searches for the satisfaction of elemental wants. The reasoning follows that whereas man could satisfy his wants by warring on his neighbor, he soon learned that trading was an alternative possibility that had merit from the standpoint of group survival.[19]

This hypothesis has many faults, not the least of which is that it leads us into the difficult path of analyzing the origins of war, a path that is as rugged and unmarked as any

---

[12] Charles H. Fernald, *Salesmanship* (New York: Prentice-Hall, 1937), pp. 44ff.

[13] Werner Sombart, *The Quintessence of Capitalism* (London: T. Fisher Unwin, 1915), p. 205.

[14] Melville J. Herskovits, *op. cit.*, pp. 17–19.

[15] Elizabeth Ellis Hoyt, *Primitive Trade, its Psychology and Economics* (London: Kegan Paul, Trench, Trubner, 1926), p. 141.

[16] W. I. Thomas and F. Znaniecki, *The Polish Peasant in Europe and America*, 1927, as quoted by E. L. Thorndike, *Human Nature and the Social Order* (New York: Macmillan, 1940), p. 633.

[17] Melville J. Herskovits, *op. cit.*, pp. 133 ff.

[18] William Henry Chamberlin, "The Planned Economy," *Red Economics* (Boston: Houghton, Mifflin, 1932), pp. 9 ff. See also M. Ilin, *New Russia's Primer* (Boston: Houghton Mifflin, 1931), II, and XIII.

[19] It is interesting that the opposite view is widely held also; namely, that trading inevitably leads to warfare. Elizabeth Ellis Hoyt cites evidence to support both views, *op. cit.*, VII.

The fact that war and trade often appeared together as effect and cause may have been attributable to the fact that the traders (foreigners) were usually more advanced culturally than those on whom they called and thus had a higher capacity to injure [cf. Max Radin, *Manners and Morals in Business* (New York: Bobbs-Merrill, 1939), pp. 89 ff]. But they also should have had a higher capacity to serve, which may well have prevented conflicts!

other that goes in the direction of primeval origins. It is sufficient here to record that the hostility notion runs afoul of evidence of trading where war is unknown, as well as testimony pointing to the conclusion that both war and trading appear to develop from the same circumstances, and independently of each other. War was unknown among some primitives who carried on a rudimentary form of trade, notably the Eskimo and the Semang of the Malay Peninsula.[20]

The Arapesh tribe of New Guinea, naturally easy-going and yet pitted against physical barrenness that might be expected to produce strong rivalry for survival, finds great adventure in producing for others and actually regards it as a sin to eat one's own kill. Motivation is achieved without competitive rivalry or war by a custom of having an official "insulter" for each man to taunt him publicly for his failure to produce feasts. So dreadful is this torture in the face of his peaceful nature, that a man looks forward to his reward— release from his "insulter" and retirement when his son reaches puberty. Thus, at least one primitive culture has institutionalized its lack of aggressiveness and self-interest, both of which seem to be of some importance in the origin of either competitive trading or war.[21]

Nor is it easy to relate war and trading in the face of the fact that in many primitive peoples the rewards for war are personal and psychological rather than economic, and take the form of prestige supported by the evidence of another feather in the cap or another enemy's scalp on the belt. And the persistence of war, not only among primitives but in our own society, is difficult to explain if it is to be argued that trading supplanted war because of its demonstrated superior contributions to group survival; for wars have almost always provided a serious interference with economic life. Indeed, it seems well to avoid any attempt to relate trade to war as a fruitless inquiry in which observable data are altogether too lacking to support reasonable conclusions.[22]

(3) Trading Originated in Predation

The "predatory" hypothesis is closely allied with the hostility notion. Because there are a few primitive tribes, such as the Bushman and the Apache, whose economies were regularly dependent upon the capture of wealth from other tribes,[23] and because there are a few evidences that modern business "is a complex and well-integrated series of frauds,"[24] some observers may conclude that trading began with the extraction of tribute and has never succeeded in getting away from the original predatory pattern.

The difficulty here lies in the abundance of evidence, historical and anthropological, that trading flourished between peoples who were entirely friendly and to whom the idea of tribute never seemed to occur. Moreover, predatory activities are not confined to the economic institution, but pervade the other social institutions as well. Indeed, political leaders, whether they be the heads of primitive tribes or of literate nations, have been among the most notorious tribute-extracting racketeers of history, and their predacity on merchants has all too often throttled trade.[25]

(4) Trade Grew Out of Friendly Gift-Giving

This "friendship" hypothesis is an explanation in diametrically the opposite vein. Professor Hoyt cites many examples of friendly gift-giving in primitive society and suggests that this practice may have led to learning the utility of exchange.[26] In primitive societies where the ownership of things was strongly identified with personal or group spiritual entity, the giving of gifts to neighboring tribal chiefs must indeed have stemmed from a genuine gregarious feeling

[20] Margaret Mead, "Primitive Society," *Planned Society* (New York: Prentice-Hall, 1937), p. 16.
[21] *Ibid.*, p. 23.
[22] A more fruitful approach to the question of war and trade will be found in Lionel Robbins, *The Economic Causes of War* (London: J. Cape, 1940).

[23] Margaret Mead, *op. cit.*, pp. 17 ff.
[24] J. B. Matthews and R. E. Shallcross, *Partners in Plunder* (Washington, New Jersey: Consumers' Research, 1935), p. 400. See also Clarence Darrow, *op. cit.*
[25] N. S. B. Gras, *Business and Capitalism* (New York: F. S. Crofts, 1939), pp. 307 ff. See also Miriam Beard, *A History of the Business Man* (New York: Macmillan, 1938), *passim*.
[26] *Op. cit.*, p. 104 and Part IV.

and friendly goodwill.[27] The cynical view that a wise chieftain would buy off the predatory nature and power of his neighbor with gifts is not sufficient to explain the facts of anthropological research.

It is perhaps sufficient here to note that both war-making and gift-giving were means of communication, either or both of which may have been helpful in the discovery of trading. Professor Hoyt's emphasis on gift-giving as an origin of trading is supported by logic; for the atmosphere of gift-giving is a congenial one in which man may learn to perceive the utility of exchange.

(5) Trading Originated with the "Silent Trade"

Silent trade is well-known to anthropologists as an early means of economic communication, and it appears in many isolated places among primitives. In this crude form, trade is initiated when one group leaves its wares on a promontory and retires from sight to permit another group to come out of hiding to inspect the goods and deposit its offering in return.[28]

Silent trade seems to have prevailed (1) where contact was between peoples of widely different cultures, (2) where languages were different, and (3) where fear or distrust was even more highly felt than were the economic motives of the intercourse. While the silent trade is an important fact in early communication, it throws little light on the real origins of trading. Its existence proves, however, that trading did occur between peoples who were motivated by neither the desire to make friends nor the will to annihilate.

It should also be recognized that neither party to the silent trade would have acted had he failed to develop an evaluation of the exchanged wares entirely apart from his own spirit or soul. Some degree of objectivity was implicit. Moreover, it is not plausible that this form of trading was an expression of instinct; it was discovered, developed, and learned as a crude but effective usage in the framework of the existing social institutions.

(6) Trading Arose from Surpluses

Some students have suggested that trading originated because of the pressure of surplus goods resulting from the early division of labor in the primitive family or tribe.[29] Presumably the relative scarcity of goods was apparent in the periodic surpluses made available either through the efforts of nature or man. The plethora of cattle against the dearth of fodder may have suggested a gain from the exchange of cattle for fodder that was plentiful in a neighboring area.

This explanation fails on a number of grounds. There is practically no evidence that surpluses were accumulated by primitive families or clans excepting for anticipated emergencies.[30] Indeed, it is probable that excesses of things to eat or wear or use were regarded as "free goods" with respect to which transferable control did not even suggest itself until after trading as an instrument of communication developed. Moreover, much of the early trade in all parts of the world was in rare and exotic items "for which the demand was largely an expression of arbitrary value."[31] The primitive trading in ornaments and trinkets which gave their owners social prestige can hardly be said to stem from surpluses.

Too, a rational and administrative division of labor in primitive tribes, assumed in this hypothesis, cannot conceivably have preceded the need for it; and this need certainly compels outside markets as a *sine qua non*. The superficial explanation posed by the surplus hypothesis is to be found in the contemporary and popular notion that foreign trade exists because of surpluses resulting from the division of labor when in fact it is quite the other way around.

---

[27] To say that gift-giving is entirely a matter of goodwill or altruism, however, is to overstate the matter; for no matter how freely a gift is given, its presentation in primitive societies appears nearly always to create an obligation which, if neglected by the recipient, leads to loss of prestige or social disapprobation, which is a strong factor in shaping action. Cf. Herskovits, *op. cit.*, p. 134.

[28] N. S. B. Gras, "Barter," *The Encyclopaedia of the Social Sciences* (New York: Macmillan 1933), II, pp. 468 ff. Elizabeth Ellis Hoyt, *op. cit.*, pp. 133 ff. Max Radin, *op. cit.*, pp. 81 ff.

[29] Edward D. Page, *Trade-Morals*, 2nd rev. ed. (New Haven: Yale University Press, 1918), p. 58. See also Charles H. Fernald, *op. cit.*, pp. 44 ff.

[30] Max Radin, *op. cit.*, pp. 85 ff.

[31] *Ibid.*

(7) Trading Grew Out of the Development of the Property Concept

Tracing the origin of trading to the growth of the concept of property is a preoccupation of those who see in the exaggerated manifestations of trading in our society an overemphasis on private ownership. It is not appropriate to our purposes here to enter the controversy over the inequalities of property ownership or over the ways by which the function of property may be molded in the interests of social progress and public welfare.

It is merely essential to point out that in the manner in which the function of property is conceived as an end in terms of private advantage, special privilege, and exploitation will have a profound bearing on the practices in the market place. That many of these practices are subject to question today is not gainsaid; but to attack trading as a major evil growing out of the property concept is to engage in ardent speculation.

If by property we refer to the claim which gives transferable control over things,[32] then the property concept is best explained by the relative scarcity of these things in terms of the contest for individual and group survival.[33] While it is true that the extensive and complex exchange in our society presupposes a well-developed concept of property, it is far from true that crude trading could never have existed without even a simple property concept. Indeed, the very definition of property as anything with exchange value implies clearly that it is the need and practice of trading which called the property concept into use and aided materially in shaping its character. To say that property value existed before the fact of exchange is to indulge in a hopeless confusion of ideas and terms.

Trading and property concepts are both man-made and have developed in close relationship. They have certain characteristics in common: (1) both are dependent on the recognition of scarcity values; (2) both presuppose a divorcement of possessions from the individual's spiritual identity—an objective valuation of things; (3) both emerge from the same set of factors and must be explained in terms of a larger institutional concept.

Hence, to say that trading originated in the property concept and is a usage of property is to misinterpret the origins of both while leaving the essential character of each shrouded in confusion. In short, it is another example of the futility of tracing origins without the supporting evidences of observable data.

A RATIONAL EXPLANATION OF TRADING

The one thing in common which all of these hypotheses of the origins of trading have is a high degree of speculation unsupported by the accumulation of empirical data. It should be clear that any logic based upon premises like these is not acceptable to the social scientist. Indeed, social science has long since abandoned the methodology suggested by such speculations as those we have been examining.

If an explanation of trading is needed, it is to be found in the nature of man and of his adaptation to his environment through the institutions he builds. The universal, abiding, and repetitive characteristics of man to learn, to explore, to satisfy his curiosity, and to live with groups of other men have led him into an everexpanding circle of experiences from which he has developed his learning and his patterns of associated living.[34] These attributes undoubtedly stem from the character of man's genes as distinguished from those of other animals. The explanation of trading lies neither in man's instincts nor his intelligence alone, but must be seen in terms of the patterns of the accumulated deposits of his activities in associated living.[35]

The essential prerequisite to trading, original or otherwise, is the development of the ability to valuate things in terms of other things rather than in terms of spiritual or mystical beliefs—to objectify and emancipate one's belongings from his spiritual self and

---

[32] Frederic B. Garver and Alvin H. Hansen, *Principles of Economics*, rev. ed. (Boston: Ginn, 1937), pp. 29 ff.

[33] Constantine Panunzio, *op. cit.*, p. 216.

[34] A highly imaginative, yet penetrating essay on this fundamental character of man as opposed to other animals is to be found in Clarence Day, *This Simian World* (New York: A. A. Knopf, 1936).

[35] Constantine Panunzio, *op. cit.*, pp. 143 ff.

soul.[36] But this ability is by no means a guarantee that trading will be carried on in a society unless the folkways and mores are receptive to the changes which it imposes in the patterns of living.

Trading may be said to have been a slow discovery, made at a relatively early stage by peoples the world over, that followed the intellectual advance of valuation and which, in turn, vastly stimulated that advance, that grew out of the practices of associated living and, in turn, greatly affected these practices.

As contrasted with the other means of acquiring things, trading is by all odds the most complex. It is unique in that it alone is a two-way transaction.[37] The fact that trading has grown to such prominence and complexity as one of the dominant means of acquiring things is attributable, in part at least, to its relative survival value and to the character of the prevailing institutional patterns of which it is a part.

---

[36] Elizabeth Ellis Hoyt, *op. cit.*, Pt. IV. That this emancipation is universally or wholly accomplished today (or, indeed, should be) is not suggested. Contemporaries have "priceless" trinkets and sometimes order them interred with their remains. Businessmen have been known to defy the logic of the case by insisting on the use of their own photographs as trademarks.

[37] The other means are strictly one-way: appropriation from nature, seizure from others, cultivation and making with the hands, gifts and inheritance, and gambling. H. K. Nixon, *Principles of Selling* (New York: McGraw-Hill, 1942), pp. 41 ff.

CONCLUSION

The answers to our original questions may now be seen in better perspective. Although it would be the height of pedantic scepticism to deny validity to a hypothesis because of the absence of all conceivable verification, nevertheless, the main assumptions examined all fall in the same category of speculation without adequate verification, and they involve an outmoded methodology in the social sciences.

Even by the most tolerant sense of proportion and broad feeling for the evidence, any conceivable proof of the kinship of modern competitive trading to the earliest forms of barter and exchange would fail to offer a basis for a discussion of either ethics or efficiency of trading unless it be considered in a particular institutional framework. Consequently, it is not to be argued that the ethics of selling in our own society can be related to that of the societies in which origin may have occurred.

As a basis for the evaluation of the ethics of selling and buying in our own society, the concept that trading is a cooperative organization in communication for the purpose of achieving economic ends is one that properly expresses the internal logic of trading. For it implies in trading a concept in the economic institution whose usages entail a continuing contest and conflict with other concepts and usages prevailing in all of the social institutions. This view of trading permits one to proceed with an examination of the ethics of trading in our own society without the hindrance of a cloak of prejudgment drawn about it by speculation with respect to the ultimate origins of trading usages.

2. The Commercial Environment

PHILIP WAGNER

The environment through which the nomad gatherers make their rounds remains, although its vegetation may be altered radically, almost as vast and empty as nature made it. In farming country, the cultivated fields and gardens display the handiwork of man, but the environments that they provide for crops remain ruled more by nature than by man. The city and the road are altogether artificial features, though, and commercial urban people live and work within environments that they impose on nature.

The wanderers live "off the land," garnering a livelihood from wild plants and animals; and farmers live "on the land," feeding themselves from their crops and livestock; but urban specialists live under highly artificial circumstances, lack the means of producing crops for themselves, and thus rely on rural populations to supply their food in exchange for other goods and services. We have observed that specialized commercial production of the kind associated with cities is possible only when, in addition to the food-producing symbiosis, there is a further symbiosis of exchange within the society that allows some of its members to engage in pursuits other than cultivation.

Large differences in artificial spatial arrangements are related to differences in economic forms. In subsistence societies, which have no appreciable exchange, all the various stages of production are carried out by the

◆ SOURCE: Reprinted by permission of Macmillan Publishing Co., Inc. from *The Human Use of the Earth* by Philip Wagner. © The Free Press, a Corporation 1960, pp. 191–200.

members of one very small household group in a small area. The complex of artificial features associated with production is "telescoped," and its component elements are little differentiated. Resource sites are few; routes of circulation are short and hardly improved; manufacture is carried on around the dwelling, and specialized services are few in number. Many parallel systems of production exist with little reciprocal effect, and the complexity and size of any one of them are limited by the small numbers of workers and the slight degree of specialization of the household group.

Societies in which much exchange is practiced display a different character. There, routes of transport link the many sites of resource exploitation, manufacture, and service; and along these routes are specialized installations for various kinds of commercial production. The artificial complex serves a large area, and tends to be connected with other like complexes. The productive system commands the labor and highly specialized skills of a large number of workers. The uses made of particular places, the equipment and installations devoted to particular tasks, and the working roles of individuals are all well differentiated and specialized.

A system organized around only the single symbiosis of food supply (subsistence) develops a multitude of unconnected, parallel economic units, each with its small complex of artificial productive features. The double symbiosis involving exchange in addition creates a single economic unit of wide scope, having one large and more or less unitary complex of highly specialized productive installations. The particular nature of this complex depends upon the degree of commercialization attained, i.e., the extent to which various commodities are subject to exchange.

CONSUMERS' AND PRODUCERS' ECONOMIES

An *economy* regulates the circulation of goods and services, the physical means for which are embodied in the transport and communications system. The character of the economic organization therefore tends to be reflected in the material features of the man-made environment.

When exchange is absent, highly specialized production does not occur, and no commodities are made and moved to serve a general consumer class. The routes of circulation are, then, hardly developed, and practically no sites are set aside especially for manufacture or services (except those dedicated to ceremonial and political activity). There is no general economy among the social group, and there is no one system of artificial features deployed to serve an economic function for the whole society.

In a *peasant society*, one observes exchange relations between food producers and specialists in service and in manufacture. The cultivator grows food both for his own household and for an urban consumer population. In the city, specialized craftsmen devote themselves to the production of goods to be distributed throughout the society; services are performed for all by recognized specialists. One finds a general economic bond extending throughout the society, and an appropriate network of artificial sites and routes serving the economic life.

The economic system of a society of peasants and urban specialists typically rests upon an exchange of finished commodities among their specialized producers. Each unit of production, or *firm*, acquires command of land or raw resources and processes commodities until they are ready for the consumer as final products. Exchange is a relation in this case among possessors of finished goods which can be traded for other finished goods. Although some of the commodities subject to exchange may serve productive purposes, as in the case of cultivating tools or cooking vessels, they are intended for permanent or terminal use in the form in which they are acquired, and not for incorporation into more evolved and complex products subject to further exchange. The handicraft shop is the characteristic manufacturing enterprise in such an economy. In it, all the necessary steps in the production of the finished article are accomplished, and often the services of retail trade are performed. The work is done by skilled craftsmen using traditional tools and simple machines. These artisans are closely integrated socially into one organized and fairly permanent group with a distinctive place in the society; often the many small handicraft enterprises are located side by side in a special quarter of the city. Raw materials are acquired by trade with the exploiters of natural resources or with cultivators of "industrial" crops, or are secured from properties controlled by the same enterprise that runs the shop. Typically, the tools and machines employed are designed, and are often even made, by the members of the shop group itself.

The situation of the peasant is closely analogous to that of the craftsman. He makes many of his tools and uses his own land or that of a proprietor. In an economy of peasants and craftsmen, therefore, exchange hardly intervenes in the productive process, but primarily affects finished commodities of consumption. An economy of this sort is a *consumers' economy*.

The *consumers' economy* represents an incompletely developed exchange economy. In it, land is seldom subject to frequent transfers of control. Land ownership and usufruct are usually hereditary rights closely linked with a stratified social order, and money or other mobile media of exchange cannot command them. Similarly, the equipment and installations used and occupied by productive enterprise are held by virtue of traditional claims. The actual processes of production, especially, are jealously kept secret by the guilds or other craftsmen's organization. The rights and the skills enabling a man to exercise a particular craft are difficult to acquire, and elaborate social arrangements rule the assignment of occupations. Neither land, nor capital, nor labor is subject to free exchange, and industrial processes are not subdivided into separate spatial stages carried on by different enterprises. There is almost no mobility of the factors of production. Limitations of skill rather than cost primarily govern the character and volume of commodities produced. The nature of the products offered in trade reflects the ability of single craft enterprises to command all the necessary techniques, materials, and equipment to carry through all steps in manufacture—all within a restrictive social milieu.

The limited scope for organization and control afforded by the consumer's economy restricts the availability of diverse and highly specialized producer's equipment and installations. These can be produced only at great expense and are not available through an exchange system under which only finished consumer goods circulate. Pre-modern textile and flour manufacturers built their own machines in the shop, and situated their wind- or water-mills in places where the enterprise could command adjacent inanimate power supplies. There were no true "public utilities" and almost no enterprises devoted exclusively to the supply of producers' goods. Few craftsmen worked entirely as producers of component parts for other enterprises' finished products.

The spatial order of the consumers' economy differs in many respects from that of subsistence economies. Consumers' economies possess concentrated urban settlements whose populations engage in manufacturing crafts and in services, and depend upon exchange with peasants for their food. A system of roads, sea routes, and sometimes canals, facilitates the movement of people and commodities. Natural resources are exploited to supply manufacturing units. Many service agencies, especially "public" ones, are concentrated in the urban settlements. The flow of production runs from the resource sites and farms over the roads to handicraft shops where the finished commodities are made; thence to the consumer through shops or the workshops themselves.

The types of installations made in these societies of peasants and craftsmen are, therefore, such as: *primary resource sites* at which raw materials for manufacture are produced: *public roads* and *canals* over which goods and people move; *workshops* in which the entire sequence of manufacture is centered; *cultivated lands* on which food for both their tillers and an urban populace is grown; *service centers* where goods are exchanged, public and private services offered, and social, religious, and administrative functions concentrated; and *settlements,* which vary from clusters of rustic huts to palaces, temples, and great cities. Residential buildings, civic and religious centers, monuments, and military fortifications are typically the most imposing artificial features of the landscape. Manufacturing enterprises are small and have no installations supplying them with large amounts of inanimate power. Their equipment is confined to numerous ingenious implements and utensils, machines built mostly from wood and driven by human or animal power, or at most by wind- and waterpower, and containers. Merchandising is carried on at the handicraft shops or small specialty stores; most retail agencies deal in a single kind of goods or services. Only in consumers' forms of *redistributive* exchange economies are great stores of diverse goods found. Pedestrians, pack animals, animal-drawn vehicles, and towed or wind-propelled watercraft travel the circulation routes. No special accommodations carry messages—with the exception of such things as lighthouses and signal beacons.

The manufacturing crafts still employ such materials as clay, wood, bone, hide, hair and fiber, though more complex products are developed from them, and the work is finer than where specialized crafts are absent. Metals are also in regular use, mainly for making small implements and utensils. Mineral fuels and wood are used in limited quantities for space-heating or in a few industries such as metallurgy. Water supply and sanitation are served by a network of conduits, reservoirs, and sewers, but little effort is made to protect the purity of water or to safeguard the population against dangerous wastes.

The same essential form of artificial environment develops wherever the consumers' economy occurs. It was characteristic of medieval Europe; the Islamic world at its height; millennial China; and, until recently, of Eastern Europe; it is even found, residually, in Latin America, and lives on here and there in the Old World. Although the peasants are still numerous, however, the old handicraft cities are rapidly disappearing, and are being replaced by modern industrial-urban complexes.

The consumers' economy, in which trade takes on great importance, requires certain conditions in order to function. Peaceful conditions must obtain to allow persons and goods to move with relative security. In some places, like Berber North Africa where there is a "market truce," or as in many Islamic countries where there is an annual period of moratorium on raids and warfare, the conditions suitable for trade are found only exceptionally. In other instances, trade flourishes within a circumscribed area where law and order are maintained by the power of a ruler. The value and volume of commodities entering trade respond to these conditions; and when risk is high, the profit sought is high, so that only goods of high value and low bulk are carried about for exchange. Military conquest, by extending favorable conditions of exchange, can promote prosperous trade, and the power of administrative agencies to guarantee the security of goods and persons within a state is of similar benefit to trade.

Bartering can be successful when just finished goods are offered, but it functions clumsily where a large and diverse assortment of products is involved. Some few accepted media of exchange, or one general medium, serve better; and where weights and measures, and especially the currency standard, are guaranteed by a central public agency, trade is favored.

Another requirement for exchange closely related to the above mentioned is the security of contractual relations. Trade is facilitated when a good or service can be exchanged not only against any other commodity at a given moment, but also by contract against future payment, services, or stocks of goods. Contract allows the exchange of future for present values. The contractual relationship also relies upon the guarantee of law and order, and upon some common medium for transacting exchanges. Contractual obligations are usually subject to enforcement by legal means.

Exchange under a consumers' economy demands, we see, not only physical means like the lines of communication, but also some degree of support and guarantee by public agencies. These must furnish at least a modicum of law and order, a monetary standard, and some legal protection of contractual relations. Although one or more of these conditions may be lacking at times, all of them and other like guarantees are ordinarily present in the consumers' economies. They are commonly provided by a comprehensive administrative and political unit, the state. Trade is, indeed, known in periods and places which lack the state organization, but the developed consumers' economy comprising symbiotic urban and rural sectors is closely dependent on the stability provided by organized political systems.

One of the distinctive features of *producers' economies* is that they are organized to effect a transfer of goods from one producer to another in unfinished form, as well as to govern transfers between producers and consumers. A firm now acquires goods, subjects them to partial preparation, and passes them on to other firms. Exchange enters into the regulation of the productive process itself, and there is a circulation not merely of finished goods, but of all the factors of production—land, labor, capital; and a single product is created in a number of different productive stages which take place successively in different locations, and are carried out by different firms. Production is serialized as well as specialized; and for each stage of production, the necessary materials and means are often assembled separately through exchange mechanisms.

The organization of production under a producers' economy differs from that under a consumers' economy. In the handicraft production associated with a consumers' economy, the technical basis of working organization is the complete product. Each enterprise commands all the tools, materials, and skills required to produce a given kind of article or a number of similar articles. Raw materials are turned, within the shop, into the final product. Leatherworkers in such enterprises may acquire raw hides which they clean, tan, dye, cut, fashion, and decorate to bring forth boots, garments, or saddles ready for use. They often sell them in the shop.

The factory enterprises of producers' economies are typically organized not to turn out a complete product ready for the consumer, but to perform only a part of the operations that produce it—the "job." A single factory may produce only the bolts that belong to a particular automobile assembly, or may only assemble pieces, already made elsewhere, into a toy. In many large enterprises, work is allocated among a number of different shops, each of which executes one or a few of the many operations that go to create the complex final product. An automobile factory, for instance, is a compound of many such shops, and in addition relies upon small independent plants to furnish certain of the parts it assembles.

Production is broken down into a series of many separate jobs, and the whole process is spread out among many agencies over some distance. Different equipment and facilities are assembled at various points; all are connected by transport lines; and each is served by its own labor force. Skillful organization of the movement of materials through the proper sequence replaces skilled handiwork as the crucial element in production. Workers are readily trained, moved, discharged, or hired, and men take and leave jobs with little concern; no social traditions exclude all but a few groups from employment at a particular job, as is true with the crafts system. Equipment is not made on the spot, but purchased from special enterprises which design and produce it according to need. In some countries, the processes used in production are restricted to whatever enterprise can acquire legal rights over them, but eventually they become common property. Equipment and processes frequently change, personnel turns over rapidly, and even the nature of the product is constantly developing.

Since exchange makes available to producers services and goods that are created by other producers expressly for their use, a supply of specialized means of production, inanimate energy, component parts, and materials becomes accessible to any enterprise, regardless of its size. The large aggregate demand for productive goods and services supports the growth of a large producers' goods industry and of public utilities. A relatively high proportion of the factories and other manufacturing plants is devoted to the production (more technically, the conversion) of energy to operate other plants, to the production of materials—like pig-iron, sulfuric acid, and lumber—that are basic to other industries, and to the building of production equipment—like machine tools and chemical plants. A relatively small number of the manufacturing plants in operation under a producers' economy actually turn out only finished consumers' goods.

The spatial order associated with factory production reflects, the great diversity of agencies concerned not only in production, but in the service of other production, and recently also in the service of urban populations employed in these activities. In the fully commercialized producers' economy, the unparalleled volume of exchange on which production rests, the intricate division of tasks in manufacture, and the variety of services require an altogether unprecedented development of artificial facilities. . . .

3. The Economic Organization of a P.O.W. Camp

R. A. RADFORD

INTRODUCTION

After allowance has been made for abnormal circumstances, the social institutions, ideas and habits of groups in the outside world are to be found reflected in a Prisoner of War Camp. It is an unusual but a vital society. Camp organisation and politics are matters of real concern to the inmates, as affecting their present and perhaps their future existences. Nor does this indicate any loss of proportion. No one pretends that camp matters are of any but local importance or of more than transient interest, but their importance there is great. They bulk large in a world of narrow horizons and it is suggested that any distortion of values lies rather in the minimisation than in the exaggeration of their importance. Human affairs are essentially practical matters and the measure of immediate effect on the lives of those directly concerned in them is to a large extent the criterion of their importance at that time and place. A prisoner can hold strong views on such subjects as whether or not all tinned meats shall be issued to individuals cold or be centrally cooked, without losing sight of the significance of the Atlantic Charter.

One aspect of social organization is to be found in economic activity, and this, along with other manifestations of a group existence, is to be found in any P.O.W. camp.

◆ SOURCE   Reprinted by permission from *Economica*, November 1945, pp. 189-201.

True, a prisoner is not dependent on his exertions for the provision of the necessaries, or even the luxuries of life, but through his economic activity, the exchange of goods and services, his standard of material comfort is considerably enhanced. And this is a serious matter to the prisoner: he is not "playing at shops" even though the small scale of the transactions and the simple expression of comfort and wants in terms of cigarettes and jam, razor blades and writing paper, make the urgency of those needs difficult to appreciate, even by an ex-prisoner of some three months' standing.

Nevertheless, it cannot be too strongly emphasised that economic activities do not bulk so large in prison society as they do in the larger world. There can be little production; as has been said the prisoner is independent of his exertions for the provision of the necessities and luxuries of life; the emphasis lies in exchange and the media of exchange. A prison camp is not to be compared with the seething crowd of higglers in a street market, any more than it is to be compared with the economic inertia of a family dinner table.

Naturally then, entertainment, academic and literary interests, games and discussions of the "other world" bulk larger in everyday life than they do in the life of more normal societies. But it would be wrong to underestimate the importance of economic activity. Everyone receives a roughly equal share of essentials; it is by trade that individual preferences are given expression and comfort increased. All at some time, and most people regularly, make exchanges of one sort or another.

Although a P.O.W. camp provides a living example of a simple economy which might be used as an alternative to the Robinson Crusoe economy beloved by the text-books, and its simplicity renders the demonstration of certain economic hypotheses both amusing and instructive, it is suggested that the principal significance is sociological. True, there is interest in observing the growth of economic institutions and customs in a brand new society, small and simple enough to prevent detail from obscuring the basic pattern and disequilibrium from obscuring the working of the system. But the essential interest lies in the universality and the spontaneity of this economic life; it came into existence not by conscious imitation but as a response to the immediate needs and circumstances. Any similarity between prison organisation and outside organisation arises from similar stimuli evoking similar responses.

The following is as brief an account of the essential data as may render the narrative intelligible. The camps of which the writer had experience were Oflags and consequently the economy was not complicated by payments for work by the detaining power. They consisted normally of between 1,200 and 2,500 people, housed in a number of separate but intercommunicating bungalows, one company of 200 or so to a building. Each company formed a group within the main organisation and inside the company the room and the messing syndicate, a voluntary and spontaneous group who fed together, formed the constituent units.

Between individuals there was active trading in all consumer goods and in some services. Most trading was for food against cigarettes or other foodstuffs, but cigarettes rose from the status of a normal commodity to that of currency. RMk.s existed but had no circulation save for gambling debts, as few articles could be purchased with them from the canteen.

Our supplies consisted of rations provided by the detaining power and (principally) the contents of Red Cross food parcels—tinned milk, jam, butter, biscuits, bully, chocolate, sugar, etc., and cigarettes. So far the supplies to each person were equal and regular. Private parcels of clothing, toilet requisites and cigarettes were also received, and here equality ceased owing to the different numbers despatched and the vagaries of the post. All these articles were the subject of trade and exchange.

THE DEVELOPMENT AND ORGANISATION OF THE MARKET

Very soon after capture people realised that it was both undesirable and unnecessary, in view of the limited size and the equality of supplies, to give away or to accept gifts of cigarettes or food. "Goodwill" developed into trading as a more equitable means of maximising individual satisfaction.

We reached a transit camp in Italy about a fortnight after capture and received ¼ of a Red Cross food parcel each a week later. At once exchanges, already established, multiplied in volume. Starting with simple direct barter, such as a non-smoker giving a smoker friend his cigarette issue in exchange for a chocolate ration, more complex exchanges soon became an accepted custom. Stories circulated of a padre who started off round the camp with a tin of cheese and five cigarettes and returned to his bed with a complete parcel in addition to his original cheese and cigarettes; the market was not yet perfect. Within a week or two, as the volume of trade grew, rough scales of exchange values came into existence. Sikhs, who had at first exchanged tinned beef for practically any other foodstuff began to insist on jam and margarine. It was realised that a tin of jam was worth ½ lb. of margarine plus something else; that a cigarette issue was worth several chocolate issues, and a tin of diced carrots was worth practically nothing.

In this camp we did not visit other bungalows very much and prices varied from place to place; hence the germ of truth in the story of the itinerant priest. By the end of a month, when we reached our permanent camp, there was a lively trade in all commodities and their relative values were well known, and expressed not in terms of one another—one didn't quote bully in terms of sugar—but in terms of cigarettes. The cigarette became the standard of value. In the permanent camp people started by wandering through the bungalows calling their offers—"cheese for seven" (cigarettes)—and the hours after parcel issue were Bedlam. The inconveniences of this system soon led to its replacement by an Exchange and Mart notice board in every bungalow, where under the headings "name", "room number", "wanted" and "offered" sales and wants were advertised. When a deal went through, it was crossed off the board. The public and semi-permanent records of transactions led to cigarette prices being well known and thus ending to equality throughout the camp, although there were always opportunities for an astute trader to make a profit from arbitrage. With this development everyone, including nonsmokers, was willing to sell for cigarettes, using them to buy at another time and place. Cigarettes became the normal currency, though, of course, barter was never extinguished.

The unity of the market and the prevalence of a single price varied directly with the general level of organisation and comfort in the camp. A transit camp was always chaotic and uncomfortable: people were overcrowded, no one knew where anyone else was living, and few took the trouble to find out. Organisation was too slender to include an Exchange and Mart board, and private advertisements were the most that appeared. Consequently a transit camp was not one market but many. The price of a tin of salmon is known to have varied by two cigarettes in 20 between one end of a hut and the other. Despite a high level of organisation in Italy, the market was morcellated in this manner at the first transit camp we reached after our removal to Germany in the autumn of 1943. In this camp—Stalag VIIA at Moosburg in Bavaria—there were up to 50,000 prisoners of all nationalities. French, Russians, Italians and Jugo-Slavs were free to move about within the camp: British and Americans were confined to their compounds, although a few cigarettes given to a sentry would always procure permission for one or two men to visit other compounds. The people who first visited the highly organised French trading centre, with its stalls and known prices, found coffee extract—relatively cheap among the tea-drinking English—commanding a fancy price in biscuits or cigarettes, and some enterprising people made small fortunes that way. (Incidentally we found out later that much of the coffee went "over the wire" and sold for phenomenal prices at black market cafés in Munich: some of the French prisoners were said to have made substantial sums in RMk.s. This was one of the few occasions on which our normally closed economy came into contact with other economic worlds.)

Eventually public opinion grew hostile to these monopoly profits—not everyone could make contact with the French—and trading with them was put on a regulated basis. Each group of beds was given a quota of articles to offer and the transaction was carried out by accredited representatives from the British compound, with monopoly rights. The same method was used for trading with sentries elsewhere, as in this trade secrecy and reasonable prices had a peculiar importance, but as is ever the case with regulated companies, the interloper proved too strong.

The permanent camps in Germany saw the highest level of commercial organisation. In addition to the Exchange and Mart notice boards, a shop was organised as a public utility, controlled by representatives of the Senior British Officer, on a no profit basis. People left their surplus clothing, toilet requisites and food there until they were sold at a fixed price in cigarettes. Only sales in cigarettes were accepted—there was no barter—and there was no higgling. For food at least there were standard prices: clothing is less homogeneous and the price was decided around a norm by the seller and the shop manager in agreement; shirts would average say 80, ranging from 60 to 120 according to quality and age. Of food, the shop carried small stocks for convenience; the capital was provided by a loan from the bulk store of Red Cross cigarettes and repaid by a small commission taken on the first transactions. Thus the cigarette attained its fullest currency status, and the market was almost completely unified.

It is thus to be seen that a market came into existence without labour or production. The B.R.C.S. may be considered as "Nature" of the text-book, and the articles of trade—food, clothing and cigarettes—as free gifts—land or manna. Despite this, and despite a roughly equal distribution of resources, a market came into spontaneous operation, and prices were fixed by the operation of supply and demand. It is difficult to reconcile this fact with the labour theory of value.

Actually there was an embryo labour market. Even when cigarettes were not scarce, there was usually some unlucky person willing to perform services for them. Laundrymen advertised at two cigarettes a garment. Battle-dress was scrubbed and pressed and a pair of trousers lent for the interim period for twelve. A good pastel portrait cost thirty or a tin of "Kam". Odd tailoring and other jobs similarly had their prices.

There were also entrepreneurial services. There was a coffee stall owner who sold tea, coffee or cocoa at two cigarettes a cup, buying his raw materials at market prices and hiring labour to gather fuel and to stoke; he actually enjoyed the services of a chartered accountant at one stage. After a period of great prosperity he overreached himself and failed disastrously for several hundred cigarettes. Such large-scale private enterprise was rare but several middlemen or professional traders existed. The padre in Italy, or the men at Moosburg who opened trading relations with the French, are examples: the more subdivided the market, the less perfect the advertisement of prices, and the less stable the prices, the greater was the scope for these operators. One man capitalised his knowledge of Urdu by buying meat from the Sikhs and selling butter and jam in return: as his operations became better known more and more people entered this trade, prices in the Indian Wing approximated more nearly to those elsewhere, though to the end a "contact" among the Indians was valuable, as linguistic difficulties prevented the trade from being quite free. Some were specialists in the Indian trade, the food, clothing or even the watch trade. Middlemen traded on their own account or on commission. Price rings and agreements were suspected and the traders certainly co-operated. Nor did they welcome newcomers. Unfortunately the writer knows little of the workings of these people: public opinion was hostile and the professionals were usually of a retiring disposition.

One trader in food and cigarettes, operating in a period of dearth, enjoyed a high reputation. His capital, carefully saved, was originally about 50 cigarettes, with which he bought rations on issue days and held them until the price rose just before the next issue. He also picked up a little by arbitrage; several times a day he visited every Exchange or Mart notice board and took advantage of every discrepancy between prices of goods offered and wanted. His knowledge of prices, markets and names of those who had received cigarette parcels was phenomenal. By these means he kept himself smoking steadily—his profits—while his capital remained intact.

Sugar was issued on Saturday. About Tuesday two of us used to visit Sam and make a deal; as old customers he would advance as much of the price as he could spare then, and entered the transaction in a book. On Saturday morning he left cocoa tins on our beds for the ration, and picked them up on Saturday afternoon. We were hoping for a calendar at Christmas, but Sam failed too. He was left holding a big black treacle issue when the price fell, and in this weakened state was unable to withstand an unexpected arrival of parcels and the consequent price fluctuations. He paid in full, but from his capital. The next Tuesday, when I paid my usual visit he was out of business.

Credit entered into many, perhaps into most, transactions, in one form or another. Sam paid in advance as a rule for his purchases of future deliveries of sugar, but many buyers asked for credit, whether the commodity was sold spot or future. Naturally prices varied according to the terms of sale. A treacle ration might be advertised for four cigarettes now or five next week. And in the future market "bread now" was a vastly different thing from "bread Thursday." Bread was issued on Thursday and Monday, four and three days' rations respectively, and by Wednesday and Sunday night it had risen at least one cigarette per ration, from seven to eight, by supper time. One man always saved a ration to sell then at the peak price: his offer of "bread now" stood out on the board among a number of "bread Monday's" fetching one or two less, or not selling at all—and he always smoked on Sunday night.

THE CIGARETTE CURRENCY

Although cigarettes as currency exhibited certain peculiarities, they performed all the functions of a metallic currency as a unit of account, as a measure of value and as a store of value, and shared most of its characteristics. They were homogeneous, reasonably durable, and of convenient size for the smallest or, in packets, for the largest transactions. Incidentally, they could be clipped or sweated by rolling them between the fingers so that tobacco fell out.

Cigarettes were also subject to the working of Gresham's Law. Certain brands were more popular than others as smokes, but for currency purposes a cigarette was a cigarette. Consequently buyers used the poorer qualities and the Shop rarely saw the more popular brands: cigarettes such as Churchman's No. 1 were rarely used for trading. At one time cigarettes hand-rolled from pipe tobacco began to circulate. Pipe tobacco was issued in lieu of cigarettes by the Red Cross at a rate of 25 cigarettes to the ounce and this rate was standard in exchanges, but an ounce would produce 30 home-made cigarettes. Naturally, people with machine-made cigarettes broke them down and re-rolled the tobacco, and the real cigarette virtually disappeared from the market. Hand-rolled cigarettes were not homogeneous and prices could no longer be quoted in them with safety: each cigarette was examined before it was accepted and thin ones were rejected, or extra demanded as a make-weight. For a time we suffered all the inconveniences of a debased currency.

Machine-made cigarettes were always universally acceptable, both for what they would buy and for themselves. It was this intrinsic value which gave rise to their principal disadvantage as currency, a disadvantage which exists, but to a far smaller extent, in the case of metallic currency—that is, a strong demand for non-monetary purposes. Consequently our economy was repeatedly subject to deflation and to periods of monetary stringency. While the Red Cross issue of 50 or 25 cigarettes per man per week came in regularly, and while there were fair stocks held, the cigarette currency suited its purpose admirably. But when the issue was interrupted, stocks ran out, prices fell, trading declined in volume and became increasingly a matter of barter. This deflationary tendency was periodically offset by the sudden injection of new currency. Private cigarette parcels arrived in a trickle throughout the year, but the big numbers came in quarterly when the Red Cross received its allocation of transport. Several hundred thousand cigarettes might arrive in the space of a fortnight. Prices soared, and then began to fall, slowly at first but with increasing rapidity as stocks ran out, until the next big delivery. Most of our economic troubles could be attributed to this fundamental instability.

PRICE MOVEMENTS

Many factors affected prices, the strongest and most noticeable being the periodical currency inflation and deflation described in the last paragraphs. The periodicity of this price cycle depended on cigarette and, to a far lesser extent, on food deliveries. At one time in the early days, before any private parcels had arrived and when there were no individual stocks, the weekly issue of cigarettes and food parcels occurred on a Monday. The non-monetary demand for cigarettes was great, and less elastic than the demand for food: consequently prices fluctuated weekly, falling towards Sunday night and rising sharply on Monday morning. Later, when many people held reserves, the weekly issue had no such effect, being too small a proportion of the total available. Credit allowed people with no reserves to meet their non-monetary demand over the week-end.

The general price level was affected by other factors. An influx of new prisoners, proverbially hungry, raised it. Heavy air raids in the vicinity of the camp probably increased the non-monetary demand for cigarettes and accentuated deflation. Good and bad war news certainly had its effect, and the general waves of optimism and pessimism which swept the camp were reflected in prices. Before breakfast one morning in March of this year, a rumour of the arrival of parcels and cigarettes was circulated. Within ten minutes I sold a treacle ration, for four cigarettes (hitherto offered in vain for three), and many similar deals went through. By 10 o'clock the rumour was denied, and treacle that day found no more buyers even at two cigarettes.

More interesting than changes in the general price level were changes in the price structure. Changes in the supply of a commodity, in the German ration scale or in the make-up of Red Cross parcels, would raise the price of one commodity relative to others. Tins of oatmeal, once a rare and much sought after luxury in the parcels, became a commonplace in 1943, and the price fell. In hot weather the demand for cocoa fell, and that for soap rose. A new recipe would be reflected in the price level: the discovery that raisins and sugar could be turned into an alcoholic liquor of remarkable potency reacted permanently on the dried fruit market. The invention of electric immersion heaters run off the power points made tea, a drug on the market in Italy, a certain seller in Germany.

In August, 1944, the supplies of parcels and cigarettes were both halved. Since both sides of the equation were changed in the same degree, changes in prices were not anticipated. But this was not the case: the non-monetary demand for cigarettes was less elastic than the demand for food, and food prices fell a little. More important however were the changes in the price structure. German margarine and jam, hitherto value-less owing to adequate supplies of Canadian butter and marmalade, acquired a new value. Chocolate, popular and a certain seller, and sugar, fell. Bread rose; several standing contracts of bread for cigarettes were broken, especially when the bread ration was reduced a few weeks later.

In February, 1945, the German soldier who drove the ration wagon was found to be willing to exchange loaves of bread at the rate of one loaf for a bar of chocolate. Those in the know began selling bread and buying chocolate, by then almost unsaleable in a period of serious deflation. Bread, at about 40, fell slightly; chocolate rose from 15; the supply of bread was not enough for the two commodities to reach parity, but the tendency was unmistakable.

The substitution of German margarine for Canadian butter when parcels were halved naturally affected their relative values, margarine appreciating at the expense of butter. Similarly, two brands of dried milk, hitherto differing in quality and therefore in price by five cigarettes a tin, came together in price as the wider substitution of the cheaper raised its relative value.

Enough has been cited to show that any change in conditions affected both the general price level and the price structure. It was this latter phenomenon which wrecked our planned economy.

PAPER CURRENCY—BULLY MARKS

Around D-Day, food and cigarettes were plentiful, business was brisk and the camp in an optimistic mood. Consequently the Entertainments Committee felt the moment opportune to launch a restaurant, where food and hot drinks were sold while a band and variety turns performed. Earlier experiments, both public and private, had pointed the way, and the scheme was a great success. Food was bought at market prices to provide the meals and the small profits were devoted to a reserve fund and used to bribe Germans to provide grease-paints and other necessities for the camp theatre. Originally meals were sold for cigarettes but this meant that the whole scheme was vulnerable to the periodic deflationary waves, and furthermore heavy smokers were unlikely to attend much. The whole success of the scheme depended on an adequate amount of food being offered for sale in the normal manner.

To increase and facilitate trade, and to stimulate supplies and customers therefore, and secondarily to avoid the worst effects of deflation when it should come, a paper currency was organised by the Restaurant and the Shop. The Shop bought food on behalf of the Restaurant with paper notes and the paper was accepted equally with the cigarettes in the Restaurant or Shop, and passed back to the Shop to purchase more food. The Shop acted as a bank of issue. The paper money was backed 100 per cent by food; hence its name, the Bully Mark. The BMk. was backed 100 per cent by food: there could be no over-issues, as is permissible with a normal bank of issue, since the eventual dispersal of the camp and consequent redemption of all BMk.s was anticipated in the near future.

Originally one BMk. was worth one cigarette and for a short time both circulated freely inside and outside the Restaurant. Prices were quoted in BMk.s and cigarettes with equal freedom—and for a short time the BMk. showed signs of replacing the cigarette as currency. The BMk. was tied to food, but not to cigarettes: as it was issued against food, say 45 for a tin of milk and so on, any reduction in the BMk. prices of food would have meant that there were unbacked BMk.s in circulation. But the price of both food and BMk.s could and did fluctuate with the supply of cigarettes.

While the Restaurant flourished, the scheme was a success: the Restaurant bought heavily, all foods were saleable and prices were stable.

In August parcels and cigarettes were halved and the Camp was bombed. The Restaurant closed for a short while and sales of food became difficult. Even when the Restaurant reopened, the food and cigarette shortage became increasingly acute and people were unwilling to convert such valuable goods into paper and to hold them for luxuries like snacks and tea. Less of the right kinds of food for the Restaurant were sold, and the Shop became glutted with dried fruit, chocolate, sugar, etc., which the Restaurant could not buy. The price level and the price structure changed. The BMk. fell to four-fifths of a cigarette and eventually farther still, and it became unacceptable save in the Restaurant. There was a flight from the BMk., no longer convertible into cigarettes or popular foods. The cigarette reestablished itself.

But the BMk. was sound! The Restaurant closed in the New Year with a progressive food shortage and the long evenings without lights due to intensified Allied air raids, and BMk.s could only be spent in the Coffee Bar—relict of the Restaurant—or on the few unpopular foods in the Shop, the owners of which were prepared to accept them. In the end all holders of BMk.s were paid in full, in cups of coffee or in prunes. People who had bought BMk.s for cigarettes or valuable jam or biscuits in their heyday were aggrieved that they should have stood the loss involved by their restricted choice, but they suffered no actual loss of market value.

PRICE FIXING

Along with this scheme came a determined attempt at a planned economy, at price fixing. The Medical Officer had long been anxious to control food sales, for fear of some people selling too much, to the detriment of their health. The deflationary waves and their effects on prices were inconvenient to all and would be dangerous to the Restaurant which had to carry stocks. Furthermore, unless the BMk. was convertible into cigarettes at about par it had little chance of gaining confidence and of succeeding as a currency. As has been explained, the BMk. was tied to food but could not be tied to cigarettes, which fluctuated in value. Hence, while BMk. prices of food were fixed for all time, cigarette prices of food and BMk.s varied.

The Shop, backed by the Senior British Officer, was now in a position to enforce price control both inside and outside its walls. Hitherto a standard price had been fixed for food left for sale in the Shop, and prices outside were roughly in conformity with this scale, which was recommended as a "guide" to sellers, but fluctuated a good deal around it. Sales in the Shop at recommended prices were apt to be slow though a good price might be obtained: sales outside could be made more quickly at lower prices. (If sales outside were to be at higher prices, goods

were withdrawn from the Shop until the recommended price rose: but the recommended price was sluggish and could not follow the market closely by reason of its very purpose, which was stability.) The Exchange and Mart notice boards came under the control of the Shop: advertisements which exceeded a 5 per cent departure from the recommended scale were liable to be crossed out by authority: unauthorised sales were discouraged by authority and also by public opinion, strongly in favour of a just and stable price. (Recommended prices were fixed partly from market data, partly on the advice of the M.O.)

At first the recommended scale was a success: the Restaurant, a big buyer, kept prices stable around this level: opinion and the 5 per cent tolerance helped. But when the price level fell with the August cuts and the price structure changed, the recommended scale was too rigid. Unchanged at first, as no deflation was expected, the scale was tardily lowered, but the prices of goods on the new scale remained in the same relation to one another, owing to the BMk., while on the market the price structure had changed. And the modifying influence of the Restaurant had gone. The scale was moved up and down several times, slowly following the inflationary and deflationary waves, but it was rarely adjusted to changes in the price structure. More and more advertisements were crossed off the board, and black market sales at unauthorised prices increased: eventually public opinion turned against the recommended scale and authority gave up the struggle. In the last few weeks, with unparalleled deflation, prices fell with alarming rapidity, no scales existed, and supply and demand, alone and unmellowed, determined prices.

PUBLIC OPINION

Public opinion on the subject of trading was vocal if confused and changeable, and generalisations as to its direction are difficult and dangerous. A tiny minority held that all trading was undesirable as it engendered an unsavoury atmosphere; occasional frauds and sharp practices were cited as proof. Certain forms of trading were more generally condemned; trade with the Germans was criticised by many. Red Cross toilet articles, which were in short supply and only issued in cases of actual need, were excluded from trade by law and opinion working in unshakable harmony. At one time, when there had been several cases of malnutrition reported among the more devoted smokers, no trade in German rations was permitted, as the victims became an additional burden on the depleted food reserves of the Hospital. But while certain activities were condemned as antisocial, trade itself was practised, and its utility appreciated, by almost everyone in the camp.

More interesting was opinion on middlemen and prices. Taken as a whole, opinion was hostile to the middleman. His function, and his hard work in bringing buyer and seller together, were ignored; profits were not regarded as a reward for labour, but as the result of sharp practices. Despite the fact that his very existence was proof to the contrary, the middleman was held to be redundant in view of the existence of an official Shop and the Exchange and Mart. Appreciation only came his way when he was willing to advance the price of a sugar ration, or to buy goods spot and carry them against a future sale. In these cases the element of risk was obvious to all, and the convenience of the service was felt to merit some reward. Particularly unpopular was the middleman with an element of monopoly, the man who contacted the ration wagon driver, or the man who utilised his knowledge of Urdu. And middlemen as a group were blamed for reducing prices. Opinion notwithstanding, most people dealt with a middleman, whether consciously or unconsciously, at some time or another.

There was a strong feeling that everything had its "just price" in cigarettes. While the assessment of the just price, which incidentally varied between camps, was impossible of explanation, this price was nevertheless pretty closely known. It can best be defined as the price usually fetched by an article in good times when cigarettes were plentiful. The "just price" changed slowly; it was unaffected by short-term variations in supply, and while opinion might be resigned to departures from the "just price", a strong feeling of resentment persisted. A more satisfactory definition of the "just price" is impossible. Everyone knew what it was, though no one could explain why it should be so.

As soon as prices began to fall with a cigarette shortage, a clamour arose, particularly against those who held reserves and who bought at reduced prices. Sellers at cut prices were criticised and their activities referred to as the black market. In every period of dearth the explosive question of "should nonsmokers receive a cigarette ration?" was discussed to profitless length. Unfortunately, it was the non-smoker, or the light smoker with his reserves, along with the hated middleman, who weathered the storm most easily.

The popularity of the price-fixing scheme, and such success as it enjoyed, were undoubtedly the result of this body of opinion. On several occasions the fall of prices was delayed by the general support given to the recommended scale. The onset of deflation was marked by a period of sluggish trade; prices stayed up but no one bought. Then prices fell on the black market, and the volume of trade revived in that quarter. Even when the recommended scale was revised, the volume of trade in the Shop would remain low. Opinion was always overruled by the hard facts of the market.

Curious arguments were advanced to justify price fixing. The recommended prices were in some way related to the caloric values of the foods offered hence some were overvalued and never sold at these prices. One argument ran as follows:—not everyone has private cigarette parcels: thus, when prices were high and trade good in the summer of 1944, only the lucky rich could buy. This was unfair to the man with few cigarettes. When prices fell in the following winter, prices should be pegged high so that the rich, who had enjoyed life in the summer, should put many cigarettes into circulation. The fact that those who sold to the rich in the summer had also enjoyed life then, and the fact that in the winter there was always someone willing to sell at low prices were ignored. Such arguments were hotly debated each night after the approach of Allied aircraft extinguished all lights at 8 p.m. But prices moved with the supply of cigarettes, and refused to stay fixed in accordance with a theory of ethics.

CONCLUSION

The economic organisation described was both elaborate and smooth-working in the summer of 1944. Then came the August cuts and deflation. Prices fell, rallied with deliveries of cigarette parcels in September and

December, and fell again. In January, 1945, supplies of Red Cross cigarettes ran out: and prices slumped still further: in February the supplies of food parcels were exhausted and the depression became a blizzard. Food, itself scarce, was almost given away in order to meet the non-monetary demand for cigarettes. Laundries ceased to operate, or worked for £s or RMk.s: food and cigarettes sold for fancy prices in £s, hitherto unheard of. The Restaurant was a memory and the BMk. a joke. The Shop was empty and the Exchange and Mart notices were full of unaccepted offers for cigarettes. Barter increased in volume, becoming a larger proportion of a smaller volume of trade. This, the first serious and prolonged food shortage in the writer's experience, caused the price structure to change again, partly because German rations were not easily divisible. A margarine ration gradually sank in value until it exchanged directly for a treacle ration. Sugar

slumped sadly. Only bread retained its value. Several thousand cigarettes, the capital of the Shop, were distributed without any noticeable effect. A few fractional parcel and cigarette issues, such as one-sixth of a parcel and twelve cigarettes each, led to momentary price recoveries and feverish trade, especially when they coincided with good news from the Western Front, but the general position remained unaltered.

By April, 1945, chaos had replaced order in the economic sphere: sales were difficult, prices lacked stability. Economics has been defined as the science of distributing limited means among unlimited and competing ends. On 12th April, with the arrival of elements of the 30th U.S. Infantry Division, the ushering in of an age of plenty demonstrated the hypothesis that with infinite means economic organisation and activity would be redundant, as every want could be satisfied without effort.

B. Identification of Markets and Market Institutions

4. Marketing Myopia

THEODORE LEVITT

Every major industry was once a growth industry. But some that are now riding a wave of growth enthusiasm are very much in the shadow of decline. Others which are thought of as seasoned growth industries have actually stopped growing. In every case the reason growth is threatened, slowed, or stopped is *not* because the market is saturated. It is because there has been a failure of management.

FATEFUL PURPOSES

The failure is at the top. The executives responsible for it, in the last analysis, are those who deal with broad aims and policies. Thus:

The railroads did not stop growing because the need for passenger and freight transportation declined. That grew. The railroads are in trouble today not because the need was filled by others (cars, trucks, airplanes, even telephones), but because it was *not* filled by the railroads themselves. They let others take customers away from them because they assumed themselves to be in the railroad business rather than in the transportation business. The reason they defined their industry wrong was because they were railroad-oriented instead of transportation-oriented; they were product-oriented instead of customer-oriented.

Hollywood barely escaped being totally

◆ SOURCE: Reprinted by permission from *Modern Marketing Strategy*, edited by Edward C. Bursk and John F. Chapman (Harvard University Press, 1964, by the President and Fellows of Harvard College): pp. 24–48.

ravished by television. Actually, all the established film companies went through drastic reorganizations. Some simply disappeared. All of them got into trouble not because of TV's inroads but because of their own myopia. As with the railroads, Hollywood defined its business incorrectly. It thought it was in the movie business when it was actually in the entertainment business. "Movies" implied a specific, limited product. This produced a fatuous contentment which from the beginning led producers to view TV as a threat. Hollywood scorned and rejected TV when it should have welcomed it as an opportunity— an opportunity to expand the entertainment business.

Today TV is a bigger business than the old narrowly defined movie business ever was. Had Hollywood been customer-oriented (providing entertainment), rather than product-oriented (making movies), would it have gone through the fiscal purgatory that it did? I doubt it. What ultimately saved Hollywood and accounted for its recent resurgence was the wave of new young writers, producers, and directors whose previous successes in television had decimated the old movie companies and toppled the big movie moguls.

There are other less obvious examples of industries that have been and are now endangering their futures by improperly defining their purposes. I shall discuss some in detail later and analyze the kind of policies that lead to trouble. Right now it may help to show what a thoroughly customer-oriented management *can* do to keep a growth industry growing, even after the obvious opportunities have been exhausted; and here there are two examples that have been around for a long time. They are nylon and glass—specifically, E. I. duPont de Nemours & Company and Corning Glass Works:

Both companies have great technical competence. Their product orientation is unquestioned. But this alone does not explain their success. After all, who was more pridefully product-oriented and product-conscious than the erstwhile New England textile companies that have been so thoroughly massacred? The DuPonts and the Cornings have succeeded not primarily because of their product or research orientation but because they have been thoroughly customer-oriented also. It is constant watchfulness for opportunities to apply their technical know-how to the creation of customer-satisfying uses which accounts for their prodigious output of successful new products. Without a very sophisticated eye on the customer, most of their new products might have been wrong, their sales methods useless.

Aluminum has also continued to be a growth industry, thanks to the efforts of two wartime-created companies which deliberately set about creating new customer-satisfying uses. Without Kaiser Aluminum & Chemical Corporation and Reynolds Metals Company, the total demand for aluminum today would be vastly less than it is.

Error of Analysis

Some may argue that it is foolish to set the railroads off against aluminum or the movies off against glass. Are not aluminum and glass naturally so versatile that the industries are bound to have more growth opportunities than the railroads and movies? This view commits precisely the error I have been talking about. It defines an industry, or a product, or a cluster of knowhow so narrowly as to guarantee its premature senescence. When we mention "railroads," we should make sure we mean "transportation." As transporters, the railroads still have a good chance for very considerable growth. They are not limited to the railroad business as such (though in my opinion rail transportation is potentially a much stronger transportation medium than is generally believed).

What the railroads lack is not opportunity, but some of the same managerial imaginativeness and audacity that made them great. Even an amateur like Jacques Barzun can see what is lacking when he says:

I grieve to see the most advanced physical and social organization of the last century go down in shabby disgrace for lack of the same comprehensive imagination that built it up. [What is lacking is] the will of the companies to survive and to satisfy the public by inventiveness and skill.[1]

SHADOW OF OBSOLESCENCE

It is impossible to mention a single major industry that did not at one time qualify for the magic appellation of "growth industry." In each case its assumed strength lay in the apparently unchallenged superiority of its product. There appeared to be no effective substitute for it. It was itself a runaway substitute for the product it so triumphantly replaced. Yet one after another of these celebrated industries has come under a shadow. Let us look briefly at a few more of them, this time taking examples that have so far received a little less attention:

Dry cleaning—This was once a growth industry with lavish prospects. In an age of wool garments, imagine being finally able to get them safely and easily clean. The boom was on.

Yet here we are 30 years after the boom started and the industry is in trouble. Where has the competition come from? From a better way of cleaning? No. It has come from synthetic fibers and chemical additives that have cut the need for dry cleaning. But this is only the beginning. Lurking in the wings and ready to make chemical dry cleaning totally obsolescent is that powerful magician, ultrasonics.

Electric utilities—This is another one of those supposedly "no-substitute" products that has been enthroned on a pedestal of invincible growth. When the incandescent lamp came along, kerosene lights were finished. Later the water wheel and the steam engine were cut to ribbons by the flexibility, reliability, simplicity, and just plain easy availability of electric motors. The prosperity of electric utilities continues to wax extravagant as the home is converted into a museum of electric gadgetry. How can anybody miss by investing in utilities, with no competition, nothing but growth ahead?

But a second look is not quite so comforting. A score of nonutility companies are well advanced toward developing a powerful

---

[1] Jacques Barzun, "Trains and the Mind of Man," *Holiday*, February 1960, p. 21.

chemical fuel cell which could sit in some hidden closet of every home silently ticking off electric power. The electric lines that vulgarize so many neighborhoods will be eliminated. So will the endless demolition of streets and service interruptions during storms. Also on the horizon is solar energy, again pioneered by nonutility companies.

Who says that the utilities have no competition? They may be natural monopolies now, but tomorrow they may be natural deaths. To avoid this prospect, they too will have to develop fuel cells, solar energy, and other power sources. To survive, they themselves will have to plot the obsolescence of what now produces their livelihood.

Grocery stores—Many people find it hard to realize that there ever was a thriving establishment known as the "corner grocery store." The supermarket has taken over with a powerful effectiveness. Yet the big food chains of the 1930's narrowly escaped being completely wiped out by the aggressive expansion of independent supermarkets. The first genuine supermarket was opened in 1930, in Jamaica, Long Island. By 1933 supermarkets were thriving in California, Ohio, Pennsylvania, and elsewhere. Yet the established chains pompously ignored them. When they chose to notice them, it was with such derisive descriptions as "cheapy," "horse-and-buggy," "cracker-barrel storekeeping," and "unethical opportunists."

The executive of one big chain announced at the time that he found it "hard to believe that people will drive for miles to shop for foods and sacrifice the personal service chains have perfected and to which Mrs. Consumer is accustomed."[2] As late as 1936, the National Wholesale Grocers convention and the New Jersey Retail Grocers Association said there was nothing to fear. They said that the supers' narrow appeal to the price buyer limited the size of their market. They had to draw from miles around. When imitators came, there would be wholesale liquidations as volume fell. The current high sales of the supers was said to be partly due to their novelty. Basically people wanted convenient neighborhood grocers. If the neighborhood stores "cooperate with their suppliers, pay attention to their costs, and improve their service," they would be able to weather the competition until it blew over.[3]

It never blew over. The chains discovered that survival required going into the supermarket business. This meant the wholesale destruction of their huge investments in corner store sites and in established distribution and merchandising methods. The companies with "the courage of their convictions" resolutely stuck to the corner store philosophy. They kept their pride but lost their shirts.

Self-Deceiving Cycle

But memories are short. For example, it is hard for people who today confidently hail the twin messiahs of electronics and chemicals to see how things could possibly go wrong with these galloping industries. They probably also cannot see how a reasonably sensible businessman could have been as myopic as the famous Boston millionaire who 50 years ago unintentionally sentenced his heirs to poverty by stipulating that his entire estate be forever invested exclusively in electric streetcar securities. His posthumous declaration, "There will always be a big demand for efficient urban transportation," is no consolation to his heirs who sustain life by pumping gasoline at automobile filling stations.

Yet, in a casual survey I recently took among a group of intelligent business executives, nearly half agreed that it would be hard to hurt their heirs by tying their estates forever to the electronics industry. When I then confronted them with the Boston streetcar example, they chorused unanimously, "That's different!" But is it? Is not the basic situation identical?

In truth, *there is no such thing* as a growth industry, I believe. There are only companies organized and operated to create and capitalize on growth opportunities. Industries that assume themselves to be riding some automatic growth escalator invariably descend into stagnation. The history of every dead and dying "growth" industry shows a self-deceiving cycle of bountiful expansion and undetected decay. There are four conditions which usually guarantee this cycle:

1. The belief that growth is assured by an expanding and more affluent population.

2. The belief that there is no competitive substitute for the industry's major product.

3. Too much faith in mass production and in the advantages of rapidly declining unit costs as output rises.

4. Preoccupation with a product that lends

[2] For more details see M. M. Zimmerman, *The Super Market: A Revolution in Distribution* (New York: McGraw-Hill, 1955), p. 48.

[3] *Ibid.*, pp. 45–47.

itself to carefully controlled scientific experimentation, improvement, and manufacturing cost reduction.

I should like now to begin examining each of these conditions in some detail. To build my case as boldly as possible, I shall illustrate the points with reference to three industries —petroleum, automobiles, and electronics— particularly petroleum, because it spans more years and more vicissitudes. Not only do these three have excellent reputations with the general public and also enjoy the confidence of sophisticated investors, but their managements have become known for progressive thinking in areas like financial control, product research, and management training. If obsolescence can cripple even these industries, it can happen anywhere.

POPULATION MYTH

The belief that profits are assured by an expanding and more affluent population is dear to the heart of every industry. It takes the edge off the apprehensions everybody understandably feels about the future. If consumers are multiplying and also buying more of your product or service, you can face the future with considerably more comfort than if the market is shrinking. An expanding market keeps the manufacturer from having to think very hard or imaginatively. If thinking is an intellectual response to a problem, then the absence of a problem leads to the absence of thinking. If your product has an automatically expanding market, then you will not give much thought to how to expand it.

One of the most interesting examples of this is provided by the petroleum industry. Probably our oldest growth industry, it has an enviable record. While there are some current apprehensions about its growth rate, the industry itself tends to be optimistic. But I believe it can be demonstrated that it is undergoing a fundamental yet typical change. It is not only ceasing to be a growth industry, but may actually be a declining one, relative to other business. Although there is widespread unawareness of it, I believe that within 25 years the oil industry may find itself in much the same position of retrospective glory that the railroads are now in. Despite its pioneering work in developing and applying the present-value method of investment evaluation, in employee relations, and in working

with backward countries, the petroleum business is a distressing example of how complacency and wrongheadedness can stubbornly convert opportunity into near disaster.

One of the characteristics of this and other industries that have believed very strongly in the beneficial consequences of an expanding population, while at the same time being industries with a generic product for which there has appeared to be no competitive substitute, is that the individual companies have sought to outdo their competitors by improving on what they are already doing. This makes sense, of course, if one assumes that sales are tied to the country's population strings, because the customer can compare products only on a feature-by-feature basis. I believe it is significant, for example, that not since John D. Rockefeller sent free kerosene lamps to China has the oil industry done anything really outstanding to create a demand for its product. Not even in product improvement has it showered itself with eminence. The greatest single improvement, namely, the development of tetraethyl lead, came from outside the industry, specifically from General Motors and DuPont. The big contributions made by the industry itself are confined to the technology of oil exploration, production, and refining.

Asking for Trouble

In other words, the industry's efforts have focused on improving the *efficiency* of getting and making its product, not really on improving the generic product or its marketing. Moreover, its chief product has continuously been defined in the narrowest possible terms, namely, gasoline, not energy, fuel, or transportation. This attitude has helped assure that:

1. Major improvements in gasoline quality tend not to originate in the oil industry. Also, the development of superior alternative fuels comes from outside the oil industry, as will be shown later.

2. Major innovations in automobile fuel marketing are originated by small new oil companies that are not primarily preoccupied with production or refining. These are the companies that have been responsible for the rapidly expanding multipump gasoline stations, with their successful emphasis on large and clean layouts, rapid and efficient drive-

way service, and quality gasoline at low prices.

Thus, the oil industry is asking for trouble from outsiders. Sooner or later, in this land of hungry inventors and entrepreneurs, a threat is sure to come. The possibilities of this will become more apparent when we turn to the next dangerous belief of many managements. For the sake of continuity, because this second belief is tied closely to the first, I shall continue with the same example.

Idea of Indispensability

The petroleum industry is pretty much persuaded that there is no competitive substitute for its major product, gasoline—or if there is, that it will continue to be a derivative of crude oil, such as diesel fuel or kerosene jet fuel.

There is a lot of automatic wishful thinking in this assumption. The trouble is that most refining companies own huge amounts of crude oil reserves. These have value only if there is a market for products into which oil can be converted—hence the tenacious belief in the continuing competitive superiority of automobile fuels made from crude oil.

This idea persists despite all historic evidence against it. The evidence not only shows that oil has never been a superior product for any purpose for very long, but it also shows that the oil industry has never really been a growth industry. It has been a succession of different businesses that have gone through the usual historic cycles of growth, maturity, and decay. Its over-all survival is owed to a series of miraculous escapes from total obsolescence, of last-minute and unexpected reprieves from total disaster reminiscent of the Perils of Pauline.

Perils of Petroleum

I shall sketch in only the main episodes:

First, crude oil was largely a patent medicine. But even before that fad ran out, demand was greatly expanded by the use of oil in kerosene lamps. The prospect of lighting the world's lamps gave rise to an extravagant promise of growth. The prospects were similar to those the industry now holds for gasoline in other parts of the world. It can hardly wait for the underdeveloped nations to get a car in every garage.

In the days of the kerosene lamp, the oil companies competed with each other and against gaslight by trying to improve the illuminating characteristics of kerosene. Then suddenly the impossible happened. Edison invented a light which was totally nondependent on crude oil. Had it not been for the growing use of kerosene in space heaters, the incandescent lamp would have completely finished oil as a growth industry at that time. Oil would have been good for little else than axle grease.

Then disaster and reprieve struck again. Two great innovations occurred, neither originating in the oil industry. The successful development of coal-burning domestic central-heating systems made the space heater obsolescent. While the industry reeled, along came its most magnificent boost yet—the internal combustion engine, also invented by outsiders. Then when the prodigious expansion for gasoline finally began to level off in the 1920's, along came the miraculous escape of a central oil heater. Once again, the escape was provided by an outsider's invention and development. And when that market weakened, wartime demand for aviation fuel came to the rescue. After the war the expansion of civilian aviation, the dieselization of railroads, and the explosive demand for cars and trucks kept the industry's growth in high gear.

Meanwhile centralized oil heating—whose boom potential had only recently been proclaimed—ran into severe competition from natural gas. While the oil companies themselves owned the gas that now competed with their oil, the industry did not originate the natural gas revolution, nor has it to this day greatly profited from its gas ownership. The gas revolution was made by newly formed transmission companies that marketed the product with an aggressive ardor. They started a magnificent new industry, first against the advice and then against the resistance of the oil companies.

By all the logic of the situation, the oil companies themselves should have made the gas revolution. They not only owned the gas; they also were the only people experienced in handling, scrubbing, and using it, the only people experienced in pipeline technology and transmission, and they understood heating problems. But, partly because they knew that natural gas would compete with their own sale of heating oil, the oil companies pooh-poohed the potentials of gas.

The revolution was finally started by oil pipeline executives who, unable to persuade their own companies to go into gas, quit and organized the spectacularly successful gas transmission companies. Even after their success became painfully evident to the oil companies, the latter did not go into gas transmission. The multibillion dollar business which should have been theirs went to others. As in the past, the industry was blinded by its narrow preoccupation with a specific product and the value of its reserves. It paid little or no attention to its customers' basic needs and preferences.

The postwar years have not witnessed any change. Immediately after World War II the oil industry was greatly encouraged about its future by the rapid expansion of demand for its traditional line of products. In 1950 most companies projected annual rates of domestic expansion of around 6% through at least 1975. Though the ratio of crude oil reserves to demand in the Free World was about 20 to 1, with 10 to 1 being usually considered a reasonable working ratio in the United States, booming demand sent oil men searching for more without sufficient regard to what the future really promised. In 1952 they "hit" in the Middle East; the ratio skyrocketed to 42 to 1. If gross additions to reserves continue at the average rate of the past five years (37 billion barrels annually), then by 1970 the reserve ratio will be up to 45 to 1. This abundance of oil has weakened crude and product prices all over the world.

Uncertain Future

Management cannot find much consolation today in the rapidly expanding petrochemical industry, another oil-using idea that did not originate in the leading firms. The total United States production of petrochemicals is equivalent to about 2% (by volume) of the demand for all petroleum products. Although the petrochemical industry is now expected to grow by about 10% per year, this will not offset other drains on the growth of crude oil consumption. Furthermore, while petrochemical products are many and growing, it is well to remember that there are nonpetroleum sources of the basic raw material, such as coal. Besides, a lot of plastics can be produced with relatively little oil. A 50,000-barrel-per-day oil refinery is now considered the absolute minimum size for efficiency. But a 5,000-barrel-per-day chemical plant is a giant operation.

Oil has never been a continuously strong growth industry. It has grown by fits and starts, always miraculously saved by innovations and developments not of its own making. The reason it has not grown in a smooth progression is that each time it thought it had a superior product safe from the possibility of competitive substitutes, the product turned out to be inferior and notoriously subject to obsolescence. Until now, gasoline (for motor fuel, anyhow) has escaped this fate. But, as we shall see later, it too may be on its last legs.

The point of all this is that there is no guarantee against product obsolescence. If a company's own research does not make it obsolete, another's will. Unless an industry is especially lucky, as oil has been until now, it can easily go down in a sea of red figures—just as the railroads have, as the buggy whip manufacturers have, as the corner grocery chains have, as most of the big movie companies have, and indeed as many other industries have.

The best way for a firm to be lucky is to make its own luck. That requires knowing what makes a business successful. One of the greatest enemies of this knowledge is mass production.

PRODUCTION PRESSURES

Mass-production industries are impelled by a great drive to produce all they can. The prospect of steeply declining unit costs as output rises is more than most companies can usually resist. The profit possibilities look spectacular. All effort focuses on production. The result is that marketing gets neglected.

John Kenneth Galbraith contends that just the opposite occurs.[4] Output is so prodigious that all effort concentrates on trying to get rid of it. He says this accounts for singing commercials, desecration of the countryside with advertising signs, and other wasteful and vulgar practices. Galbraith has a finger on something real, but he misses the strategic point. Mass production does indeed generate great pressure to "move" the product. But what usually gets emphasized is selling, not marketing. Marketing, being a more sophisticated and complex process, gets ignored.

The difference between marketing and selling is more than semantic. Selling focuses on the needs of the seller, marketing on the needs of the buyer. Selling is preoccupied

---

4 *The Affluent Society* (Boston: Houghton Mifflin, 1958), pp. 152–160.

with the seller's need to convert his product into cash; marketing with the idea of satisfying the needs of the customer by means of the product and the whole cluster of things associated with creating, delivering, and finally consuming it.

In some industries the enticements of full mass production have been so powerful that for many years top management in effect has told the sales departments, "You get rid of it; we'll worry about profits." By contrast, a truly marketing-minded firm tries to create value-satisfying goods and services that consumers will want to buy. What it offers for sale includes not only the generic product or service, but also how it is made available to the customer, in what form, when, under what conditions, and at what terms of trade. Most important, what it offers for sale is determined not by the seller but by the buyer. The seller takes his cues from the buyer in such a way that the product becomes a consequence of the marketing effort, not vice versa.

Lag in Detroit

This may sound like an elementary rule of business, but that does not keep it from being violated wholesale. It is certainly more violated than honored. Take the automobile industry:

Here mass production is most famous, most honored, and has the greatest impact on the entire society. The industry has hitched its fortune to the relentless requirements of the annual model change, a policy that makes customer orientation an especially urgent necessity. Consequently the auto companies annually spend millions of dollars on consumer research. But the fact that the new compact cars are selling so well in their first year indicates that Detroit's vast researchers have for a long time failed to reveal what the customer really wanted. Detroit was not persuaded that he wanted anything different from what he had been getting until it lost millions of customers to other small car manufacturers.

How could this unbelievable lag behind consumer wants have been perpetuated so long? Why did not research reveal consumer preferences before consumers' buying decisions themselves revealed the facts? Is that not what consumer research is for—to find out before the fact what is going to happen? The answer is that Detroit never really researched the customer's wants. It only researched his preferences between the kinds of things which it had already decided to offer him. For Detroit is mainly product-oriented, not customer-oriented. To the extent that the customer is recognized as having needs that the manufacturer should try to satisfy, Detroit usually acts as if the job can be done entirely by product changes. Occasionally attention gets paid to financing, too, but that is done more in order to sell than to enable the customer to buy.

As for taking care of other customer needs, there is not enough being done to write about. The areas of the greatest unsatisfied needs are ignored, or at best get stepchild attention. These are at the point of sale and on the matter of automotive repair and maintenance. Detroit views these problem areas as being of secondary importance. That is underscored by the fact that the retailing and servicing ends of this industry are neither owned and operated nor controlled by the manufacturers. Once the car is produced, things are pretty much in the dealer's inadequate hands. Illustrative of Detroit's arm's-length attitude is the fact that, while servicing holds enormous sales-stimulating, profit-building opportunities, only 57 of Chevrolet's 7,000 dealers provide night maintenance service.

Motorists repeatedly express their dissatisfaction with servicing and their apprehensions about buying cars under the present selling setup. The anxieties and problems they encounter during the auto buying and maintenance processes are probably more intense and widespread today than 30 years ago. Yet the automobile companies do not *seem* to listen to or take their cues from the anguished consumer. If they do listen, it must be through the filter of their own preoccupation with production. The marketing effort is still viewed as a necessary consequence of the product, not vice versa, as it should be. That is the legacy of mass production, with its parochial view that profit resides essentially in low-cost full production.

What Ford Put First

The profit lure of mass production obviously has a place in the plans and strategy of business management, but it must always *follow* hard thinking about the customer. This is one of the most important lessons that we can learn from the contradictory behavior of

Henry Ford. In a sense Ford was both the most brilliant and the most senseless marketer in American history. He was senseless because he refused to give the customer anything but a black car. He was brilliant because he fashioned a production system designed to fit market needs. We habitually celebrate him for the wrong reason, his production genius. His real genius was marketing. We think he was able to cut his selling price and therefore sell millions of $500 cars because his invention of the assembly line had reduced the costs. Actually he invented the assembly line because he had concluded that at $500 he could sell millions of cars. Mass production was the *result* not the cause of his low prices.

Ford repeatedly emphasized this point, but a nation of production-oriented business managers refuses to hear the great lesson he taught. Here is his operating philosophy as he expressed it succinctly:

Our policy is to reduce the price, extend the operations, and improve the article. You will notice that the reduction of price comes first. We have never considered any costs as fixed. Therefore we first reduce the price to the point where we believe more sales will result. Then we go ahead and try to make the prices. We do not bother about the costs. The new price forces the costs down. The more usual way is to take the costs and then determine the price, and although that method may be scientific in the narrow sense; it is not scientific in the broad sense, because what earthly use is it to know the cost if it tells you that you cannot manufacture at a price at which the article can be sold? But more to the point is the fact that, although one may calculate what a cost is, and of course all of our costs are carefully calculated, no one knows what a cost ought to be. One of the ways of discovering . . . is to name a price so low as to force everybody in the place to the highest point of efficiency. The low price makes everybody dig for profits. We make more discoveries concerning manufacturing and selling under this forced method than by any method of leisurely investigation.[5]

Product Provincialism

The tantalizing profit possibilities of low unit production costs may be the most seriously self-deceiving attitude that can afflict

a company, particularly a "growth" company where an apparently assured expansion of demand already tends to undermine a proper concern for the importance of marketing and the customer.

The usual result of this narrow preoccupation with so-called concrete matters is that instead of growing, the industry declines. It usually means that the product fails to adapt to the constantly changing patterns of consumer needs and tastes, to new and modified marketing institutions and practices, or to product developments in competing or complementary industries. The industry has its eyes so firmly on its own specific product that it does not see how it is being made obsolete.

The classical example of this is the buggy whip industry. No amount of product improvement could stave off its death sentence. But had the industry defined itself as being in the transportation business rather than the buggy whip business, it might have survived. It would have done what survival always entails, that is, changing. Even if it had only defined its business as providing a stimulant or catalyst to an energy source, it might have survived by becoming a manufacturer of, say, fanbelts or air cleaners.

What may some day be a still more classical example is, again, the oil industry. Having let others steal marvelous opportunities from it (e.g., natural gas, as already mentioned, missile fuels, and jet engine lubricants), one would expect it to have taken steps never to let that happen again. But this is not the case. We are now getting extraordinary new developments in fuel systems specifically designed to power automobiles. Not only are these developments concentrated in firms outside the petroleum industry, but petroleum is almost systematically ignoring them, securely content in its wedded bliss to oil. It is the story of the kerosene lamp versus the incandescent lamp all over again. Oil is trying to improve hydrocarbon fuels rather than to develop *any* fuels best suited to the needs of their users, whether or not made in different ways and with different raw materials from oil.

Here are some of the things which nonpetroleum companies are working on:

Over a dozen such firms now have advanced working models of energy systems which, when perfected, will replace the internal combustion engine and eliminate the demand for gasoline. The superior merit of each of these systems is their elimination of

---

[5] Henry Ford, *My Life and Work* (New York: Doubleday, Page, 1923), pp. 146–147.

frequent, time-consuming, and irritating refueling stops. Most of these systems are fuel cells designed to create electrical energy directly from chemicals without combustion. Most of them use chemicals that are not derived from oil, generally hydrogen and oxygen.

Several other companies have advanced models of electric storage batteries designed to power automobiles. One of these is an aircraft producer that is working jointly with several electric utility companies. The latter hope to use off-peak generating capacity to supply overnight plug-in battery regeneration. Another company, also using the battery approach, is a medium-size electronics firm with extensive small-battery experience that it developed in connection with its work on hearing aids. It is collaborating with an automobile manufacturer. Recent improvements arising from the need for high-powered miniature power storage plants in rockets have put us within reach of a relatively small battery capable of withstanding great overloads or surges of power. Germanium diode applications and batteries using sintered-plate and nickel-cadmium techniques promise to make a revolution in our energy sources.

Solar energy conversion systems are also getting increasing attention. One usually cautious Detroit auto executive recently ventured that solar-powered cars might be common by 1980.

As for the oil companies, they are more or less "watching developments," as one research director put it to me. A few are doing a bit of research on fuel cells, but almost always confined to developing cells powered by hydrocarbon chemicals. None of them are enthusiastically researching fuel cells, batteries, or solar power plants. None of them are spending a fraction as much on research in these profoundly important areas as they are on the usual run-of-the-mill things like reducing combustion chamber deposit in gasoline engines. One major integrated petroleum company recently took a tentative look at the fuel cell and concluded that although "the companies actively working on it indicate a belief in ultimate success . . . the timing and magnitude of its impact are too remote to warrant recognition in our forecasts."

One might, of course, ask: Why should the oil companies do anything different? Would not chemical fuel cells, batteries, or solar energy kill the present product lines? The answer is that they would indeed, and that

is precisely the reason for the oil firms having to develop these power units before their competitors, so they will not be companies without an industry.

Management might be more likely to do what is needed for its own preservation, if it thought of itself as being in the energy business. But even that would not be enough if it persists in imprisoning itself in the narrow grip of its tight product orientation. It has to think of itself as taking care of customer needs, not finding, refining, or even selling oil. Once it genuinely thinks of its business as taking care of people's transportation needs, nothing can stop it from creating its own extravagantly profitable growth.

Creative Destruction

Since words are cheap and deeds are dear it may be appropriate to indicate what this kind of thinking involves and leads to. Let us start at the beginning—the customer. It can be shown that motorists strongly dislike the bother, delay, and experience of buying gasoline. People actually do not buy gasoline. They cannot see it, taste it, feel it, appreciate it, or really test it. What they buy is the right to continue driving their cars. The gas station is like a tax collector to whom people are compelled to pay a periodic toll as the price of using their cars. This makes the gas station a basically unpopular institution. It can never be made popular or pleasant, only less unpopular, less unpleasant.

To reduce its unpopularity completely means eliminating it. Nobody likes a tax collector, not even a pleasantly cheerful one. Nobody likes to interrupt a trip to buy a phantom product, not even from a handsome Adonis or a seductive Venus. Hence, companies that are working on exotic fuel substitutes which will eliminate the need for frequent refueling are heading directly into the outstretched arms of the irritated motorist. They are riding a wave of inevitability, not because they are creating something which is technologically superior or more sophisticated, but because they are satisfying a powerful customer need. They are also eliminating noxious odors and air pollution.

Once the petroleum companies recognize the customer-satisfying logic of what another power system can do, they will see that they have no more choice about working on an efficient, long-lasting fuel (or some way of delivering present fuels without bothering the motorist) than the big food chains had a choice about going into the supermarket business, or the vacuum tube companies had a choice about making semiconductors. For their own good the oil firms will have to destroy their own highly profitable assets. No amount of wishful thinking can save them from the necessity of engaging in this form of "creative destruction."

I phrase the need as strongly as this because I think management must make quite an effort to break itself loose from conventional ways. It is all too easy in this day and age for a company or industry to let its sense of purpose become dominated by the economies of full production and to develop a dangerously lopsided product orientation. In short, if management lets itself drift, it invariably drifts in the direction of thinking of itself as producing goods and services, not customer satisfactions. While it probably will not descend to the depths of telling its salesmen, "You get rid of it; we'll worry about profits," it can, without knowing it, be practicing precisely that formula for withering decay. The historic fate of one growth industry after another has been its suicidal product provincialism.

DANGERS OF R & D

Another big danger to a firm's continued growth arises when top management is wholly transfixed by the profit possibilities of technical research and development. To illustrate I shall turn first to a new industry—electronics—and then return once more to the oil companies. By comparing a fresh example with a familiar one, I hope to emphasize the prevalence and insidiousness of a hazardous way of thinking.

Marketing Shortchanged

In the case of electronics, the greatest danger which faces the glamorous new companies in this field is not that they do not pay enough attention to research and development, but that they pay *too* much attention to it. And the fact that the fastest growing electronics firms owe their eminence to their heavy emphasis on technical research is completely beside the point. They have vaulted to affluence on a sudden crest of unusually strong general receptiveness to new technical ideas. Also, their

success has been shaped in the virtually guaranteed market of military subsidies and by military orders that in many cases actually preceded the existence of facilities to make the products. Their expansion has, in other words, been almost totally devoid of marketing effort.

Thus, they are growing up under conditions that come dangerously close to creating the illusion that a superior product will sell itself. Having created a successful company by making a superior product, it is not surprising that management continues to be oriented toward the product rather than the people who consume it. It develops the philosophy that continued growth is a matter of continued product innovation and improvement.

A number of other factors tend to strengthen and sustain this belief:

1. Because electronic products are highly complex and sophisticated, managements become topheavy with engineers and scientists. This creates a selective bias in favor of research and production at the expense of marketing. The organization tends to view itself as making things rather than satisfying customer needs. Marketing gets treated as a residual activity, "something else" that must be done once the vital job of product creation and production is completed.

2. To this bias in favor of product research, development, and production is added the bias in favor of dealing with controllable variables. Engineers and scientists are at home in the world of concrete things like machines, test tubes, production lines, and even balance sheets. The abstractions to which they feel kindly are those which are testable or manipulatable in the laboratory, or, if not testable, then functional, such as Euclid's axioms. In short, the managements of the new glamourgrowth companies tend to favor those business activities which lend themselves to careful study, experimentation, and control—the hard, practical, realities of the lab, the shop, the books.

What gets shortchanged are the realities of the *market*. Consumers are unpredictable, varied, fickle, stupid, shortsighted, stubborn, and generally bothersome. This is not what the engineer-managers say, but deep down in their consciousness it is what they believe. And this accounts for their concentrating on what they know and what they can control, namely, product research, engineering, and production. The emphasis on production becomes particularly attractive when the product can be made at declining unit costs. There is no more inviting way of making money than by running the plant full blast.

Today the top-heavy science-engineering-production orientation of so many electronics companies works reasonably well because they are pushing into new frontiers in which the armed services have pioneered virtually assured markets. The companies are in the felicitous position of having to fill, not find markets; of not having to discover what the customer needs and wants, but of having the customer voluntarily come forward with specific new product demands. If a team of consultants had been assigned specifically to design a business situation calculated to prevent the emergence and development of a customer-oriented marketing viewpoint, it could not have produced anything better than the conditions just described.

Stepchild Treatment

The oil industry is a stunning example of how science, technology, and mass production can divert an entire group of companies from their main task. To the extent the consumer is studied at all (which is not much), the focus is forever on getting information which is designed to help the oil companies improve what they are now doing. They try to discover more convincing advertising themes, more effective sales promotional drives, what the market shares of the various companies are, what people like or dislike about service station dealers and oil companies, and so forth. Nobody seems as interested in probing deeply into the basic human needs that the industry might be trying to satisfy as in probing into the basic properties of the raw material that the companies work with in trying to deliver customer satisfactions.

Basic questions about customers and markets seldom get asked. The latter occupy a stepchild status. They are recognized as existing, as having to be taken care of, but not worth very much real thought or dedicated attention. Nobody gets as excited about the customers in his own backyard as about the oil in the Sahara Desert. Nothing illustrates better the neglect of marketing than its treatment in the industry press.

The centennial issue of the *American Petroleum Institute Quarterly*, published in 1959 to celebrate the discovery of oil in Titusville, Pennsylvania, contained 21 feature articles proclaiming the industry's greatness. Only one of these talked about its achievements in marketing, and that was only a pictorial record of how service station architecture has changed. The issue also contained a special section on "New Horizons," which was devoted to showing the magnificent role oil would play in America's future. Every reference was ebulliently optimistic, never implying once that oil might have some hard competition. Even the reference to atomic energy was a cheerful catalogue of how oil would help make atomic energy a success. There was not a single apprehension that the oil industry's affluence might be threatened or a suggestion that one "new horizon" might include new and better ways of serving oil's present customers.

But the most revealing example of the stepchild treatment that marketing gets was still another special series of short articles on "The Revolutionary Potential of Electronics." Under that heading this list of articles appeared in the table of contents: "In the Search for Oil," "In Production Operation," "In Refinery Processes," "In Pipeline Operations."

Significantly, every one of the industry's major functional areas is listed, *except* marketing. Why? Either it is believed that electronics holds no revolutionary potential for petroleum marketing (which is palpably wrong), or the editors forgot to discuss marketing (which is more likely, and illustrates its stepchild status).

The order in which the four functional areas are listed also betrays the alienation of the oil industry from the consumer. The industry is implicitly defined as beginning with the search for oil and ending with its distribution from the refinery. But the truth is, it seems to me, that the industry begins with the needs of the customer for its products. From the primal position its definition moves steadily backstream to areas of progressively lesser importance, until it finally comes to rest at the "search for oil."

Beginning and End

The view that an industry is a customer-satisfying process, not a goods-producing process, is vital for all businessmen to understand. An industry begins with the customer and his needs, not with a patent, a raw material, or a selling skill. Given the customer's needs, the industry develops backwards, first concerning itself with the physical *delivery* of customer satisfactions. Then it moves back further to *creating* the things by which these satisfactions are in part achieved. How these materials are created is a matter of indifference to the customer, hence the particular form of manufacturing, processing, or what-have-you cannot be considered as a vital aspect of the industry. Finally, the industry moves back still further to *finding* the raw materials necessary for making its products.

The irony of some industries oriented toward technical research and development is that the scientists who occupy the high executive positions are totally unscientific when it comes to defining their companies' over-all needs and purposes. They violate the first two rules of the scientific method—being aware of and defining their companies' problems, and then developing testable hypotheses about solving them. They are scientific only about the convenient things, such as laboratory and product experiments. The reason that the customer (and the satisfaction of his deepest needs) is not considered as being "the problem" is not because there is any certain belief that no such problem exists, but because an organizational lifetime has conditioned management to look in the opposite direction. Marketing is a stepchild.

I do not mean that selling is ignored. Far from it. But selling, again, is not marketing. As already pointed out, selling concerns itself with the tricks and techniques of getting people to exchange their cash for your product. It is not concerned with the values that the exchange is all about. And it does not, as marketing invariably does, view the entire business process as consisting of a tightly integrated effort to discover, create, arouse, and satisfy customer needs. The customer is somebody "out there" who, with proper cunning, can be separated from his loose change.

Actually, not even selling gets much attention in some technologically minded firms. Because there is a virtually guaranteed market for the abundant flow of their new products, they do not actually know what a real market is. It is as if they lived in a planned economy, moving their products routinely from factory to retail outlet. Their successful concentration on products tends to convince them of the soundness of what they have been doing, and they fail to see the gathering clouds over the market.

CONCLUSION

Less than 75 years ago American railroads enjoyed a fierce loyalty among astute Wall Streeters. European monarchs invested in them heavily. Eternal wealth was thought to be the benediction for anybody who could scrape a few thousand dollars together to put into rail stocks. No other form of transportation could compete with the railroads in speed, flexibility, durability, economy, and growth potentials. As Jacques Barzun put it, "By the turn of the century it was an institution, an image of man, a tradition, a code of honor, a source of poetry, a nursery of boyhood desires, a sublimest of toys, and the most solemn machine—next to the funeral hearse—that marks the epochs in man's life."[6]

Even after the advent of automobiles, trucks, and airplanes, the railroad tycoons remained imperturbably self-confident. If you had told them 60 years ago that in 30 years they would be flat on their backs, broke, and pleading for government subsidies, they would have thought you totally demented. Such a future was simply not considered possible. It was not even a discussable subject, or an askable question, or a matter which any sane person would consider worth speculating about. The very thought was insane. Yet a lot of insane notions now have matter-of-fact acceptance—for example, the idea of 100-ton tubes of metal moving smoothly through the air 20,000 feet above the earth, loaded with 100 sane and solid citizens casually drinking martinis—and they have dealt cruel blows to the railroads.

What specifically must other companies do to avoid this fate? What does customer orientation involve? These questions have in part been answered by the preceding examples and analysis. It would take another article to show in detail what is required for specific industries. In any case, it should be obvious that building an effective customer-oriented company involves far more than good intentions or promotional tricks; it involves profound matters of human organization and leadership. For the present, let me merely suggest what appear to be some general requirements.

---

[6] *Op. cit.*, p. 20.

Visceral Feel of Greatness

Obviously the company has to do what survival demands. It has to adapt to the requirements of the market, and it has to do it sooner rather than later. But mere survival is a so-so aspiration. Anybody can survive in some way or other, even the skid-row bum. The trick is to survive gallantly, to feel the surging impulse of commercial mastery; not just to experience the sweet smell of success, but to have the visceral feel of entrepreneurial greatness.

No organization can achieve greatness without a vigorous leader who is driven onward by his own pulsating *will to succeed*. He has to have a vision of grandeur, a vision that can produce eager followers in vast numbers. In business, the followers are the customers. To produce these customers, the entire corporation must be viewed as a customer-creating and customer-satisfying organism. Management must think of itself not as producing products but as providing customer-creating value satisfactions. It must push this idea (and everything it means and requires) into every nook and cranny of the organization. It has to do this continuously and with the kind of flair that excites and stimulates the people in it. Otherwise, the company will be merely a series of pigeon-holed parts, with no consolidating sense of purpose or direction.

In short, the organization must learn to think of itself not as producing goods or services but as *buying customers*, as doing the things that will make people *want* to do business with it. And the chief executive himself has the inescapable responsibility for creating this environment, this viewpoint, this attitude, this aspiration. He himself must set the company's style, its direction, and its goals. This means he has to know precisely where he himself wants to go, and to make sure the whole organization is enthusiastically aware of where that is. This is a first requisite of leadership, for *unless he knows where he is going, any road will take him there.*

If any road is okay, the chief executive might as well pack his attaché case and go fishing. If an organization does not know or care where it is going, it does not need to advertise that fact with a ceremonial figurehead. Everybody will notice it soon enough.

5. Research and the Marketing Concept

W. B. REYNOLDS

Marketing literature has for some time devoted space to the so-called total marketing concept in American business and has developed a substantial rationale for the benefits which potentially can be derived through the intelligent application of the concept. I emphasize the words "intelligent application of the concept" since a few marketing experts seem to feel that total marketing concept means turning over management of all aspects of the company's business to them. These people are delighted by articles such as that by Theodore Levitt entitled "Marketing Myopia" which appeared in the *Harvard Business Review* of July-August, 1960. That this article is filled with sweeping generalizations based upon factual distortion seems to escape them.

If the total marketing concept is an opportunity to reappraise marketing thinking, it at the same time makes demands upon marketing organizations which they must realistically face. One of the most important of these demands is the understanding of the proper relationship between the total marketing concept and the intelligent use of research and development.

A successful manufacturing corporation today rests upon three essential bases—(1) an informed, aggressive and intelligent executive management, (2) sound marketing concepts

administered by superior marketing management, and (3) sound technology developed by superior scientific and technological personnel. Enlightened executive management will see to it that a proper partnership develops between marketing and technology and that neither becomes subservient to the other. Each has an important and easily defined area of basic contribution requiring a high degree of creativity and innovation. Creativity thrives best when free of undue pressure and domination.

Since authors like Mr. Levitt are reaching unwarranted conclusions based upon irrelevant or incorrect facts, I should like to reexamine the general area of the Marketing-Research relationship.

At the outset I want to make it clear that I agree thoroughly with Mr. Levitt's thesis that marketing has been frequently neglected and that many companies and even a few industries have declined because of what Levitt terms "marketing myopia." Levitt's basic fallacy is not that he emphasizes the marketing concept but that he suffers from acute technological myopia.

Permit me to illustrate by referring to the petroleum industry which seems to be Mr. Levitt's favorite whipping boy. Although Levitt's "Perils of Pauline" analogy is clever journalism, it completely begs the question of the greatness of today's industry. What happened during the first 50 years after Col. Drake spudded in his first well at Titusville is rather academic at this stage. Any new industry in a nineteenth-century environment was likely to experience growing pains. But

◆ SOURCE Reprinted by permission from *Marketing Innovations*, Proceedings of the 8th Biennial Marketing Institute, American Marketing Association, Minnesota Chapter, November 1961, pp. 14–21.

the petroleum industry was never in any real danger of demise as Levitt implies because petroleum was then and still is inherently the cheapest practical source of energy and it will continue to be so in the forseeable future. And modern civilization, friend Levitt, is based upon cheap energy. The petroleum industry has developed to its present enormous strength and virility because it has used sound technology to provide a better product at lower prices. And it has never lost sight of its basic mission of finding and exploiting the cheapest sources of fossil carbonaceous deposits.

To assert that the petroleum industry is in the energy business and should, therefore, quickly jump into atomic energy, fuel cell technology or any other energy producing or converting innovation that happens along without regard for the technological "fitness" for so doing is an error as grave as marketing myopia. Take the fuel cell.

Mr. Levitt castigates the petroleum industry for its "watch and wait" attitude on fuel cell technology. To quote: "We are now getting extraordinary new developments in fuel systems specifically designed to power automobiles. . . . Over a dozen firms now have advanced working models of energy systems which, when perfected, will replace the internal combustion engine and eliminate the demand for gasoline." end quote. Specifically this weird generalization seems to be based upon the fuel cell, storage batteries, and solar energy converters. And Mr. Levitt complains that none of the oil companies are enthusiastically researching fuel cells, batteries, or solar power plants. Here his technological myopia is quite evident.

In the first place, none of these represents a serious immediate threat to gasoline as the prime fuel for automobiles. A moment's reflection should make this obvious. The only presently developed practical fuel for the fuel cell is hydrogen. Can you imagine an automobile powered with hydrogen? Hydrogen is a light gas which cannot be liquified under any practical conditions for use in automobiles. Even under very high pressures which would require enormously heavy cylinders a practical amount of hydrogen could not be carried in an automobile. And to cap it all, hydrogen is one of the most highly explosive substances known, when mixed with air. A hydrogen cylinder leak in a home garage could blow a whole neighborhood apart. In short, hydrogen will not be used to power automobiles. If it is ever used to power stationary engines or generate electrical power, it will doubtless be obtained from methane, a petroleum product.

Because of these considerations the oil companies have worked with hydrocarbons as fuel for cells. This is the only practical approach for moving power plant use and was motivated by sound technical considerations, not an obsession with their basic raw material as Levitt contends.

The use of batteries and solar cells to power automobiles is equally impractical. The last time I used a battery-powered golf cart both the battery and my patience gave out on the fourteenth fairway. The new gasoline-powered golf carts are rapidly taking over. Even assuming great technical progress in batteries and solar cells, they cannot be regarded as more than very long-range technical possibilities. The petroleum industry has quite correctly adopted a wait-and-see attitude. In the first place, the odds are strongly in favor of petroleum fuels, and in the second place the technology involved in batteries and solar cells doesn't fit. A company should move into an entirely new field of technology only when there are compelling reasons such as unusual profit opportunities or a dire and imminent threat to present lines. Finally, the timing of potential obsolescence of motor fuel by *anything* is such that the oil industry will have at least ten years warning of a serious threat. To dilute its efforts today by moving away from established technology into an entirely new technology (in this instance electronics and electrical equipment) because of a minor and long-range threat just doesn't represent sound business judgment for the petroleum industry.

The petroleum industry is basically engaged in finding, producing and upgrading fossil deposits. In this they have had preeminent success. Mr. Levitt is quite incorrect in his statement that ". . . major improvements in gasoline quality tend not to originate in the oil industry." On the contrary, *all* major improvements in gasoline quality, with the possible exception of tetra ethyl lead, have originated in the oil industry, e.g., thermal cracking, catalytic cracking, catalytic reforming, alkylation, etc., etc. The octane rating and other performance characteristics of unleaded gasolines have consistently improved from year to year. Tetra ethyl lead was discovered by Thomas Midgeley, who took it to DuPont for production because DuPont was technologically qualified to produce it. It remained in the chemical industry because that was where it belonged technologically. On the other hand, petrochemical technology does fit the petroleum industry and many petroleum companies now derive a substantial percentage of their profit from petrochemicals. Levitt feels that petroleum management cannot find much consolation today in the rapidly expanding petrochemical industry since petrochemicals represent only 2% of the volume of oil processed. But, in fact, petrochemicals represent a much higher percentage of the *value* of hydrocarbons processed. It is not unusual for a petrochemical to sell for 50 to 100 times the value of the hydrocarbon from which it was made. The oil companies have moved rapidly into petrochemicals because the technology is right.

To emphasize the marketing myopia of the oil industry Levitt points out that gasoline users strongly dislike the bother, delay and experience of buying gasoline. Hence, the industry must quickly develop an efficient, long-lasting fuel to eliminate filling-station stops. I might point out to Mr. Levitt that there is also great popular demand for a safe, economical magic carpet and a really workable Aladdin's lamp. Where does Mr. Levitt suggest we look for this magic fuel? Atomic energy? Fuel cell? Solar devices? The petroleum companies are in the business of producing and upgrading *oil*. A company must put its research dollars into technological areas with the maximum chance of success. Otherwise like Ponce de Leon, they will die withered and frustrated. In connection with the utility of that great American institution, the filling station, I might parenthetically ask Mr. Levitt if he has ever taken a motor vacation with a carload of youngsters.

I have dwelt upon Levitt's treatment of the petroleum industry for the purpose of making a single point, namely, that the total marketing concept cannot be successful unless it is administered wisely in the light of sound technological considerations. As marketing men you have not only an opportunity but a compelling responsibility to know and understand important aspects of the technology underlying your field of interest and to benefit by what that technology can bring to your company in the way of new product opportunities.

Levitt says that an industry begins with the customer and his needs, not with a patent, a raw material or a selling skill. But I submit, on the contrary, that most new industries have grown out of technological progress leading to the development of new products which fulfill basic human needs. Dr. Wallace Carothers developed nylon, not because marketing people were clamoring for a synthetic fiber, but because his fundamental research on polyamide resins revealed that these resins had interesting fiber-forming characteristics. The great, modern plastics industry has grown from exploratory research on high polymers which, for the most part, was not slanted toward any particular market needs. Once these new products were developed, effort was then directed toward their place in the market and, if no need was apparent, extensive applications research and market development soon found many customers, frequently in unexpected places.

For some time after polyethylene was discovered there was little demand for it. Little by little, new uses were found and, most important, the price was brought down through intensive research until today sales of this product approach half a billion dollars annually. This achievement was brought about by a successful marriage of marketing and technology. And the flow was fundamental research, new products, applications research, new end product, marketing and sales to the customer, not the Levittized or backward process. The customer demand for most polyethylene products did not exist until it was created by creative applications research and marketing. And I might say parenthetically that most of the creative marketing in polyethylene and polypropylene has been carried out by the petroleum industry, whose development of low-cost olefins has made the whole thing possible.

Please do not interpret my strong disagreement with Mr. Levitt's version of the marketing concept as a lack of appreciation for the value of an enlightened total marketing concept. Whereas Levitt castigates technology and scientists in management and downgrades unreasonably the position of technology in the profit picture, an enlightened marketing concept will exploit to the utmost the contributions of technology.

In my discussion today I have been asked to emphasize the decision-making process in new product development. One of the most basic decisions executive management and marketing management must make relative to new products is whether or not *all* research projects should arise from consumer studies and marketing research. If this decision is affirmative, I submit that executive and marketing management suffer from techno'◟ical myopia and have, per se, cut themselves away from tremendous profit possibilities. As I have pointed out, many of the most highly profitable new products have resulted from unexpected discoveries made during the course of fundamental and exploratory research. These products would never have been developed as an answer to consumer wants arising from marketing research for the twofold reason that the consumer want often was not recognized *a priori* and usually the product grew out of developing technology which would not have developed in response to a defined product need.

On the other hand, many profitable new products *have* developed as a result of clearly-defined consumer needs. Frequently, but by no means always, these consumer needs have received corporate notice as a result of marketing research. Others, such as synthetic rubber, have been so obviously needed that they became prime objects of technology, itself.

The point to be emphasized is that new products arise in *two* ways; one, in response to clearly-defined consumer needs and, two, from fundamental and exploratory research, i.e., developing technology. The first and most important management decision relative to new products is to take full advantage of both sources of new products and to organize so that products and concepts from each source can and will be fully evaluated as to both marketing and technological appropriateness. This will avoid the pitfalls of (a) trying to sell a new product out of technology for which no basic need exists or (b) senselessly spending research money to develop a product which might satisfy a need but for which the technological chances of success are nil or very small.

Once a product has been placed on the market it must be supported continuously thereafter by aggressive research to improve quality and lower cost. This is the technological input that keeps a product on the market long after it otherwise would have become obsolete. But simultaneously, vigorous exploratory research must be carried out to develop new products and processes which will make the old ones obsolete. This is a continuing responsibility of research and development and here, at least, it seems that Mr. Levitt and I are on common ground. Except, and the exception is very important, I would emphasize that the limited research dollar be aimed toward programs that make technological sense both from the standpoint of technical feasibility and proper fit with the company's established technology and marketing capabilities.

If I have managed to make the point that technology, itself, has a major contribution to make to the product development function, the question naturally arises as to how this can be accomplished in a consumer, marketing oriented company. Assuming that executive and marketing management are aware of this gold in the technological rainbow, its exploitation becomes an easy organizational matter. Fundamental and exploratory research from which these products arise is set up as a corporate function, financed by the corporation and responsible only to executive corporate management. Here we are dealing with the creative talents of skilled scientists and, in the words of Mr. James F. Bell, "We must follow where research leads."

This is the kind of research that led to nylon, to the transistor, to polyethylene and to a host of other new products. True, these products were successful only because they fulfilled basic needs, but the scientists who developed them were not consciously slanting their efforts toward the fulfillment of those needs. They were pushing forward the frontiers of science simply to find out what was there. Since no one knows *a priori* what is there, it is a bit ridiculous to say that this aspect of the research program should be market directed or even strongly influenced by market considerations.

On the other hand, once the outline of a definable product begins to emerge from this black box of technology, an enlightened market research becomes as important as the product itself. The decision to perfect the product through further applied research should be made only in the light of basic marketing considerations. Through this stage of the development marketing plays an important supporting role. Once the product is perfected, the final decision to manufacture and sell becomes a dominant marketing function. The important factor in the decision-making process relating to these technology-nurtured products is proper liaison between research, marketing, and executive management. It is important that this liaison be at the highest research and division management level.

As already noted, the other prime source of new product concepts comes directly from studies of consumer wants and needs. Usually the product can be reasonably well visualized and its development becomes a matter of short-term, applied research. This type of product-development may be carried out by the operating department, itself, or it may be carried out by the corporate research function under conditions assuring the satisfaction of marketing needs. Decisions regarding new products arising in this way are straight-forward and relatively easy to make. If the economics are right and the original marketing input was right, the product should make money.

However, not all consumer wants and needs can be met by easily defined products. For example, it doesn't require a very erudite marketing study to know that one of the most urgent human needs is a cure for cancer. This does not at all mean that the chemical and pharmaceutical industry should (on the basis of business judgment) devote their major research efforts toward chemotherapy agents for cancer. A mature scientific evaluation of the difficulty of the problem and hence the chances for success requires prudence in research expenditures in this field. In fact, the technology is so difficult, even though the potential rewards are great, that most cancer research has been carried out with government or non-profit foundation funds. The point here is that a compelling market need is not per se an adequate reason for an extensive product development program. This is the point missed by Theodore Levitt in his castigation of the petroleum industry for not developing a "permanent" motor fuel to eliminate filling station stops. Technical considerations practically eliminate this idea as something to be taken seriously. Thus another of the basic decisions regarding new product research must be that purely marketing considerations must be fully evaluated in the light of sound technology.

This again emphasizes the corporate tripod of sound management, sound marketing and sound technology. My marketing friends tell me there is little consumer interest in a two-legged stool. And my corporate experience tells me that there are few if any successful companies balancing on a bipod. Strong marketing doesn't offset weak technology, and strong technology cannot offset marketing myopia.

Since product decisions are based in substantial part upon market research and since in a short run research and development manpower and budgets are relatively fixed, marketing managements have an increasing responsibility to be sure that the wants and needs which they are communicating to research and development personnel are more real than imagined. These must be supplemented with a rigorous examination of factors such as competition, trends in the industry, investment requirements, advertising appropriations necessary, channels of distribution, and a host of other critical factors. For despite the wants and needs of the consumer, and they are many and varied, corporate managements are asking for a more realistic assessment of the total risk.

In its final form the identification and interpretations of consumer wants lead ultimately to a prediction problem; and the information which managements are really asking of marketing management is prediction of consumer behavior at some future point in time. Under these conditions, and if research and development effort is not to be misdirected, it would appear that the tools and techniques to be applied in predicting consumer behavior now need the same kind of scrutiny that predictive mechanisms in the physical sciences have undergone for a hundred years.

The question becomes one of maximizing the corporation's opportunity for being right, since once the decision has been made to move in any given product area with the research and development program, valuable manpower and time is committed. If this commitment is made, and if it later develops that the commitment was improperly made, then not only has the research and development time and manpower been used unwisely but valuable time has been lost which could have been devoted to more adequately thought-through projects.

Both marketing and research managements are sensitive, to greater or lesser degrees, to the action of competitors. To a reasonable extent, this is necessary. However, the most desirable situation would be one in which the consumer's wants were being interpreted on a constant and rolling basis with an applied development program closely geared to these wants and the capacity of the individual corporation. Research and development programs cannot be all things to all men and there must come a point at which management makes a series of judgments as to what will and will not be researched. These decisions are critical to the well being of the organization and demand more complete evaluative techniques.

Even assuming that the ability to predict future consumer behavior becomes more sensitive as we learn to live with the marketing concept, the responsibilities of marketing managements do not end here. The reason for this is that the purpose of predicting and interpreting is to provide intelligent outlines for research and development programs which, if successful, will find acceptance with the consumer. The consumer, however, is not the only governing factor. Research managements must at the same time evaluate their applied projects in view of a total evaluation of the future climate in which the proposed products will find themselves competing. Research and deveolpment departments have a real responsibility in technological forecasting just as marketing managements have a responsibility in demand and business forecasting. The rate at which technology is growing has accelerated to the point where decisions must be made today on the possible impact of tomorrow's technology. The rate at which our decisions can be made obsolete is truly staggering.

An enlightened total marketing concept requires three major technical programs. These are a fundamental research program engaged in a search for new knowledge, an exploratory research program which becomes more immediate than the fundamental program, and an applied product development program aimed specifically at introducing new products in time and with particular characteristics which will satisfy consumer wants as interpreted through marketing managements. With these three programs, it is possible to work not only from the consumer back toward development, but also to work from a developing technology toward the consumer.

It is important for marketing people to understand what the research and development process is. Accustomed as they are to dealing with the uncertainties of human nature, they frequently fail to understand the uncertainties of technology. A new product should not be ordered from research as one would order a toothbrush from the drug store. There are many difficult uncertainties in product development both as to timing and quality. Frequently undue pressure from marketing leads to hastily conceived products of questionable quality. It takes a great deal of time and painstaking effort to develop good products, and requests from marketing to research should be most carefully considered and documented. Otherwise there is tremendous spinning of wheels and little forward motion.

Marketing is in the van of corporate thinking and action. The responsibility is very great as are the potential rewards. An enlightened marketing management will seek neither to direct the methodology of product development nor to dominate the conception of new products. Rather will it recognize the joint responsibility of marketing and research and seek to make its corporate contribution through supporting and promoting exploratory research and constructive guidance and mature understanding of the problems of applied research.

As one of my colleagues puts it, research is not sheer adrenalin. It is a mechanism through which the corporation can satisfy consumer wants at a profit.

6. New Criteria for Market Segmentation

DANIEL YANKELOVICH

The director of marketing in a large company is confronted by some of the most difficult problems in the history of U.S. industry. To assist him, the information revolution of the past decade puts at his disposal a vast array of techniques, facts, and figures. But without a way to master this information, he can easily be overwhelmed by the reports that flow in to him incessantly from marketing research, economic forecasts, cost analyses, and sales breakdowns. He must have more than mere access to mountains of data. He must himself bring to bear a method of analysis that cuts through the detail to focus sharply on new opportunities.

In this article, I shall propose such a method. It is called *segmentation analysis*. It is based on the proposition that once you discover the most useful ways of segmenting a market, you have produced the beginnings of a sound marketing strategy.

UNIQUE ADVANTAGES

Segmentation analysis has developed out of several key premises:

In today's economy, each brand appears to sell effectively to only certain segments of any market and not to the whole market.

Sound marketing objectives depend on knowledge of how segments which produce

◆ SOURCE: Reprinted by permission from *Harvard Business Review*, Vol. 42, No. 2, March-April 1964, pp. 83–90.

the most customers for a company's brands differ in requirements and susceptibilities from the segments which produce the largest number of customers for competitive brands.

Traditional demographic methods of market segmentation do not usually provide this knowledge. Analyses of market segments by age, sex, geography, and income level are not likely to provide as much direction for marketing strategy as management requires.

Once the marketing director does discover the most pragmatically useful way of segmenting his market, it becomes a new standard for almost all his evaluations. He will use it to appraise competitive strengths and vulnerabilities, to plan his product line, to determine his advertising and selling strategy, and to set precise marketing objectives against which performance can later be measured. Specifically, segmentation analysis helps him to:

1. Direct the appropriate amounts of promotional attention and money to the most potentially profitable segments of his market;

2. Design a product line that truly parallels the demands of the market instead of one that bulks in some areas and ignores or scants other potentially quite profitable segments;

3. Catch the first sign of a major trend in a swiftly changing market and thus give him time to prepare to take advantage of it;

4. Determine the appeals that will be most effective in his company's advertising; and, where several different appeals are significantly effective, quantify the segments of the market responsive to each;

5. Choose advertising media more wisely and determine the proportion of budget that should be allocated to each medium in the light of anticipated impact;

6. Correct the timing of advertising and promotional efforts so that they are massed in the weeks, months, and seasons when selling resistance is least and responsiveness is likely to be at its maximum;

7. Understand otherwise seemingly meaningless demographic market information and apply it in scores of new and effective ways.

These advantages hold in the case of both packaged goods and hard goods, and for commercial and industrial products as well as consumer products.

Guides to Strategy

Segmentation analysis cuts through the data facing a marketing director when he tries to set targets based on markets as a whole, or when he relies primarily on demographic breakdowns. It is a systematic approach that permits the marketing planner to pick the strategically most important segmentations and then to design brands, products, packages, communications, and marketing strategies around them. It infinitely simplifies the setting of objectives.

In the following sections we shall consider nondemographic ways of segmenting markets. These ways dramatize the point that finding marketing opportunities by depending solely on demographic breakdowns is like trying to win a national election by relying only on the information in a census. A modern census contains useful data, but it identifies neither the crucial issues of an election, nor those groups whose voting habits are still fluid, nor the needs, values, and attitudes that influence how those groups will vote. This kind of information, rather than census-type data, is the kind that wins elections—and markets.

Consider, for example, companies like Procter & Gamble, General Motors, or American Tobacco, whose multiple brands sell against one another and must, every day, win new elections in the marketplace:

These companies sell to the whole market, not by offering one brand that appeals to all people, but by covering the different segments with multiple brands. How can they prevent these brands from cannibalizing each other? How can they avoid surrendering opportunities to competitors by failing to provide brands that appeal to all important segments? In neither automobiles, soaps, nor cigarettes do demographic analyses reveal to the manufacturer what products to make or what products to sell to what segments of the market. Obviously, some modes of segmentation other than demographic are needed to explain why brands which differ so little nevertheless find their own niches in the market, each one appealing to a different segment.

The point at issue is not that demographic segmentation should be disregarded, but rather that it should be regarded as only one

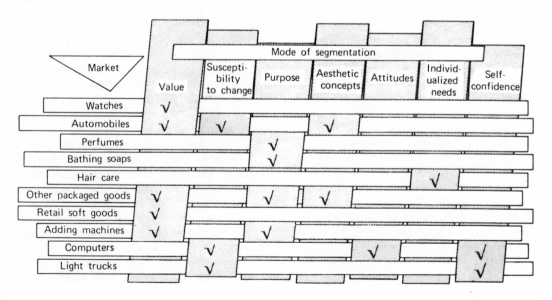

EXHIBIT 1. Example of segmentation in different industries.

among many possible ways of analyzing markets. In fact, the key requirement of segmentation analysis is that the marketing director should never assume in advance that any one method of segmentation is the best. His first job should be to muster all probable segmentation and *then* choose the most meaningful ones to work with. This approach is analogous to that used in research in the physical sciences, where the hypothesis that best seems to explain the phenomena under investigation is the one chosen for working purposes.

TEN MARKETS

In the following discussion we shall take ten markets for consumer and industrial products and see how they are affected by seven different modes of nondemographic segmentation. The products and modes are shown schematically in Exhibit 1. Of course, these segments are not the only ones important in business. The seven I have picked are only *examples* of how segmentation analysis can enlarge the scope and depth of a marketer's thinking.

I. Watches

In this first case we deal with a relatively simple mode of segmentation analysis. The most productive way of analyzing the market for watches turns out to be segmentation by *value*. This approach discloses three distinct segments, each representing a different value attributed to watches by each of three different groups of consumers:

1. *People who want to pay the lowest possible price for any watch that works reasonably well.* If the watch fails after six months or a year, they will throw it out and replace it.
2. *People who value watches for their long life, good workmanship, good material, and good styling.* They are willing to pay for these product qualities.
3. *People who look not only for useful product features but also for meaningful emotional qualities.* The most important consideration in this segment is that the watch should suitably symbolize an important occasion. Consequently, fine styling, a well-known brand name, the recommendation of the jeweler, and a gold or diamond case are highly valued.

In 1962, my research shows the watch market divided quantitatively as follows:

Approximately 23% of the buyers bought for lowest price (value segment #1).

Another 46% bought for durability and general product quality (value segment #2).

And 31% bought watches as symbols of some important occasion (value segment #3).

Defining and quantifying such segments is helpful in marketing planning—especially if a watch company's product happens to appeal mostly to one segment or if the line straddles the three segments, failing to appeal effectively to any. Without such an understanding, the demographic characteristics of the market are most confusing. It turns out, for example, that the most expensive watches are being bought by people with both the highest and the lowest incomes. On the other hand, some upper income consumers are no longer buying costly watches, but buying cheap, well-styled watches to throw away when they require servicing. Other upper income consumers, however, continue to buy fine, expensive watches for suitable occasions.

Timex's Timely Tactics. The planning implications in value segmentation are very broad for the industry. For one thing, many of the better watch companies in the years between 1957 and 1962 were inadvertently focusing exclusively on the third segment described—the 31% of the market that bought a watch only as a gift on important occasions—thus leaving the bulk of the market open to attack and exploitation.

The U.S. Time Company took advantage of this opening and established a very strong position among the more than two-thirds of America's watch buyers in the first two segments. Its new low-price watch, the Timex, had obvious appeal for the first segment, and it catered to the second segment as well. At that time, higher-price watches were making the disastrous mistake in their advertising of equating product quality with water-proof and shock-resistant features. The Timex also offered these low-cost features, at lower prices, thus striking at a vulnerable area which the competition itself created. When Timex pressed its attack, it was able within a few years to claim that "Timex sells more watches than any other watch company in the world."

Even the *timing* of Timex's watch advertising was involved. Much of the third segment was buying watches only during the Christmas season, and so most of Timex's competitors concentrated their advertising in November and December. But since buying by the other two segments went on all the time, Timex advertised all year-round, getting exclusive attention ten months of the year.

Thus, nondemographic segmentation in the watch industry has directly affected almost every phase of marketing, including the composition of the product line. Major watch companies know that they must plan product line, pricing, advertising, and distribution within the framework of the three basic value segments of this market.

II. Automobiles

The nondemographic segmentation of the automobile market is more complex than that of the watch market. The segments crisscross, forming intricate patterns. Their dynamics must be seen clearly before automobile sales can be understood.

Segmentation analysis leads to at least three different ways of classifying the automobile market along nondemographic lines, all of which are important to marketing planning.

Value Segmentation. The first mode of segmentation can be compared to that in the watch market—a threefold division along lines which represent how different people look at the meaning of *value* in an automobile:

1. *People who buy cars primarily for economy.* Many of these become owners of the Falcon, Ford, Rambler American, and Chevrolet. They are less loyal to any make than the other segments, but go where the biggest savings are to be found.

2. *People who want to buy the best product they can find for their money.* These prospects emphasize values such as body quality, reliability, durability, economy of operation, and ease of upkeep. Rambler and Volkswagen have been successful because so many people in this segment were dissatisfied.

3. *People interested in "personal enhancement (a more accurate description than "prestige").* A handsomely styled Pontiac or Thunderbird does a great deal for the owner's ego, even though the car may not serve as a status symbol. Although the value of an automobile as a status symbol has declined, the personal satisfaction in owning a fine car has not lessened for this segment of the market. It is interesting that while both watches and cars have declined in status value, they have retained *self-enhancement* value for large portions of the market.

Markets can change so swiftly, and the size of key segments can shift so rapidly, that great sensitivity is required to catch a trend in time to capitalize on it. In the automobile market, the biggest change in recent years has been the growth in segment two—the number of people oriented to strict product value. Only a few years ago, the bulk of the market was made up of the other segments, but now the product-value segment is probably the largest. Some automobile companies did not respond to this shift in the size of these market segments in time to maintain their share of the market.

Aesthetic Concepts. A second way of segmenting the automobile market is by differences in *style* preferences. For example, most automobile buyers tell you that they like "expensive looking" cars. To some people, however, "expensive looking" means a great deal of chrome and ornamentation, while to others it means the very opposite—clean, conservative lines, lacking much chrome or ornamentation.

Unfortunately, the same *words* are used by consumers to describe diametrically opposed style concepts. Data that quantify buyers according to their aesthetic *responses*—their differing conceptions of what constitutes a goodlooking car—are among the most useful an automobile company can possess.

The importance of aesthetic segmentation can be pointed up by this example:

When Ford changed from its 1959 styling to its 1960 styling, the change did not seem to be a radical one from the viewpoint of formal design. But, because it ran contrary to the special style expectations of a large group of loyal Ford buyers, it constituted a dramatic and unwelcome change to them. This essential segment was not prepared for the change, and the results were apparent in sales.

Susceptibility to Change. A third and indispensable method of segmenting the automobile market cuts across the lines drawn by the other two modes of segmentation analysis. This involves measuring the relative susceptibility of potential car buyers to changing their choice of make. Consider the buyers of

Chevrolet during any one year from the point of view of a competitor:

At one extreme are people whose brand loyalty is so solidly entrenched that no competitor can get home to them. They always buy Chevrolets. They are closed off to change.

At the other extreme are the open-minded and the unprejudiced buyers. They happened to buy a Chevrolet because they preferred its styling that year, or because they got a good buy, or because someone talked up the Fisher body to them. They could just as easily have purchased another make.

In the middle of this susceptibility continuum are people who are predisposed to Chevrolet to a greater or lesser degree. They can be persuaded to buy another make, but the persuasion has to be strong enough to break through the Chevrolet predisposition.

The implications of this kind of a susceptibility segmentation are far-reaching. Advertising effectiveness, for example, must be measured against each susceptibility segment, not against the market as a whole. Competitors' advertising should appear in media most likely to break through the Chevrolet predisposition of the middle group. In addition, the wants of those who are not susceptible must be factored out, or they will muddy the picture. Marketing programs persuasive enough to influence the uncommitted may make no difference at all to the single largest group—those who are predisposed to Chevrolet but still open enough to respond to the right stimulus.

If the marketing director of an automobile company does not break down his potential market into segments representing key differences in susceptibility, or does not clearly understand the requirements of each key segment, his company can persevere for years with little or no results because its promotion programs are inadvertently being aimed at the wrong people.

III. Perfume

A segmentation analysis of the perfume market shows that a useful way to analyze it is by the different *purposes* women have in mind when they buy perfume.

One segment of the market thinks of a perfume as something to be added to what nature has supplied. Another segment believes that the purpose of fragrance products is to help

a woman to feel cleaner, fresher, and better groomed—to correct or negate what nature has supplied. In the latter instance, the fragrance product is used to *cancel out* natural body odors; in the former, to *add* a new scent. To illustrate this difference in point of view:

One woman told an interviewer, "I like a woodsy scent like Fabergé. It seems more intense and lingers longer, and doesn't fade away like the sweeter scents."

But another woman said, "I literally loathe Fabergé. It makes me think of a streetcar full of women coming home from work who haven't bathed."

These differences in reaction do not indicate objective differences in the scent of Fabergé. They are subjective differences in women's attitudes; they grow out of each woman's purpose in using a perfume.

Purposive segmentation, as this third mode of analysis might be called, has been of great value to alert marketers. For instance:

A company making a famous line of fragrance products realized that it was selling almost exclusively to a single segment, although it had believed it was competing in the whole market. Management had been misled by its marketing research which had consistently shown no differences in the demographic characteristics of women buying the company's products and women buying competitors' products.

In the light of this insight, the company decided to allocate certain lines to the underdeveloped segments of the market. This required appropriate changes in the scent of the product and in its package design. A special advertising strategy was also developed, involving a different copy approach for each product line aimed at each segment.

In addition, it was learned that visualizations of the product in use helped to create viewer identification in the segment that used perfume for adding to nature's handiwork, but that more subtle methods of communication produced better results among the more reserved, more modest women in the second segment who want the "cancelling out" benefits of perfume. The media susceptibilities of women in the two segments were also found to be different.

Thus, from a single act of resegmentation, the advertising department extracted data critical to its copy platform, communication strategy, and media decisions.

IV. Bathing Soap

A comparable purposive segmentation was found in the closely related bathing soap field. The key split was between women whose chief requirement of soap was that it should clean them adequately and those for whom bathing was a sensuous and enjoyable experience. The company (a new contender in this highly competitive field) focused its sights on the first segment, which had been much neglected in recent years. A new soap was shaped, designed, and packaged to appeal to this segment, a new advertising approach was evolved, and results were very successful.

V. Hair-Care Market

The Breck-Halo competition in the shampoo market affords an excellent example of another kind of segmentation. For many years, Breck's recognition of the market's individualized segmentation gave the company a very strong position. Its line of individualized shampoos included one for dry hair, another for oily hair, and one for normal hair. This line accurately paralleled the marketing reality that women think of their hair as being dry, oily, or normal, and they do not believe that any one shampoo (such as an all-purpose Halo) can meet their individual requirements. Colgate has finally been obliged, in the past several years, to revise its long-held marketing approach to Halo, and to come out with products for dry hair and for oily hair, as well as for normal hair.

Other companies in the hair-care industry are beginning to recognize other segmentations in this field. For example, some women think of their hair as fine, others as coarse. Each newly discovered segmentation contains the seeds of a new product, a new marketing approach, and a new opportunity.

VI. Other Packaged Goods

Examples of segmentation analysis in other packaged goods can be selected almost at random. Let us mention a few briefly, to show the breadth of applicability of this method of marketing analysis:

In *convenience foods*, for example, we find that the most pragmatic classification is, once again, purposive segmentation. Analysis indicates that "convenience" in foods has many different meanings for women, supporting several different market segments. Women for whom convenience means "easy to use" are reached by products and appeals different from those used to reach women for whom convenience means shortcuts to creativity in cooking.

In the market for *cleaning agents*, some women clean preventively, while others clean therapeutically, i.e., only after a mess has been made. The appeals, the product characteristics, and the marketing approach must take into account these different reasons for buying—another example of purposive segmentation.

In still another market, some people use *air fresheners* to remove disagreeable odors and others to add an odor. A product like Glade, which is keyed to the second segment, differs from one like Airwick in product concept, packaging, and type of scent.

The *beer market* requires segmentation along at least four different axes—reasons for drinking beer (purposive); taste preferences (aesthetic); price/quality (value); and consumption level.

VII. Retail Soft Goods

Although soft-goods manufacturers and retailers are aware that their customers are value conscious, not all of them realize that their markets break down into at least four different segments corresponding to four different conceptions of value held by women.

For some women value means a willingness to pay a little more for quality. For others, value means merchandise on sale. Still other women look for value in terms of the lowest possible price, while others buy seconds or discounted merchandise as representing the best value.

Retailing operations like Sears, Roebuck are highly successful because they project *all* these value concepts, and do so in proportions which closely parallel their distribution in the total population.

VIII. Adding Machines

In marketing planning for a major adding machine manufacturer, analysis showed that his product line had little relationship to the segmented needs of the market. Like most manufacturers of this kind of product, he had designed his line by adding features to one or several stripped-down basic models—each addition raising the model price. The lowest priced model could only add; it could not subtract, multiply, divide, or print, and it was operated by hand.

Since there are a great many features in adding machines, the manufacturer had an extremely long product line. When the needs of the market were analyzed, however, it became clear that, despite its length, the line barely met the needs of two out of the three major segments of the market. It had been conceived and planned from a logical point of view rather than from a market-need point of view.

The adding machine market is segmented along lines reflecting sharp differences in value and purpose.

One buyer group values accuracy, reliability, and long life above all else. It tends to buy medium-price, full-keyboard, electric machines. There are many banks and other institutions in this group where full-keyboard operations are believed to ensure accuracy.

Manufacturing establishments, on the other hand, prefer the ten-key machine. Value, to these people, means the maximum number of laborsaving and timesaving features. They are willing to pay the highest prices for such models.

Both these segments contrast sharply with the third group, the small retailer whose major purpose is to find a model at a low purchase price. The small retailer does not think in terms of amortizing his investment over a period of years, and neither laborsaving features nor full-keyboard reliability count for as much as an immediate savings in dollars.

Despite the many models in the company's line, it lacked those demanded by both the manufacturer and small retailer segments of the market. But, because it had always been most sensitive to the needs of financial institutions, it had developed more models for this segment than happened to be needed. Product, sales, and distribution changes were required to enable the company to compete in the whole market.

IX. Computers

One pragmatic way of segmenting the computer market is to divide potential customers between those who believe they know how to evaluate a computer and those who believe they do not. A few years ago only about 20% of the market was really open to IBM's competitors—the 20% who believed it knew how to evaluate a computer. By default, this left 80% of the market a virtual captive of IBM—the majority who did not have confidence in its own ability to evaluate computers and who leaned on IBM's reputation for personal appraisal.

Another segmentation in this market involves differences in prospects' attitudes toward the inevitability of progress. Although this factor has been widely ignored, it is a significant method for qualifying prospects. People who believe that progress is inevitable (i.e., that change is good and that new business methods are constantly evolving) make far better prospects for computers than those who have a less optimistic attitude toward progress in the world of business.

X. Light Trucks

The market for light trucks affords us another example of segmentation in products bought by industry. As in the computer example, there are both buyers who lack confidence in their ability to choose among competing makes and purchasers who feel they are sophisticated about trucks and can choose knowledgeably. This mode of segmentation unexpectedly turns out to be a key to explaining some important dynamics of the light truck market:

Those who do not trust their own judgment in trucks tend to rely very heavily on both the dealer's and the manufacturer's reputation. Once they find a make that gives them reliability and trouble-free operation, they cease to shop other makes and are no longer susceptible to competitive promotion. Nor are they as price-sensitive as the buyer who thinks he is sophisticated about trucks. This buyer tends to look for the best price, to shop extensively, and to be susceptible to the right kind of competitive appeals, because he puts performance before reputation.

These ways of looking at the truck market have far-reaching implications for pricing policy, for product features, and for dealers' sales efforts.

CONCLUSION

To sum up the implications of the preceding anaysis, let me stress three points:

1. *We should discard the old, unquestioned assumption that demography is always the best way of looking at markets.*

The demographic premise implies that differences in reasons for buying, in brand choice influences, in frequency of use, or in susceptibility will be reflected in differences in age, sex, income, and geographical location. But this is usually not true. Markets should be scrutinized for important differences in buyer attitudes, motivations, values, usage patterns, aesthetic preferences, or degree of susceptibility. These may have no demographic correlatives. Above all, we must never assume in advance that we know the best way of looking at a market. This is the cardinal rule of segmentation analysis. All ways of segmenting markets must be considered, and *then* we must select out of the various methods available the ones that have the most important implications for action. This process of choosing the strategically most useful mode of segmentation is the essence of the marketing approach espoused in this article.

In considering cases like those described, we must understand that we are not dealing with different types of people, but with differences in peoples' *values*. A woman who buys a refrigerator because it is the cheapest available may want to buy the most expensive towels. A man who pays extra for his beer may own a cheap watch. A Ford-owning Kellogg's Corn Flakes-eater may be closed off to Chevrolet but susceptible to Post Toasties; he is the same man, but he has had different experiences and holds different values toward each product he purchases. By segmenting markets on the basis of the values, purposes, needs, and attitudes relevant to the product being studied, as in EXHIBIT I, we avoid misleading information derived from attempts to divide people into types.

2. *The strategic-choice concept of segmentation broadens the scope of marketing planning to include the positioning of new products as well as of established products.*

It also has implications for brand planning, not just for individual products but for the composition of a line of competing brands where any meaningful segment in the market can possibly support a brand. One explanation of the successful competing brand strategy of companies like Procter & Gamble is that they are based on sensitivity to the many different modes of market segmentation. The brands offered by P & G often appear very similar to the outsider, but small, marginal differences between them appeal to different market segments. It is this rather than intramural competition that supports P & G successes.

3. *Marketing must develop its own interpretive theory, and not borrow a ready-made one from the social sciences.*

Marketing research, as an applied science, is tempted to borrow its theoretical structures from the disciplines from which it derives. The social sciences offer an abundance of such structures, but they are not applicable to marketing in their pure academic form. While the temptation to apply them in that form is great, it should be resisted. From sociology, for example, marketing has frequently borrowed the concept of status. This is a far-reaching concept, but it is not necessarily the most important one in a marketing problem, nor even one of the important ones. Again, early psychoanalytic theory has contributed an understanding of the sexual factor. While this can sometimes be helpful in an analysis of buying behavior in a given situation, some motivation researchers have become oversensitive to the role of sex and, as a result, have made many mistakes. Much the same might be said of the concept of social character, that is, seeing the world as being "inner-directed," "other-directed," "tradition-directed," "autonomous," and so forth.

One of the values of segmentation analysis is that, while it has drawn on the insights of social scientists, it has developed an interpretive theory *within* marketing. It has been homegrown in business. This may explain its ability to impose patterns of meaning on the immense diversity of the market, and to provide the modern marketing director with a systematic method for evolving true marketing objectives.

7. Some Problems in Market Distribution

ARCH W. SHAW

THE ACTIVITIES OF BUSINESS

When a workman in a factory directs the cut of a planer in a malleable steel casting, he applies motion to matter with the purpose and result of changing its form.

When a retail clerk passes a package of factory-cooked food over the counter to a customer, he applies motion to matter with the purpose and result of changing its place.

When a typist at her desk makes out an invoice covering a shipment, she influences the motion of that material or merchandise, not directly to change its form or place, but indirectly to facilitate changes of one or both kinds.

Isolate any phase of business, strike into it anywhere, and invariably the essential element will be found to be the application of motion to matter. This may be stated, if you will, as the simplest ultimate concept to which all the activities of manufacturing, selling, finance and management can be reduced.

Starting with this simple concept, it is at once evident that we have an obvious and easy basis for the classification of business activities—a simplifying, unifying principle from which to proceed rather than some mere arrangement by kind or characteristic of the materials, men, operations and processes in the various departments of a business enterprise.

The nature of the motion does not of itself supply the key to this basic classification. For

◆ SOURCE: Reprinted from *Changing Perspectives in Marketing*, edited by Hugh G. Wales (University of Illinois Press, 1951), pp. 32–52.

while the action may be characteristic of one part of a business and not duplicated elsewhere, like the pouring of molten metal in a foundry or the making up of a payroll, it may, in contrast, be common to all the departments into which the organization is divided, such as the requisition of a dozen pencils or a box of paper clips. It is not until we single out the common fundamental element and inquire, "What is the purpose of this motion?", that we find the key.

I do not wish to exaggerate the importance of this simple and apparently obvious concept; but for me it has opened a way to locate the activities of business and disclose their relations to one another and to their common object, and so has proved a device of daily use. For the final function of the classification, as it is the practical problem of all business, is to identify those motions which are purposeless, so that they may be eliminated, and to discover those motions, old or new, which are of sound purpose, so that they may be expedited.

When, upon studying an individual motion or operation in itself and in relation to the other associated activities, no satisfactory answer can be found to the question, "What is its purpose?", you have strong grounds for assuming that it is a non-essential and useless motion. It may have the sanction of house tradition or trade custom, but its superfluous character persists and the wisdom of eliminating it becomes plain. Conversely, a new motion proposed for adoption, though never before tried in the trade, may still have value. Purpose again is the decisive test. From the social standpoint, any motion which has no valid purpose or result is economically useless and wrong. The effect of employing such a motion in business, like the effect of omitting a useful motion, is to limit profits that otherwise might rise.

So the purpose of the analysis, from the manager's point of view, is not alone to position the activities of business and develop their relationship, but also to order his thinking so that he can more readily see what activities he should discontinue and what others he should encourage, perfect, or add.

This does not always mean a reduction in the total number of motions. In our roundabout system of production, with its minute subdivision of labor, it is possible to make a greater number and variety of motions and distribute them over a longer period of time, yet increase the eventual output or decrease the cost through the group effectiveness of all the motions.

In the three operations already mentioned—those of the factory workman, the retail clerk, and the office typist—each application of motion was for an economically valid purpose and each instance was typical of one of the three great groups of business activities:

1. The activities of production, which change the form of materials.

2. The activities of distribution, which change the place and ownership of the commodities thus produced.

3. The facilitating activities, which aid and supplement the operations of production and distribution.

Whatever the nature or kind of any business activity, its final effect is one of these three.

METHODS OF DISTRIBUTION

In the early stages of our industrial history, sales were made in bulk. At all stages in distribution, the purchasers saw the actual goods before the sale was made.

Later sale by sample appeared. The purchaser bought goods represented to be identical with the sample he was shown. The introduction of this method of sale was necessitated by the widening of the market and was made possible by improvement in commercial ethics and increasing standardization of product. The purchaser had to have con-

fidence not only in the producer's honest intention to furnish goods identical with the sample, but also in his ability to produce identical goods. Hence, increasing uniformity in product through machine methods of applying standard materials in its manufacture was a factor in the increase of sale by sample.

Sale by description is the most modern development in distribution. Here an even higher ethical standard is required than for sale by sample. Moreover, sale by description requires a higher level of general intelligence than sale in bulk or sale by sample. Sale by description in its modern development is, in a sense, a by-product of the printing press.

All three methods of sale are in use in modern commercial life. The consumer still makes a large part of his purchases under a system of sale in bulk. He sees the goods before he buys them. The middleman, buying in large quantities, generally purchases from sample. But sale by description becomes each year more important in every stage of the distribution system.

The root idea in sale by description is the communication of ideas about the goods to the prospective purchaser by spoken, written or printed symbols and facsimiles. This method takes the place of the sight of the goods themselves or a sample of them. It is obvious that this requires that the purchaser shall have sufficient intelligence to grasp ideas either through spoken, written or printed symbols.

The ideas to be conveyed to the prospective purchaser in sale by description are such as will awaken an effective demand for the commodity in question. The awakening of demand is the essential element in selling. It must be remembered, however, that the distributor has the further task of making it possible to gratify that demand by making the goods physically available to the buyer.

With sale in bulk, this problem merges with the selling, since the goods are physically present when the sale is made; while in sale by description the physical distribution of the goods is a problem distinct from the awakening of demand. And it is a problem that requires equal attention, for it is obviously useless to awaken the demand unless the goods to satisfy it are available.

As demand creation is the initial step in distribution, it is necessary to consider the agencies for this purpose available to the merchant-producer. There are three general agencies to be considered: (1) middleman, (2) the producer's own salesman, and (3) advertising, direct and general. The business man faces the problem of what agency or combination of agencies is the most efficient for the creation of demand and the physical supply of his particular commodity.

The number of possible combinations of methods and agencies renders the problem of the producer-merchant an intricate one. It will be seen that he has a difficult task in analyzing the market with reference to his goods, and in working out that combination of methods and agencies which will give him the most efficient system of applying motion to achieve distribution.

The middleman is a by-product of a complex industrial organization. The chart of Fig. 1 shows in rough outline the evolution of the middleman from the early period when producer dealt directly with consumer, to the appearance of the orthodox type of distribution (late in the Eighteenth Century and in the first quarter of the Nineteenth Century) when a complicated series of middlemen existed.

In the more primitive barter economy, the producer deals directly with the consumer, and middlemen take no part in the transaction. In the medieval period, as the handicrafts become specialized occupations under a town-market regime, the producer is a retailer and sells directly to the consumers. As the market widens, a division of labor becomes necessary, and the merchant appears as an organizer of the market.

Steadily the market widens until business confronts both national and world-wide markets. The merchant is no longer a single intermediary between the producer and the consumer. The merchant who takes the goods from the producer disposes of them to retail merchants who in turn distribute them to consumers. After a long period, we find the producers gradually strengthening their financial position, and freeing themselves from the control of a single merchant. They become merchant-producers. They assume the burden of production, and dispose of the product to various wholesalers, who in turn sell to retailers and they to the consumers. As a world market appears, the producer disposes of a part of his product to the export merchant.

In the early days of the factory system, shown in the chart of Fig. 2, we find that the producers have lost their character as merchants and are devoting themselves to the problems of production. The selling agent appears as a link in the chain of distribution to relieve the producer from the task of selling his product. He distributes it among wholesalers, who in turn distribute it to retailers, and the retailers to the consuming public. This may be termed the orthodox

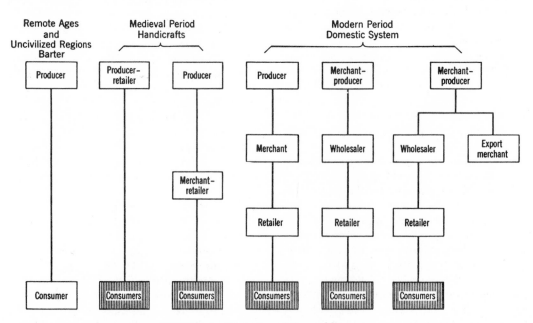

FIGURE 1. Evolution of the middleman.

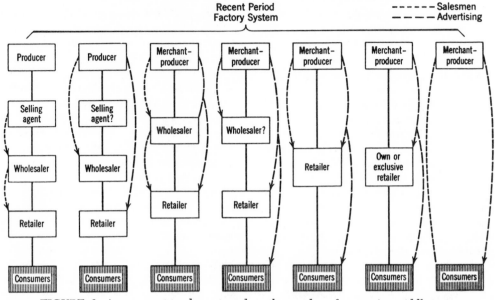

FIGURE 2. An apparent tendency to reduce the number of successive middlemen.

pattern in distribution, a pattern almost universal thus far in the Nineteenth Century.

Conversely, as the long period of development from a system of barter economy to the early decades of the factory system showed a continuous tendency toward increase in the number of middlemen intervening between the producer and the consumer, so recent years have shown a growing tendency to decrease the number of successive steps in distribution. Fig. 2 is an attempt to show diagrammatically the development of this apparent tendency to decrease the number of middlemen.

The most extreme step in the process is the complete elimination of middlemen, and the sale direct from the merchant-producer to the consumer, either by advertising alone or by salesmen supplemented by advertising.

It should be emphasized that the analogy between direct salesmen and advertising is very close. Each agency is largely used to enable the producer to take over one function of the middleman, that is, the selling function. And in each case the root idea is the same. The producer seeks to communicate most directly to the prospective purchaser, through one or the other agency, or a combination of the two, such ideas about his goods as will create a conscious demand for them. The direct salesman and advertising are different modes of accomplishing the same end.

Advertising, then, may properly be regard-ed either as a substitute for middlemen and salesmen, or as auxiliary to them in the exercise of the selling function. Owing to the rise of sale by description and the increasing differentiation of commodities, it tends to displace in whole or in part these other agencies in many lines of distribution.

Advertising may be said to build up three general classes of demand: (1) expressed conscious demand, (2) unexpressed conscious demand, and (3) subconscious demand. Expressed conscious demand means present sales; unexpressed conscious demand means future sales; subconscious demand means a fertilizing of the field so that future selling efforts will be more fruitful. Unexpressed .conscious demand and subconscious demand are difficult to measure but must always be taken into account in any consideration of the efficiency of advertising as a selling agency.

What has gone before has been by way of analysis. The general problem of distribution, the present-day differentiation of products, the price policies open to the producer, the methods of sale, and the three chief selling agencies have all been subjected to brief review. This has been essential because neither economists nor business men have previously made such an analysis.

The social significance of the problem calls for emphasis also. While a more systematic handling of distribution means to the business man greater business success, a better organization of distribution with maximum economy of motion means to society the prevention of an enormous annual waste.

CONSIDERATIONS OF THE MARKET

The business man faces a body of possible purchasers, widely distributed geographically, and showing extremes of purchasing power and felt needs. The effective demand of the individual consumer depends not alone upon his purchasing power but also upon his needs, conscious or latent, resulting from his education, character, habits, and economic and social environment. The market, therefore, splits up into economic and social strata, as well as into geographic sections.

The producer cannot disregard the geographic distribution of the consuming public. He may be able to sell profitably by salesmen where the population is dense, while that method of sale would be unprofitable where population is sparse. If a sound system of distribution is to be established, the business man must treat each distinct geographic section as a separate problem. The whole market breaks up into differing regions.

Equally important is a realization of what may be termed the market contour. The market, for the purposes of the distributor, is not a level plain. It is composed of differing economic and social strata. Too seldom does the business man appreciate the market contour in reference to his product.

Nor does the merchant-producer always realize how intricate is his problem as to the agency or combination of agencies that will be most efficient in reaching his market.

The business man often adopts one method of reaching his market and becomes an advocate of it, entirely disregarding other methods. While the method adopted may be more efficient than any other single method, it is apparent that a method which is relatively efficient in reaching one area may be inefficient in reaching another. So a system of distribution which has proved effective in reaching one economic stratum may be relatively inefficient when employed to reach a different economic stratum in society. Each distinct area and economic stratum may have to be treated as a separate problem.

A sound selling policy will require as its basis a careful analysis of the market by areas and strata, and a detailed study of the proper agency or combination of agencies to reach each area and stratum, taking into account always the economic generalizations expressed in the law of diminishing returns. It must also take into account not only the direct results obtained from the use of one or another agency over a short period, but also the less measurable results represented by the unexpressed conscious demand and subconscious demand which may facilitate future selling campaigns.

The crux of the distribution problem is the proper exercise of the selling function. The business man must convey to possible purchasers through one agency or another such ideas about the product as will create a maximum demand for it. This is the fundamental aim whatever the agency employed.

Editor's Note: The reader may be interested to know that Shaw's original material was published in the *Quarterly Journal of Economics* (1912) and in a book by Arch W. Shaw. *Some Problems in Market Distribution* (Harvard University Press, 1915).

8. Some Concepts of Markets and Marketing Strategy

ROLAND S. VAILE

THE BASIC DEFINITION OF MARKETING

"Marketing covers all business activities necessary to effect transfers in the ownership of goods and to provide for their physical distribution."[1] "Marketing includes all the activities involved in the creation of place, time, and possession utilities."[2] "Marketing, in the full sense of the word, must involve change in ownership; physical movements merely facilitate this change or make possible the use of the commodity by the new owner. All the rights, privileges, and responsibilities, either of use or of further sale, attach to ownership and are passed on with change in ownership."[3]

These three definitions, taken from many, pretty well represent the concept of marketing although perhaps sale of services merits more specific inclusion. Change in ownership is all important. Physical movement is facilitating. Place, time, and possession utilities are involved, but their development requires marketing only when change of ownership is also involved.

[1] T. N. Beckman and others, *Principles of Marketing* (New York: Ronald Press, 1957), p. 4.
[2] P. D. Converse and others, *Elements of Marketing* (New York: Prentice-Hall, 1952), p. 1.
[3] Roland S. Vaile and others, *Market Organization* (New York: Ronald Press, 1930), p. 43.

♦ SOURCE: Reprinted by permission from *Changing Structure and Strategy in Marketing*, edited by Robert V. Mitchell (Bureau of Economic and Business Research, University of Illinois, 1958), pp. 17–29.

There are many other instances in which the creation of place utility does not involve marketing. For example, place utility and only place utility is created in bringing crude oil from the bottom of a deep well to a surface tank, and yet that process is not usually included in marketing. Actually the sinking of an oil well and pumping oil from it have much in common with the laying of a pipeline and pumping oil through it. Both result in place utility, but one pair is classed with marketing and the other with production. The same point might be made with coal mining, potato digging, and many other activities which result only in place utility, but which are commonly thought of as part of production rather than marketing.

CONCEPT OF A MARKET

The term "market" may be used to designate:

1. The place where a sale is made.
2. The area in which a particular supply usually is sold, or the area from which a particular supply generally is procured.
3. The particular institutions or channels that carry on the marketing processes.
4. The complex set of forces that result in a certain price being paid for a particular bill of goods or service.

Legal controversy exists concerning the locus of a market in the geographic sense. Is the market for cement, for example, at the point where it is made, or where it is used? The primary focus of the forces of demand is at the latter point, surely, although some of the basing-point discussions seem to contend otherwise. One basic question involved is whether different proportions of common costs may properly be covered by identical sales in markets with differing demands. Retail pricing certainly results in differing contributions to common costs from the sale of different items. To what extent and under what conditions would similar leeway be appropriate between different geographic markets? In other words, is there anything necessarily nefarious in "freight absorption" per se? No completely satisfying answer has been given to this question.

A conspicuous change during the past generation is seen in the growth of individual firms through integration, both horizontal and vertical. Firms that have expanded horizontally have tended also to integrate vertically. According to data summarized in *Fortune*, six merchandising firms each had sales of over $1 billion in 1956. Each of these is engaged predominantly in retailing, but each also has undertaken many activities usually considered as wholesaling, as well as some manufacturing. Our concepts and definitions in this field are made archaic by these developments, and our statistics do not permit precise chronological comparison. Moreover, the question still is moot as to the conditions under which a firm should be permitted to own or control its principal customers so that a large portion of its "sales" are merely paper transactions.

The growth of our great suburban shopping centers and of supermarket self-service retailing is made possible, of course, by the high-income, automobile age. Rather than a move toward economy in the use of total social resources, it appears to be grossly inefficient, as is, in fact, practically every do-it-yourself program. These movements are reversions away from the principle of specialization. They can be tolerated only because specialized technology already has resulted in high productivity and considerable unused personal time and energy, together with widely dispersed ownership of idle capacity in quasi-industrial goods like washing machines and automobiles. (The importance of the automobile in our abundant economy is highlighted by the fact that six of the ten national firms with largest 1956 sales are engaged in automobile manufacture and petroleum production while three others have the automobile business as a principal customer).

Of course there are some sociological considerations connected with do-it-yourself programs, and perhaps the sociological gains outweigh any economic inefficiency. Measurement of the net effect on our culture involves value judgment that is beyond the scope of this paper. Suffice it to say that the opportunity cost of many do-it-yourself programs is pretty low while some economic use is made of otherwise unemployed labor and equipment. The alternative use of that potential capacity may be a rather low-grade consumption activity. In any case the public seems to have accepted the trend philosophically and with considerable enthusiasm.

Melvin Copeland suggested a generation ago that consumer goods are purchased as convenience, shopping, or specialty goods, and that stores tend to concentrate on one of these lines.[4] This tendency has led to a mixing of the conventional lines of groceries, drugs, and household gadgets into a fairly complete stock of convenience goods in modern supermarkets. That this development has been going on for some time is shown by the following quotation from Chester Haring:

Of course, lines are being added to the stocks of nearly all retail merchants, but the greatest change is taking place in the drug, grocery, cigar, and five-and-ten-cent stores. While each of these groups is doing its largest business in its natural field, each is encroaching upon the fields of others , and also into entirely new fields. In short these four classes of stores seem to be making up a new class which we may call "convenience stores."[5]

In the nearly thirty years since that statement was written, change in the concept of the most appropriate market institutions has continued. The supermarkets and the suburban shopping centers are dominant in the fashion of the moment. Completely automatic service in supermarkets is in the pilot stage and may become the fashion for tomorrow. Evidently the ultimate physical and institutional pattern for market distribution still is to be conceived and evolved. As one result our retail statistics are badly muddled, and for most useful analysis they should be reported in much greater detail.

---

[4] *Principles of Merchandising* (New York: A. W. Shaw, 1924).

[5] *The Manufacturer and His Outlets* (New York: Harper, 1929), p. 176.

Changes in the commodity mix are not confined to retailing. In many cases manufacturers are taking on new lines. This may be done to give more price lines as in the case of the Edsel. It may be done to improve the seasonal distribution of demand or because the firm has funds to invest and decides to spread its risks. Whatever the reasons, it appears that the concept of the market for an individual firm is broadening and specialization by manufacturers on a limited line of commodities is being reduced.

Of course many manufacturers have long undertaken to reach different segments of their market with differentiated products. For example, canners, flour millers, some tire manufacturers, and others have sold their products both under their own brands and under wholesaler or retailer brands. Sometimes the product offered under several brands has been essentially identical, but through this multiple-brand strategy additional segments of the total market have been reached. This practice constitutes a form of semisecret, intra-firm competition, often with only minor physical differences among the products.

As individual firms have grown in size and have added to their lines of products, many of them have undertaken more direct and obvious intra-firm competition. This strategy is conspicuous, of course, in the automobile field. General Motors, for example, not only offers different named cars in different price lines, but there is considerable overlap of prices among the different makes. Strenuous rivalry exists among the retail agents that sell the several makes—as strenuous, perhaps, among the separate units of GM as between them and the members of the Ford or Chrysler families. Competition among the products of a single company is well illustrated, also, in Procter and Gamble where the sales division is organized on a competitive product basis. Recently, intra-firm product competition has become keen with cigarette manufacturers, especially following the wide introduction of the filter and mentholated brands. This practice of differentiating the products of a single seller makes it possible to satisfy the tastes and whims of segregated markets. One result is an increase in total company sales, as illustrated by the huge volume of such organizations as General Motors or Procter and Gamble. Sometimes, but not always, it permits some price discrimination.

Money makes markets. This aspect of markets deserves and receives close attention. The flow of income is of great importance to market potentials. Changes in the flow of income are reflected closely by changes in retail purchases. Forecasts of future changes in income directly affect the volume of industrial expenditures. Increases in income generally are accompanied by changes in the percentage of savings and investment. Conversely, neither increases nor decreases in income flow result immediately in equal changes in consumption expenditure. Increases and decreases in credit have much the same immediate effects as do changes in income flow. Thus when income falls, an increase in consumer credit may temporarily offset the effect of the fall. These points are elementary, of course, and call for no amplification here.

It may be pointed out, however, that both government and private agencies have made available an increasing amount of data on income, past, present, and future. These data include the well-known estimates of GNP, national income, disposable personal income, average individual and family income, and so on. Of considerable use to some branches of marketing is the MacFadden estimate of discretionary purchasing power. All these data are available in both current and constant-value dollars. Studies in consumer economics are available to indicate many of the relations between changes in income and the accompanying changes in its use. These correlations are of great value in the planning of business decisions affecting marketing.

Perhaps it almost goes without saying, however, that relationships between income and expenditures change over the years. This is illustrated, for example, by the well-known fact that until recently the percentage of consumer income spent on food has decreased as income increased, while the reverse seems to have occurred in the past decade. Perhaps this is merely a statistical illusion due to changes in the form in which food is bought, but at least it points a finger of caution against stubborn adherence to past or present relations.

CONCEPT OF COMPETITION

Discussions among economists have been fruitful in developing, modifying, and clarifying concepts that are useful in the description and understanding of marketing as well as in the making of marketing decisions. (I am impressed by the extent to which recent management research has been devoted to how management decisions are made rather than to the decisions themselves.) A sharp dichotomy between competition and monopoly was neither realistic nor very useful in practical affairs. The newer concepts of monopolistic competition, oligopoly, workable competition, and administered prices are much more pertinent to actual business situations. The idea of cross-elasticity of demand has gained in acceptance and application to the analysis of specific market situations. So also has the idea of the kinked demand curve.

Understanding of these concepts seems to have an increasing influence on pricing policies of individual firms. However, the relation of costs to pricing policy and the influence of full costs, marginal costs, allocation of common costs, break-even analysis, and similar matters on specific prices still is somewhat moot.

In 1927 Wesley Mitchell wrote as follows: "The prices ruling at any moment for the infinite variety of commodities, services, and rights which are being bought and sold constitute a system in the full meaning of that term. That is, the prices paid for goods of all sorts are so related to each other as to make a regular and connected whole. Our knowledge of these relations is curiously inexact. . ."[6] Our knowledge of these relations is still inexact, but the economists' clarification and market research have at least helped toward an understanding of how some of them come about.

The concept or strategy suggested by Edwin G. Nourse in *Price Making in a Democracy*[7] is still hotly argued. Who should get how much of the advantage from technological improvements in production—stockholders of large firms, owners of small businesses, wage earners through wage increases, or consumers through lowered prices? Nourse argues for a large share to the consumer directly, Walter Reuther favors higher wages, some neo-Keynesians want high dividends to attract capital for an ever expanding economy. The consensus has not jelled yet. Relative prices unquestionably are of major importance in marketing strategy, but no one knows

just how or to what extent they should be used.

One of the changes in the applied use of a concept as a marketing strategy is seen in the case of the single price. The basic policy of one price to all was introduced by many merchants in the nineteenth century. It gained considerable acceptance, enough so that it was considered the general policy. Trade-in allowances, package deals, trading stamps, and other devices have eroded some of the rigidity so that a recent article carried the title "One Price—Fact or Fiction?" and the implication that fiction was more nearly the case. Marshall Field is using trade-in allowances even with pots and pans!

The distinction between price competition, product-quality competition, and non-price competition still is somewhat foggy. Marketing strategies include attempts to increase sales (and profits) through lowering price, through change in product, or through mere sales effort with no change in either price or product. Perhaps the latter is the true non-price competition. Probably in most real-life situations two or more of the three strategies are in use at the same time, but it is useful for the marketing analyst to consider their effects separately.

SALES PROMOTION

For the purposes of this paper I have divided marketing strategies into three classes, namely:

1. Direct price competition (just discussed briefly).
2. Product development and change (merely mentioned).
3. Sales promotion (now to be discussed).

Attempts to sell an existing product at an established price involve many sophisticated strategies. Included are such obvious things as personal selling, advertising, and merchandise fairs. Specific tactics may change with time. In 1923, for example, Daniel Starch defined advertising as "selling in print."[8] Since the advent of radio and TV, new methods of advertising have been adopted and the definition has been broadened.

As I wrote in 1927, however, "It must be clearly recognized that 'advertising' is but a

---

[6] *Business Cycles* (New York: National Bureau of Economic Research, 1927).
[7] Washington: The Brookings Institution, 1944.

[8] *Principles of Advertising* (New York: A. W. Shaw, 1923), p. 5.

convenient name for certain forms of persuasion applied to buying and selling. At many points the economic arguments would apply with equal force to the arousing of desire . . . whether the technique used was 'advertising' or 'personal selling.' In such cases the choice between the two would be merely one of relative costs. With this in mind it seems unnecessary to define advertising; each reader may include in this category whatever technical activities suit his fancy."[9]

Probably it is likewise unnecessary to define sales promotion. It may be pointed out, however, that in addition to various forms of publicity, the extension of credit, as in installment selling, may be used as a sales-promoting stratagem. When consumer credit is expanded, consumer purchasing is stimulated as with any other form of sales promotion. Moreover, it follows that there is an increase in inflationary pressure.

In 1928 Paul Nystrom wrote that "there seems to be little to indicate that any important trend of fashion has ever been changed by any form of sales promotion."[10] Probably this statement still holds so far as the *direction* of any trend is concerned. On the other hand, the *rate* of acceptance or decline of a fashion may be affected by sales promotion. Because of these phenomena, sales-promoting effort usually is correlated directly with industrial fluctuations, with increased effort when sales are easy to make, and with decreased effort when selling is difficult. This holds true, certainly, both for advertising and for extension of installment credit. Thus instability of economic activity is furthered by sales promotion. The over-all data suggest little change in this situation over the years. The burden placed on the monetary system and other possible devices for the control of industrial fluctuations is increased by sales promotion. The question may well be raised whether, as a general concept or stratagem, sales promotion should or could be used as an aid toward industrial stability. Some individual firms appear to have successfully used it in this manner.

"In December 1923 there were no less than ten manufacturers of milk chocolate who unqualifiedly advertised their products as 'the best.' Such a condition is possible because there is no definite standard of 'best.' "[11] Today an equal number of cigarette brands are advertised as having "the best taste." Apparently the use of claims that can neither be proven nor disproven is a continuing stratagem. This is one way that advertisers continue to play up what Borden has called the "hidden qualities" of goods.

Another stratagem that seems, if anything, to have grown in use is reference to scientific evidence. This is an age in which science is popular—as Anthony Standen tells us, Science is a Sacred Cow! Unfortunately, not all of the evidence used by advertisers is actually pertinent to the consumer's problem, but if it helps persuade him to buy, it has accomplished its purpose. Thus sales promotion continues to be opportunistic and to prey upon the gullible.

So long as these practices are continued it is doubtful that consumers are helped by advertising to make wiser or more rational choices in their general purchasing. In fact, I see little in today's advertising strategy, at least at the consumer level, to modify my 1927 statement that "if education were the principal claim of advertising as it is now practiced, it would be an enormously wasteful enterprise."[12] Of course, as George French said years ago, "The major function of advertising is to persuade,"[13] and this it seems to do pretty effectively with categorical and emotionally slanted claims.

In 1926 Clare Griffen wrote, "The third phase of the [automobile] industry will be one in which . . . annual sales will go largely to replace cars that have been eliminated from use. A majority of the industries of the United States have been in this . . . stage for a long time. . . ."[14] In 1927 I made a companion point in connection with the sales promotion of the California Fruit Growers Exchange.[15] In this case a wide expansion of supply was possible. In fact, while sales promotion had successfully expanded demand, supply had increased at about the

[9] Vaile, *Economics of Advertising* (New York: Ronald Press, 1927), p. 3.

[10] *Economics of Fashion* (New York: Ronald Press, 1928), p. 36.

[11] Vaile, *op. cit.*, p. 49.

[12] *Ibid.*, p. 59.

[13] *Advertising* (New York: Ronald Press, 1924).

[14] "The Evolution of the Automobile Market," *Harvard Business Review*, July, 1926, pp. 407–408.

[15] Vaile, *op. cit.*, Chap. 7.

same rate, leading to the conclusion that individuals who had owned orange orchards in 1905 had just about maintained a status quo so far as the purchasing power of the net income from these orchards was concerned. More recent data indicate that this result has been continued for another thirty years. In other words, in the long run, at least in this case, the rate of return on invested capital has not been increased by sales promotion.

Perhaps in each of these cases the professor was overly conservative or even pessimistic. Certainly the automobile industry has not yet, thirty-one years later, reached a mere replacement basis; and when control of supply is more practical, some brand advertising continues to be accompanied by high rates of return on invested capital even after more than thirty years of continuous promotion. While the two illustrations suggest the inevitable long-range result of specific sales promotion, aggressive businessmen refuse to accept the inevitable, thank goodness!

This discussion is both too broad and too episodic for successful summary or statement of specific conclusions. In closing, therefore, let me merely say that marketing is a living, growing organism. As it grows, its behavior sometimes is erratic and whimsical. Our understanding of its problems has increased materially, as has our ability to direct its further development. As with much of evolution, however, constructive and lasting change often is slow in coming.

C. Comparative Marketing

9. *The Russian Decision Process Governing Trade*

LYMAN E. OSTLUND
and
KJELL M. HALVORSEN

The 24th Congress of the Communist Party of the Soviet Union (C.P.S.U.)[1] reconfirmed the liberalized policy of increased economic ties with the Western world, which progressively have been strengthened during the last five-year plan covering 1965 to 1970.[2] Expanding trade relations have not only been limited to countries of the council of Mutual Economic Assistance, the Eastern "Common Market," but have also included Western countries. Increasingly, Russia is turning to the West as a source of production capacity and technology in order to accelerate its own economic development. The foreign trade allocation was 80% and 20% between Socialist and Western nations only ten years ago. Currently it is 60% and 40%, indicating Russia's serious intention to form major economic ties with the Western world. Therefore, it is of interest to examine the decision-making mechanism, both as to structure and process, within the U.S.S.R. concerning trade.

The most pronounced U.S.S.R. import policy changes that have taken place since 1965 are a willingness to buy production capacity through licensing agreement, capital equipment, entire factories on a turn-key basis, and to participate in joint ventures. Russians no longer merely copy Western technology, because it would create a time lag.

European and Japanese firms have been active in the formation of joint ventures within Russia. Such joint ventures do not involve foreign ownership, but are intended strictly to foster exports. The Western partner typically obtains his compensation through selling the factory output in Western markets while production is carried out by the Russians with a contractual transfer price. A management consultant fee may also be paid to the Western partner. If a Western equipment manufacturer has the ability and interest to generate export sales for the U.S.S.R., it can be used to facilitate payment for the equipment. For example, Russian chemical exports are now being used to purchase entire chemical factories.

Along with Moscow's invitation to improve trade relations, Washington has made certain concessions on the exportation of previously restricted equipment. These improved Russian-U.S. trade relations have led to the first substantial, although preliminary, export contract of equipment to Russia. According to a trade protocol signed on May 18, 1971 by the U.S.S.R. and Mack Trucks, Inc., Mack was to sell machinery and technology for a truck manufacturing plant on the Kama River with a capacity larger than that of all U.S. or U.S.S.R. truck producers combined. The protocol estimated the project to cost between $700 million and $1 billion.

The U.S.S.R. has also expressed interest in an additional $1 billion worth of machinery and technology for consumer goods, specifi-

---

[1] March 30 to April 10, 1971.
[2] Twenty-fourth Congress of the Communist Party of the Soviet Union, *Soviet Life*, June, 1971.

◆ SOURCE: Reprinted by permission from the *Journal of Marketing* (National Quarterly Publication of the American Marketing Association), Vol. 36, No. 2, April 1972, pp. 3–11.

cally razor blades, furniture, and electrical appliances. This purchase would involve buying entire factories for their own production.[3] Mack has recently withdrawn from the Kama project as the main contractor primarily caused by its delay in approaching Washington.[4] The Russians still want U.S. participation, and if licenses for industrial exports of such magnitudes are granted, it may open up a vast line of bilateral trade. Last year's total U.S.-U.S.S.R. trade of $160 million was very low relative to the trading potential of these two large economic powers. U.S. exports to the U.S.S.R. were $110 million (primarily soya beans, wheat, and natural resources), and imports from the U.S.S.R. were $50 million (primarily chromium ore).

Now that the political atmosphere has improved to the point that sizable and important projects are being discussed, it becomes vital for Western countries to examine the anatomy of the Russian capital goods decision-making process. While the formalized structure is extensive and complex, its comprehension alone is not sufficient. The informal decision processes are at least of equal importance. This formal decision structure is described in this article and then contrasted with the informal decision process.

THE FORMAL DECISION-MAKING STRUCTURE

The formal structure for capital goods decision making in Russia differs considerably from that of the West. It is rigid and reflects all the bureaucratic intricacies expected in such a highly centralized government. The production-oriented economy with central planning does not respond to conventional marketing activities appealing to the end user. The centralized character of the Russian planned economy also becomes visible in trade as a result of Russian interest in entire lines of equipment rather than of individual products. U.S. industrial suppliers are often unable to provide complete production systems unless several related manufacturers are brought together to make a package offer.

In order to describe the formal decision-making structure, the governmental units senior to the economic planning ministries will be briefly examined (Fig. 1). The first of these is the Supreme Soviet.

The Supreme Soviet

The Supreme Soviet, the highest representative body, is divided into two chambers, the Soviet of the Union and the Soviet of Nationalities. Both chambers are vested with the same broad powers covering all major issues of national and foreign policy. The Supreme Soviet adopts and amends the constitution of the U.S.S.R. and passes all union laws. It exercises state administration over the political, economic, and cultural life; therefore, it approves the annual and five-year economic plans, the state budget, and reports on their implementation. These very important documents define the primary trend of the country's economic development.[5] The Supreme Soviet also designates the composition of other senior governmental bodies. It elects the Presidium of the Supreme Soviet (executive branch to the Supreme Soviet), forms the Council of Ministers, the Government of the U.S.S.R., and elects the Supreme Court.

Standing Committees of the Supreme Soviet

There are ten standing committees in each of the two chambers. They include planning and budget, legislative proposals, foreign affairs, as well as various committees on economics and cultural developments. Approximately 50% of the Supreme Soviet deputies are members of these committees. The committees study all proposed laws submitted to them, and generally any amendments suggested by these committees are approved by the Supreme Soviet. The committees also act on their own accord drafting and submitting legislative proposals to the Supreme Soviet. Another important function of the committees is to influence the activity of administrative bodies; i.e., ministries and departments connected with the approval of economic development plans, including trade allocations and the state budget.

---

[3] "The Big Breakthrough in East-West Trade," *Business Week* (June 19, 1971), pp. 84-90.

[4] "Picking Up Where Mack Left Off," *Business Week* (September 25, 1971), pp. 42–43.

[5] B. Bayanov, Y. Umansky, and M. Shafir, *Soviet Socialist Democracy* (printed in the U.S.S.R., 1968), pp. 104–105.

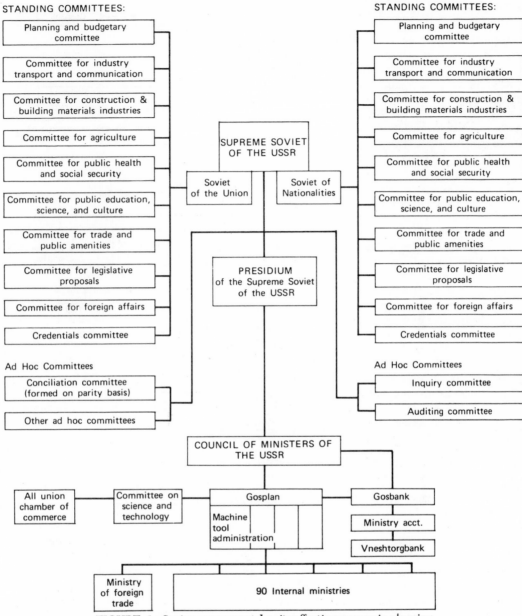

STANDING COMMITTEES:

- Planning and budgetary committee
- Committee for industry transport and communication
- Committee for construction & building materials industries
- Committee for agriculture
- Committee for public health and social security
- Committee for public education, science, and culture
- Committee for trade and public amenities
- Committee for legislative proposals
- Committee for foreign affairs
- Credentials committee

Ad Hoc Committees

- Conciliation committee (formed on parity basis)
- Other ad hoc committees

STANDING COMMITTEES:

- Planning and budgetary committee
- Committee for industry transport and communication
- Committee for construction & building materials industries
- Committee for agriculture
- Committee for public health and social security
- Committee for public education, science, and culture
- Committee for trade and public amenities
- Committee for legislative proposals
- Committee for foreign affairs
- Credentials committee

Ad Hoc Committees

- Inquiry committee
- Auditing committee

SUPREME SOVIET OF THE USSR

Soviet of the Union — Soviet of Nationalities

PRESIDIUM of the Supreme Soviet of the USSR

COUNCIL OF MINISTERS OF THE USSR

All union chamber of commerce — Committee on science and technology — Gosplan — Gosbank

Machine tool administration

Ministry acct.

Vneshtorgbank

Ministry of foreign trade

90 Internal ministries

FIGURE 1. Senior governmental units affecting economic planning.

The Council of Ministers

The Council of Ministers is a collective body with clearly defined executive and administrative powers. The Council coordinates and directs the work with various ministries and adopts measures to execute economic plans, the state budget, and the credit and monetary system. The chairman of this executive branch of government is A. Kosygin. The executive branch is responsible for the maintenance of law and order. It exercises guidance in the sphere of foreign policy and is in charge of the military and the banking system.

The Gosplan

The State Planning Committee of the Council of Ministers of the U.S.S.R. prepares and implements the Gosplan, a five-year overall plan describing the output goals, allocation of resources, and investment plans for the internal ministries in charge of different

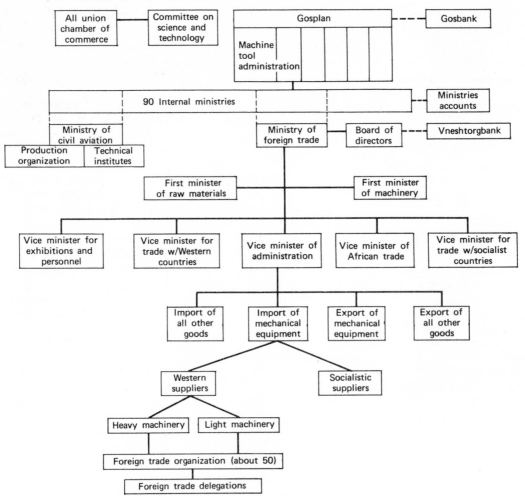

FIGURE 2. The formal structure of key economic planning units.

industries (Fig. 2). The term Gosplan is also often applied to the committee. The overall five-year plan is divided into annual plans and selected three- and six-month plans where needed. The five-year plan which is very detailed will often contain complete specifications for equipment that must be imported. Unfortunately, these plans and specifications are not available, even in summary form, to outsiders because only sketchy output goals are published. Due to the high degree of secrecy and unavailability of data, information about the total Russian demand for any given product is not easily obtained.

Requests for foreign equipment originate at the factory level and are then forwarded to the appropriate internal ministry which, in turn, will include the equipment in its budget, assuming the foreign equipment is essential for meeting output goals. The internal minis-

try's budget permits a certain amount of foreign import; however, the ministry places priorities on such equipment requests.

The ministry's budget and equipment requests are submitted to the State Planning Committee for approval and inclusion in the Gosplan. The exact specifications, if already known, will be included in each equipment request. The State Planning Committee eventually issues authorization for these equipment purchases to the Ministry of Foreign Trade.

The State Planning Committee has two agencies which collect technological intelligence from abroad. The Committee on Science and Technology's main function is to keep abreast of foreign scientific progress and technological innovation. The All Union Chamber of Commerce has offices outside the U.S.S.R. and is the worldwide extension of the State Planning Committee. In addition to collecting commercial information, the All Union Chamber of Commerce also arranges trade exhibitions in the U.S.S.R. and invites selected foreign companies to participate. The trade exhibitions provide the Westerner with a valuable source of information about the current industrial priorities in Russia. There are two annual exhibitions, one in June and one in September, of which the latter is of greater importance.

The Internal Ministries

There are currently 90 internal ministries in the U.S.S.R., plus many corresponding local ministries in each Soviet republic. The ministries include, for example, the Ministry of Foreign Trade, the Ministry of Civil Aviation, the Ministry of the Merchant Marine, the Ministry of Railways, the Ministry of the Gas Industry, and the Ministry of Tractor and Farm Machinery Building. Within each republic of the U.S.S.R., factories are directed by local offices of the various ministries. Each internal ministry is divided into a production organization and a technical institute. The production organization is responsible for the achievement of specific output objectives. Each technical institute conducts all necessary research for a given industry, from "pure" research to industrial engineering. The centralization of applied research at the ministry rather than at the factory level has led to work duplication among the ministries and the inefficient application of research findings.

The internal ministries closely coordinate equipment needs and share information concerning current foreign equipment innovations reported by the Committee on Science and Technology or the All Union Chamber of Commerce. During this planning process, there is an information flow between the internal ministry requesting the equipment and the State Planning Committee. In addition, information is sent to other ministries which might need similar equipment and the Ministry of Foreign Trade regarding price and quality.

The Ministry of Foreign Trade

The Foreign Trade Ministry directs Russian export efforts in order to balance exports against expected imports by country. Appar-
ently, the Ministry of Foreign Trade must identify a large enough quantity of export potential to balance the import requirements of the internal ministries. The export plan is communicated to the Gosplan which in turn must see that production capability exists to furnish the required quantity of exports. Production for domestic consumption is merely adjusted to match export requirements. While this process varies substantially from Western procedures, it should be remembered that Russia's trade accounts for only 2 to 3% of her gross national product. Thus, the process may not have sharply dislocating effects. Exports can be assured by pricing them below world prices. This planning process is not singularly sequential, but rather is undertaken by way of simultaneous exchanges of informal plans among the planning units.

The Foreign Trade Ministry is organized according to both geographic trade areas and products classified as machinery, raw material, and all other goods. This ministry will often ignore specific equipment requests and buy comparable products from some other sources in order to obtain a lower price. The buying decision lies with the Foreign Trade Ministry alone which is run like a profit-making organization. The Ministry has to show not only an overall annual profit generated from trade surplus, but also a substantial gain from buying foreign currency and selling it at a profit in rubles to the other internal ministries. This process has created some friction between the Foreign Trade Ministry and the other internal ministries since the latter are generally more interested in quality than price.

Foreign Trade Organizations

Foreign Trade Organizations are subordinate to the Ministry of Foreign Trade. They act as semi-autonomous purchasing agents which initiate and participate in the actual trade negotiation on behalf of their ministry. Each of the approximately 50 different Foreign Trade Organizations has a buying monopoly over a given set of end uses for a specific equipment class.

The Foreign Trade Delegations are ad hoc groups which travel the world to gather information and make preliminary contractual import commitments, after which the supplying company must negotiate the details with the appropriate central planning offices. Each delegation is composed of individuals from the requesting internal ministry which sometimes includes engineers from the factory level and Foreign Trade Ministry representatives. Occasionally the Gosplan will have representatives on the delegation.

The recent Russian trade delegation which signed the protocol with Mack Trucks, Inc. was clearly a high-level group. It included a deputy minister from the Gosplan, a deputy minister from the Ministry of Automobiles, as well as three presidents of Foreign Trade Organizations (Autoimport, Metallurgimport, and Stankoimport).[6]

There is a permanent trade delegation in New York, representing the Foreign Trade Organizations called Amtorg. Amtorg is a New York State corporation with its stock held in escrow. Its primary purpose is to gather information, locate U.S. suppliers, and submit proposals from U.S. firms to Moscow. Amtorg is frequently bypassed by U.S. firms, and its importance as a trade intermediary is uncertain.

The Russian Banking System

Gosbank is not only the world's largest bank, but also, the entire banking industry of Russia, with over eighty thousand branch offices. The banking system, like the State Planning Committee, is subordinate to the Council of Ministers. The Gosbank coordinates the budgets and the cash-flow of the Gosplan. An account is set up with the Gosbank for each ministry based upon its import requirements; a portion of that account is transferred to the Vneshtorgbank, which is the foreign banking division for Gosbank. The Ministry of Foreign Trade which has exclusive authority to deal in foreign currency and wholesale it to the internal ministries for rubles, coordinates its activities with the Vneshtorgbank.

Marketing Strategies Under the Formal Trade Structure

In view of the formal Russian trade structure, there are several marketing strategies available to the Western supplier depending on the industry and the products involved and whether initial contact is made by the Russians or by the Western supplier. Russian

institutions that can be contacted directly in the U.S. are Amtorg, the All Union Chamber of Commerce which arranges exhibits and represents the Gosplan, and the Russian Embassy. Unfortunately, this process can be very time-consuming. For example, an American shoe machinery manufacturer invested three years of effort from the initial contact to its first equipment sale. On the other hand, an Illinois manufacturer of concrete block equipment, who had been requested through Amtorg to send a representative to Moscow, was able to consummate its first sale within six months.

The two annual trade exhibitions sponsored by the All Union Chamber of Commerce have been disappointing for many U.S. businessmen who frequently complain that only a 40 to 50% chance exists of making a sale after having attended such an exhibition. This occurred in spite of obvious interest among visiting Russian managers and ministry officials in the Western products.

The reasons for not making a sale usually lie with the Western businessman who is unfamiliar with the correct procedures for pursuing personal negotiations with all the relevant planning units. For example, Western businessmen frequently send information or price quotations to the wrong ministry or planning office within Russia. This mistake, although easily made, is most serious because a Russian ministry will usually not take the time to forward such correspondence to the appropriate ministry, nor will it inform the correspondent of his mistake. The primary reason for this unreliable information flow appears to be understaffed offices in the various ministries.

INSIDE THE FORMAL STRUCTURE

A Western supplier can obtain results, however, if he follows the formal trade decision structure. Increasingly, success in negotiating a sale with the U.S.S.R. depends upon reaching the appropriate Russian ministries and committees that control the different aspects of a trade decision (Figure 3). In effect, this approach calls for a high degree of empathy concerning the informal dealings which go on among these ministries and committees as to their responsibilities and conflicts. The trade promotion task must be broken down into a series of necessary steps and, depending upon the particular trade package envisioned,

---

[6] Same reference as footnote 3.

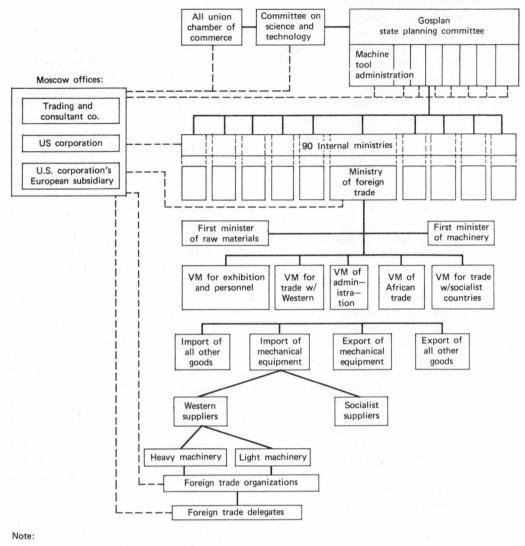

Note:

— — — Western traders communicating, obtaining information and influencing important administrative offices to increase present trade and generate new trade contracts.

FIGURE 3. Inside the formal structure.

these steps must be time ordered and related to each ministry and committee that must be influenced. Certain steps must be sequential, others can be undertaken simultaneously.

If it is known, or strongly suspected, that a current purchase interest exists in Russia for foreign equipment of a given type, a foreign supplier can maximize his probability of success by presenting the relevant information and selling appeals to several of the state agencies at approximately the same time. In this instance the most important agency to reach first is the particular internal ministry

within which the equipment will be used. It may be necessary to present equipment performance data—even conduct demonstrations—to production unit managers in order to stimulate interest among the end users and convey the message of quality and dependability up through the internal ministry. Price and delivery terms will not be of primary importance at this stage of negotiations. Since the internal ministry will rely, in part, on the recommendations of the Committee on Science and Technology, product specifications must simultaneously be submitted to that agency. The All Union Chamber of Commerce can also be of assistance in communicating information to both the internal ministry and the Committee on Science and Technology. Once an internal ministry has selected a particular foreign supplier, the supplier's promotional emphasis should shift to the Ministry of Foreign Trade since foreign currency will be involved. Here, the negotiation will center primarily on price and contractual terms. Given the internal ministry's interest in quality and the Ministry of Foreign Trade's interest in price, conflict can and frequently does arise between the two ministries. The Foreign Trade Ministry will usually have its way, unless the specific internal ministry involved is able to present a very strong case for its recommendation. The foreign supplier must be prepared to mitigate such conflicts by providing the internal ministry with compelling arguments of product superiority, so as to overcome any price dispute of the Foreign Trade Ministry.

A difficult although highly successful long-term strategy for generating sales orders from the U.S.S.R. involves the Gosplan. Through informal contacts with Gosplan representatives, the foreign supplier may succeed in having his equipment specified in one or more of the Gosplan industrial sector plans. While such a strategy could involve one to five years of preliminary work, success could mean recurring sales for many years without interference from the Ministry of Foreign Trade, as the same equipment is utilized in an increasing number of factories and requests for replacement parts are generated. Because of the lengthy time requirement, this approach almost necessitates some form of extended representation in Moscow.

These two examples represent the extreme points on the negotiation-time continuum. The elapsed time from start to finish in a contract negotiation may range from six months to several years. Once the trade link is established, however, business can often continue on virtually a routine reorder basis.

The larger multinational corporations interested in Russian trade are turning increasingly toward initiating direct contacts with the several state agencies rather than gambling on being "discovered" according to the formalized decision scheme. The necessary communication task can be undertaken in one of three ways. The first may involve sending a delegation of corporate-level executives to Moscow. However, unless a definite interest has already been expressed by the Russians, this "gate-crashing" approach is unlikely to succeed, if only due to the normal bureaucratic delays which will affect the enthusiasm of any delegation. A second approach uses European subsidiaries as representatives, particularly in countries already active in Russian trade. For example, a large U.S. manufacturer sold $100 million worth of earth-moving equipment to the U.S.S.R. over a short period of time through its distributor in Finland. For several years, many U.S. companies, while unwilling to trade directly with the U.S.S.R. for fear of negative public reaction, have encouraged their European subsidiaries to produce merchandise to be sold to the East Block countries.

The third approach to stimulating Russian trade has been to rely upon a company specializing in Russian trade. One of these companies is Satra of New York (a subsidiary of the privately held Greg Gary Corporation) which engages in both its own import/export operations and acts as intermediary for entire groups of U.S. corporations interested in specific trade sectors. It was Satra which arranged the protocol between Mack Trucks, Inc. and Russia for the Kama River project. Satra is the intermediary for a substantial volume of business; however, the exact amount is unknown. Another trading corporation is Novosider of Italy. It was responsible for negotiations on the Fiat automobile factory recently erected in Russia. Novosider has represented U.S. as well as European clients, including Textron and Corning Glass International.

The three approaches to the same basic communication task are shown on the left of Fig. 3, with the broken lines representing communication flows to the key state agencies for foreign trade. The informal relations between the trading companies and state agencies seem to be particularly close and effective.

PLANNING FOR TRADE NEGOTIATIONS

Researching the Russian Marketplace

The secrecy surrounding Russian state administration and activities makes it difficult to obtain relevant data pertaining to their import requirements because published internal data are frequently inaccurate. An additional problem is the West's basic ignorance of the Russian marketplace.

Fedderson has provided a set of questions designed to aid Westerners in analyzing East European markets.[7] In practice, answers to these questions are seldom if ever obtainable for Russia. Information regarding national production goals, specific production plans, priority lists for equipment to be imported, and national industrial capacity is not published. A Westerner can only estimate the priorities attached to given production sectors as reflected in sponsored exhibitions, articles in trade publications, and press releases about general production goals. The only way to obtain direct information is to hope for a "leak" from staff members of the internal ministries or the Gosplan to a Western representative located in Moscow. Occasionally, however, trade journals will reveal industries where difficulties exist in meeting production goals.

There are, of course, sources of macrostatistics on Russian trade such as in U.S. Department of Commerce publications and United Nations yearbooks. Statistical information from Russia is generally not very detailed, and is sometimes inaccurate. The Russian periodicals, *Ecotass*[8] and *Foreign Trade*[9] publish helpful information about recently signed trade contracts, upcoming exhibitions, and some statistics.

Emphasis on "Best" Price

Russians are tough bargainers on price, even beyond the point of reason at times. First, the thorough investigations of prevailing world suppliers and prices contribute to the long time delays in arriving at a decision. Next, most of the state agencies involved in the transaction will try to lower the price at each successive stage in the negotiation. For example, the president of a major U.S.

shirt manufacturer saw Russian shirts of comparable quality for sale at $40 in Russia. He offered to export his shirts at $2.50 each. The Russians replied they would pay $2.26 per shirt. His actual cost was $2.25 per unit. In another case, involving highly specialized industrial equipment widely known to be available from only one source, the Russians proceeded as usual to push for price cuts. Their position changed abruptly when the supplier politely told them to "take it or leave it." Because of this preoccupation with receiving the best price, it is not at all uncommon for Western companies familiar with Russian negotiation tactics to present an inflated price in the expectation of granting concessions in order to keep the negotiations moving. As with most any customer, the Russians want delivery as soon as possible; however, this is seldom an obstacle.

Terms of Payment

Sale terms usually are for cash, payable upon receipt of goods or confirmation of shipment. However, the Russians will occasionally ask for some form of barter agreement to cover at least part of the purchase price. The barter is intended to compensate for their continual shortage of hard Western currency. U.S. producers are usually ill-equipped to engage in barter transactions, although bartered products can often be marketed through switch-dealers in Austria or Switzerland. In the case of barter, trading companies have a definite advantage as they take title to goods and distribute them through their own organization. A trading company may also generate exports for the Russians, which is one of the most powerful financial tools in trading with the U.S.S.R.

Contractual Agreements and Their Enforcement

Russian trade contracts are usually more detailed than U.S. contracts, particularly with respect to performance and performance penalties. Generally, the location where a contract is signed determines the legal jurisdiction under which it could be enforced. As a practical matter, however, litigation seldom, if ever, takes place. First, the extreme detail of the contract mitigates the chances of disruptive ambiguities. A simple purchase con-

---

[7] Berend H. Fedderson, "Markets Behind the Iron Curtain," JOURNAL OF MARKETING, Vol. 31 (July, 1967), pp. 1–5.

[8] *Ecotass* is published in English by Tass News Agency which has an office in New York; the magazine is available on subscription.

[9] *Foreign Trade*, published in Russian and English, is available from Four Continent Book Corporation, New York.

tract could cover 30 pages. Second, enforcement of the contract entails possible political difficulties. For example, Russian contracts typically carry liquidated damage clauses calling for performance penalties larger than the amount of the demonstrated damages. Such clauses are enforceable under Russian law, but not under U.S. law. If a U.S. company should fail in the delivery of goods, regardless of strike, acts of God, or any other cause, Russian law would allow confiscation of goods already delivered plus liquidated damages of perhaps two times the total contract amount. However, if the Russians attempted to enforce a contract signed within the U.S. with respect to such performance penalties, U.S. courts would be unlikely to accept the relevance of Russian law in the case. Similarly, a U.S. firm could not expect a Russian court to accept the relevance of U.S. law. Seldom will U.S. companies consider litigation or even arbitration as means of enforcing a contract; instead, differences are settled through compromise.

CONCLUSION

The improved East-West political and trade atmosphere may bring a substantial trade expansion between the U.S. and Russia in the next decade. The large demand for increased productive capability existing in Russia provides a tempting opportunity for the West.

The characteristics of the Russian economy make it important to understand how to work with and around the central planning units which only recently have become accessible to the Western supplier. While the initiative can be taken through the formal political and economic structure of the U.S.S.R., the probability of success can be greatly increased and the necessary lead time reduced by working within the informal decision process. If U.S. marketers do not move quickly in pursuing trade opportunities with the U.S.S.R. their counterparts in Western Europe and Japan will do so. Therefore, the U.S. government must act now to facilitate increased trade by promptly granting export licenses for a wider variety of goods.

10. A Firsthand Study of Marketing in Communist China

BARRY M. RICHMAN

Relatively little has been written about Communist China's domestic trade or marketing system as compared to her other economic sectors such as industry, agriculture, or banking. Few published studies on the Chinese economy are based on firsthand research, and firsthand studies dealing with marketing and domestic trade are particularly rare.[1]

This research project was conducted in Communist China during the April-June period of 1966. It involved eleven major Chinese cities and a few rural areas. While the focus of this project was on the industrial sector, a fair amount of information on China's marketing system emerged, including data on the wholesaling and retailing spheres.

Key executives and other personnel were interviewed at three of China's largest retail department stores (in Shanghai, Peking, and Tientsin); also interviewed were the managers of five smaller retail stores and about fifteen key personnel employed by the Ministry of Commerce, local bureaus of commerce, and a variety of other commercial, wholesaling, and distribution organizations. In addition, quite a bit of information on marketing was obtained from the 38 industrial enterprises and various higher level industrial organizations visited.

The focus of this article is on the marketing of manufactured consumer goods at the wholesale and retail levels of the Chinese economy. This emphasis was chosen since the author's other published works on China focus on the industrial sector.[2]

ORGANIZATION OF CHINA'S DOMESTIC TRADE

China's domestic trade sector is essentially comprised of the country's myriad retail

* The author wishes to acknowledge the financial support provided by The Ford Foundation for this research.

[1] I know of no firsthand Western studies that focus on marketing in Communist China. Two significant works based on secondary sources are: A. Donnithorne, *China's Economic System* (London: Allen and Unwin, Ltd., 1967), chapter Xi; Yu-min Chou, "Wholesaling in Communist China," in R. Bartels (ed.), *Comparative Marketing* (Homewood, Ill.: Richard D. Irwin, Inc., 1963), pp. 253–70. The latter study deals with the 1950's.

◆ SOURCE: Reprinted by permission from the *Journal of Retailing*, Vol. 46, No. 2, Summer 1970, pp. 27–47, 59.

[2] See Barry M. Richman, *A Firsthand Study of Industrial Management in Communist China* (Los Angeles, Calif.: Division of Research, Graduate School of Business Administration, University of California, Los Angeles, 1967): "Managerial Decision-making and Performance at the Enterprise Level in Communist Chinese Industry," in *Mainland China in the World Economy* (Washington, D.C., United States Government Printing Office, 1967), pp. 60–99; "Capitalists and Managers in Communist China," *Harvard Business Review* (January-February 1967), pp. 57 ff.

See in particular Barry M. Richman, *Industrial Society in Communist China* (New York: Random House, 1969).

establishments, and the thousands of wholesaling organizations which serve as intermediary links in the distribution of consumer goods from the industrial sector to the retail sector. At virtually all levels of the trade sector—in fact at virtually all levels of all sectors—Communist Party organizations and committees parallel the state administrative hierarchy. Officially, at least, ultimate authority rests with the party organs at each level rather than with the administrative-governmental organs.

Communist Party cadres are often referred to as Reds, and their major concerns normally involve basic policy and objectives, as well as personnel matters, particularly those relating to political education and the ideological remolding of people. The managers, administrators, and specialists who are in their jobs largely because of professional or technical competence, formal training, education, and/or considerable work experience, are often referred to as the experts. They are primarily concerned with drawing up and implementing plans within the framework of basic policies and objectives determined by the party, as well as by technical and other day-to-day operating decisions.

The top-level Communist Party organs concerned directly with domestic trade are the Finance and Trade Work Department, and the more recently established Finance and Trade Political Department, both of them being under the Secretariat of the party's Central Committee and Politburo in Peking. The latter department was created just a few years ago to deal with ideological education in the trade and finance sectors, with the primary aim of merging "redness" and expertise along the lines desired by the regime.

The top-level government organ directly concerned with China's domestic trade is the Office for Finance and Trade under the State Council. There are four ministries under this office: Commerce, Foreign Trade, Finance, and Food. The director of this office, Li Hsien-nien, has been also Minister of Finance, as well as a member of the State Council and the party's Politburo.

The Ministry of Commerce is the central ministry in charge of the domestic trade sector on a national scale. This ministry is concerned with supply, sales, and inventory-level planning primarily in financial terms, although it also deals with the physical balancing and pricing of a limited number of commodities on a national scale. It also approves and broadly controls the inflow and outflow of major consumer goods among different provinces and major cities, and tries to ensure proper financial and critical commodity balancing among local bureaus of commerce.

There are about twenty or so specialized national trading corporations under this ministry, most of which have branches in different cities, and in some cases at the provincial level as well. Most of these corporations are organized along product lines—for example, drugs, chemicals, textiles, leather products—and each performs wholesaling and distribution functions. There is also the China General Department Store Corporation under the Ministry of Commerce, and it is involved in the management and operations of a limited number of the largest retail department stores. This national department store corporation allocates a number of major commodities for retail trade through its branches in different parts of the country.

National commercial corporations also allocate and distribute various major commodities—such as cotton, textiles, sports equipment, drugs—for retail trade among the different provinces and cities. The branches of these corporations, as well as other local wholesaling organizations, deal with products not under central control—for instance glassware, cosmetics, various synthetic leather items, sweets, handicrafts.

The local bureaus of commerce balance commodity flows and finances within their locality. There are wholesaling "stations," organized along product lines, under local bureaus of commerce which balance the inflows and outflows of goods to and from the district or province. Local commerce bureaus also deal with such matters as personnel, wages, welfare, and product prices not subject to higher level control. In some larger cities and provinces there are two bureaus of commerce. One deals with manufactured consumer goods, and the other with food, hotels, and restaurants.

There are bureaus of commerce and pricing commissions at the provincial, municipal, and district (within cities) levels, as well as branches of national trading corporations, local commercial corporations, and other wholesaling organizations at these levels. The vast majority of China's retail stores are under municipal and district control, although as indicated above a few are under the China

General Department Store Corporation— usually one of its branches—for certain matters. The author is not sure whether any retail stores are directly under provincial control, but did not learn of any that were.

The bulk of consumer goods distributed from factories to retail outlets pass through commercial wholesaling organizations, although it is not uncommon for retail stores to negotiate product orders directly with industrial organizations. National consumer goods exhibitions, organized along product lines, are usually held several times a year for each major consumer product group. In many instances similar exhibitions are held at the local levels as well. One set of exhibitions involves industrial organizations and commercial wholesaling organizations (chiefly corporations and wholesaling stations) with only limited direct participation by retail stores (mainly large ones). The other type of exhibition involves commercial wholesaling organizations and retail stores, with only minor participation by the industrial sector. The primary purpose of these consumer product exhibitions is to negotiate detailed supply and sales orders and finalize contractual agreements. Wholesaling organizations play major roles in both kinds of exhibitions since they are the key link in the distribution of consumer goods from industry to retail trade.

In general, China's domestic trade sector is characterized by complex networks of dual subordination. For example, municipal level commerce bureaus are typically subordinate to the municipal people's council for various matters—particularly those involving personnel, welfare, and the pricing of various products—as well as under provincial commerce bureaus, and even under the Ministry of Commerce, in such areas as broad planning and control, the allocation of various commodities, the pricing of major products, and key financial matters. Municipal branches of national commercial corporations are commonly subordinate to the municipal bureau of commerce for such things as personnel, while they are under central corporate control for other matters involving planning, supply allocation, and financial control. At the same time there are also commercial organizations entirely under the control of local bureaus of commerce. For instance, in Tientsin the First Light Industry Commercial Corporation is largely under the control of the municipal commerce bureau, but also is subordinate to

one of the central trading corporations in certain spheres. The same is true of the leather and chemical commercial corporations in Tientsin, but the Tientsin Daily Usage Commercial Corporation is wholly subordinate to the Tientsin Bureau of Commerce.

In general, where a municipal level commercial corporation, including branches of national corporations, is located in a city which is quite self-sufficient in the products that it handles it is likely to be subject to significantly less central control than if the reverse were true. The same seems to hold true with regard to the degree of control exerted over a municipal—or district or provincial—bureau of commerce by higher level commerce bureaus and/or the Ministry of Commerce.

It is also common for retail stores to be subject to dual control. For example, department stores are often subordinate to the municipal commerce bureau for personnel and welfare matters, as well as the retail prices charged for various products, but at the same time they are under the control of commercial corporations for other business affairs. The same is true for smaller retail stores which are under the dual control of district level commerce bureaus and local commercial organizations.

All in all, it seems that China's domestic trade sector is organizationally very complex. Executives interviewed were quite candid about organizational and other problems in the trade sector. They admitted that there is too much overlapping and duplication of activities, as well as too many links, unclear relationships, and outdated procedures and regulations.[3] They pointed out that much "experimentation" and many organizational changes have been and were still being undertaken in the trade sector in order to constantly improve the organizational setup and operations.

TRADE ORGANIZATION IN CHINA'S LEADING CITIES

In Shanghai the First Bureau of Commerce —under the Municipal People's Council—is in charge of trade involving manufactured

---

[3] See also, *Ta Kung-pao* (*The Impartial Daily*, Peking), September 10 and 13, 1965; *Joint Publications Research Service*, Washington, No. 33893, January 23, 1966.

consumer goods. Under this bureau in 1966 there were about ten commercial corporations each one concerned with the wholesaling and distribution of a specific commodity. They also operate networks of warehouses. There were also about ten wholesale stations corresponding in product lines to the commercial corporations. In fact, on a formal organization chart the corporations are likely to be reflected in a directly subordinate position to the wholesale stations, with these stations coming directly under the commerce bureau. These wholesale stations are concerned with balancing the inflow and outflow of commodities to and from Shanghai. They deal with corresponding wholesale stations in other cities and provinces. The commercial wholesaling corporations balance, distribute, and control the flow of goods and serve the market within Shanghai. They have their own product group departments and sections.

Under Shanghai's First Bureau of Commerce there is also a corporation in charge of a number of larger retail stores. Most of the smaller stores in Shanghai are under the control of district bureaus of commerce which are in turn subordinate to the Shanghai Municipal Bureau. There are also smaller and specialized district level commercial corporations and wholesaling organizations.

Shanghai's twelve largest department stores —including Wing On, China's largest joint state-private store—are under the dual control of the Municipal First Bureau of Commerce and the Shanghai Branch of the China General Department Store Corporations, which is under the Ministry of Commerce. The Shanghai Branch of this corporation deals with products that come under the local bureau of commerce for balancing purposes. This branch employs around 3,000 people, with over 100 in its head office. It has seven departments—basically similar to those found in large retail department stores—five major product group wholesale balancing sections, and over a dozen warehouses.

The trade setup in Peking and Tientsin was basically similar to that in Shanghai in 1966. Mention has already been made of some of Tientsin's commercial organizations in an earlier section. Under Peking's Bureau of Commerce in 1966 there were the following six major wholesale stations:

1. Textiles.
2. Clothing, Shoes, and Other "Daily Life Products" (e.g., soap).
3. Groceries.
4. Stationery, Sports Equipment, and Other Cultural Goods.
5. Metals, Appliances, Chemicals, and Telecommunications.
6. Local Products (including handicrafts, porcelain, toys, brooms, bamboo and straw items, glassware, etc.).

As in Shanghai, the Peking wholesale stations are concerned with interarea procurement and sales. For example, the Peking Textile Wholesale Station deals directly with textile wholesale stations, and in some cases textile commercial corporations, in other cities and provinces. This station, like most, does not employ a large number of people since its main job is commodity balancing rather than operational management. There were no more than a dozen people working for the Peking Textile Wholesale Station in 1966.

There was a commercial corporation under each of Peking's wholesale stations, each one dealing with similar product lines as its organizationally superior station. The Peking Textile Commercial Corporation employed "well over 100 people," and had several large warehouses in Peking. This corporation had cotton cloth, woolen goods, and silk commodity sections, as well as a few others. It also had departments for supply and sales, planning, finance and accounting, general administration, and one or two others.

There were five major retail department stores directly under Peking's Bureau of Commerce. Whether or to what extent these stores were also subordinate to the China General Department Store Corporation or one of its local branches is not definite. In Peking there were seven district bureaus of commerce under the municipal bureau. Most of the small stores in the city—including small joint state-private retail outlets, private shops, and cooperatives—were under district commerce bureaus. At the district level there were also branches of municipal commercial corporations, some district level corporations, as well as various other district level wholesaling organizations.

*　*　*

IDEOLOGY IN CHINA'S TRADE SECTOR

China's trade sector has been subject to the same swings in the ideological pendulum, and the same forms of ideological extremism, as the industrial sector.[4] In fact, when the pendulum has swung in the direction of extremism, domestic trade, commerce, and finance have tended to be the first spheres to come under attack. For these sectors have been regarded as politically very sensitive because they employ a large number of *bourgeois* personnel; e.g., capitalists and former private merchants or employees of former private local and foreign firms in China. Moreover, in traditional Marxian and Marxist terms, trade and commerce are viewed as rather parasitic and relatively unproductive spheres of activity.

This viewpoint may explain why trade and finance were chosen as the first spheres in 1964 in which special party political departments were established at all levels in addition to the regular party works departments, committees, and branches in the trade and finance organizational hierarchies. The party political departments in industry and communications were not established until later.

The most recent pervasive ideological campaign involving the domestic trade sector began to accelerate in September 1965 and continued through 1966.[5] It apparently petered out in 1967. This campaign began some six or seven months before the Cultural Revolution burst into the open, and also before the ideological pendulum began shifting significantly in the direction of extremism in the industrial sector.

During the period of September 1965 to April 1966, in particular, the Communist Chinese press was filled with articles calling for "ideological revolution" and much greater adherence to Mao's Thought in trade and commerce. The major themes of these articles involved merging Redness and expertness; self-interest versus serving the customer wholeheartedly; profit versus service; materialism versus altruism; attacks against localism (especially the reluctance to sell goods in short supply to other cities and provinces); improper business hours; poor product planning, stocking wrong goods, and poor quality repair work because of inadequate concern for customers and their needs, and so on. Socialist educational campaigns and ideological sessions were frequently organized by party political departments at all levels of the trade hierarchy. Model trade workers—such as Yang Chen-yu, a salesclerk at the Fong Chi-cheng Department Store—were exalted in the press.[6] Yang, and others, were praised for "serving the people with one's whole being" under Mao's guidance, and for putting customer and state interests above their own.

By the time that I surveyed three of China's largest retail department stores, and a number of smaller shops, the ideological campaign in the trade sector may have already passed its peak. The stores surveyed seemed to be functioning quite well. I was much more impressed with them than with the Soviet stores that I visited in the early 1960's; and there were no obvious symptoms of very serious inefficiencies resulting from ideological extremism. However, the Tientsin State Department Store had abolished its system of extra rewards (bonus payments) at the end of 1965, and the manager of the Peking Department Store said in April 1966 that they were considering a similar move. I did not learn enough about the Tientsin store to determine whether the end of its bonus system was having any negative impacts on operating efficiency.

---

[4] There are four identifiable basic features of this ideological pendulum: (1) Reds versus experts; (2) self-interest and material incentives versus altruism, self-sacrifice and moral stimuli; (3) class struggle and the elimination of class distinctions; (4) amount of working time spent on political education and ideological indoctrination. During periods of ideological extremism, policies and programs are launched in the above sphere with the chief aim of rapidly transforming the Chinese people into a nation of pure Communist men, as interpreted by Mao.

For a detailed analysis of China's ideological pendulum, *see* the sources cited in footnote 2 above.

[5] Cf., the sources cited in footnote 2. *Ta Kung-pao* carried articles on China's trade sector continuously through September and October 1965. See also, *Jen-min Jih-pao* (*People's Daily*, Peking), September 25 and December 30, 1965; many articles on Chinese trade and commerce have been translated in *JPRS*, IV, No. 8 (February 4, 1966), Reel No. 52 (on microfilm).

[6] See *Hung Ch'i* (Red Flag), No. 2 (February 11, 1966), 36-41.

SOME SINO-SOVIET COMPARISONS[7]

It appears that domestic trade is substantially more decentralized down to the municipal and district levels in China than in the Soviet Union. In both countries considerably greater powers were pushed down to the provincial level, or in the Soviet Union to the republic level. The Chinese, however, have apparently carried this decentralization down to the municipal level to a greater degree than have the Soviets.

In China's domestic trade sector there are clearly serious and widespread deficiencies in marketing research and analysis of consumer demand, consumer satisfaction, product planning, and sales promotion. Few statistics are available, particularly in rural areas. However, the Chinese began paying serious attention to these problems before the Soviets did, and the Chinese may well have made more effective progress in some of these areas to date. Perhaps Red China, as a nation, has better commercial instincts, as well as a greater flare for and interest in marketing and consumer satisfaction than does the Soviet Union. There certainly seemed to be substantially more direct contact between the trade and industrial sectors—including contact between factories and retail stores—in China. There also seems to be greater concern for consumer satisfaction and customer service at the retail level in China.

The Red Chinese have also been involved with advertising and sales promotion longer and more extensively than have the Soviets, although advertising in China is still basically informative rather than persuasive. There have been special advertising organizations in Red China for some years, while they have only recently been created in Russia. The press, magazines, billboards, telephone directories, and the cinema are the major advertising media in China. Greatest use is made of them in major cities such as Shanghai, Canton, Tientsin, and to a lesser extent Peking and Wuhan. While much of the advertising is aimed at wholesale and retail organizations—and carries the producer's names—there is also a fair amount aimed at the ultimate consumer. Shanghai is China's leading and best-run commercial and retailing center, and it is held up by the regime as a model for other parts of the country to emulate.

From the very sparse data that was obtained from the handful of Chinese retail stores surveyed, it does appear that pay differentials between industrial and retail or other trade personnel may be substantially smaller in China than in the Soviet Union where industrial employees have received considerably more pay on the average.[8] It also seems likely that on the average, in large stores at least, a somewhat greater proportion of employees have higher education in China than in the U.S.S.R.[9] It is quite possible that the Chinese regime has been allocating a larger proportion of higher education graduate to the trade sector than has the Soviet Union.

All in all, the author was surprisingly impressed by the merchandise and by the activities at the Chinese department stores visited and by Chinese marketing in general, especially considering that this is both a poor and a Communist country.

---

[7] In my opinion the two best sources on Soviet marketing and domestic trade are M. Goldman, *Soviet Marketing* (New York: Free Press of Glencoe, 1963); and J. Felker, *Soviet Economic Controversies: The Emerging Marketing Concept and Changes in Planning 1960–65* (Cambridge, Mass.: Massachusetts Institute of Technology Press, 1966).

[8] This statement is based on pay data obtained in Russia in the early 1960's. Soviet wage figures can be found in N. Dewitt, *Education and Professional Employment in the USSR* (Washington, D.C.: National Science Foundation, 1961), pp. 810–13, Appendix VI-w. See also Felker, *op. cit.*, especially chapter 7.

[9] For Soviet figures, see Dewitt, *op. cit.*, pp. 474 and 536. B. Richman, *Management Development and Education in the Soviet Union* (East Lansing: Division of Research, Graduate School of Business Administration, Michigan State University, 1967), pp. 61-69, Tables III-15 through III-22.

The Environmental Forces
of Marketing

As noted earlier this book places emphasis on the environmental forces of marketing. This approach recognizes that the nature of marketing, marketing policies and practices, and the operation of marketing are all a reflection of the environment in which they are carried out. The environment of marketing represents the forces of change and the shaping of the character of marketing activities. Just what are these forces? They are, in the opinion of the editors, the physical environment, the competitive environment, the legal dimension, technological developments, and consumer demand. Part II is organized so that the student more clearly can conceive of the *why* of marketing phenomena and also better appreciate the interrelationships of marketing behavior in modern society.

The physical environment of marketing takes on special significance today and will undoubtedly be of major concern of most thinking citizens throughout the 1970s. Edmunds' article clearly exposes the failure of marketing regarding the environment. These failures create a dilemma for marketing in almost all facets of marketing activity—especially products, pricing, and market communication. With our goals of consumer satisfaction narrowly defined, we have failed to recognize the higher-order needs that we derive from our biological and natural environment. The day is here for marketing practitioners and academicians to revise their thinking.

The next article ("Bottles-Cans-Energy") demonstrates what can be done when some logical alternative to a bad environmental situation is well studied and analyzed. In this same vein, the student may want to review some of the articles in subsequent sections of this book and particularly "Recycling Solid Wastes: A Channels-of-Distribution Problem" and "Criteria for a Theory of Responsible Consumption."

A most-pervasive marketing force is the legal dimension. These readings provide the reader with the impact of government upon our marketing system and some of the more-advanced views concerning the consumer and the dilemmas that he faces on a day-to-day basis. Of particular note are the rights of consumers as cited by the late President John F. Kennedy.

One of the greatest influences on the lives of all of us is technology and the fact that this force exerts great and rapid change on the social and economic environment. The management of this important modern-day phenomenon and how it relates to marketing is discussed.

Consumer demand is the focus of much marketing planning. Often we concentrate our analyses of consumer demand on economic factors. The selection by George Katona recognizes the noneconomic variables as especially influential in determining consumer demand. The reader can particularly isolate the major social and psychological influences affecting consumer demand. Katona's reading undoubtedly adds another dimension to the major constructs of consumer behavior. The remaining selections deal with voluntary poverty as cited by a university student and the identifiable consumption patterns in developing economies.

The environmental forces of marketing set the stage for a more-comprehensive understanding and appreciation of buyer behavior and marketing management.

D. The Physical Environment

11. Market Failure in the Environment

STAHRL W. EDMUNDS

The marketing function has encountered difficulties regarding the environment in three senses:

1. The environment has undergone serious degradation which presents hazards to biological balance, species survival, and human health itself.

2. Market pricing does not include all of the external or social costs of private products; and economists speak of this as a "market failure" because resources cannot be allocated to optimize consumer wants.

3. The marketing concept has not sought to optimize all consumer satisfactions, including environmental quality, but only product or service satisfactions.

These three "failures" can all be remedied; but their origins lie deep in historical assumptions which, to change, could require a considerable revolution in marketing thought.

ENVIRONMENTAL HAZARDS AND DEGRADATION

An environmental crisis has emerged suddenly on the American scene, as a result of population growth, increasing urbanization, and a rising gross national product. Population increased by 18 million people from 1960 to 1970, and another 23 million is in prospect

◆ SOURCE: Reprinted by permission from *Marketing Education and the Real World* and *Dynamic Marketing in a Changing World*, edited by Boris W. Becker and Helmut Becker, Combined Proceedings of the Spring and Fall Conferences of the American Marketing Association, 1972, Series No. 34, pp. 208–212.

by 1980. More than half of the 205 million people are presently crowded into 1% of the land space and two-thirds of the people on 9% of the land. At the same time, gross national product increased 50% in the past decade, and is expected to increase another 50% in the next. Rough estimates indicate that the amount of wastes are about equal to the amount of usable product, or about 6 pounds of waste per dollar of GNP. This constitutes about 6 trillion pounds of residuals per year, or 15 tons per person. When 15 tons of residuals per person are disposed for 100 million people on 1% of the land, the environment deteriorates from toxic substances, pollution of air and water, and the reduction of the life-support capability of the surrounding ecological systems.

The President of the United States has reported to the Congress: "Unless we arrest the depredations that have been inflicted so carelessly on our natural systems—which exist in an intricate set of balances—we face the prospect of ecological disaster.[1]

The Administrator of Environmental Health, in the U.S. Department of Health, Education and Welfare, has testified before Congress:

"The almost incredible advances in science and technology during recent history have produced tremendous benefits to human life. These benefits, however, have been accompanied by frightening changes in the balance of the ecological system of which man is an integral part but to which he has been com-

[1] "Environmental Quality," *First Annual Report of the Council on Environmental Quality*, August 1970, Supt. of Documents, Wash., D.C., p. v.

placent. . . . We are at a point where death, injury and diseases are measures of the pollution of air, land, and water."[2]

A medical task force for the U.S. Public Health Services identified the following environmental hazards to health:

1. Respiratory diseases and elevated death rates for those with respiratory ailments from air pollution.

2. Hazards of food and water-borne diseases from new processes and increased residuals.

3. Noise levels associated with hearing damage.

4. Toxic hazards due to chemicalization of the environment.

5. Half the population lives in a microwave exposure environment far higher than permitted by European standards.

6. Increasing exposure to cancer, cell mutation, and birth defects from new products which are introduced faster than their safety can be ascertained.[3,4]

The human health costs of air pollution are estimated at $6 billion per year, plus another $10 billion annual damage to vegetation and property. Compared to this total damage cost of $16 billion per year, an investment of about $5 billion per year would be needed for air pollution abatement.[5]

Every major stream in the United States is polluted and water quality continues to deteriorate. Fish kills in streams run from 6 million to 40 million per year. Marine life is declining in estuaries. Mercury contamination is world-wide, and fishing areas have been closed in Sweden and Finland as well as in the U.S.[6] One hypothesis for the widespread mercury contamination is from burning of fossil fuels for electric power production.[7] Mercury poisoning is not alone among the toxic metal hazards, which include compounds of nickel, berylium, barium, cadmium, lead, selenium, arsenic, molybdenum, and antimony. The consumption of all these metals, as well as other synthetic chemicals alien to the natural environment, are increasing rapidly.[8]

These, then, are a few among the many reasons why government reports say that death and disease are the measures of air, water, and land pollution; we are introducing new products into the environment faster than their safety can be assured.

FAILURE IN THE MARKETING CONCEPT

Industry and technology are among the principal sources of residuals and waste loads in the environment, particularly the toxic wastes. The toxic wastes are dispersed by air and water circulation, enter the nutrient chain, and eventually return through human diet and respiration to damage human health. Many of these hazardous residuals occur by the introduction of new products faster than their safety can be assured. Marketing is the principal instrument through which new products are introduced into consumption. Hence, the marketing function initiates, unknowingly perhaps, the process of ecological degradation and biological damage.

The consequence of unknowingly being the initiator of biological damage is not consonant with the marketing concept. The marketing concept presumes to concern itself with: (1) realizing consumer orientation and satisfactions; (2) integrating total business operations toward consumer satisfactions; and (3) earning a profit from operations. A conflict exists among these objectives as to whether the real goal is to optimize consumer satisfactions or maximize profits. The faltering of the marketing concept, as seen by academic and practicing marketing men, has been that

[2] Senate Hearings Before the Committee on Appropriations, Dept. of HEW Appropriations, HR18515, 91st Congress, Second Session, Fiscal Year 1971, Part IV, p. 2090, Supt. of Documents, Wash., D.C.

[3] "Man's Health and the Environment," Report of the Task Force on Research Planning in Environmental Health Science, U.S. Public Health Service, March, 1970, Supt. of Documents, Wash., D.C., pp. 11–15.

[4] B. Jennings and J. Murphy, eds., "Interactions of Man and His Environment," Proceedings of the Northwestern University Conference, Plenum Press, N.Y., 1966, pp. 131–135.

[5] "Environmental Quality," Second Annual Report of the Council on Environmental Quality, August 1971, Supt. of Documents, Wash., D.C., pp. 106–117, 218.

[6] "Hazards of Mercury," Environmental Research, Vol. 4 (March, 1971), p. 6.

[7] Oiva J. Joensuu, "Fossil Fuels as a Source of Mercury Pollution," Science, Vol. 172 (4 June, 1971), p. 1027.

[8] Council for Environmental Quality, "Toxic Substances," Supt. of Documents, Wash., D.C., April, 1971, pp. 2–10.

all too often profit dominates the goal structure so that consumer satisfactions are secondary. Thus, there has been growing academic skepticism in the literature of the efficacy of the marketing concept.[9] This skepticism is not shared by top executives, who continue to believe in the marketing concept and their own operational adherence to its tenets in their decisions.[10]

Meantime, the marketing manager faces a double jeopardy. His management has partially adopted a marketing concept which is faltering. Second, he has sold new products to his customers faster than biological safety can be ascertained. The marketer may need to unsell both his boss and the consumer on what he has been doing, or face the erosion of his marketing function. The erosion has already appeared in the form of consumer activism and political regulation. In truth, the marketer has unknowingly been put into an incongruous situation.

What does one do in an incongruent situation? One solution, suggested by Bettman, is to expand the decision model.[11] That is, new information and branches need to be added to the decision loops.

The simplified logic under which the marketing concept functions is that rising standards of living increase consumer needs; therefore, the maximization of consumer satisfactions is to produce more and better goods. The prevailing condition now is not too few goods, but too much waste. Too many people and too many residuals are causing an environmental deterioration which is threatening to health, ecological balance, diversity, living space, and aesthetics.

There lies the incongruity; the waste loads are concomitants of rising living standards. Industrial technology and the marketing process deliver equal parts of unwanted and wanted goods simultaneously. The consumer gets an automobile plus air pollution, electricity plus mercury contamination, more food plus pesticides in the food chain, communication plus microwave exposure, and chemical cure-alls plus carcinogens. The incongruity is that the marketer, in maximizing satisfactions, is also maximizing dissatisfactions by the high waste loads, residuals, and toxic materials placed in the environment.

FAILURE IN THE MARKET PRICING STRUCTURE

High waste loads are disposed into the environment as though such disposal is costless; and this is on the presumption that air, water, oceans, sometimes land, are "free goods." True, the environment can assimilate considerable organic wastes through decomposition in the soil; but the excess organic residuals, and many inorganic chemicals, cannot be assimilated, with the consequence of damage and deterioration.

The problem, then, is that the environment is treated as "free" when it is not. If there is not a monetary cost, there is often a biological cost. The air is free to the internal combustion engine; but the emissions from the internal combustion engine are not breathable by man. The water in a stream is "free" to the chemical plant, although the effluent is toxic to biological species. The oceans are free to dumping, although the marine species may decline in population.

The overuse and misuse of the—supposedly free—environment is what Hardin has called "the tragedy of the commons."[12] The commons (commonly used resources) has been abused from time immemorial by the inexorable drive of every person to make the maximum use of that which is free.

The historic solution to ruination of the commons has been to close it and put a price on it. Most of the common lands have long since been closed; water rights are closing and water is being repriced. The air is still "free," but high quality air acquires a price when pollution begins to cause health damage which must be remedied. The price of breathable air is the cost of reducing emissions from stationary sources and new cars, cost of re-equipping old cars with exhaust controls, costs of inspection and maintenance of cars on the road, costs of alternate forms of transporta-

[9] Bell and Emory, "The Faltering Marketing Concept," *Journal of Marketing*, Vol. 35, (October, 1971), pp. 37–42. Also, Carlton P. McNamara, "The Present Status of the Marketing Concept," *Journal of Marketing*, Vol. 36 (January, 1972) p. 50 ff.

[10] Barksdale and Darden, "Marketer's Attitudes Toward the Marketing Concept," *Journal of Marketing*, Vol. 35 (October, 1971), pp. 29–36.

[11] James R. Beltman, "The Structure of Consumer Choice Processes," *Journal of Marketing Research*, Vol. 8 (November, 1971), pp. 465–471.

[12] G. Hardin, "The Tragedy of the Commons," *Science*, Vol. 162 (13 December, 1968), pp. 1243–1248.

tion, costs in convenience of travel time. Either pollution control costs such as these will be added to the price of private products, or the opportunity cost will be felt in some other form of sacrifice, such as taxation, social costs, or biological damage.

REPRICING AS A REMEDY

The problem is, essentially, that marketers and businessmen have taken a narrow view of their costs. The income statement records only the short-term costs of production for materials, labor, factory and management overhead. It does not include the costs of disposing of all its wastes and residuals, nor the use of the air, nor the biological damage in streams and oceans. The profit and loss statement is a means of recording the direct operating costs of the business, but it shifts much of the social and biological costs, inherent in its production technology, elsewhere. The costs appear elsewhere in the form of ecological damage.

A remedy for such environmental degradation is to reprice industrial products to include all their social and environmental costs. The repricing might be in the form of recovering costs for investment in better pollution control equipment. It might be in the form of taxation to clean up effluents or emissions which presently are not technologically controllable. Or it might take the form of indemnification, such as restoring strip mine sites to usable form.

The proposition before the marketer, then is that satisfying consumer wants, in terms of environmental quality as well as products, requires a restructuring of the market pricing mechanism to include social and environmental costs as well as direct product costs. This means, in effect, that the marketer may need to raise his product costs and prices sufficiently to reduce residuals below the level of environmental hazard; and by this means the marketer would be satisfying consumer needs, both material and ecological.

If, however, the marketer seeks to cover the external environmental costs in the product, he is putting the faltering marketing concept to the test again; for he will then be increasing the tension between the profit goal and the consumer satisfaction goal. The marketer will be advocating, in effect, that the firm may have to reduce its profits by incurring costs which improve environmental quality and enhance consumer satisfactions, but may not be recoverable immediately in volume or price. This advocacy on the part of the marketer could place him in conflict with other executives seeking financial goals. Can the marketing man take that chance? Is he in a strong enough position in the hierarchy to take the risk? These are hard questions, but less hard approached from the reverse. Can the marketer afford not to take the chance? Can he afford the defensive posture?

IMPLICATIONS OF A DEFENSIVE STRATEGY

Suppose the marketer decides that he is not in a strong enough position internally to fight a battle for enhancing consumer environmental satisfactions because the increased costs would put him at odds with other executives. He chooses survival and abandons the faltering marketing concept. He feels it is easier to defend himself against consumers than other executives, so he adopts an externally defensive strategy.

The strategy consists of defending his company products on their techno-economic merits, regardless of their ecological effects. That is to say, he advertises and rationalizes the maximization of consumers' material wants as taking precedence over biological or aesthetic wants. Thus, when government regulation seeks to remove lead from gasoline, the marketer would argue that lead is the most economical and effective anti-knock additive, and the death of animals in the Staten Island Zoo from lead poisoning[13] is not of primary concern, even if zoo animals may be indicator species of human health hazard.

Or, in another example, when a consumer activist alleges that a particular automobile is unsafe at any speed, the role of the marketer would be to compile a dossier to discredit the allegations. Or suppose the government questions whether automobile tires are safe at high speeds, the defensive role of the marketer is to go before a federal agency hearing and prove they are indeed safe. Or, perhaps, the Food and Drug Administration finds that some substance, like tobacco or a drug or a persistent pesticide in food, is harmful to health, then the defensive marketer develops proof which justifies their use and counters the charges.

The role of the marketer, in a world of consumer activism and environmental regu-

---

[13] Robert Bazell, "Lead Poisoning," *Science*, Vol. 173 (9. July, 1971), p. 130.

lation, is that of a defender and publicist. The marketer turned defender thus has taken care of himself. The question is, then, who takes care of the consumer? Whose function is it, then, to seek the satisfaction of consumer wants? The politicians? The consumer activists? That is to say, the marketing concept becomes externalized from the firm, alienated, separated, done by those outside of management who gain votes or public accord by prosecuting business enterprise. And so, marketing becomes an adversary to what public policy alleges to be in the consumer interest; and it is a substantial reversal of roles for the marketing function to become an opponent of consumers.

IMPLICATIONS OF AN ENVIRONMENTAL STRATEGY

Assume for a moment that the adversary role is not a congenial outcome for the marketing concept; the marketer decides to take the riskier but more positive stance, which is to optimize consumer satisfactions, material and ecological, even if it results in internal conflict with other executives over profit and financial results. How would the scenario then read?

The marketer would use his considerable survey research skills to ascertain the relative priorities of consumer wants, both environmental and material. Some evidence suggests that consumers do perceive environmental problems and are willing to pay premium prices for its improvement.[14] The marketer would seek answers to such questions as: How much in cost and convenience in travel time is the consumer willing to pay for cleaner air? What change in life style and behavior is the consumer willing to contemplate to improve the design, transport, and amenities of urban living? What health hazards has the consumer perceived or experienced from environmental exposure to pollutants or hazardous material?

With findings from survey research in hand, the marketer would then turn to the technical departments to find out what alternatives there are in performance and cost to such problem products as automobiles, persistent pesticides, detergents, industrial effluents, microwave radiation, noise, food and

toxic hazards. The marketer's technical inquiry would not stop at the plant door nor at the retail store, but he would investigate the dispersion of chemicals and residuals in the environment to see whether they enter the food chain or where they finally repose.

The marketer, armed with findings on consumer satisfactions and technical alternatives, would then propose product development choices with their relative financial costs. He would recommend programs which optimize consumer satisfactions, both ecological and material, with a satisfactory long-term return.

In short, a positive marketing strategy in environmental affairs is the same thing that the marketer was supposed to be doing under the marketing concept in the first place. The only difference, perhaps, is that the marketer and management recognize the incongruence of their position in trying to satisfy consumer wants, under the circumstance where they produce about as much unwanted residuals as wanted products. The problem, then, is to enlarge the decision model. The kind of market which is compatible with the environmental quality is one in which products are repriced to cover all their social and ecological costs, and in which these internalized costs become part of the decision structure used by management.

SUMMARY

The market failure in the environment is seen in: (1) biological damage which presents hazards to ecological balance and human health; (2) failures in the marketing concept to optimize all consumer satisfactions including environmental quality as well as product volume; and (3) failure in the market price mechanism to cover social and biological costs of product decisions. The consequence of the market failures is that the marketing function is becoming externalized from business, and falling into the hands of politicians and consumer activists who seek to prosecute enterprise for its product decisions.

The marketer can respond by defending company products on techno-economic grounds, regardless of biological effects, in which case marketing may become adversary to consumer interests. Or, the marketer can attempt to make the marketing concept work, by trying to realize all of the consumers' needs, biological as well as material, by creating a new decision model which internalizes social and environmental costs.

---

[14] Harold H. Kassarjian, "Incorporating Ecology into Marketing Strategy," *Journal of Marketing,* Vol. 35 (July, 1971), at p. 61.

12. Bottles Cans Energy

BRUCE M. HANNON

American consumers paid about $25 billion in 1966 for packaging, 90 percent of which was discarded.[1] By 1971 the packaging industry had become an even larger, multibillion dollar interest opposed to reduction of the amount of materials used in wrapping, sacking, canning, bottling, and otherwise protecting and selling merchandise to the consuming public. Advertising campaigns sponsored principally by container manufacturers and based on convenience appeal have largely convinced our increasingly mobile society that the throwaway container works in the public's best interest. But litter, problems of solid waste disposal, high consumer purchase cost, and resource drain are fostering opposition to the packaging syndrome.

Nowhere is this conflict more clearly underscored than in the packaging of beer and soft drinks. These two commodities alone constitute a major portion of the food and beverage consumed by the U.S. public. About one-half of all beverage and food containers are for beer and soft drinks.[1]

The purchase price of soft drinks in throwaway glass is 30 percent more than when it is sold in returnable containers.[2] Added to this are litter pickup, hauling, and landfill costs paid by the consumer through monthly billings from trash haulers and state and municipal taxes. There are, in addition, the environmental costs of material and energy production paid in terms of health and aesthetic losses such as lung damage from power plant emissions and land strip-mined for coal. Were these costs tabulated and presented to the consumers at the time of purchase, the public would at least know the true cost of packaging convenience and might choose to buy less expensive returnable containers. (The Illinois consumer seems to prefer the returnable soft drink bottle to the throwaway.)[3]

On the other hand the packaging people have wedged themselves into the economic web, causing a redistribution of labor. Now labor, as well as the packaging industry, is opposed to a reduction in the volume of throwaway containers. One wonders if a reduction in the use of the earth's capital supplies of fuels for the production of energy might actually mean an increase in the need for human energy and consequently fuller employment. Indeed, Professor Hugh Folk

[1] Bureau of Solid Waste Management, *The Role of Packaging in Solid Waste Management*, Environmental Protection Agency, Washington, D.C., 1969.

◆ SOURCE: Reprinted by permission of The Committee For Environmental Information, Inc., *Environment*, Vol. 14, No. 2, March, 1972, pp. 11-21. © 1972 by The Committee For Environmental Information, Inc.

[2] "Fact Sheet 3," Press Release, Crusade for a Cleaner Environment, 1900 L Street, N.W., Washington, D.C., Spring 1970.

[3] "An Investigation of the Effects on Society and the Environment of Alternative Methods of Food and Beverage Packaging," National Science Foundation Student Orginated Studies, GY-9164, Jan. 1972.

has studied the effects of a conversion of the beverage container system to returnables in Illinois and found a net increase of 6,500 jobs.[4]

RETURNABLES AND RECYCLING

The use of returnables is one form of resource recycling, which almost everyone agrees promotes a more desirable environment. We recognize that the materials which constitute most of our goods are finite. The dispersal of these materials into landfills is therefore increasingly viewed as wasteful of both land and materials. These materials should somehow be reintroduced into our system of consumption. A simplistic view of such a system is to return the used item to its point of manufacture; i.e., an abandoned auto is dismembered and the steel is returned to the steel companies, discarded glass bottles are returned to the bottle manufacturer, etc. This is a highly simplified recognition of the law of conservation of mass. However, little public or scientific environmental attention has been given to a companion physical law, that of conservation of energy. Energy resources are also finite and also cause environmental degradation when consumed too rapidly. Full pollution control may ultimately be achieved, but there is no alternative to resource depletion.

A consideration of both laws lets us decide when and where to reintroduce the used material or whether a material needed to have been created in the first place.

The object of this article is to present an example of the use of these physical laws to describe recycling in the packaging industry. If any generality can be gained from the example it is that recycling of mass should be accomplished at the earliest opportunity, in order to use the least mass and the least energy of the alternatives available to perform a desired service.

Analyses such as these become very important if we are facing shortages of energy or materials. The rising cost of energy due to recognition of environmental costs, to the fluctuation of foreign supplies, and to the decrease in certain proved energy reserves in

the U.S.[5] may have the effect of an energy shortage.

In an energy shortage, the most efficient energy systems should dominate, but we must also soon question the need for the quantity consumed in providing a given quality of life. In other words, there is an extremely important distinction between evaluating system efficiency and evaluating the amount of and purposes of the energy consumed; the former is primarily an engineering matter, the latter is mainly a societal one.

Had energy not been so accessible and therefore so cheap in the U.S., many systems might not be so extensive and in use today, e.g., the automobile, the aluminum industry, the packaging industry. But energy is rapidly becoming expensive. Dr. David Schwartz, assistant chief of the Office of Economics of the Federal Power Commission, estimates that environmental costs alone will raise the cost of electricity about one cent per kilowatt-hour, which should more than double current industrial prices. We therefore must plan for least-energy-consuming systems. In fact, some hold that energy is the real currency in human societies as well as in ecosystems.[6] Under this view, items would have as their true value the resource energy committed in their manufacture. This type of pricing reflects wasted energy and dwindling energy resources, as well as the scarcity of the mass involved.

THE ORIGIN OF THROWAWAYS

The first efforts at market conversion to one-way beverage containers were made by the steel industry in the late forties and early fifties. Together with the major can companies, they viewed the beer and soft drink market as the last major expansion area for steel cans. With returnable bottles averaging about 40 trips from the consumer to the bottler, it was clear that 40 cans would be needed to replace each returnable bottle over a period of six to eight months. Aluminum companies made their entrance into the market in the mid- to late fifties by introducing the all-aluminum beer can. Aluminum has since appeared in the tops of steel beer and soft drink cans to facilitate opening.

---

[4] Folk, Hugh, "Employment Effects of the Mandatory Deposit Regulation," Illinois Institute for Environmental Quality, 189 W. Madison St., Chicago, Ill., Jan. 1972.

[5] Hubbert, M. King, "Energy Resources," Ch. 8 of *Resources and Man*, National Academy of Sciences, New York, 1969.

[6] Odum, Howard, *Environment, Power, and Society*, John Wiley and Sons, New York, 1970.

A surprising early success of cans was found in the ghetto areas of major cities. Because inner-city dwellers generally travel on foot and have small family storage and cooling space, they often purchase one cooled package per visit to the market; the three to four cent deposit per single returnable bottle lacks the appeal of a case of returnable bottles. Further, the process of reacquiring the deposit appears to be very demeaning for the inner-city resident.[7] There was also stiff retailer resistance to accepting returned bottles because of diminishing retail storage space. In 1960, for example, 40 percent of the roofed supermarket space was devoted to nonselling storage, and in 1970 only 10 percent of such space was for storage.[7] However, the bottler's storage space has increased significantly due to the diversity of containers.[8]

Suburbanites tend to favor returnable bottles much more than do inner-city residents. Suburbanites usually do their grocery shopping by auto, and also can exert more influence over the retailer. As a result, returnable bottles make significantly more trips back to the grocer in the suburbs.

Since the beverage makers and bottlers were not selling containers to the public, they were indifferent to the needs of the steel and can companies. Nevertheless, the beverage wholesalers and retailers had their own inducements toward conversion of the market to throwaway containers; the reduction of storage space and the elimination of the labor of sorting and stacking returnables had obvious appeal.

At about the same time, glass bottle manufacturers realized the impact of cans on their market, and competition between glass and steel throwaways began. With these pressures from both sides, the bottlers revised their bottling lines to handle throwaway containers.

Therefore, the decline in return rate and retreat from the market place of the returnable is not caused by bottle fragility but is due to general affluence, competition from other packages, and advertising, the mechanism for change in consumer habits.

The container manufacturer uses advertising not only on the consumer but on the other key parts of the industry. The Glass Container Manufacturers Institute's advertising program was described by an official of that organization as "three-pronged, directed at the packer, the retailer, and the ultimate consumer."[9]

In the face of this campaign, the market share of the returnable bottle has declined appreciably, as shown in Table 1, with further declines expected. While beverage consumption rose 1.6 times from 1958 to 1970, beverage *container* consumption rose 4.2 times during the same period, a further reflection of the increasing use of throw-away containers. While fewer returnable containers are being sold, those which are used make fewer return trips to the bottler. From a high of 40 return trips per soft drink container for example, the national average has declined to about 15 trips.

Table 1. A Comparison of the Returnable Bottle Market Share (Percent) for Beer and Soft Drink Beverages[1]

	1958	1966	1976
Soft drink	98	80	32
Beer	58	35	20

The market share of returnables remains higher for soft drinks than for beer. There are several probable reasons for the lag of the soft drink market conversion to throwaway containers. The relatively high cost ratio of the throwaway container to the total soft drink product is probably the most important reason. Another possible force which slows the throwaway intrusion is the housewife's generally excellent grasp of the unit cost of soft drinks. This probably occurs because she is an experienced shopper while the beer purchaser is less familiar with the importance of such calculations. The relatively high refill rate on beer containers is largely due to the type of retail outlet (tavern) and to the fact that market percentages are more nearly stable relative to soft drinks. Finally, because of the corrosive qualities of soft drinks (due to their relatively high acidity and oxygen content), introduction of cans has been slower.

---

[7] The Joyce Bottling Company, 1970-71 data, 4544 W. Carroll Ave., Chicago, Ill.

[8] Trebellas, John, The Champaign (Illinois) Pepsi Bottling Company, personal communication, Mar-Apr. 1971.

[9] United States vs. Continental Can Co., 378 U.S. 441, 1964, p. 441.

There is still reluctance among some bottlers to continue the throwaway practice because the one-way container increases the cost of consumption and therefore reduces sales and consequently profit. Many claim, however, that the throwaway container has increased their sales volume and accordingly improved their competitive position.

But the bottlers are succumbing to the "economies of scale" and following the centralizing tendencies of other industries. For example, there were 8,000 soft drink bottlers in 1960; a decade later their numbers had dwindled to only 3,600.[7] The centralized bottlers tend to the one-way container because of the inefficient return shipping of empty returnable bottles.

The only force opposing this centralizing tendency is the franchising procedure used by the major beverage makers. These franchises provide each bottler an exclusive territory, a practice which tends to irritate the large food wholesalers who are then required to buy soft drinks locally. This procedure breaks up the food wholesalers' economy of scale and has consequently produced the "private-label" soft drink. These brands are packaged exclusively in cans and sold over extremely large areas from very large centralized plants. The private-label soft drinks are sometimes sold with the wholesalers' or retailers' label and tend to be priced much lower than the major brands. The price difference is in the beverage, however, not the container.

Recently the Federal Trade Commission filed a complaint with the U.S. Justice Department to break up the major soft drink franchise operations, charging that these operations tend to exclude competition. The small bottlers are quite opposed to this complaint as they feel it will lead to large centralized canning plants.[8]

Although the beverage container industry is small compared to the economy as a whole, it has been estimated that a return to returnable bottles from throwaway beverage bottles and cans would reduce the purchase costs by $1.4 billion per year.[2]

A plethora of bottle and carton sizes has accumulated on the market. Beverages are sold in 7-, 10-, 12-, 16-, and 28-ounce containers and sold singly, in 6-packs, in 8-packs or in 24-bottle cases. This great variety tends to conceal the unit cost from all but the most calculating consumer. For example, six 12-oz.

soft drink returnables sell for $1.04, including a 30 cent deposit, while six 12-oz. cans sell for 99 cents. The marked price encourages can sales, but the beverage in returnable bottles is actually about 30 percent less expensive than in cans or throwaways. A recent court ruling in Illinois declared it illegal to tax the consumer on the deposit charge. This has had the effect of requiring a clear display of the deposit charge.

A 12-ounce returnable soft drink bottle costs the bottlers about nine cents; a 12-ounce throwaway bottle costs about four cents and a 12-oz. can costs about five cents.[10] Even though the glass throwaway costs less than a can, it is heavier and subject to inconvenient breakage. Cans can be shipped more compactly than one-way glass bottles and are much less difficult to dispose of.[11] Throwaway glass containers can be returned to the bottle maker as waste glass (cullet), although color separation is a considerable problem. The small percentage of returned cans are not remelted but chemically dissolved to obtain copper, which is currently very scarce in natural form.[12]

Besides the decrease in number of trips made by the returnable bottle, other results of heavy emphasis on throwaway packaging were a sharp increase in roadside litter and a significant increase in solid waste. In particular, those who became committed to the one-way container were quite concerned with the adverse advertising provided by a labeled discarded container. The agencies that had formed to promote their throwaway container interests now joined together to form an anti-litter organization. The Can Manufacturers Institute and the Glass Container Manufacturers Institute teamed with the U.S. Brewers Association and the National Soft Drink Bottlers Association to form the vehicle for public education against littering, "Keep America Beautiful, Inc." It was through advertising campaigns by these agencies that I became interested in the packaging industry. It initially seemed a paradox that these same

---

[10] Joyce, Tom, "Solid Waste—Litter," Release to State of Illinois Subcommittee on Solid Waste Source Reduction, The Joyce Bottling Company, Chicago, Aug. 10, 1971.

[11] "Reports on Packaging Wastes to Mayor John V. Lindsay," New York City Environment Protection Agency, New York, Jan. 28, 1971.

[12] Grisimer, Robert, Continental Can Company, Chicago, personal communication, Aug. 10, 1970.

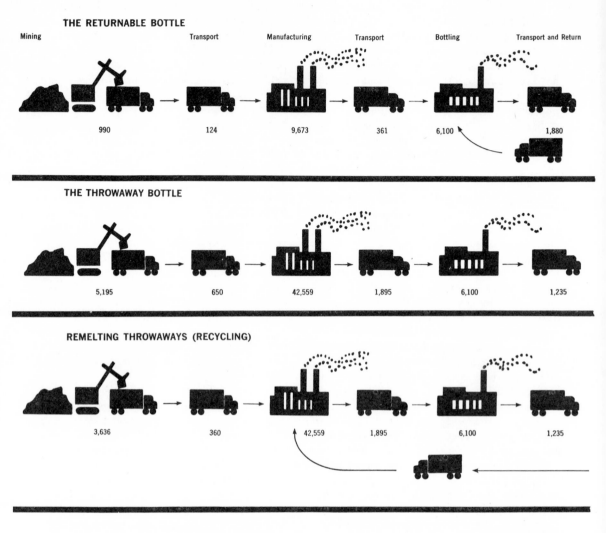

FIGURE 1. The energy costs of three different soft-drink container systems: returnable bottles (without recycling of scrap bottles), throwaway bottles (without recycling) and throwaway bottles with recycling. The figures given for each step of the process are in British Thermal Units (BTUs) per gallon of beverage for soft drinks in 16-ounce bottles. Returnables are assumed to make eight trips each.

agencies would vigorously and successfully oppose the reduction in generation of solid waste and litter and at the same time promote anti-littering campaigns.

In answer to the solid waste problems, the above agencies have actively supported a solid waste collection system which would gather household and commercial waste and separate the waste into recyclable components from which new products could be made. This proposed solution closes, with the exception of lost materials, the mass flow loop in packaging beer and soft drinks. The industry calls this "remelting" concept "recycling,"

and it is. But returnable bottles are also a form of "recycling," perhaps best called "refilling." However, the system in use today seems to be tending toward exclusive use of the one-way container without the collection, sorting, and remelting system. Thus, we have three systems, two of which claim to be recycling and all of which satisfy the same consumer demand with respect to beverage consumption.

Since the economic differences between the systems go relatively unnoticed and the recycling of mass is available for each system, we need some better device for underscoring

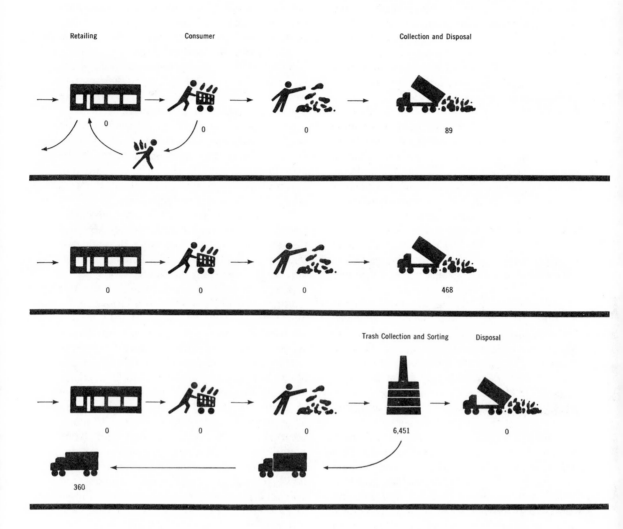

Retailing   Consumer   Collection and Disposal

Trash Collection and Sorting   Disposal

the system differences. No more suitable means exists to my knowledge than to examine the total resource energy required to operate these systems for a given quantity of beverage, an energy-effectiveness analysis.

THE ENERGY ANALYSIS

An energy analysis has been completed on the entire soft drink, beer, and milk container systems. Bottles, cans, paper, and plastic containers were considered. The analysis is here described in detail only for the soft drink industry and only the energy asso-

ciated with the containers, not the beverage, has been tabulated.

The analysis is a comparison of two systems—that which delivers a given quantity of soft drinks in throwaway containers, and that which delivers in returnable glass containers. Each system is evaluated with and without a remelting loop for discarded containers; the containers may be ultimately thrown away and/or collected and remelted. The energy required to operate each system for one gallon of beverage is calculated and the results compared.

I have neglected the indirect energy commitments in the process mainly because they seem small and difficult to calculate. Such energies would be those required to make the bottling machines, delivery trucks, paper and plastic packaging of the metal and glass containers, etc. As an example of the order of magnitude of such energies, the energy required to build an automobile is about 5 percent of the energy consumed in gasoline in the car's lifetime. Likewise, the energy of human labor is neglected as negligibly small. Rough calculations by the author indicate that this indirect energy is about 0.5 percent of the fossil mechanical energy expended in the container industry. This figure is supported by M. Tribus and E. C. McIrvine, who calculate the ratio at 0.4 percent.[13] The total energy consumed by the industry, including such things as building, heating and lighting, is given in this study.

The energy calculations are based on the quantity of basic energy resource removed from the ground. Thus, a kilowatt-hour of electricity is taken as 11,620 British Thermal Units (BTUS) since the coal-, oil-, or gas-fired steam-electric plants are only about 29.4 percent efficient (1968) in converting and delivering the resource energy to the user, and these are the major (99 percent) electricity sources in the Midwest.[14] (About 150 BTUS are needed to bring one pint of water to a boil from room temperature.) The amount of electricity generated by nuclear power is quite small relative to coal, oil, and gas, and can be neglected.[15] Since mining and transportation of coal to a power plant take about 0.25 percent of the mined coal energy, we assume this factor is also small for petroleum, and the resource energies of a gallon of gasoline and of diesel fuel were taken at their stated values of 125,000 BTUS per gallon and 138,000 BTUS per gallon respectively.[16] The

natural gas net energy value used was 1,000 BTUS per cubic foot. Propane has an energy content of 88,800 BTUS per gallon (at 30 inches of mercury and 60 degrees F.).[17]

The resource energy required to ship one ton-mile of freight by rail was taken as 640 BTUS.[18] An inner-city diesel truck consumes 2,400 BTUS per ton-mile of cargo.[19]

The number of trips per returnable bottle is of key importance in the analysis. According to the Illinois bottling industry,[10] the average return rate in the state is about ten; in rural areas the average is about thirteen, while the Chicago average is eight.

A study of a downstate Illinois small-city bottler revealed a return rate of 24. Much of his returnable bottle sales were through gasoline service stations, milk delivery routes, and drink dispensing machines.

The bottler who supplied the data for this study sells over 70 million soft drinks annually. His all-urban data is so extensive that it allowed an accurate comparison between the 16-ounce returnable, the 16-ounce throwaway bottle, and the 12-ounce can. These are the major sale items, with several million fillings annually in each form. The average number of refills for the 16-ounce returnable is 8.[7] The average unit weight of the 16-ounce returnable bottle is 1.0 pound and 0.656 pound for the 16-ounce throwaway bottle.[7] Thus, for each gallon of beverage which flows through the soft drink industry, one 16-ounce returnable or eight 16-ounce throwaway bottles are required. These bottle groups would weigh 0.0005 tons and 0.002625 tons respectively. The complete systems for both returnable and throwaway containers are described in Fig. 1 (above).

The returnable bottle materials are acquired from the raw materials and transported to the glass manufacturer, who blends new materials with recycled glass to make new bottles which are transported to the bottler. The returnable bottle makes a number of cycles through the outlet and consumer and back to the filler before breakage or loss

[13] Tribus, M., and E. C. McIrvine, "Energy and Information," Scientific American, p. 179, Sept. 1971.

[14] Edison Electrical Institute Statistical Handbook, 1969, Edison Electrical Institute, New York.

[15] Hubbert, loc. cit. Gast, Peter, Atomic Energy Commission, Argonne National Laboratory, letter to Bruce Hannon, June 23, 1971.

[16] Bureau of Census, 1963 Census of Mineral Industries, vol. 1, U.S. Dept. of Commerce, Washington, D.C., 1968. Bureau of Mines, IC 8411 and IC 8401, U.S. Dept. of Interior, Washington, D.C., 1969.

[17] National Tank Company Handbook, National Tank Company, New York, 1959.

[18] Transportation Statistics in the U.S. for 1969, Interstate Commerce Commission, Washington, D.C.

[19] Ibid. Rice, R. A., System Energy as a Factor in Considering Future Transportation, American Society of Mechanical Engineers, New York, 70 WA/ENER-8, Nov. 1970.

requires its transport to the collected waste system. Here the household and commercial wastes are separated from their glass content at about 50 percent efficiency. Further sorting and cleaning has 60 percent efficiency, and thus 30 percent of the glass in the received waste is returned to the glass manufacturer for reprocessing. The nonsalvageable glass goes on to other uses or to a landfill disposal site. The separation, cleaning, and sorting operations are presently in pilot-plant stage, but the container manufacturers insist that this is the method of the future. The Bureau of Mines of the U.S. Department of the Interior has a process which removes glass from the ash residue of a solid waste incinerator.

The throwaway bottle has a similar history except that the entire flow goes through the collection, separation, cleaning, and sorting process. A small percentage of the throwaway containers is also currently being disposed of in glass collection centers and sent to the container manufacturers for reprocessing.

ENERGY COSTS

In Table 2 I have summarized the results of my calculations of the energy resources needed for each step in the manufacturing, distribution, and return or disposal of glass soft drink containers. The numbers are given in terms of energy per gallon of beverage, and are stated in BTUs per gallon. The estimates are based on Chicago-area statistics,

where a returnable bottle makes an average of eight return trips. These data are later scaled to reflect fifteen fillings, which is the national average (Table 4).

As noted earlier, I have calculated energy requirements in terms of the energy value of the resource—coal, oil, or natural gas—required for each step of the container system. Where electrical energy is used, I have calculated the fuel needed to produce the energy used.

The energy costs of *material acquisition* are the costs of mining sand, limestone, soda ash and feldspar, the raw materials for glass manufacture, in the quantities and proportions needed[20] to manufacture one 16-ounce returnable bottle, which weighs 1.0 pound and in eight return trips would carry a gallon of beverage, and to manufacture eight throwaway 16-ounce bottles which weigh 5.25 pounds. *Transportation energy* for carrying these raw materials to the manufacturer is based on statistics, provided by one of the nation's largest glass container manufacturers,[21] which indicate that the average distance between the manufacturing site and the source of raw materials is 245 miles, and that 79 percent of these materials was moved by rail and 21 percent by truck. In the process of *container manufacturing*, 15 to 20

[20] *The Glass Industry* (a trade magazine), p. 31, Jan. 1971.
[21] The container manufacturer wishes to remain anonymous; verifiable records are in the author's file.

Table 2. Energy Expended (in BTUs) for One Gallon of Soft Drink in 16-Ounce Returnable or Throwaway Bottles

Operation	Returnable (8 Fills)	Throwaway
Raw material acquisition	990	5,195
Transportation of raw materials	124	650
Manufacture of container	7,738	40,624
Manufacture of cap (crown)	1,935	1,935
Transportation to bottler	361	1,895
Bottling	6,100	6,100
Transportation to retailer	1,880	1,235
Retailer and consumer	——	——
Waste collection	89	468
Separation, sorting, return for processing, 30% recycle	1,102	5,782
Total energy expended in BTUs per gallon:		
Recycled	19,970	62,035
Not recycled	19,220	58,100

percent of the newly made glass comes from internally recycled glass, or cullet, the scraps generated in the manufacturing process itself (this, by the way, is the basis for the statement occasionally heard that 20 percent of the glass in this industry is already being recycled). According to the container manufacturer already cited, there would be no significant increase in energy costs to increase the proportion of cullet from internal (bottle manufacturers) or external (consumer) sources. The total energies of the container industry were derived from a detailed examination of overall industry data.[22] The cost of cap or *crown manufacturing* was calculated separately.[23]

From the Census of Transportation[24] it was found that the average distance between the bottle manufacturer and the bottler was 345 miles, and that 70.2 percent of the empty bottles was shipped by truck, 16.3 percent by rail. (The remainder was shipped by trucks belonging to the container industry; therefore, this energy has already been included.) These data were in turn used in calculating the energy of *transportation to the bottler*, with an added correction for the fact that, according to the inner-city trucking companies, a single truck capacity averages 1,500 cases of throwaways but only 1,200 cases of returnable bottles.[25]

Heating and lighting account for a large share of the energy cost of *bottling*—filling the empty bottles with soft drink. Because of this there are no economies of scale in energy costs of bottling; the major urban bottler used in this study was compared to a small local bottler with one-tenth the sales, and it was found that the major bottler used 6.3 percent more resource energy per gallon of beverage than the small firm.

Eight gallons of water are needed to wash each returnable bottle before refilling, but only about one-half gallon of water is needed to wash a freshly manufactured throwaway.[10] This would lead to a higher energy cost for

returnables in this regard, but the major bottler used in this study is required by municipal law to wash returnables and throwaways in the same manner. From our study of the small bottler, we estimate that about 7 percent of the throwaway bottling energy could be saved if the less extensive rinse cycle were employed. Warehousing is included in the total bottling figure.

Transportation to the bottler was weighted to reflect the more space-consuming returnable bottles, which were assigned 55 percent of the allocated energy for storing and moving. According to the Census of Transportation, the average trip from bottler to retailer is 231 miles, 74 percent of which is by private truck.

No energy charge has been made for the *retailer and consumer;* soft drinks account for less than 1 percent of supermarket space, and storage and labor costs are small compared both to the total for the containers and to other demands on the retailer. No effort has been made to estimate the energy costs of the return of reusable bottles by the consumer, since it is assumed that only rarely would a trip to the supermarket or grocery store be made solely for the purpose of returning empty bottles.

The costs of *collection* of discarded bottles are based on information provided by local sanitary haulers,[26] who say that the average truck capacity is four tons, that trucks have a 50 percent load factor and average seven miles to a gallon of gasoline.

It should be noted that can and glass collection centers, which are now a major interest of some environmental groups, are economically infeasible.[1] Can and bottle manufacturing companies subsidize these intense activities, which in any case require donated labor and free transportation. (Paper collection and recycling is, fortunately, economically feasible.)

Rather than concluding this analysis with the costs of disposal of discarded or broken bottles, I have calculated the additional costs of returning this glass to the bottle manufacturer—what is most often called "recycling." This is done in two steps: glass must be separated from other trash in the municipal waste system, and then decontaminated and sorted. Only one firm is now making the equipment to perform these tasks. The unit is

---

[22] Bureau of Census, *1967 Census of Manufacture,* U.S. Dept. of Census, Washington, D.C., 1971.

[23] Bureau of Solid Waste Management, *loc. cit.* Bureau of Census, *1967 Census of Manufacture, op. cit.* Bureau of Census, *1967 Census of Transportation,* U.S. Dept. of Commerce, Washington, D.C., 1971.

[24] Bureau of Census, *Ibid.*

[25] Stout Trucking Company, Urbana, Illinois, 1971; McVey Trucking, Oakwood, Illinois, 1971.

[26] McLaughlin and Sons, Cumins & Wetmore, Sanitary Haulers, Urbana, Illinois, 1971.

called the Hydrosposal and is capable of reclaiming paper, glass, metal, textiles, and plastics. Pilot-plant operations (150 tons per day) have begun in Franklin, Ohio,[27] and it is data from this plant I have used for my calculation.

Half the glass is lost in the *separation* from trash, and only 60 percent of the remainder is recovered from the *sorting and decontamination* steps. Hence, 70 percent of the discarded bottles, both returnable and throwaway, must be disposed of into a nearby landfill. The cost of sorting and separating all of the glass is assigned to the 30 percent which is returned for remanufacture. No energy charge is made to landfilled material.

The *transportation* energy to return scrap glass back to the manufacturer is estimated as the transportation energy of the raw materials which it would replace.

It is important to note that the energy cost of retrieving scrap glass from waste is far higher than the energy cost of mining raw materials, and that therefore, from an energy standpoint, it makes little sense to recycle, in the sense of remelt, either returnable or throwaway bottles. The only energy savings are realized in reuse of the container; retrieving it as raw material is wasteful of energy. Substantially more (sixty times) energy is used to obtain waste glass as a replacement for crushed stone in making road-pavement materials.

[27] Black Clawson Co., Middleton, Ohio, letter to Bruce Hannon, Mar. 17, 1971.

Without reviewing the calculations in detail, I have tabulated a similar analysis for the soft drink can, which is given in Table 3. These data were derived principally from the Bureau of Census records.[28]

The energy estimates for steel and aluminum are for "finished shapes and forms" manufactured from ore; the estimates consequently do not distinguish between structural steel and tin plate sheet steel. About 30 percent of the finished steel came from scrap, while no aluminum scrap is included in the calculations.

SUMMARY

Adding the energy costs in the various categories in Tables 2 and 3, we find that returnable bottles are far superior from an energy standpoint to throwaways, either bottles or cans. From Table 2 we can see that remelting scrap bottles, while returning about 30 percent of the glass, would consume more energy than manufacturing all of the glass from raw materials. Removing this item from the total, therefore, and assuming that all bottles eventually find their way into landfills, we see that the energy cost of returnable bottles is 19,220 BTUs per gallon of beverage, assuming each bottle makes eight return trips, the case in Chicago. This compares with 58,100 BTUs

[28] Bureau of Census, *1963 Census of Mineral Industries*, vol. 1, *loc. cit.* Bureau of Census, *1967 Census of Manufacture, loc. cit.* Bureau of Census, *1967 Census of Transportation, loc. cit.*

Table 3. Energy Expended (in BTUs) for One Gallon of Soft Drink in 12-Ounce Cans

Operation	BTUs per Gallon
Mining[30] (2.5 lbs. of ore per lb. of finished steel)	1,570
Transportation of ore (1,000 miles by barge)[31]	560
Manufacture of finished steel from ore[22]	27,600
Aluminum lid (11.9% of total can weight; 4.7 times the unit steel energy)[22]	12,040
Transportation of finished steel 392 miles[32]	230
Manufacture of cans[22] (4% waste)	3,040
Transportation to bottler (300 miles average)[32]	190
Transportation to retailer	6,400
Retailer and consumer	—
Waste collection[26]	110
Total energy for can container system[a]	**51,830**
Total energy for 12 oz. returnable glass system	**17,820**
Ratio of total energy expended by can container system to that expended by 12 oz. returnable glass:	**2.91**

[a] The all-aluminum can system consumes 33% more energy than the bimetal (steel and aluminum) can system.

Table 4. Energy Ratios for Various Beverage Container Systems
(The Energy per Unit Beverage Expended by a Throwaway Container System Divided by the Energy per Unit Beverage Expended by a Returnable Container System)[a]

| Container Type | | | | | |
Throwaway	Returnable	Quantity	Beverage	Returnable Fills	Energy Ratios
Glass	Glass	16 oz.	Soft drink	15	4.4
Can	Glass	12 oz.	Soft drink	15	2.9
Glass	Glass	12 oz.	Beer	19	3.4
Can	Glass	12 oz.	Beer	19	3.8
Paper	Glass	½ gal.	Milk	33	1.8
Plastic[b]	Plastic	½ gal.	Milk	50	2.4

[a] Without remelting loop (discarded bottles and cans are not returned for remanufacture).
[b] High-density polyethylene.[3]

per gallon for throwing bottles, and 51,830 BTUS per gallon for cans. In other words, throwaway bottles use 3.11 times the energy of returnable bottles, and cans use 2.70 times the energy of returnables.

If we extrapolate these data to the nation as a whole, we assume that each returnable bottle is used fifteen times, the present national average, instead of eight. In this case, the energy cost of each gallon of soft drink in returnable bottles would drop to about 13,150 BTUS per gallon, and the throwaway bottle and can would still be more expensive by comparison. Throwaway bottles would then require 4.4 times the energy of returnables (both 16-ounce), and 12-ounce cans would use 2.9 times the energy of 12-ounce returnable bottles.

Although soft drink containers consumed nationwide slightly less than 0.17 percent of the nation's total energy in 1970 (beer containers consumed the same amount),[29] much can be learned from analyses such as this one. It is possible to show that a complete conversion to returnable bottles would reduce the demand for energy in the beverage (beer and soft drink) industry by 55 percent, without raising the price of soft drinks to the consumer (indeed, returnables are cheaper than throwaways). A complete turn to throwaways, of course, would substantially increase the energy demand of beverage containers.

Finally, we should point out that dollar costs do not reflect energy, a result of the cheapness of energy as compared to other inputs in manufacturing (although these costs are increasing). A ratio of the cost of

the returnable 16-ounce glass bottle system, in dollars per gallon of beverage, to the cost of the throwaway system was found to be 2.1.[8] To compare consumer costs the beverage costs must be included. Thus, with an average of fifteen returns for each returnable, throwaways cost about 1.2 times as much as returnables to make and distribute in Illinois. As noted earlier, the actual ratio of prices is now 1.3 as an Illinois average, which indicates that a significantly higher profit is being made on throwaways than on returnables. H. Folk indicates that a complete return to returnables in Illinois would save consumers of the state $71 million annually.[4]

Similar energy calculations have been made for beer bottles and cans, and for plastic, paper, and glass milk containers. The results are generally similar to the case of soft drinks. The energy ratios (that is, the energy expended by a returnable container system) are presented in Table 4.

In short, from dollar-cost and energy-cost standpoints, returnable bottles are preferable to cans or throwaway bottles. Can systems require approximately the same energy as throwaway bottles. Throwaways provide convenience to the consumer and additional profits to manufacturers and retailers. The question of which system is preferable to society as a whole cannot be resolved until both sides of the balance are known, and until there is some means of securing the system most desirable to society as whole, rather than the one most profitable to manufacturers and retailers.

[29] Hubbert, *loc. cit.* Abrahamas, J. H., "Utilization of Waste Container Glass," *Waste Age* (trade magazine), p. 72, July-Aug. 1970.

Acknowledgement: I wish to thank George Voss, John Hrivnak, and James Benton for their efforts in this systems analysis.

E. The Competitive Environment

13. What is Competition?
JOHN MAURICE CLARK

Competition is an indispensable mainstay of a system in which the character of products and their development, the amount and evolving efficiency of production, and the prices and profit margins charged are left to the operation of private enterprise.[1] In our conception of a tenable system of private enterprise, it is a crucial feature that the customer should be in a position (as Adam Smith put it) to exert effective discipline over the producer in these respects. Otherwise, government would feel constrained to undertake discipline over these matters—as it does in the field of public-service industries. It is competition that puts the customer in this strategic position, hence its crucial character. It is the form of discipline that business units exercise over one another, under pressure of the discipline customers can exercise over the business units by virtue of their power of choosing between the offerings of rival suppliers. Competition presupposes that businesses pursue their own self-interest, and it harnesses this force by their need of securing the customer's favor. By reason of this discipline, business, which is profit minded, has to become production minded as a means of earning profits dependably.[2]

This has its seamy side, as when the pressures of competition toward reducing money costs of production lead to substandard wages and working conditions, which increase the human costs of industry or lead to deterioration of the quality of products. These defects arise from a variety of causes: handicapped or relatively inefficient employers may be forced to make up for their disadvantages by lower money wages and may be able to do so because the competition they face as hirers of labor is less compelling than their competition as sellers of products; or customers may be poor judges of products, or certain qualities of products may be inscrutable. These are defects of a serviceable institution. In an impossibly perfect, omnipresent, and equal competition, they would presumably not arise; but that is an unattainable ideal. In the actual market place they have to be dealt with, and mitigated, by a variety of public and private measures adapted to the causes at work, including the "countervailing power" of organized labor, which uses anticompetitive pressures and has its own seamy side. Many of the remedies are themselves subject to abuse.

These defects are responsible for the view held in some quarters that it is the inherent

---

[1] The reader need hardly be reminded that this system includes many public controls to protect such values as safety, health, conservation, and truth in advertising.

◆ SOURCE: Reprinted by permission from *Competition as a Dynamic Process* by John Maurice Clark, (© 1961 by the Brookings Institution, Washington, D.C.), pp. 9–18.

[2] The phrase "profit minded" is used deliberately, to avoid the implication that business is solely and uniquely governed by an unrealistically precise "maximization" of profits.

tendency of competition to sacrifice service-ability to "vendibility" and to debase or impair the human values it touches. These things can happen; but if they were the whole story, the system of private business would not exhibit the strength it does today. Remedies that sustain the "level" of competition are in the interest of the business community, as well as the broader community of citizens. This is a more generally applicable course of action than the one envisioned a half-century ago by Gerald Stanley Lee, in a small volume entitled *Inspired Millionaires*, based on the idea that there existed men of wealth whose dominant motive was to use it to benefit humanity. To such a person, his first prescription was: "get a monopoly." Free yourself from the competitive compulsions that force you to squeeze down costs and prevent you from putting human values first.

The attraction of this procedure might have been somewhat dimmed by a hard-headed contemplation of the methods by which monopolies are established and defended. The element of truth in the prescription might better have been expressed in terms of organizing one's processes of production efficiently enough to give a margin of superiority affording leeway for experiments in promoting human values, not all of which need justify themselves by increasing profits. This, being consistent with competitive checks, would have been more clearly defensible.

A secure monopoly—if such a thing exists or can exist in industry or trade—might be able to save some of the wastes of competitive marketing. After spending part of the savings on public-relations advertising, it might choose to give the public some share of the resulting net economy. Indeed, there are quite cogent reasons why it might do this, or at least might refrain from exploiting to the utmost its immediate power over profits. Nevertheless, we would oppose such a monopoly, regardless of its good performance, because this performance would rest on its arbitrary choice. It would have power, if it chose, to make larger profits by giving the customer less for his money rather than more. The choice to give him more would depend too much on its enlightenment and good will.

While the good performance of our economy is more dependent on such qualities than many of us realize, our resources in this direction are limited. They are already heavily taxed or overtaxed by the requirements of good faith and responsibility in many relationships essential to the economic process and concerned with maintaining the level of competition. They would surely be overtaxed by laying upon them the whole burden of making economically correct decisions in the central matter of amounts produced and prices charged. In such decisions the opposition between private and community interest, is direct and powerful. Hence we do well to seek to keep these decisions subject to forces that are visibly and tangibly cogent, after the fashion of impersonal and competitive "economic law." So we are unwilling to leave in uncontrolled private hands the kind of power that goes with monopoly.

The patent system, with its grant of temporary legal monopoly, is less of an exception than might seem on the surface, as will appear later when we discuss innovation. Innovations are first selected and their value tested by their success in competition with existing practice. If innovation is to be stimulated by public policy, it is hard to devise a totally different system that would not depend more on arbitrary or bureaucratic judgment. Imperfections in the operation of the system present difficult problems, as we shall see, but do not destroy this general principle.

When an industry is recognized as a "natural monopoly," controls of the public utility kind are resorted to, imposing an enforceable obligation to render adequate service at reasonable charges. But we would quite rightly shrink from extending this system to the whole of industry and trade. And where effective competition exists, the customer does not need this sort of protection. Given a chance to choose between the offers of rival producers, his protection rests with his own ability to make an intelligent choice, plus his willingness to take the trouble involved. As to his ability, when he is faced with the inscrutable qualities of many products of modern applied science, there are difficulties, as we shall see, and there are various things that can be done about them, starting with various ways of giving the customer the most appropriate kinds of information. Minimum standards of quality may be set, publicly or privately, and some harmful products may be prohibited. But public control of output and price is not called for to meet this kind of need.

The customer can put pressure on the producer to create a supply corresponding to demand, produced at economical cost and sold at a price reasonably related to cost. "Consumer sovereignty" may be effective in this primarily quantitative sense; but it should be noted with some emphasis that this is not all there is to serviceability. Serviceability depends on how well the customer's patronage reflects those needs and interests that are properly identified with his welfare—using the term in its generally accepted meaning. This is more than an economic problem—a fact which is often used as a pretext for ignoring its economic aspects. The forces shaping our wants include the arts of salesmanship, at a time when our increased consuming power makes it disturbingly easy to become so preoccupied with the *mélange* of trifles or worse that salesmanship offers that we lose something really indispensable—a sense of worthwhile purpose in life.[3] At the utilitarian level, we shall accept consumer sovereignty as an agency that is demonstrably limited and fallible, in need of practical aids to getting what is wanted—aids that can be furnished. Yet with all its defects this agency is indispensable in a society in which the task of shaping worthwhile lives is basically voluntary, rather than dictated by central authority.[4]

So far we have been speaking of the effect of competition, from the standpoint of the alternative choices it offers to the customer, but without trying to define competition as an activity of the producers. For the present purpose, the most useful kind of definition is one that is full enough to suggest some of the

---

[3] Cf. Barbara Ward, *New York Times Magazine*, May 8, 1960. She said that in the frivolous and ridiculous choices we make, "the modern moralists see . . . more than the virtuosity of the ad man . . . a society corrupted . . . by a scale of choice that . . . finally extinguishes all sense of the proper ends of man." Here the economic goal of affluence is indicated, jointly with the failure of individuals to meet the moral challenge that arises as material necessities are conquered and marginal striving moves on to things of less and less human importance.

[4] Cf. the symposium on our national purpose, *Life, The National Purpose* (1960). Here, because our society is of the sort indicated above, the problem of individual purpose is largely bypassed, and with it the problem of national purpose relative to the individual citizen. As J. K. Galbraith has indicated, the affluent society presents its own special problems and is not an unambiguous gain.

important differences in degree and kind of situation, objective, and activity that the realistic student should be prepared to encounter. This kind of definition might also help to explain why competition is so many things to so many different people. They may take hold of it at different points and encounter different aspects, like the blind men and the elephant. Our elephant should have legs, tail, trunk, tusks, and ears. The following definition is framed with this in mind.

Competition between business units in the production and sale of goods is the effort of such units, acting independently of one another (without concerted action), each trying to make a profitable volume of sales in the face of the offers of other sellers of identical or closely similar products. The pursuit of profits includes attempting to minimize losses if that is the best the situation permits. The process normally involves rivalry, though this may or may not be direct and conscious. In perhaps the chief example, the case of staple farm products sold on organized exchanges, the rivalry of the growers is indirect and for the most part unconscious. In contrast, business units consciously attempt to get customers away from their rivals by the relative attractiveness of their offers. To the extent that the customer does his choosing effectively, the way to secure his business is to offer him good value for his money, backed by dependable information about the product. To the extent that he is incompetent or otherwise unable to choose effectively, specious selling appeals and scamped products have their opportunity. Business firms as buyers are better equipped and more competent than most consumers, and the methods of selling to them reflect this. But even with business buyers, the seller must bring his product to their attention. There may be rivalry between products not closely similar—this is ordinarily called "substitution" rather than "competition."

Rivalry may be active or latent. In the latter case it has its most visible effect when it becomes active; but if this possibility influences the conduct of active competitors without waiting for the latent rivalry to become active, then latent competition as such has some effectiveness. It may come from the potential entry of new firms, but it is nowadays often a matter of an existing producer branching out into a new type of product or a new market. Much of the most formidable competition takes this form.

Where profits are attainable, competitors may aim at the largest feasible short-run profit, or at a profit thought of as reasonable and probably the best attainable in the long run. The point in either case is that the feasible profit and the methods of pursuing it are limited by the return for which other competitors are willing and able to produce goods and offer them to buyers. The aim may be to excel the attractiveness of their offerings, or to equal it, or to come as near equaling it as possible, in cases in which the rival has something that is, at least for the time being, inescapably superior as a sales appeal. In the latter case, the first firm is under pressure to find ways of improving the appeal of its offerings. Or the aim may be merely to secure enough business to survive.

The attempt to excel may be called aggressive competition, in effect if not in intent; it may or may not be aimed at a particular rival's business. The attempt to equal a competitor's offer or minimize a rival's advantage is clearly defensive. Under competition the one implies the other, and it takes both kinds to make an effectively competitive situation—certainly in industry and trade and probably in agriculture. A proper understanding of the processes of competition in industry and trade requires a recognition of the different and complementary roles of aggressive and defensive actions. This distinction has been recognized, but its basic importance does not appear to have been developed.

Overlapping this, but not coextensive with it, is the distinction between moves of an initiatory character, including moves responding merely to the general situation in which a competitor finds himself, and responses precipitated by specific moves of a rival or rivals —responses of the nature of parries or ripostes. They may imitate the rivals' moves, or may be countermoves of a different sort. Initiatory moves may be aggressive, as defined above; or they may be made by a competitor who is in a defensive situation, in an attempt to improve his position by trying something fresh. This distinction between initiation and response has been more fully recognized than the distinction between aggression and defense. In fact, it is the basis of that theory which claims that effective competition occurs only when firms making initiatory moves disregard the responses their rivals will make. Where competitors are few and a competitive action by one has a substantial impact on his rivals, they are virtually certain to make some kind of response. If the initiator of the move does not have foresight enough to anticipate this, experience will soon drive it home to him. To assume that he ignores it requires him to be far more stupid than businessmen are. If competition really depends on this kind of stupidity on the part of businessmen, its prospects are not good.

Fortunately, this pessimistic view contains only part of the truth, and a part that is seldom fully controlling. Businessmen are not only able to anticipate that rivals will respond, but to devise moves of sorts that cannot be easily and quickly neutralized by rivals' responses. And it is not necessary that all should initiate such moves; if some do, resulting competitive pressures will spread, not instantly or in precisely predictable forms, but, in general, effectively. For this purpose, it is important that firms differ in situations and perspectives. Fewness does not eliminate the incentive to improve productive efficiency or to increase the attractiveness of the product; and the resulting differences tend to spill over into price competition, often of irregular sorts. Anticipation that rivals will respond does not carry certainty as to how prompt or effective the responses will be. This uncertainty allows some firms to hope that, as the outcome of initiating a competitive move, they may end with an improved relative market position, which will mean increased profits for them, after profits in the industry as a whole have reached a normal competitive state. There are a variety of conditions that may lead some firms to this kind of an expectation, including the hope of avoiding a worsening of the firm's market position if it fails to make competitive moves when other firms are doing so. At the best, gains may be progressive over time. This, in nonmathematical language, is a rudimentary explanation of the paradox of competition, whereby single firms see an advantage in actions that tend to eventuate in reduced profits for the entire industry. This explanation supplies some essential elements that are left out of the simplified theoretical model that runs in terms of an "individual demand function" substantially more elastic than the industry function.

The forms which this condition may take hinge on the different means competitors may use in making their offerings attractive to customers. These include the selection and design of a product, selling effort to bring it to the favorable notice of potential customers, and price. The appeal of a seller's offer is a joint resultant of all three. Nevertheless, it has meaning to distinguish "competition in price" from competition in selling effort or product design. Any one of the three may change while the others do not. Indeed, estimates of the probable effects of such single variations are implied in the attempt to devise the most effective joint combination. But all three are tied together by the fact that they all need to be appropriate to one another and to the type and level of market demand the seller is aiming to reach.

The attempt to attract the customer's trade, in this three-sided appeal, costs money, whether it takes the shape of a high-quality product, an expensive selling campaign, or a low price. To make a profit on this money outlay or sacrifice, efficient and economical production is needed; and the more economical the production, the more effective the selling inducements can be made, consistently with profits. Therefore, though low-cost production is not a direct act of rivalry (a producer *may* reduce his costs and pass none of the benefit on to his customers), it is an essential enabling factor and as such is part of the whole process. A struggling competitor may have to reduce his costs if he is to stay in business at all. So it may be added as a fourth means of competitive appeal.

Most of these responses take time and involve uncertainty, starting with the responses of the customers that determine how effective the initial move is, after which rivals' responses take further time. The outstanding exception is an openly quoted reduction in the price of a standardized product. Here response can be prompt and precise; and the expectation of such responses can interfere with the competitive incentive to reduce prices and tends to shift price action to the more irregular forms, which create problems of their own, or to increase competitive emphasis on moves in the field of product and selling effort, which present a different array of problems as to the conditions of effective and serviceable competition. Competition over distance also presents its special problems in identifying serviceable forms of competitive price behavior. All in all, the conditions of serviceable competitive behavior in price, product, or selling effort leave much to be defined.

For example, does competition improve or deteriorate quality? Actually, it can do either or both. How can we judge the conditions determining whether the range of quality offered corresponds to the range desired or misrepresents it? By what criteria can we appraise the productiveness or wastefulness of the indispensable function of advertising or balance its informative and perverting effects on the guidance of demand? Would genuine competition drive prices down to marginal cost? Whose marginal cost, and short-run or long-run? The simplified formulas of abstract theory have too-often bypassed such questions. Or would genuine competition cause prices to fluctuate continually with every change in the relation of "demand and supply" (or rather, of demand and productive capacity)? If a given price remains unchanged for weeks or months, is price competition non-existent during those intervals?

To answer the last question first, the decisive fact seems to be that the purpose of a firm in setting a price on its goods is to sell the goods at the price that has been set. If a price is set competitively, it would be absurd to claim that the price competition ended with the setting of the price and before any goods had been sold. The selling of the goods is part of the price competition. What remains is an arguable question how often prices should change, and such questions do not belong in a definition. The same applies to the other controversial questions about how competitive prices should behave. A definition should facilitate the study of such questions, not foreclose it by purporting to give a final answer.

Perhaps some of the difficulties can be reduced by accepting the consequences of the proposition that effective competition requires both aggressive and defensive actions. A second saving consideration is that price competition must, in reason, include some way in which prices can rise, on occasion, without concerted action. Some conceptions appear to leave room only for price reductions except when demand exceeds capacity. As to specific behavior, it is clear that price competition is something different for a wheat grower, a cement manufacturer, an automobile producer, or Macy's department store.

For the competition to be effective, the crucial thing seems to be that prices be independently made under conditions that give some competitors an incentive to aggressive action that others will have to meet, whenever prices are materially above the minimum necessary supply prices at which the industry would supply the amounts demanded of the various grades and types of products it produces. What profit or loss a given competitor will individually make will depend on whether he is a high-cost or a low-cost producer, and on whether the industry is shrinking or expanding.

It may be worth while calling attention to certain things that this definition does *not* set up as essential characteristics of competition. It does not limit it to cases in which the seller merely accepts a going price, which he has no power to influence. It does not define competition as a struggle to excel, after the simile of a race, in which there can be only one winner. It does not incorporate the effort to maximize profits—still less their actual maximization—as part of the definition of competition. The definition needs to leave room for competing firms that may conceive their aims in ways not necessarily inconsistent with the attempt to maximize profits, but including elements that are formulated in different terms. Perhaps the chief trouble with the conception of maximization is its implication of a precision which is unattainable and can be misleading. Secondarily, the meaning of profit maximization is ambiguous unless the time perspective that controls the firm's policy is carefully specified. Incidentally, and paradoxically, the producer who is likely to be trying hardest to maximize his profits is the one who is not making any—he is struggling for survival.

Finally, the definition does not require that each form of competition should be active at every moment, in the sense of new technical methods, new products, new selling tactics, or changed prices. All these may remain unchanged between active moves and may still embody the resultant of active and effective competitive forces. If so, this implies that preparedness is under way for further moves as occasion may present the need or the opportunity. Of course, this preparedness may lapse into ineffectiveness; but the producer who allows this to happen in his own establishment is likely to find himself fatally outclassed. And if preparedness is active, it is likely to eventuate in action.

14. Competition as Seen by the Businessman and by the Economist

JOEL DEAN

RESEARCH METHODS

The two people who ought to know most about competition are the economist, whose profession it is to study it, and the businessman, whose profession it is to practice it. The purpose of this little disquisition is to contrast the views of these two experts.

Economists, of course, differ greatly among themselves, and their views on this subject range over a broad continuum. Any attempt to lump together the opinions of such a notoriously discordant group of people must, therefore, be at best a bold simplification, and more probably a foolhardy caricature. Business executives also cover a wide spectrum of attitudes toward competition and differ strikingly in their penchant for looking at the economic mechanism as a whole. Hence, any attempt to speak about the views of "the businessman" necessarily abstracts from the great variation among individual executives, and runs the risk of merely reflecting the prejudices of the generalizer.

Instead of attempting to mitigate these hazards, I have accentuated them. No effort has been made to survey systematically a wide range of businessmen's opinions on the subject, and no effort has been made to present a central tendency of the views of the typical executive. Dr. Kinsey has established that statistics can make anything dull. So I have

◆ SOURCE: Reprinted by permission from *The Role and Nature of Competition in Our Marketing Economy,* edited by Harvey W. Huegy (Bureau of Economic and Business Research, University of Illinois, 1954,) pp. 8–15.

steered clear of statistics and confined my inquiries to businessmen whose views intrigued me.

I have maintained the same high standards of statistical thoroughness and Olympian objectivity in summarizing my dinner table findings with respect to economists. Observing that the inner soul of the academician is seldom bared in the learned journals, I have religiously abstained from any examination of the literature on the subject and instead have gone out into the byways and the unbeaten paths of casual conversation and taking my cocktail in hand, have coaxed cozy confidences from my cloistered colleagues.

Economists, doubtless as a consequence of the rigor of the scientific method and the broad factual foundation for their science, vary in their views on competition over a vast range. One can move along this continuum from the managerial economist with intimate participation in the highest policy decisions of huge corporations (like myself) along a trajectory of marginal futility down through the geologic strata of sophistication to the neoclassical, welfare economist who still takes the model of atomistic competition seriously.

A simple, scientific, and completely satisfactory solution for the annoying individuality of economists has been found. It consists of classifying them into two groups: (a) sophisticated industrial economists and (b) foolish cloistered economists. Following the pattern of our scientific treatment of the businessman, we shall ignore altogether the views of the sophisticated economists and confine ourselves to the foolish ones.

What Competition Is

By these research methods we obtained impressions about the economist's and the businessman's view of the characteristics of a competitive situation.

Hallmarks of Competition Listed by Businessman

Generally speaking, competition, to the businessman, is whatever he has to do to get business away from his rivals and whatever they do to take sales away from him. To be more specific let us look at nine hallmarks of an intensely competitive situation, as seen through the eyes of our businessman:

1. *Price uniformity.* Close similarity of quoted prices of rivals, usually accompanied by undercover price shading.
2. *Price differentiation.* A structure of price discounts characterized by wide spreads between the lowest and the highest net price, e.g., the discount structure that is usual for suppliers of fairly standardized products to the automobile industry.
3. *Selling activities.* Substantial promotional outlays, i.e., much advertising, point-of-sale merchandising, and direct personal salesmanship.
4. *Product differentiation.* Preoccupation with the modernity, quality, and style of the company's products as compared with rivals' products and with "good service."
5. *Product research.* Large outlays on product research that is focused on creation of new products and continuous improvement in the firm's existing products.
6. *Selective distribution.* A strong dealer organization, i.e., rivalry through and for sponsored, franchised (and often exclusive) distributors.
7. *Market share.* Acute consciousness of the activities and position of competitors, and preoccupation with the company's market share and with the market occupancy of individual rivals.
8. *Market raiding.* Uninhibited efforts to detach big customers from rivals, often by price shading, or special concessions, business patronage, and "services." Sporadic penetration of the market by distant rivals, who frequently dump, so that their net-back is much lower than from sales in their own backyard territory. The converse is customer-freezing, i.e., the use of sewing-up devices such as requirements contracts, reciprocity, and lavish gifts, which make good customers hard to alienate.
9. *Customer sharing.* Widespread acceptance of the strike-born doctrine that for each important material or component the buyer needs the protection of having at least two suppliers.

Economist's View—Appraisal

Influenced by fashionable doctrines of "imperfect competition" and "monopolistic competition" many neoclassical economists have taken the view that only atomistic competition is the real thing; that any form of rivalry that departs from the paragon of perfect competition falls from grace, i.e., is monopoly. Classifying all departures from the purity of atomistic rivalry as monopolistic is a simplifying analytical device of proven pedagogical value. The inference drawn by many students and, unfortunately, by some of their teachers is that all aspects of rivalry among sellers which deviate from "perfect" competition are "monopolistic," and therefore, are not competition at all.

The result of this doctrinaire dissection of the geometry of competition is the unconscious conviction on the part of many young economists that monopoly, rather than competition, is now the dominant characteristic of American capitalism. The impression that competition has been "declining" is a frequent, though not necessary, corollary.

A weird consequence is that the same behavior traits which the businessman sees as hallmarks of competition are viewed by many economists as indicia of monopoly.

Price Uniformity. To many economists close similarity of prices quoted or bid by rivals is an almost classic indication of a monopoloid situation. Some economists view "price matching" as conclusive proof of culpable collusion. Undercover price concessions have been regarded not only as buttressing the evidence of collusion but also as pernicious in themselves because they are a particularly insidious kind of price discrimination.

The businessman sees uniformity of official prices as evidence that rivals' products are such close substitutes that competition is driven underground, where dark and terrible subterranean struggles produce differences in quality, service, and terms which work out to differences in real prices.

The businessman sees no practical competitive alternative to similarity of quoted prices where products are standardized and competitors are few. Each seller knows that official price cuts will be promptly met. Overt price reduction is, therefore, a futile device for extending a firm's market share. And since open price reductions are not easily reversible undercover concessions provide the necessary mechanism for flexible adjustment to rapid changes in economic and competitive environment.

Price Differentiation. Charging different prices to different people makes the economist suspect price discrimination, roughly defined as price differences that are not "justified" by cost differences. Price discrimination is an indication of monopoly power, since it is unthinkable under atomistic competition. Price discrimination may also be employed to acquire, perpetuate, or abuse market power. Accordingly, most economists have been "agin" it. But few have recognized that under modern technology it is very difficult to define price discrimination, and almost impossible to measure, detect, or avoid it. (See *Managerial Economics*, pp. 504-10.)

The businessman sees his structure of price discounts as an instrument of competitive strategy in fighting for position in different sectors of the market. Aware of the furious consequences of failing to meet rivals' net prices as they differ among market sectors and aware of the impossibility of finding the full cost of serving different sectors he sees the sort of cost-price disparity (price discrimination) that distresses the economist as an everyday unavoidable and not particularly culpable practice. He is amazed that price differentiation that is so directly geared to market conquest and defense should be viewed as a symptom of monopoly and is even more puzzled that it should be viewed as culpable or as avoidable.

Selling Activities. By our economist, all sales effort has characteristically been viewed with serious misgivings. His ire has been concentrated on the purest forms of selling cost, such as advertising, but it has slopped over into every aspect of promotional effort. Economists, particularly of the more dedicated neoclassical persuasion, have seen in selling efforts a device for enhancing the monopoly power of the firm by differentiating the product in the minds of the prospective buyers. According to this view, the resulting "consumer franchise" is an island of monopoly power largely created by selling efforts.

To the businessman, selling activities seem the essence of competition. Pained by the unfamiliarity and indifference of consumers to the virtues of his product and service, he sees sales effort as dissolving the rigidities of ignorance and inertia that block access to substitutes. Thus it converts the incipient rivalry of substitutes into effective competition.

Product Differentiation. Physical differences among sellers' products have come under opprobrium similar to psychological differentiation. These economists consider that commercially successful product competition which develops a distinctive product that people want creates a monopoly power. This power is limited, to be sure, by the adequacy of substitutes, but nevertheless product innovation and adaptation to consumers' desires bears the opprobrium of monopoly. Thus these economists see in each new product and each improvement of an existing product an effort to escape from the competitive struggle into a stronghold of monopoly. In contrast, the businessman, in industries where product innovation and improvement is a dominant aspect of rivalry, would look upon it as the very core of competition. (Witness the workings of real-world rivalry in the automobile industry.)

Product Research. Many neoclassical economists have looked on the outlays of large corporations for technological research with apprehension. The results of research are patented; patents constitute legalized monopolies, and patents build barriers to entry. Hence research expands and perpetuates a firm's monopoly power in the view of some economists.

The businessman sees whatever monopoly power he succeeds in building up by technological research as being transient. It is eternally threatened by the competitive inroads of rivals. His experience indicates that perpetuation of his power to compete can be achieved only by research which creates new products and which keeps existing products abreast of the technological innovations of his rivals. He properly sees his existing products and methods threatened, to an extent never experienced before, by inborn substitutes that may provide dramatically cheaper solutions for his customers' problems. He see patents as poor protection in today's dynamic, fluid technology.

Selective Distribution. Flowing the product to consumers through an organization of sponsored, franchised (and sometimes exclusive) dealers has been viewed by some economists not only as evidence of monopoly power but also as an unwarranted extension and consolidation of the market power of product differentiation. The businessman, in contrast, sees an effective dealer organization as a major weapon of competition. In some industries a dealer organization appears essential to make the manufacturer's competition operational at the point where competition counts, namely, in the decisions of the ultimate consumer.

Economists have not only feared the distributive power conferred by a strong dealer organization, they have also looked upon exclusive dealershps as a grant of locational monopoly and as a monopolistic denial of access to rival sellers. To the businessman, exclusive dealerships are a means of assuring single-minded and dedicated effort to compete with dealers of rival manufacturers.

Market Share. Preoccupation with the company's market share has ominous monopolistic overtones to the neoclassical economist. For a firm to have market occupancy big enough to make its market share perceptible is in itself a significant departure from the standard of perfect competition. Making market-share goals pivotal for pricing and promotional policy is, to these economists, a sure sign of a monopoloid situation. Similarly, when the very awareness of rivals as individuals is a sinful slip from atomistic competition, overt study of rivals' reactions to the firm's market thrusts is to these economists clear litmus of "monopoly power." To the businessman who watches his market share apprehensively and at considerable cost and who frequently sacrifices immediate profits for long-run strengthening of his sinews for market-share rivalry, it is incredible that his concern about his "competitive position" should be damned as monopolistic.

Even more culpable in the eyes of the economist is industry-wide cohesion in the face of threatened encroachment by rival industries (for example, the movie industry's battle with television and radio for consumer attention and for the amusement dollar). The businessman, more painfully impressed with the realities of substitute competition, sees industry solidarity as improving his competitive effectiveness in this wider arena and hence as intensifying rather than diminishing competition.

Market Raiding. Muscling in on stable and satisfied (established) customers is to the businessman proof of voracious competition.

To the neoclassical economists, however, the very existence of long-lived, uninterrupted commercial relationships with individual large customers is an indication of monopoly power, since it is unthinkable under perfect competition. And the subterranean efforts to dislodge the favored supplier smack of discriminatory tactics.

Similarly, raiding by suppliers who are geographically (or in other ways) distant strikes the businessman as indicating that the arena of competition has been widened and hence intensified. Also, the hit-and-run tactics of the raider disturb the price peace and may force a substantial realignment of market occupancy. To the neoclassical economist, in contrast, raiding demonstrates the existence of a private preserve to raid, and raiding tactics produce disparity in the net revenue between backyard and distant sales which have discriminatory results, presumably possible only with the substantial degree of monopoly power.

Customer freezing is in a sense the converse of market raiding. To the businessman it indicates the length to which he must go to keep his established customer relationships intact and protect them against the heartless and ceaseless competitive efforts of his rivals. To some economists these sewing-up devices look like the creation of noncompetitive nooks which impose barriers to the access of rivals.

Customer Sharing. Customer sharing is to many economists proof that rivalry is imperfect. Predetermined sharing of the business even of an individual customer is a departure from the essentially anonymous and happenstance division of patronage that is assumed under perfect competition.

To the businessman, who is forced by the growing acceptance of the dual-supplier doctrine to share his established customers with rival suppliers, customer sharing shows the essential equivalence of their products and services and often sales volume, thereby intensifying competition.

Sad Conclusion

No plaudits had been expected by our businessman for his little foray into economics. But it is downright discouraging to find that his nine telltales of a tough competitive setup are to our economist sure symptoms of monopoly. Recognizing that competition is clearly just the opposite of what it seems, our business friend sadly climbs back through the looking glass.

F. The Legal Dimension

15. Impact of Government upon the Market System

E. T. GRETHER and ROBERT J. HOLLOWAY

The maintenance of a strong, widespread and varied private enterprise base in a society requires that the myriads of private choices and decisions mesh into and through an effective market system. In the United States, the highest judicial tribunals have insisted on the maintenance of the "rule of competition" through the market system by reiterating that the alternatives are direct governmental operation and regulation or private cartelization.

An acceptably effective general market system must have the capacities to:

1. Respond to the free choices of buyers at all levels.
2. Respond to general and specific *external* environment influences, forces, and conditions (that is, the system must be open ended).
3. Interact among the elements of the system *internally*, including particularly the adjustment of resources from lesser advantaged uses to products, services, or geographical areas of greater advantage.
4. "Regulate" in the sense of placing the participants in the marketing processes under strong compulsions for both (a) the efficient use of resources in production and in marketing and (b) the effective fulfillment of the wants and desires of the members of the society.

The market system as a whole and its specific subsystems are under the continuing and increasing intervention of governmental policies and programs; that is, the market system, while "regulating," is also being "regulated." Most likely, the interventions by government at all levels (especially by the federal government) and the high rate of scientific and technological change are the two most significant external environmental forces affecting the market system. It is proposed, therefore, that both empirical and normative research studies be encouraged on the effects of governmental policies and programs on the functioning of the market system as a whole and on specific subsystems. Such studies should focus sharply upon the impacts of public policies and intervention upon the capacities of the market system as a whole to fulfill its basic functions of communication, coordination and organization, adjustment to strategic environmental forces and conditions, and internal interaction and regulation.

Obviously many thousands of helpful studies could be made with this general orientation and from its vantage points. Such studies, regardless of their number or whether they were essentially empirical or normative, would have accumulative value if focused as proposed. But since research resources are not infinite and there is high urgency for basic knowledge and wisdom to guide public policies, the following topical areas are highlighted:

I. Quantitative and qualitative analyses of the extent to which the economy is under the aegis of the competitive market system.

II. The influence of governmental policies

◆ SOURCE: Reprinted by permission from the *Journal of Marketing* (National Quarterly Publication of the American Marketing Association), Vol. 31, No. 2, April 1967, pp. 1–7.

and programs upon the leading classes of managerial decision making in marketing in the perspective of the requirements of an acceptable competitive general market system.

III. Special strategic topical issues in the context of current public policies affecting the functioning of the market system in the United States.

EMPIRICAL AND NORMATIVE STUDIES

The traditional, classical models of the market system as a whole are derived from assumptions under which the market system and the economy are synonymous. There is a complete lack of quantitative measures of the extent to which the economy of the United States or other countries is, in fact, under the regulation of the market system. There are those who believe that even in the United States with its avowed policies in favor of regulation under the market system, the drift is inexorably away from the market system and hence away from a society with a private enterprise base. No systematic endeavors have been made to measure quantitatively or even to judge qualitatively the extent to which our economy is regulated by the market system. It is difficult to conceive of a study of greater potential significance for public policy than a careful quantitative and qualitative interpretive analysis of the extent to which the market system is operationally effective. A general or holistic approach, of course, would have to be considered only as tentative or preliminary. But it could have an enormous influence in guiding and stimulating research into special topics and areas and subsystems.

A possible approach would be through a breakdown of the components of the GNP in terms of the derivative relationship to or removal from the market system. A very difficult problem of appraisal arises in the areas of shared rule as between competition through the market system and governmental direct regulation. It would be most helpful to have such areas highlighted with some indications of the quantitative nature of the sharing. Ideally, a general approach should be under the direction of a task force composed of persons with varied backgrounds and interests. Useful, preliminary studies, however, could be done under a single aegis by persons of broad background and experience. It is inconceivable, however, that definitive measures

or judgments could be developed, since the bewildering labyrinths of governmental intervention now probably defy full charting and appraisal.

THE INFLUENCE OF GOVERNMENTAL POLICIES AND PROGRAMS

The influence of governmental policies and programs is to be considered in the dual perspective of the requirements of effective private decision making and the requirements of an acceptable, competitive general market system. Under this approach some orderly trails would be blazed through a few of the labyrinths of public regulations from the point of view of business enterprises in making strategic decisions. Five broad areas of research are proposed.

Vertical Marketing Organization and Relationships (the Market Channels)

It is almost universally agreed that vertical organization and relations are uniquely the central area of the field or discipline of marketing. It is agreed also that it is a field of high and overlooked importance both in terms of private managerial decision making and of public policies affecting marketing. It has become increasingly evident that in modern complex industrial societies, competitive forces operate vertically as well as horizontally. But there is a great dearth of systematic knowledge and insight into the patterns and significance of vertical organization and relationships.

In the meantime, governmental policies and programs have intervened into this complex of relationships more or less haphazardly under antitrust enforcement, the Robinson-Patman Act, laws governing resale price maintenance ("fair trade"), special laws and actions affecting relationships between manufacturers and their dealers, actions affecting vertical integration and semi-integration, exclusive and selective dealer arrangements, franchising, and so on. But such legislative, judicial, or other interventions have not been investigated systematically in terms of the functioning of the market system. Thus, for example, regulation under the Robinson-Patman Act has never been examined in this framework and context. The Robinson-Patman cases and actions provide an almost ideal opportunity for research along these lines because of the focus upon primary, secondary and tertiary levels in the perspective of broad conflicting conflicts between types of enterprises. Yet the Act is couched and enforced in terms of a specific-commodity type of regulation of pricing almost guaranteed to avoid the most important issues. The effect of the Robinson-Patman Act is merely one example of fruitful areas awaiting research in terms of this approach. For example, there are the enormously important problems in numerous industries such as the automotive industries, involving not only the dealer structures and arrangements of manufacturers, but relations with suppliers. A very important area, of course, would be vertical integration upstream and downstream, in which there are great bodies of law, action, and judicial interpretation.

Geographical Marketing Organization and Relationships

A primary test of the marketing system is its ability to support the geographical adjustment of market forces and conditions. This horizontal expression is the corollary of vertical organization and relationships. Involved here are governmental policies affecting sales territories, especially territorial confinement, laws and regulations affecting geographical pricing (as the basing point and other delivered price systems), interstate trade barriers (as through licensing and differential tax treatment), the favoritism of state and local government jurisdictions toward local industry, especially through subsidies, and other forms of differential treatment, and so on.

Product Policies, Including Innovation, Diversification, Differentiation, and the "Product Mix"

In many ways, the area of product decisions is the most important of all. Possibly, too, it is the brightest spot of all in terms of the impacts of governmental policies and programs, except, perhaps, in a small number of industries under special legislation (as food and drug legislation). It would appear, however, that the enormous impacts of governmentally supported and encouraged research and development in relation to private efforts and programs, have fostered rapid technolog-

ical advances and changes with respect to product innovation.

But there are conflicting interests and unsettled problems in connection with the patent system. And there are continuing problems in the endeavors to trademark, brand, package, and promote the *differentiated* products of particular enterprises. Antitrust implications and applications are becoming increasingly important in this area. Furthermore, product line diversification by the processes of acquisition are being questioned, increasingly, under antitrust. There is no doubt that the area of product policies in all of its expressions is basic and lends itself to a wide variety of research studies.

Promotion

Promotion is of the essence in marketing, and particularly in an environment of (1) rapid product development and (2) antitrust enforcement intended to optimize the rule of competition and to forbid cartelization. Hence, the character and impacts of the governmental policies and regulations affecting personal selling, advertising, trademarking, branding, packaging, labeling, the use of credit, etc., are basic. Research could be focused upon the impact of the enforcement of specific statutes (as food and drug legislation, or alcoholic beverages legislation), or as affecting functional areas (as advertising), or specific practices (as packaging, labeling, credit terms and practices). Important also would be the impact of public mores, standards and attitudes in general and upon specific regulations.

Research in this area could become a testing ground for relating the functioning of the market system broadly and specifically to ethical standards and precepts by reference to the host of common law or other more specific statutory and judicial constraints upon market behavior and practices. Research in this area could test product differentiation and brand promotion empirically in relation to the prevalent conceptualization under much of economical analysis derived from the theory of monopolistic competition and assumptions as to effects upon entry. It is likely that, in the main, in the United States, governmental regulations affecting promotion do not now inhibit managerial decision making and implementation in a strategic manner. One of the purposes of the research would be to check this generalization in general and in specific situations.

Pricing

Pricing is the "holy of holies" of both economic analysis and of antitrust enforcement in the United States. Consequently, there is a large literature of economic analysis and of public policy. From this standpoint, research needs are not as high as in other areas. What is needed, however, is empirical research into the exact nature of pricing and of its relationship to other aspects of decision-making and behavior in marketing. Many, perhaps most, economic analyses, make prices, pricing, and price structures and the price system the central aspects of the functioning of the market system and of the economy. Such emphasis, of course, is appropriate for the production and marketing of the great staple homogeneous products. This approach, however, is less appropriate for the modern, diversified business enterprise with rapid product innovation, which stresses product differentiation and promotion. Under these conditions, the totality of market offerings, practices, services, facilities, and relations affect market results—not merely the determination of the *basic price* of specific products. Obviously pricing and the "price system" in the case of well-known homogeneous commodities has one set of connotations for the functioning of the market system, whereas a broader, more flexible conceptualization and analysis are required for firms in other situations. Research studies focused upon pricing in this latter context could be exceedingly illuminating in terms of the actual functioning of the market system in areas other than staple, homogeneous commodities.

SPECIAL, STRATEGIC TOPICAL AREAS AND ISSUES

The Definition of the Market and Industry Under Various Types of Regulation

In many types of governmental regulation a basic aspect of regulation is the definition or determination of the "market" or "industry" or "product" or "line of commerce" or "area of effective competition," and so on. Such determinations have been and are being made unilaterally, statute by statute and in individual cases and situations. There has been no full endeavor to investigate such determinations for consistency and significance in relation to the impacts upon the regulation of the market system as a whole or upon specific subsystems. Thus, for example, under the Robinson-Patman Act, the various provisions apply to commodities of "like grade and quality," and a physical characteristic test has been used for the most part instead of the economic test of market behavior.

All statutes governing specific industries require the delimitation of the areas of coverage—an increasingly difficult matter under our changing technologies and tendencies toward product and functional diversification. It would be exceedingly helpful to examine all governmental regulations involving such determinations (as tariff regulations, internal revenue definitions, the various antitrust statutes, Robinson-Patman, and the host of special statutes) in the dual contexts of consistency and significance in relation to the maintenance of a flexible, acceptable market system.

It is possible that the market system is being fragmented into segments by contradictory and arbitrary determinations and special regulations that run counter to the requirements of both effective, flexible adjustments and the inherent forces of modern technology which are tending increasingly to obliterate or break down traditional boundaries.

Character and Impacts of Governmental Subsidies and of Subsidy-like Differential Treatment

Very likely, the most general, most insidious, and least understood of the various types of intrusions into the market system, as a whole and into specific subsystems, arise through govermental subsidies and subsidy-like differential treatment. The use of subsidies goes back deeply into American history, for the federal and state and local governments have engaged in a wide variety of such programs, intended often to expand local industry and to encourage foreign trade or to foster the provision of basic facilities. Thus, the railroads were the beneficiaries of land grants from 1850 to 1871 intended to encourage and speed railroad construction. Thus, too, the agricultural industries have received and still receive a wide variety of direct and indirect subsidies that have had and continued to have an enormous impact upon these industries.

Currently, almost all major and minor sectors and segments of our economy are receiving or are under the impacts of various open or disguised forms of subsidies and differential, favored treatment. The worth of a congressman is often measured in terms of his ability to obtain federal assistance for his district. State and local governmental bodies are also deeply involved in similar programs. Thus many states and local governmental units try to influence the location of industry by tax exemptions and tax favoritism, financial assistance in building plants, tax exempt bonds, the provision of special facilities without cost or below cost, and so on.

The market system in general and specific sub-systems are affected by a broad variety of impacts, influences, and interventions intended to serve special interests or areas. The number, character, and variety of such interventions are too great to allow simple generalizations. Subsidies and differential treatment might actually strengthen the market system. There is no guarantee or likelihood that this is so—in fact, to the contrary. There is a challenging opportunity here for special studies as well as for general analysis and interpretation. It is difficult to conceive of any other area so widely open for productive research.

Governmental Policies and Regulations Affecting the Growth of Individual Business Enterprises

In a society with a private enterprise base, it is of highest importance whether the total net effects of governmental policies and programs affect the growth of business enterprises favorably or adversely. All regulations intruding into the market system (such as subsidies and subsidy-like differential treatment) or affecting decision making in marketing by individual enterprises may affect their growth—one way or another. In general, there are strong positive endeavors to foster the growth of small business and to circumscribe or constrain the growth of large, powerful enterprises. Thus, there is the special Small Business Administration in the federal government dedicated to the interests of small business. Thus, too, the Supreme Court of the United States in recent decisions, especially *Brown Shoe*, has made the preservation of viable small business a standard of action

superior both to efficiency and the maintenance of competition in an abstract sense. Conversely, powerful well-established corporations find it increasingly difficult to grow by the simple processes of acquisition or merger.

The enforcement of the revised 1950 Section 7 of the Clayton Act is increasingly affecting the opportunities of growth by acquisition. Consequently, large enterprises are forced increasingly to plan growth through internal expansion—horizontally, vertically, functionally, and through conglomerate diversification. Possibly in the near future such avenues of internal growth may be under increasing questioning. Finally, the weight and specific character of taxes affect growth plans and opportunities.

Public Policies and Programs Affecting Consumer-buyer Decision Making and Behavior

The character and relative effectiveness of the free choices of consumer-buyers are the most basic factors in the functioning of the market system in general and throughout its myriad of subsystems. Hence it is of highest importance to investigate the impacts of the host of governmental regulations, facilities, aids, and interventions upon the quality and efficiency of consumer-buyer decision making. Of course, all forms of marketing regulations will have some influence upon consumers' choices by affecting the relative qualities, availabilities, and competitiveness of market supplies and offers. In addition, there are the specific laws and regulations governing weights and measures, packaging, labeling, deceit and misrepresentation, credit terms, and so on.

There is a common generalization that we are moving steadily away from the ancient doctrine of *caveat emptor* to an emerging *caveat venditor*. Regardless of the exact nature of our drift, there is no doubt that abundant basic research opportunities and needs exist in this general area both in general terms and in sharp focus upon specific industries (as foods, drugs, and alcoholic beverages).

In a sense, research studies in the general area of consumer-buyer behavior and decision making could be means of summing up the effects of the other areas of research.

Commentary on "Impact of Government upon the Market System"

SEYMOUR BANKS

This is an extremely well-written and interesting paper, directing attention to issues of undoubted importance. However, its very clarity, scope, and depth of perception raise questions of value judgment as much as research information and, perhaps, this is all to the good. It seems to this reviewer that Grether and Holloway are clearly on the side of private enterprise operating through what seems like the classical competitive system. Their phraseology makes their philosophy quite clear: governmental operations are "interventions." Are governmental actions "interventions"?

The value of Grether and Holloway's extremely lucid presentation is that it permits the reader with an opposing point of view to come to grips immediately with the concepts and facts at issue.

Grether and Holloway make the claim that the American market system, as a whole, as well as specific subsystems, is under the continuing and increasing intervention of governmental policies and programs. Thus this point takes for granted the very question under research. What indeed are the "facts"? First of all, one must decide on the nature of what is taken as facts—are the facts legal documents or responses to them? One can raise the question whether a feeling of confinement and intervention arises less from actual governmental legal and administrative regulatory framework and more from the frame of mind of any entrepreneur, as he sees the "rules of the game" under which he operates. Typically, one accepts the rules of the game and does not regard them as inhibiting performance or freedom of choice. What may be regarded as intervention by one generation may be accepted as part of the rules of the game by the next generation.

POSSIBLE RESEARCH INTO INTERVENTION: HISTORICAL AND CROSS-SECTIONAL

Perhaps several different research studies are required. Basic are the documentary facts; there is opportunity for historical analysis of the scope—both in broad coverage and detailed application within industries—of actual governmental regulations or inhibition of business practices.

16. Are Planning and Regulation Replacing Competition in the New Industrial State?

JOHN KENNETH GALBRAITH, WALTER ADAMS,
WILLARD F. MUELLER, and DONALD F. TURNER

Editor's note: The Select Committee on Small Business, United States Senate, invited four eminent scholars to appear before it on the question: "Are Planning and Regulation Replacing Competition in the New Industrial State?" The seminar discussion included statements by each of the noted scholars. This Senate Committee and its several sub-committees have been conducting hearings for several years on questions of distribution, marketing practices, monopoly, and competition. Each of these issues raises important questions about the antitrust laws, their enforcement and effectiveness. The statements of each scholar present diversity of views and particularly raise questions about Dr. Galbraith's thesis presented in his book, *The New Industrial State.*

STATEMENT OF
DR. JOHN KENNETH GALBRAITH[*]

I am very happy to be here this morning. And while all of us take a natural pleasure in debate, I trust that no one will consider these to be adversary proceedings. I have long been a close and admiring student of Attorney General Turner's writings, as equally those of Professor Adams. I regard, as all of us do, Professor Mueller as one of the most distinguished of our colleagues in the Federal Service. As will become evident, Mr. Turner's position, fully explored, provides comprehensive and much appreciated support for mine.

This is perhaps especially true of his position before he became subject, however slightly, to the intellectual constraints of high public office. I would like to begin by defining this area of agreement, as I venture to see it. Then I will proceed to the, by comparison, much smaller area of argument.

In the lectures that precipitated this discussion and the book I have just published,[1] I took it for granted that American business has become very big.

The element of surprise in this conclusion is very small; I doubt that this conclusion will be much disputed. There are still a large number of small firms and small farms in the United States. They are, however, no longer characteristic of the American economy. In 1962, the five largest industrial corporations in the United States, with combined assets in

---

[*] Paul M. Warburg Professor of Economics, Harvard University, Cambridge, Mass.

◆ SOURCE: Reprinted from "Planning, Regulation and Competition." Hearings before Subcommittees of the Select Committee on Small Business, U.S. Senate, Ninetieth Congress, First Session, June 29, 1967, (U.S. Government Printing Office, Washington, D.C.).

[1] *The New Industrial State* (Boston: Houghton Mifflin, 1967).

excess of $36 billion, possessed over 12 percent of all assets used in manufacturing. The 50 largest corporations had over a third of all manufacturing assets. The 500 largest corporations had well over two-thirds. Corporations with assets in excess of $10 million, some 2,000 in all, accounted for about 80 percent of all the resources used in manufacturing in the United States.[2]

In the mid-1950's, 28 corporations provided approximately 10 percent of all employment in manufacturing, mining, and retail and wholesale trade. Twenty-three corporations provided 15 percent of all the employment in manufacturing. In the first half of that decade—June 1950-June 1956—a hundred firms received two-thirds by value of all defense contracts; 10 firms received one-third.[3] In 1960 four corporations accounted for an estimated 22 percent of all industrial research and development expenditure. Three hundred and eighty-four corporations employing 5,000 or more workers accounted for 85 percent of these research and development expenditures; 260,000 firms employing fewer than 1,000 accounted for only 7 percent.[4]

If I might continue this somewhat exagger-

ated dose of statistics for just a minute, in 1965, three industrial corporations, General Motors, Standard Oil of New Jersey, and Ford Motor Co., had more gross income than all of the farms in the country. This is relevant to my statement that these are the typical, characteristic parts of the economy. The income of General Motors, of $20.7 billion, about equalled that of the 3 million smallest farms in the country—around 90 percent of all farms. The gross revenues of each of the three corporations just mentioned far exceed those of any single State. The revenues of General Motors in 1963 were 50 times those of Nevada, eight times those of New York, and slightly less than one-fifth those of the Federal Government.[5]

These figures, like all statistics, are subject to minor query on matters of detail. As orders of magnitude they are not, I believe, subject to any serious question. Nor are the consequences.

The large firms that dominate the nonservice and nonagricultural sector of the economy have extensive power over their prices. They have large influence over the prices that they pay—at least those costs that are important to their operations. And also the wages they pay. They supply themselves with capital; some three-quarters of all savings now come from the retained earnings of corporations, which is to say that the latter have largely exempted themselves from dependence on the capital market. And, with varying degrees of success firms with the resources to do so go beyond the prices that they set to persuade their customers as to what they should buy. This is a persuasion that, in various and subtle ways, extends to the State. There is great room for difference of opinion, and accordingly for debate, on how decisive are these several manifestations of power. But nearly all will agree that "There is a large correlation between the concentration of output in the hands of a small number of large producers and the existence of firms with significant degrees of market power." The observation just cited is that of Mr. Carl Kaysen and Mr. Donald F. Turner in their authoritative volume, "A Policy for Antitrust Law."[6]

They add, as would I, that a policy that

[2] Hearings before the Subcommittee on Antitrust and Monopoly of the Committee of the Judiciary, U.S. Senate, 88th Cong., 2d sess., pursuant to S. Res. 262. Pt. I. "Economic Concentration. Overall and Conglomerate Aspects" (1964), p. 113. Data on the concentration of industrial activity in the hands of large firms, and especially any that show an increase in concentration, sustain a controversy in the United States that, at times, reaches mildly pathological proportions. The reason is that much of the argument between those who see the market as a viable institution and those who feel that it is succumbing to monopolistic influences has long turned on these figures. These figures are thus defended or attacked according to predilection. However, the general orders of magnitude given here are not subject to serious question.

[3] Carl Kaysen, "The Corporation: How Much Power? What Scope?" in The Corporation in Modern Society, Edward S. Mason, ed. (Cambridge: Harvard University Press, 1959), pp. 86–87.

[4] M. A. Adelman, hearings before the Subcommittee on Antitrust and Monopoly of the Committee on the Judiciary, U.S. Senate, 89th Cong., 1st sess., pursuant to S. Res. 70, pt. III. "Economic Concentration. Concentration, Invention and Innovation" (1965), pp. 1139–1140.

[5] Data from Fortune, U.S. Department of Agriculture and Statistical Abstract of the United States.

[6] Harvard University Press, 1959, pp. 8–9.

deals with "the existence and significance of market power is not aimed at *merely marginal or special phenomena, but at phenomena spread widely through the economy.*"[7] Still quoting Professor Kaysen and Mr. Turner.

In my own volume I have gone on, at no slight length, to argue that this trend to the large corporation and this resulting exercise of substantial power over the prices, costs, wages, capital sources, and consumers is part of the broad sweep of economic development. Technology; the extensive use of capital; affluent and hence malleable customers; the imperatives of organization; the role of the union; the requirements imposed by public tasks, including arms development and space exploration, have all weakened the authority of the market. At the same time, these developments have both enabled and required firms to substitute planning with its management of markets for a simple response to the market. Bigness and market power, in other words, are but one part of a much larger current of change. To see them in isolation from other change is artificial. In part it is what results when a social discipline passes however partially from the custody of scholars to that of specialists and mechanics.

I have also been concerned in this book with the problem of how we are to survive, and in civilized fashion, in a world of great organizations which, not surprisingly, impose both their values and their needs on the society they are assumed to serve. But these further matters are not directly at issue this morning. In any case they do not directly involve the question of the antitrust laws.

The issue of the antitrust laws arises in response to a prior question. That question is whether we can escape the concentration and the attendant market control and planning which I have outlined and whether the antitrust laws, as now used, are an effective instrument for this escape. The present hearings materialized when I urged the contrary— when I said that the trend to great size and associated control was immutable, given our desire for economic development, and that the present antitrust efforts to deal with size and market power were a charade. I noted that the antitrust laws legitimatize the real exercise of market power on the part of the large firms by a rather diligent harassment of

those who have less of it. Thus, they serve to reassure us on the condition they are assumed to correct.

The facts which lead to the foregoing conclusions are not at all obscure. Nor are they matters of great subtlety. They are accepted by most competent economists and lawyers including the very distinguished men here this morning. Only the rather obvious conclusions to be drawn from these facts encounter a measure of resistance. This, no doubt, is purely temporary, but while it persists it does cause a measure of confusion.

The most effective manifestation of economic power, all must agree, is simply the big firm. To be big in general and big in an industry[8] is by far the best way of influencing prices and costs, commanding capital, having access to advertising, and selling resources, and processing the other requisites of market power. And, as we have seen, by common agreement the heartland of the industrial economy is now dominated by large firms. The great bulk of American business is transacted by very large corporations.

And here enters the element of charade in the antitrust laws. If a firm is already large it is substantially immune under the antitrust laws. If you already have the basic requisite of market power, you are safe. The Assistant Attorney General in Charge of the Antitrust Laws in the distinguished book to which I have already adverted argues that the market power of the large firm should now be made subject to the antitrust laws. This indeed is the main thrust of Mr. Turner's and Mr. Kaysen's book. If something needs to be done, he would not, of course, argue that it has been done. And in responding to the questions of this committee on May 2 of this year he affirmed the point, if in slightly more cautious language:

It is more difficult under present law to bring a case attacking *existing* concentration in an industry than to prevent further concentrations which firms attempt to realize through merger.[9]

But this we see is no minor qualification. If firms are already large—if concentration

---

[7] *Ibid.*, p. 41. (Emphasis is Dr. Galbraith's.)

[8] The two go together although some economists, in a desire to exculpate size while indicting monopoly, have, curiously enough, asserted the **contrary.**

[9] Letter to the Honorable Wayne Morse, May 2, 1967 (his emphasis).

is already great—if the resulting power to use Mr. Turner's own words, is not "merely marginal" but is "spread widely through the economy" as he says, then it means that all so favored have won immunity or virtual immunity from the antitrust laws. And this, of course, is the case.

Meanwhile, the antitrust laws are effective in two instances where the firms do not have market power but are seeking to achieve it. Where firms are few and large they can, without overt collusion, establish and maintain a price that is generally satisfactory to all participants. Nor is this an especially difficult calculation, this exercise of power. This is what we economists with our genius for the neat phrase have come to call oliogopolistic rationality. And this market power is legally immune or very nearly so. It is everyday practice in autos, steel, rubber, and virtually every other industry shared or dominated by, relatively, a few large firms. But if there are 20 or 30 or more significant firms in the industry, this kind of tacit pricemaking—this calculation as to what is mutually advantageous but without overt communication—becomes more difficult, maybe very difficult. The same result can only be achieved by having a meeting or by exchanging information on prices and costs and price intentions. But this is illegal. It is also legally vulnerable. And it is, in fact, an everyday object of prosecution as the Department of Justice will confirm. What the big firm in the concentrated industry can accomplish legally and effortlessly because of its size, the small firm in the unconcentrated industry does at the pain of civil and even criminal prosecution. Moreover, with this my colleagues will, I believe, agree.

The second manifestation of the charade has to do with mergers. If a firm is already large, it has as a practical matter nothing to fear under antimerger provisions of the Clayton Act. It will not be demerged. It can continue to grow from its own earnings; if discreet, it can even, from time to time, pick up a small and impecunious competitor, for it can reasonably claim that this does little to alter the pattern of competition in the industry. But if two medium-sized firms unite in order to deal more effectively with this giant, the law will be on them like a tiger. Again if large, you are exempt. If you seek to become as large, or even if you seek to become somewhat larger, although still much smaller, you are in trouble. And again I doubt that the

committee will encounter a great deal of dissent.

Here we have the nature of modern antitrust activity. It conducts a fairly effective war on small firms which seek the same market power that the big firms already, by their nature, possess. Behind this impressive facade the big participants who have the most power bask in nearly total immunity. And since the competitive market, like God and a sound family life, is something that no sound businessman can actively oppose, even the smaller entrepreneurs who are the natural victims of this arrangement do not actively protest. It is possible that they do not know how they are being used.

As I say all of this is agreed—or at least is supported by the past writings and speeches of participants in this discussion. All I have done—I wish I could lay claim to greater novelty—is to state the rather disagreeable conclusion flowing from this agreement. The antitrust laws give the impression of protecting the market and competition by attacking those who exercise it most effectively. I wonder if the committee thinks that charade is an unjust word?

Now let me clear up two or three secondary matters which may seem to affect this discussion but really do not. The first requires me, I think for the first time—in substance as distinct from terminology—to quit company with Attorney General Turner. Mr. Turner, while conceding that the law is largely helpless in attacking achieved as distinct from aspired-to power, holds that it is important to act preventatively to keep smaller firms from getting larger. This he has emphasized in his responses to this committee. It will surely have occurred to the committee, as it must have occurred to Mr. Turner, that this does not meet the issue of gross discrimination as between those who already have and those who aspire to market power. Nor, one imagines, can a major law officer of the Government be entirely happy about such discrimination. It condones professional and accomplished wrongdoing, as it were, but stresses the importance of cracking down on amateur wickedness. Surely this is bad law. Also, given the size and market power that has already been achieved, and given its immunity, it will be evident that this justification amounts to locking the stable door not alone after the horse has been stolen but after the entire stud has been galloped away.

Next, I must correct a misapprehension of Attorney General Turner. His responses to the committee and his extremely interesting lecture attacking my general position in London convey the impression that I am concerned with making the economic case for the large corporation. I am, he suggests, especially concerned to defend its efficiency and technical virtuosity. To this he responds by arguing that, while the big corporation is more efficient than the small firm, there is no great difference between the big corporation and the giant corporation. He doesn't make altogether clear, incidentally, how big a big as distinct from a giant corporation is. All would, I imagine, be among the five hundred or thousand firms that dominate industrial activity. But I have a more fundamental objection. He attacks me on a point that concerns me little and which is of no importance for my case.

I am not concerned with making the case for big business. Nor am I especially concerned about its efficiency or inefficiency. Doubtless efficiency is worth having. But, like truth, regular bathing and better traffic regulation, it has an adequate number of exponents. I have always thought it unwise to compete with the commonplace. Mr. Turner may be correct in his conclusions about the giants. I am content to argue that we have big business, and that the antitrust laws notwithstanding, we will continue to have it, and that they give an impression of alternative possibilities that do not exist.

I conclude also that while big business and giant business may not be more efficient, their market power as manifested only on what they sell and what they buy and over buyers does give them advantages in planning their own future and insuring their own survival. Since big business is inevitable and will not be affected by the antitrust laws, I naturally go on to consider how we may come to terms with it. Much of my book is concerned with that. If my colleagues this morning disagree, as is their right, they must tell you how the antitrust laws are to be brought effectively to bear on the large corporation. Otherwise— and here let me interpolate an important point—there is no escape from the conclusion that the antitrust laws, so far from being a threat to big business are a facade behind which it operates with yet greater impunity. They create the impression, the antitrust laws, that the market is a viable control.

Then, if a drug firm has exorbitant profits, it can say this is what the market allows. Or if an automobile firm does not want to install safety appliances, it can say that the market does not demand it. Or if there is resistance to Government price guideposts to prevent inflation, it can be said that these interfere with the market.

In each case, the antitrust laws effectively protect the large business from social pressure or regulation by maintaining the myth that the market does the regulating instead.

Finally, I agree that the antitrust laws have purposes other than those related to the structure of industry and the resulting power and planning. I agree in particular they are a code of what is deemed fair and decent as between seller and buyers. They exclude the resort to activities—naked aggression, as in the case of the old Standard Oil Co. in the last century—based on superior economic resources, favoritism, surreptitious and unfair discounts, numerous other practices which the civilized commercial community holds in disesteem. I have no complaint about these aspects of the antitrust laws. On the contrary, I consider them serviceable. But only in the most marginal fashion do they thus affect the structure of industry. They are, in large part, a separate matter and do not affect the discussion here.

To what then does this all lead? It is possible that my distinguished colleagues here this morning will call for an all-out attack on achieved market power along the lines which Attorney General Turner has adumbrated in his book, which Prof. Walter Adams has long favored, and which I have just said would be necessary if they disagree with my conclusions on the inevitability of market power. This means action, including enabling legislation leading to all-out dissolution proceedings against General Motors, Ford, the oil majors, United States Steel, General Electric, IBM, Western Electric, Du Pont, Swift, Bethlehem, International Harvester, North American Aviation, Goodyear, Boeing, National Dairy Products, Procter & Gamble, Eastman Kodak, and all of comparable size and scope. For there can be no doubt: All are giants. All have market power. All enjoy an immunity not accorded to those who merely aspire to their power. Such an onslaught, tantamount, given the role of the big firms in the economy as I described it, to declaring the heartland of the modern economy illegal, would go far to make legitimate the objections to my position. It would mean that achieved market power was subject to the same legal attack as that which is only a matter of aspiration.

But I will be a trifle surprised if my distinguished colleagues from the Government are willing to proclaim such a crusade. I am frank to say I would not favor it myself; as I indicated at the outset, I do not think that the growth of the modern corporation can be isolated from other and intricately related changes in modern economic development. I doubt that one can operate on one part of this fabric. The political problems in proclaiming much of the modern economy illegal will also strike many as impressive.

If this crusade is not to be launched, then my good friends have no alternative but to agree with me. They are good men; they cannot acquiesce in a policy which by their own admission attacks the small man for seeking what the big firm enjoys with impunity. I readily concede that it would be quixotic to ask the repeal of the antitrust laws although other industrial countries function quite competently without them. But the antitrust laws are part of the American folklore. They receive strong support from the legal profession and vice versa. They have a reserve value for dealing with extreme and sanguinary abuse of power as occasionally occurs. I would be content were we simply to withdraw our faith from the antitrust laws—were we to cease to imagine that there is any chance that they will affect the structure of American industry or its market power and, having in mind the present discrimination in their application, were we then to allow them quietly to atrophy. Then we would face the real problem, which is how to live with the vast organizations—and the values they impose—that we have and will continue to have. This being so, nostalgia will no longer be a disguise for that necessity.

STATEMENT OF
DR. WALTER ADAMS*

Time precludes more than a cursory tribute to an eminently civilized and literate political economist—a leader in that small but brave army of men who "prefer to see the truth imperfectly and obscurely rather

than to maintain error, reached indeed with clearness and consistency and by easy logic, but based on hypotheses inappropriate to the facts." It is Galbraith's cardinal virtue to focus on real problems and vital issues. His questions are invariably to the point. Regrettably, his answers are sometimes wrong.

In the "New Industrial State," Galbraith once again examines the reality of corporate giantism and corporate power, and outlines the implications for public policy. He finds that the giant corporation has achieved such dominance of American industry, that it can control its environment and immunize itself from the discipline of all exogenous control mechanisms—especially the competitive market. Through separation of ownership from management it has emancipated itself from the control of stockholders. By reinvestment of profits (internal financing), it has eliminated the influence of the financier and the capital market. By brainwashing its clientele, it has insulated itself from consumer sovereignty. By possession of market power, it has come to dominate both suppliers and customers. By judicious identification with, and manipulation of the state, it has achieved autonomy from government control. Whatever it cannot do for itself to assure survival and growth, a compliant government does on its behalf—assuring the maintenance of full employment; eliminating the risk of, and subsidizing the investment in, research and development; and assuring the supply of scientific and technical skills required by the modern technostructure.

In return for this privileged autonomy, the industrial giant performs society's planning function. And this, according to Galbraith, is not only inevitable (because technological imperatives dictate it); it is also good. The market is dead, we are told; and there is no need to regret its passing. The only remaining task, it seems, is to recognize the trend, to accept it as inexorable necessity, and, presumably, not to stand in its way.

Mr. Chairman, here is a blueprint for technocracy, private socialism, and the corporate state. The keystone of the new power structure is the giant corporation, freed from all traditional checks and balances, and subject only to the countervailing power of the intellectual in politics—those Platonic philosopher-kings who stand guard over the interests of the Republic. Happily, this blueprint need not cause undue alarm: first, because Gal-

---

* Professor of Economics, Michigan State University, East Lansing, Mich.

braith's analysis rests on an empirically un-substantiated premise; and second, even if this analysis were correct, there would be more attractive public policy alternatives than Galbraith suggests.

Galbraith's contention that corporate giant-ism dominates American industry requires no adumbration. On that there is consensus. But Galbraith fails to prove that this dominance is the inevitable response to technological imperatives, and hence beyond our control. Specifically, he offers little evidence to dem-onstrate that Brobdingnagian size is the pre-requisite for, and the guarantor of:

1. Operational efficiency.
2. Invention, innovation, and technologi-cal progress.
3. Effective planning in the public interest.

Let me comment briefly on each of these points, and in so doing indicate that the com-petitive market need not be condemned to the euthanasia which Galbraith thinks is inexorable, and perhaps even desirable.

Efficiency

In the mass-production industries, firms must undoubtedly be large, but do they need to assume the dinosaur proportions of some present-day giants? The unit of technological efficiency is the plant, not the firm. This means that there are undisputed advantages to large-scale integrated operations at a single steel plant, for example, but there is little technological justification for combining these functionally separate plants into a single administrative unit. United States Steel is nothing more than several Inland Steels strewn about the country, and no one has yet suggested that Inland is not big enough to be efficient. A firm producing such divergent lines as rubber boots, chain saws, motorboats, and chicken feed may be seeking conglom-erate size and power; it is certainly not re-sponding to technological necessity. In short, one can favor technological bigness and op-pose administrative bigness without incon-sistency.

Two major empirical studies document this generalization. The first, by Dr. John M. Blair, indicated a significant divergence be-tween plant and company concentration in major industries dominated by oligopoly. It indicates, moreover, that between 1947 and 1958, there was a general tendency for plant concentration to decline, which means that in many industries technology may actually militate toward optimal efficiency in plants of "smaller" size.[10]

The second study, by Prof. Joe Bain, pre-sents engineering estimates of scale econ-omies and capital requirements in 20 indus-tries of above-average concentration. Bain finds that:

. . . Concentration by firms is in every case but one greater than required by single-plant economies, and in more than half of the cases very substantially greater.

In less precise language, many multiplant industrial giants have gone beyond the op-timal size required for efficiency. Galbraith acknowledges the validity of Bain's findings, but dismisses them by saying:

The size of General Motors is in the service not of monopoly or the economies of scale, but of planning. And for this planning . . . there is no clear upper limit to the desirable size. It could be that the bigger the better.[11]

If size is to be justified, then, this must be done on grounds other than efficiency. I shall return to this point in a moment.

Technological Progress

As in the case of efficiency, there is no strict correlation between giantism and progressive-ness. In a study of the 60 most important inventions of recent years, it was found that more than half came from independent inventors, less than half from corporate re-search, and even less from the research done by large concerns.[12] Moreover, while some highly concentrated industries spend a large share of their income on research, others do not; within the same industry, some smaller firms spend as high a *percentage* as their larger rivals. As Wilcox points out:

The big concern has the ability to finance innovation; it does not necessarily do so. There is no clear relationship between size and investment in research.[13]

Finally, as this committee well knows, roughly two-thirds of the research done in

---

[10] U.S. Senate Antitrust and Monopoly Subcom-mittee, Economic Concentration, pp. 1541–1551.
[11] *Id.*, p. 76.
[12] Jewkes, Sawers, and Stillerman, *The Sources of Invention,* chapter IV.
[13] *Public Policies Toward Business,* 3d ed., p. 258.

the United States is financed by the Federal Government, and in many cases the research contractor gets the patent rights on inventions paid for with public funds. The inventive genius which ostensibly goes with size would seem to involve socialization of risk and privatization of profit and power.

The U.S. steel industry, which ranks among the largest, most basic, and most concentrated of American industries, certainly part of the industrial state that Professor Galbraith speaks of, affords a dramatic case in point. It spends only 0.7 percent of its revenues on research and, in technological progressiveness, the giants which dominate this industry lag behind their smaller domestic rivals as well as their smaller foreign competitors. Thus, the basic oxygen furnace—considered the "only major breakthrough at the ingot level since before the turn of the century" was invented in 1950 by a miniscule Austrian *firm* which was less than one-third the size of a single *plant* of the United States Steel Corp. The innovation was introduced in the United States in 1954 by McLouth Steel which at the time had about 1 percent of domestic steel capacity—to be followed some 10 years later by the steel giants: United States Steel in December 1963, Bethlehem in 1964, and Republic in 1965. Despite the fact that this revolutionary invention involved an average operating cost saving of $5 per ton and an investment cost saving of $20 per ton of installed capacity, the steel giants during the 1950's according to *Business Week*, "bought 40 million tons of the wrong capacity —the open-hearth furnace" which was obsolete almost the moment it was put in place.[14]

Only after they were subjected to actual and threatened competition from domestic and foreign steelmakers in the 1960's did the steel giants decide to accommodate themselves to the oxygen revolution. Thus, it was the cold wind of competition, and not the catatonia induced by industrial concentration, which proved conducive to innovation and technological progress.[15]

Planning in the Public Interest

Modern technology, says Galbraith, makes planning essential, and the giant corporation is its chosen instrument. This planning, in turn, requires the corporation to eliminate risk and uncertainty, to create for itself an environment of stability and security, and to free itself from all outside interference with its planning function. Thus, it must have enough size and power not only to produce a "mauve and cerise, air-conditioned, power-steered, and power-braked automobile"[16]— unsafe at any speed—but also enough power to brainwash customers to buy it. In the interest of planning, producers must be able to sell what they make—be it automobiles or missiles—and at prices which the technostructure deems remunerative.

Aside from the unproved premise—and I keep coming back to this: technological necessity—on which this argument rests, it raises crucial questions of responsibility and accountability. By what standards do the industrial giants plan, and is there an automatic convergence between private and public advantage? Must we, as a matter of inexorable inevitability, accept the proposition that what is good for General Motors is good for the country? What are the safeguards other than the intellectual in politics— against arbitrary abuse of power, capricious or faulty decision making? Must society legitimize a self-sustaining, self-serving, self-justifying, and self-perpetuating industrial oligarchy as the price for industrial efficiency and progress?

This high price need not and should not be paid. The competitive market is a far more efficacious instrument for serving society— and far more viable—than Galbraith would have us believe. Let me illustrate:

1. In the electric power industry, a network of local monopolies, under Government regulation and protection, was long addicted to the belief that the demand for electric power was inelastic—that rates had little to do with the quantity of electricity used. It was not industrial planning, carried on by private monopolists under public supervision, but the yardstick competition of TVA which demonstrated the financial feasibility of aggressive rate reductions. It was this competitive experiment which proved that lower electric rates were not only possible but also profitable—both to the private monopolists and to the customers they served.

---

[14] *Business Week*, Nov. 16, 1963, pp. 144–146.
[15] Adams and Dirlam, "Big Steel, Invention, and Innovation," *Quarterly Journal of Economics*, May 1966.

[16] *The Affluent Society*, p. 253.

2. In the airline oligopoly, also operating under the umbrella of Government protectionism, the dominant firms long suffered from the same addiction. They refused to institute coach service on the grounds that it would eliminate first-class service and—through a reduction in the rate structure—bring financial ruin to the industry. Again it was the force and discipline of competition—from the small, nonscheduled carriers, operating at the margin of the industry—which proved that the giants and their overprotective public regulators were wrong. As this committee observed, it was the pioneering and competition of the nonskeds which "shattered the concept of the fixed, limited market for civil aviation. As a result, the question is no longer what portion of a fixed pie any company will get, but rather how much the entire pie can grow."[17]

Again, a bureaucracy-ridden, conservative, overcautious, overprotected industry was shown to have engaged in defective planning—to its own detriment as well as the public's.

3. In the steel industry, after World War II, oligopoly planning resulted in truly shabby performance. There was an almost unbroken climb in steel prices, in good times and bad, in the face of rising or falling demand, increasing or declining unit costs. Prices rose even when only 50 percent of the industry's capacity was utilized. Technological change was resisted and obsolete capacity installed. Domestic markets were eroded by substitute materials and burgeoning imports. Steel's export-import balance deteriorated both in absolute and relative terms; whereas the industry once exported about five times as much as it imported, the ratio today is almost exactly reversed, and steel exports are confined almost exclusively to AID-financed sales guaranteed by "Buy American" provisos. We may be confident that if this deplorable performance is to be improved, it will come about through the disciplining force of domestic and foreign competition, and not through additional planning or an escalation of giant size. It will come about through an accommodation to the exigencies of the world market, and not by insensitive monopolistic pricing, practiced under the protectionist shelter of the tariffs which the industry now seeks.

Without multiplying such examples, it is safe to say that monopoloid planning is done in the interest of monopoly power. Seldom, if ever, is society the beneficiary.

In conclusion, I would note that industrial giantism in America is not the product of spontaneous generation, natural selection, or technological inevitability. In this era of "Big Government," it is often the end result of unwise, manmade, discriminatory, privilege-creating governmental action. Defense contracts, R. & D. support, patent policy, tax privileges, stockpiling arrangements, tariffs, subsidies, etc., have far from a neutral effect on our industrial structure. Especially in the regulated industries—in air and surface transportation, in broadcasting and communications—the writ of the State is decisive. In controlling these variables the policymaker has greater freedom and flexibility than is commonly supposed; the potential for promoting competition and dispersing industrial power is both real and practicable.[18]

It seems to me that Professor Galbraith keeps coming back to the charade of antitrust, but a competitive society is the product not simply of negative enforcement of the antitrust laws; it is the product of a total integrated approach on all levels of government—legislative, administrative, and regulatory. An integrated national policy of promoting competition—and this means more than mere enforcement of the antitrust laws—and is not only feasible but desirable. No economy can function without built-in checks and balances which tend to break down the bureaucratic preference for letting well enough alone—forces which erode, subvert, or render obsolete the conservative bias inherent in any organization devoid of competition. Be it the dictates of the competitive market, the pressure from imports or substitutes, or the discipline of yardstick competition, it is these forces which the policymaker must try to reinforce where they exist and to *build into* the economic system where they are lacking or moribund. The policy objective throughout must be to promote market *structures* which will *compel* the conduct and performance which is in the public interest.

The disciplining force of competition is superior to industrial planning—by the private or public monopolist, the benevolent or

---

[17] Senate Report No. 540, 82d Cong., first sess., 1951.

[18] Adams and Gray, *Monopoly in America*, (New York: Macmillan, 1955).

authoritarian bureaucrat. It alone provides the incentives and compulsions to pioneer untried trails, to explore paths which may lead to dead ends, to take risks which may not pay off, and to try to make tomorrow better than the best.

STATEMENT OF
DR. WILLARD F. MUELLER[*]

It is, indeed, an awesome challenge to cope with the ideas of the Goliath of the economics profession, one who gracefully moves from a high post in that most criticized of Government wartime agencies, the OPA, to the editorial desk of *Fortune* magazine and the halls of Harvard; one who is as much at home with the problems of the underdeveloped nations as with his so-called "new industrial state." Few in the fraternity of economists can match Professor Galbraith in his facility of expression and capacity to create provocative insights into the great issues of the day.

His recent Reith lectures on "The New Industrial State" caused a mild sensation in some circles.[19] I understand that among some segments of the European industrial community Galbraith's ideas fell like new rain on seeds already sprouted. But I suspect American economists will be less receptive to his ideas.

The heart of his thesis is that over the past 75 years certain "technological imperatives" have wrought great changes in the basic arrangement of modern economic life, the ultimate consequence of which is the "diminished effectiveness of the market." As a result, "the market is replaced by planning."

He argues that modern technological imperatives make the vast, "mature" industrial enterprise a perfect mechanism for planning the invention, innovation, and production process. But market power is not only an end result, it is prerequisite to the success of

the system. The requirements of large-scale production, heavy capital commitments, and sophisticated technology demand elaborate planning. Successful planning, in turn, requires management of consumer wants to suit the needs of the business enterprise. The planning process is carried on by what Galbraith labels "the technostructure," which encompasses all the technicians and professionals required for effective group decision-making.

Additionally, modern technology requires increasing participation by the state in the planning process, for many jobs are too big even for the largest private industrial complex. Finally, Galbraith believes that public policy aimed at maintaining competition is based on a 19th-century conception of the economy. He, therefore, would abandon our traditional policy of relying on market forces to limit and discipline the use of private economic market power.

Where is the new industrial state taking us? Galbraith predicts that the mature corporation is increasingly becoming a part of the administrative complex of the state and that there will be a gradual convergence of capitalistic and communistic societies.[20] What will be the quality of life in the new industrial state? Should we continue to subordinate all to material welfare, that is what we will get. On the other hand, should we raise our sights to more esthetic goals, the industrial system will become "responsive to the larger purposes of society." He has shown us, in his words, "wherein the chance for salvation lies."[21] So, in the end, it will be up to us to choose. (This is a surprise ending in view of the irrespressible economic determinism which led to all his earlier conclusions.)

Although I shall emphasize points of difference, there is much in Galbraith's "new industrial state" with which I agree. In fact, much of what he says has become a part of the conventional economic wisdom—Berle and Means articulated in 1934 the thesis of separation of business ownership and control.[22] But Galbraith has put together these and other old ideas—some accepted and some rejected by economists—into a new and bigger package. And as always when Galbraith

---

[*] Chief Economist and Director, Bureau of Economics, Federal Trade Commission, Washington, D.C.

[19] John Kenneth Galbraith capsuled his views of "The New Industrial State" in six Reith lectures delivered over the British Broadcasting Corporation. These lectures, delivered during November and December 1966, appeared in "The Listener," published by BBC. A fuller exposition of his views appears in his book, *The New Industrial State*, published June 26, 1967, by Houghton Mifflin Co.

---

[20] *The New Industrial State*, pp. 389 ff.
[21] *Ibid.*, p. 399.
[22] Adolf A. Berle and Gardiner C. Means, *The Modern Corporation and Private Property*, 1934.

goes over even familiar ground, he discovers new things and paints a different and grander landscape than his forbears. But as one not so friendly reviewer observed, "novelty isn't everything: one can make a decent case for the proposition that it is more important to be right than different."

At the outset, let there be no mistake about it: Although Galbraith has articulated a provocative thesis concerning the causes and implications of "the new industrial state," he has not borne the burden of mustering the evidence to validate this thesis.

Time permits joining issues on only his key points. I shall challenge three of his major contentions:

1. Technological imperatives dictate vast industrial concerns and high levels of market concentration and, hence, the death of the market.

2. Public policy aimed at maintaining a market economy has failed in the past and is doomed to fail in the future.

3. The necessity for State planning in certain areas further diminishes the need for reliance on the market as a regulating and planning agent.

The Technological Imperatives

Most fundamental to Galbraith's thesis are the so-called technological imperatives which he views as the root causes of modern industrial organization. He asserts that we must have very large industrial complexes and high market concentration because of the requirements of large-scale production, invention, and innovation. As he puts it, "The enemy of the market is not ideology but technology." But what are the facts on this point?

Recent studies of this subject are almost unanimous in concluding that productive efficiency dictates high concentration in only a small and declining share of all manufacturing industries. On this point, there seems to be little disagreement.

There is a growing body of research into the extent to which economies of large scale dictate large business enterprise and high market concentration. The evidence is sharpest in the area of productive efficiency. This is an especially crucial area because of the public policy dilemma posed by industries with increasing returns to large scale. In clear-cut cases where large-scale production dictates monopoly, as with telephone and electric power, the American answer has been either regulation or Government ownership. But, if such industries prove the rule rather than the exception, this raises a basic question as to the compatability of productive efficiency and a competitively structured economy. It is, therefore, extremely significant that recent studies are unanimous in concluding that productive efficiency dictates high concentration in only a small—and declining—share of all manufacturing industries.[23]

But Galbraith does not rest his case on the requirement of large-scale production. He further argues that economies of scale in research and innovation make high concentration and near monopoly an inevitable outcome of modern capitalism. Since Joseph Schumpeter first set forth this doctrine in 1942[24] and Galbraith expanded upon it in 1952,[25] it has been subjected to extensive empirical testing. There has been a virtual flood of studies in recent years. All students of the subject are not in complete agreement. But as a minimum, a careful reading of the evidence shows that the theory has no general validity in explaining inventive and innovative activity in American experience. Indeed, recent studies indicate that the thesis is on the verge of collapse. One of Schumpeter's disciples recently discovered no systematic relationship between the degree of market power and inventive success. He concluded:

---

[23] Some of the key studies on this subject are the following: Joe S. Bain, "Barriers to New Competition," 1956, John M. Blair, "Analysis of Divergence Between Plant and Firm Concentration." Hearings on Economic Concentration. Senate Subcommittee on Antitrust and Monopoly, Sept. 12, 1966. The FTC staff study, "The Structure of Food Manufacturing," Technical Study No. 8, National Commission on Food Marketing, June 1966, 83–99, summarizes the studies done on this subject in the food industries. Also, see various statements in hearings cited in footnote 9.

[24] Joseph Schumpeter, *Capitalism, Socialism, and Democracy*, 1942.

[25] John Kenneth Galbraith, *American Capitalism, The Concept of Countervailing Power*, 1952, p. 91. There are important differences, however, between the arguments of Schumpeter and Galbraith. Whereas Galbraith argues that technological imperatives make great market power inevitable, thereby destroying the market, Schumpeter thought "the process of creative distinction" would continually erode market power of those holding it.

These findings among other things raise doubts whether the big, monopolistic conglomerate corporation is as efficient an engine of technological change as disciples of Schumpeter (including myself) have supposed it to be. Perhaps a bevy of fact-mechanics can still rescue the Schumpeter engine from disgrace, but at present the outlook seems pessimistic.[26]

Students of the problem owe a debt of gratitude to the Senate Subcommittee on Antitrust and Monopoly, chaired by Senator Philip A. Hart, for the exhaustive hearings it has held on the subject of the role of technology and industrial organization.[27] Over the past 3 years these hearings have reviewed systematically nearly all of the recent authoritative work on this subject. I shall not review this evidence here, but it is must reading for anyone genuinely interested in getting at the facts in this area. Regrettably, Professor Galbraith apparently has failed to explore this and other authoritative work on the subject. Until he, or others, can come up with contrary evidence, the chief pillar of his thesis lacks an empirical foundation.

I think his use of illustration betrays his case. He illustrates, as you will recall from his Reith lectures and also his books, the matchless capability of the vast enterprise in planning inventive and innovative activity by a hypothetical example of how General Electric would go about the conception and birth of a new popup toaster.[28] But insight into this process is better revealed by experience than by hypothetical example. What support in experience is there for predicting that vast size is prerequisite to the development and introduction of new products and processes? Let's consider the electrical home appliances sold

by General Electric. Perhaps the past is prolog to the future.

To begin, the electric toaster was not invented or introduced by a great corporation such as General Electric, which would fit so nicely Galbraith's invention-innovation-planning framework. On the contrary, according to the late T. K. Quinn, former vice president of General Electric, it was developed and brought into the market by a relatively small firm, the McGraw Co. And, according to Mr. Quinn, "for many years none of the giant companies were able to come near to matching [McGraw's] toaster."[29] This is no exception. Mr. Quinn credited small companies with discovery and initial production of electric ranges, electric refrigerators, electric dryers, electric dishwashers, the hermetically sealed compressor, vacuum cleaners, clothes-washing machines, deep freezers, electric hot irons, and electric steam irons.[30] Indeed, Mr. Quinn summarized his own experience with GE in this way:

I know of no original product invention, not even electric shavers or hearing aids, made by any of the giant laboratories or corporations, with the possible exception of the household garbage grinder, developed not by the research laboratory but by the engineering department of General Electric. But the basic idea of this machine came from a small concern producing commercial grinders.[31]

He concluded:

The record of the giants is one of moving in, buying out, and absorbing the smaller concerns.

Nor is this record unique to household appliances. In many other industries smaller companies generate at least their proportionate share of inventions and innovations, and

---

[26] F. M. Scherer, "Firm Size, Market Structure, Opportunity and the Output of Patented Inventions," *American Economic Review*, December 1965, 1121–22.

[27] Hearings before the Subcommittee on Antitrust and Monopoly of the Committee on the Judiciary. U.S. Senate, 89th Cong., first sess., Economic Concentration, pt. 3. Concentration, Invention, and Innovation, 1965; pt. 4, Concentration and Efficiency, 1965.

[28] "The central characteristics of modern industry are illustrated by this culturally exciting invention. It would require a large organization, embracing many specialists, to get this product to consumers. Considerable capital would be required. While it is conceivably open to an indi-

vidual entrepreneur, such as myself, to have an inspiration, no one would expect a one-man firm to produce such a product. It could be floated only by a big firm. All decisions on the toaster—those involving initiation, development, and ultimate acceptance or rejection—are the work of teams of specialists and are exercised deep down in the company. And no one would think of leaving price or demand to the market. The price would be subject to careful advance calculation * * *." (Second Reith lecture, p. 754.) He also uses this illustration in his book at pp. 68–69.

[29] T. K. Quinn, *Giant Business*, 1953, p. 117.

[30] *Ibid.*, pp. 116–117.

[31] *Ibid.*, p. 177.

frequently they do a good deal better than the industrial giants.[32]

Perhaps Galbraith's "technological imperatives" assumption has greater validity in areas where invention and innovation costs are higher and the planning horizons are more distinct than they are in consumer goods products. But here, too, Galbraith's premises are based more on sands of fancy than rocks of evidence. Perhaps no industry fits as snugly the Galbraith model for ideal planning as the American steel industry. Since the creation of United States Steel in 1901, the American steel industry has been highly concentrated and dominated by big enterprises. Presumably this market structure provided what Galbraith views as the "prime requirement" of planning: "control over decision."

There can be no doubt but that the market structure of the industry gave big steel considerable discretion in planning. But the relevant question is whether this discretion was used as Galbraith's theory predicts. Fortunately in this case we need not rely on speculation. The leading steel companies clearly had a lackluster record as inventive and innovative forces in this most basic industry. The accomplishments of United States Steel have been especially disappointing. After an exhaustive study of the corporation, an engineering consulting firm reported to United States Steel in 1939 that it was lagging badly in many respects.[33] Nor have United States Steel or other large steel companies performed much better since 1939. A study of the 13 major innovations in the American steel industry between 1940 and 1955 reveals none was the outgrowth of American steel companies.[34] Four were based on inventions of European steel companies

(generally small by American standards) and seven came from independent inventors.

Especially instructive is the postwar record concerning the introduction of the oxygen steelmaking process by dominant American steel firms. The basic oxygen process has been called the only major technological breakthrough at the ingot level of steelmaking since before 1900.[35]

Not only did the largest steel companies play no role in the discovery and initial development of this important innovation, but they lagged badly in introducing it.[36] A small Austrian steel company (which was one-third the size of a single plant of United States Steel) perfected and introduced the oxygen process. The first American company to adopt the new process was McLouth Steel, which had less than 1 percent of industry capacity. Although other smaller companies followed McLouth's lead, not until 1964 did United States Steel and Bethlehem introduce the process. This was fully 10 years after McLouth and 14 years after the small pioneering Austrian firm had introduced this revolutionary process.

Does Galbraith really want more industries structured like the American steel industry? Would he have permitted this industry to become even more concentrated through mergers among small enterprises (e.g., Bethlehem and Youngstown, which you will recall was one of the first merger cases) so that they could better emulate the performance of U.S. Steel?

Is the Market Dead?

As a corollary of his assumptions concerning technology, Galbraith argues that we can no longer rely on market forces to allocate resources. Because of this, he continues, the struggle to maintain competition alive "has obviously been a losing one. Indeed, it has been lost." These assertions go to the heart of Galbraith's thesis, for it is because the market has perished that we must be saved by extensive extra market planning. Should this

---

[32] See especially summary of literature by Prof. Daniel Hamburg in "Economic Concentration," pt. 3, op. cit., pp. 1281–92. Also see Jewkes, Sawers and Stillerman, *Sources of Invention*, 1958; and W. S. Comanor, "Research and Technical Change in the Pharmaceutical Industry," *Rev. of Econ. and Stat.*, May 1965, p. 190.

[33] George W. Stocking, *Basing Point Pricing and Regional Development*, The University of North Carolina Press, 1954, p. 140.

[34] A study by Edwin Mansfield found that the leading steel companies also lagged in the innovation process. Edwin Mansfield, "Size of Firm, Market Structure, and Innovation," *Jr. of Pol. Econ.*, December 1963, pp. 556–76.

[35] Walter Adams and Joel B. Dirlam, "Big Steel, Invention and Innovation," *Quarterly Journal of Economics*, May 1966, p. 169. The following discussion of the introduction of the basic oxygen process is based on the highly important study by Adams and Dirlam, *Ibid.*

[36] *Ibid.*

premise prove faulty, Galbraith's thesis comes tumbling down.

We have already seen that the evidence does not support his thesis that as a general rule technological imperatives require high levels of industrial concentration. It should therefore come as no surprise that in many industries competitive forces are considerably stronger than Galbraith suggests and that in many industries where concentration is highest, the market position of industry leaders is being eroded. I recently presented to this committee a rather comprehensive summary of postwar concentration trends.[37] Very briefly, during the post-war years—between 1947 and 1963—market concentration tended to decline across a broad front in the producer goods sector of manufacturing. While this is in direct conflict with the predictions of Galbraith's thesis, it is entirely consistent with the empirical evidence referred to earlier and which Professor Adams has mentioned. While in some industries technology may make it impossible for very small companies to operate efficiently, it does not dictate mammoth size and high levels of market concentration. Most American markets have become so large that they can sustain a rather considerable number of efficient-size enterprises.

Surprisingly, it is in consumer goods manufacturing industries where concentration has been on the rise in the postwar years. Surprisingly, I say, because the technological requirements in these industries demand relatively smaller enterprises than in producer goods manufacturing. Of course, the reasons for increasing concentration in consumer goods manufacturing are to be found in the requirements of product differentiation (especially the costs of large-scale promotion) and distribution, not in the technological imperatives that Galbraith assumes to be the kingpins of market power.

When postwar concentration trends are viewed together with the recent findings concerning the relationship between technology and industrial organization, we have a valuable insight into the future viability of the market as a regulator and planner of economic activity. Modern technology has not made obsolete our competitive, market-oriented economy. For it is precisely in the producer goods manufacturing industries where econo-

mies of large-scale invention, innovation, and production are most pronounced. Yet these industries have experienced a significant drop in market concentration. This has occurred because many industrial markets have grown more rapidly than have the requirements of large-scale business organization.

These trends in market concentration may yet be irrelevant if Galbraith's concept of market power is correct. Throughout his discussion he implies that, "characteristically," American industries are concentrated "oligopolies," and that the firms operating in them have great discretionary pricing power independent of the market.[38] But like Gertrude Stein, Galbraith has difficulties with shades of difference. Fortunately, however, all oligopolies are not alike and there are important differences in the degree of market power conferred by varying market structures. The accumulating evidence of the relationship between an industry's structure[39] and its performance leaves little room for agnosticism concerning the powerful role played by the market in limiting discretionary pricing power.[40] And, importantly, there is now persuasive evidence demonstrating that in the

---

[38] Galbraith not only wrongly implies that market concentration is increasing, but also overstates the levels of market concentration. He says, ". . . in the characteristic market of the industrial system there are only a handful of sellers." He then lists the automobile and 17 other industries, and says that there are a "host" of others. *The New Industrial State*, pp. 180–181. Galbraith has not selected "characteristic" industries. In each industry cited the top 4 did two-thirds or more of the business. But of the "host" of other industries not cited, more than 3 out of 4 had lower levels of concentration. Also, 13 of the 18 high concentration industries which he cites experienced declines in concentration in recent years. The big exceptions were consumer goods items— most notably, automobiles, a favorite example of Galbraith.

[39] The key structural elements are market concentration, ease with which new competitors can enter the market, and the degree to which the products of individual sellers are "differentiated."

[40] See, for example, Joe S. Bain, "Relation of Profit Rate of Industry Concentration: American Manufacturing, 1936–40," *Quarterly Journal of Economics*, August 1951: L. W. Weiss, "Average Concentration Ratios and Industrial Performance," *Journal of Industrial Economics*, July 1963. Norman R. Collins and Lee Preston, "Concentration and Price Margins in Food Manufacturing Industries," *The Journal of Industrial Economics*, July 1966, 226. A report by the staff of the Fed-

---

[37] Willard F. Mueller, statement before the Select Committee on Small Business, U.S. Senate, March 15, 1967.

larger part of American manufacturing industry market forces limit quite severely the discretionary pricing power of firms.[41] But, again, Galbraith has ignored the mounting evidence which runs counter to one of his central premises.[42]

This isn't to imply that there are no strong positions of entrenched power in our economy—there are. Again, however, Galbraith greatly overstates his case. But, importantly, whereas he pays tribute to the firms with substantial market power—indeed, he believes such power is essential—the evidence indicates that firms with great power perform less admirably than he assumes. Hence, the facts support a precisely opposite public policy than that advocated by Galbraith—we need more competition, not less.

The rising concentration in consumer-goods industries at first blush seems to bear out Galbraith's thesis of managing consumer wants to suit the needs of the business enterprise. But the causes of developments here are not rooted in Galbraith's technological imperatives. As noted earlier, the requirements of large-scale production, invention, and innovation are less demanding in the manufacture of consumer goods than in other areas of manufacturing. It is true that many sellers try to manage consumer wants. But this is because of the form which competition takes where opportunities for product differentiation exist. True, the market operates less perfectly as a result—though I suspect it operates better than Galbraith assumes. If Americans really are strongly dissatisfied, however, they can do something about this problem; though they probably won't. Nor will Galbraith's "new industrial state" change things on this score.

Despite its shortcomings, particularly in the area of some consumer goods, the market clearly has not disappeared as the key coordinating and integrating force in allocating resources in most of the economy. The picture that emerges when one studies the entire industrial landscape is not that painted by Galbraith. Whereas he concedes his thesis does not encompass the entire economy, close inspection shows it captures only a small part of the real world.[43]

eral Trade Commission, "The Structure of Food Manufacturing," Technical Study No. 8, National Commission on Food Marketing, June 1966, pp. 202–210. H. Michael Mann, "Seller Concentration, Barriers to Entry, and Rates of Return in Thirty Industries, 1950–1960," *Review of Economics and Statistics*, August 1966, pp. 296–307. Unpublished study by Norman R. Collins and Lee Preston, "Concentration and Price-Cost Margins in Manufacturing Industries," April 1, 1966.
[41] Empirical evidence indicates that discretionary pricing power becomes quite severely limited when the top 4 firms in an industry control less than half and the top 8 less than 70 percent of industry output. See Bain, op. cit., "FTC Staff Study," op. cit., Mann, op. cit. The greater part of all manufacturing occurs in industries where the top 4 firms control less than 50 percent of industry output. See Mueller, Statement before Senate Small Business Committee, op. cit., p. 63. Kaysen and Turner estimated that 23 percent of manufacturing industry shipments were made in industries where the top 8 firms controlled 40 percent or more of industry shipments. Kaysen and Turner, "Antitrust Policy," 1959. These authors used rather broad definitions of industries and therefore understate somewhat the level of market concentration.
[42] In his two chapters on "Prices in the Industrial System," Galbraith does not cite a single empirical study to support his assertions *The New Industrial State*, pp. 178–197.
[43] Galbraith says that he is not concerned with "the world of the independent shopkeeper, farmer, shoe repairman, bookmaker, narcotics peddler, pizza merchant, streetwalker, and the car and dog laundries." He feels obliged to emphasize this point, he says, because, "One should always cherish his critics and protect them where possible from foolish error. The tendency of the mature corporation in the modern industrial system to become part of the administrative complex of the state cannot be refuted by appeal to contrary tendencies elsewhere in the economy." Sixth lecture, p. 916. But as I explained earlier, his thesis explains only a small part of the manufacturing sector of the economy. Moreover, his technological imperatives obviously are even less important in wholesale and retail trade, in the services industry and in agriculture, which today comprise about 35 percent of national income outside the Government sector. Nothing drastically new has occurred in the other segments of the economy which suggest a trend toward decreasing importance of market forces. Competition in transportation and finance, etc.—which generate another 13 percent of national income—is probably as effective today as in prewar years. This leaves communications and public utilities, which provide 5 percent of national income. But they, of course, have been subject to a degree of regulation since at least the 1930's.

Is Antitrust a Charade?

But the mere absence of factors requiring high market concentration does not guarantee that excessive concentration will not arise or that it will decline in industries where it already is too high. Simply put, effective competition is not a flower that thrives unattended. Powerful firms may engage in competitive strategies which counteract the forces working toward deconcentration. Specifically, until the passage of the Celler-Kefauver Act in 1950, horizontal and vertical mergers often had the effect of offsetting these forces, with the result that in many industries concentration remained unchanged or even increased.

Again, I feel that Professor Galbraith has neglected his homework. He has not kept abreast of contemporary antitrust policy or its effects. He asserts that it is a "charade" acted out, "not to prevent exploitation of the public," but, "to persuade people in general and British Socialists and American liberals in particular, that the market is still extant."[44] He sums up his views of current antitrust policy as follows (he has already mentioned them this morning):

A great corporation wielding vast power over its markets is substantially immune. . . . But if two small firms seek to unite, this corporate matrimony will be meticulously scrutinized. And, very possibly, it will be forbidden.[45]

These assertions simply do not square with the facts. Antimerger effort has been directed almost exclusively against the largest industrial concerns.[46] It has not, as he suggested, been an attack on industrial midgets. Over 60 percent of the largest, those with over a billion dollars, and merely a third of the top 200 have been subjects of antimerger complaints. Practically all of these complaints have not involved the challenging of miniscule mergers, but rather have involved an attack upon mergers by large concerns. I have discussed this at greater length elsewhere.[47] My major conclusion, however, is that there has been an enormous effort. Perhaps Professor Galbraith would say that my intellectual outlook has been affected somewhat by the techno-structure within which I now operate. But even if I were back at the University of Wisconsin—or even at Harvard—I would still come to the same conclusion, as I am sure he will when he reads my other statement. In my opinion, this enforcement effort represents a great victory for competition, as well as a clear demonstration that antitrust policy can be an effective instrument of public policy in the last half of the 20th century.

It is true that antitrust policy cannot easily —and certainly not quickly—solve problems of deeply entrenched power. Fifty years of ineffective public policy toward mergers resulted in unnecessarily high concentration in many industries. But recent developments show that much can be accomplished. I say categorically: Whether or not the market survives in the greater part of our economy, or is destroyed by vast aggregations of market power, will not be determined by technological imperatives but by public policy toward the achievement and retention of power. The market may well be destroyed in the next generation as Galbraith predicts, but not for his reasons. It will be a matter of public will or neglect, not technology.

Planning and the State

In the "new industrial state" the Government plays a central role in economic planning with a concomitant diminution in reliance upon the market. Specifically, it stabilizes aggregate demand, underwrites expensive technology, restrains wages and prices in limiting inflation, provides technical and educational manpower, and buys upwards of a fifth of our economic output.

It is true that the Government does these things, and more. But Galbraith exaggerates the role of the state (as opposed to the market) in the planning process.[48] He points out correctly that one of the main responsibilities of the modern state is to sustain aggregate de-

---

[44] Third lecture, p. 794.

[45] *Ibid.*

[46] The great bulk of merger complaints challenged mergers by the country's 500 largest concerns. Fully 62 percent of the 52 $1 billion industrial corporations have been subjects of complaints as have 35 percent of the top 200. Mueller, "The Celler-Kefauver Act," *op. cit.*

[47] *Ibid.*

[48] He also is incorrect in implying that the great role of the state as a customer of goods and services is mainly related to technological imperatives. It is true that the state buys nearly a fifth of our economic output. But what are these purchases? In 1967 expenditures related to our military and international commitments and the cost of past wars accounted for fully 79 percent of the Federal budget: National defense (54 perecnt), space research and technology (5 percent), international affairs and finance (4 per-

mand and stimulate economic growth. He fails to perceive, however, that the state's planning in this respect is neither in competition with, nor a substitute for, planning by business enterprise, and it certainly does not require abandonment of the market. On the contrary, the basic philosophy of the Employment Act of 1946 is that the state create a general economic environment within which private enterprise can generate economic growth.[49] Within this environment the basic "planning" decisions of what and how much of each product to produce are left to private enterprise responding to aggregate demand.

Experience increasingly demonstrates the heavy role played by the market in implementing or frustrating monetary and fiscal policy aimed at full employment. Only if competition is effective are extensive price controls not a necessary adjunct to planning for rapid economic growth without inflation.

The wage and price guideposts of the Council of Economic Advisers are a symptom of the absence of effective competition in some segments of the economy.[50] But, happily, these segments are in the minority. Were it otherwise, it probably would be impossible to push toward full employment without implementing extensive wage and price controls.

None appreciate these facts of life so keenly as those economists responsible for public policy in this area. Dr. Walter Heller, the former Chairman of the Council of Economic Advisers and prime mover in gaining public acceptance for the "new economics," has emphasized the importance of keeping competition alive. He does not believe that planning for rapid economic growth requires abandonment of the market. Rather, he argues forcibly in his recent book that we must make competition more, not less, effective. As he puts it:

There are substantial differences among economists on how far the government should go in protecting consumers or setting guide-

posts for wages and prices. But there is little difference—at least among the vast majority of economists—in supporting strong measures to protect the free play of market forces against monopoly and price-fixing, and in strongly opposing direct wage and price controls as inefficient and inequitable substitutes for market forces, to be considered only as a last resort in a war economy.[51]

In a similar vein, the Joint Economic Committee of the Congress has repeatedly emphasized the importance of maintaining effectively competitive markets, and I do not think they are merely playing charades. Its most recent report on the Economic Report of the President concluded, "Antitrust must be assigned a central role in national economic policy of no less significance than monetary and fiscal policy."[52]

Do not misunderstand me. Certainly, many of the most pressing problems of the day—water and air pollution, job retraining, urban and rural poverty, preservation of our natural resources, promotion of basic research, to name a few—require action and planning by the state. But it is wrong to infer that the failure of the market to solve these kinds of problems represents a fatal flaw in the system. Unfortunately, many persons are inclined to damn the market—which to them means the businesses operating within it—for failing to do jobs better left to the state. And, unfortunately, the defensively hostile responses of some business leaders to every social welfare proposal lend credence to the argument that the real issue at stake is the market system. Actually, however, the real issue usually is whether or not a particular job should be done at all, and who is going to pay for it. Once it is agreed that there is nothing inherently un-American or antimarket in admitting that some things are best left to the state, the state and the market can live in happy coexistence. In truth, they are indispensable complements of one another, rather than rivals or substitutes. But this has little to do with

cent), veterans' benefits (5 percent), and interest on the national debt (11 percent). Thus the growing size of the Federal budget is not the outcome of technological imperatives but of international imperatives of being the world's leading power.

[49] The Employment Act of 1946 states in its "Declaraion of Policy" that the Federal Government shall "coordinate and utilize all its plans, functions, and resources for the purpose of creating and maintaining, in a manner calculated to foster and promote free competitive enterprise

and the general welfare * * *." Employment Act of 1946, As Amended, with Related Laws, 60 Stat. 23, Public Law 304—79th Cong.

[50] Walter W. Heller, *New Dimensions of Political Economy*, 1966, p. 43.

[57] *Ibid*, pp. 8–9

[52] Report of the Joint Economic Committee, Congress of the United States, on the January 1967 Economic Report of the President, 90th Cong., 1st sess., Report. No. 73, Mar. 17, 1967, p. 25.

economic imperatives and the abandonment of the market.

STATEMENT OF
HON. DONALD F. TURNER*

I do not believe that Professor Galbraith's evaluation of our economy's market structure is accurate. I subscribe almost in toto to the points that have been made previously by Dr. Mueller and Dr. Adams. They have spread me the task of dealing in detail with those aspects of the argument.

But in any event, I think it would be more suitable for me to discuss the charges that have been made against antitrust law and the characterization that has been put upon it.

On the impact of antitrust law, I think it is undeniable that it has been more vigorous and more effective in attacking price fixing, other restrictive agreements and mergers than in dealing directly with existing market power. I suppose that may even be characterized as a massive understatement. But, on the failure of antitrust law to deal adequately with undue existing market power, I do have a few comments.

The first is that to some extent this failure to deal with existing market power makes sense. I think it clearly makes sense to the extent that size and whatever market power that happen to go with it truly reflects economies of scale. I think it may also make some sense, although in my opinion perhaps less, where market power was acquired by initial competitive superiority and has been maintained without exclusionary behavior of any kind.

We have here, at least arguably, a problem of incentive. The fundamental purpose of the antitrust laws is to encourage competitive striving. It would be a little paradoxical, to say the least, to turn on the winner when he wins. If that were regular practice, one might anticipate some disincentive problems which may reach serious proportions.

I do not know the answer to that argument, but I just suggest, as I said, that it may make some sense to permit some conditions of market power which may be acquired and maintained in unexceptional ways. Beyond this, I agree it would be desirable to increase the effectiveness of antitrust in dealing directly with existing market power. Of course,

in saying so, I am proceeding on the premise that my friends Mueller and Adams more accurately assess the current validity of the competition than Professor Galbraith has. There may be some ways of expanding the scope of antitrust within the confines of existing legislation. That is worth probing, and it is being probed.

I would also add that I still subscribe to the views Professor Kaysen and I set forth, now some 8 years ago, in which we urged additional legislation which would make it easier to deal with monopoly and oligopoly problems. However, I suppose it is highly likely that if I sent such a proposal forward to the administration, it would not be rushed over to the Hill the following morning.

Even assuming, however—and I will make that assumption for the purposes of the balance of my remarks—that our present relative inactivity in dealing with existing undue market power shall continue for the indefinite future, I do not agree that it is bad public policy or bad law or bad anything to continue to attack price fixing and other restrictive agreements and mergers likely to increase market power in those areas where we still have hope.

To put it somewhat differently, the fact that for historical reasons of one sort or another we have had to accept a measure of unfortunate development in one or more areas of our economy does not mean, it seems to me, that we are compelled to make things worse by permitting more.

It seems to me that to describe the kind of policy we have been carrying on as "discrimination" is to apply a most inappropriate term. In antitrust or in any other area of public policy it has always been true that even though we cannot undo the past we can try to do better for the future, and we cannot rationally measure prospective public policy by past mistakes. Past mistakes by no means compel repetition.

In this regard, while monopoly and oligopoly are, indeed, a problem, I think we should be careful not to overstate it, as I believe Mr. Galbraith has. To quote from his book, "Oligopoly is not a special but a general case. It is the market structure of the industrial system."

Now, unaccustomed as I am to calling attention to the nonoligopolistic sector of our economy, I do feel compelled to put Professor Galbraith's remarks in perspective. Taking mining and manufacturing together with

---

* Assistant Attorney General, Antitrust Division, Department of Justice, Washington, D.C.

transportation and public utilities, Professor Kaysen, a man whom we both view with high regard, estimates that the oligopolistic sectors produce around 20 percent or probably 25 percent of national income. Concededly, this is not a trivial figure. But neither does it amount to the domination that Professor Galbraith's remarks suggest.

That being so, we have wide areas of economy which have not been afflicted or badly afflicted, and it seems clear to me that it makes good public policy sense to endeavor to preserve competition where it can be preserved in those areas. I see no reason why we should not continue to attack outright price-fixing agreements, even though, in some industries, concentration is so high and the nature of the product is such that the sellers, as Mr. Galbraith indicates, can achieve close to the kind of price determination that an outright agreement would.

I have already given some general reasons for this. I would add a particular one. That is that price-fixing agreements involving a rather large number of firms in a way is the worse of all possible worlds. You get all of the disadvantages of price fixing and the kind of interference with competition and allocation of resources that gives you without any of the economies of size that come from growth of firms—except, I should say, perhaps some planning advantage. But I doubt very much the episodic kind of price fixing that we have seen really makes any significant contribution to this.

Now, turning to mergers, where industries are currently relatively unconcentrated, why permit further concentration by merger? There may, indeed, be some economic changes taking place in some industries which tend to indicate that the current size of firms is below that which would be necessary for the achievement of economies. But typically, substantial economies will be developed by internal growth, and without having any figures, I would guess that internal growth has been the means by which most economies of scale have been achieved in the past.

Where there is already a fair degree of concentration in an industry, even where there may be one or two or three dominant firms, the problem posed by merger involving firms other than the largest is indeed a somewhat more difficult problem than it appears to be in the unconcentrated industry. But it is also, I suggest, much more complicated than Pro-

fessor Galbraith suggests by using the term "discrimination."

Let me give you a specific example: In the steel industry, several years ago, Bethlehem, the No. 2 firm, and Youngstown—I forget which, No. 5 or No. 6—proposed to merge. Both were substantially smaller than the United States Steel Corp. and the merged company was still considerably smaller. Indeed, the argument was made that we should have permitted those two companies to merge in order that they could more adequately deal with United States Steel. It seems perfectly plain to me that apart from any moral reason, which I reject, there was no persuasive economic reason to permit this merger, and the decision was eminently correct. I will only give a couple of reasons.

Even assuming that the merger would have increased the competitive ability of the merged firms, which was disputable, there was no reason to suppose that the merger would have made the industry in fact any more competitive than it was or, to put it somewhat differently, that a merged Bethlehem-Youngstown would have embarked upon a competitive pricing spree or any kind of other competitive spree as a consequence of the merger. Moreover, to have permitted the merger would have made it much less likely that future technological changes, if they came, that would have lowered the size of firm necessary for economies of scale, would have led to an appropriate deconcentration of that industry.

Now, in all of these activities, as in attacks on patent licensing restrictions and the like, the purpose of the antitrust laws, even assuming that we can do nothing about existing concentration, is to preserve the opportunity for declining concentration in the future as new developments take place—new entry, new products, and the like. And I would cite in this connection, lest there be doubt that any such happy developments will ever take place, that Dr. Mueller's figures over the past 15 years show more often than not, many more oftentimes than not, there has been declining concentration in the producer-goods industries.

To sum up, even if we did nothing more than we now do in directly attacking undue market power, I am firmly convinced that a strong antitrust preventive policy makes economic sense and, on the basis of evidence now available to us, would still appear to promote longrun benefits for the economy.

17. Consumers' Protection and Interest Program

JOHN F. KENNEDY

To the Congress of the United States:

Consumers, by definition, include us all. They are the largest economic group in the economy, affecting and affected by almost every public and private economic decision. Two-thirds of all spending in the economy is by consumers. But they are the only important group in the economy who are not effectively organized, whose views are often not heard.

The Federal Government—by nature the highest spokesman for all the people—has a special obligation to be alert to the consumer's needs and to advance the consumer's interests. Ever since legislation was enacted in 1872 to protect the consumer from frauds involving use of the U.S. mail, the Congress and executive branch have been increasingly aware of their responsibility to make certain that our Nation's economy fairly and adequately serves consumers' interests.

In the main, it has served them extremely well. Each succeeding generation has enjoyed both higher income and a greater variety of goods and services. As a result our standard of living is the highest in the world —and, in less than 20 years, it should rise an additional 50 percent.

Fortunate as we are, we nevertheless cannot afford waste in consumption any more than we can afford inefficiency in business or

Government. If consumers are offered inferior products, if prices are exorbitant, if drugs are unsafe or worthless, if the consumer is unable to choose on an informed basis, then his dollar is wasted, his health and safety may be threatened, and the national interest suffers. On the other hand, increased efforts to make the best possible use of their incomes can contribute more to the well-being of most families than equivalent efforts to raise their incomes.

The march of technology—affecting, for example, the food we eat, the medicines we take, and the many appliances we use in our homes—has increased the difficulties of the consumer along with his opportunities; and it has outmoded many of the old laws and regulations and made new legislation necessary. The typical supermarket before World War II stocked about 1,500 separate food items— an impressive figure by any standard. But today it carries over 6,000. Ninety percent of the prescriptions written today are for drugs that were unknown 20 years ago. Many of the new products used every day in the home are highly complex. The housewife is called upon to be an amateur electrician, mechanic, chemist, toxicologist, dietician, and mathematician—but she is rarely furnished the information she needs to perform these tasks proficiently.

Marketing is increasingly impersonal. Consumer choice is influenced by mass advertising utilizing highly developed arts of persuasion. The consumer typically cannot know whether drug preparations meet minimum standards of safety, quality, and efficacy. He

◆ SOURCE: Message from *The President of the United States* Relative to Consumers' Protection and Interest Program, Document No. 364, House of Representatives, 87th Congress, 2d Session, March 15, 1962.

usually does not know how much he pays for consumer credit; whether one prepared food has more nutritional value than another; whether the performance of a product will in fact meet his needs; or whether the "large economy size" is really a bargain.

Nearly all of the programs offered by this administration—e.g., the expansion of world trade, the improvement of medical care, the reduction of passenger taxes, the strengthening of mass transit, the development of conservation and recreation areas and low-cost power—are of direct or inherent importance to consumers. Additional legislative and administrative action is required, however, if the Federal Government is to meet its responsibility to consumers in the exercise of their rights. These rights include:

1. The right to safety—to be protected against the marketing of goods which are hazardous to health or life.

2. The right to be informed—to be protected against fraudulent, deceitful, or grossly misleading information, advertising, labeling, or other practices, and to be given the facts he needs to make an informed choice.

3. The right to choose—to be assured, wherever possible, access to a variety of products and services at competitive prices; and in those industries in which competition is not workable and Government regulation is substituted, an assurance of satisfactory quality and service at fair prices.

4. The right to be heard—to be assured that consumer interests will receive full and sympathetic consideration in the formulation of Government policy, and fair and expeditious treatment in its administrative tribunals.

To promote the fuller realization of these consumer rights, it is necessary that existing Government programs be strengthened, that Government organization be improved, and, in certain areas, that new legislation be enacted.

I. STRENGTHENING OF EXISTING PROGRAMS

This administration has sponsored a wide range of specific actions to strengthen existing programs. Major progress has already been achieved or is in prospect in several important areas. And the 1963 budget includes recommendations to improve the effectiveness of almost every major program of consumer protection.

(1) Food and Drug Protection

Thousands of common household items now available to consumers contain potentially harmful substances. Hundreds of new uses for such products as food additives, food colorings, and pesticides are found every year, adding new potential hazards. To provide better protection and law enforcement in this vital area, I have recommended a 25-percent increase in staff for the Food and Drug Administration in the budget now pending before the Congress, the largest single increase in the agency's history. In addition, to assure more effective registration of pesticides, a new division has been established in the Department of Agriculture; and increased appropriations have been requested for pesticide regulation and for meat and poultry inspection activities.

(2) Safer Transportation

As Americans make more use of highway and air transportation than any other nation, increased speed and congestion have required us to take special safety measures.

(a) The Federal Aviation Agency has reexamined the Nation's air traffic control requirements and is designing an improved system to enhance the safety and efficiency of future air traffic.

(b) The Secretary of Commerce has established an Office of Highway Safety in the Bureau of Public Road, to promote public support of highway safety standards, coordinate use of highway safety research findings, and encourage cooperation of State and local governments, industry, and allied groups—the Department of Health, Education, and Welfare is likewise strengthening its accident prevention work—and the Interstate Commerce Commission is strengthening its enforcement of safety requirements for motor carriers.

(c) In addition, I am requesting the Departments of Commerce and of Health, Education, and Welfare, to review, with representatives of the automobile industry, those changes in automobile design and equipment which will help reduce the unconscionable toll of human life on the highways and the pollution of the air we breathe. Additional legislation does not appear required at this time in view of the automobile industry's action to incorporate in the new model design changes which will reduce air pollution.

(3) Financial Protection

Important steps are being taken to help assure more adequate protection for the savings that prudent consumers lay aside for the future purchase of costly items, for the rainy day, for their children's education, or to meet their retirement needs.

(a) Legislation enacted last year has strengthened the insurance program of the Federal Savings and Loan Insurance Corporation.

(b) The Securities and Exchange Commission has undertaken at the request of the Congress a major investigation of the securities market which should provide the basis for later legislation and administrative measures.

(c) The Postmaster General and the Department of Justice have stepped up enforcement of the mail fraud statutes. Arrests for mail fraud last year set an alltime record; and convictions increased by 35 percent over the previous year.

(4) More Effective Regulation

The independent regulatory agencies also report increased emphasis on programs directly helpful to consumers.

(a) The Interstate Commerce Commission has instituted proceedings designed to prevent excessive charges for moving household goods in interstate commerce.

(b) The Civil Aeronautics Board has recently taken action to protect air travelers from abuses of overbooking.

(c) The Federal Trade Commission has intensified its actions against deceptive trade practices and false advertising affecting a variety of goods, including refrigerators, house paint, sewing machines, vacuum cleaners, kitchen utensils, food wrapping, and carpets.

(d) The Federal Power Commission is initiating a vigorous program to assure consumers of reasonable natural gas prices while assuring them of adequate supplies—revitalizing all of its regulatory programs in the

electric power field—and undertaking a national power survey designed to identify ways of bringing down power costs in the decades ahead by making the best possible use of our capital and energy resources; and I recommend that the Congress enact legislation and make available funds to enable the Commission to provide for 34 million natural gas consumers the information similar to that now provided electrical consumers on typical bills in various areas, thus spotlighting abnormally high rates and stimulating better industry performance.

(e) The Federal Communications Commission is actively reviewing the television network program selection process and encouraging the expanded development of educational television stations; and it will also step up in fiscal year 1963 its enforcement program to prevent interference with air navigation signals, distress calls, and other uses of radio important to public safety.

(f) For all of the major regulatory agencies, I am recommending increased appropriations for 1963 to provide the increased staff necessary for more effective protection of the consumer and public interest.

(g) Of the important changes in agency organizational procedure recommended last year to eliminate delays and strengthen decisionmaking, the great majority have been authorized by reorganization plans or legislation and are being put into practice by agency heads; and, to permit similar improvements in the operations of the Securities and Exchange Commission and the Federal Power Commission through greater delegation of assignments, I recommend enactment this year of legislation along the lines of S. 2135 for the SEC and S. 1605 and H. R. 6956 for the FPC.

(5) Housing Costs and Quality

The largest purchase most consumers make in their lifetimes is a home. In the past year, significant steps have been taken to reduce the cost of financing housing and to improve housing quality. The level of interest rates and other charges on mortgage loans has been reduced by a variety of Federal actions. Under authority provided by the Housing Act of 1961, new programs have been started (a) to encourage experimental construction methods likely to develop better housing at lower cost, (b) to provide lower interest rates and longer maturities on loans for rehabilitation of existing housing, (c) to provide especially low cost rental housing for moderate income families, and (d) to provide housing for domestic farm labor. The same legislation also authorized demonstration grants to develop better methods of providing housing for low income families.

(6) Consumer Information and Research— and Consumer Representation in Government

Government can help consumers to help themselves by developing and making available reliable information.

(a) The Housing and Home Finance Agency will undertake, under the budget proposed for fiscal 1963, new studies to discover ways of reducing monthly housing expenses, lowering the cost of land for homebuilding, and minimizing financing charges.

(b) The Department of Agriculture is undertaking similar research designed to help raise rural housing standards and reduce costs.

(c) The Food and Drug Administration will expand its consumer consultant program which, together with the home demonstration program of the Agriculture Extension Service, now provides valuable information directly to consumers on product trends, food standards, and protection guides.

(d) The Bureau of Labor Statistics is now conducting a nationwide survey of consumer expenditures, income, and savings, which will be used to update the widely used Consumer Price Index and to prepare model family budget.

Too little has been done to make available to consumers the results of pertinent Government research. In addition to the types of studies mentioned above, many agencies are engaged—as aids to those principally concerned with their activities, in cooperation with industry or for Federal procurement purposes—in testing the performance of certain products, developing standards and specifications, and assembling a wide range of related information which would be of immense use to consumers and consumer organizations. The beneficial results of these efforts—in the Departments of Agriculture, Commerce, Defense, and Health, Education, and Welfare, and in the General Services Administration and other agencies—should

be more widely published. This is but one part of a wider problem: the failure of governmental machinery to assure specific consideration of the consumer's needs and point of view. With this in mind, I am directing:

First, that the Council of Economic Advisers create a Consumers' Advisory Council, to examine and provide advice to the Government on issues of broad economic policy, on governmental programs protecting consumer needs, and on needed improvements in the flow of consumer research material to the public; this Consumers' Council will also give interested individuals and organizations a voice in these matters;

Second, that the head of each Federal agency whose activities bear significantly on consumer welfare designate a special assistant in his office to advise and assist him in assuring adequate and effective attention to consumer interests in the work of the agency, to act as liaison with consumer and related organizations, and to place increased emphasis on preparing and making available pertinent research findings for consumers in clear and usable form; and

Third, that the Postmaster General undertake a pilot program by displaying in at least 100 selected post offices, samples of publications useful to consumers and by providing facilities for the easier purchase of such publications.

II. NEW LEGISLATIVE AUTHORITY FOR ADDED CONSUMER PROTECTION

In addition to the foregoing measures, new legislative authority is also essential to advance and protect the consumer interest.

(A) Strengthen Regulatory Authority Over Foods and Drugs

The successful development of more than 9,000 new drugs in the last 25 years has saved countless lives and relieved millions of victims of acute and chronic illnesses. However, new drugs are being placed on the market with no requirement that there be either advance proof that they will be effective in treating the diseases and conditions for which they are recommended or the prompt reporting of adverse reactions. These new drugs present greater hazards as well as greater potential benefits than ever before—

for they are widely used, they are often very potent, and they are promoted by aggressive sales campaigns that may tend to overstate their merits and fail to indicate the risks involved in their use. For example, over 20 percent of the new drugs listed since 1956 in the publication "New and Non-Official Drugs" were found, upon being tested, to be incapable of sustaining one or more of their sponsor's claims regarding their therapeutic effect. There is no way of measuring the needless suffering, the money innnocently squandered, and the protraction of illnesses resulting from the use of such ineffective drugs.

The physician and consumer should have the assurance, from an impartial scientific source, that any drug or therapeutic device on the market today is safe and effective for its intended use; that it has the strength and quality represented; and that the accompanying promotional material tells the full story—its bad effects as well as its good. They should be able to identify the drug by a simple, common name in order to avoid confusion and to enable the purchaser to buy the quality drugs he actually needs at the lowest competitive price.

Existing law gives no such assurance to the consumer—a fact highlighted by the thorough-going investigation led by Senator Kefauver. It is time to give American men, women, and children the same protection we have been giving hogs, sheep, and cattle since 1913, under an act forbidding the marketing of worthless serums and other drugs for the treatment of these animals.

There are other problems to meet in this area:

1. An extensive underground traffic exists in habit-forming barbiturates (sedatives) and amphetamines (stimulants). Because of inadequate supervision over distribution, these drugs are contributing to accidents, to juvenile delinquency and to crime.

2. Two billion dollars worth of cosmetics are marketed yearly, many without adequate safety testing. Thousands of women have suffered burns and other injuries to the eyes, skin, and hair by untested or inadequately tested beauty aids.

3. Factory inspections now authorized by the pure food and drug laws are seriously hampered by the fact that the law does not clearly require the manufacturer to allow inspection of certain records. An uncooperative small minority of manufacturers can engage in a game of hide-and-seek with the Government in order to avoid adequate inspection. But protection of the public health is not a game. It is of vital importance to each and every citizen.

4. A fifth of all the meat slaughtered in the United States is not now inspected by the Department of Agriculture, because the coverage of the Meat Inspection Act is restricted to meat products moving across State lines. This incomplete coverage contributes to the diversion of unhealthy animals to processing channels where the products are uninspected and can, therefore, be a threat to human health.

In short, existing laws in the food, drug, and cosmetic area are inadequate to assure the necessary protection the American consumer deserves. To overcome these serious statutory gaps, I recommend:

1. First, legislation to strengthen and broaden existing laws in the food-and-drug field to provide consumers with better, safer, and less expensive drugs, by authorizing the Department of Health, Education, and Welfare to:

(a) Require a showing that new drugs and therapeutic devices are effective for their intended use—as well as safe—before they are placed on the market;

(b) Withdraw approval of any such drug or device when there is substantial doubt as to its safety or efficacy, and require manufacturers to report any information bearing on its safety or efficacy;

(c) Require drug and therapeutic device manufacturers to maintain facilities and controls that will assure the reliability of their product;

(d) Require batch-by-batch testing and certification of all antibiotics;

(e) Assign simple common names to drugs;

(f) Establish an enforceable system of preventing the illicit distribution of habit-forming barbiturates and amphetamines;

(g) Require cosmetics to be tested and proved safe before they are marketed; and

(h) Institute more effective inspection to detemine whether food, drug, cosmetics, and therapeutic devices are being manufactured and marketed in accordance with the law;

2. Second, legislation to authorize the Federal Trade Commission to require that advertising of prescription drugs directed to physicians disclose the ingredients, the efficacy, and the adverse effects of such drugs; and

3. Third, legislation to broaden the coverage of the Meat Inspection Act administered by the Department of Agriculture, to promote adequate inspection—in cooperation with the States and industry—of all meat slaughtered in the United States.

(B) Require "Truth in Lending"

Consumer debt outstanding, including mortgage credit, has almost tripled in the last decade and now totals well over $200 billion. Its widespread availability has given consumers more flexibility in the timing of their purchases. But, in many instances, serious abuses have occurred. Under the chairmanship of Senator Douglas, a subcommittee of the Senate Banking and Currency Committee has been conducting a detailed examination of such abuses. The testimony received shows a clear need for protection of consumers against changes of interest rates and fees far higher than apparent without any real knowledge on the part of the borrowers of the true amounts they are being charged. Purchasers of used cars in one study, for example, paid interest charges averaging 25 percent a year, and ranging well above this; yet very few were aware of how much they were actually paying for credit.

Excessive and untimely use of credit arising out of ignorance of its true cost is harmful both to the stability of the economy and to the welfare of the public. Legislation should therefore be enacted requiring lenders and vendors to disclose to borrowers in advance the actual amounts and rates which they will be paying for credit. Such legislation, similar in this sense to the truth-in-securities laws of 1933-34, would not control prices or charges. But it would require full disclosure to installment buyers and other prospective credit users, and thus permit consumers to make informed decisions before signing on the dotted line. Inasmuch as the specific credit practices which such a bill would be designed to correct are closely related to and often combined with other types of misleading trade practices which the Federal Trade Commission is already regulat-

ing, I recommend that enforcement of the new authority be assigned to the Commission. The Government agencies most concerned in this area have been cooperating with the subcommittee in developing the information necessary to prepare a workable and effective bill; and in view of the exhaustive hearings already held, I hope that the Congress can complete action on this important matter before it adjourns.

(C) Manufacture of All-Channel Television Sets

Five out of six home television receivers today are equipped to receive programs on only the 12 very-high frequency (VHF) channels. As a result, in most areas, stations desiring to operate on any of the 70 ultrahigh frequency (UHF) channels would usually have such small audiences that there is little incentive to make the substantial initial investment and continuing expenditures that effective broadcasting requires. The result is a sharply restricted choice for consumers.

After extensive study, the Federal Communications Commission has concluded that an effective and genuinely competitive nationwide television service, with adequate provision for local outlets and educational stations, is not possible within the narrow confines of 12 VHF channels. Legislation now before the Congress would authorize the Commission to prescribe the performance characteristics of all new television receivers shipped in interstate commerce to assure that they can receive both VHF and UHF signals. I strongly urge its passage as the most economical and practical method of broadening the range of programs available. This step, together with the Federal aid for construction of educational television stations which is nearing final passage by the Congress, will speed the full realization of television's great potential.

(D) Strengthen Laws Promoting Competition and Prohibiting Monopoly

The most basic and longstanding protections for the right of consumers, to a choice at a competitive price, are the various laws designed to assure effective competition and to prevent monopoly. The Sherman Act of 1890, the Clayton Act of 1914, and many related laws are the strongest shields the consumer possesses against the growth of un-checked monopoly power. In addition to the measure now nearing final passage which would provide subpoena powers for civil as well as criminal antitrust investigations, several other improvements are needed:

1. The Federal Trade Commission should be empowered to issue temporary cease-and-desist orders against the continuance of unfair competitive practices while cases concerned with permanent relief from such practices are pending before the Commission. Under the present law, smaller competitors may be driven into bankruptcy or forced to accept merger on adverse terms long before present remedies become effective, thus reducing the competitive safeguards vital for the consumer. Similarly, deceptive trade practices in consumer goods may do their damage long before the Commission can "lock the barn door." I, therefore, reiterate my previous recommendation that the Congress give prompt consideration to effective legislation to accomplish this purpose.

2. The consumer's right to a reasonable price can also be adversely affected by mergers of two business firms which substantially reduce effective competition. As in the case of unfair methods of competition, damage once done is often irreparable, and the Government, acting through the courts, cannot readily restore the degree of competition existing prior to the merger. Accordingly, I strongly recommend advance notice to the Department of Justice and to the appropriate commission or board of any merger expected to result in a firm of substantial size. This will enable the businessman to obtain advice in advance, without litigation, as to whether a proposed merger would be regarded as contrary to the public interest. In addition, along with the recommended authority for the FTC to issue cease- and-desist orders, it is an essential safeguard against combinations which might cause unwarranted increases in consumer prices.

3. In view of the potentially anticompetitive abuses to which the use of patents and trademarks are by nature subject, I recommend:

(a) Enactment of legislation requiring publication of the terms of all settlement agreements between different persons applying for patent rights on the same invention— for recent hearings have shown that such agreements may include features designed to weaken future competition at the expense of the consumer; and

(b) Enactment of legislation authorizing the FTC to apply for the cancellation of any trademark which is, or becomes, the common descriptive name of an article and thus should be in the public domain.

While a competitor has such a right today, it is important—if the FTC is to have clear authority to halt this kind of unfair commercial advantage—that the Senate insert this provision in its review of trademark legislation (H.R. 4333) already approved by the House.

(E) "Truth in Packaging"

Just as consumers have the right to know what is in their credit contract, so also do they have the right to know what is in the package they buy. Senator Hart and his subcommittee are to be commended for the important investigation they are now conducting into packaging and labeling practices.

In our modern society good packaging meets many consumer needs, among them convenience, freshness, safety, and attractive appearance. But often in recent years, as the hearings have demonstrated, these benefits have been accompanied by practices which frustrate the consumer's efforts to get the best value for his dollar. In many cases the label seems designed to conceal rather than to reveal the true contents of the package. Sometimes the consumer cannot readily ascertain the net amount of the product, or the ratio of solid contents to air. Frequently he cannot readily compute the comparative costs per unit of different brands packed in odd sizes, or of the same brand in large, giant, kingsize, or jumbo packages. And he may not realize that changes in the customary size or shape of the package may account for apparent bargains, or that "cents-off" promotions are often not real savings.

Misleading, fraudulent, or unhelpful practices such as these are clearly incompatible with the efficient and equitable functioning of our free competitive economy. Under our system, consumers have a right to expect that packages will carry reliable and readily useable information about their contents. And those manufacturers whose products are sold in such packages have a right to expect that their competitors will be required to adhere to the same standards. Upon completion of our own survey of these packaging and labeling abuses, in full cooperation with the Senate subcommittee, I shall make recommendations as to the appropriate roles of private business and the Federal Government in improving packaging standards and achieving more specific disclosure of the quantity and ingredients of the product inside the package in a form convenient to and useable by the consumer.

As all of us are consumers, these actions and proposals in the interest of consumers are in the interest of us all. The budgetary investment required by these programs is very modest—but they can yield rich dividends in strengthening our free competitive economy, our standard of living and health, and our traditionally high ethical patterns of business conduct. Fair competition aids both business and consumer.

It is my hope that this message, and the recommendations and requests it contains, can help alert every agency and branch of Government to the needs of our consumers. Their voice is not always as loudly heard in Washington as the voices of smaller and better organized groups—nor is their point of view always defined and presented. But under our economic as well as our political form of democracy, we share an obligation to protect the common interest in every decision we make. I ask the Congress, and every department and agency, to help in the fulfillment of that obligation.

G. Technology

18. *Management and the Challenge of Change*
FRANK K. SHALLENBERGER

The greatest fact of life in the next 20-30-40 years—the remaining years of the twentieth century—will be the fact of change, rapid, accelerating technological, social and economic change. And nowhere will change have greater impact than on business and the management job.

* * *

Scientists tell us that the world is five billion years old. The mammal we call man has been on earth for about 250,000 years. Recorded history dates back only about 5,000 years. All but a very few of the products that we buy and sell and use today had their origins less than 50 years ago. Items of major current interest and discussion—automation, the computer, management sciences, guided missiles, antibiotics, executive development, electronic data processing, television and the Common Market—these are post-war developments of the last 20 years. Eighty per cent of the prescriptions filled today at the corner drugstore could not have been filled ten years ago. Sputnik was launched only eight years ago—yet already we are sending probes to the moon and to Mars and to Venus, and are orbiting man around the earth and building hardware for his trip to the moon. In *eight* years out of *five billion* years!

If the earth's history is equated to the distance around the world, the last fifty years, the period of our lifetimes, the period of most rapid development, would be *one foot!*

Consider the earth's history as a book of 100,000,000 pages, a book 25,000 feet (or almost five miles) thick. The period of technological discovery and development would be the *last page!*

Of compress the earth's history into one calendar year. From January to August there was no life. Between August and November there was only single-celled life, elementary virus, primitive bacteria, jelly-fish. Mammals first came into the world December 15. Man arrived December 31, 11:45 P.M. Written history dates back only to December 31, 11:59 P.M. The last 100 years, in which period practically all modern science has developed, occupies only the last one-half second of the year. The post-war period is the last one-tenth second!

Now ask yourselves what is going to happen on the next page, in the next one-fifth second, the next 30-40 years of our time, the remainder of the twentieth century, the period of your business careers. By any measure you wish, virtually all the technological progress of mankind has been crowded into a mere instant of time. And the acceleration is continuing. The next few years will see the creation of more new knowledge, new technology, new change, than the world has ever seen.

THE IMPACT OF CHANGE

Technological and social and economic changes have, in the past, revolutionized or destroyed industries, cultures, mores, living standards, religions, empires and even civilizations. Will the increasingly rapid change of the immediate future have any less impact? No. Change will be just as disrupting, just as revolutionizing, just as destructive to our present way of life and to our industries and business as the more leisurely change of the past—in all probability, much more so.

Does it not follow, therefore, that a major responsibility, perhaps *the* major responsibility, of top executives, into whose hands has been placed responsibility for the success and preservation of the corporation, will be that of sensing change, of predicting it, of adapting to it, of taking advantage of it, and— for the true executive—*creating* change, to his own company's advantage and his competitor's disadvantage, using change itself as a major competitive weapon?

What areas of change can best dramatize our prediction of rapid technology in the next few years? Technology advances on extremely broad and varied fronts; we have space to discuss only a few out of very many.

Atomic Energy

First developed and used only twenty years ago for destructive military purpose, *atomic energy* is now widely used for peaceful power generation, analysis and detection, propulsion, medical purposes and research. Its potential for power or heat generation, anywhere in the world, with complete freedom from dependence on hydroelectric or fuel resources, is almost unlimited.

A fascinating proposed use of atomic energy has been termed "geographical engineering," the massive changing of the face of the earth—creating a harbor or an island where none existed before, building canals and tunnels, creating valleys or removing mountains. Currently under serious consideration are a new canal across Central America paralleling the Panama Canal, one across the foot of the Aleutian Chain, and the so-called Kra Canal across the Malay Peninsula.

The use of atomic energy to blast a series of tunnels or valleys through the Andes to bring water from the rain forests to the arid coast would revolutionize the economy of Peru. Underground blasts could be used to create vast storage reservoirs in areas of high evaporation and low rainfall, such as North Africa, the Middle East, Central Australia. Atomic energy may enable us to convert sea water to fresh water in unlimited amounts, doubling or tripling the food-producing capacity of the world. Or through the heat and pressure of atomic energy we may be able to exploit the 700 billion barrels of oil in the Athabasca tar fields of western Canada and oil shale deposits throughout the world. Mining as done today differs from that of ancient times. We burrow like moles under the ground to extract minute bits of metal from the earth. Could atomic energy be used to break up the ore so we might leach out the minerals? Could we even smelt some ores underground and bring only concentrates to the surface?

The Oceans

One of the truly great industrial frontiers, an untapped treasure house of wealth and knowledge, is the *ocean,* "the bountiful sea." No single area of technology, including space, offers greater opportunities for research and industrial exploitation by man.

The oceans cover three-fourths of the earth's surface to an average depth of two miles. They have unknown and virtually inexhaustible food resources—fish, animal and plant life. They are the only feasible source of protein to feed the world's exploding population. Since time began, the rivers of the land world have been carrying the chemicals and minerals of the land to the sea. Now, dissolved in its waters, or lying on its floor, is more mineral wealth than we have ever mined—probably more than exists on or under all the land areas. We are already starting to mine the ocean for gold, tin, diamonds, manganese, coal, phosphorites, iron ore and oil. Every cubic mile of the ocean holds over 6 million tons of valuable minerals, salts and chemicals. And there are *390 million cubic miles!* There is reason to believe we may find in the minute plankton, in fish and in the plants of the sea, the mechanisms and the secrets of extracting and concentrating these chemicals and minerals.

The oceans have currents equal to thousands of Mississippis. They have temperature differentials, tides and waves which produce more energy than all the power of the winds, coal, oil and natural fuels. They have all the power of the winds, coal, oil and natural fuels. They have all the water necessary for any conceivable human or agricultural consumption and perhaps within themselves the energy to break it free.

Yet we know almost less about the bottom of the sea than we know about the surface of the moon. We can instantly detect a missile thousands of miles away in the atmosphere— it took us months to find a submarine lost at 8,000 feet. We fish the sea like the hunters of old—with crude weapons, ancient hit-or-miss methods, steeped in tradition and superstition. We don't produce—we hunt. We use none of the techniques of modern agriculture or animal husbandry—planting, cultivation, fertilization, feeding, selective breeding.

We spend less than one-twelfth as much on ocean sciences as we do on space. When industry and government awake to the danger and opportunity in the ocean and start investing substantial sums in marine research, the knowledge that will come from the sea will stagger us. And the new knowledge will create an impact on the economy far greater than has the space program, for the wealth of the oceans is at our doorstep. There is threat and promise here for transportation, food products, communications, metals, chemicals, drugs, power, electronics and many other industries.

Bionics

Bionics is one of the most exciting of the new technologies. In the past, engineering and design problems have been tackled as problems in physics or chemistry or mechanics. Now we have suddenly awakened to the fact that Nature has solved many of these problems long before we even knew they existed. She has, for the last billion years or so, in the vast laboratory of the evolutionary world, been carrying on an untold number of trial and error experiments, keeping solutions that worked, rejecting those that failed. In this way she has developed practical answers to many technical problems we are only now facing.

If you want to know how to live in the hostile environment of other planets we will visit, study the ecology of mammal life in the Arctic, or the desert, or the tropics, or the sea, and observe nature's adaptation to life in such environments.

Do you want to know how to develop better sonar for underwater detection or to develop electronic "eyes" for the blind? Study the porpoise and determine how while blindfolded it can detect an object an eighth inch in diameter 50 feet away, distinguish between a square object and a round object, a smooth object and a rough object, a soft object and a hard object. Or study the bat and its amazing ability to fly blindfolded at high speed through a maze of closely spaced wires.

Do you want to know how to propel a ship or a submarine faster with less power? Again, study the porpoise. Why can it swim 40 percent faster than its size and energy theoretically should permit?

Do you want to learn how to build a miniature computer? Study the brain and its fantastic storage and logic capacity. Do you want a machine to read printing or writing or movement for computer or radar input? Study the frog's or pigeon's eye to determine how they preprocess information and filter out all except the limited critical information their tiny brains can handle. All this priceless knowledge is there for the taking, if and when we learn how to read and understand it.

Population

The advance of technology is deeply intertwined with social and economic change, much of which technology creates. One of the most important and interesting changes, one whose genesis lies largely in technology, and a great "tide in the affairs of men," is the popularly-called population explosion. What will be the impact on business of a doubling of the population every 35 years? Of 7,000 births every hour? Of 10,000 births during the reading time of this article? Of adding *every two months* another New York City to feed, to clothe, to house, to sell to, to find jobs for?

The world's population today is slightly over 3 billion. Before the end of the century it will be 6 billion. A hundred years from now it will be 25 billion, eight times the present population! What will this mean in terms of a drain on our already largely depleted resources? Many basic resources already face the need for substitution, secondary working of reserves, increased recycling, improved recovery techniques if we are to avoid exhaustion in the next 10-20 years. At the end of this century we will consume as much power in one year as has been consumed to date in all the history of mankind. Will the "have" nations become the "have nots"?

Can technology, which created the population explosion, also support it? Economic welfare is a fraction—output over population. In spite of the millions India has invested in economic development her people have less to eat today than twenty years ago—their numbers have grown faster than the production of food. Egypt's great new Aswan dam will add 2 million acres of new farmland by 1972—yet the Egyptians will not eat any better, for the population growth will have added 13 million new mouths to feed. Little wonder a report of the National Science Foundation states, "Other than the search for lasting peace, no problem is more urgent than the control of population growth."

Some Others

To be conservative is dangerous, because all but the wildest dreamers tend to far underestimate the future. Who, in light of an anticipated rate of change far greater than anything we have experienced in the past, can possibly put *any* limitations on what we may see in our lifetimes or our children's lifetimes?

Supersonic jets promise within the next ten years flights from South America to Europe or the United States in two or three hours. Who can say what is beyond? One hour? One-half hour? Then what happens to our concepts of administration, decentralization, branch plants, markets, free trade areas, lines of communication, span of control? We are also promised world-wide video communication as realistic as face-to-face contact. Why travel, when you can hold a world-wide conference in your office?

Who can say that within our children's lifetime we won't have a cure for all diseases, fully replaceable body organs, control of aging and death only by accident? Until several years ago we could transplant only corneas. Now we have transplanted kidneys, and in animals—hearts, lungs, and other organs. We have successfully constructed artificial arteries, heart valves, and heart pacers, and thousands of lives are today extended by such devices. How far away are artificial or transplanted lungs, stomachs, eyes, hearts, even brains? A Stanford scientist describes the transplant of hearts as only a matter of "simple plumbing," and asks what are the economics of a market in which many people want to buy, at any price, and no one wants to sell? To how many hearts is a man entitled? Having worn out his own, and a replacement, should he, if he has the wealth, be allowed to purchase a third? Or a fourth?

Medical science has successfully conquered most of the communicable diseases of childhood. Assume then that it attacks and overcomes with equal success the diseases of old age, and where it cannot overcome the disease it replaces the diseased or worn-out organ with a transplant or artificial device. Assume we successfully conquer aging itself? Suppose life expectancy is extended by these means to 100, 150, 200 years, and useful working life proportionately?

What then of your retirement and pension and social security plans? Will industry still relegate people to the scrap heap at 65? Who will support them for the remaining half of their lives? What will happen to our tax bills, insurance rates, pension funds? In what security markets could we conceivably invest enough money to support a third or more of our population in retirement and another third in childhood and college? To what level must the remaining work force raise its output to support such a non-working population? What new markets will be created for airlines, railroads, oil companies, pharmaceuticals or leisure products.

Assume we do not retire them at 65. Suppose we keep managers, engineers, scientists working productively until they reach 80. What if you don't tap this reservoir of experience and maturity and judgment and your competitor does? How can we provide challenge and opportunity and experience for our younger employees? How will we maintain the necessary influx of imagination, daring, willingness to try new approaches, to challenge tradition, dogma, the old way of doing things? Can adequate managerial opportunities and challenge and experience for the younger executives be created through growth and expansion and diversification and decentralization?

What effect would a doubling of life expectancy have upon the world's accumulated wisdom and culture and ethics? What would be the impact on the pattern and rate and direction of change itself if a Galileo, or Newton, or Einstein could live and work productively for 150 years?

The Mind

The *human mind*, like the oceans, is a virtually untapped frontier, of whose ultimate potential we have absolutely no concept. The mind weighs only a few pounds and yet, in many ways, its capacity exceeds that of the largest and most complex computer. It can do many things a computer can never do.

Like the computer, it can think, it can remember, it can reason. But it can also create, it can invent, it can dream, it can feel, and it can love. Who can say that it cannot also communicate freely with other minds? Who can say we will not someday, perhaps even in our own lifetime, have effective and widely used thought transmission? Then what of your newspapers, periodicals, telephone, telegraph, radio, television, transportation industries? What will be the impact on education, company organization, advertising, collective bargaining, business morality, and a thousand and one other areas? Who can say—with certainty—that we will not someday have useable, effective, planned clairvoyance, the ability to foresee the future? What effect on planning, inventories, markets, economic, military affairs? Impossible? The airplane, in its infancy, was "proven" impossible by competent scientists.

Can anyone say we will not someday, perhaps soon, and through some force of whose existence we may not even know, develop control of mind over matter, psychokinetics? Who can say we might not someday transfer intelligence and learning from one being to another—by injection, by drugs, perhaps by brain transplants or genetic manipulation? Attempts are now under way to transplant the brains of mice, to determine whether training or intelligence can be transferred from one body to another. Experiments with planaria, or flatworms, indicate possible transfer of knowledge and learning by other means.

We have pills that induce sleep, relax, tranquilize, stimulate, anesthetize. We have drugs that slow metabolism, drugs that kill pain, drugs that expand consciousness, induce dreams, hallucinations and euphoria. How far away are drugs that improve concentration, expand memory, speed up the thinking process by a factor of 2, or 10, or 100? Education is a distressingly inefficient process, why not learning pills? We spend a third of our lives asleep—can we learn during sleep? Or can we eliminate or reduce the need for sleep? Could a drug, or perhaps hypnosis, substitute for sleep?

Other Planets

Now, a little farther out, who can say that we may not soon communicate with intelligent beings on other planets? Impossible? Intelligent life on other planets appears to be a virtual certainty. At least 600 million other planets are said to be capable of supporting life. By what stretch of imagination and probability can we presume that the particular combination of pressure, chemicals, and temperature that generated the first spark of life on this planet occurred here and on no other planet?

Assume that on at least *one* other planet, life began a mere forty years before that on earth, one-fifth second on our condensed time scale. If we assume also that evolution proceeded there at the same rate that it has on earth, that planet would be forty years ahead of us, and all the technological development which we have just predicted for our own immediate future on earth, plus much more, would already have taken place. Suppose we could communicate with the beings on this other planet and draw from them today the details of our next forty years' achievements! Is such speculation only wild dreaming? Is it any more impossible than atomic fission was fifty years ago?

You might argue that the speed of light, the speed of electromagnetic waves, places an insurmountable time barrier against practicable communication with any but the nearest planets. What is the speed of thought transmission?

If it is agreed that even some of what has been suggested may come to pass, then we must face the hard and practical questions of how we as citizens and as businessmen live with, adapt to, make the most of changing technology.

A basic decision for any individual, any manager, any corporation, is whether to participate in the rat race or not. It can't be avoided completely. You can't "Stop the world, I want to get off." But you can choose for yourself or for your company those industries least subject to change. Thus you can obtain lower than average risk—and must thereby reconcile yourself to lower than average gains.

Within any industry, even the most technical, there are both leaders and followers. You can let the others do the pioneering, break with the past, take the risks, while you ride their coattails. Again you "play it safe," but for more modest stakes. (The long-run risks may of course be even greater than those taken by the leaders. You may fall off the coattails, may be lost by the wayside in the competitive race.)

You can attempt to protect yourself by diversification—by spreading your risks, by placing your bets on all the horses in the race. (Here again you may risk more—by dividing your attention, by averaging your organization to a level of mediocrity unable to compete in a changing world.)

But these are defensive actions, taken to protect *against* change. The great excitement and big rewards will go to those who welcome and capitalize on change, those who themselves lead and create, rather than accept, technological advance. How does one organize to join this club? How does one foster alertness, pioneering, imagination, receptivity to change? How do you overcome the normal pressures toward stability, mediocrity, caution, playing it safe, the red tape, the checks and balances, that characterize so many organizations? How do you attract, encourage, appraise, and reward daring creativity, vision?

One leader in the technological race has developed an organization structure, procedures and policies specifically geared to the challenge of changing times and changing technologies. It has tried to create an environment which encourages the flow of new ideas, and waters and cultivates and protects and helps new ideas grow. It has encouraged vision and wide-ranging thinking and imagination by spreading individual responsibility throughout the organization, right down to the lowest supervisory authority. It has tried to capture the initiative, the motivation, the creativity of the small firm. It has tried to attract truly entrepreneurial executives and to encourage them at all levels to function as managers in business for themselves. It gives them full responsibility for their own area and for its profits and growth. It provides opportunity for individual growth and self-expression. And it offers commensurate rewards, big rewards—"you can't catch a tiger with a worm on a hook." (Note the difference between this environment and that in which other writers describe the one most likely to succeed as the dedicated, loyal, deferential, adaptable, well-bred, well-poised conformist—the "grade A corporation creep.")

This company has been outstandingly successful. Thirteen years ago it didn't exist; today it has 140 plants, located throughout the world. Its average annual growth rate has been over 50 percent, and profits have kept pace. It is presently operating at a sales level of over one billion dollars per year.

The problem seems to be that in the years ahead, "the future will come sooner." The future will be no easier to predict but it will be far more important to predict. The time for evaluation and appraisal of developments in the marketplace and in the laboratory, as well as for taking corrective action, will be drastically shortened. The problem will be not just one of keeping up with current technology, but rather one of keeping well *ahead* of technology, of developing a corporate foresight or vision, a sense of direction or movement and corporate destiny, an ability to know what's ahead and to plan and prepare in the same manner that a gunner leads his target.

This is far different from random jumping on the technological bandwagon *after* the trends become apparent. It implies making goals, plans and decisions *in anticipation of trends*. It implies a continuous, objective, and at the same time intuitive, analysis of where the profit opportunities lie, not today, but tomorrow and the day after tomorrow. It means even more than before planning and organizing, not in generalities but in specifics, with consistent, realistic, integrated research, investment and marketing goals, programs and time-tables, fully communicated and accepted throughout the organization. And it means continuous follow-up, evaluation and control of performance against the plan.

How can we resolve the conflict between planning and flexibility? How can we plan and organize and invest against anticipated trends and at the same time retain our ability to adjust to the unpredictable? Can we choose our research and development projects so well, even before the trends become clear, that we are consistently in the winning circle? Can we maintain bridges behind us to allow for a fast retreat or adjustment? How can we maintain profits and growth, and write off costs of development and capital investment and promotion when product lives are measured in months or years rather than decades?

What changes in organization, recruitment, training, appraisal, and rewards are ahead? A recent study by *Scientific American* indicates that among top U.S. corporation executives the proportion having degrees or equivalent experience in science or engineering rose from 6.8 per cent in 1900 to 13.5 per cent in 1925, 20 per cent in 1950, and 36 per cent in 1963. Among managers in the age group 35–45, the pool from which tomorrow's top managers will be drawn, *51 per cent* have such background!

How, in the technological age, will small business fare in competition with the magnificent laboratories, the generous development and promotional budgets of large industry? Hold no fear for the smaller firm; it seems well able, if it utilizes its natural advantages of flexibility, specialization, resourcefulness, creativity, enthusiasm and high motivation, to succeed. One can better fear for the future of many larger firms "too paralyzed by their own bureaucratic structures to survive in the swift cross-currents of contemporary affairs."

THE DEVELOPING WORLD

The problems created by technological change are even more challenging in the newly developing countries than in the more advanced countries. We of the industrialized world face merely an *adjustment* in the rate of change—the developing countries face a complete *revolution* in their way of life.

Technology is highly transportable. It is at least theoretically possible to impose on a primitive agrarian economy, virtually overnight, the highest level of industrial sophistication—to leap from handcrafts to full automation, from the canoe to jets, from the wooden plow to the bulldozer, from the witch doctor to antibiotics, from drums to television. The Manu tribe of Papua and New Guinea has in one generation literally come from the Stone Age to the 20th Century! Think of it! People who spent their youth in an age which did not even know metals, now spending their adult years in the age of jets, nuclear power and space exploration!

In another generation or two the developing countries will make the transition from a world where the greatest problems are hunger, disease and ignorance, to a world where their greatest problems may be affluence and the constructive use of leisure time. How do peoples or countries adjust to such change? How much change—in his environment, his culture, his ambitions, his problems—can man stand?

Every resource of the developing countries is threatened by obsolescence—cheap labor by automation, fiber and food products by synthetics, hydroelectric power by nuclear power, minerals by new materials. How does a country which competes in world markets with cheap labor defend itself against modernized plants which produce with *no* labor? Nothing is safe from obsolescence.

Countries, like companies, must look ahead, must anticipate unfolding technology, must "lead the target," must act now in anticipation of the technology of the future. Peru has an ambitious and exciting program under way for the colonization of its vast jungle area. Highways are the primary and most costly element in this program. How far should Peru lead the target? How soon will it be cheaper to fly fruits and meat and lumber and livestock and oil and grain and cement over the Andes and jungle by cargo plane than to make the long and difficult haul by truck or rail? Should Peru be building highways? Or airports?

The proposed railroad across Tanzania to haul Zambian copper to the coast raises the same question. Will the railroad be obsolete before it is completed? Reportedly, a politician insisted 200 years ago that unless a mammoth program of planting oak trees were undertaken to provide oak for ships, England's dominance of the seas would end. How far should you lead the target?

What are the economic, social, political consequences of bringing *three-fourths* of the world's population from a level only slightly above animal existence to one of material comfort and nourishment and education? This is a Pandora's box of problems and possibilities. It implies fantastic changes in the world's economy, a quadrupling of the world's markets, an upsetting of all the present economic and political and social relationships. Coupled with the population explosion and its demands for food, fibers, minerals, transportation, jobs, power, products, capital investment, markets, competition, it promises economic changes of a magnitude never before seen.

At the individual company level it brings many new opportunities, but also extremely difficult short-term uncertainties stemming from continually changing governmental policy on planning, controls, protection, ownership, taxes, labor, fiscal affairs, economic cooperation.

THE COST

Unfortunately, technological and scientific advance does not always benefit mankind. In all the glamour and excitement of "the brave new world," we must recognize that in return for all that science offers us in freedom from disease, relief from heavy physical labor, longer life, plentiful food, we pay a terrible price.

We pay in jammed freeways, highway slaughter, slums, urban sprawl, sleazy, cheap, unimaginative subdivisions. We pay through the loss of human individuality in every phase of life. We pay in the loss of pride and challenge and meaning in work. We pay in ulcers, neuroses, coronary disease, emphysema, lung cancer. We pay in synthetic, bland, canned, frozen, dehydrated, premixed foods. We pay in a flood of equally synthetic television and radio programs, magazines and paperbacks geared to the lowest intellectual level. We pay in distorted and confused mass education, stifling the excellent, the dissenter, the protester, and emphasizing academic performance rather than learning and understanding, and science at the expense of the humanities.

We submit willingly to outrageous intrusions on our personal lives by Madison Avenue, motivating us to purchase things we neither want nor need. We pay in the wastage of sound values through planned obsolescence. We tolerate the widespread destruction of our natural heritage—the hills, the fields, the streams—by billboards, highways, dams, mines, factories, powerlines. We accept the slaughter of our wildlife through obliteration of grazing lands, forests and streams. We are suffocating ourselves in our own wastes—smog, stream pollution, pesticides, detergents, sewage.

We pay through technological unemployment and obsolescence of individual skills that took lifetimes to build. We tolerate tragic poverty in the midst of plenty. We are enmeshed in an economic-political system so complex that we can't find a way to distribute our disgraceful food surpluses to a starving world—instead we continue exhausting our land resources to produce even greater surpluses. It sometimes doesn't seem to matter where we're going so long as we get there quickly. Our materialistic orientation, our worship of the god of efficiency and produc-

tivity, distorts or destroys our more fundamental human values. We live in fear of a technology that could destroy the world.

Some observers think we pay much too high a price, and who can say they are wrong? Many express deep concern with the direction and emphasis of technology:

Technique, efficiency, management, results! But what does the poor man in these countries live for? . . . Nobody asks the fundamental question as to what is the whole blooming thing for. Nobody cares to find out what spirit pervades the whole thing. Nobody has the time to ascertain whether Man, in his freedom and in his fullness, exists at all.

Just because we can do something, does this mean we should do it? Technology develops to answer human needs, but what human needs does the supersonic transport answer?

What is growth? Is it getting bigger or getting better? What is a good standard of living? More things to consume or better things to appreciate and discriminate? What is a better use of the moon? To hit it with a rocket or just to look at it? What are the frontiers of human enterprise? Should people build and pioneer always outwards, or sometimes inwards?

At a fantastic cost—$30 billion—mankind puts a man on the moon—to impress mankind. Where is our sense of priorities?

With $30 billion we could give a 10 per cent raise in salary over a ten-year period to every teacher in the U.S. from kindergarten through universities (about $9.8 billion); give $10 million each to 200 of the best smaller colleges ($2 billion); finance seven-year fellowships (freshman through Ph.D.) at $4,000 per person per year for 50,000 new scientists and engineers ($1.4 billion); contribute $200 million each toward the creation of ten new medical schools ($2 billion); build and largely endow complete universities with medical, engineering and agricultural faculties for—fifty-three of the nations which have been added to the United Nations since its original founding ($13.2 billion); create three more permanent Rockefeller Foundations ($1.5 billion); and still have $100 million left over to popularize science.

IN CONCLUSION

We cannot stop the advance of technology. We can do very little to slow it. As citizens

—and managers—of the twentieth century we cannot escape its impact. But we can guide it, we can direct and control it with wisdom and understanding to maximize the social gain and minimize the social cost. We have been given the unique and boundless blessing of the human mind. We were given it not to destroy ourselves but to develop and use for the greater understanding and improvement of ourselves and our surroundings. Surely this gift promises mankind a much higher destiny than to wallow in problems he has created himself, to drown himself in his own stupidity, to blow himself off the face of the earth, and to destroy all that a billion years of evolution and labor and thought have thus far accomplished. Surely we are more than links in a grand experiment about to come to an end.

What a paradox! Technology has given us the technique—the threat—and the promise. Military technology provided us with a new and powerful research capability. This in turn has brought us to an unstable truce enforced by the threat of mutual annihilation, by "equal fear equally shared." And now the truce gives us the opportunity to turn our immense new problem-solving capability to the *right* questions, to the search for new sources of food, water, and energy, to the exploration of the oceans, to the threat of nuclear war, to the conquering of disease—and beyond these to the human mind, man's relationship with his fellow man.

These problems are far too important to leave to politicians. Nor can they be left to the scientists who create the new technology. Society and business, the exploiters of technology, must choose whether it will be used for the benefit or detriment of mankind.

If private enterprise is to survive as a viable, independent, self-directed force, business executives must accept responsibility for leadership, not only in directing the use of science and technology to constructive ends, but also in seeking solutions to problems of poverty, old age, population, leisure time, diminishing resources and to those relating to spiritual and moral values. These are *your* problems, *your* responsibility. You are executives in your companies, in your jobs—you are also executives in the progress of the universe.

The journey of mankind is a wonderful journey, an "immense journey," out of darkness. Since mankind first emerged, his first preoccupation has been the fight against hunger, disease, and physical want. Now for the first time in history he holds the technology necessary to erase these problems—or himself—from the face of the earth. We have come to the fork in the road—one branch leads back to darkness, the other to the elimination of human want and ignorance. What a wonderful choice! What a wonderfully exciting thrill to stand as travelers at the crossroad, to stand where no man has stood before—to hold such power for good or evil—and as business executives to have both the responsibility and the opportunity of directing and continuing the journey to understanding and man's destiny.

19. Integrating Science, Technology, and Marketing: An Overview
ROBERT L. CLEWETT

Science has become a pervasive force in modern society, as can be seen in the profound social, cultural, economic, and technological changes that have been occurring ever more rapidly during recent decades. Many benefits to mankind have already come from these changes, but the potential benefits for man's future are still virtually unlimited. It is my conviction that a primary role of business enterprise is to transform or convert the knowledge of science into useful products and services that contribute to a higher standard of living for mankind. Further, it is important that, through business, society should support the widest possible expansion, dissemination, and application of scientific knowledge, within the limits imposed by our democratic form of government and the private enterprise economic system.

In this paper the role of marketing in working toward this goal is presented. Briefly, marketing's role is to facilitate the translation of scientific and technological knowledge into profitable, want-satisfying products, processes, services, and distributive arrangements. To intelligently discuss and explore this transformation, one's view of science, technology, and marketing needs to be explained. Having defined these, we shall deal with the relationships among them; and most importantly, we shall offer some alternative orientations of

◆ SOURCE: Reprinted by permission from *Science Technology, and Marketing*, edited by Raymond M. Hass, Proceedings of the Fall Conference of the American Marketing Association, August-September 1966, pp. 3-20.

management which facilitate the integration of marketing, science, and technology.

SCIENCE AND TECHNOLOGY

Science, as the term is used here, embraces both the accumulated knowledge about man and his environment and the work of extending this knowledge.[1] In the words of Karl Pearson, written in the late nineteenth century:

The field of science is unlimited; its material is endless, every group of natural phenomena, every phase of social life, every stage of past or present development is material for science. *The unity of all science consists alone in its method, not in its material.*[2]

Technology, according to Webster's Dictionary, is the science of applying knowledge to practical purposes. As used here, technology embraces the application of scientific knowledge to the creation of plans, designs,

---

[1] Based on *Webster's Third New International Dictionary, Unabridged,* 1964; M. P. O'Brien, "Technological Planning and Misplanning," in James R. Bright (ed.), *Technological Planning on the Corporate Level* (Boston: Harvard University Graduate School of Business Administration, 1962), p. 73; and James M. Gavin, "Science, Technology, Market Affairs and World Peace," In Peter D. Bennett (ed.), *Marketing and Economic Development* (Chicago: American Marketing Association, 1965), pp. 22–23.

[2] Karl Pearson, *The Grammar of Science* (London: J. M. Dent & Sons, Ltd., 1937), p. 16. The italics are Pearson's.

and means for achieving desired results. It also includes the tools and techniques for carrying out plans.[3]

The Conquest of Nature

Science and technology, as Kast and Rosenzweig have suggested,[4] are concerned with accelerating the conquest of nature which began in pre-history. This conquest, they say, has proceeded in spite of superstitions, magic, and other restrictions. It has continued through many centuries when Western thought was dominated by Aristotelian science, which sought to explain *why* things happened. It has advanced at an accelerating rate during the 300 years since the beginning of modern science, which now seeks to explain *how* things happen.

The Application of Science and Technology

In his book, *The Research Revolution*, Silk states that some scholars see the application of science and technology to industry as having developed in three stages. He suggests these might be called the stages of the isolated inventor, the organized investigators, and the organized scientists.[5]

When isolated inventors began to use the scientific method in the eighteenth century, the result was the industrial revolution. Starting in Britain, large-scale mechanical manufacturing spread technology around the world. In this country, whole new industries sprang up from the inventions of such men as Eli Whitney, Robert Fulton, Samuel F. B. Morse, Cyrus McCormick, and Thomas A. Edison.

Organized investigators began to work in Germany toward the end of the nineteenth century. Institutes were established, with the support of the Kaiser, that encouraged German science to improve the industrial process. The American effort in this second phase

took the form of organized research laboratories, initiated primarily by private industrial firms such as Eastman Kodak, B. F. Goodrich, General Electric, and DuPont. Starting slowly late in the nineteenth century, the organized application of science to manufacturing in the United States during the 1920's and 1930's far exceeded such efforts by competing countries.

Organized scientists, brought together in this country through the Office of Scientific Research and Development to meet the needs of World War II, made tremendous strides in expanding and applying scientific and technological knowledge. The most important and dramatic of these organized efforts was the Manhattan project—benefiting from the earlier work of such scientists as Einstein, Lawrence, and Fermi, the co-ordinated talents of many specialists lead to success in the quest for the atom bomb. Other technological advances achieved during the war effort by scientists organized in terms of projects include, for example, the development of synthetic rubber, radar, and the antibiotics. Illustrations of technological advances achieved through organized research and development activities since World War II are such things as atomic reactors, electronic computers, jet transports, earth satellites, and space ships. In addition to spectacular achievements such as these, there is also a long fast-growing list of new products and new services based on technological progress.

Social Implications of Science and Technology

The social implications of science and technology are emphasized by Boulding in his thoughtful little book, *The Meaning of the 20th Century*.[6] He suggests that the continuous process of scientific and technological development which began about the sixth century A.D. has brought us the second great transition in the history of mankind. The first was that from pre-civilized to civilized society, which began to take place five (or ten) thousand years ago. The second, he says, may be called the transition from civilized to post-

---

[3] This concept of technology brings together "engineering" and "technology" as defined in the *Encyclopedia of Science and Technology* (New York: McGraw–Hill Book Co., Inc., 1966), Vol. 13, p. 406.

[4] Fremont E. Kast and James E. Rosenzweig (eds.), *Science, Technology and Management* (New York: McGraw–Hill Book Co., 1963), pp. 16–17.

[5] This section is based on Leonard S. Silk, *The Research Revolution* (New York: McGraw–Hill Book Co., Inc., 1960), pp. 49–59.

[6] Kenneth E. Boulding, *The Meaning of the 20th Century: The Great Transition* (New York: Harper & Row, Publishers, 1964).

civilized, technological, or developed civilization, which may be expected to last a million or so years.[7] This great transition is not only something that takes place in science, technology, the physical makings of society, and the utilization of physical energy; it is also a transition in social institutions.[8] Boulding thinks that both of these great transitions in the state of mankind may be identified primarily with changes in the state of human knowledge.[9]

It is generally agreed that society has failed to use great scientific discoveries fully for the benefit of man. The following statement made by John Dewey some thirty years ago continues to be relevant today:

We have displayed enough intelligence in the physical field to create the new and powerful instrument of science and technology. We have not as yet enough intelligence to use this instrument deliberately and systematically to control social operations and consequences.[10]

In citing Dewey's statement, Mesthene, of the Harvard Program on Technology and Society, proposes optimistically that the most significant of all social implications of today's rapid advance in science and technology may be the determination which is now present to do something about it.[11]

MARKETING

It was posited earlier that "marketing" has a role in advancing the effort to reach the individual and collective goals of mankind by facilitating the translation of scientific and technological knowledge into profitable want-statisfying products, processes, services, and distributive arrangements. In this section, the meaning of marketing will first be identified, then attention will be directed to two approaches to marketing—the social and the entrepreneurial—that are relevant to the effective utilization of scientific and technological knowledge.

Marketing as a Matching Process

Over the years, the term "marketing" has come to mean many different things for the same and different individuals and groups. It is essential, therefore, that I make clear what it means to me and the ways in which I intend to use it. In my view, marketing is concerned primarily with matching the needs and wants of potential buyers with products, processes, services, and distributive arrangements which will improve the relative position of both buyer and seller in exchange. According to this concept, the needs and wants of potential buyers and the means to satisfy them are separated in one or more ways, such as by differences in form, space, time, perception, ownership, and value. In seeking to understand fully both the needs and wants of potential buyers and the capabilities and resources of sellers in meeting them, a contribution is made toward meeting individual and collective goals through actualizing market potential.[12] This appears to be what Drucker had in mind in his frequently quoted statement that the purpose of a business is the creation of customers.

The major elements implied in the above concept of marketing include: (1) the needs and wants of potential buyers and the capabilities and resources of potential sellers; (2) a market mechanism operating effectively to facilitate exchange; (3) an effective energizing force or catalyst which provides motivation for exchange, such as business enterprise which focuses on meeting the needs and wants of potential buyers; (4) aggressive competition among business organizations for differential advantage in meeting the needs and wants of potential buyers; and (5) government regulation designed to maintain the environment of free competition to the extent that this is possible in a world of dramatic change and shrinking dimensions.

"The matching concept of marketing," described above, is based primarily on the work

---

[7] *Ibid.*, pp. 1, 2.

[8] *Ibid.*, p. 9.

[9] *Ibid.*, p. 27

[10] Quoted in Emmanuel G. Mesthene, "Technological Change and Social Development," a paper presented to The Institute of Management Sciences 1965 Eastern Meeting, October 14, 1965, Rochester, New York.

[11] *Ibid.*

[12] The idea of actualizing market potential was formulated by William McInnes. See "A Conceptual Approach to Marketing," in Reavis Cox, Wroe Alderson and Stanley J. Shapiro (eds.), *Theory in Marketing, Second Series* (Homewood, Ill.: Richard D. Irwin, 1964), pp. 51–57; and "Discussion," in Stewart J. Rewoldt (ed.), *Frontiers in Marketing Thought* (Bloomington: Indiana University Bureau of Business Research, 1955), pp. 187–96.

of Alderson.[13] In my view, it suggests the nature of marketing as a field of study with sufficient clarity to be generally understood by most marketing scholars and executives. At the same time, it is sufficiently broad to accommodate most of the analytical frameworks, processes, and concepts proposed by marketing scholars concerning their field of study; the analytical tools and techniques now available; and the growing inventory of data.

Once the central focus of a discipline is clear, then its essential elements can be identified. Hence, "the matching concept of marketing," briefly described above, suggests two approaches that appear fruitful in considering the integration of science, technology, and marketing. These are (1) the social process approach and (2) the entrepreneurial approach. The latter builds upon one part of the former. A firm grasp of both appears to me to be essential to a real understanding of the role of marketing, the marketing philosophy as a way of business life, the marketing concept, or marketing as a business function.

The Social Process Approach to Marketing. The social process approach to marketing first assumes the point of view suggested by Drucker in his 1957 Parlin Memorial Lecture —that marketing is a dynamic process of society through which business enterprise is integrated productively with society's purposes and human values. By focusing on the individual making decisions within a social structure and within a personal and social value system, the customer's individual and social values, needs, and wants are satisfied.[14]

Using Drucker's formulation as a general overview, the social process approach then utilizes some basic concepts formulated by Alderson as essential elements. In his last book, *Dynamic Marketing Behavior*, Alder-

son suggests (1) that marketing consists of activities of organized behavior systems, such as households and business firms, in heterogeneous markets; (2) that the marketing process begins with conglomerate resources in the natural state and ends with meaningful assortments in the hands of consumers; and (3) that this change consists of an alternating sequence of sorts and transformations, facilitated by market transactions.[15] The energizing force in Alderson's formulation of the marketing process appears to be competition among firms for differential advantage in terms of characteristics of products, services, geographic location, or specific combinations of these features. Alderson assumes that every firm occupies a position which is unique in some respects, and that for some groups of buyers it enjoys a differential advantage over all other suppliers. Since differential advantage is subject to change and neutralization by competitors, survival and growth for marketing organizations depend upon the preservation of differential advantage through continuous innovation.[16]

My view of the catalyst and energizing force for the social process approach to marketing is derived from McInnes,[17] Nicosia,[18] and the Alderson position. It is the effort made by business enterprise both in attempting to perceive accurately the needs and wants of potential buyers and in attempting to meet these effectively with appropriate goods and services through market transactions. It is business enterprise that takes the initiative in reducing the separation between potential buyers and the products and services which will satisfy their needs and wants.

The social process approach to marketing presumes an ultimate goal which is the satisfaction of human needs and wants. This is accomplished through effective utilization of scientific and technological knowledge to aid in transforming resources of all kinds into products, services, and distributive arrangements which when facilitated through market transactions will improve the relative position of both buyer and seller. From this point of

---

[13] Wroe Alderson, especially *Dynamic Marketing Behavior* (Homewood, Ill.: Richard D. Irwin, Inc., 1965); "The Analytical Framework for Marketing," in Delbert J. Duncan (ed.), *Conference of Marketing Teachers from Far Western States, Proceedings* (Berkeley: University of California Press, 1958); *Marketing Behavior and Executive Action* (Homewood, Ill.: Richard D. Irwin, Inc., 1957); and discussions in the annual Marketing Theory Seminars.

[14] Peter F. Drucker, "Marketing and Economic Development," *The Journal of Marketing*, Vol. XXII, No. 3 (January, 1958), pp. 252–59 at p. 252.

[15] *Dynamic Marketing Behavior*, p. 26.

[16] "The Analytical Framework for Marketing," p. 18.

[17] "The Conceptual Approach to Marketing," pp. 60–4.

[18] F. M. Nicosia, "Marketing and Alderson's Functionalism," *The Journal of Business*, Vol. XXXV, No. 4 (October, 1962), pp. 403–13 at p. 411.

view, profit is a measure of how effectively a business organization operating in a private enterprise economic system meets the needs and wants of buyers in competition with other firms.

In passing, it should be noted that the social process approach to marketing can be useful in understanding the role of marketing in developing economies, as well as in those more highly developed. In discussing "The Concept of a National Market and Its Economic Growth Implications," Rostow emphasizes the need to encourage business enterprise in agriculture and food processing as a means of modernizing the expensive marketing arrangements which now exist for many commodities in developing countries and as a means of breaking down the "Chinese Wall" between city and the countryside.[19] Sears Roebuck's entry into Latin America is an example which points up the contribution business enterprise is making there in meeting human needs and wants through modern marketing methods.[20]

The Entrepreneurial Approach to Marketing. Business enterprise, the catalyst and energizing force of the social process approach to marketing, is concerned with two major activities. One focuses attention on the human organization of a business. The other, which is central to the entrepreneurial approach to marketing, is the economic task of business enterprise. The nature of the economic task is suggested by the three dimensions identified by Drucker, in *Managing for Results*. These include: (1) making the present business more effective; (2) identifying and realizing its potential; and (3) making a different business for a different future.[21]

The entrepreneurial approach to marketing is based on the premise that the economic task of business enterprise can be performed effectively, in all three of its dimensions, only when based on appropriate strategic market-oriented planning. Logically, the focus of

such planning is on marshalling, allocating, and administering the capabilities and resources of a business to accomplish the economic objectives which it seeks. These are usually accomplished through profitable market transactions involving want-satisfying products. The three major phases of this complex process which are relevant for the purpose at hand include: (1) selecting appropriate strategic "market opportunities" to receive major marketing effort; (2) formulating competitive market-oriented strategies, designed to exploit successfully those "market opportunities" selected to receive major effort; and (3) formulating broad strategy for administering programs designed to implement the market-oriented strategies which have been formulated.

I have discussed "the concept of market opportunity" in a previous paper and will point out here only that both specific market requirements and the capabilities of an individual firm to meet these requirements are essential elements of a "market opportunity."[22] Since each firm is unique, competing firms are confronted with market opportunities which are different in degree, if not in kind. Each firm, therefore, seeks to match what it has to offer with particular market requirements relevant to the general areas of its market activity. It does this in competition with other firms with similar orientation, but with dissimilar differential advantage.

While not always fully recognized, most firms are usually confronted with many potential market opportunities, some with brighter prospects than others. The entrepreneurial approach to marketing focuses attention on those which will improve the economic performance of the business, and generally it elevates for major effort those market opportunities which fulfill unmet needs and wants of potential buyers through innovation in products, processes, services, and distributive arrangements.

INTEGRATING SCIENCE, TECHNOLOGY, AND MARKETING

If science is knowledge about man and his environment; if technology is the application of this knowledge to achieve desired results; and if marketing is concerned with matching

[19] Walt W. Rostow, "The Concept of a National Market and Its Economic Growth Implications," Bennett, *Marketing and Economic Development*, pp. 11–20, at pp. 15–16.

[20] Drucker, *op. cit.* p. 257.

[21] Peter F. Drucker, *Managing for Results* (New York: Harper & Row, 1964) distinguishes between the function of managing the human organization and the entrepreneurial function of business management (p. 227). With reference to the latter he sets out (p. 4) the dimensions of the economic task referred to above.

[22] Robert L. Clewett, "Market Opportunity and Corporate Management," Bennett, *Marketing and Economic Development*, pp. 187–99.

the needs and wants of potential buyers with profitable want-satisfying products and services through market transactions, then clearly, it is in the general interest of mankind everywhere to seek integration of science, technology, and marketing. The entrepreneurial approach to marketing, which emphasizes the concept of strategic market-oriented planning sketched below, is a step in this direction.

The problem lies not with a lack of objectives nor with a lack of recognition of the potential benefits available, for executives are keenly aware of the necessity to integrate marketing, science, and technology. I feel that the primary deterent to more successful integration resides in management attitude and posture toward marketing, science, and technology.

In the following sections, I will briefly describe the research and development (R&D) problem and R&D expenditures and results. Two different concepts of integrating science, technology and marketing—"the R&D" and the "entrepreneurial"—will then be presented.

Industrial Research and Development: Expenditures versus Results

U.S. industry has long sought new products and processes through the application of scientific and technological knowledge, as was described earlier in this paper. It is impressive to note that expenditures for industrial R&D have increased dramatically during the last four decades. American industry spent less than $100 million for this purpose in 1928. In 1964, according to the National Science Foundation, the funds for industrial R&D amounted to $13.4 billion, about three-fourths of the entire national R&D effort. Between 1953 and 1964, the amount of these funds expanded more than two and one-half times.[23] Another source reports that between 1946 and 1961, investment in industrial plants and equipment increased by 135 percent, whereas R&D expenditures grew 735 percent. And, by 1962 the total U.S. dollar expenditure for R&D was roughly 40 percent of that for plant and equipment.[24] Increased

funds for industrial R&D reflect, in part, work being done by private industry for the Department of Defense, the National Aeronautics and Space Administration, the Atomic Energy Commission, and other Federal agencies. But they also reflect recognition by industrial leaders of the tremendous opportunities and threats which technological progress holds for the individual business firms which they represent and for U.S. industry in world markets.

Sometimes management expectations have not been met by expenditures of large sums for R&D. This is not surprising since many firms without understanding the basic nature of the R&D process, have made very large outlays for R&D in the hope that such effort would solve the company's problems. In his article, "Science on Park Avenue," Stewart (himself a scientist) discusses some of the reasons behind managements' almost unbounded faith in scientists, and some of the difficulties that scientists have encountered in working in industry. He observes that it becomes ever more apparent that the bloom is off the rose.[25] There has been a growing disenchantment on the part of management with the idea that out of R&D expenditures there will somehow almost automatically flow a stream of profitable new products.

The Increasing Complexity of Corporate R&D Decisions

Corporate decisions concerning R&D can be expected to become increasingly complex as the search for new products through industrial R&D activities becomes more competitive, as the lives of products become shorter, and as shortages of technically trained people become ever more acute. Business executives will find it more difficult to determine how much to spend on R&D, which particular projects to support, and to what extent each should be supported. In addition, rising R&D costs themselves will further complicate business decisions.[26] R&D decisions by private industry must also take into account market dynamics and, ironically,

---

[23] *Reviews of Data on Science Resources*, No. 7, Jan., 1966 (NSF 66–6), p. 1.

[24] H. Igor Ansoff, "The Firm of the Future," *Harvard Business Review*, Vol. 43, No. 5 (September-October, 1965), pp. 162–78, at p. 163.

[25] Albert C. Stewart, "Science on Park Avenue," *International Science and Technology*, No. 28 (April, 1964), pp. 38–42, at pp. 39–40.

[26] "Company R & D: Status and Outlook," *The Conference Board Record*, February, 1966, pp. 7–17, at p. 8.

one source of market change is product innovation which, of course, is stimulated by
technological progress itself. Another significant source of market dynamics is the global
restructuring of the marketplace.[27]

On the other hand, there is an unprecedented market for the products and services
of U.S. industry. Quinn points out three aspects of the U.S. market as being especially
noteworthy: (1) its relative technological
sophistication; (2) its sheer size; and (3) its
general homogeneity.[28] He suggests that such
aspects have strongly stimulated the growth
in the United States of giant companies
which can develop overwhelming technological and marketing strengths in domestic and
global markets when technologies grow
more complex, markets expand and standardize, and economies of scale increase.

From an economic point of view, then, a
critical problem confronts corporate management in making R&D expenditures on the
basis of contribution to a stream of profitable
new products. In general, it is important that
the contribution of such expenditures be
measured in terms of profitable sales. Not
only does this contribute to an enhanced
profit position for the firm, but it suggests
that the needs and wants of buyers are being
more closely met than if it were otherwise.
This, in turn, contributes to economic growth
through expansion of demand.

The R&D Concept of Integrating Science, Technology and Marketing

The recent attempts by many firms to improve the management of their R&D efforts
are symptomatic of dissatisfaction with the
results obtained from past R&D expenditures.
Attention is increasingly being given to improving criteria for the allocation of R&D
funds as well as for improving R&D administration. With respect to the latter, a recent
survey by The Industrial Conference Board
suggests that management efforts are increasingly being directed toward improving
communication and coordination of R&D with
other company functions.[29]

---

[27] Ansoff, op. cit. p. 163.
[28] James B. Quinn, "Technological Competition:
Europe vs. U.S.," Harvard Business Review. Vol.
44, No. 4 (July-August, 1966), pp. 113–30 at
p. 114.
[29] "Company R & D: Status and Outlook," p. 12.

These and similar steps are in the right
direction and will hopefully contribute to increased productivity of R&D expenditures.
In my view, however, they are merely steps
in the refinement of what I refer to as "the
R&D concept of integrating science, technology, and marketing." This concept, as I see
it, is based on the relatively narrow view
that available technology should be translated into new products. This logic is a
natural outgrowth of the work done by organized scientists working on wartime projects geared to clearly defined objectives in
terms of defense needs. From this experience
management has taken a similar view of
R&D's role in industry and has for the most
part emphasized the translation of technological advances into new products. Earlier,
when relatively few firms were influenced by
this concept, the results were sometimes very
profitable. In general, however, as more firms
aggressively seek clearly visible markets for
new products that represent readily available
technological spin-offs, the probability of an
individual firm finding them can be expected
to decrease.

I should hasten to add that the "R&D concept of integrating science, technology, and
marketing" is far superior to what could be
labeled the "automatic, R&D, new-product
machine concept of integrating science, technology, and marketing." With this notion,
management expected, for example, after
World War II, that nearly any new product
they offered could be marketed successfully.

As change increasingly becomes a way of
life, as competition for profitable sales becomes more intense, and as the problems of
corporate management become more complex, indications grow stronger that "the
R&D concept of integrating science, technology, and marketing" has severe weaknesses.
It appears that a more comprehensive concept is needed. The entrepreneurial concept,
to which attention is turned next, is such a
concept.

The Entrepreneurial Concept of Integrating Science, Technology, and Marketing

The "entrepreneurial concept of integrating
science, technology, and marketing" elevates
to a central position the satisfaction of the
needs and wants of mankind everywhere as
the desired goal for the utilizaiton of scientific and technological knowledge of all kinds

within the limits imposed by our democratic form of government and the private enterprise economic system. Emphasis is placed on utilizing scientific and technological knowledge of all kinds to translate capabilities and resources of all kinds into profitable want-satisfying products, services, and distributive arrangements. This is very different from translating technological advances into products, which we have described as the "R&D concept of integrating science, technology, and marketing."

The entrepreneurial concept of integrating science, technology, and marketing is based on the entrepreneurial approach to marketing previously described. Both emphasize the three dimensions of the economic task formulated by Drucker which has been set out above. Similarly, both are based on the premise that the economic task of business enterprise can be performed effectively, in all of its dimensions, only when based on appropriate strategic market-oriented planning. Moreover, they both assume the position that, logically, such planning focuses on marshalling, allocating, and administering the capabilities and resources of a business to accomplish the economic objectives which it seeks. Both emphasize selecting appropriate strategic "marketing opportunities" to receive major marketing effort.[30]

The entrepreneurial approach to marketing as a field of study is just that—a particular approach to the study of the subject matter of marketing as defined earlier. The entrepreneurial concept of integrating science, technology, and marketing is a particular orientation useful in working toward solutions to the market-oriented problems of a firm. It is based on a comprehensive frame of reference which elevates for major consideration by corporate planners and decision-makers the key market-oriented elements in working toward corporate survival and profitable growth. It assumes that in the planning process, appropriate attention will be given to corporate objectives and to corporate capabilities in terms, for example, of production, finance, and managerial perspective.

The Entrepreneurial Concept and the R&D Concept

The entrepreneurial concept and the R&D concept of integrating science, technology,

and marketing differ in several important ways, only a few of which will be outlined here. Perhaps the most important concerns orientation. The entrepreneurial concept focuses on utilizing scientific and technological knowledge of all kinds to translate corporate capabilities and resources of all kinds into profitable want-satisfying products, processes, services, and distributive arrangements, which in exchange will leave both buyer and seller better off. In contrast, the R&D concept, as I view it, focuses on translating developing and advanced technology into new products. The former receives direction from what will satisfy human needs and wants. Direction for the latter is provided by technological advances. Both concepts necessarily embrace both satisfying human wants and needs on one hand and technological capabilities on the other—but these are viewed with different emphasis.

Under the entrepreneurial concept all kinds of scientific and technological knowledge are utilized imaginatively to translate corporate capabilities and resources into meeting the needs and wants of mankind everywhere. This is done through market transactions which involve innovations in products, processes, services, and distributive arrangements. In contrast, the R&D concept focuses attention on translating scientific and technological knowledge primarily identified with the "hard sciences" into profitable new products. The talents of all kinds of scientists are used in the former, whereas primarily those of the physical scientists are used in the latter. The former seeks to utilize the available body of scientific and technological knowledge in its entirety to fulfill human needs and wants by reducing the differences which separate buyers and sellers, such as space, time, perception, ownership, and value. The latter, as I view it, seeks primarily to translate into new products specialized technological knowledge about important but relatively limited areas.

Another important difference between these two concepts concerns marketing research. The entrepreneurial concept assumes that all the talents of all kinds of scientists plus the total body of scientific and technological knowledge will be brought to bear on market-oriented problems of all kinds however they relate to whatever "offers" are eventually made to potential buyers. In addition to products, this includes, for example, the

---

[30] See Clewett, passim.

choice of corporate goals, the selection of corporate fields of endeavor, and so on down through the selection of strategic market opportunities, the formulation of competitive market-oriented strategies and specific marketing programs, to the administration of these programs day by day. In contrast, the R&D concept utilizes marketing research to study whether markets exist for products which may be developed through the technological R&D process. The former concept assumes a marketing R&D process which is similar to the technological R&D process. The latter concept reduces marketing research activities to a subsidiary role which is much more restricted than that under the entrepreneurial concept.

It is important to note and to emphasize that under both concepts the measure of performance is profit through market transactions involving products and services.

The entrepreneurial concept of integrating science, technology, and marketing does not relegate the R&D process to the limbo of management concepts, devices, strategies, and so forth; which after a period of popularity fade away. Rather, the entrepreneurial concept views the role of the R&D process in a comprehensive frame of reference which integrates all aspects of business enterprise to mankind profitably and effectively through the market mechanism of a private enterprise economic system. It views marketing as ". . . a dynamic process of society through which business enterprise is integrated productively with society's purposes and human values."[31]

The Entrepreneurial Concept in an Operational Setting

By way of viewing the entrepreneurial concept of integrating science, technology, and marketing in an operational setting, I will first present a hypothetical example based on the actual experience of a large U.S. firm and will then give brief attention to some organizational considerations.

Recognizing several years ago that the social, economic, political, and technological changes that were then taking place in the United States and in other parts of the world

would undoubtedly accelerate, the firm's management assumed a posture which they hoped would result in survival and profitable growth of their company. Perhaps without full appreciation of what it meant, a program was then initiated which today appears to be similar in many respects to what I have described as the entrepreneurial concept of integrating science, technology, and marketing.

A research group under the direction of capable market-oriented staff executives first analyzed the task and then formulated a plan which included a series of interrelated research projects. They directed attention first to the question, what should marketing do? For the planning group this was essential since they felt it was the only way to provide an adequate home for the entrepreneurial decisions concerning what business objectives to pursue and what strategies of implementation to apply. Attention was then directed toward determining what marketing work would be required to carry out the business strategy; what organization and allocation of marketing resources would be appropriate for this work; and, finally, what measurements of results were indicated in order to control the entire process of formulating ends and choosing marketing means. In this manner they initially developed a rather abstract structure for the decisions of a business, which could be used to identify and explore the question of supporting whatever research might be needed.

The things that were relevant to these decisions were then identified and organized into a classification suited to the problems of carrying out research. This lead to delineation of subjects, each of which constituted a separate work program (to be handled by a specific group of people) that, in turn, would feed into the previously described structure of marketing decisions. The subjects chosen were: first, the future of society as a setting for the performance of the business; second, the identity of the company viewed both as a social institution with certain characteristics and as a collection of capabilities with certain values; third, the behavior of customers, be they households or other groups of buyers; fourth, the characteristics of markets viewed both as systems requiring adaptation, and as structures capable of evolution and susceptible to influence; and fifth, the attributes of marketing instruments,—warehouses, computers, salesmen, advertising agencies, dealers,— things with changing performance characteristics and costs which would be used to produce marketing effects. Finally, a sixth

---

[31] Drucker, "Marketing and Economic Development," p. 252.

research program was established to develop methods to research these bodies of substantive knowledge, and to apply the results to business decisions in actual practice.[32]

Although useful in showing how one company initially moved in the direction of the entrepreneurial concept of integrating science, technology, and marketing, the illustration is not complete, since R&D has not been treated explicitly from either the technological or marketing point of view. What should be emphasized, however, is that this hypothetical example suggests the orientation which is the essence of the entrepreneurial concept of integrating science, technology, and marketing; that is, the utilization of scientific and technological knowledge of all kinds to translate capabilities and resources of all kinds into profitable want-satisfying products, processes, services, and distributive arrangements—not just new products based on technological advances.

Results are not achieved by means of an orientation only, however. Of the many areas that are relevant here, I will comment briefly on two: organization and information. Earlier I suggested that the entrepreneurial concept of integrating science, technology, and marketing embraces a marketing R&D process similar to the technological R&D process. Both Levitt, in "Growth and Profits Through Marketing Innovation,"[33] and Talley,[34] in "Marketing R&D: Neglected Way to Profit," suggest that a separate department be set up to implement such a process. The responsibility for the administration of such a unit and the co-ordination of its activities would be expected to rest with a member of top management. Levitt suggests that for marketing R&D a special breed of energetic men will be needed—men who have no interest in perpetuating the present marketing scheme. I think this also applies to technological R&D. He also suggests that these men must not be put into a position of jeopardizing their own personal futures because they are pushing ideas which may offend or threaten persons who are in a position to affect their careers. Levitt takes the position that besides being at home in the world of ideas, marketing R&D men must also have an active interest in the broadest spectrum of the business view of life; the physical, social, and life sciences; aesthetics; mass culture; and technology. In summary, Levitt has said:

. . . they must have a restless need to be on top of things—of the whole panoramic cluster of ideas, theories, facts, and events that constantly reshape our lives, tastes, values, and needs. They must be the type of people who regularly read widely and avidly and exhibit an enthusiastic flair for business.[35]

Again, I would suggest that Levitt's comments apply not only to desirable characteristics for marketing R&D men, but also generally to technological R&D men—especially to those concerned with development phases of R&D work and to a lesser degree to those involved in applied and basic research. Also, I assume Levitt suggests these characteristics over and above a high degree of competence in one or more specialized fields of knowledge.

Organizational devices, information flows, and working relations designed to achieve integration of marketing R&D, technological R&D, and all other relevant corporate activities must, of course, be provided. . . . In addition to a particular orientation and competent men, the effective use of the entrepreneurial approach also depends upon an information system which makes available relevant information from widespread sources both internal and external to the firm. A total management information system might conceivably be made up of several subsystems. For example, one might be a marketing information subsystem which would serve both marketing R&D and marketing operations. I have previously outlined the kind of information which would be needed from such a subsystem.[36] Another subsystem might be concerned with technological R&D. Company information subsystems for technological R&D could expect to benefit from a national

---

[32] From a paper delivered to personnel of the firm which is the subject of my hypothetical example. For this reason I prefer not to identify the company.

[33] Theodore Levitt, "Growth and Profit Through Planned Marketing Innovation," *Journal of Marketing*, Vol. 24, No. 4 (April, 1960), pp. 1–8, at p. 4. See also "Needed Marketing R & D," in Levitt's *Innovation in Marketing* (New York: McGraw-Hill Book Company, Inc., 1962), pp. 97–113.

[34] Walter Talley, "Marketing R & D; Neglected Way to Profit Growth," *Business Horizons*, Fall, 1962, pp. 31–40, at p. 37.

[35] Levitt, "Growth and Profit Through Planned Marketing Innovation," p. 4.

[36] Clewett, op. cit. pp. 193–4.

system of technical information such as is discussed by Rosenbloom in "Technology Transfer—Process and Policy"[37]. I assume that individual firms who are heavy users of technological information already have found technological information systems essential. Such a system appears to be needed if these firms are to take full advantage of the efforts of Federal agencies such as NASA's Technology Utilization Division and its support of Indiana University's Aerospace Research Applications Center. The new Technical Services Act, as I understand it, is also in-

tended to facilitate the transfer of information generated through the technological R&D activities of the Federal Government to private industry.

SUMMARY

Integrating science, technology, and marketing has been the central point of focus throughout this paper. First, background material concerning science and technology was presented briefly. My own view of marketing was then set out, followed by two approaches to it—the "social process" and the "entrepreneurial." After introducing the problem of integrating science, technology, and marketing, two different management viewpoints concerning its solution were developed —one emphasizes R&D activities and the other emphasizes market requirements.

[37] Richard S. Rosenbloom, *Technology Transfer —Process and Policy: An Analysis of the Utilization of Technological By-Products of Military and Space R & D* (Washington, D. C.: National Planning Association, 1965), Special Report No. 62, p. 31.

H. Consumer Demand

20. Rational Behavior and Economic Behavior
GEORGE KATONA

While attempts to penetrate the boundary lines between psychology and sociology have been rather frequent during the last few decades, psychologists have paid little attention to the problems with which another sister discipline, economics, is concerned. One purpose of this paper is to arouse interest among psychologists in studies of economic behavior. For that purpose it will be shown that psychological principles may be of great value in clarifying basic questions of economics and that the psychology of habit formation, of motivation, and of group belonging may profit from studies of economic behavior.

A variety of significant problems, such as those of the business cycle or inflation, of consumer saving or business investment, could be chosen for the purpose of such demonstration. This paper, however, will be concerned with the most fundamental assumption of economics, the principle of rationality. In order to clarify the problems involved in this principle, which have been neglected by contemporary psychologists, it will be necessary to contrast the most common forms of methodology used in economics with those employed in psychology and to discuss the role of empirical research in the social sciences.

◆ SOURCE: Reprinted by permission from the author and the American Psychological Association, *Psychological Review*, Vol. 60, No. 5, 1953, pp. 307–317. Copyright © 1953 by the American Psychological Association.

THEORY AND HYPOTHESES

Economic theory represents one of the oldest and most elaborate theoretical structures in the social sciences. However, dissatisfaction with the achievements and uses of economic theory has grown considerably during the past few decades on the part of economists who are interested in what actually goes on in economic life. And yet leading sociologists and psychologists have recently declared "Economics is today, in a theoretical sense, probably the most highly elaborated, sophisticated, and refined of the disciplines dealing with action" (*15, p. 28*).[1]

To understand the scientific approach of economic theorists, we may divide them into two groups. Some develop on a priori system from which they deduce propositions about how people *should* act under certain assumptions. Assuming that the sole aim of businessmen is profit maximization, these theorists deduce propositions about marginal revenues and marginal costs, for example, that are not meant to be suited for testing. In developing formal logics of economic action, one of the main considerations is elegance of the deductive system, based on the law of parsimony. A wide gap separates these theorists from economic research of an empirical-statistical

---

[1] The quotation is from an introductory general statement signed by T. Parsons, E. A. Shils, G. W. Allport, C. Kluckhohn, H. A. Murray, R. R. Sears, R. C. Sheldon, S. A. Stouffer, and E. C. Tolman. The term "action" is meant to be synonymous with "behavior."

type which registers what they call aberrations or deviations, due to human frailty, from the norm set by theory.

A second group of economic theorists adheres to the proposition that it is the main purpose of theory to provide hypotheses that can be tested. This group acknowledges that prediction of future events represents the most stringent test of theory. They argue, however, that reality is so complex that it is necessary to begin with simplified propositions and models which are known to be unreal and not testable.[2] Basic among these propositions are the following three which traditionally have served to characterize the economic man or the rational man:

1. The principle of complete information and foresight. Economic conditions—demand, supply, prices, etc.—are not only given but also known to the rational man. This applies as well to future conditions about which there exists no uncertainty, so that rational choice can always be made. (In place of the assumption of certainty of future developments, we find nowadays more frequently the assumption that risks prevail but the probability of occurrence of different alternatives is known; this does not constitute a basic difference.)

2. The principle of complete mobility. There are no institutional or psychological factors which make it impossible, or expensive, or slow, to translate the rational choice into action.

3. The principle of pure competition. Individual action has no great influence on prices because each man's choice is independent from any other person's choice and because there are no "large" sellers or buyers. Action is the result of individual choice and is not group-determined.

Economic theory is developed first under these assumptions. The theorists then introduce changes in the assumptions so that the theory may approach reality. One such step consists, for instance, of introducing large-scale producers, monopolists, and oligopolists, another of introducing time lags, and still another of introducing uncertainty about the probability distribution of future events. The question raised in each case is this: Which of the original propositons needs to be changed, and in what way, in view of the new assumptions?

The fact that up to now the procedure of gradual approximation to reality has not been completely successful does not invalidate the method. It must also be acknowledged that propositions were frequently derived from unrealistic economic models which were susceptible to testing and stimulated empirical research. In this paper we shall point to a great drawback of this method of starting out with a simplified a priori system and making it gradually more complex and more real—by proceeding in this way one tends to lose sight of important problems and to disregard them.

The methods most commonly used in psychology may appear at first sight to be quite similar to the methods of economics which have just been described. Psychologists often start with casual observations, derive from them hypotheses, test those through more systematic observations, reformulate and revise their hypotheses accordingly, and test them again. The process of hypotheses-observations-hypotheses-observations often goes on with no end in sight. Differences from the approach of economic theory may be found in the absence in psychological research of detailed systematic elaboration prior to any observation. Also, in psychological research, findings and generalizations in one field of behavior are often considered as hypotheses in another field of behavior. Accordingly, in analyzing economic behavior[3] and trying to understand rationality, psychologists can draw on (a) the theory of learning and thinking, (b) the theory of group belonging, and (c) the theory of motivation. This will be done in this paper.

---

[2] A variety of methods used in economic research differ, of course, from those employed by the two groups of economic theorists. Some research is motivated by dissatisfaction with the traditional economic theory; some is grounded in a systematization greatly different from traditional theory (the most important example of such systematization is national income accounting); some research is not clearly based on any theory; finally, some research has great affinity with psychological and sociological studies.

[3] The expression "'economic behavior" is used in this paper to mean behavior concerning economic matters (spending, saving, investing, pricing, etc.). Some economic theorists use the expression to mean the behavior of the "economic man," that is, the behavior postulated in their theory of rationality.

HABITUAL BEHAVIOR AND
GENUINE DECISION MAKING

In trying to give noneconomic examples of "rational calculus," economic theorists have often referred to gambling. From some textbooks one might conclude that the most rational place in the world is the Casino in Monte Carlo where odds and probabilities can be calculated exactly. In contrast, some mathematicians and psychologists have considered scientific discovery and the thought processes of scientists as the best examples of rational or intelligent behavior.[4] An inquiry about the possible contributions of psychology to the analysis of rationality may then begin with a formulation of the differences between (a) associative learning and habit formation and (b) problem solving and thinking.

The basic principle of the first form of behavior is repetition. Here the argument of Guthrie holds: "The most certain and dependable information concerning what a man will do in any situation is information concerning what he did in that situation on its last occurrence" (4, p. 228). This form of behavior depends upon the frequency of repetition as well as on its recency and on the success of past performances. The origins of habit formation have been demonstrated by experiments about learning nonsense syllables, lists of words, mazes, and conditioned responses. Habits thus formed are to some extent automatic and inflexible.

In contrast, problem-solving behavior has been characterized by the arousal of a problem or question, by deliberation that involves reorganization and "direction," by understanding of the requirements of the situation, by weighing of alternatives and taking their consequences into consideration and, finally, by choosing among alternative courses of action.[5] Scientific discovery is not the only example of such procedures; they have been demonstrated in the psychological laboratory as well as in a variety of real-life situations. Problem solving results in action which is new rather than repetitive; the actor may have never behaved in the same way before and may not have learned of any others having behaved in the same way.

Some of the above terms, defined and analyzed by psychologists, are also being used by economists in their discussion of rational behavior. In discussing, for example, a manufacturer's choice between erecting or not erecting a new factory, or raising or not raising his prices or output, reference is usually made to deliberation and to taking the consequences of alternative choices into consideration. Nevertheless, it is not justified to identify problem-solving behavior with rational behavior. From the point of view of an outside observer, habitual behavior may prove to be fully rational or the most appropriate way of action under certain circumstances. All that is claimed here is that the analysis of two forms of behavior—habitual versus genuine decision making—may serve to clarify problems of rationality. We shall proceed therefore by deriving six propositions from the psychological principles. To some extent, or in certain fields of behavior, these are findings or empirical generalizations; to some extent, or in other fields of behavior, they are hypotheses.

1. Problem-solving behavior is a relatively rare occurrence. It would be incorrect to assume that everyday behavior consistently manifests such features as arousal of a problem, deliberation, or taking consequences of the action into consideration. Behavior which does not manifest these characteristics predominates in everyday life and in economic activities as well.

2. The main alternative to problem-solving behavior is not whimsical or impulsive behavior (which was considered the major example of "irrational" behavior by nineteenth century philosophers). When genuine decision making does not take place, habitual behavior is the most usual occurrence: people act as they have acted before under similar circumstances, without deliberating and choosing.

3. Problem-solving behavior is recognized most commonly as a deviation from habitual behavior. Observance of the established routine is abandoned when in driving home from

---

[4] Reference should be made first of all to Max Wertheimer who in his book *Productive Thinking* uss the terms "sensible" and "intelligent" rather than "rational." Since we are mainly interested here in deriving conclusions from the psychology of thinking, the discussion of psychological principles will be kept extremely brief.

[5] Cf. the following statement by a leading psychoanalyst: "Rational behavior is behavior that is effectively guided by an understanding of the situation to which one is reacting." French adds two steps that follow the choice between alternative goals, namely commitment to a goal and commitment to a plan to reach a goal.

my office, for example, I learn that there is a parade in town and choose a different route, instead of automatically taking the usual one. Or, to mention an example of economic behavior: Many businessmen have rules of thumb concerning the timing for reorders of merchandise; yet sometimes they decide to place new orders even though their inventories have not reached the usual level of depletion (for instance, because they anticipate price increases), or not to order merchandise even though that level has been reached (because they expect a slump in sales).

4. Strong motivational forces—stronger than those which elicit habitual behavior—must be present to call forth problem-solving behavior. Being in a "crossroad situation," facing "choice points," or perceiving that something new has occurred are typical instances in which we are motivated to deliberate and choose. Pearl Harbor and the Korean aggression are extreme examples of "new" events; economic behavior of the problem-solving type was found to have prevailed widely after these events.

5. Group belonging and group reinforcement play a substantial role in changes of behavior due to problem solving. Many people become aware of the same events at the same time; our mass media provide the same information and often the same interpretation of events to groups of people (to businessmen, trade union members, sometimes to all Americans). Changes in behavior resulting from new events may therefore occur among very many people at the same time. Some economists (for instance, Lord Keynes, see 9, p. 95) argued that consumer optimism and pessimism are unimportant because usually they will cancel out; in the light of sociopsychological principles, however, it is probable, and has been confirmed by recent surveys, that a change from optimistic to pessimistic attitudes, or vice versa, sometimes occurs among millions of people at the same time.

6. Changes in behavior due to genuine decision making will tend to be substantial and abrupt, rather than small and gradual. Typical examples of action that results from genuine decisions are cessation of purchases or buying waves, the shutting down of plants or the building of new plants, rather than an increase or decrease of production by 5 or 10 per cent.[6]

Because of the preponderance of individual psychological assumptions in classical economics and the emphasis placed on group behavior in this discussion, the change in underlying conditions which has occurred during the last century may be illustrated by a further example. It is related—the author does not know whether the story is true or fictitious—that the banking house of the Rothschilds, still in its infancy at that time, was one of the suppliers of the armies of Lord Wellington in 1815. Nathan Mayer Rothschild accompanied the armies and was present at the Battle of Waterloo. When he became convinced that Napoleon was decisively defeated, he released carrier pigeons so as to transmit the news to his associates in London and reverse the commodity position of his bank. The carrier pigeons arrived in London before the news of the victory became public knowledge. The profits thus reaped laid, according to the story, the foundation to the outstanding position of the House of Rothschild in the following decades.

The decision to embark on a new course of action because of new events was then made by one individual for his own profit. At present, news of a battle, or of change of government, or of rearmament programs, is transmitted in short order by press and radio to the public at large. Businessmen—the manufacturers or retailers of steel or clothing, for instance—usually receive the same news about changes in the price of raw materials or in demand, and often consult with each other. Belonging to the same group means being subject to similar stimuli and reinforcing one another in making decisions. Acting in the same way as other members of one's group or of a reference group have acted under similar circumstances may also occur without deliberation and choice. New action by a few manufacturers will, then, frequently or even usually not be compensated by re-reverse action on the part of others. Rather the direction in which the economy of an entire country moves—and often the world economy as well—will tend to be subject to the same influences.

---

[6] Some empirical evidence supporting these six propositions in the area of economic behavior has been assembled by the Survey Research Center of the University of Michigan.

After having indicated some of the contributions which the application of certain psychological principles to economic behavior may make, we turn to contrasting that approach with the traditional theory of rationality. Instead of referring to the formulations of nineteenth century economists, we shall quote from a modern version of the classical trend of thought. The title of a section in a recent article by Kenneth J. Arrow is "The Principle of Rationality." He describes one of the criteria of rationality as follows: "We can imagine the individual as listing, once and for all, all conceivable consequences of his actions in order of his preference for them" (1, p. 135). We are first concerned with the expression "all conceivable consequences." This expression seems to contradict the principle of selectivity of human behavior. Yet habitual behavior is highly selective since it is based on (repeated) past experience, and problem-solving behavior likewise is highly selective since reorganization is subject to a certain direction instead of consisting of trial (and error) regarding all possible avenues of action.

Secondly, Arrow appears to identify rationality with consistency in the sense of repetition of the same choice. It is part and parcel of rational behavior, according to Arrow, that an individual "makes the same choice each time he is confronted with the same set of alternatives" (1, p. 135).[7] Proceeding in the same way on successive occasions appears, however, a characteristic of habitual behavior. Problem-solving behavior, on the other hand, is flexible. Rationality may be said to reflect adaptability and ability to act in a new way when circumstances demand it, rather than to consist of rigid or repetitive behavior.

Thirdly, it is important to realize the differences between the concepts action, decision, and choice. It is an essential feature of the approach derived from considering problem-solving behavior that there is action without deliberate decision and choice. It then becomes one of the most important problems of research to determine under what

conditions genuine decision and choice occur prior to an action. The three concepts are however, used without differentiation in the classical theory of rationality and also, most recently, by Parsons and Shils. According to the theory of these authors, there are "five discrete choices (explicit or implicit) which every actor makes before he can act"; before there is action "a decision must always be made (explicitly or implicitly, consciously or unconsciously)."

There exists, no doubt, a difference in terminology, which may be clarified by mentioning a simple case: Suppose my telephone rings; I lift the receiver with my left hand and say, "Hello." Should we then argue that I made several choices, for instance, that I decided not to lift the receiver with my right hand and not to say "Mr. Katona speaking"? According to our use of the terms decision and choice, my action was habitual and did not involve "taking consequences into consideration."[8] Parsons and Shils use the terms decision and choice in a different sense, and Arrow may use the terms "all conceivable consequences" and "same set of alternatives" in a different sense from the one employed in this paper. But the difference between the two approaches appears to be more far-reaching. By using the terminology of the authors quoted, and by constructing a theory of rational action on the basis of this terminology, fundamental problems are disregarded. If every action by definition presupposes decision making, and if the malleability of human behavior is not taken into consideration, a one-sided theory of rationality is developed and empirical research is confined to testing a theory which covers only some of the aspects of rationality.

This was the case recently in experiments devised by Mosteller and Nogee. These authors attempt to test basic assumptions of economic theory, such as the rational choice among alternatives, by placing their subjects

---

[7] In his recent book Arrow adds after stating that the economic man "will make the same decision each time he is faced with the same range of alternatives": "The ability to make consistent decisions is one of the symptoms of an integrated personality."

[8] If I have reason not to make known that I am at home, I may react to the ringing of the telephone by fright, indecision, and deliberation (should I lift the receiver or let the telephone ring?) instead of reacting in the habitual way. This is an example of problem-solving behavior characterized as deviating from habitual behavior. The only example of action mentioned by Parsons and Shils, "a man driving his automobile to a lake to go fishing," may be habitual or may be an instance of genuine decision making.

in a gambling situation (a variation of poker dice) and compelling them to make a decision, namely, to play or not to play against the experimenter. Through their experiments the authors prove that "it is feasible to measure utility experimentally" but they do not shed light on the conditions under which rational behavior occurs or on the inherent features of rational behavior. Experiments in which making a choice among known alternatives is prescribed do not test the realism of economic theory.

MAXIMIZATION

Up to now we have discussed only one central aspect of rationality—means rather than ends. The end of rational behavior, according to economic theory, is maximization of profits in the case of business firms and maximization of utility in the case of people in general.

A few words, first, on maximizing profits. This is usually considered the simpler case because it is widely held (*a*) that business firms are in business to make profits and (*b*) that profits, more so than utility, are a quantitative, measurable concept.

When empirical research, most commonly in the form of case studies, showed that businessmen frequently strove for many things in addition to profits or in place of profits, most theorists were content with small changes in their systems. They redefined profits so as to include long-range profits and what has been called nonpecuniary or psychic profits. Striving for security or for power was identified with striving for profits in the more distant future purchasing goods from a high bidder who was a member of the same fraternity as the purchaser, rather than from the lowest bidder—to cite an example often used in textbooks—was thought to be maximizing of nonpecuniary profits. Dissatisfaction with this type of theory construction is rather widespread. For example, a leading theorist wrote recently:

If *whatever* a business man does is explained by the principle of profit maximization—because he does what he likes to do, and he likes to do what maximizes the sum of his pecuniary and non-pecuniary profits—the analysis acquires the character of a system of definitions and tautologies, and loses much of its value as an explanation of reality.

The same problem is encountered regarding maximization of utility. Arrow defines rational behavior as follows: ". . . among all the combinations of commodities an individual can afford, he chooses that combination which maximizes his utility or satisfaction" (1, p. 135) and speaks of the "traditional identification of rationality with maximization of some sort" (2, p. 3). An economic theorist has recently characterized this type of definition as follows:

The statement that a person seeks to maximize utility is (in many versions) a tautology: it is impossible to conceive of an observational phenomenon that contradicts it. . . . What if the theorem is contradicted by observation: Samuelson says it would not matter much in the case of utility theory; I would say that it would not make the slightest difference. For there is a free variable in his system: the tastes of consumers. . . Any contradiction of a theorem derived from utility theory can always be attributed to a change of tastes, rather than to an error in the postulates or logic of the theory (16, pp. 603 f.).[9]

What is the way out of this difficulty? Can psychology, and specifically the psychology of motivation, help? We may begin by characterizing the prevailing economic theory as a single-motive theory and contrast it with a theory of multiple motives. Even in case of a single decision of one individual, multiplicity of motives (or of vectors or forces in the field), some reinforcing one another and some conflicting with one another, is the rule rather than the exception. The motivational patterns prevailing among different individuals making the same decision need not be the same; the motives of the same individual who is in the same external situation at different times may likewise differ. This approach opens the way (*a*) for a study of the relation of different motives to different forms of behavior and (*b*) for an investigation of changes in motives. Both problems are disregarded by postulating a single-motive theory and by restricting empirical studies to attempts to confirm or contradict that theory.

The fruitfulness of the psychological approach may be illustrated first by a brief reference to business motivation. We may rank the diverse motivational patterns of businessmen by placing the striving for high immediate profits (maximization of short-run

---

[9] The quotation refers specifically to Samuelson's definition but also applies to that of Arrow.

profits, to use economic terminology; charging whatever the market can bear, to use a popular expression) at one extreme of the scale. At the other extreme we place the striving for prestige or power. In between we discern striving for security, for larger business volume, or for profits in the more distant future. Under what kinds of business conditions will motivational patterns tend to conform with the one or the other end of the scale? Preliminary studies would seem to indicate that the worse the business situation is, the more frequent is striving for high immediate profits, and the better the business situation is, the more frequent is striving for nonpecuniary goals (see 8, pp. 193–213).

Next we shall refer to one of the most important problems of consumer economics as well as of business-cycle studies, the deliberate choice between saving and spending. Suppose a college professor receives a raise in his salary or makes a few hundred extra dollars through a publication. Suppose, furthermore, that he suggests thereupon to his wife that they should buy a television set, while the wife argues that the money should be put in the bank as a reserve against a "rainy day." Whatever the final decision may be, traditional economic theory would hold that the action which gives the greater satisfaction was chosen. This way of theorizing is of little value. Under what conditions will one type of behavior (spending) and under what conditions will another type of behavior (saving) be more frequent? Psychological hypotheses according to which the strength of vectors is related to the immediacy of needs have been put to a test through nationwide surveys over the past six years.[10] On the basis of survey findings the following tentative generalization was established: Pessimism, insecurity, expectation of income declines or bad times in the near future promote saving (putting the extra money in the bank), while optimism, feeling of security, expectation of income increases, or good times promote spending (buying the television set, for instance).

Psychological hypotheses, based on a theory of motivational patterns which change with circumstances and influence behavior, thus stimulated empirical studies. These studies, in turn, yielded a better understanding of past developments and also, we may add, better predictions of forthcoming trends than did studies based on the classical theory (see footnote 10). On the other hand, when conclusions about utility or rationality were made on an a priori basis, researchers lost sight of important problems.[11]

DIMINISHING UTILITY, SATURATION, AND ASPIRATION

Among the problems to which the identification of maximizing utility with rationality gave rise, the measurability of utility has been prominent. At present the position of most economists appears to be that while interpersonal comparison of several consumers' utilities is not possible, and while cardinal measures cannot be attached to the utilities of one particular consumer, ordinal ranking of the utilities of each individual can be made. It is asserted that I can always say either that I prefer A to B, or that I am indifferent to having A or B, or that I prefer B to A. The theory of indifference curves is based on this assumption.

In elaborating the theory further, it is asserted that rational behavior consists not only of preferring more of the same goods to less ($2 real wages to $1, or two packages of cigarettes to one package, for the same service performed) but also of deriving diminishing increments of satisfaction from successive units of a commodity.[12] In terms of an old textbook example, one drink of water has tremendous value to a thirsty traveler in a desert; a second, third, or fourth drink may still have some value but less and less so; an

---

[10] In the Surveys of Consumer Finances, conducted annually since 1946 by the Survey Research Center of the University of Michigan for the Federal Reserve Board and reported in the *Federal Reserve Bulletin*. See also 8 and a forthcoming publication of the Survey Research Center on consumer buying and inflation during 1950–52.

[11] It should not be implied that the concepts of utility and maximization are of no value for empirical research. Comparison between maximum utility as determined from the vantage point of an observer with the pattern of goals actually chosen (the "subjective maximum"), which is based on insufficient information, may be useful. Similar considerations apply to such newer concepts as "minimizing regrets" and the "minimax."

[12] This principle of diminishing utility was called a "fundamental tendency of human nature" by the great nineteenth century economist, Alfred Marshall.

nth drink (which he is unable to carry along) has no value at all. A generalization derived from this principle is that the more of a commodity or the more money a person has, the smaller are his needs for that commodity or for money, and the smaller his incentives to add to what he has.

In addition to using this principle of saturation to describe the behavior of the rational man, modern economists applied it to one of the most pressing problems of contemporary American economy. Prior to World War II the American people (not counting business firms) owned about 45 billion dollars in liquid assets (currency, bank deposits, governmental bonds) and these funds were highly concentrated among relatively few families; most individual families held no liquid assets at all (except for small amounts of currency). By the end of the year 1945, however, the personal liquid-asset holdings had risen to about 140 billion dollars and four out of every five families owned some bank deposits or war bonds. What is the effect of this great change on spending and saving? This question has been answered by several leading economists in terms of the saturation principle presented above. "The rate of saving is . . . a diminishing function of the wealth the individual holds" (5, p. 499) because "the availability of liquid assets raises consumption generally by reducing the impulse to save."[13] More specifically: a person who owns nothing or very little will exert himself greatly to acquire some reserve funds, while a person who owns much will have much smaller incentives to save. Similarly, incentives to increase one's income are said to weaken with the amount of income. In other words, the strength of motivation is inversely correlated with the level of achievement.

In view of the lack of contact between economists and psychologists, it is hardly surprising that economists failed to see the relevance for their postulates of the extensive experimental work performed by psychologists on the problem of levels of aspiration. It is not necessary in this paper to describe these studies in detail. It may suffice to formulate three generalizations as established in numerous studies of goal-striving behavior (see, for example, 12):

1. Aspirations are not static, they are not established once for all time.
2. Aspirations tend to grow with achievement and decline with failure.
3. Aspirations are influenced by the performance of other members of the group to which one belongs and by that of reference groups.

From these generalizations hypotheses were derived about the influence of assets on saving which differed from the postulates of the saturation theory. This is not the place to describe the extensive empirical work undertaken to test the hypotheses. But it may be reported that the saturation theory was not confirmed; the level-of-aspiration theory likewise did not suffice to explain the findings. In addition to the variable "size of liquid-asset holdings," the studies had to consider such variables as income level, income change, and savings habits. (Holders of large liquid assets are primarily people who have saved a high proportion of their income in the past!)[14]

The necessity of studying the interaction of a great number of variables and the change of choices over time leads to doubts regarding the universal validity of a one-dimensional ordering of all alternatives. The theory of measurement of utilities remains an empty frame unless people's established preferences of A over B and of B over C provide indications about their probable future behavior. Under what conditions do people's preferences give us such clues, and under what conditions do they not? If at different times A and B are seen in different contexts—because of changed external conditions or the acquisition of new experiences—we may have to distinguish among several dimensions.

The problem may be illustrated by an analogy. Classic economic theory postulates a one-dimensional ordering of all alternatives; Gallup asserts that answers to questions of choice can always be ordered on a yes-uncertain (don't know)—no continuum; are both arguments subject to the same reserva-

---

[13] The last quotation is from the publication of the U.S. Department of Commerce, *Survey of Current Business*, May 1950, p. 10. This quotation and several similar ones are discussed in 8, pp. 186 ff.

[14] The empirical work was part of the economic behavior program of the Survey Research Center under the direction of the author. See (8) and also (10) and (11).

tions? Specifically, if two persons give the same answer to a poll question (e.g., both say "Yes, I am for sending American troops to Europe" or "Yes, I am for the Taft-Hartley Act") may they mean different things so that their identical answers do not permit any conclusions about the similarity of their other attitudes and their behavior? Methodologically it follows from the last argument that yes-no questions need to be supplemented by open-ended questions to discern differences in people's level of information and motivation. It also follows that attitudes and preferences should be ascertained through a multi-question approach (or scaling) which serves to determine whether one or several dimensions prevail.

ON THEORY CONSTRUCTION

In attempting to summarize our conclusions about the respective merits of different scientific approaches, we might quote the conclusions of Arrow which he formulated for social science in general rather than for economics:

To the extent that formal theoretical structures in the social sciences have not been based on the hypothesis of rational behavior, their postulates have been developed in a manner which we may term *ad hoc*. Such propositions . . . depend, of course, on the investigator's intuition and common sense (1, p. 137).

The last sentence seems strange indeed. One may argue the other way around and point out that such propositions as "the purpose of business is to make profits" or "the best businessman is the one who maximizes profits" are based on intuition or supposed common sense, rather than on controlled observation. The main problem raised by the quotation concerns the function of empirical research. There exists an alternative to developing an axiomatic system into a full-fledged theoretical model in advance of testing the theory through observations. Controlled observations should be based on hypotheses, and the formulation of an integrated theory need not be delayed until all observations are completed. Yet theory construction is part of the process of hypothesis-observation-revised hypothesis and prediction-observation, and systematization should rely on some empirical research. The proximate aim of scientific research is a body of empirically validated generalizations and not a theory that is valid under any and all circumstances.

The dictum that "theoretical structures in the social sciences must be based on the hypothesis of rational behavior" presupposes that it is established what rational behavior is. Yet, instead of establishing the characteristics of rational behavior a priori, we must first determine the conditions a_1, b_1, c_1 under which behavior of the type x_1, y_1, z_1 and the conditions a_2, b_2, c_2 under which behavior of the type x_2, $y_{,2}$ z_2 is likely to occur. Then, if we wish, we may designate one of the forms of behavior as rational. The contributions of psychology to this process are not solely methodological; findings and principles about noneconomic behavior provide hypotheses for the study of economic behavior. Likewise, psychology can profit from the study of economic behavior because many aspects of behavior, and among them the problems of rationality, may be studied most fruitfully in the economic field.

This paper was meant to indicate some promising leads for a study of rationality, not to carry such study to its completion. Among the problems that were not considered adequately were the philosophical ones (rationality viewed as a value concept), the psychoanalytic ones (the relationships between rational and conscious, and between irrational and unconscious), and those relating to personality theory and the roots of rationality. The emphasis was placed here on the possibility and fruitfulness of studying forms of rational behavior, rather than the characteristics of *the* rational man. Motives and goals that change with and are adapted to circumstances, and the relatively rare but highly significant cases of our becoming aware of problems and attempting to solve them, were found to be related to behavior that may be called truly rational.

21. Four Reasons for Voluntary Poverty

JAMES PARK

Being poor by choice means refusing high-paying jobs or taking them at lower pay, and intentionally spending and consuming less than the average American. It is totally different from involuntary poverty, which results when people are unable to earn or spend as much as they would like. Nor is voluntary poverty a "sour grapes," temporary decision which is immediately abandoned when easy money presents itself. It is not a postponement of the American Dream but a rejection of it. In the midst of our affluent culture some people are choosing to avoid earning and spending. Why? The following are my personal reasons for opting out of the money game:

1. I do not want to exploit people. Exploitation is a very slippery concept; few people would ever consider themselves exploiters. But this is precisely where the questions should be raised: "Am I exploiting other people? Am I using other people for my own advantage? Is my work self-serving, doing me more good than anyone else?" Periodically I must ask myself if I would continue my work even if I received no benefits from it: "Is my work important enough to pursue without pay? If all the selfish reasons were eliminated, would I still continue my activities because they are intrinsically worthwhile?"

We all know what exploitation feels like from the bottom: when we have to pay outrageous prices for goods and services or when an employer makes huge profits from our work. But such open and blatant exploitation is often turned into more subtle channels. The marvelous advances of our technocratic civilization have minimized face-to-face exploitation and replaced it with impersonal, mass exploitation. The six-figure salaries of corporate executives cannot be seen as the exploitation of just a few people. This exploitation is spread over the masses of employes, consumers and taxpayers. The selfish use of each victim may be relatively insignificant, but it is exploitation nevertheless. Can any one man do $250,000 worth of work in one year? I think not. Perhaps, then, he is collecting money for someone else's work, using other people's efforts to line his own pockets, skimming off the money which should have gone to the people who actually produced the goods or performed the services.

This exploitation by big businessmen is obvious to all (except these exploiters themselves), but there are more subtle kinds of exploitation being practiced even by the critics of these big exploiters.

Lest all the exploiters seem to be members of the establishment, let me hasten to add that a lot of exploitation takes place in the counter culture too: rock bands charge thousands of dollars for a single performance: records sell for several times their cost of production: drug pushers make fantastic profits.

Each person will have to examine himself to determine to what degree he might be exploiting other people. Some people suggest that any high income depends on exploitation—whether direct or indirect. Objection:

◆ SOURCE: *The Minnesota Daily*, November 28, 1972, pp. 7–8.

"But if I stop exploiting people through my job or profession, someone else will simply step into my place and continue the exploitation: it is the system that is responsible for exploitation and not the individuals within it."

This is probably true; the exploitation is likely to continue. But if you agree that anyone who takes more money than he really needs is an exploiter, then the only sure way to avoid being an exploiter yourself is to avoid excessive income. If you want to reduce your personal exploitation, instead of looking for ways to increase your income, look for ways to earn and exploit less. This turns the American Dream of unlimited personal aggrandizement rightside up: instead of pursuing money as a status symbol, you can give yourself to goals that you really value.

On the collective levels, we can avoid exploiting by creating and supporting nonexploitive, alternative organizations to meet people's needs: cooperatives for housing, food, bicycles, learning, etc.

Let everyone examine himself instead of his brother. Figure out what you really need for comfortable survival. The rest of your income is exploitive. Personally, if ever again I make over $2,000 a year, I will consider myself an exploiter.

2. I do not want to pollute the environment.
If earning causes exploitation, spending creates pollution. I used to think that I contributed very little to the pollution problem because I spent my income very carefully—over half of it for rent. But then I realized that even money I spent on rent and human services is spent again by my dentist and landlord on whatever they please—doubtless producing a great deal of pollution. So the only way for me to control my burden on the environment is to limit my spending and consuming.

An American child is as great a burden on the environment as 17 children born in India. This is not because he will eat or breathe as much as 17 Indians during his lifetime, but because he will spend that much more. The basic needs of life are the same for all human beings: air to breathe, food to eat, a place to live, water to drink and wash with. Most of these necessities are relatively inexpensive, and getting them produces little pollution. The greatest damage to the environment is caused by the things we pay the most for. Every American uses 27,000,000 gallons of water during his lifetime—not because he

drinks that much but because he spends thousands of dollars on foolish products which require a lot of water to manufacture.

Recycling your bottles and cans, riding a bicycle, giving up cigarettes and babies will all help reduce pollution, but this is tokenism if you still continue to spend at a high level. Don't believe the hired advocates of consumerism—life can be beautiful and happy lived in simplicity. The person who spends $10,000 a year pollutes as much as five people spending $2,000 a year each. Each person's contribution to pollution probably rises even faster than his spending because a dollar spent on basic necessities probably pollutes less than a dollar spent on luxuries.

If this is so, the most effective way to reduce your burden on the environment is to reduce the total amount of money you spend each year. Not only will spending less reduce your exploitation of others, but it will also reduce your contribution to pollution.

Your personal decision to be poor may not have a noticeable impact on the total amount of pollution, but this decision may have some effect on the other people you know, and people can change. Beyond the foreseeable future, something may happen to we human beings that will completely reverse our mad rush for greater and greater spending and which will bring pollution down to tolerable limits. In the meantime, voluntary poverty is only your personal decision to reduce your share of environmental pollution.

3. I do not want to finance government policies of which I do not approve. History will record the American War in Indochina (1965-1972) as the most absurd and evil event in the recent history of mankind. Not since the extermination of 6,000,000 Jews a quarter of a century earlier has genocide been practiced so openly and meaninglessly. One and a half million people are known to be dead and millions more have been maimed and displaced. One hundred and ten billion dollars has been blown up—uselessly, senselessly. The very soil of Vietnam has been destroyed for a generation. All for what? This has been done for political reasons so obscure that few of the unwilling executioners understood them. Is the government of South Vietnam any less totalitarian and repressive than the government of North Vietnam? Are we trying to "save the peoples of Indochina from Communism" by killing them?

Now that our diabolical passion for killing Southeast Asian people who disagree with us seems to have nearly spent itself, the American nation, like the German nation after World War II, will have to take stock of its guilt. And each American will have to think of his own life's story: "What did I do during those dark years? What part did I play in killing those nearly defenseless peasants of Indochina?" More than 1 percent of the American people (2.7 million) have been in Vietnam participating directly in this atrocity; millions more have been helping with the killing from a distance; and all 200 million of us have paid for this absurd carnage with our taxes. If our income was too small to be paying taxes, we could not finance this immoral war.

Until there is a radical change in our system of government there will be more Vietnamese wars waged by that self-appointed world policeman, the United States of America.

The issue of financing government policies is much deeper than Vietnam, although Vietnam is the best historical example. The problem resides in the overcentralization of power in the American system. Too much money and too much power resides in the hands of too few men. "Power corrupts and absolute power corrupts absolutely." The ultimate solution to this problem is the decentralization of power. If the American people had been asked individually to finance the war in Indochina, it would have been over years ago. The penultimate solution is the reestablishment of balancing powers in the government. Congress must reassert its responsibility for spending the people's money wisely.

Until either of these events occurs, there is still something we can do individually: We can take control of our own money by living below the taxable level. Voluntary poverty provides a way of separating ourselves from policies with which we do not agree. If we are willing to make some personal sacrifices, give up come of the comforts of our affluent lives, then we can reduce our incomes below the taxable level and become personally disengaged from the policies of the American government. I haven't paid any federal income taxes since 1968. And my method of avoiding taxes is perfectly legal: I avoid excessive income. For an individual, federal income taxes now start at about $2050. For four years I have been living very comfortably below the taxable level.

Living in voluntary poverty is the best way to be free. I regard myself as a citizen of the world and a resident of the United States, of Minnesota and of Minneapolis. As more people join the voluntary poverty movement, we can form a nation within a nation—a people who have not been corrupted by the system around us. Even if this does not prove to be the rebirth of freedom at least we will be among the free people who saw and acted while most of the others stood blindly by.

Acting against the overcentralization of power begins at home. If you refuse to take power over anyone else's life, then freedom will be a little closer.

4. I do not want to sell myself. Freedom is the greatest gift of voluntary poverty. Freedom is the possibility of using one's 600,000 hours of life precisely as he pleases. Most people are not free to decide how they will use their time because they have locked themselves into the System. They are forced to spend the best hours of the best days of every week doing things that they would not voluntarily do if they were not paid.

But the person who is willing to live at a subsistence level can be essentially free from what everyone else regards as the economic necessity of selling their minds and bodies in order to survive.

The easiest way to live in freedom is never to start playing the money game. If you never have been consumed by consumerism, you won't have to change your style of life. College students should seriously ask themselves how much of their education is really technical training for joining the money game. If you find that you are working toward a degree in order to get a high-paying job, perhaps you should reexamine your whole philosophy of life.

Those who are already addicted to money will have withdrawal pains, but I think they will be happier after they have been liberated. If you have a high-paying job which causes you to exploit other people, to pollute the environment, to finance government policies with which you do not agree, and to sell yourself, simply quit your job and do something worthwhile for a change. You only have one life to live; why not make it good? If you are a doctor, heal for less—serve those who need your services the most instead of those who are able to pay the most. If you are a teacher, help people to learn and grow in the most effective way—without considering your salary first. If you are a lawyer, serve people without exploiting them. If you are willing to earn less, you will have greater control over your own life—the people who pay you will not have a stranglehold on you.

Never were so many benefits so simply achieved: Work less—spend your life on things that really matter to you instead of having your life governed by the powers that control the money. Experience the joy of giving instead of exploiting. Know what it is to own your existence once again. Become free to decide your life not by how best you can make money, but by how best you can contribute to your fellow man.

Voluntary poverty, unlike most other kinds of social reform, has the great advantage of being an actual possibility for anyone right now. Becoming poor does not require a reorganization of government or a change of public policy. Each individual can become voluntarily poorer in whatever degree he wants.

Voluntary poverty need not be a retreat from social responsibility; it permits you to become an authentic and effective person, pursuing your own goals and values instead of committing your time and energy to something that merely generates income.

22. Future Consumption Patterns in the Developing Countries

ANDRÉ VAN DAM

1. CAN THINKERS AND DOERS MEET?

The encounter between the prestigious International Marketing Federation futurologists of world renown may be the right place and time to search for common denominators between corporate and central planners on the one hand, and future-oriented scientists on the other hand.

In their forward planning, private enterprise and governments habitually work with a timespan of a few years, seldom more than five. Futures research, however, is generally concerned with at least a decade, often as much as an entire generation. In fact, their dramatic benchmark is the year 2000.

In all likelihood, the future will be mostly shaped by people who have the powers of decision. Whether they hold private or public office, they only have pragmatic use for conjectures that confine themselves to the 1970s. At best, the 1980s can serve as some vague framework of reference for their think tanks, if any. If we wish to strive seriously for the optimum of the possible futures, then futures research must be brought within the reach of corporate and central planners—and firmly within the grasp of captains of industry and leading civil servants.

One of my objectives is to build a bridge, however rudimentary, between futurology

◆ SOURCE: Reprinted by permission of the author from a paper submitted to the third world conference on futures research, Bucharest, September 4–9, 1972, in conjunction with the International Marketing Federation.

and pragmatic planning. Within that objective, the central message is that the future consumption patterns of the developing countries may well be different from past and present consumption patterns in the market-oriented and centrally planned economies—why, how, and where.

Indeed, I limit myself to the third world, in which we find three-fourths of our planet's population—although they use up only one-seventh of the world's resources. Sooner or later the developing countries will have to be integrated to some extent into the global economic system, for the benefit and survival of spaceship earth. It may, therefore, constitute a valuable service to the two halves of our world to reconcile the practical requirements of international marketing executives and the scientific aspirations of the world's futurologists. Hence our proposal to shrink the timespan of futurology and stretch that of business planning.

Consumption, as we shall analyze, can be a basic instrument of development. The central theme of this conference—"The future of consumption"—is therefore applied to about one hundred developing countries in Africa, Asia, and Latin America. In a large portion of these continents many consumption patterns are rather primitive. Thus, multinational corporations and intergovernmental agencies often face a virgin territory for the application of their huge resources.

However, there are constraints. First, half the population of the third world is under nineteen years of age, which originates peculiar consumption patterns, of interest to the young participants in this conference. Second, future consumption patterns of the developing countries hinge partly on their ability to develop human resources and achieve a profound social transformation of their structures. Finally, the third world is fully aware of the modern world's search for a balance between material affluence and the quality of life, and its myriad implications.

2. CONSUMPTION IN THE CONTEXT OF DEVELOPMENT

The term "third world"—coined for the sake of brevity—is to be used with caution. The one hundred nations under review here present a kaleidoscope image of consumption patterns and levels of development. Compared to Canada, Argentina for instance is a developing country. From the Argentine viewpoint, however, Yugoslavia is an underdeveloped country, being half as rich or poor as Argentina. To the average Yugoslav, on the other hand, Egypt looks like a backward country, since it is half as rich or poor as Yugoslavia. In a similar vein, Egypt must consider Indonesia a poor country. Yet Afghanistan may well look up to Indonesia with quite some envy. These few examples demonstrate the relativity of the term "underdevelopment." Inevitably when one scrutinizes the problems of the third world, one wonders: "developed —compared to what or to whom?"

We must therefore search for measurable criteria that can guide us into the forecasts of consumption patterns, based upon development potentials. (There are also, as we shall appraise at a later stage, noneconomic facets of consumption patterns).

The availability of natural resources— which comprise soil, forests, water, minerals, and so forth — greatly influence consumption patterns. Their utilization can be translated into consumption of dairy products, fiber, grains, meat, lumber, metals and nonmetalic minerals, oil, and pulp. The discovery of petroleum can substantially boost the development potential in a relatively short time span, as witnessed by Libya and Venezuela. Yet, the presence of adequate natural resources does not ensure prosperity, as demonstrated by Chile and Zaire—nor does their absence necessarily impede affluence: for example Hong Kong and Lebanon. A variety of natural resources can accelerate balanced growth, as in the case of Ecuador and Greece.

How great the gap between resource utilization can become is illustrated among other things, by the per-capita consumption of steel, where Tanganyika uses 4, Iraq 40, and Australia 400 kilos per year. Similarly, this is exemplified in the per-capita annual use of energy: Ethiopia 20, Algeria 200, and Romania 2000 kilos of coal equivalent.

Energy—like telephones, cement, foreign trade, and literacy, for instance—tends to become a key indicator of consumption. However, the equation may be affected one way or another by the presence of heavy industry, the abundance of cheap water power, the preponderance of mining, or a low proportion of arable land.

Consumption patterns are also influenced by the mobility of products and services. In this respect rail, road, air, maritime, or fluvial communications can become essential, because the economic development of many a nation depends partly on the reduction—in miles and days—of the distance between harvest and consumption. In countries like India and Nigeria up to one-sixth of the crops can be lost for consumption because of deficient transportation or lack of storage facilities.

Access to the sea is, in principle, advantageous to consumption. However, Switzerland is wealthy whereas Haiti and the Dominican Republic are still fairly poor. Experts of the United Nations anticipate that futures research in the area of sea culture (ocean farming) may particularly favor consumption patterns of those developing countries that enjoy relatively long coastlines.

In our studies of the future the modernization of the rural sectors may well hold the key to the quintessence of consumption. However long and painful—and here, of course, one cannot be confined to one decade—the transition from traditional, primitive farming to some degree of modern agriculture is essential to development. In countries where traditional farming is predominant, mass consumption of industrialized products remains dramatically low, as witnessed by Burma and Senegal. On the other hand, Israel and Puerto Rico prove that the low propensity of arable land is no obstacle to rapidly growing modern consumption patterns.

In the final analysis, I believe that human resources will prove the most decisive factor in the crystallizing of adequate consumption patterns in the third world. It may well be that the economies of various African nations were doomed to stagnation because their human resources were wholly inadequate—the result of heat, disease, and centuries of isolation.

The mere size of population has little bearing on consumption, as witnessed by populous Pakistan and empty Ireland, except maybe for the reduced ability of a small nation to diversify its manufacturing industry. Nor does density of population seem to correlate with scarcity or abundance, as illustrated by sparse Bolivia and the densely inhabited Philippine Islands. However, the national distribution of population is significant as it can be decisive in the level and pattern of consumption.

Futures research will also center around the possible correlations between consumption patterns and such factors as fertility and mortality rates and the ensuing life expectancy at birth. Variations between countries are indeed huge. The lowest country on the scale of life expectancy, Chad I believe, reaches half that of the world's leader, Norway—with 74 years. Fertility rates vary all the way from 1.5 percent in Hungary to 5.5 percent in the Ivory Coast. Birth rates usually change very gradually only—in contrast to death rates that can be halved, as in the case of Ceylon, in the time span of one generation, for example, by the eradication of malaria. The fact that this is a mixed blessing has been ascertained by the employment studies of the International Labor Office.

The consequence of high-fertility rates is a young population, half of which is under 19 years of age. This influences the labor market, the need for and cost of education, the size of families and, inevitably, the demand for food, housing, and other essential consumption items. In fact, education becomes, in this youthful third world, the magic key to the utilization of its human resources. In very low stages of development, each family tends to produce its own food, clothing, work tools, and shelter, for which no formal education is required. However, as a country moves from a farm economy through a small-town economy to a regional and finally a national economy, educational requirements change and widen tangibly.

Given the overwhelming importance of the human element to consumption Asia, Latin America and Africa, futures research should reckon with the quantity and quality of human resources that are to develop these con-tinents. To these topics we now discuss before analyzing the changes in consumption as the central thesis—are to beckon and challenge multinational corporations and intergovernmental organizations.

3. THE POPULATION EXPLOSION

One of the most vehemently discussed subjects is the so-called exponential growth of the population that preoccupies environmentalists, economists, and political scientists. This topic has no bearing, however, upon the problems dealt with here—a statement that in no way belittles the magnitude of the problem beyond the 1980s.

Most babies born today will reach the labor market in about 15 years. They will be at the age of marriage 5 or 10 years afterwards. Even if it were feasible to curb the growth of population in the next few years, the pressure on employment, family formation, and the ensuing consumption patterns cannot physically be assessed before the 1990s! If, faithful to our objective, we wish to influence the decision process of corporations and governments by our futures research, then it would be a futile exercise to relate consumption patterns in 1970s to the eventual saturation of the exponential growth curve in demography.

Nevertheless, it may be useful at this stage to suggest to business executives and civil servants that the future ratio of rich to poor populations is important in today's decision process. Barring nuclear holocaust or acts of God, we are moving towards a world that, at the end of this century, may consist of five billion people in the third world versus two billion in the industrialized countries.

This future ratio of 5:2 means this: the time may come when the consumption of resources in absolute numbers should, for geopolitical if not for humane motives, become subordinated to the proportion of haves and have-nots. If this happens in the lifetime of the next generation, it may be up to the decision makers—and the futurologists—of this generation to pave the way for a different global outlook on consumption. To this end, different research seems warranted.

4. THE IFES AND THE BVANIS

Such research may well be concerned as much with the quality of human resources as with the quantity. Introducing his Unesco-sponsored book, Dr. Wilbur Schramm depicts, in *Mass Media and Development,* the life of two typical rural families,—the Ifes in Africa and the Bvanis in Asia. Regardless of the degree of typification of these families, they do give us a deep insight into what has to be changed—and how—in order to arrive at desirable and possible consumption patterns in the rural sectors of the developing countries. Some of these observations may also apply to consumption in small towns.

The Ife family is composed of father, mother, and two children (out of five born) plus Mr. Ife's father, too old and sick to work. Although improductive, he is fully taken care of by the poor family. What is remarkable is the warmth of the Ifes' family life, the affection for each other, and the kindness towards the useless grandfather. The Ifes are bright, tender people. They have never walked more than 10 miles away from home.

They are not ambitious, not upward mobile people, primarily because they are often sick due to undernourishment and tropical parasites. They usually go without lunch, except for nuts they are sucking to soothe their hungry stomachs. They eat very little meat, some roots, beans, peanuts, rice, and fruit. Their low-protein, high-carbohydrate diet may still the pains of hunger but does not make for energetic and hardworking people. At any rate, there is not much scope for employment on the land because of a lack of seeds, implements, and perhaps water.

These people have special talents; father Ife in repairing the frail "house"; mother Ife in weaving artistic frames and colorful baskets. The boy has a remarkable memory, but illness prevents him often from walking quite a few miles from home to school. In sum, the Ife family represents incompletely used resources. With medical care, a balanced diet, and some education—and boiled water—they could make use of their talents and have access to the basic amenities of life.

Economically the Bvanis are as underdeveloped as the Ifes, but they have a richer heritage of religion, philosophy, and arts. The Bvanis raise rice, the basic meal, which they combine with beans and hot pepper-sauces. The Bvanis are more vigorous, fine-looking people who are short, dark, and clear-eyed, and who have intelligent faces. Chronic illnesses are rarer but they suffer from more epidemics than the Ifes do. They have lost many children to cholera and smallpox.

In the family compound the children play together, the men work together, and the women chatter together. In the evenings, they sit and sing together. In summer they all sleep outside the compound, together with the animals under the bright sky. They farm together a few acres of land. The patriarch makes the family decisions, which does not always please the sons. When they become upset, they go to town for jobs and never return. Changes threaten traditional village life, and tensions arise.

In the Bvani family the old people make the decisions, slowing down change. Until the rigid mores and customs of village life are broken down, improvement is unlikely to come. Of course, the margin of livelihood is slim, and the risk of innovation looms large. Survival is uppermost in their mind. The Bvanis are limited by conservative leadership, the social system, and tradition. These factors limit their use of native intelligence and vigor.

Economic development will require, first, a social transformation, which is essentially a human transformation. The goal is to educate and inform people to change some attitudes and values and to imbue and rethink social behavior.

5. DEVELOPMENT—PAST, PRESENT, AND FUTURE

In the famous Founex report—in preparation for the Stockholm conference on the human environment—it is clearly spelled out that many developing countries are fast turning from a preoccupation with "how much to produce and how fast" to "what is produced and how is it distributed." Previously, development was primarily a matter of quantities of production and of growth. In the future, it is anticipated, the emphasis will be on specific priorities—based on human needs—and a more adequate distribution of the output. It is essential for futures research into consumption patterns to be familiar with past developments in order to break away from them if, where, and when needed.

A century ago, per-capita product in the now-industrialized countries did not exceed US$ 300—measured in today's prices. It may well be that Rhodesia and South Korea are now where Italy and New Zealand were in 1872. A century ago the now-advanced countries moved from the iron age into the steel and machine age. Half the population of Europe and the United States was then engaged in agriculture, as compared with less than 10 percent today. The muscles of men and animals provided some 90 percent of all available energy, versus 10 percent now. Therefore, the economics of the United States and Europe were then not dramatically superior to those of the average developing country today.

In these 100 years, world population rose 2.5 times, world output increased tenfold, and per-capita output 4 times. In the now industrialized countries alone, production rose as much as 25 times, or sevenfold on a per-capita basis. These growth rates look extremely impressive—but if we compound them, these rates barely reach a 2 percent per-capita output each year.

This, today, is a low growth rate—since developing countries average 3 percent per year. In fact, small countries like Malaysia and large countries like Brazil set and reach targets of 5 percent or more. In view of the demographic expansion of the third world, Gross National Products have been rising to the tune of 6 percent per year—and some countries, such as Panama and Taiwan, have reached 7 and 8 percent over a prolonged period of time.

These growth rates should be scrutinized, however, in order to initiate meaningful futures research. It may be specifically important for world business and governments to realize that agriculture—the "home" of half the third world—has mostly been a Cinderella of development, with growth rates barely ahead of population increases. Manufacturing industry has been the general favorite because of an economic and psychological obsession with import substitution: economic independence. Some dynamic sectors in the upper half of the developing countries—such as automotive, chemicals, construction, electronics, metal mechanics, paper, and plastics—have shown growth rates of between 10 and 15 percent per year. Yet, these valuable industries are not necessarily the great national priorities of many developing countries.

This is really the quintessance of what may separate the future from the past. In bygone times—and even nowadays—the preoccupation with economic growth stemmed partly from a genuine anxiety about the widening gap between rich and poor countries. This concern, however understandable and laud-

able, risks confusing the real issue of the future of consumption. One major reason why this is so is that it seems difficult for a human being to visualize the reversal of an existing trend. This is precisely what we anticipate to occur in a good part of the third world. It is, indeed, my central message.

I anticipate the possible reversal of existing trends in various sectors. These are delicate, sometimes controversial issues that can only be touched on briefly. If they strike a responsive chord with business and government executives, as also with university professors and futurologists, the foundation may be laid for interdisciplinary research in these changes. If they occur as prophesied, they will profoundly affect consumption patterns in the third world.

First, new development models may upset the best forecasts. In the book *The Year* 2000, Dr. Herman Kahn and Dr. Anthony Wiener expect per-capita incomes, at the end of this century, of US$ 15,000 in the United States and US$ 500 in Brazil, in today's purchasing power. Yet, Brazil's particularly successful development model may well lift its per-capita income above US$ 1500 at the end of this century, since it is already close to US$ 500 now. On the other hand, the growing preoccupation with the quality of life, the reaction to consumerism, the new concern about the "limits of growth," and the cost of cleaning up the human environment may all translate into a U.S. per-capita income below the US$ 10,000 mark—perhaps to the satisfaction of most U.S. citizens.

Second, the gap between rich and poor countries is expressed in terms of Gross National Product, which tends to have a somewhat misleading interpretation. Statistics in the third world omit a substantial portion of the national product such as farm produce consumed on the farm, the housework of a married woman, the rental value of an owner-occupied dwelling, and earnings not disclosed to the fiscal authorities. Neither can data on Gross National Products take into consideration the economic value of climes and mores. Sunshine in Africa is free whereas Scandinavians spend a sizeable portion of their income on protection against cold, in the form of clothing, food, fuel and housing. In addition, the use of the U.S. dollar or any other reserve currency is a deceptive measurement of income because exchange rates are partly a matter of balance of trade and payments instead of a reflection of internal purchasing power.

Third, the widening gap between rich and poor countries—after rectification for the above factors—should not give rise to excessive anxiety. Some countries will no doubt enter the industrial world and will be "promoted" from UNCTAD to OECD, so to speak. This should not distract from the growing awareness that Gross National Product does not necessarily equate with gross national happiness or gross national usefulness. However great the importance of access to the basic material necessities of life—one factor that everybody must have constantly in mind —futures research into consumption patterns will have to introduce noneconomic values, such as the amenities of life.

Dr. Rodrigo Gutiérrez, a Costa Rican physiologist, hinted at this potential development— which is still a gleam in few eyes—at a seminar on "Technology, faith and the future of man," sponsored by the World Council of Churches. Somewhat utopically, Dr. Gutiérrez urged the human being to turn his gaze to the simple and fundamental things of his existence: shelter, food, clothing, education for living, and recreation. This would allow man to once again find his own fate: the gratifying of the basic and fundamental needs of his existence.

It may be opportune for those who profess a global outlook to contrast the above faraway thesis with four-color pages in *Time* magazine, picturing how affluent people bathe. *Time* pointedly reminded its readers all over the world that the Greek and Roman civilizations went down the drain when their bathing facilities reached a zenith of opulence. *Time*'s essay does not fall on deaf ears in countries that presently aspire to Cornucopia.

Fourth, international marketing executives will no doubt dismiss Dr. Gutiérrez' vision of a consumer society. Instead, they will be inclined to rely on the demonstration effect and advertising to introduce fairly modern consumption patterns into the developing countries. This is what Peter Drucker anticipates in his thesis on the global shopping center. Yet, despite man's thirst for the material goods of life, there is a growing awareness that planet earth may simply not have the ecological power to allow five or six or seven billion people to reach levels of living now prevailing in the lesser developed of the industrial countries, for example, Poland or Portugal.

Scientists Barbara Ward and René Dubos, on behalf of over 100 environmentalists, anticipate that consumption patterns will be molded, in rich and poor countries, by the dictates of ecological reality. Reluctantly they admit a threshold called the "poverty of affluence," which is also termed the tyranny of goods and services. This has induced some sociologists to confound the freedom from want with the freedom from consumption—a thesis with which world business leaders and vote-conscious political leaders are likely to disagree wholeheartedly. It does assist futures research, however, in reconciling the desirable consumption patterns with the possible consumption levels.

Fifth, in addition to ecological constraints, there are human ones. In the tradeoff between available resources and pressing human needs, many developing countries will be compelled to set priorities for consumption and production. International marketing executives may consider such priorities as an infringement upon the mechanism of free market forces as advocated by Professor Milton Friedman et al. This is so—but then economic benefits and sociopolitical costs of development (and vice versa!) cannot always be considered in the same coin. This was one of the themes at the congress of the International Chamber of Commerce in Istanbul—and a theme that futures research should be seriously concerned with.

For between the third world and ours there are environmental differences, based on climate and history and geography. In marketing —certainly in the third world—these noneconomic factors may play a growingly important role. Love and friendship, contemplation of beauty and truth, enjoyment of nature, artistic expressions, and nonpurposive behavior do not constitute part of the Gross National Product. According to Lewis Mumford, these values have been conserved in large parts of the third world, whereas, according to Alvin Toffler in "Future Shock," they are being eroded somewhat in the technetronic society as a result of affluence, technology, and urbanization. What matters is that many "consumption items" that render life meaningful are free —but on the other hand they can only be free to those Ifes and Bvanis who are no longer unemployed sick, and hungry.

To international-marketing executives, the possible development of consumption patterns in the third world constitutes both a challenge and a threat. We may not be able to reach the state of a global shopping village whereby the consumption patterns of the advanced countries are likely to be sooner or later copied in or even adapted to the third world. At the same time, entirely new vistas open up for different patterns of demand, which innovative and flexible multinational corporations may be able to meet—and which warrants on-the-spot futures research.

6. TOWARDS DIFFERENT DEVELOPMENT PATTERNS

Indeed, the basic difference between the future development pattern of the third world and the past development of our world is that they hold good for noncomparable time periods. One illustration may suffice. It happens to be in the area of industry, but it is also applicable to other fields of endeavor.

It is only 50 years ago that President Calvin Coolidge reflected the spirit of the entire Western world when he remarked that "the business of America is business." A third of a century later, a leading captain of industry spoke for most of the industrial world when he observed that "the business of business is America." That trend is visible in Europe, Japan, and in other areas too—even in the developing countries. Why?

It is likely that something went awry in the pursuit of economic growth for the sake of growth. The obnoxious by-products of "growth" proved to be a waste or underutilization of manpower and a stranger distribution of income. This has given rise to a new range of development priorities that tend to shape consumption patterns, directly or indirectly.

For instance, India's bottleneck is, inter alia, its foreign trade to finance the production goods that can manufacture massive consumption goods. This problem does not exist in oil-rich Iran—which, on the other hand, suffers from great mobility problems that hamper distribution and, therefore, consumption. Jamaica, which has fairly well solved its pressing distribution problems, faces serious unemployment, a problem that is apparently all but wiped out in China.

Sanitation no longer rates a priority in Kenya but remains a high priority in Cameroon. Guatemala and Sudan may build family planning into their national development programs—which will be absent from the ob-

jectives in Bulgaria and Uruguay. Education at all levels deserves a real priority in Morocco, a medium priority in Thailand, but no longer a priority in Trinidad.

Perhaps the most dramatic evidence that consumption patterns will be different in the third world is the fact that there consumption can be truly productive. An understanding of this complex phenomenon is essential to my central message and to our plea for interdisciplinary research into the future.

In the advanced countries, a rise in the level of living tends to have little or no effect on human productivity. People normally consume enough to maintain an optimum level of labor input and efficiency that more consumption can hardly raise, nor would a lessened consumption, within limits, reduce labor input and efficiency because the standards of nutrition are high. More and better food does not improve labor output. In fact, more and better food might lower rather than increase labor productivity.

On the other hand, for the largest portion of people in Asia, Latin America and Africa, even today's calorie, vitamin, and protein intake is wholly inadequate to reach and maintain optimum levels of health, energy, and labor productivity. Undernourishment and malnutrition, from which two-thirds of people in the developing countries suffer, reduce labor input and productivity. The same fact is true for sanitation and education. The general mortality rate is falling rapidly as a result of medical care. However, the frequency of illnesses lowers the stamina and the energy, and reduces the resistance to disease. All this affects productivity negatively. There is, therefore, a very pronounced correlation between consumption and production.

This focus on consumption is fairly new in the third world. A case in point is Mexico. Twenty years of uninterrupted high rates of economic growth and monetary stability have almost quadrupled its Gross National Product but in the process the proportion of marginal consumers (partly outside the modern economy) rose. Marginal consumers now consist of 40 to 50 percent of the population. In other words, substantial emphasis on modernization may have relatively worsened the consumption capacity in half the country. Now the government reverses the pattern. It seems bent on integrating—through employment, consumption and fiscal measures—the marginated population into the mechanism of consumption.

What we witness is a new trend from pure economic growth and development—in the classical sense—toward human growth and development.

7. THE MANAGEMENT OF CONSUMPTION

This new trend—the reversal of an existing one—is likely to astonish or perplex many international marketing executives. They may be challenged by the numerically huge, essentially consumer-oriented third world that experiences a fast growth albeit from a small base. On the other hand, relatively poor countries shrug off development models that met with an astounding success in the United States and Europe and instead experiment with new models in which economic policies are mixed with human needs and emotional attitudes.

Yet, on close scrutiny, we find that many developing countries face limited options. It is entirely different to manage consumption under conditions of abundance or scarcity. Many developing countries that "imported" Western development models discovered that, notwithstanding an overall success, this process gave rise to the emergence of a modern urban enclave in a generally backward rural country.

It was no doubt the avowed aim of the policy makers and the marketers to gradually widen the enclave geographically and horizontally—and to penetrate the lower masses vertically. The practical experience of some high-growth countries such as Brazil and Mexico, and even Spain and South Africa, is that it may be neither feasible nor desirable to extrapolate this apparently successful model of economic growth. This awareness has been spurred by the effects of prosperity on the resource utilization and the human environment in North America, Europe, and Japan.

It may be up to the young and not-so-young entrepreneurs, politicians, and economists of the developing countries to start their thinking on the management of resources, and on consumption, afresh. They will have to muster the courage to discard, where necessary, blatantly inadequate doctrines and theoretical approaches. Above all they may wish to remember that when the now-industrialized countries were in their own takeoff stage—back in 1870 or 1910 or 1930—they did not have to deal with population explosion, mass com-

munications, the revolution of rising expectations, degradation of biosystem and ecosphere, burgeoning world trade, United Nations agencies, and very stringent social legislation. To the contrary, the countries that take off in the 1970s must build most of these environmental factors into their management of consumption under conditions of scarcity.

In the above task, foreign firms and intergovernmental agencies can play a catalytic and rewarding role. Dr. Mahbub Ul Haq, senior economic advisor to the World Bank, provides us with one example of such a role. He anticipates that more-stringent controls over pollution in the rich countries may tend to drive out such industries as petroleum refining, chemicals, metal extracting and processing, and paper and pulp, to the huge open and sparsely populated spaces of the third world. This would present a considerable opportunity to the developing countries that, at this stage of their development, may argue that employment and exports must take precedence over the environment.

Similarly at the Ottawa world conference of the Society for International Development, I urged the affluent countries to move their labor-intensive industries to the developing countries where rampant unemployment threatens to play havoc with political world equilibrium. The resulting redundant labor in North America and other areas could be trained to employment of much higher caliber. Socially, the removal of industry from rich to poor countries seems a more compensating solution than the wholesale migration of blue-collar workers from developing to advanced countries — as is presently practiced in Europe.

The above two suggestions are only illustrative examples of what interdisciplinary futures research may come up with. What we search for is a modus vivendi—a reconcilement of the positive and dynamic elements in our own development strategy (hygiene, education, mass food production, modern management, and technology) with the pressing requirements of employment, income distribution, and rural modernization in order to ensure the satisfaction of the basic requirements of a decent life in half our world. This, too, can be illustrated very briefly.

From the picture of the Ifes and the Bvanis it becomes crystal clear that the greatest transformation is bound to occur in the daily diet. Today diet is monotonous and wholly inadequate and sometimes unhealthy. In managing future consumption patterns in foods, multinational corporations and government agencies can be guided by the Food and Agricultural Organization's avant-garde magazine *Ceres* and the FAO/Industry Cooperative Programme. They constitute, among other things, suitable platforms for futures research.

Another area for managed change is housing. Many people in the third world live in poorly built, overcrowded, unsanitary, and scantily furnished dwellings that become a social ill when they constitute urban slums whether they are called favelas, shantytowns, bidonvilles, or barriadas. Water and sewage facilities are inadequate; fresh air and light can be scarce. This may not be true in the rural areas, but housing there is often blended with animal life—a mixed blessing.

Housing in the third world thus presents one typical example of what is called "cumulative causation": lack of productivity for lack of education for lack of light. Most villages are indeed dark after sunset. Even if they could read and had newspapers and books, adults would be often incapable of reading for want of light. After food and sanitation, adult education is a pressing priority. Although it can hardly widen employment in the short term, it is likely to increase productivity substantially. In addition, the social impact of adult literacy is deep, as witnessed by the satisfaction and delight of adults who after half a lifetime of illiteracy suddenly discover that they can read and write.

The reversal of priorities has an endless number of multiplying factors. The most visible result may be a chain reaction in other areas of consumption, such as agricultural implements, construction materials, transportation, textiles, and paper and household goods. Less visibly, priority reversal will create accelerating demands for a wide array of intermediate and capital goods for mass markets. The practical implication of the reversal of the existing trend to international marketing executives and government agencies will emerge from interdisciplinary futures research—which is the hard core of our recommendation.

8. INTERDISCIPLINARY FUTURES RESEARCH

Multinational corporations, intergovernmental organizations, and universities and foundations may indeed find a common denominator for futures research. This function can be performed by the so-called taxonomic appraisal, recently developed by Dr. F. H. Harbison et al. for Princeton University. Previously, similar analyses had been worked out by Marketing Science Institute, the Organization for Economic Cooperation and Development, and Columbia University. In fact, eight years ago I used a comparable method in futures research for CPC International, Inc.

In a nutshell, this method allows researchers to anticipate the degree of development of the third world in accordance with many criteria of economic, social, technical, and cultural nature, which can be interrelated. Causal relationships do not always emerge, however. Yet it is the correlation between a wide range of different measurements that allows the "reading" of the relative future development of a country.

Of course, the objectives of the research determine the selection of pertinent criteria: agriculture, development, finance, industry, labor, leisure, services, and trade. Communications, construction, manufacturing, and mobility—to name but a few "consumption" areas that affect virtually all corporations—can thus be translated into the potential demand for a given product or service. The causal relationships have the same feedback —greatly simplified, however— as stated in Professor Jay Forrester's "systems dynamics" upon which the Club of Rome had its "limits of growth" construed. In fact, the feedback follows Dr. Barry Commoner's first law of ecology: that everything is connected with everything.

Many correlations are obvious. We acknowledge that consumption determines productivity; sanitation affects family size and longevity; urbanization has an impact on work and leisure; energy affects literacy; literacy in turn determines productivity; roads widen the consumption of foods; taboos restrict the diet; and sunshine, proximity to the sea, distribution of population, and natural resources determine consumption patterns of food, textiles, and housing. A cross-linkage of these data allows a fairly reliable forecast for the demand of, for example, animal feeds, bicycles, cement, contraceptives, lamp bulbs, milk, paper, soap, starch, and tractors.

After all, we also detect a tendency in the affluent societies whereby more and more the consumers dictate, or at least influence, what the producers will manufacture or service. Such moves are also, albeit in a still-insipid, manner, on the horizon of developing areas, for example:

Ford Motor Company's low-cost automobile, specially developed for the rugged terrain and economy of Asia; Honda's marketing of a two-wheeled, walk-behind tractor competing economically with oxen and ploughs; British Petroleum's conversion of petroleum into yeast proteins for low-cost foods; and Philips' pilot factory, scaled down to the level of manpower, technology, and market size of the lesser developed nations. International food companies, experienced in freeze-drying in their sophisticated markets, successfully engage in sun-drying in African countries. In China, a plant manufactures fertilizers and insecticides out of the liquid waste of a nearby paper factory. The use of sugar-cane waste for paper making in Peru is another illustration of a trend that may snowball—once a deeper understanding of the giant yet peculiar opportunities of the developing countries emerges from pragmatical futures research.

This is the central suggestion to business leaders, politicians and planners in the United States, the Soviet Union, the enlarged European Economic Community, Japan, Canada, and other advanced countries: to adapt, where necessary and possible, their product mix and marketing techniques and financial aid, in fact the sum total of their approach, to the inevitably changing priorities of the third world. To this end, interdisciplinary research may be *sine qua non*.

Presently, thousands of research assignments into (future) consumption patterns of the third world are undertaken by foundations, multinational corporations, intergovernmental agencies, and universities. Many as-signments reach publication. Yet not enough of them seem to penetrate effectively the powers of decision, especially in the private sector. In order to ensure action, two proposals are put forward:

One, to cross-communicate and cross-fertilize, between public and private sectors, non-confidential research into consumption of the third world, if possible through an existing international clearing house of such information.

Two, to fund and initiate future oriented-research as much as possible on a truly interdisciplinary basis, for example, the FAO/Industry Cooperative Programme that sends mixed teams of experts into developing countries to study specific projects that fit into the priorities and absorption power of the host countries.

To sum up: we expect that it may become necessary and possible for pragmatical business executives and down-to-earth politicians and international civil servants to work effectively in conjunction with future-oriented scientists of many disciplines. In order to unleash this catalytic force, we should all be imbued with the concept and vision of the late U.S. statesman Adlai Stevenson:

We travel together, passengers on a little spaceship dependent on its vulnerable reserves of air and soil; all committed for our safety to its security and peace; preserved from annihilation only by the care, the work and the love we give our fragile craft. We cannot maintain it half fortunate, half miserable; half confident, half despairing; half slave of the ancient enemies of man, half free in a liberation of resources undreamed of until this day. No craft, no crew can safely travel with such vast contradictions.

Buyer Behavior-Household and Industrial

A great deal of the marketing effort is focused on the buyer in an attempt to persuade him and her to buy a specific product or service. A prerequisite to doing an efficient marketing job is the understanding of buyer behavior. This is true, of course, for the industrial and institutional buyer as it is for the household buyer. An enormous amount of buyer research is performed each year in an effort to learn a bit more about the buyer.

Six readings have been selected from among hundreds that are available. Philip Kotler presents five models that show different conceptions of how the buyer translates buying influences into purchases. These five models illustrate the complexity as well as the diversity of the buying process.

Broad questions of social classes are raised by Pierre Martineau. These classes have their psychological differences and their differences in consumption and buying patterns. Though Martineau's work was performed some years ago it remains a classic in its field. Another approach to understanding buyer behavior is to examine the buyer's referents—the people to whom the buyer refers in various ways. James Stafford develops the concept of reference theory as related to buyer decisions.

Marketers have studied buyers in every way they thought made sense. One of the attempts has included the study of personality in the hopes that buyer behavior would relate to personality types. However, Harold Kassarjian concludes that personality studies have been equivocal. A more-recent psychological development has been life-style analysis or psychographics. William Wells distinguishes between these terms and then discusses seven questions about their utilization by marketers.

William Yoell points out some of the difficulties in studying the buyer. Marketers would like an easy way to identify kinds of buyers, but is it possible to answer buyer behavior questions without studying the complete and total behavior of the individual? This is one of the questions discussed in this reading.

Since the professional buyer in government, institutions, and industry would be expected to behave quite differently than household buyers, two selections have been included to shed some light on the nonhousehold buyer. Frederick Webster and Yoram Wind, who have made a number of studies of the industrial buyer, present a model of industrial buyer behavior and show how buying takes place within a formal organization such as the business firm. Patrick Robinson includes a conceptual framework as an aid to understanding industrial buyer behavior and also illustrates the buying action with a study of a specific item.

The selections on household and industrial buying behavior are meant to be sufficiently varied so that they present a good idea of the challenge to the marketer in understanding as much as possible about the buyers whom he hopes to persuade in today's marketing place.

I. The Household Consumer

23. Behavioral Models for Analyzing Buyers

PHILIP KOTLER

In times past, management could arrive at a fair understanding of its buyers through the daily experience of selling to them. But the growth in the size of firms and markets has removed many decision-makers from direct contact with buyers. Increasingly, decision-makers have had to turn to summary statistics and to behavioral theory, and are spending more money today than ever before to try to understand their buyers.

Who buys? How do they buy? And why? The first two questions relate to relatively overt aspects of buyer behavior, and can be learned about through direct observation and interviewing.

But uncovering *why* people buy is an extremely difficult task. The answer will tend to vary with the investigator's behavioral frame of reference.

The buyer is subject to many influences which trace a complex course through his psyche, and lead eventually to overt purchasing responses. This conception of the buying process is illustrated in Fig. 1. Various influences and their modes of transmission are shown at the left. At the right are the buyer's responses in choice of product, brand, dealer, quantities, and frequency. In the center stand the buyer and his mysterious psychological processes. The buyer's psyche is a "black box" whose workings can be only partially deduced. The marketing strategist's challenge to the behavioral scientist is to construct a more

specific model of the mechanism in the black box.

Unfortunately no generally accepted model of the mechanism exists. The human mind, the only entity in nature with deep powers of understanding, still remains the least understood. Scientists can explain planetary motion, genetic determination, and molecular behavior. Yet they have only partial, and often partisan, models of *human* behavior.

Nevertheless, the marketing strategist should recognize the potential interpretative contributions of different partial models for explaining buyer behavior. Depending upon the product, different variables and behavioral mechanisms may assume particular importance. A psychoanalytic behavioral model might throw much light on the factors operating in cigarette demand, while an economic behavioral model might be useful in explaining machine-tool purchasing. Sometimes alternative models may shed light on different demand aspects of the same product.

What are the most useful behavioral models for interpreting the transformation of buying influences into purchasing responses? Five different models of the buyer's "black box" are presented in the present article, along with their respective marketing applications: (1) The Marshallian model, stressing economic motivations; (2) The Pavlovian model, learning; (3) the Freudian model, psychoanalytic motivations; (4) the Veblenian model, social-psychological factors; and (5) the Hobbesian model, organizational factors. These models represent radically different conceptions of the mainsprings of human behavior.

◆ SOURCE: Reprinted by permission from the *Journal of Marketing* (National Quarterly Publication of the American Marketing Association), Vol. 29, No. 4, October 1965, pp. 37–45.

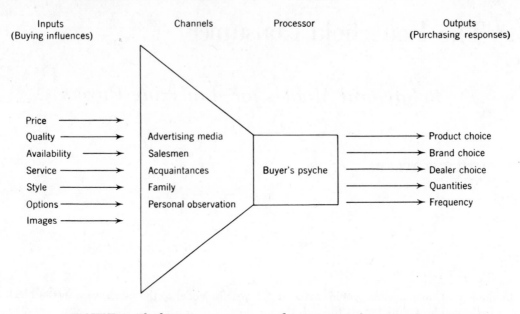

FIGURE 1. The buying process conceived as a system of inputs and outputs.

THE MARSHALLIAN ECONOMIC MODEL

Economists were the first professional group to construct a specific theory of buyer behavior. The theory holds that purchasing decisions are the result of largely "rational" and conscious economic calculations. The individual buyer seeks to spend his income on those goods that will deliver the most utility (satisfaction) according to his tastes and relative prices.

The antecedents for this view trace back to the writings of Adam Smith and Jeremy Bentham. Smith set the tone by developing a doctrine of economic growth based on the principle that man is motivated by self-interest in all his actions.[1] Bentham refined this view and saw man as finely calculating and weighing the expected pleasures and pains of every contemplated action.[2]

Bentham's "felicific calculus" was not applied to consumer behavior (as opposed to entrepreneurial behavior) until the late 19th century. Then, the "marginal-utility" theory of value was formulated independently and almost simultaneously by Jevons[3] and Marshall[4] in England, Menger[5] in Austria, and Walras[6] in Switzerland.

Alfred Marshall was the great consolidator of the classical and neoclassical tradition in economics; and his synthesis in the form of demand-supply analysis constitutes the main source of modern micro-economic thought in the English-speaking world. His theoretical work aimed at realism, but his method was to start with simplifying assumptions and to examine the effect of a change in a single variable (say, price) when all other variables were held constant.

He would "reason out" the consequences of the provisional assumptions and in subsequent steps modify his assumptions in the direction of more realism. He employed the "measuring rod of money" as an indicator of the intensity of human psychological desires. Over the years his methods and assumptions have been refined into what is now known as *modern utility theory*: economic man is bent on maximizing his utility, and does this by carefully calculating the "felicific" consequences of any purchase.

---

[1] Adam Smith, *An Inquiry into the Nature and Causes of the Wealth of Nations*, 1776 (New York: The Modern Library, 1937).

[2] Jeremy Bentham, *An Introduction to the Principles of Morals and Legislation*, 1780 (Oxford, England: Clarendon Press, 1907).

[3] William S. Jevons, *The Theory of Political Economy* (New York: The Macmillan Company, 1871).

[4] Alfred Marshall, *Principles of Economics*, 1890 (London: The Macmillan Company, 1927).

[5] Karl Menger, *Principles of Economics*, 1871 (Glencoe, Illinois: Free Press, 1950).

[6] Leon Walras, *Elements of Pure Economics*, 1874 (Homewood, Illinois: Richard D. Irwin, Inc., 1954).

As an example, suppose on a particular evening that John is considering whether to prepare his own dinner or dine out. He estimates that a restaurant meal would cost $2.00 and a home-cooked meal 50 cents. According to the Marshallian model, if John expects less than four times as much satisfaction from the restaurant meal as the home-cooked meal, he will eat at home. The economist typically is not concerned with how these relative preferences are formed by John, or how they may be psychologically modified by new stimuli.

Yet John will not always cook at home. The principle of diminishing marginal utility operates. Within a given time interval—say, a week—the utility of each additional home-cooked meal diminishes. John gets tired of home meals and other products become relatively more attractive.

John's *efficiency* in maximizing his utility depends on the adequacy of his information and his freedom of choice. If he is not perfectly aware of costs, if he misestimates the relative delectability of the two meals, or if he is barred from entering the restaurant, he will not maximize his potential utility. His choice processes are rational, but the results are inefficient.

Marketing Applications of Marshallian Model

Marketers usually have dismissed the Marshallian model as an absurd figment of ivory-tower imagination. Certainly the behavioral essence of the situation is omitted, in viewing man as calculating the marginal utility of a restaurant meal over a home-cooked meal.

Eva Mueller has reported a study where only one-fourth of the consumers in her sample bought with any substantial degree of deliberation.[7] Yet there are a number of ways to view the model.

From one point of view the Marshallian model is tautological and therefore neither true nor false. The model holds that the buyer acts in the light of his best "interest." But this is not very informative.

A second view is that this is a *normative* rather than a *descriptive* model of behavior. The model provides logical norms for buyers who want to be "rational." Although the consumer is not likely to employ economic analysis to decide between a box of Kleenex and Scotties, he may apply economic analysis in deciding whether to buy a new car. Industrial buyers even more clearly would want an economic calculus for making good decisions.

A third view is that economic factors operate to a greater or lesser extent in all markets, and, therefore, must be included in any comprehensive description of buyer behavior.

Furthermore, the model suggests useful behavioral hypotheses such as: (a) The lower the price of the product, the higher the sales. (b) The lower the price of substitute products, the lower the sales of this product; and the lower the price of complementary products, the higher the sales of this product. (c) The higher the real income, the higher the sales of this product, provided that it is not an "inferior" good. (d) The higher the promotional expenditures, the higher the sales.

The validity of these hypotheses does not rest on whether *all* individuals act as economic calculating machines in making their purchasing decisions. For example, some individuals may buy *less* of a product when its price is reduced. They may think that the quality has gone down, or that ownership has less status value. If a majority of buyers view price reductions negatively, then sales may fall, contrary to the first hypothesis.

But for most goods a price reduction increases the relative value of the goods in many buyers' minds and leads to increased sales. This and the other hypotheses are intended to describe average effects.

The impact of economic factors in actual buying situations is studied through experimental design or statistical analyses of past data. Demand equations have been fitted to a wide variety of products—including beer, refrigerators, and chemical fertilizers.[8] More recently, the impact of economic variables on the fortunes of different brands has been pursued with significant results, particularly in the case of coffee, frozen orange juice, and margarine.[9]

But economic factors alone cannot explain all the variations in sales. The Marshallian model ignores the fundamental question of

[7] Eva Mueller, "A Study of Purchase Decisions," Part 2, *Consumer Behavior, The Dynamics of Consumer Reaction*, edited by Lincoln H. Clark (New York: New York University Press, 1954), pp. 36–87.

[8] See Erwin E. Nemmers, *Managerial Economics* (New York: Wiley, 1962), Part II.

[9] See Lester G. Telser, "The Demand for Branded Goods as Estimated from Consumer Panel Data," *Review of Economics and Statistics*, Vol. 44 (August, 1962), pp. 300–324; and William F. Massy and Ronald E. Frank, "Short Term Price and Dealing Effects in Selected Market Segments, *Journal of Marketing Research*, Vol. 2 (May, 1965), pp. 171–185.

how product and brand preferences are formed. It represents a useful frame of reference for analyzing only one small corner of the "black box."

THE PAVLOVIAN LEARNING MODEL

The designation of a Pavlovian learning model has its origin in the experiments of the Russian psychologist Pavlov, who rang a bell each time before feeding a dog. Soon he was able to induce the dog to salivate by ringing the bell whether or not food was supplied. Pavlov concluded that learning was largely an associative process and that a large component of behavior was conditioned in this way.

Experimental psychologists have continued this mode of research with rats and other animals, including people. Laboratory experiments have been designed to explore such phenomena as learning, forgetting, and the ability to discriminate. The results have been integrated into a stimulus-response model of human behavior, or as someone has "wisecracked," the substitution of a rat psychology for a rational psychology.

The model has been refined over the years, and today is based on four central concepts—those of *drive, cue, response,* and *reinforcement.*[10]

Drive. Also called needs or motives, drive refers to strong stimuli internal to the individual which impels action. Psychologists draw a distinction between primary physiological drives—such as hunger, thirst, cold, pain, and sex—and learned drives which are derived socially—such as cooperation, fear, and acquisitiveness.

Cue. A drive is very general and impels a particular response only in relation to a particular configuration of cues. Cues are weaker stimuli in the environment and/or in the individual which determine when, where, and how the subject responds. Thus, a coffee advertisement can serve as a cue which stimulates the thirst drive in a housewife. Her response will depend upon this cue and other cues, such as the time of day, the availability of other thirst-quenchers, and the cue's intensity. Often a relative change in a cue's intensity can be more impelling than its absolute level. The housewife may be more motivated by a 2-cents-off sale on a brand of coffee than

the fact that this brand's price was low in the first place.

Response. The response is the organism's reaction to the configuration of cues. Yet the same configuration of cues will not necessarily produce the same response in the individual. This depends on the degree to which the experience was rewarding, that is, drive-reducing.

Reinforcement. If the experience is rewarding, a particular response is reinforced; that is, it is strengthened and there is a tendency for it to be repeated when the same configuration of cues appears again. The housewife, for example, will tend to purchase the same brand of coffee each time she goes to her supermarket so long as it is rewarding and the cue configuration does not change. But if a learned response or habit is not reinforced, the strength of the habit diminishes and may be extinguished eventually. Thus, a housewife's preference for a certain coffee may become extinct if she finds the brand out of stock for a number of weeks.

Forgetting, in contrast to extinction, is the tendency for learned associations to weaken, not because of the lack of reinforcement but because of nonuse.

Cue configurations are constantly changing. The housewife sees a new brand of coffee next to her habitual brand, or notes a special price deal on a rival brand. Experimental psychologists have found that the same learned response will be elicited by similar patterns of cues; that is, learned responses are *generalized.* The housewife shifts to a similar brand when her favorite brand is out of stock. This tendency toward generalization over less similar cue configurations is increased in proportion to the strength of the drive. A housewife may buy an inferior coffee if it is the only brand left and if her drive is sufficiently strong.

A counter-tendency to generalization is *discrimination.* When a housewife tries two similar brands and finds one more rewarding, her ability to discriminate between similar cue configurations improves. Discrimination increases the specificity of the cue-response connection, while generalization decreases the specificity.

Marketing Applications of Pavlovian Model

The modern version of the Pavlovian model makes no claim to provide a complete theory

---

[10] See John Dollard and Neal E. Miller, *Personality and Psychotherapy* (New York: McGraw-Hill, 1950), Chapter III.

of behavior—indeed, such important phenomena as perception, the subconscious, and interpersonal influence are inadequately treated. Yet the model does offer a substantial number of insights about some aspects of behavior of considerable interest to marketers.[11]

An example would be in the problem of introducing a new brand into a highly competitive market. The company's goal is to extinguish existing brand habits and form new habits among consumers for its brand. But the company must first get customers to try its brand; and it has to decide between using weak and strong cues.

Light introductory advertising is a weak cue compared with distributing free samples. Strong cues, although costing more, may be necessary in markets characterized by strong brand loyalties. For example, Folger went into the coffee market by distributing over a million pounds of free coffee.

To build a brand habit, it helps to provide for an extended period of introductory dealing. Furthermore, sufficient quality must be built into the brand so that the experience is reinforcing. Since buyers are more likely to transfer allegiance to similar brands than dissimilar brands (generalization), the company should also investigate what cues in the leading brands have been most effective. Although outright imitation would not necessarily effect the most transference, the question of providing enough similarity should be considered.

The Pavlovian model also provides guide lines in the area of advertising strategy. The American behaviorist, John B. Watson, was a great exponent of repetitive stimuli; in his writings man is viewed as a creature who can be conditioned through repetition and reinforcement to respond in particular ways.[12] The Pavlovian model emphasizes the desirability of repetition in advertising. A single exposure is likely to be a very weak cue, hardly able to penetrate the individual's consciousness sufficiently to excite his drives above the threshold level.

Repetition in advertising has two desirable

effects. It "fights" forgetting, the tendency for learned response to weaken in the absence of practice. It provides reinforcement, because after the purchase the consumer becomes selectively exposed to advertisements of the product.

The model also provides guide lines for copy strategy. To be effective as a cue, an advertisement must arouse strong drives in the person. The strongest product-related drives must be identified. For candy bars, it may be hunger; for safety belts, fear; for hair tonics, sex; for automobiles, status. The advertising practitioner must dip into his cue box—words, colors, pictures—and select that configuration of cues that provides the strongest stimulus to these drives.

THE FREUDIAN PSYCHOANALYTIC MODEL

The Freudian model of man is well known, so profound has been its impact on 20th century thought. It is the latest of a series of philosophical "blows" to which man has been exposed in the last 500 years. Copernicus destroyed the idea that man stood at the center of the universe; Darwin tried to refute the idea that man was a special creation; and Freud attacked the idea that man even reigned over his own psyche.

According to Freud, the child enters the world driven by instinctual needs which he cannot gratify by himself. Very quickly and painfully he realizes his separateness from the rest of the world and yet his dependence on it.

He tries to get others to gratify his needs through a variety of blatant means, including intimidation and supplication. Continual frustration leads him to perfect more subtle mechanisms for gratifying his instincts.

As he grows, his psyche becomes increasingly complex. A part of his psyche—the id—remains the reservoir of his strong drives and urges. Another part—the ego—becomes his conscious planning center for finding outlets for his drives. And a third part—his super-ego—channels his instinctive drives into socially approved outlets to avoid the pain of guilt or shame.

The guilt or shame which man feels toward some of his urges—especially his sexual urges—causes him to repress them from his consciousness. Through such defense mechanisms as rationalization and sublimation, these urges are denied or become transmuted into socially

---

[11] The most consistent application of learning-theory concepts to marketing situations is found in John A. Howard, *Marketing Management: Analysis and Planning* (Homewood, Illinois: Richard D. Irwin, Inc., revised edition, 1963).

[12] John B. Watson, Behaviorism (New York: The People's Institute Publishing Company, 1925).

approved expressions. Yet these urges are never eliminated or under perfect control; and they emerge, sometimes with a vengeance, in dreams, in slips-of-the-tongue, in neurotic and obsessional behavior, or ultimately in mental breakdown where the ego can no longer maintain the delicate balance between the impulsive power of the id and the oppressive power of the super-ego.

The individual's behavior, therefore, is never simple. His motivational wellsprings are not obvious to a casual observer nor deeply understood by the individual himself. If he is asked why he purchased an expensive foreign sportscar, he may reply that he likes its maneuverability and its looks. At a deeper level he may have purchased the car to impress others, or to feel young again. At a still deeper level, he may be purchasing the sportscar to achieve substitute gratification for unsatisfied sexual strivings.

Many refinements and changes in emphasis have occurred in this model since the time of Freud. The instinct concept has been replaced by a more careful delineation of basic drives; the three parts of the psyche are regarded now as theoretical concepts rather than actual entities; and the behavioral perspective has been extended to include cultural as well as biological mechanisms.

Instead of the role of the sexual urge in psychic development—Freud's discussion of oral, anal, and genital stages and possible fixations and traumas—Adler[13] emphasized the urge for power and how its thwarting manifests itself in superiority and inferiority complexes; Horney[14] emphasized cultural mechanisms; and Fromm[15] and Erikson[16] emphasized the role of existential crises in personality development. These philosophical divergencies, rather than debilitating the model, have enriched and extended its interpretative value to a wider range of behavioral phenomena.

Marketing Applications of Freudian Model

Perhaps the most important marketing implication of this model is that buyers are motivated by *symbolic* as well as *economic-functional* product concerns. The change of a bar of soap from a square to a round shape may be more important in its sexual than its functional connotations. A cake mix that is advertised as involving practically no labor may alienate housewives because the easy life may evoke a sense of guilt.

Motivational research has produced some interesting and occasionally some bizarre hypotheses about what may be in the buyer's mind regarding certain purchases. Thus, it has been suggested at one time or another that:

1. Many a businessman doesn't fly because of a fear of posthumous guilt—if he crashed, his wife would think of him as stupid for not taking a train.

2. Men want their cigars to be odoriferous, in order to prove that they (the men) are masculine.

3. A woman is very serious when she bakes a cake because unconsciously she is going through the symbolic act of giving birth.

4. A man buys a convertible as a substitute "mistress."

5. Consumers prefer vegetable shortening because animal fats stimulate a sense of sin.

6. Men who wear suspenders are reacting to an unresolved castration complex.

There are admitted difficulties of proving these assertions. Two prominent motivational researchers, Ernest Dichter and James Vicary, were employed independently by two separate groups in the prune industry to determine why so many people dislike prunes. Dichter found, among other things, that the prune aroused feelings of old age and insecurity in people, whereas Vicary's main finding was that Americans had an emotional block about prunes' laxative qualities.[17] Which is the more valid interpretation? Or if they are both operative, which motive is found with greater statistical frequency in the population?

Unfortunately the usual survey techniques —direct observation and interviewing—can be used to establish the representativeness of more superficial characteristics—age and family size, for example—but are not feasible for establishing the frequency of mental states

---

[13] Alfred Adler, *The Science of Living* (New York: Greenberg, 1929).

[14] Karen Horney, *The Neurotic Personality of Our Time* (New York: Norton, 1937).

[15] Erich Fromm, *Man For Himself* (New York: Holt, Rinehart & Winston, 1947).

[16] Erik Erikson, *Childhood and Society* (New York: Norton, 1949).

[17] L. Edward Scriven, "Rationality and Irrationality in Motivation Research," in Robert Ferber and Hugh G. Wales, editors, *Motivation and Marketing Behavior* (Homewood, Illinois: Richard D. Irwin, Inc., 1958), pp. 69–70.

which are presumed to be deeply "buried" within each individual.

Motivational researchers have to employ time-consuming projective techniques in the hope of throwing individual "egos" off guard. When carefully administered and interpreted, techniques such as word association, sentence completion, picture interpretation, and role-playing can provide some insights into the minds of the small group of examined individuals; but a "leap of faith" is sometimes necessary to generalize these findings to the population.

Nevertheless, motivation research can lead to useful insights and provide inspiration to creative men in the advertising and packaging world. Appeals aimed at the buyer's private world of hopes, dreams, and fears can often be as effective in stimulating purchase as more rationally-directed appeals.

THE VEBLENIAN SOCIAL-PSYCHOLOGICAL MODEL

While most economists have been content to interpret buyer behavior in Marshallian terms, Thorstein Veblen struck out in different directions.

Veblen was trained as an orthodox economist, but evolved into a social thinker greatly influenced by the new science of social anthropology. He saw man as primarily a *social animal*—conforming to the general forms and norms of his larger culture and to the more specific standards of the subcultures and face-to-face groupings to which his life is bound. His wants and behavior are largely molded by his present group-memberships and his aspired group-memberships.

Veblen's best-known example of this is in his description of the leisure class.[18] His hypothesis is that much of economic consumption is motivated not by intrinsic needs or satisfaction so much as by prestige-seeking. He emphasized the strong emulative factors operating in the choice of conspicuous goods like clothes, cars, and houses.

Some of his points, however, seem overstated by today's perspective. The leisure class does not serve as everyone's reference group; many persons aspire to the social patterns of the class immediately above it. And important segments of the affluent class practice conspicuous underconsumption rather than over-

consumption. There are many people in all classes who are more anxious to "fit in" than to "stand out." As an example, William H. Whyte found that many families avoided buying air conditioners and other appliances before their neighbors did.[19]

Veblen was not the first nor the only investigator to comment on social influences in behavior; but the incisive quality of his observations did much to stimulate further investigations. Another stimulus came from Karl Marx, who held that each man's world-view was determined largely by his relationship to the "means of production."[20] The early field-work in primitive societies by social anthropologists like Boas[21] and Malinowski[22] and the later field-work in urban societies by men like Park[23] and Thomas[24] contributed much to understanding the influence of society and culture. The research of early Gestalt psychologists—men like Wertheimer,[25] Köhler,[26] and Koffka[27]—into the mechanisms of perception led eventually to investigations of small-group influence on perception.

Marketing Applications of Veblenian Model

The various streams of thought crystallized into the modern social sciences of sociology, cultural anthropology, and social psychology. Basic to them is the view that man's attitudes and behavior are influenced by several levels of society—culture, subcultures, social classes, reference groups, and face-to-face groups. The challenge to the marketer is to determine which of these social levels are the most important in influencing the demand for his product.

[18] Thorstein Veblen, *The Theory of the Leisure Class* (New York: Macmillan, 1899).

[19] William H. Whyte, Jr., "The Web of Word of Mouth," *Fortune*, Vol. 50 (November, 1954), pp. 140 ff.

[20] Karl Marx, *The Communist Manifesto*, 1848 (London: Martin Lawrence, Ltd., 1934).

[21] Franz Boas, *The Mind of Primitive Man* (New York: Macmillan, 1922).

[22] Bronislaw Malinowski, *Sex and Repression in Savage Society* (New York: Meridian Books, 1955).

[23] Robert E. Park, *Human Communities* (Glencoe, Illinois: Free Press, 1952).

[24] William I. Thomas, *The Unadjusted Girl* (Boston: Little, Brown, 1928).

[25] Max Wertheimer, *Productive Thinking* (New York: Harper & Brothers, 1945).

[26] Wolfgang Köhler, *Gestalt Psychology* (New York: Liveright Publishing Co., 1947).

[27] Kurt Koffka, *Principles of Gestalt Psychology* (New York: Harcourt, Brace, 1935).

Culture

The most enduring influences are from culture. Man tends to assimilate his culture's mores and folkways, and to believe in their absolute rightness until deviants appear within his culture or until he confronts members of another culture.

Subcultures

A culture tends to lose its homogeneity as its population increases. When people no longer are able to maintain face-to-face relationships with more than a small proportion of other members of a culture, smaller units or subcultures develop, which help to satisfy the individual's needs for more specific identity.

The subcultures are often regional entities, because the people of a region, as a result of more frequent interactions, tend to think and act alike. But subcultures also take the form of religions, nationalities, fraternal orders, and other institutional complexes which provide a broad identification for people who may otherwise be strangers. The subcultures of a person play a large role in his attitude formation and become another important predictor of certain values he is likely to hold.

Social Class

People become differentiated not only horizontally but also vertically through a division of labor. The society becomes stratified socially on the basis of wealth, skill, and power. Sometimes castes develop in which the members are reared for certain roles, or social classes develop in which the members feel empathy with others sharing similar values and economic circumstances.

Because social class involves different attitudinal configurations, it becomes a useful independent variable for segmenting markets and predicting reactions. Significant differences have been found among different social classes with respect to magazine readership, leisure activities, food imagery, fashion interests, and acceptance of innovations. A sampling of attitudinal differences in class is the following:

Members of the *upper-middle* class place an emphasis on professional competence; indulge in expensive status symbols; and more often than not show a taste, real or otherwise, for theater and the arts. They want their children to show high achievement and precocity

and develop into physicists, vice-presidents, and judges. This class likes to deal in ideas and symbols.

Members of the *lower-middle* class cherish respectability, savings, a college education, and good housekeeping. They want their children to show self-control and prepare for careers as accountants, lawyers, and engineers.

Members of the *upper-lower* class try to keep up with the times, if not with the Joneses. They stay in older neighborhoods but buy new kitchen applicances. They spend proportionately less than the middle class on major clothing articles, buying a new suit mainly for an important ceremonial occasion. They also spend proportionately less on services, preferring to do their own plumbing and other work around the house. They tend to raise large families and their children generally enter manual occupations. This class also supplies many local businessmen, politicians, sports stars, and labor-union leaders.

Reference Groups

There are groups in which the individual has no membership but with which he identifies and may aspire to—reference groups. Many young boys identify with big-league baseball players or astronauts, and many young girls identify with Hollywood stars. The activities of these popular heroes are carefully watched and frequently imitated. These reference figures become important transmitters of influence, although more along lines of taste and hobby than basic attitudes.

Face-to-face Groups

Groups that have the most immediate influence on a person's tastes and opinions are face-to-face groups. This includes all the small "societies" with which he comes into frequent contact: his family, close friends, neighbors, fellow workers, fraternal associates, and so forth. His informal group memberships are influenced largely by his occupation, residence, and stage in the life cycle.

The powerful influence of small groups on individual attitudes has been demonstrated in a number of social psychological experiments.[28] There is also evidence that this influence may be growing. David Reisman and his coauthors have pointed to signs which

---

[28] See, for example, Solomon E. Asch, "Effects of Group Pressure Upon the Modification & Distortion of Judgments," in Dorwin Cartwright and

indicate a growing amount of *other-direction,* that is, a tendency for individuals to be increasingly influenced by their peers in the definition of their values rather than by their parents and elders.[29]

For the marketer, this means that brand choice may increasingly be influenced by one's peers. For such products as cigarettes and automobiles, the influence of peers is unmistakable.

The role of face-to-face groups has been recognized in recent industry campaigns attempting to change basic product attitudes. For years the milk industry has been trying to overcome the image of milk as a "sissified" drink by portraying its use in social and active situations. The men's-wear industry is trying to increase male interest in clothes by advertisements indicating that business associates judge a man by how well he dresses.

Of all face-to-face groups, the person's family undoubtedly plays the largest and most enduring role in basic attitude formation. From them he acquires a mental set not only toward religion and politics, but also toward thrift, chastity, food, human relations, and so forth. Although he often rebels against parental values in his teens, he often accepts these values eventually. Their formative influence on his eventual attitudes is undeniably great.

Family members differ in the types of product messages they carry to other family members. Most of what parents know about cereals, candy, and toys comes from their children. The wife stimulates family consideration of household appliances, furniture, and vacations. The husband tends to stimulate the fewest purchase ideas, with the exception of the automobile and perhaps the home.

The marketer must be alert to what attitudinal configurations dominate in different types of families, and also to how these change over time. For example, the parent's conception of the child's rights and privileges has undergone a radical shift in the last 30 years. The child has become the center of attention and orientation in a great number of households, leading some writers to label the modern family a "filiarchy." This has important implications not only for how to market to today's family, but also on how to market to tomorrow's family when the indulged child of today becomes the parent.

The Person

Social influences determine much but not all of the behavioral variations in people. Two individuals subject to the same influences are not likely to have identical attitudes, although these attitudes will probably converge at more points than those of two strangers selected at random. Attitudes are really the product of social forces interacting with the individual's unique temperament and abilities.

Furthermore, attitudes do not automatically guarantee certain types of behavior. Attitudes are predispositions felt by buyers before they enter the buying process. The buying process itself is a learning experience and can lead to a change in attitudes.

Alfred Politz noted at one time that women stated a clear preference for G.E. refrigerators over Frigidaire, but that Frigidaire continued to outsell G.E.[30] The answer to this paradox was that preference was only one factor entering into behavior. When the consumer preferring G.E. actually undertook to purchase a new refrigerator, her curiosity led her to examine the other brands. Her perception was sensitized to refrigerator advertisements, sales arguments, and different product features. This led to learning and a change in attitudes.

THE HOBBESIAN ORGANIZATIONAL FACTORS MODEL

The foregoing models throw light mainly on the behavior of family buyers.

But what of the large number of people who are organizational buyers? They are engaged in the purchase of goods not for the sake of consumption, but for further production or distribution. Their common denominator is the fact that they (1) are paid to make purchases for others and (2) operate within an organizational environment.

How do organizational buyers make their

Alvin Zander, *Group Dynamics* (Evanston, Illinois: Row, Peterson, 1953), pp. 151–162; and Kurt Lewin, "Group Decision and Social

[29] David Riesman, Reuel Denney, and Nathan Glazer, *The Lonely Crowd* (New Haven, Connecticut: Yale University Press, 1950).

Change," in Theodore M. Newcomb and Eugene L. Hartley, editors, *Readings in Social Psychology* (New York: Henry Holt Co., 1952).

[30] Alfred Politz, "Motivation Research—Opportunity or Dilemma?", in Ferber and Wales, same references as footnote 17, at pp. 57–58.

decisions? There seem to be two competing views. Many marketing writers have emphasized the predominance of rational motives in organizational buying.[31] Organizational buyers are represented as being most impressed by cost, quality, dependability, and service factors. They are portrayed as dedicated servants of the organization, seeking to secure the best terms. This view has led to an emphasis on performance and use characteristics in much industrial advertising.

Other writers have emphasized personal motives in organizational buyer behavior. The purchasing agent's interest to do the best for his company is tempered by his interest to do the best for himself. He may be tempted to choose among salesmen according to the extent they entertain or offer gifts. He may choose a particular vendor because this will ingratiate him with certain company officers. He may shortcut his study of alternative suppliers to make his work day easier.

In truth, the buyer is guided by both personal and group goals; and this is the essential point. The political model of Thomas Hobbes comes closest of any model to suggesting the relationship between the two goals.[32] Hobbes held that man is "instinctively" oriented toward preserving and enhancing his own well-being. But this would produce a "war of every man against every man." This fear leads men to unite with others in a corporate body. The corporate man tries to steer a careful course between satisfying his own needs and those of the organization.

Marketing Applications of Hobbesian Model

The import of the Hobbesian model is that organizational buyers can be appealed to on both personal and organizational grounds. The buyer has his private aims, and yet he tries to do a satisfactory job for his corporation. He will respond to persuasive salesmen and he will respond to rational product arguments. However, the best "mix" of the two is not a fixed quantity; it varies with the nature of the product, the type of organization, and the relative strength of the two drives in the particular buyer.

Where there is substantial similarity in what suppliers offer in the way of products, price, and service, the purchasing agent has less basis for rational choice. Since he can satisfy his organizational obligations with any one of a number of suppliers, he can be swayed by personal motives. On the other hand, where there are pronounced differences among the competing vendors' products, the purchasing agent is held more accountable for his choice and probably pays more attention to rational factors. Short-run personal gain becomes less motivating than the long-run gain which comes from serving the organization with distinction.

The marketing strategist must appreciate these goal conflicts of the organizational buyer. Behind all the ferment of purchasing agents to develop standards and employ value analysis lies their desire to avoid being thought of as order-clerks, and to develop better skills in reconciling personal and organizational objectives.[33]

SUMMARY

Think back over the five different behavioral models of how the buyer translates buying influences into purchasing responses.

Marshallian man is concerned chiefly with economic cues—prices and income—and makes a fresh utility calculation before each purchase.

Pavlovian man behaves in a largely habitual rather than thoughtful way; certain configurations of cues will set off the same behavior because of rewarded learning in the past.

Freudian man's choices are influenced strongly by motives and fantasies which take place deep within his private world.

Veblenian man acts in a way which is shaped largely by past and present social groups.

And finally, Hobbesian man seeks to reconcile individual gain with organizational gain.

Thus, it turns out that the "black box" of the buyer is not so black after all. Light is thrown in various corners by these models. Yet no one has succeeded in putting all these pieces of truth together into one coherent instrument for behavioral analysis. This, of course, is the goal of behavioral science.

---

[31] See Melvin T. Copeland, *Principles of Merchandising* (New York: McGraw-Hill, 1924).

[32] Thomas Hobbes, *Leviathan*, 1651 (London: G. Routledge and Sons, 1887).

[33] For an insightful account, see George Strauss, "Tactics of Lateral Relationship: The Purchasing Agent," *Administrative Science Quarterly*, Vol. 7 (September, 1962), pp. 161–186.

24. Social Classes and Spending Behavior

PIERRE MARTINEAU

All societies place emphasis on some one structure which gives form to the total society and integrates all the other structures such as the family, the clique, voluntary association, caste, age, and sex groupings into a social unity.

Social stratification means any system of ranked statuses by which all the members of a society are placed in some kind of a superordinate and subordinate hierarchy. While money and occupation are important in the ranking process, there are many more factors, and these two alone do not establish social position. The concept of social class was designed to include this process of ranking people in superior and inferior social position by any and all factors.

CLASS SYSTEM

It has been argued that there cannot be a class system existent in America when most individuals do not have the slightest idea of its formal structure. Yet in actuality every individual senses that he is more at home with and more acceptable to certain groups than to others. In a study of department stores and shopping behavior, it was found that the Lower-Status woman is completely aware that, if she goes into High-Status department stores, the clerks and the other customers in the store will punish her in various subtle ways.

"The clerks treat you like a crumb," one woman expressed it. After trying vainly to be

◆ SOURCE: Reprinted by permission from the *Journal of Marketing* (National Quarterly Publication of the American Marketing Association), Vol. 23, No. 2, October 1958, pp. 121–130.

waited on, another woman bitterly complained that she was loftily told, "We thought you were a clerk."

The woman who is socially mobile gives considerable thought to the external symbols of status, and she frequently tests her status by shopping in department stores which she thinks are commensurate with her changing position. She knows that, if she does not dress correctly, if she does not behave in a certain manner to the clerks, if she is awkward about the proper cues, then the other customers and the clerks will make it very clear that she does not belong.

In another study, very different attitudes in the purchase of furniture and appliances involving this matter of status were found. Middle-Class people had no hesitancy in buying refrigerators and other appliances in discount houses and bargain stores because they felt that they could not "go wrong" with the nationally advertised names. But taste in furniture is much more elusive and subtle because the brand names are not known; and, therefore, one's taste is on trial. Rather than commit a glaring error in taste which would exhibit an ignorance of the correct status symbols, the same individual who buys appliances in a discount house generally retreats to a status store for buying furniture. She needs the support of the store's taste.

In a very real sense, everyone of us in his consumption patterns and style of life shows an awareness that there is some kind of a superiority-inferiority system operating, and that we must observe the symbolic patterns of our own class.

Lloyd Warner and Paul Lunt have described a six-class system: the Upper-Upper or old families; Lower-Upper, or the newly arrived; Upper-Middle, mostly the professionals and successful businessmen; Lower-Middle, or the white collar salaried class; Upper-Lower, or the wage earner, skilled worker group; and Lower-Lower, or the unskilled labor group.[1] For practical purposes, in order to determine the individual's class position, Warner and his associates worked out a rating index, not based on amount of income but rather on type of income, type of occupation, house type, and place of residence.

Although the Warner thesis has been widely used in sociology, it has not generally been employed in marketing. As a matter of fact, some critics in the social sciences have held that, since Warner's thesis rested essentially on studies of smaller cities in the 10,000-25,-000 class, this same system might not exist in the more complex metropolitan centers, or might not be unravelled by the same techniques. Furthermore, many marketers did not see the application of this dimension to the individual's economic behavior, since the studies of Warner and his associates had mostly been concerned with the differences in the broad patterns of living, the moral codes, etc.

SOCIAL CLASS IN CHICAGO

Under Warner's guidance, the *Chicago Tribune* has undertaken several extensive studies exploring social class in a metropolitan city, and its manifestations specifically in family buying patterns. The problem was to determine if such a social-class system did exist in metropolitan Chicago, if the dimensions and the relationships were at all similar to the smaller cities which were studied before the far-reaching social changes of the past fifteen years. The studies were undertaken to see if there were any class significances in the individual family's spending-saving patterns, retail store loyalties, and his expressions of taste in typical areas such as automobiles, apparel, furniture, and house types.

---

[1] W. Lloyd Warner and Paul Lunt, *The Social Life of a Modern Community* (New Haven: Yale University Press, 1950). Also, W. Lloyd Warner, Marchia Meeker, and Kenneth Eells, *Social Class in America* (Chicago: Science Research Associates, 1949).

It seems that many an economist overlooks the possibility of any psychological differences between individuals resulting from different class membership. It is assumed that a rich man is simply a poor man with more money and that, given the same income, the poor man would behave exactly like the rich man. The *Chicago Tribune* studies crystallize a wealth of evidence from other sources that this is just not so, and that the Lower-Status person is profoundly different in his mode of thinking and his way of handling the world from the Middle-Class individual. Where he buys and what he buys will differ not only by economics but in symbolic value.

It should be understood, of course, that there are no hard and fast lines between the classes. Implicit in the notion of social class in America is the possibility of movement from one class to another. The "office boy-to-president" saga is a cherished part of the American dream. Bobo Rockefeller illustrates the female counterpart: from coal miner's daughter to socialite. As a corollary of the explorations in class, the study also tried to be definitive about the phenomenon of social mobility—the movement from one class to another.

There are numerous studies of vertical mobility from the level of sociological analysis, mostly by comparing the individual's occupational status to that of his father. There are also studies at the level of psychological analysis. This study attempted to combine the two levels, to observe the individual's progress and also to understand something of the dynamics of the mobile person as compared to the stable individual. The attempt was to look both backward and forward: tracing such factors as occupation, place of residence, and religion back to parents and grandparents, and then where the family expected to be in the next five or ten years, what were the educational plans for each son, each daughter, a discussion of future goals.

Because this article is confined primarily to social class, this section may be concluded by saying that the studies show a very clear relationship between spend-saving aspirations and the factors of mobility-stability.

FRAMEWORK OF STUDY

Following are Warner's hypotheses and assumptions for the study:

I. *Assumptions about symbols and values and about saving of money and accumulation of objects.*

Our society is acquisitive and pecuniary. On the one hand, the values and beliefs of Americans are pulled toward the pole of the accumulation of money by increasing the amount of money income and reducing its outgo. On the other hand, American values emphasize the accumulation of objects and products of technology for display and consumption. The self-regard and self-esteem of a person and his family, as well as the public esteem and respect of a valued social world around the accumulator, are increased or not by such symbols of accumulation and consumption.

The two sets of values, the accumulation of product symbols and the accumulation (saving) of money, may be, and usually are, in opposition.

General working hypotheses stemming from these assumptions were: (1) People are distributed along a range according to the two-value components, running from proportionately high savings, through mixed categories, to proportionately high accumulation of objects. (2) These value variations conform to social and personality factors present in all Americans.

II. *Assumptions about product symbols, savers, and accumulations.*

American society is also characterized by social change, particularly technological change that moves in the direction of greater and greater production of more kinds and more numerous objects for consumption and accumulation.

Hypothesis. New varieties of objects will be most readily accepted by the accumulators, and most often opposed by the savers.

III. *Assumptions about the social values of accumulators and savers.*

American society is characterized by basic cultural differences, one of them being social status. Social class levels are occupied by people, some of whom are upward mobile by intent and fact. Others are non-mobile, by intent and fact. The values which dictate judgments about actions, such as the kinds of objects which are consumed and accumulated, will vary by class level and the presence or absence of vertical mobility.

IV. *Assumptions about the personal values of accumulators and savers.*

The personality components are distributed through the class levels and through the mobility types. By relating the social and personality components, it is possible to state a series of hypotheses about accumulators and savers as they are related to the object world around them, particularly to objects which are new and old to the culture, those which are imposing or not and those which are predominantly for display or for consumption.

At the direct, practical level, all of these theoretical questions can be summarized by one basic question: *What kinds of things are people likely to buy and not buy if they are given class positions and if they are or are not socially mobile?* In other words, what is the effect on purchasing behavior of being in a particular social class, and being mobile or non-mobile?

If this is the crucial question, theoretically grounded, then a whole series of hypotheses can be laid out concerning values about money and values about buying various kinds of objects for consumption and for display. Some of these are:

1. There will be a relationship between values held by a particular subject and the extent to which particular products exemplify those values.

2. There is a differential hierarchy of things for which it is worth spending money.

3. Veblen's theory that conspicuous expenditure is largely applied to the Upper Class is erroneous. It runs all the way through our social system.

From these statements certain other hypotheses follow:

4. At different class levels, symbols of mobility will differ.

There is a differential hierarchy of things on which it is worth spending money. Class and mobility will be two of the dimensions that will differentiate—also personality and cultural background.

5. The place in the home where these symbols will be displayed will shift at different class levels.

The underlying assumption here is that there is a hierarchy of importance in the rooms of the house. This hierarchy varies with social class, mobility, age, ethnicity. The studies also revealed clear-cut patterns of taste for lamps, furnishings, house types, etc.

6. The non-mobile people tend to rationalize purchases in terms of cost or economy.

In other words, non-mobile people tend to be oriented more toward the pole of the accumulation of money. Purchases, then, are rationalized in terms of the savings involved.

The basic thesis of all the hypotheses on mobility is this: Whereas the stable individual would emphasize saving and security, the behavior of the mobile individual is characterized by spending for various symbols of upward movement. All of the evidence turned up indicates that this difference in values does exist, and furthermore that notable differences in personality dynamics are involved. For instance, the analysis of how families would make investments shows that stable people overwhelmingly prefer insurance, the symbol of security. By contrast, the mobile people at all levels prefer stocks, which are risk-taking. In Warner's words, the mobile individual acts as if he were free, white, and twenty-one, completely able to handle the world and perfectly willing to gamble on himself as a sure bet to succeed.

CLASS PLACEMENT

Returning to the factor of social class, in this study class placement was based on a multistate probability area sample of metropolitan Chicago, involving 3,880 households. It was found that the matter of placement could not be done by the relatively simple scoring sufficient for the smaller cities. To secure house typings, it was necessary to provide the field investigators with photographs covering a wide range of dwelling types, all the way from exclusive apartments to rooms over stores. Because of the very complexity of metropolitan life, occupations provided the biggest problem. To solve this operational problem, it was necessary to construct an exhaustive list of occupational types involving degree of responsibility and training required by each. The data finally used to calculate the Index of Status Characteristics (ISC) were:

(weighted by 5),
  Occupation (from 1 to 7 broad categories)
(weighted by 4)
    Sources of Income (from 1 to 7 types)

(weighted by 3)
    Housing Type (from 1 to 7 types)

The sum of the individual's weighted scores was used to predict his social class level as follows:[2]

ISC Scores	Predicted Social Class Placement
12-21	Upper class
22-37	Upper-middle class
38-51	Lower-middle class
52-66	Upper-lower class
67-84	Lower-lower class

The study very clearly shows that there is a social-class system operative in a metropolitan area which can be delineated. Furthermore, class membership is an important determinant of the individual's economic behavior, even more so than in the smaller city. The one department store in the smaller city may satisfy almost everyone, whereas in the metropolitan city the stores become sharply differentiated.

This is the social-class structure of Metropolitan Chicago, typifying the transformation of the formerly agrarian Midwestern cities from Pittsburgh to Kansas-City into a series of big milltowns:

Upper and upper-middle	8.1%
Lower-middle	28.4
Upper-lower	44.0
Lower-lower	19.5

While the Old Families and the Newly Arrived are still recognizable as types, they constitute less than 1 per cent of the population. A similar study in Kansas City turned up so few that they could not be counted at all. On the other hand, we see the emergence of a seventh class, the Upper-Lower "Stars" or Light-Blue Collar Workers. They are the spokesmen of the Upper-Lower Class groups —high income individuals, who have the income for more ostentatious living than the average factory worker but who lack the personal skills or desire for high status by social mobility.

---

[2] Dr. Bevode McCall helped to solve the ISC scoring problem for Metropolitan Chicago.

There is certainly a rough correlation between income and social class. But social class is a much richer dimension of meaning. There are so many facets of behavior which are explicable only on a basis of social class dynamics. For instance, this analysis of the purchase of household appliances in Chicago over a four-year period shows a very different picture by income and by class:

Nine Appliance Types–Four-Year Period
By Income

Over $7,000	36.2%
4,000-6,999	46.0
Under 4,000	17.8
By Social Class	
Upper and upper middle	16.6
Lower middle	29.2
Upper lower	45.7
Lower lower	8.5

Income analysis shows that the lowest income group represents an understandably smaller market, but nevertheless a market. Social-class analysis highlights a fundamental difference in attitudes toward the home between the two lower classes. The Upper-Lower Class man sees his home as his castle, his anchor to the world, and he loads it down with hardware—solid heavy appliances—as his symbols of security. The Lower-Lower Class individual is far less interested in his castle, and is more likely to spend his income for flashy clothes or an automobile. He is less property-minded, and he has less feeling about buying and maintaining a home.

Several *Tribune* studies have explored the way of life and the buying behavior in many new suburbs and communities. All of them quickly become stratified along social-class and mobility dimensions, and, therefore, differ tremendously among themselves. *Fortune* has reported on Park Forest, Illinois, a Middle-Class suburb of 30,000 and only ten years old. It is characterized by high degrees of both upward and geographical mobility. The people are overwhelmingly those who had moved from other parts of the United States, who had few local roots, and who consequently wanted to integrate themselves in friendship groups. But this was not typical of the new Lower-Status suburbs where the women did relatively little fraternizing. It was not typical of the new Upper-Middle Class mobile suburbs where the people were preoccupied with status symbols, not in submerging themselves in the group.

One new community had crystallized as being for Higher-Status Negroes. This was a resettlement project with relatively high rents for Negroes. Eighty-five per cent of them had come from the South where social class was compressed. But, as soon as they came to Chicago, the class system opened up and they were anxious to establish a social distance between themselves and other Negroes. Almost all of them said they enjoyed the "peace and quiet" of their neighborhood, which was their way of insisting that they were not like the "noisy" Lower-Class Negroes. They deliberately avoided the stores patronized by other Negroes.

CHOICE OF STORE

All of these studies reveal the close relation between choice of store, patterns of spending, and class membership. In the probability sample delineating social class, such questions were asked in the total metropolitan area as:

"If you were shopping for a good dress, at which store would you be most likely to find what you wanted?"
"For an everyday dress?"
"For living room furniture?"
"At which store do you buy most of your groceries?"

To assume that all persons would wish to shop at the glamorous High-Status stores is utterly wrong. People are very realistic in the way they match their values and expectations with the status of the store. The woman shopper has a considerable range of ideas about department stores; but these generally become organized on a scale ranking from very High-Social Status to the Lowest-Status and prestige. The social status of the department store becomes the primary basis for its definition by the shopper. This is also true of men's and women's apparel stores, and furniture stores, on the basis of customer profiles. The shopper is not going to take a chance feeling out of place by going to a store where she might not fit.

No matter what economics are involved, she asks herself who are the other customers in the store, what sort of treatment can she expect at the hands of the clerks, will the merchandise be the best of everything, or lower priced and hence lower quality? Stores are described as being for the rich, for the average ordinary people, or for those who have to stretch their pennies.

The most important function of retail advertising today, when prices and quality have become so standard, is to permit the shopper to make social-class identification. This she can do from the tone and physical character of the advertising. Of course, there is also the factor of psychological identification. Two people in the same social class may want different stores. One may prefer a conservative store, one may want the most advanced styling. But neither will go to stores where they do not "fit," in a social-class sense.

In contrast to the independent food retailer, who obviously adapts to the status of the neighborhood, the chain grocers generally invade many income areas with their stores. Nevertheless, customer profiles show that each chain acquires a status definition. The two largest grocery chains in the Chicago area are A. & P. and Jewel; yet they draw very different customer bodies. A. & P. is strong with the mass market, whereas Jewel has its strength among the Middle Class.

While the national brand can and often does cut across classes, one can think of many product types and services which do have social class labels. The Upper-Middle Class person rarely travels by motor coach because none of his associates do so, even though there is certainly nothing wrong with this mode of transportation. On the other hand, even with low air-coach fares, one does not see many factory workers or day laborers on vacation around airports. Such sales successes as vodka and tonic water, and men's deodorants and foreign sports cars, were accomplished without benefit of much buying from this part of the market.

COMMUNICATION SKILLS

There is also a relation between class and communication abilities which has significance for marketing. The kind of super-sophisticated and clever advertising which appears in the *New Yorker* and *Esquire* is almost meaningless to Lower-Status people. They cannot comprehend the subtle humor; they are baffled by the bizarre art. They have a different symbol system, a very different approach to humor. In no sense does this imply that they lack intelligence or wit.

Rather their communication skills have just been pressed into a different mold.

Here again, style of advertising helps the individual to make class identification. Most of the really big local television success stories in Chicago have been achieved by personalities who radiate to the mass that this is where they belong. These self-made businessmen who do the announcing for their own shows communicate wonderfully well with the mass audience. While many listeners switch off their lengthy and personal commercials, these same mannerisms tell the Lower-Status individual that here is someone just like himself, who understands him.

Social Research, Inc., has frequently discussed the class problem in marketing by dividing the population into Upper-Middle or quality market; the middle majority which combines both the Lower-Middle and Upper-Lower; and then the Lower-Lower. The distinction should be drawn between the Middle Classes and the Lower-Status groups. In several dozen of these store profiles, there is scarcely an instance where a store has appeal to the Lower-Middle and Upper-Lower classes with anything like the same strength.

It would be better to make the break between the Middle Class, representing one-third of the population and the Lower-Status or Working-Class or Wage-Earner group, representing two-thirds of metropolitan Chicago. This permits some psychological distinctions to be drawn between the Middle-Class individual and the individual who is not a part of the Middle-Class system of values. Even though this is the dominant American value system, even though Middle-Class Americans have been taught by their parents that it is the only value system, this Lower-Status individual does not necessarily subscribe to it.

WHO SAVES, WHO SPENDS?

Another important set of behavioral distinctions related to social class position was revealed in the "save-spend aspiration" study. The question was asked: "Suppose your income was doubled for the next ten years, what would you do with the increased income?" This is a fantasy question taken out of the realm of any pressing economic situation to reflect aspirations about money. The coding broke down the answers to this question into five general categories: (1) the mode of saving, (2) the purpose of saving, (3) spending which would consolidate past gains, meet present defensive needs, prepare for future self-advancement, (4) spending which is "self-indulgent-centered," (5) spending which is "house-centered."

Here are some of our findings:[3] The higher the individual's class position, the more likely is he to express some saving aspirations. Conversely, the lower his class position, the more likely is he to mention spending only. Moreover the higher the status, the more likely is the individual to specify *how* he will save his money, which is indicative of the more elaborate financial learning required of higher status.

Proceeding from the more general categories (such as saving versus spending only) to more specific categories (such as non-investment versus investment saving and the even more specific stock versus real estate investment, etc.) an increasingly sharper class differentiation is found. It is primarily *non-investment* saving which appeals to the Lower-Status person. Investment saving, on the other hand, appeals above all to the Upper-Status person.

Investors almost always specify how they will invest. And here in mode of investment are examples of the most sharply class-differentiated preferences. Intangible forms of investment like stock and insurance are very clearly distinguished as Upper-Status investments. Nearly four times as many Upper-Middles select insurance as would be expected by chance, whereas only one-fifth of the Lower-Lowers select it as would be expected by chance. By contrast, Lower-Status people have far greater preference for tangible investments, specifically ownership of real estate, a farm, or a business.

To sum up, Middle-Class people usually have a place in their aspirations for some form of saving. This saving is most often in the form of investment, where there is a risk, long-term involvement, and the possibility of higher return. Saving, investment saving, and intangible investment saving—successively each of these become for them increasingly symbols of their higher status.

The aspirations of the Lower-Status person are just as often for spending as they are for saving. This saving is usually a non-investment saving where there is almost no risk, funds can be quickly converted to spendable cash, and returns are small. When the Lower-Status person does invest his savings, he will be specific about the mode of investment, and is very likely to prefer something tangible and concrete—something he can point at and readily display.

Turning from mode of saving to purpose of saving, very significant class relationships are likewise evident. Consider the verbalization of saving purpose. Lower-Status people typically explain why one should save—why the very act of saving is important. On the other hand, Middle-Class people do not, as if saving is an end-in-itself, the merits of which are obvious and need not be justified.

Spending is the other side of the coin. Analysis of what people say they will spend for shows similar class-related desires. All classes mention concrete, material artifacts such as a new car, some new appliance. But the Lower-Status people stop here. Their accumulations are artifact-centered, whereas Middle-Class spending-mentions are experience-centered. This is spending where one is left typically with only a memory. It would include hobbies, recreation, self-education and travel. The wish to travel, and particularly foreign travel, is almost totally a Middle-Class aspiration.

Even in their fantasies, people are governed by class membership. In his daydreaming and wishful thinking, the Lower-Status individual will aspire in different patterns from the Middle-Class individual.

PSYCHOLOGICAL DIFFERENCES

This spending-saving analysis has very obvious psychological implications to differentiate between the classes. Saving itself generally suggests foresightedness, the ability to perceive long-term needs and goals. Non-investment saving has the characteristics of little risk-taking and of ready conversion, at no loss, into immediate expenditures—the money can be drawn out of the account whenever the bank is open. Investment spending, on the other hand, has the characteristics of risk-taking (a gamble for greater returns) and of delayed conversion, with possible loss, to expenditures on immediate needs.

---

[3] The saving-spending aspiration analysis was carried out by Roger Coup, graduate student at the University of Chicago.

Here are some psychological contrasts between two different social groups:

Middle-Class

1. Pointed to the future.
2. His viewpoint embraces a long expanse of time.
3. More urban identification.
4. Stresses rationality.
5. Has a well-structured sense of the universe.
6. Horizons vastly extended or not limited.
7. Greater sense of choice-making.
8. Self-confident, willing to take risks.
9. Immaterial and abstract in his thinking.
10. Sees himself tied to national happenings.

Lower-Status

1. Pointed to the present and past.
2. Lives and thinks in a short expanse of time.
3. More rural in identification.
4. Non-rational essentially.
5. Vague and unclear structuring of the world.
6. Horizons sharply defined and limited.
7. Limited sense of choice-making.
8. Very much concerned with security and insecurity.
9. Concrete and perceptive in his thinking.
10. World revolves around his family and body.

CONCLUSIONS

The essential purpose of this article was to develop three basic premises which are highly significant for marketing:

I. *There is a social-class system operative in metropolitan markets which can be isolated and described.*

II. *It is important to realize that there are far-reaching psychological differences between the various classes.*

They do not handle the world in the same fashion. They tend not to think in the same way. As one tries to communicate with the Lower-Status group, it is imperative to sense that their goals and mental processes differ from the Middle-Class group.

III. *Consumption patterns operate as prestige symbols to define class membership, which is a more significant determinant of economic behavior than mere income.*

Each major department store, furniture store, and chain-grocery store has a different "pulling power" on different status groups. The usual customers of a store gradually direct the store's merchandising policies into a pattern which works. The interaction between store policy and consumer acceptance results in the elimination of certain customer groups and the attraction of others, with a resulting equilibration around a reasonably stable core of specific customer groups who think of the store as appropriate for them.

Income has always been the marketer's handiest index to family consumption standards. But it is a far from accurate index. For instance, the bulk of the population in a metropolitan market today will fall in the middle-income ranges. This will comprise not only the traditional white collar worker, but the unionized craftsman and the semi-skilled worker with their tremendous income gains of the past decade. Income-wise, they may be in the same category. But their buying behavior, their tastes, their spending-saving aspirations can be poles apart. Social-class position and mobility-stability dimensions will reflect in much greater depth each individual's style of life.

25. Reference Theory as a Conceptual Framework for Consumer Decisions

JAMES E. STAFFORD

Reference group theory has received an unusual amount of attention in its short but eventful lifespan of twenty years. From its inception the idea of reference groups gained adherents among social scientists, but an interest in an expanded theory of reference group behavior was first manifested in Merton and Kitt's interpretation of the data in the volumes of *The American Soldier*. Since then the subject has been expanded and utilized in varied research settings, including consumer behavior. However, because of a lack of theoretical integration, scientific inquiry has often proceeded along divergent lines with consequent limitations on the significance of the findings.

In this paper I will survey the background of reference group theory and elaborate some of the problems in the development of the area which indicate the need for a theoretical revision. Then, a reformulation of reference group theory will be attempted. Finally, some attention will be focused on the implications and relevance of reference theory to the study of consumer behavior.

HISTORICAL PERSPECTIVE

Development of the Concept

The term "reference group" was coined by Herbert Hyman, although other writers had

◆ SOURCE: Reprinted by permission from *Marketing and the New Science of Planning*, edited by Robert L. King, Proceedings of the Fall Conference of the American Marketing Association, 1968, Series No. 28, pp. 280–284.

used the general idea of a "frame of reference" prior to Hyman's signal publication. The term was employed by Hyman to indicate groups which are used for the estimation of self-statuses, *i.e.*, comparison groups. At about the same time, Newcomb was studying the influence of social interaction on attitude change in a small college town. While he did not use the term directly, there is no doubt that he was studying, at least in part, the formation of reference groups.

Kelley, writing several years later, collated much of the earlier work and concluded that reference groups have two basic dimensions: 1) a comparison function and 2) a normative function. A group functions as a comparison reference group for an individual to the extent that the behavior, attitudes, circumstances, or other characteristics of its members represent standards or comparison points which he uses in making judgements and self-evaluations. In other words, a reference group is a check point or standard which an individual uses in forming a picture of the situation, particularly his own position within it. The result is that the individual may alter his behavior after comparing himself with a group of people with whom he wishes to identify and to whom he orients himself psychologically. The second major usage of "reference group" has been related to the establishment and maintenance of norms, values and perspectives—the normative function—which help guide the individual's behavior. Several well known writers, including Sherif and Newcomb, utilized and emphasized this alternative. Shibutani offered a third meaning—a group whose acceptance one seeks, but Turner retorted that this possibility is actually only a variation of the second usage. He asserted:

In the literature . . . the desire to be accepted is depicted as the mechanism which leads to the adoption of the values and perspectives of the reference group. These are not, therefore, separate usages of the term but merely definitions, on the one hand, in terms of the effect of the reference group [the adoption of values and perspectives] and, on the other hand, in terms of the mechanism of the reference group [aspiration for membership].[1]

Thus, there are two fairly distinct ways in which reference group theory has been used. The distinction between the two functions mentioned above is important because it makes explicit two main aspects of reference group theory: the motivational and the perceptual. The normative functions of reference groups are related to the more general theory of goal-setting and motivation which also includes other social determinants of standards, nonsocial factors in motivation, and the processes of self-motivation. The comparison functions, on the other hand, are part of general perceptual theory, particularly as represented by the psychological theories of frames of reference.

Problem Areas

The inability to find and utilize a single definition of reference group which would give adequate recognition to both group and individual factors is symptomatic of the muddled state of reference group theory. Sherif, for example, is representative of a group of writers who have taken a completely individualistic position. He defined reference groups as ". . . those groups to which the individual relates himself (subjectively) as a part or to which he aspires to relate himself psychologically." Sherif's conceptual scheme includes both "membership groups" and "reference groups." The first is defined in terms of objective group criteria, while the subjective orientations of individuals form the bases for reference groups. A specification of the

relationship between reference groups and membership groups was side-stepped with the comment that "usually one's reference groups and membership groups are the same." The significance of Sherif's use of both terms lies in his recognition of the importance of both individual and group dimensions, even though he did nothing to promote their integration in his theory.

On the other hand, Merton approached reference group theory as the subject for group study exclusively. His modification of the emphasis on the individual was expressed in his linking of reference group theory with functional analysis.

He advocated:

In general, then, reference group theory aims to systematize the determinants and consequences of this process of evaluation and self-appraisal in which the individual takes the values or standards of other individuals and groups as a comparative frame of reference.[2]

If primary attention is devoted to "the determinants and consequences," then the fundamental process of evaluation and self-appraisal may be, in large measure, ignored.

Another problem with reference group theory in its present state is that its ties with the concept "group" restrict the scope of applicability of the idea of reference behavior. The use of "group" does not allow the possibility that individuals orient their self-evaluations to non-group phenomena. Apparently sensing the need for a broad perspective, reference group theorists have often stretched the meaning of "group." Merton acknowledged, for instance:

Reference groups are, in principle, almost innumerable: any of the groups of which one is a member, and these are comparatively few, as well as groups of which one is not a member, and these are, of course, legion, can become points of reference for shaping one's attitudes, evaluations and behavior.[3]

Merton also classed collectivities and social categories as reference groups. Shibutani put further strain on the logical cohesiveness of

[1] R. Turner, "Role-taking, Role Standpoint, and Reference Group Behavior," American Journal of Sociology, Vol. 61, 1956, pp. 130-136.

[2] Robert K. Merton and A. S. Kitt, "Contributions to the Theory of Reference Group Behavior," in Studies in the Scope and Method of "The American Soldier," (Glencoe: Free Press, 1950), p. 92.
[3] Robert K. Merton, Social Theory and Social Structure (Glencoe: Free Press, 1957), p. 233.

the term "group" by including the possibility of reference individuals and imaginary persons. Even if we could grant the logical consistency of such illogical uses of "group," reference group theory would still lack the flexibility necessary to encompass the whole sphere of reference behavior. It seems that a theory of reference behavior should attempt to account for reference behavior which is not related specifically to groups, as well as group-related phenomena.

In conclusion, a review of the literature indicates there are several unresolved problems relative to reference group theory. In spite of the salience of the difficulties, contributions to scientific advance have been made using various interpretations of reference group theory. Yet, this does not obviate the need for a unified theory which will account for both individual orientations and the social basis of individual behavior. A reformulation of reference group theory will be attempted in the following section. I do not claim to have "discovered" any new elements, only to have put old ones together in a somewhat different fashion.

REFORMULATION OF THE THEORY

As seen in the previous section, many of the difficulties of reference group theory are intertwined with the failure to find a way to harmoniously fit the term "group" into the theory. Moreover, in view of the subject matter of the theory, this has been a misplaced concern. Since it is a theory of reference behavior, the emphasis should be on reference behavior and not on groups *per se*. In addition, the possibility that future studies would only perpetuate unnecessary conflicts can be precluded by simply dropping "group" and calling the subject "reference theory." This is not an admission that groups are unimportant, but a recognition that other sociocultural phenomena are also important in reference behavior. The more general concept, reference theory, includes both possibilities.

Reference theory is necessarily an extensive subject for its basic postulate is that people *refer* themselves and their behavior to something and/or someone else. In brief, reference theory may be said to be a logically interrelated conceptual scheme about reference behavior from which empirical propositions can be deducted. An understanding of the meaning of "referents" will furnish the background for a definition of reference behavior.

The same breadth of scope of reference theory is maintained by the term "referent" which is defined as whatever individuals employ in evaluating their own statuses, behavior, norms, and values. The following quotation from Shibutani includes part of what we designate as referents:

. . . all kinds of units may serve as reference groups. Attention should not be limited to organized groups that are readily identifiable. [One] . . . may consist of a single person, a small handful of people with whom he is in sustained contact, a voluntary association, or some broad category, of people—a social class, a profession, an ethnic group, or some community.[4]

A referent may also be an ideology, ancestors, God, Oriental marital standards, spirits, a set of laws, a future state of affairs, one's family, broader kinship groupings, or a nation. Whether these phenomena are real or imagined, extant or extinct, present or future does not alter the fact that they are referents if people refer their behavior, norms, values, and statuses to them.

Reference Behavior

Having specified the meaning of referents, we may now define reference behavior. Reference behavior is the cognitive process in which individuals evaluate their statuses, behavior, norms, and values by means of referents. The four objects of evaluation—norms, values, statuses, and behavior—may be grouped into objective (statuses and behavior) and subjective (norms and values) categories. We recognize that the contents of each category have important linkages with those of the other, but for purposes of analysis the distinction may be made.

Reference behavior is characterized by three general dimensions—knowledge, affectivity, and sanctions. These dimensions appear as interrelated variables which come into play in all forms of reference behavior and will receive the bulk of discussion in the remainder of this section.

[4] T. Shibutani, "Reference Groups and Social Control," in Arnold Rose (ed.), *Human Behavior and Social Processes* (Boston: Houghton Mifflin Co., 1962), p. 132.

For a phenomenon to be used as a referent, the individual must have knowledge of its existence, the degree and kind of knowledge serve as guides to his use of the referent. When, for example, an individual only knows the social statuses of others, he can compare his own statuses with those of the others in light of the norms of the broader social system, but he is unable to evaluate his own norms and values by means of those associated with the other statuses, because he doesn't know what they are.

A second possibility regarding knowledge is that the value and normative aspects of the referents are known, but the implications there from the statuses and behavior are not clearly defined. This would be the case if an individual selected a referent such as an ideology or a broadly defined future state of affairs. As an illustration, the potential referent, "service to mankind," has many important implications for an individual's normative system but furnishes only fuzzy direction for the selection of appropriate statuses and behavior.

The last possibility is that the individual knows both the norms and values, and the accompanying statuses and behavioral patterns. This is the type of knowledge usually conveyed in membership groups in which members interact with each other. Through the formal and informal media of communication members learn the norms and values and see how the normative structure is expressed in the status arrangements and corresponding behavioral patterns. This same kind of knowledge may be gained from non-membership groups with which there is a large amount of symbolic interaction.

The dimension of sanctions is as applicable to informal voluntary membership groups as formal membership groups. However, all referents are not alike in their sanctioning potential for there are perceived degrees of salience of sanctions. Therefore, referents possess differential importance to an individual because varying degrees of salience are associated with their respective sanctions. Sanctions are salient: 1) to the degree that the individual perceives them to be important to his own self-maintenance and/or self-enhancement; and 2) given (1), to the degree that their positive support of the individual's self-maintenance and/or self-enhancement is in doubt. To sum up, potential referents move into the sphere of actual referents when they are perceived to possess sanctions which are important to the individual and they may be ranked according to the degree of salience of the sanctions associated with each.

Affectivity is the third dimension of reference behavior and it is present in degrees of positive or negative affect. Most writers have emphasized the positive end of the continuum. Shibutani advised that the concept "reference group" be reserved for those groups whose perspectives one assumes, and Kelley suggested that a group becomes a reference group when its values are assumed. Turner proposed that reference groups be subdivided into three types and one of these, "identification group," be the group which is the source of a person's major perspectives and values. This recognition of the importance of identification or positive affect in reference behavior is very valuable, but should not obscure the other end of the dimension.

Negative Reference Groups

Many referents stimulate only negative affectivity and it is a common experience in almost all areas of life for people to be required to accommodate themselves to groups or individuals who are extremely distasteful to them. Newcomb was the first writer to introduce the notion of negative reference group as, "one which . . . (a person) is motivated to oppose, or in which he does not want to be treated as a member." In spite of criticism, the concept is needed to describe the type of referent which is undesirable in the eyes of the evaluator. Thus, a referent may be an object of identification or an alienation group, but in all cases the referent may be found along a continuum of positive to negative affect. A point of emotional neutrality along the continuum is logically but not empirically possible. The fact that potential sanctions are perceived by the actor results in his taking some kind of stance in relation to the possible threats to, or enhancement of his evaluation of himself.

Dimensions of Reference Behavior

To summarize this discussion of dimensions of reference behavior, a referent consists of anything which is utilized by an individual in his evaluation of his norms, values, statuses, and behavior. Referents may be characterized by the individual's knowledge of them, by the perceived negative or positive sanctions, and by the individual's positive or negative affectivity toward the referent.

Because of the segmentalization of life in industrialized, mass society, the perspectives of multiple referents may be used without any perceived conflicts between them. Shibutani asserted:

Those who live in a pluralistic society tend to lead compartmentalized lives, shifting from one perspective to another as they participate in a succession of transactions that are not necessarily related. In each social world they play somewhat different roles, and they manifest a different facet of their personality.[5]

When contradictions between salient referents do arise, however, the individual may choose the perspective of only one referent, but it is more probable that he would try to compromise the differences so as to achieve the most rewards and the fewest negative sanctions from the most salient referent, the next most rewards and the next fewest punishments from the next most salient referent, etc. Since many important choices involve fine shadings or degrees of difference, rather than polar alternatives, and because important decisions usually involve many sectors of an individual's life, many referents may be brought into focus on a particular decision faced by the actor. In general, the more restricted the application of the results of a process of evaluation, the more limited will be the number of referents mobilized in the process.

Social Basis of Reference Behavior

In this part of the theoretical section the social basis of reference behavior will be delineated. All social phenomena arise out of the symbolic interaction of individuals and groups. Societal norms are ultimately dependent on this interaction and may change over time as a result of changes in the patterns of interaction in the population. Within the broad context of the societal normative structure subsystem norms, values, statuses and patterns of behavior are developed. In specific situations social interaction occurs within the limits imposed by the societal norms and most behavior is consistent with these norms. Thus, individuals select as referents certain phe-

nomena which are generally consistent with the normative structure of the larger society. This statement does not conflict with the previous affirmation that referents are chosen according to the perceived sanctions associated with them, for, sanctions are also subject to the conditioning of societal norms and values. The perception of sanction which is inconsistent with societal norms and values alters the significance of the referent.

In conclusion, reference behavior is ultimately out of, shapes, and, in turn, is shaped by symbolic interaction with the social system. This broad normative environment conditions the acquisition of knowledge, perception of sanctions, and the degree and type of affectivity toward reference groups. Moreover, it has molded the subsystem norms and values he holds, his present statuses and patterns of behavior, and the way he evaluates all of these.

THE RELEVANCE OF REFERENCE THEORY TO MARKETING

Substantial evidence exists which indicates that "referents" may have considerable influence upon consumer purchase behavior. For example, Katz and Lazarsfeld suggested that the importance of personal influence, relative to the influence of mass media, was considerably greater than had been commonly accepted. Also established was the notion that different individuals were the opinion leaders or "influentials" in different situations or for different decisions. Similarly, other more marketing-oriented writers and researchers have expounded the importance of "referents" on the formation of the self, in changing attitudes, in modifying perceptions, and in actually motivating and directing purchase behavior.[6]

Whether or not reference influence is likely to come into play in the decisions of individuals depends on many interrelated factors. For descriptive-purposes, however, it is convenient to lump these factors under two major headings:

---

[5] *Ibid.*, p. 139.

[6] See, for instance, M. D. Beckman, "Are Your Messages Getting Through?," *Journal of Marketing*, July 1967, pp. 34–38; James E. Stafford, "Group Influences on Consumer Brand Preferences," *Journal of Marketing Research*, February 1966, pp. 68–75; W. T. Tucker, *The Social Context of Economic Behavior* (New York: Holt, Rinehart & Winston, 1964), Chapters 1-3.

1. Influence determinants which vary primarily according to the individual making the decision, such as the feeling of security or insecurity with respect to certain reference groups, the perception of the positions of these groups concerning kinds of behavior expected or attitudes toward specific issues, and the extent of knowledge about the matter on which a decision must be made.

2. Influence determinants which vary primarily according to the matter to be decided, such as the attributes of the product in a marketing situation.

In marketing, it is rarely practical to utilize information about individual differences (the first class above), because products must be designed and advertised with large classifications of people in mind. Also, while a great deal of purchase behavior may be an individualistic kind of activity, it may be very much socially conditioned. Consumers are often influenced by what others buy, especially those persons with whom they compare themselves, or use as referents.

While referents may have a great influence on purchase behavior, this influence is selective in that it does not apply equally to all products or brands. Bourne, for example, has shown that reference influence is potentially strong when a product has "expressive value" in distinguishing one group from another.[7] Clothing, cars, and home furnishings would fall in this category. Reference influence is also likely to be stronger on products reflecting personal taste, e.g., clothing, or in situations where the individual has little knowledge about a product or service, e.g., choosing a new doctor. However, the fact that referents do influence behavior does not satisfactorily answer the critical question according to Myers and Reynolds: How does the individual select from all present and possible groups those which he considers as referents for him?[8] While the answer is not absolute, the choice appears to be determined by some weighted combination of an internalized personal value-attitude system, coupled with current influences associated with social interaction with day-to-day referents. Each one of us has a rather structured value-attitude system, yet any of these attitudes, and resulting behavior, can be changed after being influenced by one or more referents.

The problems of the marketer, therefore, are two-fold: 1) determining whether purchases of his product are governed to any great extent by reference groups, and 2) determining which types of reference groups are most influential.

In conclusion, one of the crucial problems in the analysis of consumer behavior is ascertaining how a person defines the purchase situation, which of many referents does he use in arriving at such a definition, and who constitutes the audience whose responses provide the necessary confirmation and support for his purchase decision. The result is that we must focus our attention upon the expectations an individual imputes to others, the communications channels in which he participates, and his relations with those with whom he identifies himself. In short, reference theory should be an indispensable tool for understanding and interpreting the diversity and dynamic character of consumer behavior.

---

[7] Francis S. Bourne, "Group Influences in Marketing," in *Marketing Models, Quantitative and Behavioral*, Ralph Day (ed.) (Scranton, Pa.: International Textbook Co., 1964), pp. 63–79.

[8] J. H. Myers and W. H. Reynolds, *Consumer Behavior and Marketing Management* (Boston: Houghton-Mifflin Co., 1967), p. 176.

26. Personality and Consumer Behavior: A Review

HAROLD H. KASSARJIAN

INTRODUCTION

The past two decades, especially the last five years, have been exciting times in the field of consumer behavior. New data, theories, relationships, and models have been received with such enthusiasm that, in fact, a new field of scientific inquiry has developed. Studies such as consumer economics, rural sociology, social and mathematical psychology, social anthropology, and political science have been so churned and milled that from their amorphous mass the study of consumer behavior has become a relatively well delineated scientific discipline.

One of the more engrossing concepts in the study of consumer behavior is that of personality. Purchasing behavior, media choice, innovation, segmentation, fear, social influence, product choice, opinion leadership, risk taking, attitude change, and almost anything else one can think of have been linked to personality. The purpose of this article is to review the literature of consumer behavior and organize its contributions around the theoretical stems from which it grows.

Unfortunately, analysts do not agree on any general definition of the term "personality,"[1] except to somehow tie it to the concept of consistent responses to the world of stimuli surrounding the individual. Man does tend to be consistent in coping with his environment. This consistency of response allows us to type politicians as charismatic or obnoxious, students as aggressive or submissive, and colleagues as charming or "blah." Since individuals do react fairly consistently in a variety of environmental situations, these generalized patterns of response or modes of coping with the world can be called personality.

Personality, or better yet, the inferred hypothetical constructs relating to certain persistent qualities in human behavior, have fascinated both laymen and scholars for many centuries. The study of the relationship between behavior and personality has a most impressive history, ranging back to the earliest writings of the Chinese and Egyptians, Hippocrates, and some of the great European philosophers. In the fields of marketing and consumer behavior, the work in personality dates from Sigmund Freud and his popularizers in the commercial world, and the motivation researchers of the post-World War II era.

◆ SOURCE: Reprinted by permission from the *Journal of Marketing Research*, Vol. VIII, November 1971, (Published by the American Marketing Association), pp. 409–416.

[1] Hall and Lindzey, in attempting to deal with the dozens of approaches that exist in the literature, frustratingly submit that *personality is defined by the particular concepts which are part of the theory of personality employed by the observer.* Because this article reviews marketing literature rather than psychological literature, the various theories are not described in detail.

PSYCHOANALTIC THEORY

The psychoanalytic theories and philosophies of Freud have influenced not only psychology but also literature, social science, and medicine, as well as marketing. Freud stressed the unconscious nature of personality and motivation and said that much, if not all, behavior is related to the stresses within the personality system. The personality's three interacting sets of forces, the id, ego, and superego, interact to produce behavior.

According to Freudian theory, the id is the source of all driving psychic energy, but its unrestrained impulses cannot be expressed without running afoul of society's values. The superego is the internal representative of the traditional values and can be conceptualized as the moral arm of personality. The manner in which the ego guides the libidinal energies of the id and the moralistic demands of the superego accounts for the rich variety of personalities, interests, motives, attitudes, and behavior patterns of people. It accounts for the purchase of a four-door sedan rather than a racy sports car, the adoption of a miniskirt, and the use of Ultra-Brite toothpaste (with its promise of sex appeal) as a substitute for the rental of a motel room. The tools of the ego are defenses such as rationalization, projection, identification, and repression; its goals are integrated action.

Freud further believed that the child passes through various stages of development—the oral, anal, phallic, and genital periods—that determine the dynamics of his personality. The degree of tension, frustration, and love at these stages leads to his adult personality and behavior.

The influence of Freud and psychoanalytic theory cannot be overestimated. Most of the greatest names in psychiatry and psychology have been followers, disciples, or critics of Freud, much as many good marketing research studies have been criticisms of motivation researchers or experiments applying scientific procedures to motivation research. The work of Sidney Levy, Burleigh Gardner and Lee Rainwater, some of the projects of Martineau, and the proprietary studies of Social Research, Inc., are in the latter tradition. Although today the critics of psychoanalytic applications to consumer behavior far outweigh the adherents, Freud and his critics have contributed much to advances in marketing theory.

SOCIAL THEORISTS

In his lifetime, several members of Freud's inner ring became disillusioned with his insistence on the biological basis of personality and began to develop their own views and their own followers. Alfred Adler, for example, felt that the basic drive of man is not the channelization of the libido, but rather a striving for superiority. The basic aim of life, he reasoned, is to overcome feelings of inferiority imposed during childhood. Occupations and spouses are selected, homes purchased, and automobiles owned in the effort to perfect the self and feel less inferior to others.

Eric Fromm stressed man's loneliness in society and his seeking of love, brotherliness, and security. The search for satisfying human relationships is of central focus to behavior and motivations.

Karen Horney, also one of the neo-Freudian social theorists, reacted against theories of the biological libido, as did Adler, but felt that childhood insecurities stemming from parent-child relationships create basic anxieties and that the personality is developed as the individual learns to cope with his anxieties.

Although these and other neo-Freudians have influenced the work of motivation researchers, they have had minimal impact on research on consumer behavior. However, much of their theorizing can be seen in advertising today, which exploits the striving for superiority and the needs for love, security, and escape from loneliness to sell toothpaste, deodorants, cigarettes, and even detergents.

The only research in consumer behavior based directly on a neo-Freudian approach is Cohen's psychological test that purports to measure Horney's three basic orientations toward coping with anxiety—the compliant, aggressive, and detached types. Cohen found that compliant types prefer brand names and use more mouthwash and toilet soaps; aggressive types tend to use a razor rather than an electric shaver, use more cologne and after-shave lotion, and buy Old Spice deodorant and Van Heusen shirts; and detached types seem to be least aware of brands. Cohen, however, admitted to picking and choosing from his data, and although the published results are by no means conclusive, his work does indicate that the Horney typology may have some relevance to marketing.

Several follow-up studies using his instruments are unpublished to date.

STIMULUS-RESPONSE THEORIES

The stimulus- response or learning theory approach to personality presents perhaps the most elegant view, with a respected history of research and laboratory experimentation supporting it. Its origins are in the work of Pavlov, Thorndike, Skinner, Spence, Hull, and the Institute of Human Relations at Yale University. Although the various theorists differ among themselves, there is agreement that the link between stimulus and response is persistent and relatively stable. Personality is seen as a conglomerate of habitual responses acquired over time to specific and generalized cues. The bulk of theorizing and empirical research has been concerned with specifying conditions under which habits are formed, changed, replaced, or broken.

A drive leads to a response to a particular stimulus, and if the response is reinforced or rewarded, a particular habit is learned. Unrewarded and inappropriate responses are extinguished or eliminated. Complex behavior such as consumer decision processes is learned in a similar manner.

According to Dollard and Miller, a drive is a stimulus strong enough to impel activity; it energizes behavior but, by itself, does not direct it. Any stimulus may become a drive if it reaches sufficient intensity. Some stimuli are linked to the physiological processes necessary for the survival of the individual, others are secondary or acquired. With the concepts of cues, drives, responses, and reinforcement, complex motives such as the need for achievement or self-esteem are learned in the same manner as brand preference, racism, attitudes towards big business, purchasing habits, or dislike of canned spinach.

Marketing is replete with examples of the influence of learning theory, ranging from Krugman's work to the Yale studies on attitudes and attitude change, from lightweight discussions on the influence of repetition and reinforcement in advertising texts to Howard and Sheth's buyer behavior theory and the work in mathematical models. However, very few personality studies have used this theoretical orientation.

The reason for the lack of impact is probably that personality tests and measuring instruments using this theoretical base do not exist. Typically, clinical psychologists have developed measuring instruments, but until this past decade clinicians were not trained directly in learning theory. Recently, however, behavior modification based on the work of Skinner has become a psychotherapeutic technique. Many clinical psychologists are turning to learning theory for guidelines in the treatment of abnormality. Unfortunately, they do not seem to be predisposed to create psychological tests to measure personality in line with their definitions, but are more concerned with behavioral change. Until such instruments are developed there will be little use of these theories in relating consumer behavior to personality, irrespective of their completeness and extreme relevance.

TRAIT AND FACTOR THEORIES

As learning theory approaches to personality have evolved from the tough-minded empirical experimentation of the animal laboratories, factor theories have evolved from the quantitative sophistication of statistical techniques and computer technology. The core of these theories is that personality is composed of a set of traits or factors, some general and others specific to a particular situation or test. In constructing a personality instrument, the theorist typically begins with a wide array of behavorial measures, mostly responses to test items, and with statistical techniques distills factors which are then defined as the personality variables.

For one large group of personality instruments the researcher begins with the intent to measure certain variables, for example, need for achievement or aggressiveness. Large samples of subjects predetermined as aggressive or not agressive (say, by ratings from teachers and employers) are given the instrument. Each item is statistically analyzed to see if it discriminates aggressive from nonaggressive subjects. By a series of such distilling measures and additional validation and reliability studies, an instrument is produced which measures traits the researcher originally was attempting to gauge. Several of these variables are often embodied in, for example, a single 200-item instrument.

A second type of personality instrument is created not with theoretically predetermined variables in mind, but rather to identify a few items (by factor analysis) which account for a significant portion of the variance. Subjects are given questionnaires, ratings, or tests on a wide variety of topics, and test items are grouped in the factor analysis by how well they measure the same statistical factor. The meaning of a particular factor is thus empirically determined and a label arbitrarily attached to it that hopefully best describes what the researcher presumes the particular subset of items measures. Further reliability and validation measures lead to creation of a test instrument with several variables that supposedly account for the diversity and complexity of behavior. The theoretical structure is statistical and the variables are empirically determined and creatively named or labeled.

The concept of traits, factors, or variables that can be quantitatively measured has led to virtually hundreds of personality scales and dozens of studies in consumer behavior. Instruments of this type are discussed below.

Gordon Personal Profile

This instrument purports to measure ascendency, responsibility, emotional stability, and sociability, Tucker and Painter found significant correlations between use of headache remedies, vitamins, mouthwash, alcoholic drinks, automobiles, chewing gum, and the acceptance of new fashions and one or more of these four personality variables. The correlations ranged from .27 to .46, accounting for perhaps 10% of the variance.

Kernan used decision theory in an empirical test of the relationship between decision behavior and personality. He added the Gordon Personal Inventory to measure cautiousness, original thinking, personal relations, and vigor. Pearsonian and multiple correlations indicated few significant relationships, but canonical correlations between sets of personality variables and decision behavior gave a coefficient of association of .77, significant at the .10 level. Cluster analysis then showed that behavior is consistent with personality profiles within clusters. Kernan's results, like those of Tucker and Painter, show interesting relationships but are by no means startling.

Edwards Personal Preference Schedule

The EPPS has been used in about two dozen studies or rebuttals in consumer be-

havior from a trait and factor theory approach. The purpose of the instrument was to develop a factor-analyzed, paper-and-pencil, objective instrument to measure the psychoanalytically-oriented needs or themes developed by Henry Murray. Its popularity in consumer behavior can be traced to Evans' landmark study, in which he could find no differences between Ford and Chevrolet owners to an extent that would allow for prediction. He was, however, able to account for about 10% of the variance. Criticism of Evans' study and conclusions came from many fronts and on many grounds. Rejoinders were written, and finally Evans replicated the study. Using Evans' original data. Kuehn then concluded that predictive ability can be improved if one computes a discriminant function based on the two needs displaying the largest initial predictive ability. Kuehn improved Evans' results by using dominance scores minus affiliation scores. However, the psychological significance of dominance minus affiliation has escaped me for five years. Nevertheless, the controversy over Evans' study is in the very finest tradition of the physical and social sciences, with argument and counterargument, rejoinder and replication, until the facts begin to emerge, something very seldom seen in marketing and consumer behavior research. The final conclusion that seems to trickle through is that personality does account for some variance but not enough to give much solace to personality researchers in marketing.

Along other lines, Koponen used the EPPS scale with data collected on 9,000 persons in the J. Walter Thompson panel. His results indicate that cigarette smoking is positively related to sex dominance, aggression, and achievement needs among males and negatively related to order and compliance needs. Further, he found differences between filter and nonfilter smokers and found that these differences were made more pronounced by heavy smoking. In addition, there seemed to be a relationship between personality variables and readership of three unnamed magazines.

Massy, Frank, and Lodahl used the same data in a study of the purchase of coffee, tea, and beer. Their conclusion was that personality accounted for a very small percentage of the variance. In fact, personality plus socioeconomic variables accounted for only 5% to 10% of the variance in purchases.

In a sophisticated study, Claycamp presented the EPPS to 174 subjects who held savings accounts in banks or savings and loan associations. His results indicate that personality variables predict better than demographic variables whether an individual is a customer of a bank or a savings and loan association. These results contradict those of Evans, who concluded that socioeconomic variables are more effective than personality as measured by the same instrument. Using personality variables alone, Claycamp correctly classified 72% of the subjects.

Brody and Cunningham reanalyzed Koponen's data employing techniques like those of Claycamp and Massy, Frank, and Lodahl with similar results, accounting for 3% of the variance. Further, these results are similar to those from the Advertising Research Foundation's study on toilet paper in which 5% to 10% of the variance was accounted for by personality and other variables. Brody and Cunningham argued that the weak relationships may have been caused by an inadequate theoretical framework. Theirs consisted of three categories: perceived performance risk—the extent different brands perform differently in important ways; specific self-confidence—how certain the consumer is that a brand performs as he expects; and perceived social risk—the extent he thinks he will be judged on the basis of his brand decision. The authors concluded that, "when trying to discriminate the brand choice of people most likely to have perceived-high performance risk and to have high specific self-confidence, personality variables were very useful." For people who were 100% brand loyal, 8 personality variables explained 32% of the variance. As the minimum purchase of the favorite brand dropped from 100% to 40%, the explained variance fell to 13%.

Thurstone Temperament Schedule

This is another factor-analyzed instrument. Westfall, in a well known study that is often interpreted as a replication of Evans' study, compared personalities of automobile owners and could find no differences between brands. He further found no differences between compact and standard car owners on the Thurstone variables. However, personality characteristics did differ between owners of convertibles and standard models.

Using the same instrument, Kamen showed a relationship between the number of people who had no opinion on foods to be rated and the number of items they left unanswered on the Thurstone scale. Using a specially created questionnaire, he concluded that the dimension of "no opinion" is not related to food preference. Proneness to have an opinion does not seem to be a general trait, but rather is dependent on the content area.

California Personality Inventory

This is the newest paper-and-pencil test to be used extensively. Robertson and Myers developed measures for innovativeness and opinion leadership in the areas of food, clothing, and appliances. A multiple stepwise regression with 18 traits on the CPI indicated poor R^2's; the portion of variance accounted for was 4% for clothing, 5% for food, and 23% for appliances. The study tends to support the several dozen previous studies on innovation and opinion leadership that show a minimal relationship between personality variables and behavior toward new products. Several studies indicate that gregariousness and venturesomeness are relevant to opinion leadership. Two studies using personality inventories have found a relationship between innovation and personality, while three others could find none. Other traits, such as informal and formal social participation, cosmopolitanism, and perceived risk, are related to innovative behavior in about half a dozen studies, while an additional half a dozen studies show no differences.

A very recent study by Boone attempted to relate the variables on the California Personality Inventory to the consumer innovator on the topic of a community antenna television system. His results indicate significant differences between innovators and followers on 10 of 18 scales. Unfortunately, the statistical techniques were quite different from those employed by Robertson and Myers, so it is not possible to determine whether or not the two studies are in basic agreement.

Finally, Vitz and Johnston, using the masculinity scale of both the CPI and the Minnesota Multiphasic Personality Inventory, hypothesized that the more masculine a smoker's personality, the more masculine the image of his regular brand of cigarettes. The correlations were low but statistically significant, and the authors concluded that the results moderately support product preference as a predictable interaction between the consumer's personality and the product's image.

THEORIES OF SELF AND SELF-CONCEPT

Relationships of product image and self-image have been studied quite thoroughly by the motivation researchers and, particularly, Levy and Gardner. The theoretical base for this work, I presume, rests in the writings and philosophies of Carl Rogers, William James, and Abraham Maslow and the symbolic interactionism proposed by Susan Langer and others.

The core of these views is that the individual has a real- and an ideal-self. This *me* or *self* is "the sum total of all that a man can call his—his body, traits, and abilities: his material possessions; his family, friends, and enemies; his vocations and avocations and much else." It includes evaluations and definitions of one's self and may be reflected in much of his actions, including his evaluations and purchase of products and services. The belief is that individuals perceive products that they own, would like to own, or do not want to own in terms of symbolic meaning to themselves and to others. Congruence between the symbolic image of a product (e.g., a .38 caliber is aggressive and masculine, a Lincoln automobile is extravagant and wealthy) and a consumer's self-image implies greater probability of positive evaluation, preference, or ownership of that product or brand. For example, Jacobson and Kossoff studied self-perception and attitudes toward small cars. Individuals who perceived themselves as "cautious conservatives" were more likely to favor small cars as a practical and economic convenience. Another self-classified group of "confident explorers" preferred large cars, which they saw as a means of expressing their ability to control the environment.

Birdwell, using the semantic differential, tested the hypotheses that: (1) an automobile owner's perception of his car is essentially congruent with his perception of himself and (2) the average perception of a specific car type and brand is different for owners of different sorts of cars. The hypotheses were confirmed with varying degrees of strength. However, this does not imply that products have personalities and that a consumer purchases those brands whose images are congruent with his self-concept; Birdwell's study did not test causality. It could very well be that only after a product is purchased does the owner begin to perceive it as an extension of his own personality.

Grubb and Grubb and Grathwohl found that consumers' different self-perceptions are associated with varying patterns of consumer behavior. They claimed that self-concept is a meaningful mode of market segmentation. Grubb found that beer drinkers perceived themselves as more confident, social, extroverted, forward, sophisticated, impulsive, and temperamental than their non-beer-drinking brethren. However, the comparison of self-concept and beer brand profiles revealed inconclusive results: drinker and nondrinkers perceived brands similarly.

In a follow-up study of Pontiac and Volkswagen owners, Grubb and Hupp indicated that owners of one brand of automobile perceive themselves as similar to others who own the same brand and significantly different from owners of the other brand. Sommers indicated by the use of a Q-sort of products that subjects are reliably able to describe themselves and others by products rather than adjectives, say on a semantic differential or adjective checklist. That is, individuals are able to answer the questions, "What kind of a person am I?" and "What kind of a person is he?" by Q-sorting products.

Dolich further tested the congruence relationship between self-images and product brands and concluded that there is a greater similarity between one's self-concept and images of his most preferred brands than images of least preferred brands. Dolich claimed that favored brands are consistent with and reinforce self-concept.

Finally, Hamm and Hamm and Cundiff related product perception to what they call self-actualization, that is, the discrepancy between the self and ideal-self. Those with a small discrepancy were called low self-actualizers, a definition which does not seem consistent with Maslow's work on the hierarchy of needs. High self-actualizers describe themselves in terms of products differently from low self-actualizers, and in turn perceive products differently. For both groups, some products such as house, dress, automatic dishwasher, and art prints tend to represent an ideal-self, wife, or mother, while others such as cigarettes, TV dinners, or a mop do not.

LIFE STYLE

An integration of the richness of motivation research studies and the tough-mindedness and statistical sophistication of computer technology has led to another type of research involving personality, variously called psychographic or life-style research. The life-style concept is based on distinctive or characteristic modes of living of segments of a society. The technique divides the total market into segments based on interests, values, opinions, personality characteristics, attitudes, and demographic variables using techniques of cluster analysis, factor analysis, and canonical correlation. Wells dubbed the methodology "backward segmentation" because it groups people by behavioral characteristics before seeking correlates. Pessemier and Tigert reported that some preliminary relationships were found between the factor-analyzed clusters of people and market behavior.

Generally, the relationship of the attitude-interest-personality clusters, when correlated with actual buyer behavior, indicates once again that 10% or less of the variance is accounted for. Yet quite properly the proponents of the technique claim that very rich data are available in the analyses for the researcher and practitioner interested in consumer behavior.

MISCELLANEOUS OTHER APPROACHES

The overall results of other studies with other points of view are quite similar. Some researchers interpret their results as insignificant while others interpret similarly minimal relationships as significant, depending on the degree of statistical sophistication and the statistical tools used. A hodgepodge of other studies indicates that heavy and light users of several product classes do not differ on the McClosky Personality Inventory or Dunnette Adjective Checklist. Axelrod found a predictable relationship between the mood produced by viewing a movie—*The Nuremburg Trial*—and attitudes towards consumer products such as savings bonds, sewing machines, typewriters, and daiquiris. Eysenck, Tarrant, Woolf, and England indicated that smoking is related to genotypic personality differences. Summers found a minimal relationship between characteristics of opinion leaders and the Borgatta personality variables. Pennington and Peterson have shown that product preferences are related to vocational interests as measured on the Strong Vocational Interest Blank. Finally, Jacoby has demonstrated that Rokeach's concepts of open and closed mindedness are relevant to consumer behavior and found that low dogmatics tend to be more prone to innovation and dogmatism was −.32, the explained variance about 10%. Myers, in a study of private brand attitudes, found that Cattell's 16-Personality Factor Inventory explained about 5% of the variance. Once again, the results are in the same order—5% to 10% of the variance accounted for.

Social Character

In the usual pattern of applying psychological and sociological concepts to marketing and consumer behavior, several researchers have turned their attention to Riesman's theories, which group human beings into three types of social character: tradition-directed, inner-directed, and other-directed. A society manifests one type predominantly, according to its particular phase of development.

Riesman by no means intended his typology to be interpreted as a personality schema, yet in the consumer behavior literature social character has been grouped with personality, and hence the material is included in this review.

A society of tradition-directed people, seldom encountered in the United States today, is characterized by general slowness of change, a dependence on kin, low social mobility, and a tight web of values. Inner-directed people are most often found in a rapidly changing, industrialized society with division of labor, high social mobility, and less security, these persons must turn to inner values for guidance. In contrast, other-directed persons depend upon those around them to give direction to their actions. The other-directed society is industrialized to the point that its orientation shifts from production to consumption. Thus success in the other-directed society is not through production and hard work but rather through one's ability to be liked by others, develop charm or "personality," and manipulate other people. The contemporary United States is considered by Riesman to be almost exclusively populated by the latter two social character types and is rapidly moving towards an other-directed orientation.

Dornbusch and Hickman content analyzed consumer goods advertising over the past decades and noted a clear trend from inner- to other-direction. Kassarjian and Centers have shown that youth is significantly more other-directed and that those foreign born or reared in small towns tend to be inner-directed.

Gruen found no relationship between preference for new or old products and inner-other-direction. Arndt and Barban, Sandage, Kassarjian, and Kassarjian could find little relationship between innovation and social character; Donnelly, however, has shown a relationship between housewives' acceptance of innovations and social character, with the inner-directed being slightly more innovative. Linton and Graham indicated that inner-directed persons are less easily persuaded than other-directed persons. Centers and Horowitz found susceptible to social influence in an experimental setting than were inner-directed subjects. Kassarjian found that subjects expressed a preference for appeals based on their particular social character type. There was minimal evidence for differential exposure to various mass media between the two Riesman types.

In a similar study, Woodside found no relationship between consumer products and social character, although he did find a minimal relationship between advertising appeals and inner-other-direction.

Finally, Kassarjian and Kassarjian found a relationship between social character and Allport's scale of values as well as vocational interests but could find no relationship between inner-other-direction and personality variables as measured by the MMPI. Once again, the results follow the same pattern: a few studies find and a few do not find meaningful relationships between consumer behavior and other measures.

Personality and Persuasibility

To complete a review on the relationship between personality and consumer behavior, the wide body of research findings relating personality to persuasibility and attitude change must be included. In addition to the dozens of studies carried out under Carl Hovland, there are many relating personality characteristics to conformity, attitude change, fear appeals, and opinions on various topics. The consumer behavior literature studies by Cox and Bauer, Bell, Carey, and Barach tied self-confidence to personality in the purchase of goods. These studies indicated a curvilinear relationship between generalized self-confidence and persuasibility and between specific self-confidence and persuasibility. Venkatesan's results, however, throw some doubt on these findings. In recent reanalysis and review of much of this literature, Shuchman and Perry found contradictory data and felt these were inconsequential. The authors claim that neither generalized nor specific self-confidence appears to be an important determinant of persuasibility in marketing. Bauer, in turn, has found fault with the Shuchman and Perry reanalysis.

SUMMARY AND CONCLUSIONS

A review of these dozens of studies and papers can be summarized in the single word, *equivocal*. A few studies indicate a strong relationship between personality and aspects of consumer behavior, a few indicate no relationship, and the great majority indicate that if correlations do exist they are so weak as to be questionable or perhaps meaningless. Several reasons can be postulated to account for these discrepancies. Perhaps the major one is based on the validity of the particular personality measuring instruments used: a typically "good" instrument has a test-retest reliability of about .80 and a split-half reliability of about .90. Validity coefficients range at most from .40 to about .70; that is, when correlated against a criterion variable, the instrument typically accounts for about 20% to 40% of the variance. Too often the marketing researcher is just plain disinterested in reliability and validity criteria. *Tests validated for specific uses on specific populations, such as college students, or as part of mental hospital intake batteries are applied to available subjects in the general population.* The results may indicate that 10% of the variance is accounted for; this is then interpreted as a weak relationship and personality is rejected as a determinant of purchase. The consumer researcher too often expects more from an instrument than it was originally intended to furnish.

An additional problem for the marketing researcher is the conditions under which the test instrument is given. The instrument is often presented in the classroom or on the doorstep, rather than in the office of a psychometrician, psychotherapist, or vocational counselor. As Wells has pointed out:

The measurements we take may come from some housewife sitting in a bathrobe at her kitchen table, trying to figure out what it is she is supposed to say in answering a questionnaire. Too often, she is not telling us about herself as she really is, but instead is telling us about herself as she thinks she is or wants us to think she is.

To compound the error, consumer researchers often forget that the strength of a correlation is limited by the reliability of the measures being correlated. Not only the personality test but also the criterion itself may be unreliable under these conditions, as Wells has pointed out. Often the criterion used in these studies is the consumer's own account of her purchasing behavior. More often than not, these data are far more unreliable than we may wish to almit.

Adaptation of Instruments

Much too often, in order to adjust test items to fit specific demands, changes are made in the instrument. Items are taken out of context of the total instrument, words are changed, items are arbitrarily discarded, and the test is often shortened drastically. This adjustment would undoubtedly horrify the original developer of the instrument, and the disregard for the validity of the modified instrument should horrify the rest of us. Just how much damage is done when a measure of self-confidence or extroversion is adapted, revised, and restructured is simply not known, but it would not be a serious exaggeration to claim it is considerable. And, most unfortunately, from time to time even the name of the variable is changed to fit the needs of the researcher. For example, Cohen has pointed out that in the Koponen study male smokers scored higher than average on self-depreciation and association, variables not included in the Edwards instrument. The researcher was apparently using the abasement and affiliation scales. Such changes may or may not be proper, and although they may not necessarily violate scientific canons, they certainly do not help reduce the confusion in attempting to sort out what little we know about the relationships of personality to consumer behavior.

Psychological Instruments in Marketing Research

A second reason for discrepancies in the literature is that instruments originally intended to measure gross personality characteristics such as sociability, emotional stability, introversion, or neuroticism have been used to make predictions of the chosen brand of toothpaste or cigarettes. The variables that lead to the assassination of a president, confinement in a mental hospital, or suicide may not be identical to those that lead to the purchase of a washing machine, a pair of shoes, or chewing gum. *Clearly, if unequivocal results are to emerge, consumer behavior researchers must develop their own definitions and design their own instruments to measure the personality variables that go into the purchase decision rather than using tools designed as part of a medical model to measure schizophrenia or mental stability.*

Development of definitions and instruments can perhaps be handled in two ways. One will require some brilliant theorizing as to what variables do relate to the consumer decision process. If neuroticism and sociability are not the relevant personality variables, then perhaps new terms such as risk aversion, status seeking, and conspicuous consumption will emerge. Personality variables that in fact are relevant to the consumer model need to be theorized and tests developed and validated.

Another approach to developing such instruments might be that of the factor theorists. Dozens of items measuring behavior, opinions, purchases, feelings, or attitudes can be factor analyzed in the search for general and specific factors that in turn can be validated against the marketing behavior of the individual. The research group at Purdue, and the recent work of Wells, have made refreshingly new attempts at personality measurement and come very close to the research techniques developed by the factor theorists. Whether or not these attempts will succeed in producing a new approach to personality research is yet to be proved; the studies to date are encouraging.

Only with marketing-oriented instruments will we be able to determine just what part personality variables play in the consumer decision process and, further, if they can be generalized across product and service classes or must be product-specific instruments. At that stage, questions of the relevancy of these criteria for market segmentation, shifting demand curves, or creating and sustaining promotional and advertising campaigns can be asked.

Hypotheses

A third reason for the lackluster results in the personality and consumer behavior literature is that *many studies have been conducted by a shotgun approach with no specific hypotheses or theoretical justification.* Typically a convenient, available, easily scored, and easy-to-administer personality inventory is selected and administered along with questionnaires on purchase data and preferences. The lack of proper scientific method and hypothesis generation is supposedly justified by the often-used disclaimer that the study is exploratory. As Jacoby has pointed out:

Careful examination reveals that, in most cases, no a priori thought is directed to *how,* or especially *why,* personality should or should not be related to that aspect of consumer behavior being studied. Moreover, the few studies which do report statistically significant findings usually do so on the basis of post-hoc "picking and choosing" out of large data arrays.

Statistical techniques are applied and anything that turns up looking halfway interesting furnishes the basis for the discussion section.

An excellent example of the shotgun approach to science, albeit a more sophisticated one than most, is Evans' original study examining personality differences between Ford and Chevrolet owners. Jacoby, in an excellent and most thoughtful paper, noted that Evans began his study with specific hypotheses culled from the literature and folklore pertaining to personality differences to be expected between Ford and Chevrolet owners. He then presented the EPPS to subjects, measuring 11 variables, 5 of which seemed to be measuring the variables in question; the remaining 6 were irrelevant to the hypotheses with no a priori basis for expecting differ-

ences. If predictions were to have been made on these six scales, Jacoby says, they should have been ones of *no* difference. Using one-tailed tests of significance, since the directions also should have been hypothesized, 3 of the 5 key variables were significant at the .05 level and none of the remaining 6 were significant. In short, Evans' data could have been interpreted such that 9 of the 11 scales were "significant" according to prediction. Jacoby's interpretation leads to a conclusion quite different from Evans', that there are no personality differences between Ford and Chevrolet owners. Also, with a priori predictions, Jacoby did not have to pick and choose from his data, as Kuehn was forced to do in showing a relationship between "dominance minus affiliation" scores and car ownership.

Finally, personality researchers and researchers in other aspects of marketing seem to need simple variables which can be somehow applied in the marketplace. We seem to feel that the only function of science and research is to predict rather than to understand, to persuade rather than to appreciate. Social scientists can fully accept that personality variables are related to suicide or crime, to assassinations, racial prejudice, attitudes towards the USSR, or the selection of a spouse. They do not get upset that personality is not the only relevant variable or that the portion of the explained variance is merely 20% or 10% or 5%. Yet personality researchers in consumer behavior much too often ignore the many interrelated influences on the consumer decision process, ranging from price and packaging to availability, advertising, group influences, learned responses, and preferences of family members, in addition to personality. *To expect the influence of personality variables to account for a large portion of the variance is most certainly asking too much.* What is amazing is not that there are many studies that show no correlation between consumer behavior and personality, but rather that there are any studies at all with positive results. That 5% or 10% or any portion of the variance can be accounted for by personality variables measured on ill-chosen and inadequate instruments is most remarkable, indeed!

27. Seven Questions about Lifestyle and Psychographics

WILLIAM D. WELLS

Since work on lifestyle and psychographics is both comparatively new and eminently marketable, it is not surprising that interest in this field is high and that a covey of disagreeing experts has already assembled. In view of this healthy situation, it might be useful to pose some of the questions that have been asked about lifestyle and psychographic research, and to provide what seem to be parts of some of the answers.

The questions are arranged roughly in order of degree of seeming consensus about what the "right" answers are—from "This is pretty definitely it" to "Well, we just don't know, yet."

The questions are as follows:

1. Are lifestyle differences among groups of consumers "really" just differences along a few familiar demographic variables?

2. How does lifestyle analysis relate to product benefit segmentation and to other forms of segmentation that are in widespread use today?

3. Are the relationships between lifestyle and consumption strong enough to be used in making marketing decisions?

4. When designing a lifestyle study, is it better to tailor make questions to fit the product or to focus on more generalized traits and attributes?

5. When designing a lifestyle study, is it better to focus on a few hypothesized relationships between lifestyle and product consumption or to cast a wide net among apparently unrelated variables, hoping to catch something interesting?

6. What is the "best" way to analyze lifestyle data?

7. Once a lifestyle study has been done, how do you insure that it will be used?

LIFESTYLE AND DEMOGRAPHICS

Let us first look at the relationship between lifestyle and demographics, and address the question, "Does lifestyle data add anything that is both real and important to the standard forms of demographic analysis?" Among those who have worked with lifestyle and psychographic data at least, this question seems to have been pretty well settled. There is little doubt among those that have had experience in this field that data of this kind contain information that cannot be found in, or inferred from, demographics alone.

At times, lifestyle differences have been found where demographic differences do not exist.[1] Even in those situations where life-

◆ SOURCE: Reprinted by permission from *Marketing Education and the Real World* and *Dynamic Marketing in a Changing World*, edited by Boris W. Becker and Helmut Becker, Combined Proceedings of the Spring and Fall Conferences of the American Marketing Association, 1972, Series No. 34; pp. 462–465.

[1] Harry E. Heller, "Defining Target Markets by Their Attitude Profiles," in *Attitude Research on the Rocks*, Lee Adler and Irving Crespi, eds. (Chicago: American Marketing Association, 1970), 45–57; Thomas P. Hustad and Edgar A. Pessemier, "Will the Real Consumer Activist

style patterns can be said to be partly (or even largely) "due to" underlying demographic patterns, lifestyle data add a richness and a texture that is useful both to the product manager and to the advertising copywriter. Detailed information about consumer activities, interests, needs, attitudes and values provides a picture of the consumer that simply cannot be drawn from demographics alone.

LIFESTYLE AND BENEFIT SEGMENTATION

The second question may be stated as follows: "How does lifestyle analysis relate to benefit segmentation[2]—a type of analysis that has recently seen much use?" As Hustad and Pessemier have pointed out,[3] it is possible to think of the various kinds of data we get from consumers as forming a continuum, running from demographic characteristics and personality traits at one end to purchasing decisions at the other. This continuum is illustrated in Fig. 1.

Please Stand Up: An Examination of Consumers' Opinions About Marketing Practices and Their Relationships to Individual Attitudes and Behavior," Institute Paper No. 345, Krannert Graduate School of Industrial Administration, Purdue University, March, 1972; Alan R. Nelson, "A National Study of Psychographics," unpublished working paper delivered at the International Marketing Congress, American Marketing Association, June, 1969, Time-Life, Inc., New York; Douglas J. Tigert, "Psychometric Correlates of Opinion Leadership and Innovation," working paper, the Graduate School of Business, The University of Chicago.

[2] Russell I. Haley, "Beyond Benefit Segmentation," *Journal of Advertising Research*, 11 (August, 1971), 3–8; and "Benefit Segmentation: A Decision-Oriented Research Tool," *Journal of Marketing*, Vol. 32 (July, 1968), 30–5.
[3] Thomas P. Hustad and Edgar A. Pessemier, "The Development and Application of Psychographic Life Style and Associated Activity and Attitude Measures," Paper No. 287, Krannert Graduate School of Industrial Administration, Purdue University, March 1971.

Clearly, among these types of data, purchase intentions are closest to actual purchases, brand and product preferences are next, responses to the benefits offered by different products and different brands are next, and so on. One should therefore be able to predict purchases more accurately from intentions than from preferences; more accurately from preferences than from benefits; more accurately from benefits than from activities, interests, and opinions; and more accurately from activities, interests and opinions than from demographics and personality traits. A very substantial amount of research has now shown that the closer you get to the actual act—both temporally and psychologically—the more accurate the prediction.[4] When prediction is the name of the game, variables to the right of the diagram are virtually certain to be superior.

Unfortunately, this greater predictive accuracy is purchased at the cost of descriptive value. To describe those who purchase Brand X as "Those who intended to purchase Brand X" is not very helpful, regardless of the size of the correlation coefficient. Similarly, to say "Those who purchase Brand X are those who prefer it" usually strikes marketing managers as something less than sensational.

When we move back several spaces in the diagram, to evaluation of product benefits, the data begin to produce useful descriptions of consumers. It *does* help to know that some consumers want strength while others want safety, that some want decay prevention while others want whitening, and that some want economy while others want style. In fact, it is just such benefit differences— sharpened, publicized and sometimes even created by advertising—that distinguish the brands in many product categories. But even these benefit differences leave something to be desired as descriptions of consumers. They

[4] Frank M. Bass and Wayne Talarzyk, "An Attitudinal Model for the Study of Brand Preference," *Journal of Marketing Research*, Vol. 9 (February, 1972), 93–6.

Demographics personality traits	Activities, interests, and opinions	Evaluation of product benefits	Preferences	Intentions	Purchases

FIGURE 1. A continuum of consumer characteristics.

are frequently important clues in the analysis of consumer behavior, but they reveal little about the consumer as a person.

It is in this context that activities, interests and opinions—lifestyle data—have proved to be of significant value. By providing a detailed portrait of the consumer over a large range of interesting descriptive variables, lifestyle data bring the consumer to life in a way that is difficult to duplicate short of seeing him (or her) in person.

Are the Relationships Strong Enough to be Useful?

With Fig. 1 in mind, one can evaluate the strength of the relationships between lifestyle variables and purchasing criteria. Stated as correlation coefficients these relationships appear to be shockingly small—frequently in the .1 to .2 range, seldom higher than .3 to .4.

While one may not be prepared to argue in favor of weak prediction over strong prediction, it is important to point out that relationships of this size have been used for years in marketing research and in the selection of media. Correlations between product or brand use and demographics are of this order of magnitude or smaller, as are correlations between media use and demographics and between media use and product consumption.

The cross-tabulation in Table 1 between a homemaker's employment status and the amount she travels per day may be considered as an example. Although the relationship appears strong enough to be both meaningful and useful, the correlation is only .19.

The relationship between social class and use of a particular type of cosmetics as shown in Table 2 represents a second example. A significant and meaningful relationship seems

again present, but the product-moment correlation is only .24.

One could multiply these examples over and over, and show that the relationships upon which marketing and media decisions are *typically* made are, when expressed as r^2, seldom higher than .3 and almost never as high as .5.

The answer to the question, "Are the relationships strong enough to be useful?" is: yes, small correlations *do* provide useful information. In fact, it is on low correlations that many really important decisions—in marketing and in other areas of applied social science—are made.

GENERALIZED VS. TAILOR-MADE STUDIES

Another question often asked is, "Is it better to use a standard questionnaire to generate lifestyle data, or should a new set of questions be created to fit the subject and the circumstances of each new study?"

One part of the answer is that a tailor-made questionnaire, like a tailor-made suit, is apt both to be a better fit and more expensive. But another less obvious part of the answer is that there are some real values in using at least some of the same lifestyle questions over and over again. In addition to providing trend information, repeated use of the same question in different studies builds up a frame of reference that helps explain what answers to the question mean. After seeing a question in different contexts—in relationships to different products and different media, for example—one knows more about the meaning of a question than after seeing it the first time.

In fact one may not be confronted with a bitter choice between two mutually exclusive

Table 1. Employment Status and Travel

(Base:)	Amount of Travel Per Year			
	Very Low (207) %	Low (177) %	High (193) %	Very High (182) %
Employment of homemaker				
Full time	20	22	30	41
Part time	9	11	12	10
None	71	67	58	49

Table 2. Social Class and Cosmetic Use

	Cosmetic Use			
(Base:)	Low (120) %	Medium (155) %	High (167) %	Very High (139) %
Social Class				
Upper middle	19	14	22	23
Lower middle	18	30	40	50
Upper lower	47	43	33	25
Lower	16	13	5	2

alternatives. It is possible—and indeed quite common—to use a core set of questions time after time, supplemented by a tailor-made set designed to fit each specific problem.

FISHING EXPEDITION VS. SPECIFIC HYPOTHESES

A related issue is, "Is it better to use a wide variety of questions, many of which have no obvious relationship to the matter under consideration, or should one focus on much more limited question sets, each one designed to test some hypothesized relationship?"

The answer to this question would seem to depend upon how much one knows about the matter to begin with. If the knowledge is such that all one needs is verification, a sensible approach would be to ask specific, pointed questions.

On the other hand, if knowledge is limited and some interesting surprises might emerge, it seems a pity to avoid that opportunity. The following statements are examples of perhaps unforeseen but significant relationships:

— Use of heavy duty hand soap and agreement with the statement "There should be a gun in every home."
— Heavy usage of laundry detergent and agreement with "The next car our family buys will probably be a station wagon."
— Heavy use of all purpose liquid cleaner and agreement with "I spend a lot of time talking with my friends about products and brands."
— Recent purchases of diapers and agreement with "I am uncomfortable when my house is not completely clean."
— And, for males, ownership of at least one dog and zero cats is associated with

"I would do better than average in a fist fight."

BEST FORM OF ANALYSIS

Finally, there are two questions for which only fragmentary answers can be provided. The first is, "What is the best way to analyze lifestyle data?" And the second is, "Once a lifestyle study has been completed, what can one do to help decision makers use the results?"

In the first lifestyle studies conducted at Leo Burnett, usage rates for more than 100 products and brands were each cross-tabulated with 300 lifestyle questions, along with questions about demographic characteristics and media use. This procedure resulted in an office full of paper, only a small portion of which was of any real use.

To reduce the volume of paper, we adopted the practice of computing correlation coefficients between the lifestyle statements and the product and brand questions, and cross-tabulating only those relationships that exceeded an arbitrary cut-off point. This procedure reduced the tables to a manageable number; and, for many products, it provided interesting and useful lifestyle portraits.

At this point two additional problems appeared. For some products, so few significant relationships emerged that it was impossible to draw a lifestyle portrait. And for some other products, the cross-tabulations seemed to be producing a double or triple exposure, as it were. Instead of a single, sharp picture, two or three portraits seemed to be superimposed.

This experience led to a series of experiments employing cluster analysis as a preliminary step. With the respondents grouped into clusters, representing dramatically different lifestyles it was often possible to see that what had been thought of as "the target" —the heavy user of a product category, or the user of a specific brand, for example— frequently consisted of two or three quite distinct types of consumers. Merging these types in a general, over-all cross-tabulation had produced either no portrait at all, or the double or triple exposure effect just mentioned.

Continued experiments with different clustering routines and with Q factor analysis have remained inconclusive as to which approach yields the optimal mix of meaningfulness, stability and cost. It does seem clear, however, that in many situations almost any form of preclustering is better than no preclustering at all.

GETTING THE INFORMATION USED

Several problems may also be encountered in inducing the usage of information on the part of those who could benefit from it most. First, it sometimes happens that the information contradicts dearly held ideas. If a copy chief has committed himself to a particular stance in his advertising, and if the lifestyle data suggests that this particular stance might be wrong, it is too much to expect that the copy chief will bow gracefully to the verities of research. If a brand manager has oriented all his thinking and all his plans around "the" heavy user of a product class, and if a lifestyle segmentation suggests that "the" heavy user actually consists of several distinct types, the added complexity in an already complex situation is not likely to be warmly welcomed. These situations are much less comfortable all around than situations in which research confirms what its users already knew.

Second, lifestyle research is comparatively new, and as such it is subject to the skepticism verging on hostility that any emerging development deservedly gets. Potential users rightfully hesitate to base major decisions on something that has not yet been thoroughly explored, evaluated, tested and proved. Perhaps with time that problem will become less serious.

Finally, lifestyle data seem to be inherently complex, and trying to boil it all down to a one-page executive summary is almost certain to eliminate the detail that is the essence of the method. This means that if the sponsor of lifestyle research is to get the most for his money, he must commit major time resources to immersing himself in the findings. Frequently those who would benefit most from such immersion simply cannot afford the time to do it.

Many who have participated in lifestyle studies have found that this final step—the translation of findings into action—is the most difficult step of all. While this step may be difficult in any kind of research, it seems to be especially painful when the material is complex and subtle, and when the methodology is strange.

At Burnett, the problem has been approached by presenting data in semi-finished form as a basis for speculation and discussion. It has frequently (but not always) been found that extensive informal discussion of possible interpretations and implications has served to get the user into the data as well as to get the data into the user. As Kurt Lewin[5] discovered when he tried to persuade housewives to serve unusual cuts of meat, discussion and resolution are apt to elicit more action than a well-ordered, logical lecture does.

CONCLUSION

As noted earlier, the last two of these seven questions seem to be particularly sticky, and it is possible that neither will ever be completely solved. But lifestyle and psychographic research has attracted a good deal of attention—both in the business world and in academia—and it seems quite likely that interesting new developments will continue for some time to come. Perhaps we will even see the time when questions 6 and 7 are not as troublesome the they now are.

---

[5] Kurt Lewin, "Group Discussion and Social Change," in Maccoby, Newcomb and Hartley (eds.) *Readings in Social Psychology*, 3rd ed. (New York: Holt, Rinehart and Winston, 1958), pp. 197–212.

28. Causes of Buying Behavior: Mythology of Behavior Fact?

WILLIAM A. YOELL

I'd like to paint a mental picture for you—one which you might recognize as having seen in your own home.

Visualize a dark and dreary, rainy day. The children have become bored, restless. They break out into a streak of wildness, loud horseplay, teasing each other. Their mother has cajoled; then threatened. Nothing will quiet them down.

One mother, in such a situation, announces the intention to bake a cake.

Another announces a "soda" party.

Another serves dinky balls for lunch.

Quiet and calm is restored.

Was the behavior of these mothers caused by some kind of vague segmentation? By a life style or psychograph characterized as indulgent, leisure loving, social desirability, conformity? A value system? An aesthenic or cyclothymic personality? Or, was there a learned Response to an environmental situation based on previous conditioning and reinforcement?

Here is another picture. A housewife sees a new food product advertised. She sees it on the shelf in the store, but passes it by. Is she in the "non-leader" group? Is her non-buying behavior the result of a graph of her psyche which indicates she is not food-oriented or oriented toward family life? Or, is it because her Response to new food product appeals has been extinguished; because when she

tried new food products and new ways of cooking, her family didn't like them? When she added a particular product to the meat loaf, her family said, "Hey, Mom, what did you do to the meat loaf tonight? It's awful!" (It *is* a universal characteristic of children not to like highly spiced foods.)

Before you label new product tryers the "leader group" had you better not study the total behavior and experience of non-buyers? Maybe the new product buyers are simply first time new product tryers or haven't had the experiences of the non-buyers. Did you analyze the total behavior and experience of both buyers and non-buyers, not only in *your* product category, but in all? Perceptions and conceptions *do* transfer.

"Life style" is a coined expression that sounds nice, but which has no objective basis. It is an a priori assumption—like the Id, Ego, the Unconscious. It is no different than the attempt to put consumers into Personality categories such as cyclothymic, pyknic, choleric.

You cannot take broad, macroscopic concepts, such as life style, psychograph, or personality, and predict cake mix, dog food, dessert or deodorant, skin care or pickle eating behavior, or extend them to these microscopic areas.

One more group of pictures: An adult male is pacing up and down a New York City subway platform. He puts his money down, picks up a candy bar, a *particular* kind of candy bar.

A woman in Minneapolis visiting her daughter is doing the laundry in the Laundro-

◆ SOURCE: Reprinted by permission from *Marketing in a Changing World*, edited by Bernard A. Morin, Proceedings of the June 1969 Conference of the American Marketing Association, Series No. 29, pp. 241–248.

mat for her daughter. After a short while, she puts a dime in the candy machine and selects a *particular* kind of candy bar—the same kind the subway pacer bought.

A teen in Atlanta misses the school bus. She has to walk a mile to get home. Before she begins walking, she enters a candy store and buys two bars of candy, the same type the Grandmother and the pacer bought.

Does the psychograph of these three individuals show them to be introverted, self-indulgent, or aggressive? Or, were these behaviors a universally learned, conditioned and reinforced response that connected a long-lasting, chewy type candy with a long, arduous, unpleasant activity. On the other hand, were they compensation for the situations (environmental) in which these people found themselves?

DO these behaviors (responses) just described, occur regardless of whether the mother is outdoor "oriented"? Aware of social responsibility? Or, whether her husband is a Scotch drinker or an "intellectualist"?

In the rainy day picture, it is the rainy day plus the behavior of the children that evokes the cake-baking response. If any mother bakes a cake and dinner time brings less fussing and toying with food, she will do it again; also, she will do it again if she has baked a cake and the family eats left-overs without haggling.

I offer you a simple, but, empirically established, formula: $B = (f) \ C$

Behavior is a function of its consequences, not of psychometric measurements, graphs of the psyche, life styles or value systems. It is A-historical. What happens after a response is emitted determines whether or not it is repeated. The Response operates on the environment.

An extension of this formula indicates the probability that a particular behavior will occur.

The Probability of behavior Y occurring is a function of the individual's expectancy to be reinforced, depending on previous reinforcing situations *times* how much value is attached to reinforcement:

$$PBy = f \ (R_E y \times Rv)$$

Simply put, if good behavior has been reinforced with a candy bar, the child will behave while mother is gone, expecting a candy bar. The value to the child has been established, because in the past he has been willing to obey, perform satisfactorily.

By calling a person something as the result of a psychograph or life style measurement, you are not labeling behavior, although it *sounds* as if you are. It says nothing about what a person does. A man may be lazy around the house but a ball of fire at the bowling alley or playing with the kids. Nothing is gained by terming such a man or his value system as "outside oriented". Orientation is a posturizing, a turning toward—it is paying attention to novel or important stimuli. When this man fixes the faucet, he is inside oriented at that time. He may not LIKE to make home repairs—but that is another matter. Labeling a person depressed, or anxiety filled or a corn flake eater says nothing about what a person does—although you get the impression it is behavior that is being labeled. You must enumerate circumstances, but without description and enumeration, the label means nothing.

In order to explain and account for behavior, you must refer directly to the environment of the behaving person and the conditions under which behavior occurs. And this involves a detailed analysis of past behaviors —to account for present and to predict future behavior. Responses are emitted in a real environment which contains hundreds of stimuli, many meaningless. The individual learns to discriminate. A shining sun and the behavior of eating a banana or chewing gum are not associated.

HISTORY OF SEGMENTATION— THE PRECURSOR OF PSYCHOGRAPHS, PSYCHOMETRIC MEASUREMENTS

The history of segmentation extends back to the original "Serutan, for those over 35". This was nothing more than determining people under 35 did not experience too much difficulty with constipation. It was also perceived that people did not like to consider themselves over 40. Plus 40 had a bad connotation *then*, in the depression. Therefore, the arbitrary decision to lower the age to over 35 was simply a means of avoiding the stigma of "you are 40 plus".

Here there was justification for applying a market segment. However, the definition of segment was not really factually true. All this meant was that people over 35 had a different *need* because of their physiological system and those under 35, or in their twenties or teens did not have this need, any more than a man has the need for a sanitary napkin, or a housewife with children grown needs baby food. Those people who do not have floors do not need floor wax. Segmentation is a phantom that does not exist except in the minds of those who created it.

These are rather strong statements, but there is rather strong factual evidence. First, we must begin with the fact that regardless of how you can segment or classify or define consumers, the learning process, the way in which consumers acquire habits, attitudes, concepts is based on principles and laws of learning: The Law of Primary Reinforcement; the Law of Contiguity; of Stimulus Generalization; Extinction.

These Laws can be seen operating through a study of TOTAL behavior and experiences —today's, yesterday's, last week's, last year's; behavior in the morning, at night; on holidays, weekends; when rising time is later or earlier; when Dad is late; when mother returns late from a shopping trip. Regardless of life styles or psychographers all people respond (behave) to a soft drink, a cake mix, baked bean stimulus similarly. The same DIFFERENT Resonses are made at different times, when the environment is different—different stimulus elements and combinations of stimuli evoke different perceptions and, therefore, different responses. Yet, there are common and similar elements which are stable, and which are self-validating—even to the absence of a particular behavior when the stimuli are not operating. And all people face these situations and are capable of responding with the proper stimulus.

In the same person, responses differ in different situations. "Duck" on a ball field evokes one response—in a duck blind, another behavior.

Behavior is countable, not segmented. It is continuous, not discrete: There is

> Behavior 1
> Behavior 2
> Behavior 3

even within the same area of activity or product and brand approach or withdrawal. Responses are to stimuli which have received various orders of reinforcement. Behavior is not constant but subject to stimuli and a graph of behavior is more logical and germane to our profession and our needs than a graph of the psyche, of a life style. And this behavior graph must be with reference to A phenomenon—dish washing or breakfast or beer drinking.

What Is the Basis for Life Styles, Psychographs, Etc.?

What is a graph of the psyche? What is a life style? A graph of the mind is an impossibility. The mind is merely a reference point because the mind is in touch with nothing. Mind is an abstraction. Something is in touch with nerves—but it isn't the mind. A graph of behavior IS possible—situations and conditions under which various behaviors occur —climate, seasons, weekends, vacation; father home, not home; mother early, mother late; etc. No matter what a psychograph or life style tells you, responses are to situations.

Psychographs, segmentationism, psychometrics, life styles are all the old Personality theory of buying motivation in a new name. The techniques used are the same as those connected with Freudian theory which are connected with failure in the area in which they were supposed to resolve problems—the clinic or the therapist's office. All assume in advance that the Personality inventory, the projective test, psychometric measurement, psychographic chart, are revealing of the particular segment the test is supposed to determine!

You may as well use measurements of spiral after affect—a method for determining introversion-extroversion; neuroticism; a technique not yet well documented, but as well documented as life style, psychographic measurements, psychographs. It should be realized that psychographs, psychometric measurements were developed in order to detect neuroses, psychoses, and their personality correlates from a behavioral point of view. Our problem from the consumer point of view is not at all comparable. Moreover, the principle of response specificity has been well documented: emotionality, for example, is not a general factor pervading all of an individual's behavior—any more than a certain life style pervades the use of orange juice, hand lotions, or chocolate pudding.[1]

---

[1] (Broadhurst, P. L. and Eysenik, H. J. "Emotionality in the Rat", in Banks, C. L. and Broadhurst, P. L. Studies in Psychology, University of London Press, London, 1965).

If you are to use these theories, you must study what OVERT behavior, consistent behavior correlates with the label indulgent, aggressive, self-assertive, conforming, leisure, baked bean eating, shaving, dancing or oral hygiene. Is there a psychograph permeating toilet tissue use, face washing, toast eating with or without jelly, tying ties, smoking, making love to one's wife, drinking tea at lunch, scratching an itch—a vital, psychic invisible force permeating all this? How can this be established objectively?

A study of total behavior and experience reveals there may be ten responses (behaviors) for any ONE given stimulus situation.

Life stylists, psychographists sound as if ONE stable, unchanging basic behavior pattern existed.

Even the dysthymic neurotic does not exhibit constant anxiety behavior in ALL circumstances. Compulsions, hostilities, shyness are NOT stable.[2] We *should* be looking for a readiness to respond, not a type of person.[3] We should be looking for the kinds of responses people make in various categories of situations. A life style may well be cultural, but not at all motive, concept generating—and certainly not deodorant affecting.

If a life style or a graph of the psyche reveals an individual to be leisure or socially structured, these operate only under given general conditions and do not pertain to personal care, pretzels, luncheon meats, putting catsup on eggs.

Psychograph measures, just as the Personality theory, are extracted by market researchers from Personality Inventories, psychometric indices of anxiety neuroses, then converted into questions pertaining to people as consumers:

My home is frequently a place where my friends gather informally.

I enjoy clubs, group activities.

I'm for progress, but the new fashions are too extreme.

Our modern conveniences are fine, but people enjoyed life in the good old days.

[2] A. L. Couvrey—"Personality Factors, Compulsion, Dependence, Hostility, Neuroticism and Shyness", *Journal of Educational Psychological Measurement*, Volume 24, 1964.
[3] J. V. McHunt—"Cognitive Factors in Motivation and Social Organization"; "Traditional Personality Theory in the Light of Recent Evidence", *American Science*, Volume 53, 1965.

One conclusion to this line of questioning could be that this is not a "new product buyer".

There is no base of comparison in such measurements except against the data from the people you questioned, which is no comparison at all. There is no scientific methodology here. At least, in the development of the Minnesota Multiphase Personality Inventory and in order to determine if it was significant, data was collected over a period of years before the final Inventory was established. There *is* a base in MMPI of reference *away* from the data obtained from the individual taking the MMPI; and even then, it is apparent the MMPI test is invalid as a measurement of Personality.

Psychographs or life styles assume the questions obtain a life style and that the answers encompass sex relations, toothpaste, leisure patterns, outdoor orientation, deodorant or bath soap use. With all due respect to Mr. Kenneth Longman,[4] any factor analysis is only as good and as valid as the data and its method of collection.

What does "I like to spend evenings at home" mean? On cold nights only? Sometimes? Always? When we have friends over? When the kids are asleep?

Based on the theory of the rejection of the feminine role or aversion to it, no significance can be attached to the statement, "I wish I were a man". If this were a true indication of intention, every woman would be developing twenty-nine-inch biceps.

Behavior can be counted and is far more specific than the statement, "I often skip powdering the baby". If you studied behavior, microscopically, you would find the specific number of times and all the situations under which the behavior of not powdering the baby occurs, and that they are universal. Such situations as the number of children coming home for lunch and husband coming home for lunch (not everybody lives in New York City or works in an office) occur in some families more than in others. But then, if not these, other activities occur such as taking children to nursery school, a heavy cleaning day, a quick fill-in shopping trip, a phone call, which result in the same non-powdering behavior; and all contain the same elements including, "it's near dinner time and

[4] Kenneth Longman, "The Psychographic Fad", *Management Science*, Volume 15, No. 6, 1969.

I have to give him a bath anyway". A rushed day, caused by ANY event, results in the non-powdering behavior and regardless of life style, income, even age, psychograph or personality type, the response is to the same stimulus.

If you persist in these theories, then after you have the graph, the style, you must verify its implications and determine if it *does* permeate cleansing tissues, dessert, breakfast, toilet tissue, and shaving habits.

A life style may be late to bed, late to rise; but the dislike of snack crackers as too spicy and burny exists regardless.

You can segment consumers into 1,000 classifications—if you design the questions to break down into 1,000—just as Fourier divided personality into three classes, twelve orders, thirty-two genera, 134 species, 404 varieties, which in turn yield 810 types of personalities.

If one is going to segment markets on the basis of personality, one must explain the fact that no two psychologists have ever agreed on what personality is. How can one prove a domineering individual will select this particular make and model of car, or brand of beer? The individual may be domineering in only one environmental (stimulus situation) area, but not in all and this can hardly characterize his personality. (One might also discover the domineering individual or selector of A car drinks Scotch. If we assume a priori personality or Scotch are indicators of type purchaser, that is what we will "prove".)

Why not segment the market according to eye blinks, chromosomes, time of ovulation? This *could* be found to exist; with as much "proof" as the various and myriad segments that are assumed to exist.

The only thing that consumers are different in is ABILITY to make perceptions, and ABILITY to visualize, which is due to "training", learning, experiences. And this, of course, transcends autos, toothpaste, etc. Those consumers who never learned what to do or do not perceive how the situation can be rectified, are capable of responding to the same appeal as users, because it *is* within their response repertory; or, the frame of reference might have to be changed because they are poor perceivers, visualizers or transferers.

It would be sheer folly to assume that the 6,500 odd products on the grocer's shelves from soup to nuts, to rice, to crackers, to canned fish are on the basis of segmentation, graph of the psyche or some ephemeral classification which is only based on the researcher's a priori assumption but without any causal data. Now add autos, appliances, rugs, clothes, etc., and the list jumps to 10,000 or more.

Simply observing or seeing that different people with different characteristics buy different products does not mean their needs, wants, or their motivations are different. This is an assumption without fact. One could take anything and determine that the market is segmented in accordance with how many sunny days or how many rainy days or the length of the days, or the length of the sun shining in a given market area.

Study daily behavior in the morning and you will find people generally:

Get up at the same time.
Bathrooms are used, are crowded.
Children are awakened.
Coffee put on; breakfast prepared.
Lunches are made.
Family gotten off to school, work.
Table cleaned, floor swept.
Dishes done.
Beds made.
Personal toilette, etc.
Dust.
Vacuum.
Straighten up after the kids go.

This is LIFE—not some vague generalization called life style, a graph of family solidarity, self-indulgence. A life style is four, five, six people—not a single abstraction.

Unless you know complete and total behavior you can hypothesize any kind of segmentation or classification you want to. You are looking for differences to begin with and you'll surely find them just as Freud was looking for sexual aberrations, repressions, traumatic experiences, and he discovered them. Did the data, from the very beginning, say "there is a difference in market demand by personalities"? Or did someone assume "people buy on the basis of personality", then develop or adjust a technique whether it was the Edwards' personality scale or what have you, and decided that yes these people have these characteristics, despite all that has been written and researched: 1) against the personality factor; 2) against the subjective interpretations of consumers; 3) against projective techniques. Here we have the old rigamarole that was just as nonsensical as subliminal advertising.

Markets are called segmented because there are no facts available, that is, no empirical and no causal relationship data to establish any other cause of differences in consumer behavior.

If indeed there is market segmentation by any classification, then what in effect marketing people are saying is we must have ten different kinds of tomato soup which must be packaged in ten different ways and which must be presented in ten different media. This is not carrying the concept, ad absurdum.

The reason why I or a million other consumers use a particular remedy has nothing to do with the fact that I am a this or a that or a those. At least this cannot be proved because if these differences don't apply, you can assuredly find some differences that do exist between me and my fellow million users and the million users of some other brand or product. In other words, if you look long and hard enough you will find differences because this is what you are looking for. But whether these differences have any effect on the motivations, on the needs, the wants or the behavior is pure conjecture. You must study the history, the objective history and past experience of both groups, the one I belong to and those who are on the opposite side. Even if people are different and can be put into different clumps, on what basis are the clumps delineated? And do these differences in clumps determine whether the consumer buys a minty toothpaste or a non-minty toothpaste, or whether the consumers buy a spiced rice or not a spiced rice or a minute rice vs. a long-cooking rice? A cause and effect relationship has not been established that the differences, no matter what they may be in clumps, are related to the differences in brand preference, the size of package, the appearance or model of a car. It is after the fact that such statements are made.

We can take pipe smokers and non-pipe smokers. Of course, we can find many, many facts in the lives of each which would differentiate them. In fact they are different to begin with by virtue of the fact one smokes a pipe and another does not. But you still don't know the reasons why one does or why one does not and if you don't know the reasons why, then you cannot appeal to or even develop a product that will meet the individual's needs.

And you cannot depend on the consumer to tell you because the consumer does not know. John Locke's dictum, "Man is the poorest observer of his own behavior", still obtains today as it did in 1650. How would you segment markets—let's say for teenagers? Into disciplined and undisciplined? Into aggressive or non-aggressive? Into what? Into inferiority vs. superiority complexes?

People will conceive or perceive of the external environment and those objects in it in accordance with their learning which means their previous record of experience and behavior. Today's concepts are the result of and lie in the history of behavior and experience, which can be objectively established, whereas such fantasies as a father image, a sibling rivalry, a repressed infantile desire, personality trait, graph of the psyche—which is the basis for these measurements—are purely subjective, personal interpretation.

The life style and psychograph are just another form of the ego structure theory—despite the fact the ego is invisible, and any change and inference is based on visible change.

Behavior, learning, responses are the same —receive a gum ball from the machine and you keep putting a penny in. No gum, the behavior of putting a penny in becomes extinguished—Negro, Oriental, Caucasian, Jew, Gentile, aggressive, indulgent, etc.

It is past experience that directs and causes behavior. We deal in small units of behavior —teeth, hair, shaving—and these all have common and similar elements. Consumers do not behave isomorphically. As Einstein said, "If you want to find out anything from the theoretical physicists, about the methods they use, stick to one principle; fix attention on their deeds".

Fix your attention on consumers' deeds— behavior with respect to your product—not on subjective expressions or responses to questions.

Psychometrics and psychographics are Monte Carlo approximations.[5]

---

[5] Loehlin, J. *Computer Models of Personality*, Random House, New York, 1963.

Structure and styles imply stability and permanence. They are ambiguous measures of automatized modes of response and not measurement of substantive personality dimension. All are based on self report inventories and reflect mainly response dispositions and item characteristics that operate independently of the items.[6]

Behavioral rating scales are more objective, more germane to our profession. Let me put some behavioral data in the form of questions and you think about them; then decide whether a life style, a psychograph, a value system is responsible, or living, learned behavior.

When is this done MORE than usual?
When is this done LESS than usual?
When is this AVOIDED?
When is it done differently?
Is it being done differently than last week, last month?
Are there times, conditions, situations when it is done differently?
Etc.

Surroundings influence what is learned, done, said; so if life styles exist, it is environment and response that must be studied. But even then, it is doubtful that scratching an itch is related to psychographs or life styles any more than using a tissue to blow one's nose or the brand of tissue.

There is no life style permeating consumer behavior. There is a continuum of behaviors and unless questions are designed to obtain what this continuum is, and under what conditions a behavior on the continuum occurs, psycho charts are meaningless.

Behavior is acquired, learned.

You don't want to determine personality, emotion, aggression, submission, because it is behavior you want to change—not life styles, extroversion, aesthenic styles. You should use behavioral terminoloy, OVERT BEHAVIOR. Self-esteem means nothing unless you relate it to behavior within a given class of responses and stimuli. You must know the behavioral meaning of such terms related to responses and stimuli.

So long as a woman must subject her hands to extremely hot water, wringing out clothes, abrasive dish cloths, dust, polish, wax, cut vegetables, then that woman, no matter where she is, who she is, has the need for a hand lotion that soothes and comforts and removes hurt and pain. There is no way one can segment the market and say a particular personality type, or any kind of differentiation in terms of any part of the physical organism or segment causes the need and the use in *this* group of individuals because these things cited cross any conceivable classification, segmentation, psychograph or life style imaginable.

Do M&M's not melt in anyone's hands? And do not all parents not permit solid chocolate in the living room or in the car when their youngster is dressed up? Or, would a psychograph reveal an over anxiety ridden, compulsively clean mother and father?

With no babies the *opportunity* exists for more informal, quick meals which increases as children grow older—because total family activities increases and schedules change. A different NEED is not segmentation on any basis.

All women run out of cold cuts after the first few days of the week and face the problem, "What's for lunch"?—and nearly all respond to the situation with a particular, universally liked sandwich combination—which all mothers consider the old reliable. This behavior (response) transcends age, geographical area, outdoor value system, any personality type, and graph of any psyche.

Skin burns whether it is a teenager's or a 50-year old's. Now one thing that might be true is that it does require an older person's skin more time to heal than a younger person's, and, therefore, the ingredients of the product must be different. But now we are not talking about segmentation; we are talking about two groups, the old and young whose bodies are entirely different. There is no segmentation; there is a different consumer.

Can one say that the dirt in the hair of a 45 year old is any different than dirt in a 21-year old's hair? The 21-year old may have dirty hair more frequently, be forced to wash it more frequently, but that cleaning product must have the capacity to remove dirt and leave hair clean.

When one is sweaty, it doesn't make any difference what one's age is because the nature of sweat is to smell, stain, to cause annoyance and dissonance. If you are talking about the fact that one group of people do not sweat, or sweat more, then you are talking about physiological need, not based on any

[6] H. G. Rorer—"The Great Response Style Myth", *Psychological Bulletin* 63, 1965.

geographical, chronological, social level. A ditch digger will perspire and so will the suburban home owner who is mowing his lawn or chopping wood. The need to feel clean and to cleanse the body, and the dissonance is the same regardless of where, what, who it is. Again it may well be that because of high temperatures, some people in some areas will sweat more, but then on the other hand, the same situation occurs in the North given hot weather. And the hot weather does occur in the North albeit less frequently.

An alarm clock must serve to get people up in the morning no matter who, what, or where they are. If that clock has white dials and white numerals, it cannot be seen very clearly; if it is a four pointed corner glass clock, it will scratch ANYONE's night table, the typical place the alarm clock is situated.

The life style, psychograph, segmentation, etc., theorists, of course, eventually come down to some kind of self-concept, personality self-image kind of reasoning which is pure theory and cannot and never has been proved as an actual fact. This is a priori reasoning, but the causal connections between product use and self-concept have never been established. One might just as well take blue-eyed people, chromosomal structure, or red-haired vs. brown-haired people and make an assumptive conclusion. However, the a priori assumption will be that brown-haired people do need this, blond-haired do not. This does not prove a causal evidence to link these two. This is using Skinner's example of "we do not attribute the sun's shining to the fact that people brush their teeth", because this is something that is constantly operating in the environment.

It makes no difference again, what the life style or psychograph is, mothers will allow their children to eat only certain foods as the time for meals approaches and will prevent the children from eating other kinds. This is only determined by studying the history of behavior and experience. The consumer may not even be aware that this is a common characteristic of the foods she permits her children to eat, under given conditions, but an analysis of behavior will prove it so. Thus, we do not have market segmentation, a life style, although without the right data it would APPEAR to be.

Is peanut butter, corn flakes, mint toothpaste preference due to life styles, graphs, etc., all having a common basis? Is there causal proof? You could also ask are you a liberal, conservative, a reactionary and find a correlation between new product purchase and a Liberal, but how do you prove this is motive arousing, behavior causing?

The kids of Church goers, civic leaders, socialites, leisure or luxury lovers all like peanut butter. So does the son of an aggressive or submissive father.

Any woman can and does forget to take food out of the freezer to thaw; will serve finger foods under the same condition; serve hamburgers, baked beans and a salad for dinner under common situations. Common situations, implements, situational elements are all involved in a microscopic study of living, within a specific area.

As kids grow older, habits and needs change. Any baby needs toilet training; gets a red, sore bottom. Dirty hair itches and must be washed—irrespective of a psychograph or value system. Rainy days, wet feet evoke a soup–hot chocolate response. These behaviors resolve problems, satisfy needs for anyone under the same condition and the learning of the behavior occurred under the same conditions.

To say the consumer bought this or that, thinks this or that, is to know nothing. We only have the end result, not the cause, not the movements which are the things to be researched.

To take the end result and surround it with:

Age
Income
Occupation
Number of children
Heavy usage
Introversion
Obesity
Preference for the odd

or any other characteristic, feature, etc., and *then* decide on segmentation is not only NO PROOF, NO CAUSATIVE ANALYSIS, IT IS A NOTHING, A SHALLOW NOTHING. NEEDS, MOTIVES, CONCEPTS are revealed by behavior and were established through behavior and experience. *If there are* differences, they have been due to learning and reinforcement. The African in the Equator KNOWS nothing of keeping his body warm through the use of animal hides, but the primitive American Indian did.

People can differ in a thousand details or be similar. But only behavior and experience (response to stimuli) are common and similar and have the same causes—learning. Take in enough details and you are bound to find similarities and differences and groupings even to the effect of the sun on the number of cavities, use of hair coloring, but this *proves* or establishes no causal relation.

Anyone can get a belly ache from hot, spicy foods! Is there a liquid segment for an upset stomach? A fizz segment? A pill segment of the upset stomach remedy? Why? Because one-third buy each? Or, because *their* particular ailment, the response *when* the need occurs, the environment, etc., preclude taking *other* forms? The one drinks more coffee and smokes more. The other does not, but is a doughy foods eater. Yet, when *either* is under the same ENVIRONMENT or CIRCUMSTANCE, EACH takes the other's form. What is good for one is good for another.

Dried blood is dried blood no matter whose body it is on, and when blood dries on the body it itches. Scabs harden and itch on anyone's body unless the sedimentation or coagulant level is low.

Some skins are sensitive and some deodorant sprays burn. This again is not market segmentation in terms of any kind of environmental or social life style, etc., classification unless one wishes to see in the modest woman, a psychological quirk—but then all women are still covered.

True, there are levels of tolerance and these are different. It takes considerably more aggravation, perhaps twenty phone calls which involve running up and downstairs before one individual will "have had it" and say to her husband, "we need an extension phone", whereas another might wait until sixty-two such calls. Here we must find out what the spacing of these calls is, how many occurred in one day, etc. Even the time of the day would have an affect on these levels of tolerance so, therefore, again we have no segmentation and no classification. What kind of psychograph does a pregnant woman have, whose doctor tells her not to run up and down stairs and says to *her* husband, "we need an extension upstairs".

If, of course, by segmentation, life styles, etc., we mean that a six-month old baby's food requirements are different than 11-year old brother's, then of course in that sense you have segmentation, if this is what you want to call it. Is there segmentation in mouth washes? Does not food which remains in anyone's mouth decay and, therefore, result in a bad taste? And does this bad taste not mean to all consumers, "my breath might smell?"

Is it a market segment, life style, or psychograph that causes some to like the long, imperial size cigarette, or is it the fact that those people who use the long cigarette find themselves in a smoking situation where their cigarette burns up much too quickly; whether it is the housewife who lights a cigarette, leaves it in an ashtray and then must busy herself and comes back to find the cigarette smoked out; or the busy office executive; or the busy ditch digger, etc. We are not talking about segmentation; we are talking about degrees of intensity of need under specific environmental situations.

Segmenting consumers on the basis of any classification is the same as segmenting them on the basis of their religious, political or other beliefs or their attitude toward Viet Nam or anything else. There is no empirical evidence that could ever establish such a connection.

There is a universality in behavior simply because that behavior which is the response to environmental situations was based on the same facts and the same learning under the same conditions. We all learn to avoid stubbing our toes on rocks in the same manner. All children soon learn that by crying they can bring the mother running. Your wives go through the same balky eater, fussing and restlessness *any* mother goes through, sunrise to sunset. The housewife also learns that the promise of baking a cake is going to have a particular affect on her family and will relieve the tensions and pressures that daily living causes. This is learned and this is not market segmentation.

Limburger cheese smells up anybody's icebox and women object to it. If you believe there is segmentation, you would have to find out how many husbands and wives and children like limburger and do not object to other foods having the aroma or taste or flavor of limburger, which these other foods have absorbed. Then you do not have market segmentation at all; you have different likes and dislikes which will always exist. Some people prefer peppermint, but others do not. And the preference for peppermint is not dependent upon age or geographical area, nor on sex, nor on personality, nor on the color of hair, nor on the number of teeth left in the mouth. What may be different is the intensity of need and the intensities of the stimuli in the environment, which cause all people to respond in a similar fashion.

Even in such a case as acne, the teenager is no different than the 24-year old male or female who has blemishes and who wishes to cover them up, who wishes to eliminate them. It may well be that the teenager, because of more social contacts is more intensely aware of the need and has more time, but this does not mean she is any different than the male 25-year old who, proud of his appearance, knows that a pimple is unsightly and wishes to conceal it or get rid of it. The teenager may simply have and probably does have more pimples, and, therefore, the need is greater and it is a daily need.

If Southerners smoke more Chesterfields than Northerners, this was *not* due to personality, climate or nearness to the factory, or the Southern disposition or to slow movements. It was learned behavior—habit behavior, maybe conformity. But then, there IS a universal tendency to conform. It is a matter of history—not of personality, or bourbon territory background.

CONCLUSION

Segmented market? By Gallstone size? Horoscopes? Compulsive cleaners? Sex proclivity?

Maybe, but obtain *CAUSAL* proof. Behavior and experience is the causal proof.

J. The Industrial Buyer

29. A General Model for Understanding Organizational Buying Behavior

FREDERICK E. WEBSTER, JR. and YORAM WIND

Industrial and institutional marketers have often been urged to base their strategies on careful appraisal of buying behavior within key accounts and in principal market segments. When they search the available literature on buyer behavior, however, they find virtually exclusive emphasis on consumers, not industrial buyers. Research findings and theoretical discussions about consumer behavior often have little relevance for the industrial marketer. This is due to several important differences between the two purchase processes. Industrial buying takes place in the context of a formal organization influenced by budget, cost, and profit considerations. Furthermore, organizational (i.e., industrial and institutional) buying usually involves many people in the decision process with complex interactions among people and among individual and organizational goals.

Similar to his consumer goods counterpart, the industrial marketer could find a model of buyer behavior useful in identifying those key factors influencing response to marketing effort. A buyer behavior model can help the marketer to analyze available information about the market and to identify the need for additional information. It can help to specify targets for marketing effort, the kinds of information needed by various purchasing decision makers, and the criteria that they will use to make these decisions. A framework for analyzing organizational buying behavior could aid in the design of marketing strategy.

The model to be presented here is a *general* model. It can be applied to all organizational buying and suffers al the weaknesses of general models. It does not describe a specific buying situation in the richness of detail required to make a model operational, and it cannot be quantified. However, generality offers a compensating set of benefits. The model presents a comprehensive view of organizational buying that enables one to evaluate the relevance of specific variables and thereby permits greater insight into the basic processes of industrial buying behavior. It identifies the *classes* of variables that must be examined by any student of organizational buying, practitioner, or academician. Although major scientific progress in the study of organizational buying will come only from a careful study of specific relationships among a few variables within a given class, this general model can help to identify those variables that should be studied. It can be useful in generating hypotheses and provides a framework for careful interpretation of research results that makes the researcher more sensitive to the complexities of the processes he is studying.

TRADITIONAL VIEWS

Traditional views of organizational buying have lacked comprehensiveness. The literature of economics, purchasing, and, to a limited degree, marketing has emphasized variables related to the buying task itself and has

♦ SOURCE: Reprinted by permission from the *Journal of Marketing* (National Quarterly Publication of the American Marketing Association), Vol. 36, No. 2, April 1972, pp. 12–19.

emphasized "rational," economic factors. In these economic views, the objective of purchasing is to obtain the minimum price or the lowest total cost-in-use (as in the materials management model[1]). Some of the models focussing on the buying task have emphasized factors that are not strictly economic such as reciprocal buying agreements[2] and other constraints on the buyer such as source loyalty.[3]

Other traditional views of organizational buying err in the opposite direction, emphasizing variables such as emotion, personal goals, and internal politics that are involved in the buying decision process but not related to the goals of the buying task. This "nontask" emphasis is seen in models which emphasize the purchasing agent's interest in obtaining personal favors,[4] in enhancing his own ego,[5] or in reducing perceived risk.[6] Other nontask models have emphasized buyer-salesman interpersonal interaction[7] and the multiple relationships among individuals involved in the buying process over time.[8] The ways in which purchasing agents attempt to expand their influence over the buying decision have also received careful study.[9]

These views have contributed to an understanding of the buying process, but none of them is complete. To the extent that these models leave out task or nontask variables they offer incomplete guidelines for the industrial market strategist and researcher. The tendency in interpreting research results based on these simple models is to overemphasize the importance of some variables and to understate or ignore the importance of others.

AN OVERVIEW OF A GENERAL MODEL

The fundamental assertion of the more comprehensive model to be presented here is that organizational buying is a decision-making process carried out by individuals, in interaction with other people, in the context of a formal organization.[10] The organization, in turn, is influenced by a variety of forces in the environment. Thus, the four classes of variables determining organizational buying behavior are *individual, social, organizational,* and *environmental*. Within each class, there are two broad categories of variables: Those directly related to the buying problem, called *task* variables; and those that extend beyond the buying problem, called *nontask* variables. This classification of variables is summarized and illustrated in Table 1.

The distinction between task and nontask variables applies to all of the classes of variables, and subclasses, to be discussed below. It is seldom possible to identify a given set of variables as exclusively task or nontask; rather, any given set of variables will have both task and nontask dimensions although one dimension may be predominant. For example, motives will inevitably have both dimensions—those relating directly to the buying problem to be solved and those primarily concerned with personal goals. These motives overlap in many important respects and need not conflict; a strong sense of personal involvement can create more effective buying decisions from an organizational standpoint.

Organizational buying behavior is a complex *process* (rather than a single, instantaneous act) and involves many persons, multiple

[1] Dean S. Ammer, *Materials Management* (Homewood, Illinois: Richard D. Irwin, Inc., 1962), pp. 12 and 15.

[2] Dean S. Ammer, "Realistic Reciprocity," *Harvard Business Review*, Vol. 40 (January-February, 1962), pp. 116–124.

[3] Yoram Wind, "Industrial Source Loyalty," *Journal of Marketing Research*, Vol. 7 (November, 1970), pp. 450–457.

[4] For a statement of this view, see J. B. Matthews, Jr., R. D. Buzzell, T. Levitt, and R. Frank, *Marketing: An Introductory Analysis* (New York: McGraw-Hill Book Company, Inc., 1964), p. 149.

[5] For an example, see William J. Stanton, *Fundamentals of Marketing* Second Ed. (New York: McGraw-Hill Book Company, Inc., 1967), p. 150.

[6] Theodore Levitt, *Industrial Purchasing Behavior: A Study of Communications Effects* (Boston: Division of Research, Graduate School of Business Administration, Harvard University, 1965).

[7] Henry L. Tosi, "The Effects of Expectation Levels and Role Consensus on the Buyer-Seller Dyad," *Journal of Business*, Vol. 39 (October, 1966), pp. 516–529.

[8] Robert E. Weigand, "Why Studying the Purchasing Agent is Not Enough," JOURNAL OF MARKETING, Vol. 32 (January, 1968), pp. 41–45.

[9] George Strauss, "Tactics of Lateral Relationship," *Administrative Science Quarterly*, Vol. 7 (September, 1962), pp. 161–186.

[10] The complete model is presented and discussed in detail in Frederick E. Webster, Jr. and Yoram Wind, *Organizational Buying Behavior* (Englewood Cliffs, New Jersey: Prentice-Hall, Inc., in press).

Table 1. Classification and Examples of Variables Influencing
Organizational Buying Decisions

	Task	Nontask
Individual	desire to obtain lowest price	personal values and needs
Social	meetings to set specifications	informal, off-the-job interactions
Organizational	policy regarding local supplier preference	methods of personnel evaluation
Environmental	anticipated changes in prices	political climate in an election year

goals, and potentially conflicting decision criteria. It often takes place over an extended period of time, requires information from many sources, and encompasses many inter-organizational relationships.

The organizational buying process is a form of problem-solving, and a *buying situation* is created when someone in the organization perceives a problem—a discrepancy between a desired outcome and the present situation—that can potentially be solved through some buying action. Organizational buying behavior includes all activities of organizational members as they define a buying situation and identify, evaluate, and choose among alternative brands and suppliers. The *buying center* includes all members of the organization who are involved in that process. The roles involved are those of user, influencer, decider, buyer, and gatekeeper (who controls the flow of information into the buying center). Members of the buying center are motivated by a complex interaction of individual and organizational goals. Their relationships with one another involve all the complexities of interpersonal interactions. The formal organization exerts its influence on the buying center through the subsystems of tasks, structure (communication, authority, status, rewards, and work flow), technology, and people. Finally, the entire organization is embedded in a set of environmental influences including economic, technological, physical, political, legal, and cultural forces. An overview of the model and a diagrammatic presentation of the relationships among these variables are given in Fig. 1.

ENVIRONMENTAL INFLUENCES

Environmental influences are subtle and pervasive as well as difficult to identify and to measure. They influence the buying process by providing information as well as constraints and opportunities. Environmental influences include physical (geographic, climate, or ecological), technological, economic, political, legal, and cultural factors. These influences are exerted through a variety of institutions including business firms (suppliers, competitors, and customers), governments, trade unions, political parties, educational and medical institutions, trade associations, and professional groups. The nature of these institutional forms will vary significantly from one country to another, and such differences are critical to the planning of multinational marketing strategies.

As Fig. 1 illustrates, environmental influences have their impact in four distinct ways. First, they define the availability of goods and services. This function reflects especially the influence of physical, technological, and economic factors. Second, they define the general business conditions facing the buying organization including the rate of economic growth, the level of national income, interest rates, and unemployment. Economic and political forces are the dominant influences on general business conditions. Some of these forces, such as economic factors, are predominantly (but not exclusively) task variables whereas others such as political variables may be more heavily nontask in nature. Third, environmetal factors determine the values and norms guiding interorganizational and interpersonal relationships between buyers and sellers as well as among competitors, and between buying organizations and other institutions such as governments and trade associations. Such values and norms may be codified into laws, or they may be implicit. Cultural, social, legal, and political forces are the dominant sources of values and norms.

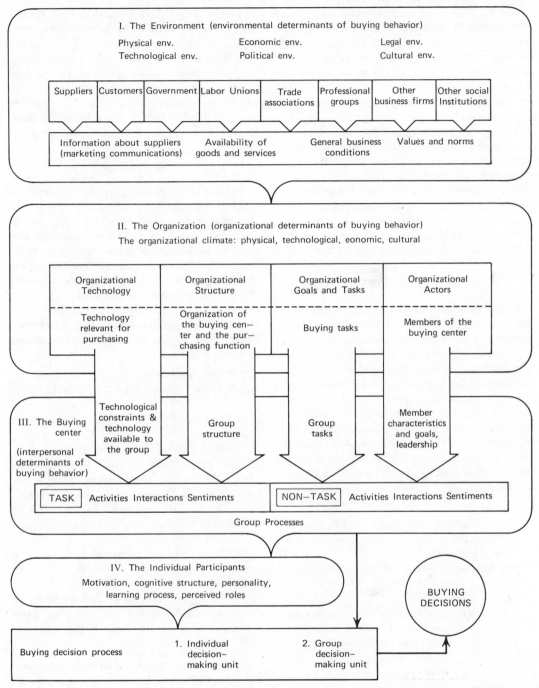

FIGURE 1. A model of organizational buying behavior.

Finally, environmental forces influence the information flow into the buying organization. Most important here is the flow of marketing communications from potential suppliers, through the mass media and through other personal and impersonal channels. Information flows reflect a variety of physical, technological, economic, and cultural factors.

The marketing strategist, whose customers are organizations, must carefully appraise each set of environmental factors and identify and analyze the institutions that exert those influences in each of the market segments served. This kind of analysis is especially important in entering new markets. For example, economic factors as revealed in measures of general business conditions must be continually assessed where market prices fluctuate and buyers make decisions to build or reduce inventories based on price expectations. Similarly, the impact of technological change in markets served must be considered as the basis for strategic decisions in the areas of product policy and promotion. The necessity of analyzing institutional forms is most readily apparent when markets are multinational in scope and require specific consideration of government policies and trade union influences. Environmental factors are important determinants of organizational buying behavior, but they can be so basic and pervasive that it is easy, and dangerous, to overlook them in analyzing the market.

ORGANIZATIONAL INFLUENCES

Organizational factors cause individual decision makers to act differently than they would if they were functioning alone or in a different organization. Organizational buying behavior is motivated and directed by the organization's goals and is constrained by its financial, technological, and human resources. This class of variables is primarily task-related. For understanding the influence of the formal organization on the buying process, Leavitt's classification of variables is most helpful.[11] According to Leavitt's scheme, organizations are multivariate systems composed of four sets of interacting variables:

Tasks—the work to be performed in accomplishing the objectives of the organization.
Structure—subsystems of communication, authority, status, rewards, and work flow.
Technology—problem-solving inventions used by the firm including plant and equipment and programs for organizing and managing work.
People—the actors in the system.

Each of these subsystems interacts with, and is dependent upon, the others for its functioning. Together, these four interacting sets

of factors define the information, expectations, goals, attitudes, and assumptions used by each of the individual actors in their decision making. This general model defines four distinct but interrelated sets of variables that must be carefully considered in the development of marketing strategies designed to influence that process: buying tasks, organization structure, buying technology, and the buying center.

Buying Tasks

Buying tasks are a subset of organizational tasks and goals that evolves from the definition of a buying situation. These are pure task variables by definition. The specific tasks that must be performed to solve the buying problem can be defined as five stages in the buying decision process: (1) Identification of need; (2) establishment of specifications; (3) identification of alternatives; (4) evaluation of alternatives; and (5) selection of suppliers.[12] Buying tasks can be further defined according to four dimensions:

1. The *organizational purpose* served—e.g., whether the reason for buying is to facilitate production, or for resale, or to be consumed in the performance of other organizational functions.

2. The *nature of demand*, especially whether demand for the product is generated within the buying organization or by forces outside of the organization (i.e., "derived" demand) as well as other characteristics of the demand pattern such as seasonal and cyclical fluctuations.

3. The *extent of programming*; i.e., the degree of routinization at the five stages of the decision process.

4. The *degree of decentralization* and the extent to which buying authority has been delegated to operating levels in the organization.

Each of these four dimensions influences the nature of the organizational buying process and must be considered in appraising market opportunities. At each of the five stages of the decision process, different members of the buying center may be involved, different decision criteria are employed, and different information sources may become

[11] Harold J. Leavitt, "Applied Organization Change in Industry: Structural, Technical, and Human Approaches," in *New Perspectives in Organization Research*, W. W. Cooper, H. J. Leavitt, and M. W. Shelly, II, eds. (New York: John Wiley and Sons, Inc., 1964), pp. 55–71.

[12] A modified version of this model is presented in P. J. Robinson, C. W. Faris, and Y. Wind, *Industrial Buying and Creative Marketing* (Boston: Allyn & Bacon, Inc., 1967), p. 14.

more or less relevant. Marketing strategies must be adjusted accordingly. There are rich research opportunities in defining the influence of different members of the buying center at various stages of the buying process.[13]

Organizational Structure

The formal organizational structure consists of subsystems of communication, authority, status, rewards, and work flow, all of which have important task and nontask dimensions. Each of these subsystems deserves careful study by researchers interested in organizational buying. The marketing literature does not include studies in this area. A beginning might be several rigorous observational or case studies.

The *communciation* subsystem performs four essential functions: (1) Information; (2) command and instruction; (3) influence and persuasion; and (4) integration.[14] The marketer must understand how the communication system in customer organizations *informs* the members of the buying center about buying problems, evaluation criteria (both task and nontask related), and alternative sources of supply. He must appraise how *commands and instructions* (mostly task-related) flow through the hierarchy defining the discretion and latitude of individual actors. The pattern of *influence and persuasion* (heavily nontask in nature) defines the nature of interpersonal interactions within the buying center. Organizational members may differ in the extent to which they prefer either commands and instructions or more subtle influence and persuasion to guide the actions of subordinates. The *integrative* functions of communication become critical in coordinating the functioning of the buying center and may be one of the primary roles of the purchasing manager.

The *authority* subsystem defines the power of organizational actors to judge, command, or otherwise act to influence the behavior of others along both task and nontask dimensions. No factor is more critical in understanding the organizational buying process because the authority structure determines who sets goals and who evaluates (and therefore determines rewards for) organizational performance. The authority structure interacts with the communication structure to determine the degree of decentralization in the decision process.

The *status* system is reflected in the organization chart and defines the hierarchical structure of the formal organization. It also expresses itself in an informal structure. Both the formal and the informal organization define each individual's position in a hierarchy with respect to other individuals. Job descriptions define positions within the organization and the associated dimensions of responsibility and authority. Knowing the responsibility, authority, and the position in the internal status hierarchy of each member of the buying center is a necessary basis for developing an account strategy for the organizational customer. A complete theory of organizational buying will permit accurate predictions of an organizational actor's influence based upon his position and role.

The *rewards* system defines the payoffs to the individual decision maker. It is intimately related to the authority system which determines the responsibilities of organizational actors for evaluating other individuals. Here is the mechanism for relating organizational task accomplishment to individual nontask objectives. Persons join organizations in anticipation of the rewards given by the organization and agree to work toward organizational objectives in return for those rewards. A careful analysis of the formal and social reward structure of the organization as it affects and is perceived by the members of the buying center can be most helpful in predicting their response to marketing effort. The key fact is that people work for organizations in order to earn rewards related to personal goals, both economic and noneconomic.[15]

Every buying organization develops task-related procedures for managing the *work*

---

[13] For research on the influence of organizational actors and information sources at various stages of the decision process, see Urban B. Ozanne and Gilbert A. Churchill, "Adoption Research: Information Sources in the Industrial Purchasing Decision," in *Marketing and the New Science of Planning*, Robert L. King, ed. (Chicago, Ill.: American Marketing Association, Fall, 1968), pp. 352–359; and Frederick E. Webster, Jr., "Informal Communication in Industrial Markets," *Journal of Marketing Research*, Vol. 7 (May, 1970), pp. 186–189.

[14] Lee Thayer, *Communication and Communication Systems* (Homewood, Ill.: Richard D. Irwin, Inc., 1968), pp. 187–250.

[15] Yoram Wind, "A Reward-Balance Model of Buying Behavior in Organizations," in *New Essays in Marketing Theory*, G. Fisk ed. (Boston: Allyn & Bacon, 1971).

flow of paperwork, samples, and other items involved in the buying decision process. The flow of paperwork also has nontask aspects which reflect the composition of the buying center as well as the authority and communciation subsystems of an organizational structure. Needless to say, marketers must understand the mechanical details of buying procedures. Such procedures also provide documentation of the buying process that can provide useful data for the academic researcher.

Buying Technology

Technology influences both what is bought and the nature of the organizational buying process itself. In the latter respect, technology defines the management and information systems that are involved in the buying decision process, such as computers and management science approaches to such aspects of buying as "make or buy" analysis. More obviously, technology defines the plant and equipment of the organization, and these, in turn, place significant constraints upon the alternative buying actions available to the organization. It is a common failing of industrial marketing strategy, especially for new product introductions, to underestimate the demands that will be placed upon existing technology in customer organizations.[16] A new material, for example, may require new dies and mixing equipment, new skills of production personnel, and substantial changes in methods of production.

Buying Center

The buying center is a subset of the organizational actors, the last of the four sets of variables in the Leavitt scheme. The buying center was earlier defined as consisting of five roles: users, influencers, deciders, buyers, and gatekeepers. Since people operate as part of the total organizations, the behavior of members of the buying center reflects the influence of others as well as the effect of the buying task, the organizational structure, and technology.

This interaction leads to unique buying behavior in each customer organization. The

---

16 Frederick E. Webster, Jr., "New Product Adoption in Industrial Markets: A Framework for Analysis," JOURNAL OF MARKETING, Vol. 33 (July, 1969), pp. 35–39.

marketing strategist who wishes to influence the organizational buying process must, therefore, define and understand the operation of these four sets of organizational variables— tasks, structure, technology, and actors—in each organization he is trying to influence. The foregoing comments provide only the skeleton of an analytical structure for considering each of these factors and its implications for marketing action in a specific buying situation. The marketer's problem is to define the locus of buying responsibility within the customer organization, to define the composition of the buying center, and to understand the structure of roles and authority within the buying center.

SOCIAL (INTERPERSONAL) INFLUENCES

The framework for understanding the buying decision process must identify and relate three classes of variables involved in group functioning in the buying center. First, the various roles in the buying center must be identified. Second, the variables relating to interpersonal (dyadic) interaction between persons in the buying center and between members of the buying center and "outsiders" such as vendors' salesmen must be identified. Third, the dimensions of the functioning of the group as a whole must be considered. Each of these three sets of factors is discussed briefly in the following paragraphs.

Within the organization as a whole only a subset of organizational actors is actually involved in a buying situation. The buying center includes five roles:

Users—those members of the organization who use the purchased products and services.

Buyers—those with formal responsibility and authority for contracting with suppliers.

Influencers—those who influence the decision process directly or indirectly by providing information and criteria for evaluating alternative buying actions.

Deciders—those with authority to choose among alternative buying actions.

Gatekeepers—those who control the flow of information (and materials) into the buying center.

Several individuals may occupy the same role; e.g., there may be several influencers. Also, one individual may occupy more than one role; e.g., the purchasing agent is often both buyer and gatekeeper.

To understand interpersonal interaction within the buying center, it is useful to consider three aspects of role performance: (1) Role *expectations* (prescriptions and prohibitions for the behavior of the person occupying the role and for the behavior of other persons toward a given role); (2) role *behavior* (actual behavior in the role); and (3) role *relationships* (the multiple and reciprocal relationships among members of the group). Together, these three variables define the individual's *role set*. An awareness of each of these dimensions is necessary for the salesman responsible for contacting the various members of the buying center. It is especially important to understand how each member expects the salesman to behave toward him and the important ongoing relationships among roles in the buying center.

As illustrated in Fig. 1, the nature of group functioning is influenced by five classes of variables—the individual members' goals and personal characteristics, the nature of leadership within the group, the structure of the group, the tasks performed by the group, and external (organizational and environmental) influences. Group processes involve not only activities but also interactions and sentiments among members, which have both task and nontask dimensions. Finally, the output of the group is not only a task-oriented problem solution (a buying action) but also nontask satisfaction and growth for the group and its members.

In analyzing the functioning of the buying center, it helps to focus attention on the buyer role, primarily because a member of the purchasing department is most often the marketer's primary contact point with the organization. Buyers often have authority for managing the contacts of suppliers with other organizational actors, and thus also perform the "gatekeeper" function. While the buyer's authority for selection of suppliers may be seriously constrained by decisions at earlier stages of the decision process (especially the development of specifications), he has responsibility for the terminal stages of the process. In other words, the buyer (or purchasing agent) is in most cases the final decision maker and the target of influence attempts by other members of the buying center.

In performing their task, purchasing agents use a variety of tactics to enhance their power which vary with the specific problems, the conditions of the organization, and the purchasing agent's personality. The tactics used by purchasing agents to influence their relationships with other departments can be viewed as a special case of the more general phenomenon of "lateral" relationships in formal organizations—those among members of approximately equal status in the formal organizational hierarchy.[17] These include *rule-oriented* tactics (e.g., appealing to the boss for the enforcement of organizational policy; appealing to rules and formal statements of authority); *rule-evading* tactics (e.g., compliance with requests from users that violate organizational policies); *personal-political* tactics (e.g., reliance on informal relationships and friendships to get decisions made and an exchange of favors with other members of the buying center); *educational* tactics (e.g., persuading other members of the organization to think in purchasing terms and to recognize the importance and potential contribution of the purchasing function); and finally, *organizational-interactional* tactics (e.g., change the formal organizational structure and the pattern of reporting relationships and information flows).

Buyers who are ambitious and wish to extend the scope of their influence will adopt certain tactics and engage in bargaining activities in an attempt to become more influential at earlier stages of the buying process. These tactics or bargaining strategies define the nature of the buyer's relationships with others of equal oranizational status and structure the social situation that the potential supplier must face in dealing with the buying organization. An understanding of the nature of interpersonal relationships in the buying organization is an important basis for the development of marketing strategy.

THE INFLUENCE OF THE INDIVIDUAL

In the final analysis, all organizational buying behavior is individual behavior. Only the individual as an individual or a member of a group can define and analyze buying situations, decide, and act. In this behavior, the individual is motivated by a complex combination of personal and organizational objec-

---

[17] Same reference as footnote 9.

tives, constrained by policies and information filtered through the formal organization, and influenced by other members of the buying center. The individual is at the center of the buying process, operating within the buying center that is in turn bounded by the formal organization which is likewise embedded in the influences of the broader environment. It is the specific individual who is the target for marketing effort, not the abstract organization.

The organizational buyer's personality, perceived role set, motivation, cognition, and learning are the basic psychological processes which affect his response to the buying situation and marketing stimuli provided by potential vendors. Similar to consumer markets, it is important to understand the organizational buyer's psychological characteristics and especially his predispositions, preference structure, and decision model as the basis for marketing strategy decisions. Some initial attempts to develop categories of buying decision makers according to characteristic decision styles ("normative" and "conservative") have been reported.[18] Cultural, organizational, and social factors are important influences on the individual and are reflected in his previous experiences, awareness of, attitudes and preference toward particular vendors and products and his particular buying decision models.

The organizational buyer can, therefore, be viewed as a constrained decision maker. Although the basic mental processes of motivation, cognition, and learning as well as the buyer's personality, perceived role set, preference structure, and decision model are uniquely individual; they are influenced by the context of interpersonal and organizational influences within which the individual is embedded. The organizational buyer is motivated by a complex combination of individual and organizational objectives and is dependent upon others for the satisfaction of these needs in several ways. These other people define the role expectations for the individual, they determine the payoffs he is to receive for

his performance, they influence the definition of the goals to be pursued in the buying decision, and they provide information with which the individual attempts to evaluate risks and come to a decision.

Task and Nontask Motives

Only rarely can the organizational buyer let purely personal considerations influence his buying decisions. In a situation where "all other things are equal," the individual may be able to apply strictly personal (non-task) criteria when making his final decision. In the unlikely event that two or more potential vendors offer products of comparable quality and service at a comparable price, then the organizational buyer may be motivated by purely personal, nontask variables such as his personal preferences for dealing with a particular salesman, or some secial favor or gift available from the supplier.

The organizational buyer's motivation has both task and nontask dimensions. Task-related motives relate to the specific buying problem to be solved and involve the general criteria of buying "the right quality in the right quantity at the right price for delivery at the right time from the right source." Of course, what is "right" is a difficult question, especially to the extent that important buying influencers have conflicting needs and criteria for evaluating the buyer's performance.

Nontask-related motives may often be more important, although there is frequently a rather direct relationship between task and nontask motives. For example, the buyer's desire for promotion (a nontask motive) can significantly influence his task performance. In other words, there is no necessary conflict between task and nontask motives and, in fact, the pursuit of nontask objectives can enhance the attainment of task objectives.

Broadly speaking, nontask motives can be placed into two categories: achievement motives and risk-reduction motives. Achievement motives are those related to personal advancement and recognition. Risk-reduction motives are related, but somewhat less obvious, and provide a critical link between the individual and the organizational decision-making process. This is also a key component of the behavioral theory of the firm[19] where uncer-

[18] David T. Wilson, H. Lee Mathews, and Timothy W. Sweeney, "Industrial Buyer Segmentation: A Psychographic Approach," paper presented at the Fall, 1971 Conference of the American Marketing Association. See also Richard N. Cardozo, "Segmenting the Industrial Market," in Marketing and the New Science of Planning, Robert L. King ed. (Chicago: American Marketing Association, 1969), pp. 433–440.

[19] Richard M. Cyert and James G. March, A Behavioral Theory of the Firm (Englewood Cliffs, N.J.: Prentice-Hall, 1963).

tainty avoidance is a key motivator of organizational actors.

The individual's perception of risk in a decision situation is a function of uncertainty (in the sense of a probabilistic assessment) and of the value of various outcomes. Three kinds of uncertainty are significant: Uncertainty about available alternatives; uncertainty about the outcomes associated with various alternatives; and uncertainty about the way relevant other persons will react to various outcomes.[20] This uncertainty about the reaction of other persons may be due to incomplete information about their goals or about how an outcome will be evaluated and rewarded.

Information gathering is the most obvious tactic for reducing uncertainty, while decision avoidance and lowering of goals are means of reducing the value of outcomes. A preference for the status quo is perhaps the most common mode of risk reduction, since it removes uncertainty and minimizes the possibility of negative outcomes. This is one explanation for the large amount of source

---

[20] Donald F. Cox, ed., *Risk Taking and Information Handling in Consumer Behavior* (Boston: Division of Research, Graduate School of Business Administration, Harvard University, 1967).

loyalty found in organizational buying and is consistent with the "satisficing" postulate of the behavioral theory of the firm.

The individual determinants of organizational buyer behavior and the tactics which buyers are likely to use in their dealings with potential vendors must be clearly understood by those who want to affect their behavior.

SUMMARY

This article has suggested the major dimensions and mechanisms involved in the complex organizational buying process. The framework presented here is reasonably complete although the details clearly are lacking. It is hoped that these comments have been sufficient to suggest a general model of the organizational buying process with important implications for the development of effective marketing and selling strategies as well as some implicit suggestions for scholarly research. The model is offered as a skeleton identifying the major variables that must be appraised in developing the information required for planning strategies. Hopefully, the model has also suggested some new insights into an important area of buying behavior presently receiving inadequate attention in the marketing literature.

30. Some Alternative Approaches to Modeling and Evaluating Industrial Marketing Strategies

PATRICK J. ROBINSON

Is the current disenchantment of industrial marketers with modern building and evaluative techniques justified? The answer obviously depends on one's point of view. But there is considerable evidence of a negative response from many modern managers. And likely many thoughtful researchers would also express concern and frustration.

Possibly, the strongest complaints center on the substantial gap that exists between prevailing practice and elusive theory. This is more apparent when coupled with managers complaints concerning obscure technical jargon and naive models used by technicians. On the other hand, many research people complain bitterly over obscure-seeming management practices and largely intuitive value judgments. Both groups cite the lack of a sense of involvement and teamwork which further hampers communication and progress. Clearly, the difficulties on both sides call for patience, and possibly a change in emphasis.

This paper is a plea for placing the emphasis on problem definition and solution using conceptual frameworks. Likely, both managers and researchers can employ the suggested approach to explore better the manager's relevant assumptions and questions, and also to satisfy the researcher's appropriate curiosity and methods. If more emphasis is

◆ SOURCE: Reprinted by permission from *A New Measure of Responsibility for Marketing*, edited by Keith Cox and Ben M. Enis, Proceedings of the June 1968 Conference of the American Marketing Association, Series No. 27, pp. 273–283.

placed on the underlying conceptual aspects of research model building and management evaluative processes then the answer to the vital (although irreverent) "so what" question may be answered with relative ease. Furthermore, non-quantitative, behavioral-science inputs should not be submerged in the current wave of mathematical statistics and computer technology.

No doubt many problems will be attacked differently if the selection of tools and techniques for modeling and evelution follows, rather than precedes, the essential reconciliation with larger issues and previous experience.

In this paper the phrase "Industrial Marketing Strategies" is considered in the context of marketing management in general. We shall assume that the are some significant differences between industrial marketing and consumer marketing practices—even though these differences may be primarily in degree rather than in kind. The essential distinction recognized here is that products and services being sold to other than the ultimate consumer involve the promotion and sale to company or institutional buyers as opposed to householders or individuals for their own consumption. Clearly, the decision making units or buying influences involved in industrial markets perform differently when in the role of consumer versus that of industrial buyer and pose operational and definitional problems which require significantly different planning and problem-solving capabilities for the marketer.

Insofar as the use of the word "strategy" is concerned, it is intended to focus attention on relatively broad decision making considerations involving choices among alternatives. Of course, many tactical details are subsumed in any given strategic plan; and these are considered merely as facilitating or implementing factors which must be taken into account to the extent necessary for considering alternatives.

The need for modeling and evaluating industrial marketing strategies can be illustrated by considering the place of these functions within the managerial process. As a framework for this analysis, we may use the Adaptive Planning and Control Sequence (APACS), which was first described in MSI's book on

PROMOTIONAL DECISION MAKING: PRACTICE AND THEORY.[1]

Following this general discussion, some functions and applications of models in industrial marketing are highlighted. Moving from the general models to a specific focus on a framework designed primarily for industrial marketing, the paper presents two such procedures which were developed at MSI.

APACS—A GENERAL STRATEGIC PLANNING AND CONTROL MODEL FOR MARKETERS

Fig. 1 presents a chart of the APACS model. It starts with the need to recognize and bound a problem and proceeds by setting realistic objectives (which are likely only subsidiary goals to some higher corporate goals), identifies the necessary tasks and feasible alternative means to achieve these ends. At each stage some form of modeling, either purely intuitive and judgmental or something much more formal and rigorous, enters the management process. Such models, whether purely mental and heuristic or strictly mathematical and analytic, are then employed to generate predictions of the probable consequences of alternative courses of action. On

the basis of such predictions, operating management evaluates and selects from among the alternatives, taking into account risks, payoffs, penalties and other considerations. Following this evaluation, implementation is necessary and as part of this, a system of monitoring performance and comparing results with plans must be available. This feedback of results may be either explicit, through delegating measurement tasks, or it may be simply relegated to accounting and other record keeping functions. In either event, on the strength of such continuing feedback, marketing adaptation or reconfirmation of plans, goals and operations can take place.

Throughout the sequence of eight APACS steps which characterizes either descriptively what goes on or prescriptively what should occur, a great deal of complexity and dynamic marketing behavior is apparent. At one time most companies had to rely almost solely upon the experience-based intuition and judgment of its manufacturing-oriented managers to plan and operate their marketing systems. Recently, we have seen an increasing emphasis on the Marketing Management Concept as the principal focus of the organization as a whole. There has also been an increasing emphasis on reducing the areas for unaided judgment wherever possible.

Undoubtedly, the advent of high-speed data handling and communication facilities, coupled with the increasing sophistication and utility of the management sciences, have had a catalytic effect in accelerating the adoption and development of more formal and quantitative instruments and models to aid management decisions. In the first industrial revolution there was a dramatic transfer to manual skills to machines, which enhanced and altered the capabilities and requirements of jobs and broadened the range and availability of products. In contrast, today we are experiencing the second industrial revolution in which a transfer of mental skills to machines is already being accomplished in many different ways. The first Industrial Revolution put a multiplier on men's muscles, while the second revolution is attempting to put a multiplier on men's minds. However, it is by no means an easy or smooth task, even though it seems to be proceeding at an accelerating pace if one judges by the increasing claims, boasts and cries of anguish coming from all concerned.

---

[1] Patrick J. Robinson and David J. Luck, *Promotional Decision Making* (New York: McGraw-Hill Book Company, 1964).

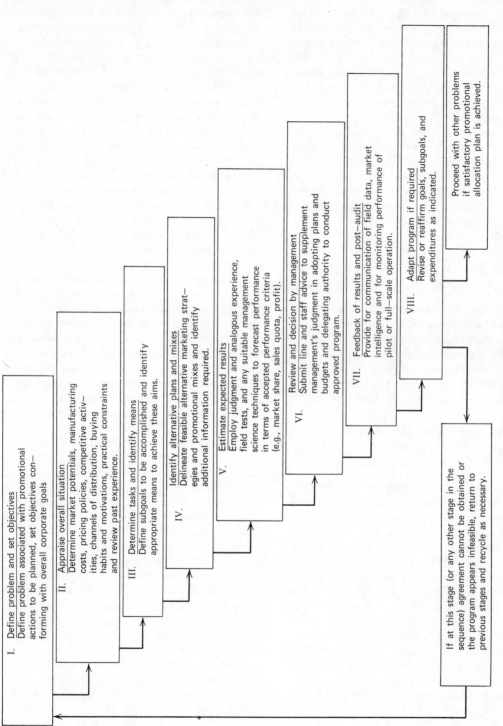

I. Define problem and set objectives
   Define problem associated with promotional actions to be planned, set objectives conforming with overall corporate goals

II. Appraise overall situation
   Determine market potentials, manufacturing costs, pricing policies, competitive activities, channels of distribution, buying habits and motivations, practical constraints and review past experience.

III. Determine tasks and identify means
   Define subgoals to be accomplished and identify appropriate means to achieve these aims.

IV. Identify alternative plans and mixes
   Delineate feasible alternative marketing strategies and promotional mixes and identify additional information required.

V. Estimate expected results
   Employ judgment and analogous experience, field tests, and any suitable management science techniques to forecast performance in terms of accepted performance criteria (e.g., market share, sales quota, profit).

VI. Review and decision by management
   Submit line and staff advice to supplement management's judgment in adopting plans and budgets and delegating authority to conduct approved program.

VII. Feedback of results and post-audit
   Provide for communication of field data, market intelligence and for monitoring performance of pilot or full-scale operation.

VIII. Adapt program if required
   Revise or reaffirm goals, subgoals, and expenditures as indicated.

Proceed with other problems if satisfactory promotional allocation plan is achieved.

If at this stage (or any other stage in the sequence) agreement cannot be obtained or the program appears infeasible, return to previous stages and recycle as necessary.

FIGURE 1. Adaptive planning and control sequence (APACS).

SOME FUNCTIONS OF MODELS IN INDUSTRIAL MARKETING

If we now think of formal model building, we generally visualize the staff specialist at work. His task is primarily one of attempting to capture the essence of the operating manager's "assumption structure" concerning a particular problem which is in the mind of the decision maker, and to mirror this problem in its proper setting. A model itself may be studied and tested for sensitivity with the reasonable expectation that a good model can absorb instructions and data and permit "dry runs" so as to generate artifacts from which reasonable inferences may be drawn. These inferences are then translated into their real-world implications for the setting being modeled. Fortunately, there need not be a one-to-one correspondence between the artifacts, as generated by the model, and the real-world facts which will be generated in the natural setting by the operations under study. Nevertheless, the essential assumption here is that the researcher and the administrator will derive some nourishment from the use of the model as a pretesting of predictive device.

Furthermore, formal models, by stating explicitly the relevant variables and their interrelationships, provide a guideline for the firm's marketing research activities. Such research efforts, being aimed at providing specific data to test the hypotheses derived from the model furnish the marketing manager with relevant information and avoid the dilemma of what to do with the data and how the research findings can be utilized. Such models can facilitate the subsequent evaluation of alternative marketing strategies by focusing on the likely outcomes of the alternating approaches under review; and so help to crystallize the assumptions and test the constraints within which planning and control must be made to function.

The process of formal modeling by researchers relies on teamwork with management and evaluation by managers. This approach entails the development of some sort of conceptual framework or structure within which a number of elements may be positioned so as to produce a reasonable analogue of the operations under study. This analogue, and the analogous reasoning which is later translated from the scale model to the full-scale operation, assumes that a good deal is known about the efficacy and nature of the methods being employed.

APPLYING MODELS IN INDUSTRIAL MARKETING

In many respects, the practical implementation problems of applying models to industrial marketing appears quite parallel to the farming situation in which we have a large inventory of farm implements available, and yet we may not have many farmers taking advantage of these tools. In effect (as cited in the *Promotional Decision Making: Practice and Theory* book) we don't appear in practice to be farming a tenth as well as we know how in theory. Of course, people must rely on their experience and it takes time to adopt and become accustomed to new technology—even to sow and harvest crops.

Clearly, the process of selecting and adopting new tools for industrial marketing is apt to be a slow process of education assimilation and adaptation; just as the introduction of a new farm implement, or a new approach to farm fertilization or to crop rotation can take a long time before changing the modus operandi of a farmer. The introduction of formal management science models can also make a substantial difference in the way in which managers consider and participate in the planning and evaluation process in business.

There are a number of classes of methodological contributions which are, so to speak, available "on the shelf"; and they may have potential applicability to various phases of the marketing management process. The accompanying chart (See Fig. 2) shows the eight APACS steps, and sets them off against a variety of methodological contributions to indicate that there are quite a number of possibilities for exploiting the new technology in the normal course of planning and control. In some companies a number of these potential applications have been realized, but with differing degrees of success. Most researchers in industrial marketing could recite a number of such successes and failures from their own experience. Likely, such reports would be of a conditional nature in that most of these approaches to modeling and evaluation of alternative marketing strategies are heavily dependent on competent teamwork between the line and staff people—plus an element of luck and experience in their use.

Such teamwork may be more apt to succeed if some general concepts and guidelines are used as a frame of reference in considering both practic and theory. APACS was only the first and most general such framework or conceptual model, and it has been used to position our opening observations. Two other different, and more specific, approaches also appear relevant.

The second conceptual approach was developed and presented in MSI's book on *Industrial Buying and Creative Marketing*[2] and is called the BUYGRID framework (see Fig. 3).

[2] Patrick J. Robinson and Charles W. Faris, *Industrial Buying and Creative Marketing* (Boston: Allyn & Bacon, Inc., 1967).

Understanding buyer behavior is the key to any creative marketing activity. The Buygrid framework is but one aid to understanding and improving Industrial Marketing strategies since it focuses directly on the nature of customer requirements buying process. This framework combines in a single matrix both the eight buying phases (BUYPHASES) and buying situations (BUYCLASSES).

THE BUYPHASES

Industrial procurement can be characterized by eight buying stages, which are termed "Buyphases." While some of these Buyphases may occur simultaneously, they tend to follow in sequence.

Methodological Contributions: (General Categories)	APACS steps	I. Define Problem & Set Objectives	II. Appraise Overall Situation	III. Determine Tasks & Identify Means	IV. Identify Alternative Plans and Mixes	V. Estimate Expected Results	VI. Review & Decision by Management	VII. Feedback of Results & Postaudit	VIII. Adopt Program if Required	No. of Contributions	
Statistical inference and estimation			X			X		X		3	Statistical inference and estimation
Econometrics			X			X				2	Econometrics
Experimental design						X		X		2	Experimental design
Stochastic processes						X				1	Stochastic processes
Analytical techniques						X	X			2	Analytical techniques
Mathematical programming						X				1	Mathematical programming
Decision and search theory				X	X	X	X	X		5	Decision and search theory
Value theory		X		X	X	X	X	X	X	7	Value theory
Behavioral models		X	X			X	X	X	X	6	Behavioral models
Simulation and gaming		X				X	X	X	X	5	Simulation and gaming
Analytical philosophy				X	X					2	Analytical philosophy
Cybernetics and servo theory								X	X	2	Cybernetics and servo theory
Number of contributions	3	3	3	3	10	5	7	4		38	Number of contributions

FIGURE 2. Scientific contributions to the adaptive planning and control sequence (APACS).

BUYCLASSES

	New Task	Modified Rebuy	Straight Rebuy
1. Anticipation or recognition of a problem (need) and a general solution.			
2. Determination of characteristics and quantity of needed item.			
3. Description of characteristics and quantity of needed item.			
4. Search for and qualification of potential sources.			
5. Acquisition and analysis of proposals.			
6. Evaluation of proposals and selection of supplier(s).			
7. Selection of an order routine.			
8. Performance feedback and evaluation.			

Notes:

The most complex buying situations occur in the upper left portion of the BUYGRID framework when the largest number of decision makers and buying influences are involved. The initial phases of a new task generally represent greatest difficulty for management.

FIGURE 3. The BUYGRID framework.

Phase One: Anticipation or Recognition of a Problem (Need).

Realization that a problem exists and that it may be solved by buying a product or service.

Phase Two: Determination of the Characteristic and Quantity of the Needed Item. Usually done within the firm, outside sources may be helpful in arriving at this decision. In this phase, the process of narrowing down the solution has begun.

Phase Three: Description of the Characteristics and Quantity of the Needed Item. An extension of Phase Two, this stage involves setting down a specific description of the item.

Phase Four: Search for and Qualification of Potential Sources.

This may consist of selecting a supplier from a list or considerable time may be spent investigating sources and suppliers.

Phase Five: Acquisition and Analysis of Proposals. This may be a routine step or involve a complicated series of proposals and counterproposals running over several months.

Phase Six: Evaluation of Proposals and Selection of Suppliers.

Analysis of offers and possible further negotiation on price, terms, delivery and other details.

Phase Seven: Selection of an Order Routine. Includes both external and internal aspects.

Among the former, preparation of purchase order and follow-up activities. Among the latter, reports to the using department, inventory management.

Phase Eight: Performance Feedback and Evaluation.

Formally or informally, an evaluation of how well the product or service solved the problem and the performance of the supplier.

According to the report, suppliers stand the best chance of doing business with a company if they get involved early in the Buyphase process. As companies move from one phase to the next, a kind of "creeping commitment" develops that tends to prevent new vendors from being considered.

In some cases, two or more phases may take place at the same time, and the significance of different phases may vary in different buying situations. The important thing, the authors suggest, is that thinking about buying decisions as a series of steps will help the industrial marketer adapt his sales effort to the buying pattern of the company and to design sales appeals to satisfy the needs of people involved in a specific Buyphase.

BUYCLASSES

The three Buyclasses are new tasks, straight rebuys, and modified rebuys. The accompanying exhibit (see Fig. 4) illustrates the decision network diagram of the buying situation for a new drill.

New task buying occurs when a company is confronted with a new need or problem. In new tasks, the narrowing down process that goes on in Phases Two and Three of the Buyphase and the qualification of new sources that occurs in Phase Four are closely interwoven.

In these situations, the buyer has little or no experience to work from and needs a great deal of information. Close communication between buying and selling personnel is vital. Buyers place considerable emphasis on the vendor's reputation for reliability, and companies which have built a sound reputation through advertising and other means often have an edge in the new task situation. Although new task situations are infrequent, they are important to marketers because they set the pattern for the more routine purchase

to follow. And new task purchases can often be anticipated or developed by the creative marketer.

A *straight rebuy* is described as a continuing or recurring need handled by the Purchasing Department on a routine basis. In these situations, the later stages of the Buyphase process are important. Since the buyers have purchased the item a number of times, they seldom look for new information. If the supplier is reliable and will get the material to them on schedule, this is usually all they ask. Because the buyers feel they know all they need to know about products in the in the straight rebuy class, calls by new suppliers are often looked upon as something as a nuisance. This can mean that products better than the one being purchased may not be considered. Consequently, the job of the marketer is essentially educational to try to overcome buyers' fixed ideas or established habits.

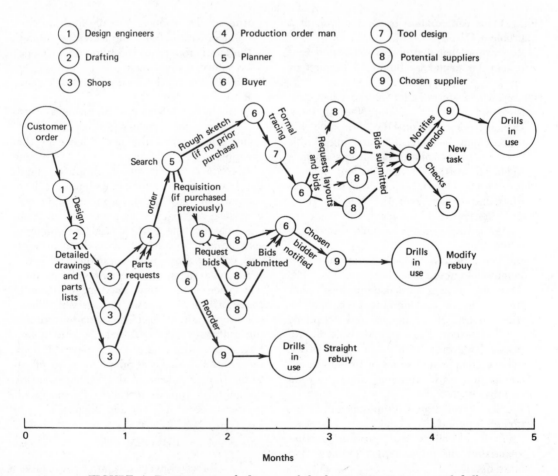

FIGURE 4. Decision network diagram of the buying situations: special drill.

The modified rebuy usually springs from a new task situation or a straight rebuy that for one reason or another is being reviewed. The modified rebuy can occur when buyers look for opportunities to save money, get better service, or find a product that will do a better job. Changes in specifications can also make it necessary for buyers to look beyond present suppliers. In these situations, buyers need information. Suppliers who can meet this need may be in a good position to create business, providing the product they offer will in fact solve the buyers' problems.

In addition to providing a model of the industrial buying process, the BUYGRID framework, by helping marketers spot critical decision points, can be a useful device for devising more effective sales programs tailored to fit the buying patterns within companies and to satisfy the needs of the people involved in different phases of the buying process. At present, we are developing a simulation of the industrial buying process which may be thought of as centering on a view of the customer under the three buying situations.

Industrial marketing executives can employ the BUYGRID framework, and a simulation model based on it, to develop an acute sensitivity to customers' needs and requirements, to the point that they can anticipate customer problems and future needs before the customer himself may be aware of them.

Even without the simulation as an aid to modeling and evaluation, the question of how much information for buyers may be relevant under different circumstances can be roughly evaluated. This is summarized in Fig. 5.

The industrial marketer's efforts to understand his customers and hence improve his marketing strategies can further be aided by models aimed at the understanding of the interaction between his organization and his customers. A framework aimed at this subject which was developed in MSI is discussed briefly next.

COMPACT—AN APPROACH TO MODELING AND EVALUATING SELLING COMPETENCE IN RELATION TO BUYER BEHAVIOR

The third conceptual model of value in industrial Marketing Strategies is taken from the MSI book *Personal Selling in a Modern*

Type of Buying Situation	Newness of The Problem	Experience and Information Requirements	Consideration of New Buying Alternatives
New Task	Problem or requirement is new to buying decision makers.	Past experience not considered relevant; great deal of information required before making decision.	Buying alternatives are not known; all solutions considered are new to buying decision makers.
Modified Rebuy	Problem or requirement is not new but is somewhat different from previous similar situations.	Past experience is relevant, but more information is required before making decision.	New alternative solutions, whether or not known, will be considered before making buying decision.
Straight Rebuy	Continuing or recurring requirement.	Past experience considered sufficient to make a buying decision with little or no additional information required.	Alternative solutions may be known but are not given serious consideration.

FIGURE 5. Distinguishing characteristics of buying situations.

Perspective.[3] This COMPACT model deals with individual conceptual and interpersonal competence applied to selling activities. The approach employs notions from communication theory and social psychology and, while it essentially starts with the micro level of individuals it has important implications for sales force, selection, training, compensation and management.

The COMPACT framework provides a standardized format for classifying and comparing observed activities of sales people and customers. However, COMPACT is not a computer model or an accounting model. It is simply a methodical approach to taking account of the kinds of activities people perform, and the level of competence with which they perform their tasks.

The analysis of these selling tasks, selling behavior, and the basic processes of persuasion between sellers and buyers is a first step to more effective planning modeling and evaluating of industrial selling strategy. More specifically it is also a model in the selection, training, organization, and compensation of salesmen. These in turn help to identify those tasks for which nonpersonal selling can prove more efficient. The COMPACT model is the key to this analysis and employs three dimensions which can be analyzed separately or together.

Starting with the first dimension—the flow of action—it is assumed that selling and buying can be viewed as a system of action. Despite the fact that they are essentially continuous behavior process, they are divisible conceptually into phases or classes of activities. Five such divisions are proposed in the COMPACT model, based on the orientation or object toward which the activities are directed (Fig. 7). These phases, applicable to an analysis of both selling and buying behavior, are:

Phase One: *Awareness* of a problem situation, and development of a commitment to action.

Phase Two: *Acquisition* of required information, products, or services to facilitate the attainment of a desired goal.

Phase Three: *Attainment* of a desired goal, including implementation of plans (man-

agers), selling (salesmen) or consumption (buyers).

Phase Four: *Harmonization* of goal-attainment activities with the existing framework (individual or organizational) of standards and values (essentially achieving satisfaction and reinforcement from experience).

Phase Five: *Commitment* to a given object or course of action (which may be reflected in a pattern of behavior such as habit formation).

The second dimension of COMPACT, which can be added to the flow of action, is based on *The Idea on Individual Conceptual and Interpersonal Competence*. The concept of competence accounts for and provides a basis on which to differentiate the varying abilities and skills of individuals in terms of *awareness, acquisition, goal attainment, harmonization,* and *commitment*.

This concept of selling and buying ability implies five levels of competence which move from the simplest physiological acts through a succession of higher levels of behavior and are illustrated in Fig. 6.

Adding a third dimension entails considering organizational hierarchy, from the "doer" through layers of supervision to top management. An example of a two dimensional matrix utilizing the first and third dimension as applied to an analysis of marketing to defense and aerospace buyers is illustrated in Fig. 7.

The COMPACT model is employed to present and to analyze seller-buyer relationships, problems in communication, information "appetites," and the importance of properly matching tasks and people in the most effective and efficient combinations. Consequently marketing is considered from the point of view of a process designed to *create, modify, exploit or maintain a communicative relationship between utility producing and utility consuming entities (individuals) of a social system.*

Utility Producing
Entities or
Systems

Marketing

Utility Consuming
Entities or
Systems

---

[3] Patrick J. Robinson and Bent Stidsen, *Personal Selling in a Modern Perspective* (Boston: Allyn & Bacon, Inc., 1967).

Direction of Competence
Direction of Control

Flow of Action	Level 1 Activity	Level 2 Behavior	Level 3 Performance	Level 4 System	Level 5 Values
Awareness	"Things to do" with regard to buyers	Types of buyers and buyer expectations	Differences between own and buyer's goals	Indicators of strategically relevant buying systems	Differences among own, buying systems', and selling system's goals
Acquisition	Memorization of presentation and rules for place and object of presentation	Development of ability to adapt to buyer's viewpoint	Acquisition of information and skills relevant to perceived goods	Acquisition of information and ability to creatively analyze buying situations	Development of information and skills relevant to achievement to buyer's, seller's, and own goals
Goal seeking	Flawless delivery of presentation, in a *prescribed* number of situations	Achievement of *prescribed* goals	Achievement of *self-approved* goals	Establishment of communicative relationships with relevant set of buying systems	Selection of strategically relevant buyer relationships
Harmonization	Quality of delivery of sales presentation	Quality of performance measured against prescribed standards	Evaluation of performance in relation to self-concept	Evaluation of communicative effectiveness in relation to own and organizational goals	Strategic effectiveness of relationships
Commitment	Rhetorical competence	Adaptive competence	Performance competence and achievement of buyer satisfaction	Buying systems and communicative relationships involved	Integrated value structure with reference to all relevant systems

FIGURE 6. Outline of the concept of selling competence.

	Buying	Supervisory	Operation	Integration	Strategy
Awareness	Rules and regulations for acquiring and processing proposals and contracts	Perceived requirements for maintenance, repair and operating supplies and other non-development products	TDP for a new or changed system, on-going projects or additions to existing systems	Strategy and doctrine analysis, threat analysis, political negotiation, and bargaining and technological developments and innovations	Political and social philosophy concerning international relations and national security
Acquisition	Procedures for invitation of bids (bid rooms, forms, etc.)	Invitation of bids by advertising (competitive) or by negotiation	Request for proposal (RFP), or initiation with contractor for all or part of contract	Development of system concepts, determination of required means, methods and resources, and exploratory developments	Analysis and assessment of international and domestic environments, possibilities of war, strategy of antagonists, peace trends and arms control
Goal Seeking	Receipt and completion of all required forms and procedures in prescribed manner	Selection of contractor and completion of contract	Selection and recommendation of contract by Source Selection Board (SSB)	Formulation of military proposal, tentative decision and development of preliminary Technical Development Plan (TDP)	Maintenance of national and (in cooperation with allies) international balance and security
Harmonization	Harmonization of contractor performance with rules and regulations	Harmonization of contractor performance with administrative and procedural rules	Harmonization of selected contract with requirements and existing systems by Program Review Board	Harmonization of desires of U.S. and international and national interests. Integration into present and planned programs	Political, technical, and military assessments of the effectiveness and success of strategic policies
Commitment	Development of commitment to rules and procedures	Development of commitment regarding contractor performance (negatively or positively)	Review and decision by chain of command in buying agency	Submission of program for change or development of systems and entry into the programming and budgeting network of DOD	Development of commitment to successful policies and methods by which they are implemented

FIGURE 7. A comparison of activities and levels of defense and aerospace procurement process.

Using the COMPACT framework the marketer can derive the conditions under which the personal selling function is potentially the most effective and efficient. These conditions are:

1. Potential buyers are unaware of a given product and no other means can achieve awareness.
2. The search patterns of potential buyers are such that no other channel will bring the given product into the purview of the buyer.
3. Potential buyers' goals are so specific and different that no general function can be established.
4. The number of potential buyers is relatively restricted and individual buying systems can be defined.
5. Potential buyers are so strongly committed, legally, economically, or psychologically to competitive suppliers or existing and traditional practices (in the case of a new product or service) that any other medium is rendered ineffective.

Central to the COMPACT framework is the premise that human behavior constitutes an integrated, continuously ongoing process, certain parts of which are directly observable or overt, while other parts are not directly observable, but overt. Some of the more important implications of this view for industrial modelers are:

1. An individual's behavior, whether as a manager, salesman, or a buyer, is not necessarily, if at all, explainable in small convenient "cause" and "effect" segments.
2. The "rationality" versus "irrationality" dichotomy, popularly made with reference to buyer behavior, becomes meaningless other than as an indicator of an outside observer's ability to identify an immediate "cause" or rationale for any other individual's observable behavior. *All behavior is in some sense* rational; so the problem facing both marketers and buyers becomes one of determining and influencing the rationale for the behavior each observes in the other.
3. An individual's behavior, for the most part, is based on concepts which are "out of consciousness." This does not necessarily imply that such behavior is either "emotional" or "irrational." It merely implies *that an individual internalizes certain behavior rules and acts upon them without necessarily re-examining them continuously.*

4. The marketer, or for that matter the salesman, cannot directly influence an individual buyer. *The sole means of influence lies in the changes which can be effected upon the individual's environment within the constraints of his ability to take account of such changes.*
5. Any individual, whether manager, salesman, or buyer, possesses an information and decision system which, by virtue of the value concepts contained in it, *develops a certain set of predilections to act in a more or less specific manner in any given situation.* The process of influence required to change such predilections is essentially different from, and more "intensive" than, one of information giving.

Following this line of reasoning it seems that the marketer can gain some strategically important insights into the relationships, interactions and key variables linking him with his markets. This should help him to construct better models of his relevant markets and their probable response to his marketing strategies. Furthermore, this can also enhance their evaluative abilities in pre- and post-testing of performance.

SUMMING UP

Just as The Scientific Method provides a rigorous conceptual framework for the design of experiments to test falsifiable hypotheses, so conceptual frameworks can help marketing model builders and evaluators in the representation and weighing of alternative strategies. By focusing on the conceptual level, and so avoiding detailed technical methodologies, we have suggested several avenues of attack on broad marketing, and specific buyer and seller aspects of strateic planning and evaluation.

The Adaptive Planning and Control Sequence (APACS) provides a dynamic framework suitable for describing and prescribing how strategic marketing decisions may be planned and implemented. The BUYGRID framework is a systems engineering type of aid to better understanding and diagnosis of key buying influences and helps to diagnose the process of creeping commitment which so often appears to characterize industrial buying decisions. Finally, the COMPACT conceptual model employs some behavioral science insights to apply in the analysis of strategies and tactics to help the seller to better understand, plan and review alternative buyer/seller interactions.

Taken together, these three aids to modeling and evaluation may help focus attention on issues of merit, and on how, what, when, where and why data are needed and additional knowledge of relationships required. Many implications for research and for management flow from these conceptual models; starting with the general and moving to the specific. Of course, the corollary to employing these frameworks is the selection of tools and measures to perform empiric studies or to affect implementation and effective control.

Subscribing to the approach described in this paper tends to minimize the risk of over-preoccupation *with detailed techniques and a "how to" cookbook approach*. Instead it stresses a more thoughtful conceptual teamwork involving industrial marketing managers and researchers in assessing and taking account of the relevant assumptions and realities of the marketplace; wherein many compromises with theoretical ideals must be accepted—but need not be haphazard or unevaluated.

IV

Marketing Management
in a Dynamic Environment

This part of the book presents most of the material on the actual management of the marketing process. The principal functions of marketing are each developed by several readings. Thus the reader should have a good picture of marketing management as he studies the overall job, marketing research, product, channels, logistics, pricing, communications, and international marketing.

The opening reading by one of the great thinkers of marketing, the late Wroe Alderson, explains the American market-oriented economy and relates it to the management of the marketing process. This is followed by a classic by the late Robert J. Keith, former president of a large food company. Keith traces the four eras of marketing management and presents a history that is useful in studying the various trends of marketing. Martin Bell and C. William Emory's reading presents an evaluation of the marketing concept, a term that unfolded during the 1950s. The three main elements of the concept are presented and the student can relate them to the eras presented in Alderson's reading.

Now that the overall picture of marketing management has been presented, the basic role of marketing research is covered. The editors prefer to stress marketing research early because it is good management sense to make decisions based on reliable information. The readings on marketing research cover its role in the firm and its relationship to top-management decision making. Then a number of the techniques of the marketing researcher are briefly discussed. These techniques relate to marketing decisions and to marketing functions that are included in the remaining readings in Part IV.

Business firms produce products that are sold to buyers, and hence the product is the center of much of marketing activities. Research, advertising, and other functions of marketing are directed at getting the product sold and delivered. In our economy there is pressure to introduce new products, and this is explained in A. C. Nielsen's reading. Then the importance of the product life-cycle concept is discussed. This is a useful concept that helps us understand the history of a product, and the product life-cycle relates to the different marketing efforts or functions. Since the goal of the company is to gain buyer acceptance for its products, an examination of new-product diffusion process also is germane to this section.

The physical aspects of marketing traditionally have not received a great deal of attention, but in recent years the importance of channel decisions and logistics has increased considerably. The many changes in physical distribution are discussed in James L. Heskett's reading, and this is followed by a discussion of channel control including the degree of coordination within a channel that is a measure of competitive position in the channel. William Zikmund and William Stanton deal with ecology—looking at the solid waste problem as a channel of distribution problem. In the past, marketing has been concerned about getting the goods down the pipeline from producer to consumer, but now the solid waste problem is demanding another kind of marketing effort.

Pricing, another ingredient of the marketing mix, is the next subject. The new products, discussed in an earlier section, are now examined from the standpoint of pricing techniques. Two principal kinds of pricing strategies are developed by Joel Dean. Then the psychological aspects of pricing are considered. A marketer cannot overlook the psychology of pricing as he sets the price of his product since each price gives clues about the seller and product.

The concept of the marketing mix is the subject of the reading by Neil H. Borden. Borden, who introduced the term, explains its derivation, meaning, and application to marketing. The communication of a corporation image is then discussed by Steuart Henderson Britt. Businessmen change their ideas about many things over any given period of time, and this holds true with advertising. A look at the businessmen's ideas is provided by Stephen Greyser and Bonnie Reece, and both the strengths and weaknesses of advertising are suggested in this examination.

The final readings in Part IV relate to the international sector. A basic approach to international business is provided by Franklin Root. He develops the environment of the international market and brings in recent developments such as the multinational corporation. Since there is a basic question concerning the application of our domestic marketing practices to international marketing, Yoshi Tsurumi's reading on doing business with Japan is included. Tsurumi suggests some of the ways the U.S. marketer should think about foreign markets. Similarly, there is debate over the marketing practices that are applied to developing nations, and this is discussed in the selection by A. Graeme Cranch.

K. Adapting to the Environment

31. A Marketing View of Business Policy

WROE ALDERSON

The American economy is a market-oriented economy. It is essential that the top management of successful companies consist of market-oriented executives.

Top management executives who accept the marketing concept must rely on marketing executives who are knowing and skillful users of the techniques of analysis and planning which are still being pioneered by the membership of this association.

What does it mean to assert that the American economy is a market-oriented economy? A market-oriented economy, to begin with, is one in which consumers obtain most goods and services through the market and in which the dynamics of the economy are governed essentially by consumer sovereignty.

Our economy today is surely not the subsistence economy of colonial times which we were still fighting our way out of when Lincoln spoke at Gettysburg. Increasingly our wives are skilled buyers, as in sharp contrast with their great-grandmothers who were primarily skilled operators of household industries.

Our economy is surely a long way from the state capitalism of Russia under which the flow of consumer goods is inadequate in quantity and dreadfully dull in character. Here we seek to maximize the production and use of consumer goods, and, incidentally, to broaden the economic base which can support essential government expenditures for civil or military requirements.

Ours is not the raw materials economy of some underdeveloped countries in which natural resources which might support a good life for all are being steadily depleted to provide luxury for a few. It is true that these raw-materials producers are dependent upon markets, but that is not market orientation.

Ours is not the economy of some European countries dominated by market-sharing cartels and by caste-bound petty tradesmen. We not only welcome change in our society but reserve our greatest rewards for the innovator. Profits in our system are for those who develop products which expand the range of consumer choice or who find better ways of bringing products to market.

Finally, ours is not the economy of classical economic theory. The theorist here typically assumes that the demand follows production rather than the reverse. In marketing we know that investment in specialized and automated capacity, to achieve greater productivity, must follow from a careful assessment of potential demand. The theorist usually assumes that exchange transactions are costless, but one of the essential tasks of the marketing practitioner is to reduce transactional costs which might otherwise be prohibitive. Another economic postulate is that perfect knowledge of markets is a prerequisite for perfect competition. Fortunately, perfect knowledge is not essential to workable competition since the quest for perfect knowledge would bankrupt any firm which adopted it as a fixed goal.

◆ SOURCE: Reprinted by permission from *Advancing Marketing Efficiency*, edited by Lynn H. Stockman, Proceedings of the Winter Conference of the American Marketing Association, December 1958, pp. 114–119.

What does it mean to say that top management must consist of market-oriented executives? Certainly, nothing is more significant to the top executive than his sales expectations. In critical situations I have even seen top management pacing the floor waiting for a report on yesterday's sales, but market orientation is more than that. If a man without a marketing background or understanding of the marketing concept is suddenly catapulted into top management responsibility and comes to realize that all of his crucial decisions are now inherently marketing decisions, he has some cause for worry.

Many top executives are star salesmen, even though they have never served in a full time sales capacity. One of their greatest values to their firm may be as charming hosts for leading customers or as shrewd negotiators of major contracts. A company president who is not consciously exerting any sale effort at all may be the ideal symbol for the corporate image the firm wishes to project as part of its effort to maximize sales. But personal selling, however effective, is only one aspect of marketing.

The highest function of the top executive is to think in terms of a system of action, to control or influence the behavior of the system in ways that are favorable to maximizing its output, and to remodel or rebuild the system should changing conditions render it obsolete. The system of action which he must try to understand and direct embraces not only the resources and employees of his firm but the actual and potential customers for its products and the distribution channels by which the firm reaches its customers. The greatest uncertainties within this system of action are those which lie beyond the limits of corporate ownership and control. The problems which will offer the greatest challenge to his creative imagination and objective judgment are problems which arise in the market place.

As he works his way into the all-embracing task of top management, the top executive may remember with some embarrassment the more limited perspective which he reflected in the past. If he comes out of production management, it would be surprising indeed if he had never censured the marketing department for not providing the firm figures on expected requirements which would facilitate his operations. If he will search his memory, he may recollect some statement to the effect that he could scarcely be expected to avoid fluctuations in production unless marketing was willing to specify the monthly or weekly quantities required for each product in the line. Similarly, when chided for swollen inventories, he may have replied that scientific inventory control was impossible unless marketing was ready to set cost figures against lost sales.

If the top executive comes out of research and development, he may now for the first time see some of his most cherished technical projects in the cold light of market acceptance and expected sales and profits. Faced with the urgencies of potential competitive developments, he may be forced to take some risks in the market introduction of products not yet fully perfected, which would have previously seemed intolerable to his scientific spirit.

If he comes out of accounting and finance, he may wonder how he could have ever been so stiff-necked in resisting pleas for functional cost analysis or statistical analysis of sales records to guide management decision. He will undoubtedly acquire a new vision as to the place of long range market forecasts in an investment program and as to degree of flexibility requisite to sound marketing in operating under an expenditure budget.

Even if the top executive comes out of sales and advertising, he will find that he now needs a greater depth of understanding of marketing rather than less. He may have interpreted his past role in terms of unwavering loyalty to his sales force in order that they in turn might be loyal to him. He may have acted as an advocate for a constantly increasing advertising budget on the assumption that the adverse forces were so strong that any budget approved would never be quite enough. As a top executive, the key issue lands squarely in his lap, namely—what is the right amount to spend for sales and advertising?—neither too little nor too much.

More and more, executive preferment will come to those production managers, controllers, research directors, sales and advertising managements who manifest some understanding of the broader marketing concept even while filling subordinate roles. More and more, training for the ultimate responsibilities of top management will include a substantial marketing component in the mix.

* * *

What does it mean to say that we need marketing executives who are knowing and skillful users of techniques pioneered by members of this association?

On the one hand, he should appreciate both the potentialities and the limitations of the analytical techniques now available in solving marketing problems. On the other hand, he should recognize that the greatest pioneering in systematic decision-making still lies ahead and that these advances cannot happen without his collaboration. I am referring particularly to the discipline of marketing planning, currently a backward art compared to the progress which has been achieved in marketing research and analysis.

The stereotype of the self-sufficient executive making one quick decision after another is no longer appropriate in complex and dynamic markets. It is characteristic of marketing decisions to be linked together in interdependent groups. Marketing decisions are linked from customer to customer, from product to product, and in time. A major decision, made in isolation, will almost inevitably make other decisions doubly difficult. Planning is the process of weighing the net effect of a group of interdependent decisions. The planning process provides a framework for strategic decision, a framework that is continuously adjusted to the state of the action system.

A systematic discipline of marketing planning will provide the future pattern of collaboration between an analytical staff and the decision-maker in marketing. This pattern will embrace all of the tested procedures of research and analysis which are now established in marketing. It will use analytical models and electronic simulation of marketing systems which we are only beginning to explore. The difference is that when this approach to planning is fully developed, our present conception of a sequential attack on one problem after another will be largely superseded.

In one sense, effective planning is the stockpiling of prefabricated or semi-fabricated decisions. By determining what should be done in a specified type of repetitious situation, a plan provides in advance for hundreds of such occasions. In another sense, planning is like a tool factory turning out the instruments of more detailed decision-making.

To summarize, a fully developed discipline of marketing planning would accomplish three things:

a. The mass production of decisions concerning repetitive situations.

b. The design of decision rules for handling less frequent and more diverse situations.

c. The maintenance of a comprehensive and up-to-date framework for guiding strategic decisions.

I am really talking here about something that is broader even than planning. I began by asserting that we live in a market-oriented economy which must be guided by market-oriented executives and then attempted to suggest how planning can and must contribute to systematic decision-making. I am attempting to speak today in prophetic mood rather than in didactic tones, to picture what can be done rather than to describe current practice.

Let us now look briefly at one more question which may have come to your minds in the course of this talk. What does all of this have to do with the American Marketing Association and its program for attracting and serving marketing management? Simply, that the subject of greatest moment for the marketing executive as well as for the marketing teacher or the market analyst is the structure of the decision-making process. The marketing executive who can see beyond the limits of his particular company or product field will find much in common with the two groups which now constitute our membership. They need his help in preparing marketing students for executive responsibility and in educating themselves to the changing needs of marketing management. He will obtain in return an enriched understanding of the marketing concept which is now in the forefront of advanced management thinking.

32. The Marketing Revolution

ROBERT J. KEITH

The consumer, not the company, is in the middle.

In today's economy the consumer, the man or woman who buys the product, is at the absolute dead center of the business universe. Companies revolve around the customer, not the other way around.

Growing acceptance of this consumer concept has had, and will have, far-reaching implications for business, achieving a virtual revolution in economic thinking. As the concept gains ever greater acceptance, marketing is emerging as the most important single function in business.

A REVOLUTION IN SCIENCE

A very apt analogy can be drawn with another revolution, one that goes back to the sixteenth century. At that time astronomers had great difficulty predicting the movements of the heavenly bodies. Their charts and computations and celestial calendars enabled them to estimate the approximate positions of the planets on any given date. But their calculations were never exact—there was always a variance.

Then a Polish scientist named Nicholas Copernicus proposed a very simple answer to the problem. If, he proposed, we assume that the sun, and not the earth, is at the center of our system, and that the earth moves around the

sun instead of the sun moving around the earth, all our calculations will prove correct.

The Pole's idea raised a storm of controversy. The earth, everyone knew, was at the center of the universe. But another scientist named Galileo put the theory to test—and it worked. The result was a complete upheaval in scientific and philosophic thought. The effects of Copernicus' revolutionary idea are still being felt today.

A REVOLUTION IN MARKETING

In much the same way American business in general—and Pillsbury in particular—is undergoing a revolution of its own today: a marketing revolution.

This revolution stems from the same idea stated in the opening sentence of this article. No longer is the company at the center of the business universe. Today the customer is at the center.

Our attention has shifted from problems of production to problems of marketing, from the product we *can* make to the product the consumer *wants* us to make, from the company itself to the market place.

The marketing revolution has only begun. It is reasonable to expect that its implications will grow in the years to come, and that lingering effects will be felt a century, or more than one century, from today.

So far the theory has only been advanced, tested, and generally proved correct. As more and more businessmen grasp the concept, and put it to work, our economy will become more truly marketing oriented.

◆ SOURCE: Reprinted by permission from the *Journal of Marketing* (National Quarterly Publication of the American Marketing Association), Vol. 24, No. 3, January 1960, pp. 35–38.

PILLSBURY'S PATTERN: FOUR ERAS

Here is the way the marketing revolution came about at Pillsbury. The experience of this company has followed a typical pattern. There has been nothing unique, and each step in the evolution of the marketing concept has been taken in a way that is more meaningful because the steps are, in fact, typical.

Today in our company the marketing concept finds expression in the simple statement, "Nothing happens at Pillsbury until a sale is made." This statement represents basic reorientation on the part of our management. For, not too many years ago, the ordering of functions in our business placed finance first, production second, and sales last.

How did we arrive at our present point of view? Pillsbury's progress in the marketing revolution divides neatly into four separate eras—eras which parallel rather closely the classic pattern of development in the marketing revolution.

FIRST ERA—PRODUCTION ORIENTED

First came the era of manufacturing. It began with the formation of the company in 1869 and continued into the 1930's. It is significant that the *idea* for the formation of our company came from the *availability* of high-quality wheat and the *proximity* of water power—and not from the availability and proximity of growing major market areas, or the demand for better, less expensive, more convenient flour products.

Of course, these elements were potentially present. But the two major elements which fused in the mind of Charles A. Pillsbury and prompted him to invest his modest capital in a flour mill were, on the one hand, wheat, and, on the other hand, water power. His principal concern was with production, not marketing.

His thought and judgment were typical of the business thinking of his day. And such thinking was adequate and proper for the times.

Our company philosophy in this era might have been stated this way: "We are professional flour millers. Blessed with a supply of the finest North American wheat, plenty of water power, and excellent milling machinery, we produce flour of the highest quality. Our basic function is to mill high-quality flour, and of course (and almost incidentally)

we must hire salesmen to sell it, just as we hire accountants to keep our books."

The young company's first new product reveals an interesting example of the thinking of this era. The product was middlings, the bran left over after milling. Millfeed, as the product came to be known, proved a valuable product because it was an excellent nutrient for cattle. But the impetus to launch the new product came not from a consideration of the nutritional needs of cattle or a marketing analysis. It came primarily from the desire to dispose of a byproduct! The new product decision was production oriented, not marketing oriented.

SECOND ERA—SALES ORIENTED

In the 1930's Pillsbury moved into its second era of development as a marketing company. This was the era of sales. For the first time we began to be highly conscious of the consumer, her wants, and her prejudices, as a key factor in the business equation. We established a commercial research department to provide us with facts about the market.

We also became more aware of the importance of our dealers, the wholesale and retail grocers who provided a vital link in our chain of distribution from the mill to the home. Knowing that consumers and dealers as well were vital to the company's success, we could no longer simply mark them down as unknowns in our figuring. With this realization, we took the first step along the road to becoming a marketing company.

Pillsbury's thinking in this second era could be summed up like this: "We are a flour-milling company, manufacturing a number of products for the consumer market. We must have a first-rate sales organization which can dispose of all the products we can make at a favorable price. We must back up this sales force with consumer advertising and market intelligence. We want our salesmen and our dealers to have all the tools they need for moving the output of our plants to the consumer."

Still not a marketing philosophy, but we were getting closer.

THIRD ERA—MARKETING ORIENTED

It was at the start of the present decade that Pillsbury entered the marketing era. The amazing growth of our consumer business as the result of introducing baking mixes provided the immediate impetus. But the groundwork had been laid by key men who developed our sales concepts in the middle forties.

With the new cake mixes, products of our research program, ringing up sales on the cash register, and with the realization that research and production could produce literally hundreds of new and different products, we faced for the first time the necessity for selecting the best new products. We needed a set of criteria for selecting the kind of products we would manufacture. We needed an organization to establish and maintain these criteria, and for attaining maximum sale of the products we did select.

We needed, in fact, to build into our company a new management function which would direct and control all the other corporate functions from procurement to production to advertising to sales. This function was marketing. Our solution was to establish the present marketing department.

This department developed the criteria which we would use in determining which products to market. *And these criteria were, and are, nothing more nor less than those of the consumer herself.* We moved the mountain out to find out what Mahomet, and Mrs. Mahomet, wanted. The company's purpose was no longer to mill flour, nor to manufacture a wide variety of products, but to satisfy the needs and desires, both actual and potential, of our customers.

If we were to restate our philosophy during the past decade as simply as possible, it would read: "We make and sell products for consumers."

The business universe, we realized, did not have room at the center for Pillsbury or any other company or groups of companies. It was already occupied by the customers.

This is the concept at the core of the marketing revolution. How did we put it to work for Pillsbury?

The Brand-Manager Concept

The first move was to transform our small advertising department into a marketing department. The move involved far more than changing the name on organizational charts. It required the introduction of a new, and vitally important, organizational concept— the brand-manager concept.

The brand-manager idea is the very backbone of marketing at Pillsbury. The man who bears the title, brand manager, has total ac-

countability for results. He directs the marketing of his product as if it were his own business. Production does its job, and finance keeps the profit figures. Otherwise, the brand manager has total responsibility for marketing his product. This responsibility encompasses pricing, commercial research, competitive activity, home service and publicity coordination, legal details, budgets, advertising plans, sales promotion, and execution of plans. The brand manager must think first, last, and always of his sales target, the consumer.

Marketing permeates the entire organization. Marketing plans and executes the sale —all the way from the inception of the product idea, through its development and distribution, to the customer purchase. Marketing begins and ends with the consumer. New product ideas are conceived after careful study of her wants and needs, her likes and dislikes. Then marketing takes the idea and marshals all the forces of the corporation to translate the idea into product and the product into sales.

In the early days of the company, consumer orientation did not seem so important. The company made flour, and flour was a staple—no one would question the availability of a market. Today we must determine whether the American housewife will buy lemon pudding cake in preference to orange angel food. The variables in the equation have multiplied, just as the number of products on the grocers' shelves have multiplied from a hundred or so into many thousands.

When we first began operating under this new marketing concept, we encountered the problems which always accompany any major reorientation. Our people were young and frankly immature in some areas of business; but they were men possessed of an idea and they fought for it. The idea was almost too powerful. The marketing concept proved its worth in sales, but it upset many of the internal balances of the corporation. Marketing-oriented decisions resulted in peaks and valleys in production, schedules, labor, and inventories. But the system worked. It worked better and better as maverick marketing men became motivated toward tonnage and profit.

FOURTH ERA—MARKETING CONTROL

Today marketing is coming into its own. Pillsbury stands on the brink of is fourth major era in the marketing revolution.

Basically, the philosophy of this fourth era can be summarized this way: "We are moving from a company which has the marketing concept to a marketing company."

Marketing today sets company operating policy short-term. It will come to influence long-range policy more and more. Where today consumer research, technical research, procurement, production, advertising, and sales swing into action under the broad canopy established by marketing, tomorrow capital and financial planning, ten-year volume and profit goals will also come under the aegis of marketing. More than any other function, marketing must be tied to top management.

Today our marketing people know more about inventories than anyone in top management. Tomorrow's marketing man must know capital financing and the implications of marketing planning on long-range profit forecasting.

Today technical research receives almost all of its guidance and direction from marketing. Tomorrow marketing will assume a more creative function in the advertising area, both in terms of ideas and media selection.

Changes in the Future

The marketing revolution has only begun. There are still those who resist its basic idea, just as there are always those who will resist change in business, government, or any other form of human institution.

As the marketing revolution gains momentum, there will be more changes. The concept of the customer at the center will remain valid; but business must adjust to the shifting tastes and likes and desires and needs which have always characterized the American consumer.

For many years the geographical center of the United States lay in a small Kansas town. Then a new state, Alaska, came along, and the center shifted to the north and west. Hawaii was admitted to the Union and the geographical mid-point took another jump to the west. In very much the same way, modern business must anticipate the restless shifting of buying attitudes, as customer preferences move north, south, east, or west from a liquid center. There is nothing static about the marketing revolution, and that is part of its fascination. The old order has changed, yielding place to the new—but the new order will have its quota of changes, too.

At Pillsbury, as our fourth era progresses, marketing will become the basic motivating force for the entire corporation. Soon it will be true that every activity of the corporation —is aimed at satisfying the needs and desires of the consumer. When that stage of development is reached, the marketing revolution will be complete.

ADDENDUM: The New Management and the Changing Role of the Corporation

ROBERT J. KEITH

I saw an article recently that suggested the times in which we live should be labeled, "Subject to change without notice."

The same thing could be said about business. Indeed, it is almost redundant to use the words "change" and "business" in the same sentence. Change is of the essence of business; it is occurring at an accelerating pace, fueled by our expanding technologies, whipped along and channeled by the growing demands of the consumer.

As a matter of fact, the biggest single change that I have observed in business has concerned change itself: It is the evolvement of the need to create and not follow change. To be sure, companies continue to have change thrust upon them by technological advances and the pressures of competition. But they have learned that it is possible to reach out and create change instead of waiting for change to come to them.

The changes in business, whether thrust upon it or created by it, are too many to be catalogued. And they are not easily summarized. In an effort to gather my observations into some kind of organized framework, however, I will discuss them:

First in terms of the changing corporate structure, and

Second in terms of the people we need to deal with and be a part of change.

◆ SOURCE: Reprinted by permission from the School of Business Administration, University of Minnesota. (A talk delivered before Annual Meeting, Mid-Continent East Region, American Association Collegiate Schools of Business, Oct. 19–20, 1967, Minneapolis, Minn.) pp. 1–9.

MANAGEMENT CHANGES

Corporations, like people, have experienced a population explosion. There are a lot more of them than there used to be, and of course, they are quite different. The men who run them have changed considerably, too.

The chief executive has evolved from a man who made all the decisions to a man who sees that all the decisions are made. He is no longer able to accomplish his goals through the use of raw power. He must now get the job done with a new set of management tools: information, prediction and persuasion.

The first two of those—information and prediction—are made possible in great measure by the computer. The third—persuasion—has not yet been computerized; it's still up to the executive, and if he had the foresight to get himself a degree in psychology, he finds that it comes in handy.

The computer, a device that does mysterious things routinely and routine things mysteriously, has contributed in a major way to the changing shape of the corporation.

While saving industry from suffocation in its own paperwork, it has—among other things—made industry a much more exciting place for a young businessman to work.

Young men joining the Pillsbury Company today, for example, are likely to find themselves making important decisions—or at least helping to make important decisions—almost as soon as they start receiving their paychecks. Within a few days or weeks they may find themselves on project-teams working on more or less equal footing with vice-presidents and others of stature and long experience.

It used to be—and not very long ago, either—that a man had to work his way up to the rank of department head before he got to decide anything more important than where to eat lunch. Not so anymore. Now he must be equipped to make business decisions when he completes his graduate education, because his apprenticeship will be brief.

ORGANIZATIONAL CHANGES

What has happened is this: The computer has made possible an information system that has largely dissolved the traditional box-and-line organizational structure of our company. The old organizational charts no longer illustrate the actual working relationships of our managers. They no longer trace the actual flow of information, reports and authority.

The information that used to filter to the Executive Office through layer after organizational layer, arriving in distorted and outdated form, is now available swiftly, almost instantaneously. The computer draws the information directly from the points of origin in production, sales, marketing and distribution. It classifies, organizes and reports simultaneously to every level of management in the company—in as much detail as desired.

This does not mean that the Executive Office is likely to use this abundance of current operating data to totally dominate operations. On the contrary: In the days when the Executive Office got 30-to-45-day-old data, it had to get a feel of the business through involvement. Now that current information is available to give us readings on how things are going, the executive officers are able to withdraw from operations to a degree not possible in the past. It has, to be frank about it, removed us as bottlenecks in the decision-making process.

NEED FOR SPECIALIST AND GENERALIST

It is not uncommon today for three, four or even five levels of management to come together in one meeting to bring to bear on a problem their various talents and perspectives. That's the way the project-team system works.

The project-team requires, of course, that we have two kinds of men: the specialist who can focus his particular expertise on the problem at hand, and the generalist who can see enough of the whole picture to quarterback the specialists.

It isn't enough for the generalist to know what the specialists are talking about, however. They must know what he's talking about, too. He must know how to use the English language—both in person and on paper. Face-to-face communication is what makes the team work. And he will have reports to write that must be concise to be effective.

UNDERSTANDING GOVERNMENT IMPORTANT

We need men trained early in life to understand business *and* government. The relationship grows ever closer. There was a time when business ignored government. But as Thomas Gates, chairman of Morgan Guaranty Trust Co., has observed, "It's safe to say that business-government relations have come out of their Ice Age."

On the government side, former Secretary of Commerce Alexander Trowbridge has said: "Business and government today jointly serve America in many ways . . . By focusing on 'public problem-solving,' business is expanding its service to the nation that yields several types of profit. Across the whole broad range of national life, nothing is more essential to continued growth and progress than a sound, balanced relationship between business and government."

It seems clear to me that we need young men trained to the thought that government will influence business and that business, through capable people, will influence government.

CREATIVITY AND APPROPRIATE REWARDS

I realize that creativity is a pretty nebulous subject to talk about, but nebulous or not I think business has established more avenues for its expression than ever before. We need men who can travel those avenues, for how can we create change without creative people?

I know there's an old saying that poverty is the step-mother of genius. But I happen to think genius should be rewarded handsomely; big salaries should go with big imaginations.

In fact, it's not hard to imagine a creator making more money than his boss—in the fashion of a star baseball player who commands a bigger salary than his manager.

I have a closing thought about the attitudes of the young business school graduate: We find too many who are interested in tours of duty rather than a career. They have been encouraged in school, I'm told, to test themselves in several companies.

Viewing changes in business is a little like looking at the world from the observation car of a passenger train: You have a better idea of where you have been than where you are going. I have presented some of the changes as I see them—past, present and future—in terms of the anatomy of the corporation and in terms of the men business needs.

My conclusion is that business now has more to offer a man with a degree than ever —and needs him more than ever. Our hope is that the degree-holder has more to offer, too.

33. The Faltering Marketing Concept

MARTIN L. BELL and C. WILLIAM EMORY

The marketing concept has been widely accepted as an adequate statement of the function and role of marketing in today's society as well as in the business firm. In recent years, however, there has been a growing indication that the concept has faltered to the point where it is no longer an adequate statement. Evidence exists to support the questioning of the marketing concept. One is organizational stress, excessive costs, and high product failure rates in some companies incurred by attempting to implement the concept.[1] Additional evidence of a breakdown in the marketing concept is found in the deterioration of relations between business on the one hand and the public and government on the other. These developments include events which are now widely called "consumerism." For example, "In the very broadest sense, consumerism can be defined as the bankruptcy of what the business schools have been calling 'marketing concept.' "[2] Is such an indictment justified?

CONSUMERISM AND THE MARKETING CONCEPT

For decades there have been outcries that the consumer has been mistreated.[3] However, the present challenge is part of a much broader and deeper concern with a variety of social problems. The new wave of social criticism started to build in the late 1950s and early 1960s. Popular books began to focus attention on the impacts of various marketing activities upon consumers and society as a whole.[4] The criticism increased and several self-appointed consumer spokesmen emerged to organize and lead the attack upon alleged marketing abuses and the companies responsible for them.

The challenges by the consumerists are not restricted to a single product, industry, or practice. Many of the leading corporations are under the strongest attacks. Automobile manufacturers, publishers, soap companies, and especially oil companies have been confronted. For example, gasoline marketers have periodically been accused of pricing irregularities. Certain commercials for long-mileage ingredients have been banned from television.

---

[1] For example, see T. L. Berg, *Mismarketing* (Garden City, N.Y.: Doubleday and Company, 1970); Theodore Levitt, *The Marketing Mode* (New York: McGraw-Hill Book Company, 1969), p. 230; and A. P. Felton, "Making the Marketing Concept Work," *Harvard Business Review*, Vol. 37 (July-August, 1959), pp. 55–65.

[2] "Business Responds to Consumerism," *Business Week* (September 6, 1969), p. 95.

◆ SOURCE: Reprinted by permission from the *Journal of Marketing* (National Quarterly Publication of the American Marketing Association), Vol. 35, No. 4, October 1971, pp. 37–42.

[3] Robert O. Herrmann, "Consumerism: Its Goals, Organizations and Future," JOURNAL OF MARKETING, Vol. 34 (October, 1970), pp. 55–60.

[4] For example, see Rachel Carson, *Silent Spring* (Boston: Houghton Mifflin Co., 1962); Jessica Mitford, *American Way of Death* (New York: Simon and Schuster, Inc., 1963); Ralph Nader, *Unsafe at Any Speed* (New York: Brossman Publishers, Inc., 1965).

The use of lotteries and games has been denied because the outcomes have been manipulated, and the chances of winning have been deceitfully promoted.[5] Their products have been severely criticized as pollutants and the slowness of the industry to develop ways of lessening the harmful waste has also come under attack.

Major food companies have been accused of feeding "empty calories" to both adults and children. One nutritionist claimed that the consumer typically receives fewer vitamins and minerals today than he did ten years ago.[6] Along with other industries, notably the toy manufacturers, the food industry has also been accused of influencing children with its television advertising.

Appliance manufacturers have been castigated for their self-serving warranties. Corporations that are closely identified with the popularization of the marketing concept have been accused of producing unsafe merchandise. The important point is that charges are not being brought against the "marginal few" who skirt the edge of the economic process using the marketing approach of the "caravan trader." The consumerists have focused on the elite of U.S. industry.

Business, however, is not without its defenders. Many claim, with much justification, that ethics in the marketplace are as high or higher today than at any time in history. Most firms try to provide good values; many firms extend themselves to offer superior services and products to the consumer. Where practices are deficient, they are often attributed to competitive pressures and sometimes even to government regulations. As a result, its defenders claim that business is the target of a witch hunt; that it is being criticized for problems that it did not create and which lie beyond its control. In fact, many businessmen see consumerism as an attack upon the free enterprise system rather than as an effort to improve it.[7]

Consumerists would probably agree that U.S. business has provided society with many benefits. However, the message is clear—society expects more. Businessmen cannot look back at their achievements; rather, they are exhorted to accept new standards by which to judge their role in society. The focus of the consumerist message is that the existing marketing concept is an inadequate standard.

THE MARKETING CONCEPT

The marketing concept is the result of an attempt to operationalize a basic philosophy of marketing held by economists and marketing theorists. Welfare economics is replete with references to the responsibility of business to provide utilities for consumers. Adam Smith, the father of enterprise economics, noted that the purpose of production is to serve consumption. The authors of early marketing texts also emphasized that the purpose of marketing is to provide consumer satisfactions. Note the following statement from an early edition of a leading marketing text.

Business functions to satisfy the needs of the consumers. The first measure of the success of any business is how well it serves the consumers. If an operation is not in the interest of the consumers, it is not justified, no matter how profitable it may be to its owners. He profits most who serves best.[8]

This philosophy of customer satisfaction was not clearly articulated in operational business terms until the 1950s. However, this situation changed as the "marketing revolution" unfolded. The need to look to the customer for guidance in the organization and direction of business was recognized.[9]

McKitterick, a leading marketing executive, presented a paper before the American Marketing Association which became one of the most widely reproduced statements on the

---

[5] Investigation of 'Preselected Winners' Sweepstakes Promotions: Hearings before the Subcommittee on Activities of Regulatory Agencies Relating to Small Business of the Select Committee on Small Business, House of Representatives, 91st Congress, 1st Session, p. 2.

[6] Dr. Jean Mayer in a speech reported in Advertising Age (March 23, 1970), p. 106.

[7] See Ralph Gaedeke, "What Business, Government, and Consumer Spokesmen Think about

Consumerism," The Journal of Consumer Affairs, Vol. 4 (Summer, 1970), p. 10; see also "Roche, Larken Views Conflict on Consumerism," Advertising Age (March 29, 1971), p. 1.

[8] P. D. Converse and H. W. Huegy, The Elements of Marketing (New York: Prentice-Hall, Inc., 1946), p. 21.

[9] R. J. Keith, "The Marketing Revolution," JOURNAL OF MARKETING, Vol. 24 (January, 1960), pp. 35–38.

marketing concept.[10] He clearly tied the emerging marketing concept to the problems of corporate growth and the need to develop a meaningful, internalized "philosophy" of business to guide the planning and profit control functions. The first contributions to marketing literature concerning the operational concept came from consultants and practitioners such as Alderson, Borch, Felton, Jewell, McKay, and Keith.[11] By 1965 practically all introductory marketing texts include some discussion of the "new" marketing concept.

What is this concept? In what respects, if any, does it differ from traditional philosophical statements of marketing's responsibility to consumers? To answer these questions it is necessary to restate the generally accepted meaning of the concept, and then to distinguish its operational from its philosophical aspects.

The marketing concept has three basic elements:

1. *Customer Orientation.* Knowledge of the customer, which requires a thorough understanding of his needs, wants, and behavior should be the focal point of all marketing action. It implies the development of products and services to meet these needs. It does not exclude the possibility that these needs may be "stimulated" by business or that aggressive selling may be needed to persuade consumers to buy goods and services which have been created for them.

---

[10] J. B. McKitterick, "What is the Marketing Management Concept?" in *The Frontiers of Marketing Thought and Science*, Frank M. Bass, ed. (Chicago: American Marketing Association, 1958), pp. 71–82.
[11] W. Alderson, "A Marketing View of Business Policy," *Cost and Profit Outlook*, Vol. VIII (December, 1955), p. 1; F. J. Borch, "The Marketing Philosophy as a Way of Business Life," *Marketing Series No. 99* (New York: American Management Association, 1957), pp. 193–195; A. P. Felton, "Conditions of Marketing Leadership," *Harvard Business Review*, Vol. 34 (March-April, 1956), pp. 117–127; A. P. Felton, "Making the Marketing Concept Work," *Harvard Business Review*, Vol. 37 (July-August, 1959), pp. 55–65; "New Marketing Concept at Westinghouse: Decentralize and Study the Consumer," *Printer's Ink* (January 24, 1958), pp. 33-35; E. S. McKay, "Blueprint for an Effective Marketing Program," *Marketing Series No. 91* (New York: American Management Association, 1954); and Keith, same reference as footnote 9, pp. 35–38.

2. *Integrated Effort.* Ultimately, the entire firm must be in tune with the market by placing emphasis on the integration of the marketing function with research, product management, sales, and advertising to enhance the firm's total effectiveness.

3. *Profit Direction.* The marketing concept is intended to make money for the company by focusing attention on profit rather than upon sales volume.

As defined here, the marketing concept is entirely operational, although the statement on customer orientation touches on elements that could be philosophical in a different context. But philosophical issues are not raised. Rather, the purpose of customer orientation is to improve the firm's selling effectiveness. Providing customer satisfaction is a means to achieving a company profit objective and does not imply protection of the consumer's welfare.

CONSUMER PROTECTION UNDER THE MARKETING CONCEPT

Those who have considerable faith in the free enterprise system tend to believe that it is not the concept that has failed the consumer but its implementation. They argue that if companies had actually designed their total marketing mix to meet the needs and wants of consumers, there would not be a "consumerism" problem today. Of course, there is no way to prove what "might have been." It is clear, however, that many companies which claim adherence to the marketing concept are presently under attack. Chemical companies, appliance and automobile manufacturers, and food processors have sought to be customer oriented, and yet they have become the principal targets of the consumerists. These industries are among the "elite" of modern marketers—leaders in marketing research, new product development, and innovative methods of merchandising. If the marketing concept could have been implemented correctly, should not these companies have been the ones to do it?

Faulty implementation is not the problem. The marketing concept as it is practiced today does not imply a commitment to the kind of consumer satisfaction that is now being demanded. Customer orientation turned the manager away from the factory to the market place. Decisions were based on what could be sold at a profit instead of on what could be manufactured to satisfy the needs and wants of society. The marketing concept was thus an operational concept, not a philosophical one.

Even as a means to business profits, the marketing concept can serve the interests of consumers. Good products, creatively promoted, adequately distributed, and fairly priced might result from an operational approach to customer orientation. But what if the seller consciously compromises product quality in order to improve profits? How is the consumer protected from inferior products, misleading promotion, and exploitative prices?

Business has relied upon a number of assumptions to bridge the gap between the operational marketing concept and its social responsibility to protect the consumer:

1. The company and its long-run survival come first. Providing the consumer with goods and services is a means to this end.

2. The consumer should and can defend his own best interest; i.e., he assures his consumption effectiveness through his own buying ability and the sanction of his market veto. In those few cases where the buyer is unwilling or unable to make rational decisions, the pressures of competition plus the generally prevalent ethical standards governing transactions will provide adequate safeguards.

3. Since the consumer can look out for himself, if a product sells well in the marketplace, this is *prima facie* evidence that it is meeting the needs of the consumer.

4. The seller recognizes that long-run survival depends upon satisfaction of the consumer; therefore, in the long run he must meet the consumers' needs. Thus, long-run survival is *prima facie* evidence of a marketer's ability to satisfy consumers.

Consumerists maintain that society can no longer accept these assumptions as a basis for an equitable relationship between buyer and seller. The following assumptions are suggested as a more equitable basis for the buyer-seller relationship:

1. The consumer comes first. If there is a conflict between the consumer and the firm's objectives, then the consumer must have priority.

2. The typical consumer is at such a dis-advantage that he cannot assure his own effectiveness. Business has the responsibility to help him, and if business fails then the government or other parties must act on the consumer's behalf.

3. Offering products and/or services that "will sell" is not an adequate measure that the seller is fulfilling his responsibility. It is the duty of business to promote proper consumption values.

4. The assumption of the long-run congruence between buyer and seller interests is neither quick enough nor certain enough. The interests of buyer and seller must be reconciled in the short run.

The key to the consumerist message may be stated as follows:

To be legitimate (business objectives) must be in conformity with public interest. An analysis of business objectives should include a study of the assumptions on which our values rest. . . . The "free enterprise" system is based on the right of the private property. Society has delegated to individual citizens the right to own and use physical property for the production and distribution of goods and services to the public. . . . Their right to a profit depends . . . on the ability of the business organization to discharge this responsibility.[12]

THE CONFLICT

The businessman's operational interpretation of customer orientation has not approached the philosophical meaning of providing customer satisfaction as the ultimate goal of marketing. One apparent reason is that the attempt to provide customer satisfaction may conflict directly with the most basic operational goal of the business—to earn a satisfactory rate of return on its shareholders' investment.

In resolving the conflict between consumer orientation and profits, one element usually dominates while the other is rationalized. The manner in which this rationalization was accomplished at one major corporation provides some evidence that the consumer's interest is secondary to the company's.

---

[12] Ralph Currier Davis, *The Fundamentals of Top Management* (New York: Harper & Brothers, Publishers, 1951), pp. 91–92.

. . . with the new marketing concept now a part of the Westinghouse operating philosophy, the customer is all important. Production is based on market forecasts. Marketing planning controls sales activities. All operations related to marketing are coordinated. The goal is improved market position and adequate return on investment . . . it is designed to insure that the customer gets what he wants, where he wants it, when he wants it—*if* these needs provide some kind of opportunity to Westinghouse. (Italics added here for emphasis.)[13]

The little "if" became the point of rationalization. Customer satisfaction yielded to corporate profit opportunity and customer orientation was accepted as an operational rather than as a philosophical guide to direct the marketing activities of the firm. It appears that customer orientation has meant little more than looking to the customer for guidance as to what can be sold at a profit. It has meant knowing the customer, knowing him even better than he knows himself. It has implied the appropriateness of using this knowledge to persuade and even to manipulate him.

There is a danger that the position taken in this article might be misunderstood because it has been overstated. Marketing is not anti-consumer. Without question, much that is good in marketing today is the result of paying more attention to consumer needs and desires. Still, the responsibility for customer welfare has existed within the marketing concepts, but not beyond the point of sale. Customer orientation has been related to the company's goals of sales and profits. The goal of marketing has been a profitable transaction, but the emergence of consumer welfare as a business goal necessitates a revision in the marketing concept.

THE MARKETING CONCEPT REVISITED

The most acceptable basis for a revised marketing concept is the set of assumptions suggested by the consumerist position. Based on these assumptions, the marketing concept would have three elements:

1. *Consumer Concern.* A positive effort by the marketer to make the consumer the focus

of all marketing decisions through service that delivers a high level of satisfaction per consumer dollar spent.

2. *Integrated Operations.* A view that the entire business is a total operational system with consumer and social problems taking precedence over operational considerations in all functional areas.

3. *Profit Reward.* Profit must be viewed as the residual that results from efficiently supplying consumer satisfactions in the marketplace.

Consumer Concern

A firm can show consumer concern by supplying more and better product information to the buyer. Although many consumers do not appreciate or use information, this is not adequate justification for denying such information or for seeking to perpetuate buyer ignorance. Packaging and advertising have often been criticized by consumerists and government regulatory spokesmen for not providing useful information.[14] These criticisms are beginning to have an effect. Demands for more nutritional information, use instructions, and content information bring responses from sellers, and this is only the beginning. Food manufacturers are providing more informative labels, the FTC has proposed that gasoline pumps display octane ratings, and it has also suggested that textiles carry product-care labels.[15] Such information will clearly serve the buyers' best interests and should benefit most sellers.

A second manifestation of more consumer concern is to revise the criteria of acceptability for promotional efforts. The selective presentation of data, the level of puffery, and the freedom of the copywriter are all being challenged by the consumerists as well as by the government's regulatory bodies.[16] Lead-

---

[13] *Printer's Ink,* same references as footnote 11, pp. 33–35.

[14] See comments of Charles Edwards, Commissioner of the Food and Drug Administration, before the annual meeting of the Toilet Goods Association, as reported in "Consumers' Product Information Demands Must Be Met, TGA Told," *Advertising Age* (January 18, 1971), p. 14.

[15] "Enforcer Pitofsky Explains FTC's New Get Tough Policy," *Advertising Age* (January 18, 1971), p. 1.

[16] "FTC to Demand Substantiation of Ads, Supply It to Consumerists," *Advertising Age* (June 14, 1971), p. 1.

ing corporations are currently accused of: (1) misleading and manipulating children—the TV advertising to children controversy; (2) producing merchandise with "miracle" ingredients which, in fact, are of little value—FTC investigation of mouthwash claims; (3) advertising ordinary or inferior features in a way to suggest that they are actually superior features—the analgesic probe; and (4) offering warranties for the consumer's protection that are not understood by the consumer and, in fact, protect the seller more than the buyer —the Consumer Products Guaranty Act now pending before Congress. These charges do not characterize all companies, but the growing list of charges brought against business suggests that more complaints are forthcoming.

The broadened responsibility for consumer concern will also require companies to allocate more resources to post-sale service. Major corporations are now establishing corporate ombudsmen to provide better feedback systems for dissatisfied customers. However, these moves have been chiefly reactive. In order for a company to adequately process consumer complaints, a formal information system with a genuine consumer concern is necessary.

Finally, out of concern for the safety of the consumer as well as for the quality of life, society demands that sellers assume more responsibility for the effects of the use of their products. Since the consumer does not always act in his own or society's best interest, the seller is now being called upon to assume more responsibility to protect the user of his products. For example, pressures developed to change detergent ingredients in order to reduce damage to the environment, particularly by the elimination of phosphates. Business efforts to do this while continuing to provide effective cleaning agents have now brought additional demands that the substitute products be labeled because their caustic ingredients may be harmful to the skin.[17] Up to now, the steps taken by business have largely been in reaction to pressures from the government and the public. The revised marketing concept, however, would include a positive business effort to advance product safety and environmental protection.

Integrated Operations

The preceding changes are some of the most obvious consequences of a revised concept of consumer concern. In addition, company managements will find that their organizations and operations must change. While the exact form of these changes will vary widely among firms, it is suggested that greater emphasis be placed upon company integration.

In the revised marketing concept, operations integration encompasses the entire firm —in some cases an entire industry—to ascertain that resources are efficiently and purposely channeled to the satisfaction of consumer wants.

Profit Reward

The implications for profit making are severe. The crux of the revised marketing concept is that any conflict between customer orientation and profit will be resolved by the rationalization of profit. Does increased concern for consumer protection mean that business should not plan for profits? Not necessarily; however, the order of the planning process should be changed. Instead of setting profit goals and then seeking means and methods of achieving them, the corporation should approach planning in the following manner:

1. What specific satisfactions *should* be provided to the consumer?
2. What specific consumer satisfactions can my company provide?
3. What is the most efficient way to provide these satisfactions?
4. Is the rate of return expected from the venture sufficient to justify the investment?
5. If the anticipated return is below the desired standard, what can still be done to supply the consumer need? For example,
  (a) Provide the services at less than normal profit?
  (b) Contribute know-how or other aid to others who might provide the services?
  (c) Pool interests with other businesses to provide the services cooperatively?
  (d) Assist government or other agencies to provide the services?

---

[17] "Detergent Makers Ordered to Initiate, Toughen Warnings," *Wall Street Journal* (June 29, 1971), p. 8.

CONCLUSIONS

In this approach, the first objective for the company is to assume more responsibility for consumer welfare. The reward for doing this should be profit. On the other hand, these dual goals will make it more difficult to evaluate the performance of corporate programs and personnel. Probably the most effective way to handle the conflict of recognizing the dual social and profit goals will be to establish explicit company criteria of social responsibility. Within such restraints executives will be charged with achieving profit goals. Some companies are beginning to move in this direction. For example, one major marketer of food products has published a list of five basic principles which are expected to guide the company in achieving its corporate objectives.[18] These principles are:

1. "We apply the highest ethical and moral standards, and strive for excellence and leadership in everything we do.

2. "We believe in a dual responsibility to shareholders:—To earn a return on their investment that compares favorably with the return for other leading companies in our industries;—To apply our corporate resources wherever practical to the solution of public

---

[18] *Principles and Objectives* (Chicago: The Quaker Oats Company, 1970), p. 2.

problems in which the interests of shareholders, employees, customers, and the general public are fundamentally inseparable.

3. "We concentrate our efforts on products and services that are useful, of good quality, and of genuine value to consumers.

4. "We conduct our operations with respect for the intelligence and good taste of consumers.

5. "We seek to provide an environment for personal development and advancement that attracts, stimulates, and rewards outstanding employees, whose integrity, ability, and ambition are essential to the Company's progress."

This type of approach will require that company managements include the consideration of social implications in their decision processes and their management control procedures. It will require a substantial increase in feedback mechanisms, more intra-industry consultation and even negotiation with competitors, government agencies, and consumers.

It will be difficult to assume the responsibility for the social implications of its operations, products, and services, but nearly every advance in marketing has made severe demands upon marketing managements. Concern for the consumer will be marketing management's greatest challenge in the next decade. A revised view of the marketing concept is one approach to meet this challenge.

L. Marketing Research

34. The Role of Research in Marketing

MURRAY CAYLEY

Marketing research is a communications activity capable of improving marketing management's understanding of, ability to communicate with or to make decisions about, the market place. Too often, however, communications between management and research personnel are poor. Studies are not clearly related to management's information needs, provide data rather than information or bury useful information under jargon. A clear and shared concept of the role of research on the part of line management and market research can enable management to organize, staff and productivity utilize a research function, while providing a sense of direction and participation for the research group.

Any member of marketing who has had contact with "research" will be able to cite examples of marketing research studies conducted for him that have been meaningless— i.e. not actionably related to his objectives or decision needs. These studies may have been interesting or informative but irrelevant; but they may have been presented as tabulations of data which, if he had the time, might be analyzed in some way helpful to him. "Research," on the other hand, will argue that: "Management doesn't let us in early enough to participate in a meaningful way," "Management objectives are not clearly stated," or "Management is not sympathetic to our efforts to tell them what conclusions the

facts seem to indicate." Situations such as the following are common:

1. The research manager has been striving to establish a cordial relation with the distribution department. He feels that such a relationship may yield an opportunity to "do" some useful studies for that department. The distribution manager calls asking for help from research: "We need to know customer attitudes towards our product and service." An ambitious research study is launched and a thorough report on consumer attitudes presented. The "client's" reaction is: "Certainly a lot of interesting stuff here that we didn't know; but how do we brand-label our trucks? General management is on our backs and we have to make a recommendation next week!"

2. The research manager, cautious about vaguely stated study objectives, has been impressing on his staff the need for clearly written research proposals including management objectives, information requirements and anticipated uses of expected results. A senior market research staff member is asked to participate in a planning meeting where research needs will be discussed. He is advised: "be sure to develop a careful specification of how the information required will be used!" The staff member returns thoroughly defeated. "They told me it wasn't any of my damn business what they were going to do with the information. We are just supposed to get it and they will decide what to do with it!"

3. The research analyst reviews a market-

◆ SOURCE: Reprinted by permission from *The Business Quarterly*, Vol. 33, No. 3, Autumn 1968, pp. 32–40.

ing plan and reports to his manager: "If they had paid any attention to my report they wouldn't be doing these things. They must be stupid up there, why I could run that program better!" The research manager has just had a call from the planning manager telling him: "If that analyst can't just report the facts and stop trying to make us look stupid, we would rather do without!"

These kind of problems arise from several common factors:

1. Lack of commonly understood marketing objectives throughout management.
2. Lack of full partnership participation by research in marketing decision making due to:
  a. absence of well defined research objectives
  b. inability of research to communicate findings in meaningful form
  c. lack of commitment by management to the research concept
  d. frustrated ("I can do it better than them") attitude by research
3. Lack of clear and shared concept of the research role.

Many of these problems would be resolved by clear definition of marketing and research objectives and research role. The purpose of this article is, therefore, to provide:

1. A definition of the role of marketing research—its place within the marketing activity—that will help management and research clarify their relationship.
2. A format for research and marketing management communications and objective setting.
3. Some suggestions for implementation.

DECISION MAKING AND RESEARCH

The management decision process includes: awareness of need for a decision, setting objectives, development and evaluation of alternatives and selection of a course of action. This process is basic to all of the prime functions of management: planning, organizing, directing, staffing and control; planning and control being paramount and interdependent. The participation of research in the process involves the provision of meaningful (i.e. decision oriented) information to management at each step in the process, with particular emphasis in the planning and control functions.

The purpose of this input is to help narrow decision making error and broaden decision making alternatives. Better decisions should result from better information. Thus we may define research with the firm as *a staff service function supplying information to aid the management decision process.*

Research is too often used, however, on an *ex post facto* basis to view the bones of failures, earning a critical and negative reputation. Often, the research manager must pound a beat in the corridors soliciting business which results in fragmentary studies and only rarely making a meaningful contribution to someone's decision problem. Well defined marketing objectives and plans, on the other hand, provide research with the opportunity to examine information needs and develop a research plan in active participation with marketing management. Here, real needs can be identified and satisfied in an organized manner.

Where do these objectives and plans come from? They emerge most dependably from a formal planning approach to business operations. Such an approach enforces discipline on the manager as he:

1. Analyzes pertinent influences in his environment relative to his product.
2. Attempts to establish specific objectives for his operation.
3. Develops marketing strategies.
4. Decides upon tactical action.
5. Evaluates operating results relative to his planned objectives.

Without such formal discipline, planning tends to be spotty at best. With it, the effort to write a plan determines quickly the information needed. Ideally, research is a pillar in such a process, becoming a support to planning. Since planning is decision oriented, then so must the research be.

THE NEED FOR RESEARCH

Why is research needed? Why is the experience of the manager not sufficient to enable him to make these kinds of decisions himself, to write a good plan based on his experience and knowledge of the market place?

1. There is too much information available for one man to stay current with it. This becomes evident when people start to write long term plans and find themselves unable

to answer critical questions about market definition, size of market and consumer buying habits.

2. The market place is changing too rapidly for the individual manager to remain "up-to-date" with his experience, or easily anticipate the future through traditional reporting forms.

3. The administrative responsibilities of "management" inhibit indirect contact between the manager and his market place—an information gulf develops.

4. Growing affluence and competition between similar products yield a less and less "rational" basis for consumer buying decisions. More information about how these decisions are currently being made is essential to meaningful communications with the potential customer.

5. The mass of current raw data to be reviewed is already greater than the individual's ability to assimilate it. This mass is growing at an increasing rate.

RESEARCH AND PLANNING

Given a planning environment and management recognition of the need for information, the problem still arises of assuring that research studies are designed and conducted so as to provide meaningful results. (By this we mean meaningful relative to meeting a planning or decision need rather than technical design.) We may begin to insure this result by first relating some of the many ways various types of research apply to the various stages in the planning-decision making process.

1. Environmental Analysis

New opportunities or innovative possibilities, competitive strengths and weaknesses may be discovered directly or as a peripheral benefit from exploratory market studies, motivation research.

Product or service total market and consumer buying habits, changes in market size and composition from consumer research, market quantification studies, competitive position and trend research.

Operating changes in regional sales performance, product line activity through sales analysis, consumer research.

Systems improvements, resource allocation, financial models, developed through operations research and systems analysis.

2. Objective Setting

Sales and market share objectives from market analysis, consumer research.

Style, design, performance objectives, product and consumer research and market testing.

Pricing and profit objectives from economic analysis, distribution research, consumer research and market testing.

Distribution channel objectives, personnel and capital deployment through operations research and systems analysis.

3. Strategic Alternatives

Advertising appeal, pricing, distribution alternatives through consumer, advertising, distribution research.

Market segmentation strategy based on consumer and motivation research.

Personnel and capital deployment from operations research and systems analysis.

4. Tactical Objectives

Probability of success of tactical alternatives may be derived from historical sales research, advertising pre-testing, package tests, market tests, consumer and motivation research.

New product and advertising planning are aided by sales analysis and market studies showing acceptance and decay curves for products and services.

Market simulations through operation research and system analysis.

5. Course of Action

Management's decision.

6. Evaluation and Control

Sales performance information from audit samples, territorial sales analysis.

Criteria for sales oriented information systems developed from historical sales analysis and consumer research.

Advertising penetration and effectiveness evaluation through post-testing, sales analysis.

Consumer perception of and attitude towards company name, brands, facilities, products relative to strategic and tactical sales and advertising objectives from consumer and motivation research.

This listing of the kinds of things various kinds of research can do at various stages of the planning-decision making process is neither complete nor definitive. Nevertheless, and disregarding any argument over definitions of "types" of research, it does illustrate that research can serve management in varied ways. Further, by eliminating the emphasis on "type" and focussing our attention on objectives, we can avoid the traditional discussion of how various kinds of research are done rather than what research should be doing for management.

MODEL

A model of the interrelationship between management and research appears on the following page. At the top are the elements of the decision process as inputs to the management function, both shown as inputs to any operation.

At the bottom is data, a large, amorphous mass consisting of small disorganized bits. This mass is growing rapidly. The broken arrow at the left shows that management cannot tap this source data by itself but requires a system to select, organize and convert the right data into meaningful information. Thus, at (4) pertinent and actionable information requirements or hypotheses about reality are developed and (5) the data required to develop this information specified. This listing of data requirements results in a filter (7) or sample description and research design prepared to screen out appropriate data from the mass of irrelevancy. *The design of the filter is the responsibility of research.* A close relationship between the researcher and his "client" is required to clearly understand and often help specify management's information requirements in order that precise and correct sample description and research designs may be prepared.

Given the filter, data assembly (8) through statistical sampling, interviews, etc. and analysis (9) may be accomplished. Research technology is highly developed in these two areas. A report written (10) which presents the data analysis and the conclusions and recommendations derived from this analysis. These results are meaningful information when they refer directly to management's decision needs.

The keystone in this system is the development of hypotheses or specification of information required. If this is done properly, the resulting information should be actionable in terms of the decision need. This can only be brought about by close collaboration between research and management. In practice, the definition of information requirements is the interface between management activities (1–3), and research activities (7–10) and is critical to the effective utilization of the research system by management.

TASK, ROLE, METHODOLOGY

The model above is helpful in defining the role of research in the organization as well as clarifying:

1. Those things that research does,
2. The kinds of people it requires, and
3. Its most meaningful alternatives.

The task of research is: to provide and maintain for management the research system, to work with management in such a way as to be able to understand its needs, to help define informational requirements, to specify the filter and generate, through application of professional methodology, meaningful information in the most efficient manner. Its role is to broaden managerial decision alternatives and reduce the range of decision error through application of the scientific method to analysis of data and evaluation of information.

It must be noted that research is *not* a decision making activity in line management terms. It can examine problems and point out opportunities, it can provide the framework for strategic planning and help evaluate tactical alternatives. Research can point out the need for a decision or specify new areas for management attention. It cannot, regardless of periodic temptations in this direction, make the decision. Such involvement would necessarily reduce objectivity by introducing vested interest. The manager, drawing on his experience, other information or policy considerations, is utimately charged with this responsibility.

WHAT RESEARCH DOES

The techniques of research used to assemble and evaluate data are found to be common to all "types" of research and are, in most cases, relatively simple. Their main emphasis is the application of probability theory

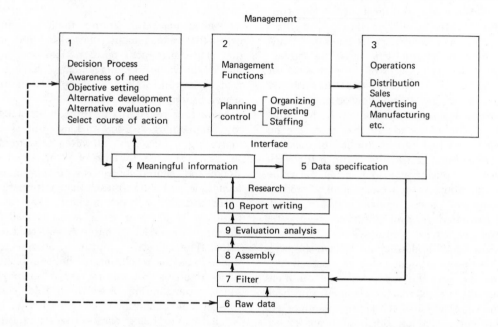

and the imposition of the scientific method to achieve objective results about which certain statements of confidence can be made. The basic tools of research are interviews, observation, published information and in-house operating data. These tools are not only common to all types of research but also to all functional and operating areas of management.

The kinds of things that research can or does do have traditionally been defined by relating them to operating areas of management rather than to the elements of the decision process. Thus we find, for example:

1. Market Characteristics Research (Qualitative)
2. Size of Market Research (Quantitative)
3. Distribution Research
4. Sales Research
5. Advertising and Promotion Research
6. Product Research
7. Competitive Position and Trend Research

Research is conducted in all of these areas, but we can see from the model that categorizing research in this manner can bypass the decision activity (1). When this happess, it becomes nearly impossible to specify information according to the requirements of our definition. Without this discipline, research output ceases to be focused on decision needs, and can quickly become reduced to being interesting but not necessarily valuable. Further, given neatly compartmented types of research, researchers have tended to split off into specialized groups. The texts and journals abound with case examples of research studies of these kinds. Specialized techniques and jargon tend to develop, inhibiting communication with non-specialists and management. For many, therefore, research has become an esoteric and nearly occult science. That this has happened is not hard to understand by the very nature of the "specialist" or technician. His major concern will always be his methodology and techniques, not necessarily with his role vis-à-vis management's need for actionable information. This concept has serious implications regarding research organizing and staffing. . . .

RESEARCH PLANNING AND EVALUATION

The objective of marketing activity is, of course, to sell products at a profit to the firm consistent with long term organizational survival. Research is part of the marketing mix dedicated to accomplishing this objective. It is difficult to attribute sales results to an ad campaign, more difficult to attribute such results to research. On the other hand, advertising that is conceived and developed in terms specifically related to consumer wishes and how they are expressed must, in the long run, provide greater benefits to the total marketing effort than otherwise. In the same manner, research productivity must be subjectively evaluated in terms of the pertinence of the information provided and its use by management, given the knowledge that better decisions tend to be made on better information. This is not to say that there are no explicit tests that can be applied to measure research input. Progress is being made with Bayesian applications to measuring the value of information in such areas of new product introduction. Using known levels of confidence around research information, greater degrees of future "rightness" may be attributed to decision alternatives. However, evaluating the gross input value of research to a marketing program must still rely on more pragmatic judgments. A planned approach to research within a marketing planning environment is perhaps the best means of obtaining a favorable judgment. Planning involves spelling out decision and informational needs over some future period. Given this specification, a research program can be planned to provide the most pertinent kinds of information to the decision maker rather than developing spot studies to fill sudden gaps. Research may then be evaluated in terms of how well it fills informational gaps in marketing plans while maintaining an effective current operating research program.

The foregoing implies a deeply involved role for research in the management process. How far this involvement will be permitted remains, to a large extent, management's decision. Consumer orientation, for example, is aided by consumer research, not "market facts." But management must be open and receptive to this kind of information. If management sees research as a fact finding function or an audit bureau, it has the power to limit research to that role. This is clear both in the nature of the interface relationship in the model and the inherent organization powers of senior management. If, on the other hand, management is consciously willing to accept its planning responsibility or function and sees research as meaningful in this context, good consumer research must necessarily provide a foundation for better decisions and even a springboard to innovation.

CONCLUSIONS

A clear need for "information" is found within the management process and the nature of the manager's position. This need indicates the value to management of having a well organized, staffed and contributing research function within the firm.

Marketing research can provide assistance to the planning-decision making process of marketing management. It often fails to do so, however, due to lack of clearly understood and shared objectives, emphasis on technique and data rather than information needs and ability to communicate. The cases illustrate problems in these areas as well as the need for effective interpersonal relationships. The effective utilization of research depends on the resolution of these problems, which depends on a mutual research-management understanding of research role, commitment and planning.

The model helps clarify the relationship between research and marketing management. If it is understood that the two must interface at the problem definition–hypothesis building stage, management may become more willing to let research "in" on its thoughts and problems and research correspondingly become more broadly aware and thoughtful about marketing problems apart from the technical aspects of data handling.

Once the concepts of the interface relationships and planning are understood by management, it should become possible to organize and staff an effective research function. Technical specialists are required to carry out the research task, but research management will require a broadly perceptive generalist able to clearly understand management's needs in order to bring research to bear in a meaningful way. Development of these latter kinds of people will become an urgent problem in the next few years.

Marketing planning serves the useful functions of forcing management's consideration of objectives, abstracted from day to day operating pressures, and focusing attention on gaps in information. Within a planning environment, therefore, management should be more easily able to understand what research can do for it while research can demonstrate usefulness more easily through a planned approach to filling the information gap.

The problem of obtaining management's commitment to the research concept and understanding of what research can do is mentioned wherever research is discussed. This is an easy demand for research to make in that it throws much of the responsibility for effective utilization of research outside the research department. Management is also broadly advised to accept the "marketing con-cept," get "consumer oriented." The time has come for marketing research to take this same advice and orient itself to the needs of its consumer, marketing management. In this way, demonstrating ability to contribute to planning-decision making problems in a meaningful way, research may help itself achieve management's enthusiastic encouragement and co-operation.

35. Some Observations on Marketing Research in Top Management Decision Making

JOHN G. KEANE

A respected source estimates that investment in marketing research will increase approximately $50 million in 1969 to almost $600 million.[1] In order to improve the return on that size investment, top management needs to use marketing research more in top level decision making.

Time is certainly appropriate for marketing research to participate in these high decision-making efforts. Never has top management decision making been riskier. Consider some of the responsible forces:

- Explosion of information and information processing.
- Intensifying competition.
- Increasing complexity of business.
- Inflationary cost trends.
- Expanding technology.
- Collapsing product life cycles.
- Increasing R&D and capital costs.
- Overall economic, financial, political, and social uncertainty.
- Ever layering management.

This is the backdrop of management at the top. Against it, there is an acknowledged need and opportunity for marketing research to play an expanded role in top management decision making. This paper (1) describes

[1] "Marketing Research Investment to Hit $600,-000,000: Dutka," *Advertising Age*, Vol. 39 (December 9, 1968), p. 88.

◆ SOURCE: Reprinted by permission of the *Journal of Marketing* (National Quarterly Publication of the American Marketing Association), Vol. 33, No. 4, October 1969, pp. 10–15.

the flow of marketing research information to top management, (2) assesses the role of marketing research in top management decision making, (3) summarizes obstacles impeding the effective use of research in decision making, and (4) offers suggestions for improving the marketing research-top management interface.

RESEARCH FLOW

Where does marketing research start? What is its path to top management?

Fig. 1 is a diagrammatic attempt to help answer these questions. While obviously not a blueprint for all companies, it is representative of current practice.

The request for research can originate almost anywhere. It can come from the top, from a nonresearch staff function, or from research itself. Sometimes the request comes from the outside (for example, advertising agency, research company) in the form of a suggested need or opportunity.

Regardless of where the request for research originates, evidence indicates that completed research may or may not reach top management. Considering the current situation regarding the flow of market research information, the following observations are noted:

1. The more directly concerned top management is with an original research request, the more likely it is to be influenced by the results.

2. The more management layers research

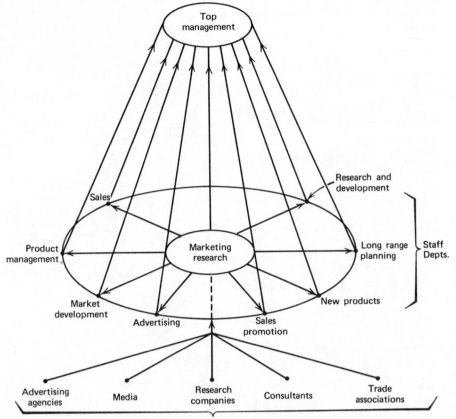

FIGURE 1. Illustrative flow of marketing research to top management.

results must pass through, the less likely results will be timely and undistorted.

3. Among potential marketing research suppliers, advertising agencies and consultants appear to be in the best position to develop direct client contact and influence top management of end-user companies.

DECISION-MAKING INFLUENCES

Top management decisions are the reconciliation of many influences. The reconciliation occurs both within and among management members. Admittedly, marketing research is but one input; however, one which should grow in impact and persuasion.

Decisions may be as perfunctory as casual observation sometimes suggests. Often they are not. Many influences may be operating as Fig. 2 suggests. Some influences such as past experience, personal bias, judgment, and intuition operate within an individual. Their *intra*-personal character belies their potential

significance in a given decision. For instance, intuition and bias can be powerful factors. In some instances, intuition is the dominant influence.

Fig. 2 portrays another set of influences. These influences are termed *extra*-personal and operate outside the individual. This group would comprise marketing research data, company considerations, group dynamics plus competition, government, stockholders, and the market. Here it becomes quite apparent that marketing research interacts with many other influences in the decision process.

Important among these influences is the interplay of group dynamics. For instance, there is the "bulldozer-type" executive who sometimes substitutes voice and title for logic and facts as he rams *his* decision home. This individual intimidates others who are perhaps more capable of moving a group toward a better decision. The bulldozer-type is a likely candidate to ignore, slant or otherwise abuse marketing research in his decision deportment.

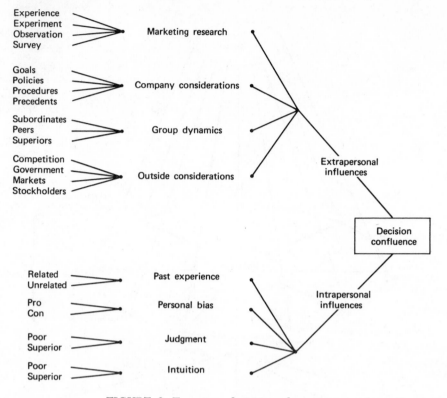

FIGURE 2. Expository decision-making tree.

Other, but less blatant, group dynamic influences exist. Disguised motivations, subtle power plays, management trades, gamesmanship, and one-upmanship may operate. When they do exist, marketing research sometimes becomes the "whipping boy" or "the executive out."

The decision-making process of top management has largely become a committee effort. This most often means decision by consensus, which frequently indicates compromise. Assuming these circumstances, research findings are usually given a rather broad interpretation.

This is the system and it seems to work satisfactorily. For the most part, marketing research does not seem generally abused. Even when it is, often it is abused unintentionally.

DOES TOP MANAGEMENT REALLY DECIDE?

A relevant question is whether or not top management makes its decisions based on research. This requires an answer to the even more basic question: Does top management *really* decide?

In many instances, top management decides things in every sense of the term. This seems particularly true in an enterprise which is not of huge proportions, technologically complex, or run by committee.

Within this kind of company, marketing research either does not formally exist or tends to be a modest staff function with a relatively small voice. Yet its role ranges widely. In some companies it provides information and little else. In other instances, recommendations are solicited and followed by top management. For other companies the case is not so clear-cut. This is the acknowledged era of conglomeration. Attempting to pinpoint who does what is tricky business. It distills down to what is meant by the term "deciding."

If the meaning refers to rendering a judgment and determining courses of action, then top managements decide. But if deciding means developing alternative courses of action, thoroughly analyzing and reconciling them before making a judgment, then top management decision making may be legitimately questioned for many of our larger enterprises.

In large corporations characterized by elaborate staff functions and committee management, top management decision making seems narrowed to approving or disapproving the recommendations of others. Among others, John K. Galbraith infers this:

In the last case, however, there must always be questions as to how much the individual is deciding and how much is being decided for him by the group which has provided the relevant information; the danger of confusing ratification with decision must again be emphasized.[2]

Within our emerging technocracy, it seems likely that top management will become increasingly dependent upon marketing research (and other staff functions) to supply conclusions and recommendations. This forecasts an expanding role for marketing research as an analytical function in *addition* to its information function. This also indicates a trend of more approving/disapproving and less true decision making by top management.

SOME INHERENT PROBLEM AREAS

What are the apparent or potential causes of top management—marketing research conflict? Pinpointing these areas of conflict may suggest appropriate remedial action.

The following areas frequently present conflict between top management and marketing research:

- Research responsibility
- Research personnel
- Budget
- Assignments
- Problem definition
- Research reporting
- Use of research

Table 1 is an attempt to indicate the typical position of respective top management and marketing research staffs on these areas of conflict when they exist.

IMPROVING TOP MANAGEMENT DECISION MAKING

Improving top management decision making through marketing research calls for tightening the interrelationship of the two groups. Fig. 3 suggests some primary opportunities for this achievement.

---

[2] John Kenneth Galbraith, *The New Industrial State* (Boston: Houghton Mifflin Company, 1967), p. 83.

Suggestions for Top Management

1. Define Research Responsibilities. A strong marketing research department wants to know what is expected of it. Top management sometimes fails to make research responsibility and limitations explicit. There should be a written explanation of the research department's overall function, limitations, and priorities. The research director's role should be defined and others should not be permitted to play research director. Vertical and lateral working and reporting relationships should be specified.

2. Budget Realistically. The supply-demand gap on highly competent researchers has boosted their salaries and mobility considerably in the last several years. Management should be aware of increasing salary trends as well as the cost of outside services. Realistic budgets should be established and periodically reviewed. The marketing research director should be involved in budget setting.

3. Be Objective. Frequently managers allow their biases to interfere with an objective appraisal of research efforts. It is important that all levels of management be open-minded in dealing with researchers. New approaches should be solicited and judged fairly.

4. Periodically Review and Plan. The research department should be reviewed periodically and informed of top management's appraisal. All facets of the research organization, that is, budgets, priorities, personnel, goals, and policies should be reviewed with the objective of improving the marketing research function. Formal sessions should be held at least once a year and should result in an operational research department plan for the ensuing year.

5. Emphasize High Yield Projects. Management often forgets to consider past research and makes repetitious assignments. Fire-fighting assignments usually waste resources and affect morale. Each research request should be questioned as to its current benefit and cost. Alternative uses of resources on other research and other areas may be more advantageous. The focus should remain on the best way to increase profitability through marketing research. It is of vital importance to first determine the business problem and then the research problem.

6. Minimize Management Filters. The number of management layers through which research information must flow lengthens the time span between research completion and

Table 1. Probable Areas of Top Management-Marketing Research Conflict

Top Management Position	Area	Marketing Research Position
MR lacks sense of accountability. Sole MR function is as an information provider.	Research Responsibility	Responsibility should be explicitly defined and consistently followed. Desire decision-making involvement with TM.
Generally poor communicators. Lack enthusiasm, salesmanship, and imagination.	Research Personnel	TM is anti-intellectual. Researchers should be hired, judged and compensated on research capabilities.
Research costs too much. Since MR contribution difficult to measure, budget cuts are relatively defensible.	Budget	"You get what you pay for" defense. Needs to be continuing, long-range TM commitment.
Tend to be over-engineered. Not executed with proper sense of urgency. Exhibit ritualized, staid approach.	Assignments	Too many nonresearchable requests. Too many "fire-fighting" requests. Insufficient time and money allocated.
MR best equipped to do this. General direction sufficient . . . MR must appreciate and respond. Can't help changing circumstances.	Problem Definition	TM generally unsympathetic to this widespread problem. Not given all the relevant facts. Changed after research is under way.
Characterized as dull with too much researchese and qualifiers. Not decision-oriented. Too often, reported after the fact.	Research Reporting	TM treats superficially. Good research demands thorough reporting and documentation. Insufficient lead-time given.
Free to use as it pleases . . . MR shouldn't question. Changes in need and timing of research are sometimes unavoidable. MR deceived by not knowing all the facts	Use of Research	TM use to support a predetermined position represents misuse. Isn't used after requested and conducted . . . wasteful. Uses to confirm or excuse past actions.

top management appraisal and tends to distort the original findings. Where possible, management layers between top management and marketin research should not impede the timely flow of original research findings to top management.

Suggestions for Marketing Research

1. **Reflect Management Viewpoint.** Marketing researchers should make every effort to understand top management thinking, particularly on company short- and long-range goal and priorities. Research planning should establish priorities to emphasize efforts geared to company profit goals.

2. **Be Decision-oriented.** Researchers tend to lack a sense of urgency in reporting. When they do report, it seems too often dull, windy, researchese, and not decision-oriented. To avoid aggravating the decision-making process, researchers should push to understand the nature and context of the decision riding on the research assignments.

3. **Improve Methodology.** Much of the continuing acceptance of research can be traced to the research director. If he combines research skills with communications skills and stimulates innovation in research methodology, he and his research organization will become an integral part of the business machinery. The research organization should investigate recent developments in management and the social sciences. Researchers should

FIGURE 3. Two-way improvement flow.

combine objectivity with imagination in employing such areas as learning theory, input-output analysis decision trees, game theory, and cost-benefit analysis.

4. Be Imaginative. Unfortunately imagination in research seems to be in short supply. There is a tendency to repeat the familiar approach rather than seek the best approach. Meanwhile pressure builds for the shorter way, the cheaper way, and the better way. Plainly there is a need for more imagination in marketing research.

5. Seek Opportunities. It is important that the research department not only react to requests for research studies, but also cast about for research opportunities which may have high company profit potential. The research department should scan and internalize relevant trends in demographics, economics, dietetics, geriatrics, technology, fashion, consumerism, income, health, etc. In this role, the researcher can initiate new research studies.

6. Communicate Persuasively. If the value of marketing research to top management decision making is to improve, communications must improve first. The research response should be tailored precisely to the problem. The presentational format should be streamlined and geared to the audience with detail presented only as necessary. An execu-tive digest style which presents the issue, facts, reasoning, conclusion, and recommendations is suggested.

CONCLUDING OBSERVATIONS

Competitive pace, management science advances, high cost of poor decisions, overall business uncertainties, need to document decisions are but some of the concentric forces which pressure for an improved role for marketing research in top management decision making. These forces appear far more likely to intensify than abate. Maximum contribution of marketing research toward top management decision making requires some basic efforts by both groups . . . and toward each other. Top management needs explicitly to define research responsibility and limitations, communicate regularly, support organizationally, use objectively and focus on research programs with high profit potential. Concurrently, marketing research should dovetail its organization, personnel, techniques, emphasis, pace, style, and communications to top management's legitimate needs and opportunities. It should reflect top management's point-of-view. Otherwise, marketing research is likely to exist as an ineffective arm of the organization, under-realized and under-rewarded.

36. Techniques in Marketing Research

JOSEPH F. DASH and CONRAD BERENSON

Two key questions management should consider in managing marketing research are:

1. Is traditional marketing research losing its relevance for the new complex processes of management decision making?

2. Have the changes in marketing research skills kept pace with the way top management isolates, analyzes, and solves its problems?

One of the criteria that the executive responsible for marketing research can use in answering these questions is whether or not members of his research group are sufficiently trained and knowledgeable in the use of the traditional and the more advanced marketing research techniques.

The objective of this article is to focus on the pivotal research marketing methodologies with which professional researchers should be familiar, hopefully removing for the reader some of the obscureness from the market researchers' arcane lexicon.

Perhaps the following discussion will place top management in a better-informed position so that when these "in" terms are spoken during a marketing research project presentation, management will have a better understanding of their meaning and use.

We have divided the techniques into two groups—mature and modern. Each technique is first explained in simple language designed

◆ SOURCE: Reprinted by permission from *Harvard Business Review*, Vol. 47, No. 5, September-October 1969, pp. 14–16, 19, 21–22, 24, 26, 155.

to inform the nonstatistically oriented manager. Next, typical problems which can be solved by the method are mentioned, followed by a glimpse into the marketing applications often associated with the particular technique under discussion. For the more adventuresome, we have suggested sources of additional reading for greater depth of discussion and clarification of each term. Businessmen should also be reminded that a number of the methods to be covered have been discussed in detail in past HBR issues.

Toward the end of the article, a grid relating each marketing research technique and its applications to marketing problems is show (*Exhibit 1*, page 296). This has been prepared to facilitate cross-referencing. Although simplified it can also serve as a kind of summary of much of this article.

MATURE TECHNIQUES

These include regression and correlation analysis, discounted cash flow, incremental analysis, multiple regression and multiple correlation, random sampling, and sampling theory. Let us take a brief look at each technique in turn.

Regression and Correlation Analysis. These are statistical techniques that measure the degree to which variables are related. In regression analysis the researcher uses his knowledge of what is called an "independent variable" (e.g., advertising) to determine the *magnitude* of a "dependent variable" (e.g., sales), which changes in magnitude as management changes the independent variable. Correlation analysis differs somewhat from regression analysis in that, although the analytical methods used are quite similar to those of regression, what the analyst is interested in is the *degree of association* between variables.

Typical problems to which these methods apply involve analyses of the effects of changes in one element of the marketing mix on the performance of the mix as a whole. Marketing applications include advertising research, sales forecasting, pricing, packaging, product strategy, and product planning.[1]

Discounted Cash Flow (DCF). This technique introduces the concept of the "time value of money" (i.e., the notion that revenues or profits in hand today are worth more than revenues of the same amount in the future) into measurement of the profitability of proposed capital investments.

Typical problems involve the evaluation and comparison of alternative investment proposals where future income and costs, and their timing, can be estimated. Marketing applications include planning, product-line analysis, investment analysis, and distribution planning.[2]

Incremental Analysis. When this value analysis concept is employed, the added cost of an investment increment is compared with the additional gain resulting from that increment. The decision on whether to accept the proposed investment is based on the net contribution expected from the investment.

Typical problems involve determinations of how much to spend on projects whose financial components and benefits can be readily defined. Marketing applications include sales staffing strategy, pricing strategies, advertising expenditure decisions, product-line planning, and the selection of distribution channels.[3]

Multiple Regression/Multiple Correlation. These statistical techniques (classified by experts as "multivariate analysis") allow the researcher to describe and measure the *interrelationships among sets* of variables. Multiple regression attempts to describe the relationships between a dependent variable and *several* independent variables, and also to measure the effect of a change in the independent variable on the value of the dependent variable. Multiple correlation is used to screen variables for inclusion in regression equations.

Typical problems involve situations in which there are a number of independent, but interrelated, variables whose effects on the "dependent" variable cannot be studied discretely. Marketing applications include brand-share analysis, advertising effectiveness, consumer preferences, and sales forecasting.[4]

Keeping Informed

Random Sampling. Sometimes referred to as a probability sample, the random sample allows every element in the "population universe," as the field of study is called, an equal chance to get included in the sample.

Typical problems include cases where the populations can be easily identified and "labeled" so that a researcher can choose from among them, using a lottery system of random numbers. Marketing applications include brand-preference studies, sales forecasting, pricing studies, and advertising research.[5]

Sampling Theory. Using this statistical technique, an analyst predicts the characteristics of a large population universe on the basis of his findings about a small selection (the "sample") taken from that population.

Typical problems involve measurements of populations that are too large to examine economically and efficiently but contain well-defined members who are easy to sample. Marketing applications include sales fore-

[1] For further discussion, see John I. Griffin, *Statistics: Methods and Applications* (New York, Holt, Rinehart and Winston, 1962), pp. 222–258.
[2] For further discussion, see Curtis J. Blecke, *Financial Analyses for Decision Making* (Englewood Cliffs, New Jersey, Prentice-Hall, Inc., 1966), pp. 27–47.
[3] For further discussion, see Milton H. Spencer and Louis Siegelman, *Managerial Economics* (Homewood, Illinois, Richard D. Irwin, Inc., 1959), pp. 123–124.

[4] For further discussion, see Samuel B. Richmond, *Statistical Analysis,* 2nd Edition (New York, Ronald Press Co., 1964), pp. 446–464.
[5] For further discussion, see Clifford H. Springer et al., *Statistical Inference,* Vol. 3 of the Mathematics for Management Series (Homewood, Illinois, Richard D. Irwin, Inc., 1966), pp. 160–202.

Techniques	Advertising Research	Acquisition Screening	Brand Strategy	Customer Segmentation	Customer Service	Distribution Planning	Market Segmentation	Pricing Strategy	Product Life-Cycle Analysis	Product-Line Analysis	Product Planning	R&D Planning	ROI Analysis	Sales Forecasting	Test Marketing	Venture Planning
Mature Techniques																
Regression & correlation analysis	X													X		
Discounted cash flow (DCF)						X		X				X	X			X
Incremental analysis	X									X		X	X			
Multiple regression/ multiple correlation	X		X											X		
Random sampling																
Sampling theory	X		X											X	X	
Modern Techniques																
Bayesian approach	X							X	X		X		X			
Cost-benefit analysis	X												X			
Critical path method (CPM)								X		X	X	X			X	X
Decision trees	X	X								X						
Dynamic programming	X							X		X		X	X			X
Exponential smoothing														X		
Industrial dynamics						X		X								
Input-output analysis										X	X	X		X		X
Linear programming	X					X										
Markov processes			X	X												
Monte Carlo simulation		X	X			X				X						X
Nonlinear programming	X					X										
Numerical taxonomy	X		X	X			X									
PERT										X	X	X			X	X
Queueing models					X	X										
Risk analysis	X	X						X		X						
Sensitivity analysis	X	X						X		X						
Technological forecasting	X						X		X	X	X	X		X		X

EXHIBIT 1. Marketing techniques and applications.

casting, brand-switching probabilities, test-marketing analysis, and advertising effectiveness.[6]

MODERN TECHNIQUES

These include the Bayesian approach, cost-benefit analysis, the critical path method, decision trees, dynamic programming, exponential smoothing, industrial dynamics, input-output analysis, linear programming, Markov processes, Monte Carlo simulation, nonlinear programming, numerical taxonomy, PERT, queueing models, risk analysis, sensitivity analysis, and technological forecasting. Let us take a brief look at these individually.

Bayesian Approach. This decision-making statistical framework helps the manager perceive the economic cost of alternative actions. It is based on probability theory, which makes use of a decision maker's estimates of the likelihood that a given event will occur. The estimates can be modified as additional data are introduced.

Typical problems involve situations with varying degrees of risk and uncertainty which cannot be estimated easily by means of normal statistical sampling devices. Marketing applications include pricing strategy, product planning, new product introductions, product life-cycle analysis, and advertising planning.[7]

Cost-Benefit Analysis. This technique is used for comparing the profits, income, or other benefits of a proposed project with the costs of obtaining them. It is generally employed when there are limitations on the company's resources or abilities to take action.

Typical problems involve situations so complex that the ultimate decision might rest on judgment or intuition along with quantitative estimates of probable costs and benefits. Marketing applications include decisions on ad-

vertising programs, research strategies, and criteria for evaluating marketing services.[8]

Critical Path Method (CPM). This tool is similar in concept to PERT, but diverges in its application by focusing on the most efficient project completion plan in terms of time and money costs.

Typical problems, like those handled by PERT, involve projects having well-defined phases and well-defined relationships between these phases. Marketing applications include new product planning and introduction, venture team planning, and advertising and marketing research planning.[9]

Decision Trees. A simple mathematical/visual tool, the decision tree depicts business decision options and the consequences of particular decisions in terms of the probability of a given event occurring. The validity of decisions can be increased by analyzing each path with the procedures of risk analysis.

Typical problems involve cases where a rough initial screening of alternative actions is to be made so that the relative merit of each action can be determined. Marketing applications are similar to risk analysis applications—these include marketing and pricing strategies, acquisition analyses, product-line extensions and divestments, and advertising investment decisions.[10]

Dynamic Programming. A researcher can use this technique to determine an optimized return from a plan of sequential decisions over a known period of time. (The final return here is a function of the cumulative effect of all the prior decisions). For example, a plastics producer might use dynamic programming to determine in what sequence and

---

[6] For further discussion, see Paul E. Green and Donald S. Tull, *Reseach for Marketing Decisions* (Englewood Cliffs, New Jersey, Prentice-Hall, Inc., 1966), pp. 220–289.

[7] For further discussion, see Paul E. Green and Donald T. Tull, *Research for Marketing Decisions* (Englewood Cliffs, New Jersey, Prentice-Hall, Inc., 1966), pp. 55–87; see also Howard Raiffa, *Decision Analysis* (Boston, Addison-Wesley Publishing Company, Inc., 1968).

[8] For further discussion, see Ralph L. Day, "Optimizing Marketing Research Through Cost-Benefit Analyses," *Business Horizons*, Fall 1966, pp. 45–54.

[9] For further discussion, see *The Critical Path Method* (New York, American Telephone and Telegraph Company, Business Research Division, 1963); see also William R. King, *Quantitative Analyses for Marketing Management* (New York, McGraw-Hill Book Company, Inc., 1967), pp. 155–161.

[10] For further discussion, see Edward M. McCreary, "How to Grow a Decision Tree," *Think* magazine (published by the International Business Machines Corporation), March–April 1967, pp. 13–18.

in what amounts he should spend R&D, advertising, and commercial development funds on the introduction of a new product during a two-year period.

Typical problems include multi-stage projects with a number of variables of different degrees of risk and uncertainty. Marketing applications include product introduction strategies, advertising and market research planning, and R&D planning.[11]

Exponential Smoothing. This statistical forecasting technique allows one to give greater weight to current data than to older data.

Typical problems contain series of figures for variables (e.g., annual consumption of cigarettes) where *all* the cyclical trends have been removed. (For example, smoothing out the normal seasonal fluctuations in cigarette sales gives more weight to the current sales picture.) Marketing applications include sales and market forecasting.[12]

Industrial Dynamics. Using this simulation technique, an analyst attempts to study the effect of decisions in industry or other large complex systems (e.g., universities and governments), and of other variables, on the growth and stability of the system studied.

Typical problems include studies of systems that have a number of interrelated variables. Marketing applications include marketing policy and strategy analysis, advertising research, marketing research, pricing decisions, and distribution planning.[12a]

Input-Output Analysis. Using this technique, the researcher builds an econometric matrix model depicting how the output of each major industrial sector (e.g., steel) is distributed among industries buying the output (e.g., autos and appliances) and other sectors of the economy. The model also shows how much the industrial sector in question is buying from other parts of the economy.

Typical problems concern descriptive analyses of supply-demand relationships in a regional or national economy where the supply-and-demand relationships between industries are reasonably stable. Marketing applications include market and sales forecasting, market share analyses, and measurement of the impact of technological changes on supply-and-demand factors.[13]

Linear Programming. These techniques apply to such problems as the optimization of profits and the reduction of production costs. The problems usually involve a number of variables, and the solutions are subject to certain constraints.

Typical problems have an objective representable by a linear function, and the restrictions on attaining the objective are known and representable as linear functions. Marketing applications include media research, promotion planning, distribution analyses, and sales territory allocations.[14]

Markov Processes. These are statistical techniques based essentially on probability theory and decision making under risk. The processes deal with event sequences over time wherein the probability of each event occurring depends, at most, only on the outcome of the event immediately preceding it.

Typical problems contain a complex of interacting elements where the relationships among the problem elements lead to particular outcomes. Marketing applications include customer brand-shifting behavior, market-share analysis, and marketing planning.[15]

Monte Carlo Simulation. This technique can be used to determine the range and implications of possible business decisions. It employs unrestricted random sampling (i.e., selecting variables from a population so that each item has an equal chance of being selected) and mixes together on a computer a host of variables (e.g., investment, price, cost, and growth in sales volume). Uncertainty is taken into account by the assignment of probability estimates to a range of possible events.

Typical problems involve situations with

[11] For further discussion, see Robert S. Ledley, *Programming and Utilizing Digital Computers* (New York, McGraw-Hill Book Company, Inc., 1962), pp. 330–333.

[12] For further discussion, see Peter R. Winters, "Forecasting Sales by Exponentially Weighted Moving Averages," *Management Science*, April 1960, pp. 324–342.

[12a] For further discussion, see Jay W. Forrester, *Industrial Dynamics* (Cambridge, The Massachusetts Institute of Technology Press, 1961).

[13] For further discussion, see William H. Miernyk, *The Elements of Input-Output Analysis* (New York, Random House, 1966).

[14] For further discussion, see A. M. Glicksman, *Linear Programming and the Theory of Games* (New York, John Wiley & Sons, Inc., 1963).

[15] For further discussion, see Wroe Alderson and Paul E. Green, *Planning and Problem Solving in Marketing* (Homewood, Illinois, Richard D. Irwin, Inc., 1964), pp. 180–191.

elements of future uncertainty which can be described in a probabilistic manner. Marketing applications include distribution planning, acquisition analysis, product introduction analyses or simulation, and ROI determinations for new products.[16]

Nonlinear Programming. This approach is a variant of linear programming; in this case, however, the incremental value of each resource in a given application need not remain constant as more of the resource is used. For example, the additional contribution from an advertising campaign may not be the same as additional advertising dollars are used; the contribution may go up or down.

Typical problems are similar to those handled by linear programming (but the objective can be represented by a nonlinear function). Marketing applications are similar, again, to those of linear programming: media research, promotion planning, distribution analyses, and sales territory applications.[17]

Numerical Taxonomy. With this statistical technique (called "multivariate" because it can be used for problems containing several independent variables), data are analyzed and assigned to groups so that there will be considerable similarities *within* groups and considerable dissimilarity *among* groups.

Typical problems involve situations where there are no obvious criteria for grouping data into entities or subsets. Marketing applications include customer classification, brand-loyalty studies, market segmentation analysis, advertising research, and TV audience profiles.[18]

PERT: The Program Evaluation Review Technique is a method of planning, replanning, and evaluating progress so that program objectives will be accomplished on time. A major benefit of this technique is that it provides a diagramming method for depicting and controlling the entire program. It is similar to CPM in that it uses the same diagraming method; but, unlike CPM, it focuses on probable project completion through the use of probability theory.

Typical problems involve projects that have well-defined phases and well-defined relationships between these phases. Marketing applications include new product planning and introduction, venture team planning, and advertising and market research planning.[19]

Queueing Models. Often referred to as "waiting-line" models, these statistical techniques are used to analyze situations where the length of a waiting line (e.g., trucks arriving at a loading dock) depends on a parameter such as time.

A typical problem that could be handled by this method is that faced by a gasoline station which serves customers who arrive at random and need services requiring varying periods of time to perform. Marketing applications include distribution planning, customer service, and facilities planning.[20]

Risk Analysis. This technique employs Monte Carlo simulation, and it enables management to identify, measure, and analyze uncertainties in investment problems.

Typical problems contain random variables whose values vary depending on time (giving rise to the term "stochastic" in technical discussions) and which are too complex to allow exact calculations of results. Marketing applications include marketing and pricing strategies, acquisition analyses, product-line extensions and divestments, and advertising investment decisions.[21]

Sensitivity Analysis. This statistical technique highlights the impact of a change in one variable on the other economic variables of a project. For example, it can show the amount of shift in various measures of return when key inputs to an economic model (e.g., price, volume, and capital) are varied, one at a time.

---

[16] For further discussion, see Paul E. Green and Ronald E. Frank, *A Manager's Guide to Marketing Research* (New York, John Wiley & Sons, Inc., 1967), pp. 127–131.

[17] For further discussion, see C. William Emory and Powell Niland, *Making Management Decisions* (Boston, Houghton-Mifflin Co., 1968), pp. 240–249.

[18] For further discussion, see Ronald E. Frank and Paul E. Green, "Numerical Taxonomy in Marketing Analyses," in *Insights Into Consumer Behavior*, edited by J. Arndt (Boston, Allyn and Bacon, Inc., 1968), pp. 101–121.

[19] For further discussion, see *General Information Manual PERT . . . a dynamic project planning and control method* (White Plains, New York, IBM Technical Publications Department, 1965).

[20] For further discussion, see C. West Churchman et al., *Introduction to Operations Research* (New York, John Wiley & Sons, 1957), pp. 391–415.

[21] For further discussion, see David B. Hertz, "Risk Analysis in Capital Investment," HBR January–February 1964, pp. 95–106.

Typical problems involve determinations of the costs of changing certain inputs. Marketing applications, often used in conjunction with risk analysis, include predictions of inventory carrying costs, demand, and marketing costs.[22]

Technological Forecasting. With this technique, the researcher attempts to look at the future, estimating the technological conditions which are likely to exist and making reasonable evaluations of the significance of other future developments and the likelihood of their occurrence.

Typical problems involve pinpointing the rapidly advancing technological and socioeconomic changes of our times. Marketing applications include R&D planning, pricing decisions, product life-cycle evaluations, marketing planning, distribution and marketing program changes, and competitive changes.[23]

In *Exhibit 1* the techniques described earlier are listed down the left-hand side, while the possible applications are listed to the right. It is interesting to note how many applications have been found in some fields (e.g., advertising research and pricing strategy)—perhaps a tribute to the ingenuity of practitioners in those areas as well as a reflection of the subject matter.

Needless to say, we have had to limit the coverage of methods and applications described in this article. We might have considered more methods, and surely some companies have devised applications with which we are not familiar. Nevertheless, in a crude way this list reflects the state of the art today. Sometime in the future a businessman, thumbing through a back issue of HBR, may come on this list and make a mental note of how far we still had to go in 1969!

---

[22] For further discussion, see C. William Emory and Powell Niland, *Making Management Decisions* (Boston, Houghton Mifflin Co., 1968), p. 266.

[23] For further discussion, see *Technological Forecasting for Industry and Government—Methods and Applications,* edited by James R. Bright (Englewood Cliffs, New Jersey, Prentice-Hall, Inc., 1968).

M. New Products and Life Cycles

37. The Mounting Pressure for New Products

A. C. NIELSEN, JR.

Time was when new products were nearly always the direct result of a new invention or new process which suddenly enabled a manufacturer to offer a brand new item to the market. As a result, the introduction of a new product for even a large corporation was a reasonably rare occurrence and many small companies seldom, if ever, had anything new to put in the window.

Times have changed, as you know, and now consumer goods manufacturers have found that a large, fully-staffed research and development department is as essential to their operations as marketing, sales, accounting, and so forth.

As a result, new products are currently appearing with what might be considered almost monotonous regularity. In fact, our New Products Services, which make a business of recording new entries into the grocery and health and beauty aid field recorded the entry of 1154 new items in 1971 alone. If this sounds like an unbelievably high figure, you must keep in mind that overall sales of grocery, drug, and health and beauty aids, both new and old, reached approximately 106 billion dollars last year in grocery and drug outlets alone. To secure just a little larger piece of this enormous pie provides some of the pressure for new product adventures.

But here, I think it would be helpful to spend a moment defining a new product, at

least in terms of my discussion this morning. It is simply any new item, not previously offered by a manufacturer, regardless of what it is. For example, if Procter & Gamble, long time makers of Crest and Gleem toothpaste, bring out a new dentifrice called Bright and Shine, it will be considered by P & G, their agency, retailers, and consumers as a new product. Or, if Heinz brings out a new type of catsup, for example, with Chili Peppers, it will be considered, and in fact is, a new product.

You can see by these examples that a new product, in this sense, scarcely represents a new scientific discovery, but from the manufacturer's viewpoint it requires a new marketing, sales, and advertising program, etc., and will hopefully provide a new source of profit in the future. Obviously, some new products are "newer" than others, but it has become virtually impossible to make a distinction that will hold up in all cases.

I'm sure all of you have seen statements to the effect that 80% of all new products fail, or 9 out of 10, or some comparable figure. One can also read that 3 out of 4 succeed or 5 out of 6, or some such number. Obviously, there are many loose or careless statements made in this area. In addition, a part of the discrepancy in these figures would no doubt depend upon the stage in the product's development when one chose to call it a new product. Is it before, during, or after the conceptual or feasibility tests; or just after the products emerge from the labs? Or is it following a successful test marketing operation? Thus, it would appear to us at Nielsen that

◆ SOURCE: Reprinted by permission from The Nielsen *Researcher* (Published by A. C. Nielsen Company), Vol. 31, No. 1, 1973, pp. 4–18.

it is possible to come up with almost any success vs. failure reading you want, depending entirely upon when the reading is taken. In addition, the performance varies widely by company depending upon its size, experience, financial capacities and marketing skill.

Regardless of how one makes his measurement, the batting average of successes is pretty low, certainly in the fast-paced consumer goods market of today. Unfortunately, management can't avoid these risks because there is almost as much of a gamble in standing-pat with established brands, as there is in developing and introducing new brands. This is true because there will always be competitors breathing down the managers neck—on both his new and old products—hoping to capture all or part of his valuable consumer franchise.

This intensified new product development work has, I believe, shortened the life cycle of many established brands. We have found that there is a curve which can be plotted and which will describe the life cycle of most products. In general most of these curves take somewhat the shape shown in Chart 1.

The product is launched, growing steadily over time until it reaches a peak, then levels off, and sooner or later will begin a decline. This appears to be a fact of life. It is virtually impossible to predict for any given product the precise shape of this curve—or how long any phase will last. Sometimes the cycle moves quickly—sometimes at a more leisurely pace. When the share level declines below 80% of peak share achieved, we judge, from experience and study of many case his-

tories, that the primary growth cycle has been terminated.

While the brand still enjoys a sizable volume and earns good profits—experience has proven that unless some corrective action is taken—the share will continue to decline, in fits and starts perhaps, but eventually it will fall to a level where it is no longer a viable product. We refer to the efforts made by the manufacturer to restore an upward trend as "recycling." This usually involves a major change; an improvement in product, the advertising claims, the package, perhaps the introduction of a new flavor, type or form, or any combination of these factors. Because of the substantial lead time required, in most cases, to institute a major change, the brand's progress must be continuously monitored so that necessary planning and implementation of improved variations can be brought out as needed.

You men who are attempting to assess the future prospects of various companies will be interested in what we have learned concerning the factors which determine how long a product can be expected to contribute to a company's growth and profitability. Chart 2 shows the results of a recent study into the length of the primary growth cycle of 70 product categories.

It indicates that the average for health and beauty aid items was just under three years —or 34 months—23 months for household products, and an even two years for food items. The composite for all items was 28 months.

As you can see, this does not offer much time for a manufacturer to rest on his laurels.

What clues can be sought which will help

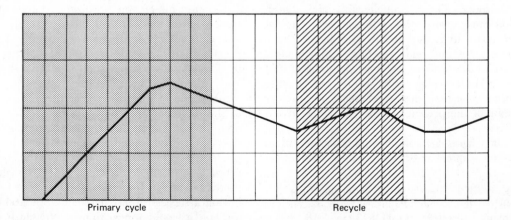

CHART 1. "Life cycle"—illustration.

CHART 2. Primary growth cycle for new brands entering market place between 1966 and 1968—70 product categories.

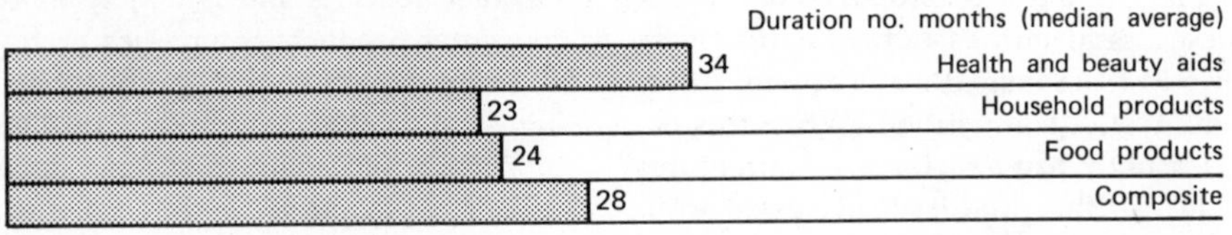

Duration no. months (median average)

34	Health and beauty aids
23	Household products
24	Food products
28	Composite

CHART 3. The higher the peak share of market achieved the longer the primary-growth cycle.

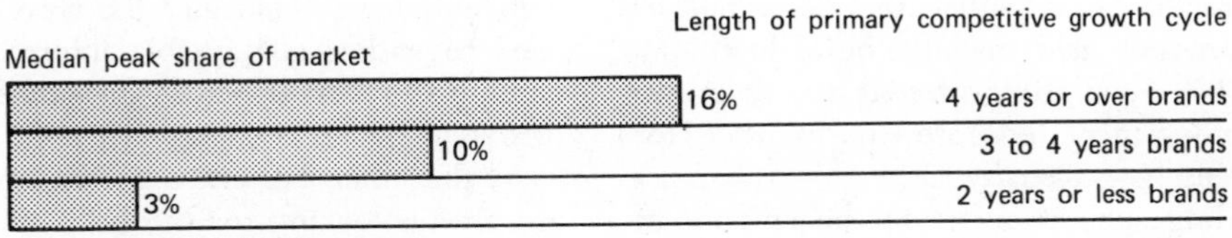

Length of primary competitive growth cycle

Median peak share of market

16%	4 years or over brands
10%	3 to 4 years brands
3%	2 years or less brands

Source: A. C. Nielsen Company

CHART 4. Primary competitive growth cycle

"reasons why" for duration.

Some primary considerations:
1. Product category characteristics
   A—Market size.
   B—Density of brand "population" in category.
   C—Relative new brand activity.

2. New brand characteristics
   A—Peak Share achieved—a "relative" to category characteristics.
   B—Spending support—relative to category "norms".
   C—Product qualities—"newness, uniqueness, convenience," etc.
   D—Other factors—segmentation, new brand entry rate price,
               exploitation of well-known line or "family"
               name, etc.

Source: A. C. Nielsen Company.

you predict whether a company's brand will enjoy a relatively long growth—or are apt to decline fairly rapidly?

One important factor is the share of market which the brand has achieved. Generally speaking, the higher the peak share of market achieved the longer the growth cycle (Chart 3). Those brands that continued to grow for four years or more, achieved a market share of 16% or more, those achieving a 10% share level had a growth cycle lasting from 3 to 4 years, and those that barely obtained a toehold, or 3%, had a correspondingly short period of growth.

Obviously, the safest investment would be in a company with products which have already carved out a sizable share in their particular market and where growth may be

expected to continue for a reasonably long period of time. As such, there would be less need to spend heavily on research and development, and the introduction of new products.

Chart 4 shows a number of primary considerations that affect life cycle duration. The size of the market or product category is of extreme importance. In the categories under examination in this study they vary from huge groups like pet food (well over a billion dollars), detergents and soft drinks on the large side, to categories such as acne remedies or eye make-up on the small side. Obviously, a market share of 10% in a large market will be worth more than 20% in a smaller group.

Point B, density of brand population in the category, and new brand activity are related and they must be judged in relation to the market's size. Product fields, like stocks in a given industry, are subject to fads. A certain category may attract a disproportionate number of new brand entries during a relatively short period of time and thus create an unusually high level of competition. When this occurs, it is usually prudent for a manufacturer to steer clear of this product field as one additional entry will usually depress earnings for all concerned, including himself.

Points A & B, under Number 2, refer to what can be expected in a given field.

A peak share in either the detergent or cereal product field may be quite low—say under 10%—and still represent a very profitable achievement because the market for these items is unusually large.

Spending support refers to the amount of promotional and advertising support ordinarily necessary to enter a given field. Some products require a substantial investment in advertising and promotional activities in order to secure retailer and consumer attention. Often times it is as difficult to persuade the retailer to handle an additional brand as it is to persuade the consumer to buy it.

C and D refer to other product qualities such as uniqueness, price, and the possibility of using the name of a previously established brand as a foundation.

Selecting the right field to enter is extremely important to the success of any new product effort. Helping companies find prom-

ising new product fields and then evaluating the chances for success, based on criteria such as these, is the primary function of our New Product Services and is widely used by many consumer products companies.

There is, after all, a proper way of studying and developing new product opportunities. Some companies have developed excellent procedures and consequently their batting average is quite good. I would characterize these companies as those taking a true research approach—in effect saying to themselves that they really know very little about a potential new field and therefore they proceed to gather all possible information concerning the market before they take even the first step.

At the other extreme are companies which are always looking for the brilliant new idea which is to make their fortune. They lack the patience to methodically persevere in the study and testing of new ideas. They fear some competitor will "steal" their hot new idea and will beat them with it to the market. So they plunge forward and the results are often erratic—if not disastrous—an occasional success surrounded by more failures.

Having been privileged to observe a great many companies attempting to find the proper approach to the development and marketing of new products, we have reproduced a composite of the procedures used in abbreviated form. In general, companies achieving the highest success ratio in the area of new prod-

CHART 5. Evaluation of product categories.

- Market size and trends
- Market vulnerability
- Market investment requirements and profitability potential
- Category compatibility with company
  - Corporate strategy
  - Production facilities
  - Distribution systems

CHART 6. Initial consumer research.

Determination of product category vulnerability in relation to consumer demands

- Consumer attitudes toward product category
- Consumer attitudes toward current brands
- Images of current brands
- Degree of satisfaction
- Improvements necessary or desired
- Areas of need for new products

ucts all appear to follow these steps in one form or the other.

You may be interested in knowing that many of our services have been designed to help manufacturers through some of these critical stages.

Once a company has made the decision to expand into new product fields, the all important question arises—what field or fields.

Thus begins the task of evaluating product categories for their size, trends, vulnerability, etc. (Chart 5). You will note how closely these points are linked to the primary considerations on the previous chart explaining why some products enjoyed a longer growth cycle than others.

Following the examination of the past and current trends of one or several product groups, most companies go directly to consumers to determine the prospects for a new brand (Chart 6). In short, how satisfied are consumers with products currently being offered and how might they possibly be improved.

If the reaction by consumers is "positive," in that there is noticeable dissatisfaction with the current brands and a general concensus that improvements can be made, for example, in either brand utility, packaging, or type, etc., further study is warranted—usually by a new product's task force.

At this point the original evaluation and consumer studies are further analyzed to seek out the possibilities for market segmentation, current brand shares, brand satisfaction and loyalty (Chart 7). This is followed by an exhaustive study of the market's characteristics based on the six basic points shown here.

Competitive sales trends are reviewed and the study is broadened to include competitive advertising, distribution, retail support and production, as well as measure forces against whom their salesmen will be competing.

From there, product concepts will be examined in terms of alternatives to fulfill the opportunities that have been uncovered (Chart 8). For example, under "quality," they will explore product appearance and performance; under "packaging" they will see what can be done relative to design, size, types and labeling; under "value," an evalaution of price vs. quality, price vs. packaging, and price vs. advertising. And, of course, these are related directly to the competitive brands currently on the market.

Again, presuming positive judgments have been made, concept tests will be ordered (Chart 9). These tests are designed to determine the strongest demand concepts originally voiced by consumers relative to what they desire in terms of a product of this type, and their dissatisfaction with the brands currently being offered. Alternatives are tested and competitive difference analyzed in relation to product quality, package and price. Following the concept tests, the investigation turns inward to an evaluation of production feasibility (Chart 10). Here technological know-how, capacity, and availability of material are judged in relation to estimated production requirements.

The same is done for financial feasibility where determinations are made relative to the funds required for the new product in rela-

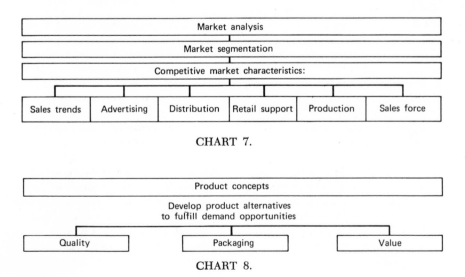

CHART 7.

CHART 8.

CHART 9. Concept tests.

Determination of strongest demand concept

- Evaulation of product alternatives
- Analysis of competitive differences
- Determination of competitive advantages
    - Product quality
    - Package
    - Price

CHART 10. Production feasibility.

Production requirements relative to

- Technological know-how
- Capacity
- Availability of materials
- Production growth capacity
- Etc.

CHART 11. Financial feasibility.

Investment requirements in relation to
corporate financial commitments

Funds required for

- Investing in new product
- Maintaining current franchise growth
- Expanding current franchise growth
- Other new product programs

tion to the corporations overall financial commitments (Chart 11).

From here, assuming again that only green lights are flashing, a complete marketing plan is devised. This will be an enlarged version of the market analysis chart but will cover a detailed plan for advertising, including creative objectives, media to be used and the costs involved, distribution, sales promotion, merchandising, brand name, pricing and the 101 other details that go into a market plan.

Once the market plan has been completed, and production geared to provide the product in sufficient quantities for test marketing needs, Nielsen again comes into the picture.

There's little question that all of the steps taken prior to this point, including the original market analysis, testing, and planning are necessary and important, but if there is one step more important than any other, it is the test marketing stage. Here the product is unveiled for the first time and allowed to sink or swim on the merits of its basic quality and the advertising and promotions used to support it.

In fact, Leo Burnett, one of the greatest advertising geniuses of our time, once stated that:

I have learned that the public does not know what it wants and there is no sure way of finding out until the idea is exposed under normal conditions of sale.

And the point here is, that if the product fails in test markets, it is possible to pull back without suffering the cataclysmic losses that are inevitable if the product fails on a much larger national scale.

In fact, when you men are assessing the future prospects for a particular company, you might consider how they conduct their new product operations. As we have noted, there has been a very high rate of failure associated with new product activity.

However, these results can be improved and in fact are quite satisfactory when proper procedures are faithfully adhered to. In Chart 12 we see that when a company follows the path of careful test marketing, the possibility of excessive losses is greatly reduced—and corporate assets are conserved.* Tests conducted in a small number of cities at low cost have predicted final results achieved on a national scale within a very close tolerance in a high percent of cases.

For example, 50 new brand introductions were followed and the first year's national share was compared with shares achieved in test markets. All tests ran for at least 10 months or more.

Note that 29% of the new brands' national shares fell within ±5% of the test market share, and another 21% were within ±10%. Thus, the odds are about 50-50 that the national performance will match test results within ±10%. But note further that another 31% were in the ±11-20% range which, on a cumulative basis, includes 81% of the brands tested. As such, the odds are 4 to 1 that national performance will match test results within a range of ±20%.

Another way of putting it is, that a brand that has achieved a 5% share level in a Nielsen test market has a 4 to 1 chance of achieving a national share ranging from 4% to 6%.

In your evaluation of a new product's chances for success you may wish to find out how long that product was kept in test markets before the final "go" decision was made.

The odds of predicting final test results

* The complete results of the study upon which Charts 12 and 13 are based originally appeared in Reseacher No. 4, 1972.

(and future national share), improve the longer the test is run. In general the item must be tested long enough for customers to try it several times, also to have an opportunity to make up their minds as to whether or not they will continue to use it in the future.

Chart 13 presents the results of nearly 100 tests made in an effort to determine how long tests should be run. They suggest that a certain degree of patience — at least 8 months of it — should be exercised prior to making a final decision.

The odds for forecasting final test results are as follows

After 2 months — 1 out of 7
After 4 months — 1 out of 3
After 6 months — 1 out of 2
After 8 months — 3 out of 4
After 10 months — 5 out of 6

Again, the amount of perseverance required is directly related to the degree of assurance necessary. But it would appear that a judgment made before 8 months had passed would be difficult to defend if there were major sums of money to be risked.

And in the new product's game, major sums are generally what we are talking about. Although it is difficult to provide a meaningful average of new product costs since they vary so widely, advertising and promotion alone will cost at least 2 million dollars to make even a minor splash nationally. In addi-

CHART 12. National share vs. test performance (50 new products).

Ratio national to test share within	Range	Cumulative
±5%	29%	29%
±6—10%	21	50
±11—20%	31	81
±21—30	13	94
±31 & over	6	100

Source: A.C. Nielsen Company.

CHART 13. Odds for forecasting test results.

After 2 months	1 out of 7
After 4 months	1 out of 3
After 6 months	1 out of 2
After 8 months	3 out of 4
After 10 months	5 out of 6

Source: A. C. Nielsen Company.

tion, there is usually an added cost for production facilities which can also run into millions of dollars.

Another important reason for test marketing is that nothing succeeds like success. When a manufacturer's sales representative asks buyers to give him an initial order for a new product—many buyers will inevitably remember what happened to the previous new product offering of the same company. If results were good, the salesman will in all probability secure an order, thereby gaining the distribution which is so essential. On the other hand, if this salesman's previous new item was a failure, the retailer or wholesaler will hesitate to buy and the number of stores stocking the new brand will be fewer—which will of itself, inhibit chances for success.

This conclusion is borne out by a study which we conducted among chain grocery buyers. We asked them to name the most important reasons for rejecting a new product. The results, as noted in Chart 14, indicated that if a salesman could not state that a

product had already been tested and accepted in test markets, there was a strong chance that the buyer would refuse to buy it.

At this point, you may again wonder why manufacturers should even think of introducing new products since the risks and the costs — in both manpower and money — are so great.

In fact, as noted in Chart 15, the success rate for new products introduced appears to have actually declined slightly.* The study in 1962 showed 54% of new products measured by us succeed whereas in 1971 the figure was 47%. Note that there were nearly twice as many new products measured in 1971 than in 1962.

The success rate, however, varied somewhat by type of product (Chart 16). About 6 out of 10 household type items succeeded—

---

* The complete study upon which Charts 15 through 18 are based originally appeared in Researcher No. 5, 1971.

CHART 14. Weak points of rejected items.

1. No evidence of item salability
2. Inadequate allowance provisions
3. Insufficient promotional back-up
4. Lack of item newness or uniqueness

Source: A. C. Nielsen Company.

CHART 15. Success rate for new products.

	54%	(103 items) 1962
	47%	(204 items) 1971

Source: A.C. Nielsen Company.

CHART 16. Success rate by general product type.

	42.4%	(106 items) HBA
	58.3%	(24 items) household
	48.6%	(74 items) grocery

Source: A.C. Nielsen Company.

CHART 17. Average sales per new brand (12 month dollar sales).

	$14,985,785	All brands
	11,451,152	HBA
	28,584,608	Household
	11,337,867	Grocery

Source: A.C. Nielsen Company

versus 4 in 10 health and beauty aids and 5 in 10 grocery items.

Further, and here is where the carrot becomes readily visible, those that did succeed obtained significant amounts of revenue and presumably profits for their company (Chart 17). Here you see the average sales achieved during the first 12 months of national sales. Sales in succeeding years were even greater as a larger percentage of stores will grant distribution to a new item once they find out that it is in demand.

Chart 18 provides a comparison between the annual sales achieved by the successful new brands in 1962 and the most recent group of product successes — the pattern is pretty much the same. Although the proportion of successful products reporting sales of $5 million and under remained essentially constant, the percent of new items in the $5 to $10 million category showed a slight decline. This was more than offset, however, by the current number of new brands that achieved sales of $15 million and over. In fact, more than half of this group reached sales of $25 million and over.

In summary I believe we can conclude that the first reason why companies are so

CHART 18. Distribution of dollar sales per volume 1962 vs. 1971.

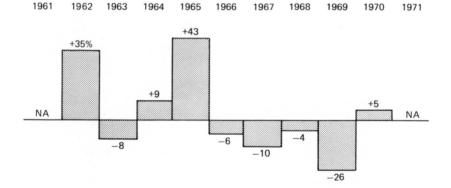

Source: A.C. Nielsen Company.

CHART 19. New brand introductions vs. Dow-Jones Industrials year-ago changes.

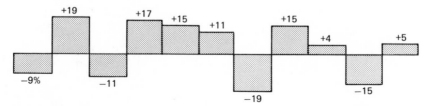

Source: A.C. Nielsen Company and D.J. averages.

deeply involved in new product development is for protection or, to state it more bluntly, for survival, since the growth cycle of many products is but a few short years.

The second reason is that the financial rewards can be very great when a new product succeeds in capturing a reasonable share of what have become very large markets.

I have tried to describe the procedures used by many well managed companies in their efforts to find and evaluate the most promising new product areas. I hope that some of our findings will be helpful to you in your own assessments of the new product activities of the companies you are responsible for investigating.

Since you are so intimately involved with the Dow Jones' averages, I thought that you would find my last chart of particular interest (Chart 19).

Here you see how the number of new product introductions has risen and fallen in comparison with the Dow Jones average over the past 10 years. The correlation, although far from perfect, is reasonably close. In brief, it suggests that confidence in the economic climate plays a large part in new product introductions.

With the Dow running well above 1,000, and corporate earnings moving up, we foresee a great many new product introductions. Consequently, I believe you will be very busy in 1973 assessing their impact on the fortunes of the companies you follow.

38. The Product Life Cycle: A Key to Strategic Marketing Planning

JOHN E. SMALLWOOD

Modern marketing management today increasingly is being supported by marketing information services of growing sophistication and improving accuracy. Yet the task remains for the marketing manager to translate information into insights, insights into ideas, ideas into plans, and plans into reality and satisfactory programs and profits. Among marketing managers there is a growing realization of the need for concepts, perspectives, and for constructs that are useful in translating information into profits. While information flow can be mechanized and the screening of ideas routinized, no alternative to managerial creativity has yet been found to generate valuable marketing ideas upon which whole marketing programs can be based. The concept of the products life cycle has been extremely useful in focusing this creative process.

The product life cycle concept in many ways may be considered to be the marketing equivalent of the periodic table of the elements concept in the physical sciences; like the periodic table, it provides a framework for grouping products into families for easier predictions of reactions to various stimuli. With chemicals—it is a question of oxidation temperature and melting; with products—it is marketing channel acceptance and advertising budgets. Just as like chemicals react in

♦ SOURCE: John E. Smallwood, "The Product Life Cycle: A Key to Strategic Marketing Planning," pp. 29–35, *MSU Business Topics*, Winter 1973. Reprinted by permission of the publisher, Division of Research, Graduate School of Business Administration, Michigan State University.

similar ways, so do like products. The product life cycle helps to group these products into homogeneous families.

The product life cycle can be the key to successful and profitable product management, from the introduction of new products to profitable disposal of obsolescent products. The fundamental concept of the product life cycle (PLC) is illustrated in Fig. 1.

In application, the vertical scale often is measured in saturation of the product (percentage of customer units using), while the horizontal scale is calibrated to represent the passage of time. Months or years are usually the units of time used in calibration, although theoretically, an application along the same concept of much shorter or longer durations (milliseconds in physical sciences, millenia in archaeology) might be found. In Figure 1 the breakdown in the time scale is shown by stages in the maturity of product life. The saturation scale, however, is a guide only and must be used accordingly. When comparing one product with another, it is sometimes best treated by use of qualitative terms, not quantitative units. It is important to the user of the product life cycle concept that this limitation be recognized and conceptual provisions be made to handle it. For example, if the basic marketing unit chosen is "occupied U.S. households," one cannot expect a product such as room air conditioners to attain 100 percent saturation. This is because many households already have been fitted with central air conditioning; thus, the potential saturation attainment falls well short of 100 percent of the marketing measurement chosen.

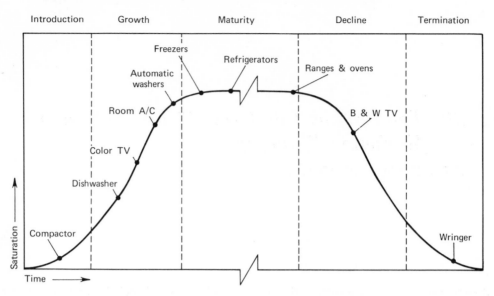

FIGURE 1 Life cycle stages of various products.

To overcome this difficulty, marketing managers have two basic options. They can choose a more restrictive, specific marketing unit such as "all occupied U.S. households that do not have forced air heating"; homes without forced air heating are unlikely candidates for central air conditioning. It can be anticipated that room air conditioners will saturate not only *that* market, but portions of other markets as well. On the other hand, on the basis of informed judgment, management can determine the *potential* saturation of total households and convert the PLC growth scale to a measurement representing the degree of attainment of potential saturation in U.S. households. The author has found the latter approach to be the more useful one. By this device, automatic washers are considered to be at 100 percent saturation when they are at their full potential of an arbitrarily chosen 80 percent.

Consider Fig. 1, where various products are shown positioned by life cycle stages: the potential saturations permit the grouping of products into like stages of life cycle, even when their actual saturation attainments are dissimilar. One can note that in Figure 1 automatic washers (which are estmated at 58 percent saturation) and room air conditioners (30 percent) are positioned in the same growth stage in Fig. 1; freezers (29 percent) and refrigerators (99 percent), on the other hand, are in the maturity stage. This occurs because, *in our judgment*, freezers have a po-

tential of only about one-third of "occupied households" and thus have attained almost 90 percent of that market. Automatic clothes washers, however, have a potential of about four-fifths of the occupied households and at about 70 percent of their potential still show some of the characteristics of the growth stage of the PLC. General characteristics of the products and their markets are summarized in Fig. 2.

The product life cycle concept is illustrated as a convenient scheme of product classification. The PLC permits management to assign given products to the appropriate stages of acceptance by a given market: *introduction, growth, maturity, decline,* and *termination*. The actual classification of products by appropriate stages, however, is more art than science. The whole process is quite imprecise; but unsatisfactory as this may be, a useful classification can be achieved with management benefits that are clearly of value. This can be illustrated by examining the contribution of the PLC concept in the following marketing activities: sales forecasting, advertising, pricing, and marketing planning.

APPLICATION OF THE PLC TO SALES FORECASTING

One of the most dramatic uses of the PLC in sales forecasting was its application in explaining the violent decline in sales of color TV during the credit crunch recession of

	Introduction	Growth	Maturity	Decline	Termination

Marketing

	Introduction	Growth	Maturity	Decline	Termination
Customers	Innovative/ high income	High income/ mass market	Mass market	Laggards/ special	Few
Channels	Few	Many	Many	Few	Few
Approach	Product	Label	Label	Specialized	Availability
Advertising	Awareness	Label superiority	Lowest price	Psychographic	Sparse
Competitors	Few	Many	Many	Few	Few

Pricing

	Introduction	Growth	Maturity	Decline	Termination
Price	High	Lower	Lowest	Rising	High
Gross margins	High	Lower	Lowest	Low	Rising
Cost reductions	Few	Many	Slower	None	None
Incentives	Channel	Channel/ consumer	Consumer/ channel	Channel	Channel

Product

	Introduction	Growth	Maturity	Decline	Termination
Configuration	Basic	Second generation	Segmented/ sophisticated	Basic	Stripped
Quality	Poor	Good	Superior	Spotty	Minimal
Capacity	Over	Under	Optimum	Over	Over

FIGURE 2. Product life cycle.

1969-70. This occurred after the experience of the 1966-67 mini-recession which had almost no effect on color TV sales that could be discerned through the usual "noise" of the available product flow data. A similar apparent insensitivity was demonstrated in 1958, in 1961, and again in 1966-67, with sales of portable dishwashers. However, it too was followed by a noticeable sales reduction in the 1969-71 period, with annual factory shipments as shown in Figure 3.

In early 1972 sales of both portable dishwashers and color TV sets showed a positive response to an improving economic climate, raising the question as to why both products had become vulnerable to economic contractions after having shown a great degree of independence of the business cycle during previous years. The answer to the question seems to lie in their stage in the product life cycle. In comparing the saturation of color TV and dishwashers, as shown in Fig. 3, consider first the case of color TV sales.

We can ascertain that as late as 1966, saturation of color TV was approximately 8 percent. By late in 1969, however, saturation had swiftly increased to nearly 40 percent.

The same observation is true in the case of dishwashers—considered a mass market appliance only since 1965. This is the key to the explanation of both situations. At the early, introductory stages of their life cycles, both appliances were making large sales gains as the result of being adopted by consumers with high incomes. Later, when sales growth depended more upon adoption by the less affluent members of the mass market whose spending plans are modified by general economic conditions, the product sales began to correlate markedly to general economic circumstances.

It appears that big ticket consumer durables such as television sets and portable dishwashers tend to saturate as a function of customer income. This fact is illustrated by

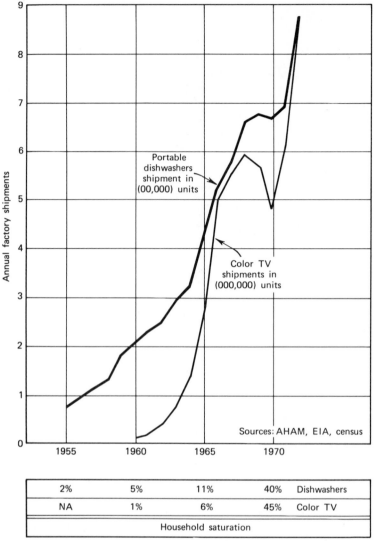

FIGURE 3. Effect of recession on product sales.

the data displayed in Fig. 4, concerning refrigerators and compactors, where one can note the logical relationship between the two products as to the economic status of their most important customers and as to their position in the product life cycle. The refrigerator is a mature product while the compactor is the newest product in the major appliance family.

The refrigerator once was in the introduction stage and had marketing attributes similar to the compactor. The refrigerator's present marketing characteristics are a good guide to proper expectations for the compactor as it matures from the *introductory* stage through *growth* to *maturity*. One can anticipate that

the compactor, the microwave oven, and even nondurables such as good quality wines, will someday be included in the middle income consumption patterns, and we will find their sales to be much more coincident with general economic cycles.

PRODUCT LIFE STAGES AND ADVERTISING

The concept of a new product filtering through income classes, combined with long-respected precepts of advertising, can result in new perspectives for marketing managers. The resulting observations are both strategic and tactical. New advertising objectives and

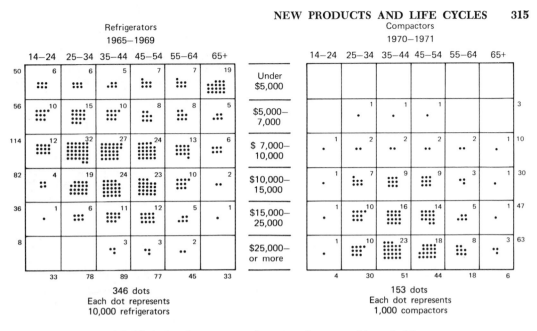

FIGURE 4. Purchase patterns by age and income of households.

new insights for copy points and media selection may be realized. Consider the advertising tasks by the following phases:

Phase 1

Introduction. The first objective is to make the best customer prospects aware that the new product or service is now available; to tell him what it does, what are the benefits, why claims are to be believed, and what will be the conditions of consumption.

Phase 2

Growth. The next objective is to saturate the mass market with the same selling points as used in Phase 1. In addition, it is to recognize that a particular brand of the product is clearly superior to other "inferior" substitutes while, at the same time, to provide a rationalization that this purchase is not merely a wasteful, luxury indulging activity but that it will make the consumer a better *something*, a better husband, mother, accountant, driver, and so forth.

Phase 3

Maturity. A new rationalization, respecability, is added, besides an intensification of brand superiority ("don't buy substitutes; get the real *XYZ* original, which incidentally, is *new* and *improved* . . ."). To a great extent, the *product* registration is dropped. Respectability is a strong requisite of the American lower class, which in this phase is the economic stratum containing the most important opportunities for sales gains. Companies do not abandon higher income customers, but they now match advertising to a variety of market segments instead of concentrating on only one theme for the market. Several distinct advertising programs are used. All elements of the marketing mix—product, price, sales promotion, advertising, trading and physical distribution channels—are focused on specific market segments.

Phase 4

Decline. Superior substitutes for a product generally will be adopted first by the people who before were the first to adopt the product in consideration. These people usually are from the upper economic and social classes. Advertising themes reflect this situation when they concentrate on special market segments such as West Coast families or "consumption societies" such as beer drinkers or apartment dwellers.

PRODUCT LIFE STAGES AND PRICING

As a product progresses through all five stages of the life cycle shown in Figure 1, the price elasticity can be expected to undergo dramatic changes. Generally speaking, price elasticity of a relatively simple product will be low at first. Thus, when customers are drawn from the higher income classes, demand is relatively inelastic. Later, when most customers are in the lower income categories, greater price elasticity will exist.

Of course, increased price elasticity will not automatically lower prices during the growth stage of the PLC. It is in this growth stage, however, that per unit costs *are* most dramatically reduced because of the effect of the learning curve in engineering, production, and marketing. Rising volume and, more important, the *forecasts* of higher volumes, justify increased capital investments and higher fixed costs, which when spread over a larger number of units, thereby reduce unit costs markedly. New competitors with great rapidity in this stage as profits tend to increase dramatically.

Pricing in the mature phase of the PLC usually is found to be unsatisfactory, with no one's profit margins as satisfactory as before. Price competition is keener within the distribution channel in spite of the fact that relatively small price differences seldom translate into any change in aggregate consumer activity.

PRODUCT PLANNING AND THE PLC

Curiously enough, the very configuration of the product takes on a classical pattern of evolution as it advances through the PLC. At first, the new device is designed for function alone; the initial design is sometimes crude by standards that will be applied in the future. As the product maturation process continues, performance sophistication increases. Eventually the product develops to the point where competitors are hardpressed to make meaningful differences which are perceptible to consumers.

As the product progresses through the product life cycle these modifications tend to describe a pattern of metamorphosis from "the ugly box" to a number of options. The adjustment cycle includes:

Part of house: the built-in look and function. Light fixtures, cooking stoves, wall safes, and furnaces are examples.

Furniture: a blending of the product into the home decor. This includes television, hi-fi consoles, radios, clocks, musical instruments, game tables, and so forth.

Portability: a provision for increased *presence* of the product through provisions for easier movement (rollers or compactness), or multiple unit ownership (wall clocks, radios, even refrigerators), or miniaturization for portability. Portability and *personalizations*, such as the pocket knife and the wristwatch, can occur.

System: a combination of components into one unit with compatible uses and/or common parts for increased convenience, lower cost, or less space. Home entertainment centers including television, radio, hi-fi, refrigerator-freezers, combination clothes washer-dryers, clock radios, pocket knife-can-and-bottle openers are illustrative.

Similar changes can also be observed in the distribution channel. Products often progress from specialty outlets in the introductory stage to mass distribution outlets such as discount houses and contract buyers during the "maturity" and "decline" phases of the PLC. Interestingly enough, the process eventually is reversed. Buggy whips can still be found in some specialty stores and premium prices are paid for replicas of very old products.

CONCLUSION

The product life cycle is a useful concept. It is the equivalent of the periodic table of the elements in the physical sciences. The maturation of production technology and product configuration along with marketing programs proceeds in an orderly, somewhat predictable, course over time with the merchandising nature and marketing environment noticeably similar between products that are in the same stage of their life cycle. Its use as a concept in forecasting, pricing, advertising, product planning, and other aspects of marketing management can make it a valuable concept, although considerable amounts of judgment must be used in its application.

39. The New Product Diffusion Process

THOMAS S. ROBERTSON

THE NEW PRODUCT DIFFUSION PROCESS

Product innovation will be critical to survival and essential to growth for American firms in the decade of the 1970s. The pace of technological advances coupled with the American consumer's receptivity to progress and "newness" will shorten the life cycles of established products and place a premium on new products, although product obsolescence rates will continue to vary among industries and among product groups. In general, the less the commodity nature of the product group, or alternatively, the more the opportunity for product differentiation, then the more rapid is innovation and, concurrently, obsolescence.

WHAT IS A NEW PRODUCT?

The concern of this paper is with consumer acceptance of product innovations (new products). A major difficulty is in defining what is a new product and at least four definitional criteria have frequently been used: (1) newness from existing products, (2) newness in time, (3) newness in terms of sales penetration level, and (4) consumer newness to the product.

1. *Newness from existing products.* Many authors argue that a "new product" must be

very *different* from established products, although there is little attempt to make such a definition operational. The Federal Trade Commission has rendered an advisory opinion that a product may properly be called "new" "only when [it] is either entirely new or has been changed in a functionally significant and substantial respect. A product may not be called 'new' when only the package has been altered or some other change made which is functionally insignificant or insubstantial." [1]

E. B. Weiss claims that over 80% of new products are not, in fact, "new" but "simply modifications" of existing products.[2] He does not, however, establish guidelines for distinguishing such modifications from new products. It is possible to extend this point of view to the thesis that all new products are modifications or recombinations of existing items. Barnett, an anthropologist who has studied innovation and its effects on cultural change, states that "No innovation springs full-blown out of nothing; it must have antecedents . . ."[3] This viewpoint, which is quite prevalent in sociological thinking, looks at innovation as

♦ SOURCE: Reprinted by permission from *Marketing in a Changing World*, edited by Bernard A. Morin, Proceedings of the June Conference, 1969, Series No. 29, pp. 80–86.

[1] Federal Trade Commission, "Permissible Period of Time During which New Product May Be Described as 'New'," *Advisory Opinion Digest*, No. 120, April 15, 1967.

[2] E. B. Weiss, "That Malarky about 80% of New Products Failing," *Advertising Age*, Vol. 36, August 2, 1965, p. 101.

[3] Homer G. Barnett, *Innovation: The Basis of Cultural Change*, New York, McGraw-Hill, 1953, p. 181.

the outcome of an evolutionary sequence. Even an innovation such as the computer can be considered to be a recombination of existing elements coupled with a measure of technological insight.

2. *Newness in time.* Length of time on the market is a second criterion in defining a new product. There has been a pronounced tendency for firms to promote a product as new for as long as two or three years after introduction, under the assumption that the word "new" in advertising or on the package is a positive and desirable sales appeal. The Federal Trade Commission advisory opinion arbitrarily limits the use of the word new to six months after the product enters regular distribution after test marketing.[4]

3. *Newness in terms of sales penetration level.* Another new product definition criterion is the sales level which the product has achieved. Bell[5] and Robertson,[6] for example, have arbitrarily defined products as innovations when they have not yet secured 10% of their total potential market.

4. *Consumer newness to the product.* Yet another criterion for defining a new product is that the consumer must *perceive* it to be new. There is, however, invariably some consumer who is "new" to the product and it is not particularly useful to talk in terms of any individual consumer; the aggregate consumer is generally what the marketer has in mind. Perhaps a product could be defined as new when a majority of consumers perceive it in such a way, but this is again arbitrary.

These definitions, unfortunately, need not yield the same determinations as to what products are new. For example, using the consumer perception of newness definition, an item can be new without being substantially different in fuction from existing products, without being particulary new to the market, and while possessing a significant sales penetration level. There is a further difficulty in the discussion to this point, and that is that a simple dichotomy is being used — a product is either new or not new. More

logically, a range of "newness" would be the case.

NEWNESS IN TERMS OF CONSUMPTION EFFECTS

The critical factor in defining a new product should be its effects upon established patterns of consumption. It is convenient to think in terms of: (1) continuous innovations, (2) dynamically continuous innovations, and (3) discontinuous innovations.

1. A *continuous* innovation has the least disrupting influence on established consumption patterns. Alteration of a product is almost always involved rather than the creation of a new product. Examples include: fluoride toothpaste, menthol cigarettes, and annual new-model automobile changeovers.

2. A *dynamically* continuous innovation has more disrupting effects than a continuous innovation, although it still does not generally involve new consumption patterns. It may mean the creation of a new product or the alteration of an existing product. Examples include: electric toothbrushes, electric hair curlers, and the Mustang automobile.

3. A *discontinuous* innovation involves the establishment of new consumption patterns and the creation of previously unknown products. Examples include: television, the computer, and the automobile.

This definitional framework, while recognizing that innovations are not all of same order of newness, does not, unfortunately, distinguish new products from non-new products. It is my opinion that this decision is always arbitrary. It may be possible to agree that new sizes, new flavors, and new packages are not new products. Does, however, the addition of sugar to corn flakes or raisins to bran constitute a new product? Is an instant oatmeal a new product or a variation of the old product? No definition of innovation satisfactorily answers these and similar questions unless we rely on consumer perception and, as suggested, accept majority consumer opinion of what is and what is not an innovation.

MOST INNOVATION IS CONTINUOUS

Most innovation in the American economy is of a continuous nature. Most innovation, especially in the consumer sector, results as

---

[4] Same reference as footnote 1.

[5] William E. Bell, "Consumer Innovators: A Unique Market for Newness," in *Proceedings of the American Marketing Association*, ed. Stephen A. Greyser, Chicago, 1963, pp. 85–95.

[6] Thomas S. Robertson, "Determinants of Innovative Behavior," in *Proceedings of the American Marketing Association*, ed. Reed Moyer, Chicago, 1967, pp. 328–332.

an attempt to differentiate products to increase market share. Few and far between are innovations of a discontinuous nature which significantly alter or create new consumption patterns. The image of innovations resulting from the inspiration of the occasional genius does not fit the typical occurrence and even discontinuous innovations are increasingly the result of planned team research. Most innovation today results from programmed, systematic research efforts.

Some Case Examples

If the first detergent on the market represented a fairly discontinuous innovation, then the succeeding proliferation of brands must represent highly continuous innovations. While one brand may be a low sudser, another possess cold water attributes, another contain bleach, and another contain disinfectant for baby clothes, all are essentially minor variations on the basic product. All of these succeeding brands are *programmed innovations*.

The automobile industry is the leading example of programmed, continuous innovations. New products appear on schedule each year and every three years major design changes occur. This planning and programming of innovation occurs across almost all industries. When a major aircraft manufacturer was considering its next venture into the commercial market, it plotted the various offerings then available in terms of such variables as runway requirements, flying range, seating capacity, and cost of operation and found the gaps in the market. These gaps were in short-range jets and high-seating-capacity jets. The company then planned to innovate in one of these areas and did so.

THE IMPORTANCE OF INNOVATION TO THE FIRM

Innovation, according to a variety of sources, occurs due to: (1) shrinking profit margins for established products, (2) shorter lives for established products, and (3) excess capacity. Schumpeter has attributed innovation to (4) a search for profit.[7] Barnett has emphasized (5) the pressure of competition

and the search for product differentiation as factors leading to innovation.[8]

These reasons for the occurrence of innovation overlap considerably. Analysis of their content also reveals their all-inclusive nature. Innovation, it would appear, is the solution to all business problems. Perhaps Schumpeter's view of innovation as a search for profit summarizes all of the other reasons; although corporate marketers generally cite growth, or forward momentum, as the most important factor encouraging new product development.

Maintaining Momentum

New products are basic to company growth and to profitability. It is seldom possible in today's economy to maintain momentum or even stability with innovations. Mattel Toymakers, for example, grew rapidly with the acceptance of Barbie Doll, but such growth could not be continued without other new products since Barbie Doll soon reached "maturity" on the product life cycle. It is also difficult to maintain profit margins when a product reaches maturity since competition intensifies and product advantages may be neutralized. The typical pattern in the food industry, for example, has been for profit margins to decline while sales are still increasing so that companies must quickly look to other new products for continued profit performance.[9]

Empirical Data

The contribution of new products to the sales growth of various industries has been researched by Booz-Allen & Hamilton, Inc. Expected growth from new products varies from 46% to as much as 100%, with an average of 75%. Innovating industries are also more likely to be high growth industries.[10]

In another study, Mansfield assessed the value of technological innovation to the growth and profitability of individual firms. His concern was with the acceptance of capital goods' innovations by firms of com-

[7] Joseph A. Schumpeter, *Business Cycles*, New York, McGraw-Hill Book Company, Inc., 1939, Vol. 1, p. 97.

[8] Same reference as footnote 3 at p. 73.

[9] Robert D. Buzzell and Robert Nourse, *Product Innovation in Food Processing: 1954–1964*, Boston, Division of Research, Harvard Business School, 1967.

[10] Booz-Allen & Hamilton, Inc., *Management of New Products*, New York, 1965.

parable initial size in the steel and petroleum refining industries. He concludes:

> In every interval and in both industries, the successful innovators grew more rapidly than the others, and in some cases, their average rate of growth was more than twice that of the others.[11]

INNOVATIVE COMPETITION

The importance of successfully marketing product innovations is today being recognized as never before. This is evidenced in the marketing trade magazines and academic journals as well as in the proliferation of consulting agencies devoted to new products and the establishment of new product divisions within existing agencies.

Yet, as more firms become committed to innovation, new product advantages exist for shorter time periods and the "monopoly" power of new products is soon overcome. When General Electric quickly followed Squibb into electric toothbrushes, for example, it added innovation to innovation by marketing a cordless version which was then a new usage concept. The new product marketplace is increasingly becoming more competitive as fairly simultaneous innovations often occur and imitation is indeed rapid. Many firms, such as Mattel Toymakers, prefer to jump from product tests to national marketing since test marketing often speeds imitation.

RISKS IN NEW PRODUCTS

Commitment to new products is not without serious problems and associated risks. Research and development expenditures for 1971 should approach $22.4 billion[12] — most of which will be spent on *unsuccessful* new product ideas. Based on responses from 51 prominent companies, Booz-Allen & Hamilton report that it takes almost 60 *ideas* to result in one commercially successful new product and that three-fourths of new product expense funds go to unsuccessful products.[13] These figures, however, must be treated as estimates only, especially since this is a sample of "prominent" companies and we can

probably assume greater sophistication in the research and development process.

Buzzell and Nourse, in an extensive study of product innovation in the food industry, report that of every 1,000 new product ideas:

810 are rejected at the idea stage
135 are rejected on the basis of product tests
12 are discontinued after test marketing
43 are introduced to the market
36 remain on the market after introduction[14]

According to these figures, food companies would appear to better the across-industry average reported by Booz-Allen & Hamilton. The Buzzell and Nourse figures suggest that over two successful new food products result from every 58 ideas.

New Product Failures

The greatest risk in new products and the greatest potential monetary loss comes at the market introduction stage. Estimates of new product failures run from 10% to 80%. This wide discrepancy in estimates is due largely to three reasons: (1) *definition* of what constitutes a new product — this is seldom stated; (2) *measurement* of what failure means — while one study may include only product withdrawals from the market, another may include all unprofitable or marginally profitable products. While one study may limit itself to measurement within one or two years of introduction, another may choose a considerably longer time span; and (3) the *sample of companies* chosen—large companies are likely to market fewer failures than small companies and companies in sophisticated consumer-oriented industries are likely to market fewer failures than companies in less sophisticated, production-oriented industries.

While it is difficult, therefore, to provide an average new product failure ratio which will uniformly apply, this failure rate can be quite high. It is probably fair to say that a majority of new products fail, although it

---

[11] Edwin Mansfield, "Entry, Gibrat's Law, Innovation, and the Growth of Firms," *American Economic Review*, Vol. 52, December, 1962, pp. 1023–1051, at p. 1036.

[12] "Research: The Cash Pours Out for Research and Development," *Business Week*, #2020, May 18, 1968, pp. 72–74.

[13] Same reference as footnote 10.

[14] Same reference as footnote 9 at p. 105 and p. 124.

would be more meaningful to present figures by *industry* if such figures could be obtained.

Why Do New Products Fail?

New product failures are seldom due to bad products. Analysis of the trade literature provides countless examples of basically sound new products failing after market introduction. General Foods failed with a Birds Eye line of frozen baby foods and rejected a forerunner of Instant Breakfast, Brim, in test markets. Ford Motor Company's Edsel is perhaps the classic example of a new product failure. Campbell proved unsuccessful in marketing fruit soup as well as a Red Kettle line of dry soup mixes. Coca-Cola, despite its strong consumer franchise in cola beverages, was initially unsuccessful in marketing a diet cola.

Reasons for new product failures could be discussed at length, but the foremost problem is in *marketing*. More tightly controlled test market and market experimentation procedures are necessary as well as a greater volume of marketing research in advance of new product introductions. Sophisticated models for predicting new product sales levels should be encouraged. The primary focus here, however, will not be on these concerns. It is the thesis of this paper that the probability of new product success can be increased by understanding the factors governing *diffusion* of new products, that is, acceptance by consumers.

NEW PRODUCT DIFFUSION

Diffusion is the process by which something spreads. Anthropologists have studied the diffusion of language, religion, and ideas among tribes and societies. Sociologists, particularly rural sociologists, have studied the diffusion of new ideas and new practices within societies. Physicists have studied the diffusion of atomic particles within elements. Marketers have implicitly studied diffusion for many years as they have sought to guide and control the spread of new products, but little research or conceptual thinking has been directed toward an understanding of the diffusion process itself.

The diffusion literature, as developed across a number of disciplines, offers for consideration a fairly well-developed theoretical framework which applies to the flow of information, ideas, and products. It is the integration of this framework with the traditional marketing framework which may advance our understanding of how new products disseminate and gain consumer acceptance and which may suggest means of improving new product marketing strategies.

Components of the Diffusion Process

The diffusion process can be conceptualized as: (1) the adoption, (2) of new products and services, (3) over time, (4) by consumers, (5) within social systems, (6) as encouraged by marketing activities.

Adoption refers to the use of a new item. *New products* and services will be considered in the broadest sense from highly continuous to highly discontinuous innovations. The *time* dimension distinguishes early adopters from later adopters. The *consumer adoption unit* may be the individual consumer or a family or buying committee, or even a city of consumers. *Social systems* constitute the boundaries within which diffusion occurs. In a broad sense the market segment as a whole can be viewed as a social system, or more narrowly defined, the consumer's friendship group can be considered his social system. Within these systems, communication will occur — both marketer-initiated and non-marketer-initiated. *Marketing activities* are defined as the mix of product, price, promotion, and distribution plans and strategies.

These several aspects of the diffusion process are interdependent. For example: the attributes of the new product will affect the rate of adoption over time, the types of consumers who will adopt, the kinds of social systems within which diffusion will take place, and the marketing efforts needed to achieve diffusion. Alternatively, successful new product diffusion is critically dependent upon the communication of relevant product information and the matching of new product attributes with social system and individual consumer characteristics. Marketing activities can guide and control, to a considerable extent, the rate and extent of diffusion.

EFFECTS OF MARKETING ACTIVITIES

The opportunities for marketing activities to affect the diffusion process *for a given new product* can be summarized as follows:

Social System

- Marketing decisions can select the social systems (market segments) in which diffusion is most likely to be successful.
- Promotion, pricing, and distribution strategies can be combined to reach specific social systems.
- Marketing activities can, in some cases, chart the diffusion path within a social system to achieve the fastest rate of diffusion. This may be possible by reaching critical individuals first — especially innovators and opinion leaders.

Consumer Adopters

- Marketing decisions can establish the consumer profile most likely to adopt the new product.
- Promotion, pricing, and distribution strategies can be oriented toward this consumer profile.
- Marketing activities can vary by penetration level to specifically reach different kinds of consumers. For example: advertising strategies to reach first adopters should usually be different than strategies to reach later adopters.

Product Meaning

- Marketing activities can help define product meaning and can encourage diffusion by emphasizing the most relevant product attributes. For example: should promotion for a new dessert product emphasize taste, convenience, low cost, or low calorie content?

Time

- Marketing activities can affect *rate* of diffusion. A low price, penetration strategy, a high level of promotional expenditures, free sampling and deal activity, and intensive distribution will generally all encourage a fast diffusion rate.

These opportunities will now be assessed briefly in turn.

Social System

The characteristics of a social system highly influence diffusion patterns for new products. This can be demonstrated by reference to a study by Graham who researched the diffusion of five innovations — television, canasta, supermarkets, Blue Cross, and medical service insurance — across social class levels. His research revealed that no single social class was consistently innovative in adopting all five innovations. Television, for example, diffused more quickly among low social classes while the card game canasta diffused more quickly among upper social classes.[15]

Graham argues that the critical factor in determining diffusion is the extent to which the attributes of the innovation are compatible with the attributes of the culture of the receiving social system. The "cultural equipment" required for the adoption of television, according to Graham, included an average education, a minimum income, and a desire for passive spectator entertainment. This cultural pattern coincided with a lower social class level.

Other researchers have distinguished between communities exhibiting modern versus traditional norms. The modern-oriented community is receptive to innovations while the tradition-oriented community relies on established ways of doing things. The norms in effect in a social system have a sizeable bearing on diffusion rates. This may vary by region of the country and from rural to urban areas.

Innovations may also diffuse at different rates within particular spheres of a social system. A number of studies show that an innovation diffuses more quickly among socially integrated social system members than among socially isolated members. For some products, diffusion may be most rapid among older people.

The marketer has at his discretion the choice of social systems in which to market his product or in which to place heaviest support behind his product. This decision must be based on a matching between the attributes of the new product and social system attributes. Should segmentation be on the basis of social class, ethnic group, age, or ecology? Given the selection of the most relevant social systems, what are the most appropriate promotional, distribution, and pricing strategies to reach these social systems? Finally, is it possible to initiate strategies to reach the most likely buyers within

[15] Saxon Graham, "Class and Conservatism in the Adoption of Innovations," *Human Relations*, Vol. 9, 1956, pp. 91–100.

a social system? While this is frequently possible in industrial selling, it is seldom possible in reaching ultimate consumers.

Consumer Adopters

Ultimately, diffusion is dependent upon the individual consumer. He must decide whether adoption of the new product is the appropriate course of action for him. The adoption process refers to the mental sequence of stages through which the consumer passes in arriving at an acceptance (adoption) or rejection decision. It can be conceptualized as awareness, knowledge, liking, preference, conviction, and adoption, although other conceptualizations are also available.

Considerable research evidence indicates that communication sources are not equally effective at different stages of the adoption process. While *advertising* generally has greatest impact at the earlier stages of awareness, knowledge, and liking, the consumer seeks more objective, evaluative information at the later stages of preference and conviction and *personal influence* (word-of-mouth) often becomes the dominant communication source. This, of course, varies by product and holds most when the consumer perceives a good amount of risk in buying. The important point is that a purchase decision results from the cumulative impact of a number of communication sources and the marketer must attempt to move consumers through an entire sequence of information needs.

Not all consumers within a social system have an equal initial propensity toward buying a new product and consumers adopt at different points in time. The earliest buyers, the "innovators," have generally been found to possess different characteristics from later adopters. (A discussion of innovator characteristics is provided by Charles W. King in a paper following this one). An initial goal before marketing a new product should be to establish the profile of the most likely consumer innovators. It may then be possible to design marketing activities in line with this profile. As the innovator level of diffusion is achieved, marketing strategies should then be re-oriented to reach later buyers.

Product Meaning

Extent of a new product's diffusion and its rate of diffusion are, of course, largely a function of the particular attributes of the product. The emphasis given particular attributes and the overall brand image created are critical marketing decision areas.

There are several attribute classification schemes to account for differential diffusion rates. Rogers proposes a set of five characteristics of innovations which he believes are generally relevant. These characteristics are: (1) relative advantage, (2) compatibility, (3) complexity, (4) divisibility, and (5) communicability.[16]

Relative advantage is the degree to which an innovation is superior to the product it supersedes or with which it will compete. While the addition of fluoride to toothpaste was considered to add extra product value, many other ingredients had previously been added to toothpaste without the consumer attaching relative advantage to the resulting "new" product. A dominant marketing management function is product differentiation to encourage the consumer to perceive greater product value.

Compatibility refers to how consistent the new product is with existing ways of doing things. The greater the need for consumers to restructure their thinking and to engage in new forms of behavior, the less quickly the item is likely to diffuse.

Complexity refers to the degree of difficulty in understanding and using the new product. In general, the more complex the item, the slower its rate of diffusion and the narrower its potential market.

Divisibility refers to the extent to which a new product may be tried on a limited scale. In-store sampling of a new food product and marketing of small sizes take account of the divisibility factor.

Communicability is the degree to which word of the new product may readily be communicated to others. Conspicuous products, such as clothes, are highest on communicability.

The important point is how these characteristics are *perceived* by consumers since this is what governs response. In summary form, it can be hypothesized that rate of diffusion is positively related to relative advantage, compatibility, divisibility, and communicability, but negatively related to complexity.

Diffusion rates of technological innovations

---

[16] Everett M. Rogers, *Diffusion of Innovations*, New York, The Free Press, 1962, Chapter 5.

among firms have been studied by Mansfield, who hypothesizes as follows:

1. Profitability of an innovation relative to others that are available will increase the rate of adoption.

2. The larger the investment required, assuming equally profitable innovations available, the slower the rate of adoption.

3. The type of industry will affect the rate of adoption depending on its aversion to risk, market competitiveness, and financial health.[17]

Considerable work remains to be done relating innovation attributes to diffusion rates and further relating innovation attributes to consumer characteristics. For example, to the extent that a product is high on complexity, this may suggest a slower rate of diffusion, but does this also suggest a certain kind of consumer adopter? Also, when is a product attribute important? Relative advantage may be irrelevant for fashion items and for many fad items since their adoption is largely related to the perception of *newness itself* rather than to better functional performance. Diffusion patterns for fashion and fad products show a much more accelerated growth and an equally accelerated decline phenomenon.

Time

The business firm in general wishes to shorten the diffusion time span consistent with profit maximization objectives. At times it may be desirable to gain maximum short-run penetration, while at other times a more deliberate segmentation strategy, often on the basis of price, may be followed. A strategy of maximum diffusion need not be most profitable. It is probably a fair generalization, however, that maximum diffusion (market share) is the goal for most new products. This is especially true for continuous and dynamically continuous innovations and less true for discontinuous innovations.

In a penetration strategy, maximum diffusion is sought as quickly as possible. Price tends to be set relatively low; promotion will lean heavily toward mass advertising; and intensive distribution will be used. This strat-

egy is most necessary if little product differentiation exists for the new product and, therefore, demand is highly elastic. This strategy is also necessary if competitors are likely to introduce similar new product offerings within a fairly short period of time, despite the continuity or discontinuity of the innovation. Rapid diffusion may discourage competition, although it could also have an encouraging effect when high sales are noted — especially if the estimated potential market is large. More importantly, however, rapid diffusion will often lead to a large and brand loyal consumer franchise which is crucial to continuing sales success given the subsequent entry of competition.

A penetration strategy has implications as to the shape of the diffusion curve and encourages high acceleration. In fact, in a number of cases for new convenience *brands,* the diffusion curve is far from S-shaped. In the pre-sweetened cereal market and in the detergent market, for example, a new brand (because of concentrated advertising and deal activity at introduction) may attain its maximum life cycle sales within a matter of a month and then settle down to a lower "maturity" level of sales. It is critical to remember that a varying proportion (sometimes very high) of beginning sales may be for *trial* purposes and need not represent *adoption,* defined in terms of acceptance and commitment to the brand as reflected in repeat purchases. A company must quickly determine its trial-adoption ratio or it can be misled into expanding production for never-to-be-realized repeat sales.

In a sales staging strategy, the typical progression is from generally high "skim the cream" pricing to relatively lower prices, from selective distribution to intensive distribution, and from limited promotion to expanded or mass promotion. Such a strategy is more likely to be successful for specialty and durable items and is generally dependent upon a differentiated product and one which competition cannot readily duplicate. The somewhat discontinuous innovation allows, in effect, a certain degree of monopoly power.

DuPont's "Corfam" shoe material was marketed using the sales staging strategy. It was deliberately introduced to manufacturers of quality shoe products before being made available on a mass basis. Management apparently felt that maximum long-run diffusion for the product would be gained if it was not

---

[17] Edwin Mansfield, "Technical Change and the Rate of Imitation," *Econometrica,* Vol. 29, October, 1961, pp. 741–766.

perceived as a cheap substitute for leather but instead as a quality improvement over leather. DuPont, therefore, by its choice of manufacturers to whom the product was made available, was governing intensity of distribution and pricing and extent of manufacturer advertising.

It is interesting to note that the marketer's diffusion strategy very much influences the shape of the diffusion curve. By the same token, however, the selection of a strategy is a function of the type of product and the competitive situation. A penetration or sales staging strategy must be based on accurate assessment of future market acceptance. Wasson, for example, argues that color television marketers unsuccessfully followed a penetration strategy for their products when sales to support such a strategy were not forthcoming. They misjudged rate of market acceptance and should have been following a sales staging strategy with selective distribution, relatively high price, and limited promotion until the growth segment of the diffusion process was attained.[18] We must also take cognizance of the fact that while a dichotomy of ideal types makes for expository efficiency, a considerable range of strategies between staging and penetration is available to the firm.

CONCLUSION

It is essentially an arbitrary decision as to what is and what is not a new product. Most "new products" on the market today, however, involve only minor changes in consumption patterns; they are of a highly *continuous* nature. Such products are the result of programmed product differentiation.

The critical value of innovation to a firm is demonstrated in many industries where over 50% of sales growth is coming from new products. Yet, the risk of new product failures is high and it is probably fair to say that a *majority* of products which are introduced to the market fail. Furthermore, these failures are seldom due to a technically unsound product but instead are largely the result of poor marketing performance.

It is the conclusion of this paper, however, that the probability of new product success can be increased by understanding the diffusion process. Successful new product diffusion is dependent upon the communication of relevant product information and the matching of new product attributes with social system and individual consumer attributes. Marketing strategies can guide and control, to a considerable extent, the rate and extent of new product diffusion.

---

[18] Chester R. Wasson, "How Predictable Are Fashion and Other Product Life Cycles?" *Journal of Marketing*, Vol. 32, July. 1968, pp. 36–43.

N. Channels and Logistics

40. Sweeping Changes in Distribution

JAMES L. HESKETT

Near the conclusion of World War II, the wartime T-2 tanker, with a rating of 15,600 tons, was thought by many to be too large for expected peacetime petroleum needs and also too large to be handled safely in most ports. Yet just 20 years later, marine architects were designing ships 20 times larger than the T-2, ships exceeding 300,000 deadweight tons which have since been built and now sail the world's oceans.

Only 25 years ago, a respectably advanced rate at which to handle bulk materials was about 500 tons per hour. Recently, a number of installations have been built capable of handling bulk materials at 40 times that rate.

Just a generation ago, there were three basic alternatives for transporting most commodities: rail, water, and truck. Since then, we have witnessed a vast increase in opportunities for transporting commodities other than petroleum by pipeline. Airfreight has become a viable alternative for many shippers. And the development of unitized freight handling and coordinated methods of transporting freight has produced a number of new modal combinations, including piggyback and trailers and containers on ships which, for all practical purposes, did not exist 20 years ago.

Since the inauguration of modern-day con-

tainerized service just 8 years ago, ocean transportation to and from the United States has seen an enormous growth of containerized freight in the general cargo sector. In the North Atlantic trade, it is estimated that 60% of all containerizable freight now moves in containers.

As late as 1950, the Interstate Highway System, although conceived, had yet to be financed for construction.

The computer, whose rapid development was another by-product of World War II, has made possible only within the past 15 years the application of techniques and managerial models so vital to the successful management of logistics activities.

Clearly, the generation just ended has produced remarkable technological advances in transportation, materials handling, and information processing.

Party in response to technological change, industrial, commercial, and governmental organizations have reorganized to improve the management of logistics activities and to make intelligent use of the newly available technology. Increased breadth, in terms of both the backgrounds of individuals attracted to the field and the scope of responsibilities which they have been given, has facilitated a trend toward the purchase of carrier services, physical facilities, and logistics equipment as elements in a broader system of related activities.

In this sense, the past decade can fairly be termed an era of organizational as well as technological change in logistics.

◆ SOURCE: Reprinted by permission from *Harvard Business Review*, Vol. 51, No. 2, March–April 1973, pp. 123–132. © 1973 by the President and Fellows of Harvard College; all rights reserved.

TOWARD INSTITUTIONAL CHANGE

If we have witnessed significant technological and organizational change in the recent past, what does the foreseeable future hold? What are the implications of the fact that the U.S. population, and to some degree the size of the market that it represents, appears to be leveling out as emphasis on birth control increases? What will be the effect if pressures for new products and product individuality continue?

Similarly, what types of responses will be required by the growing congestion in city centers and the continuing dispersion and rapid growth of suburban markets? Will new technology continue to provide the primary means with which to deal with logistics problems arising from all these and other trends?

There are signs which suggest that the answer to my last question is *no*. While technological and organizational change will, of course, continue, major challenges will be met primarily by institutional change involving the spatial reordering of functions and facilities within an organization and among cooperating organizations.

This represents a logical progression in logistics from emphasis on decision making based on *internal cost analyses* to emphasis on *internal profit analyses* and on *interorganizational cost and profit analyses* of the sort suggested in *Exhibit 1*.

FACTORS IN SHIFT OF EMPHASIS

We will turn our interest during the foreseeable future to institutional (as opposed to technological) change, for a variety of reasons. Included among these are the seven possibilities that:

1. There are physical constraints on certain methods of transportation and materials handling, as well as restrictive public attitudes toward the further technological development of others.

2. Certain technological developments appear to be "topping out," at least for the time being.

3. Existing technologies, to an increasing extent, require for their success a rationalization of activity which can be brought about largely through institutional cooperation and new types of institutions.

4. Technological advances have made institutional cooperation not only possible, but in some cases necessary.

5. There are changing attitudes toward inter-organizational coordination among individuals in business as well as government.

6. Continued emphasis on logistics management will yield information necessary to justify institutional change.

7. Perhaps of greatest importance, the economic benefits from institutional coordination and change will far exceed any that foreseeable technological developments can offer.

I shall consider each of these factors in the shift of emphasis to institutional change in the course of this article.

1. Constraints on technology. Certain transportation modes, such as rail and highway, have natural constraints imposed on them by the existing physical facilities. The height of a rail car can be increased to the point where any further increase would require massive expenditures for greater clearances at bridges, tunnels, and underpass or overpass intersections that have replaced grade-level railroad crossings.

Truckers now speak in terms of a 6-inch increase in the width of a vehicle instead of a 10-foot increase in length, which was more feasible when highway carriers were operating with 27- and 30-foot trailers. And they will have difficulty getting even that small increase in width.

Public attitude now comprises a growing constraint on the further development of other transportation technologies. The refusal to support the development of the supersonic transport, however temporary a victory for such forces it may represent, was an important indicator. It may be significantly more difficult in the future to obtain funds for the development of an ecologically and economically uncertain device such as the SST than for, say, an expanded system of bicycle paths for urban commuters.

When we throw in the growing opposition to supertankers and the fear of the potential disasters they could create, and the issues and arguments over possible ecological impacts of pipelines in the tundra of the Far North, we have a clear indication that technology in the late 1970's and 1980's may be in for close scrutiny.

2. Temporary 'topping out'. Several years

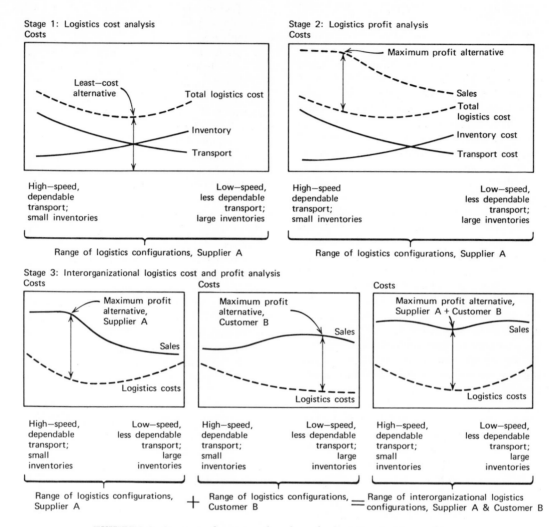

EXHIBIT 1. Stages in the scope of analyses for logistics decision making.

ago, it was popular to look ahead to the "era of the 747," the great hope of airfreight advocates. These "boxcars of the sky" were to eliminate the economic barriers to the use of airfreight. Closer analysis at the time could have shown that the most significant development, the introduction of the DC-8-63F airplane, already had occurred. Furthermore, few anticipated the problems of assembling a sufficient volume of freight in one place at one time to meet the 747's vastly greater requirements for efficient operation. Finally, with their attention diverted to developments in the sky, most airfreight advocates paid too little heed to the significant improvements needed in the problem area of handling airfreight on the ground.

The same marine architects who produced the 300,000-ton ship designs now tell us that,

although designs of 1,000,000 tons are possible, the economics of building and operating such ships quite likely precludes their construction in the foreseeable future, public attitude aside. Certain diseconomies of scale begin to assert themselves.

While ingenious devices for introducing automation in the warehouse have been developed in recent years, the promise of automated warehousing is yet to be realized. In fact, the requirements which it imposes on freight flow for effective utilization may in many cases be achieved only through the type of institutional cooperation I shall discuss later.

We now have the computers and the concepts to achieve significant savings through effective control of inventories. More important, economical computer and communication capacity will make possible the use of models offering more individual attention to product-line items, inventory locations, and customers. But the gains which improved technology in this area could make possible are small compared with the improvements in operations that could be achieved through proper application of currently available machines and methods.

3. **Rationalization of activity.** Typified by improved allocation of effort and responsibility among cooperating and even competing institutions, rationalization of activity has been required by the introduction of certain technologies. Conversely, technological advances have so badly outstripped institutional changes that the absence of the latter now imposes significant constraints on the former.

Perhaps the best example of this is the introduction of containerization on a wholesale basis in North Atlantic shipping several years ago.

Prospective container-ship operators planned for massive capital investment in fast, expensive ships, and the containers they would carry. Even the most forward-looking ship operators, however, did not provide for the numbers of containers which would ultimately be required for the service. They did not properly anticipate the problems of controlling container usage in the hinterlands surrounding the ports which they would serve. And they paid dearly for their traditional lack of interest in, and institutional separation from, freight before it arrived and after it left the docks.

In response to this problem, operators are making extensive efforts to: (a) acquire freight-forwarding, trucking, and other organizations which control freight in the hinterlands; (b) seek out arrangements under which containers can be jointly owned; (c) collect and transmit information in such a way that more effective control can be maintained over container usage.

4. **Necessity for institutional cooperation.** We have already noted that effective utilization of the 747 jetliner requires the assembly of large quantities of freight at a given place and time for shipments to a common destination. It is quite possible that, until airfreight volume increases significantly on a general front, self-organized groups of shippers with common origins and destinations may offer the best potential for providing this kind of volume.

In view of current computer capabilities and concepts, perhaps the most acute need in inventory control activities has been for more accurate data on which to base forecasts of future demand. As we have seen, the data have always existed. They needed to be collected and transmitted in a timely way. This has led to the establishment of direct line of communications between customers and suppliers.

Production technologies have made possible smaller, lighter products that perform jobs better than their larger, heavier predecessors. At the same time, improvements in our intercity transportation systems have made it easier and less expensive to transport larger quantities of these smaller products, at least to the outskirts of large metropolitan areas.

Yet, in a growing number of cities, we have congestion and chaos.

This is clearly a case in which technology has contributed to a problem that will be solved either by more technological development, perhaps in the form of subterranean freight-access routes, or by institutional cooperation to create more efficient freight flows.

5. **Changing attitudes.** Many forms of organizational coordination not only are legal, but are becoming more and more attractive as problem-solving means to businessmen and government officials alike. The growing interest in coordinating inbound freight movements to congested city centers is just one example of a response by government and industry leaders to a difficult problem. Recently, this has led to the organization of the first symposium in this country to explore approaches to the problem of urban freight movements.[1]

Efforts in other countries are more advanced. For example, a recent study of freight movements into Utrecht, Holland, disclosed that the consolidation and systematic delivery of certain types of freight moving typically in small shipments could reduce the number of delivery vehicles in the city center from over 600 to 6.[2]

The Supermarket Institute has supported

---

[1] Results of this symposium were reported in *Urban Commodity Flow,* Special Report 120 (Washington, D.C., Highway Research Board, National Academy of Sciences, 1971).

[2] Described in *Nieuwe Wegen Naar Bevoorrading* (Rotterdam, Holland, Transport Advies Groep Trag, 1971).

investigation into the feasibility of consolidated distribution facilities which might be operated as a joint venture by competing grocery product manufacturers and chain food-store organizations utilizing the same regional distribution centers. Essentially, such facilities would enable manufacturers and retailers to eliminate duplicated warehouse space.

In commenting on the concept of consolidated distribution facilities, the president of a large retail food chain recently remarked that "the idea may not be so farfetched, and it might have advantages to both segments of the industry." Of course, the concept will have arrived when a manufacturer of a store organization closes all or a part of its own warehouse facility to take advantage of a consolidated distribution service.

6. Continued organizational development. In the past 15 years, there has been a rebirth in the concern for coordinated management of transportation, warehousing, materials handling, inventory-control, order-processing, and procurement activities. Evidence for this can be found in the rapidly increasing number of job titles like Physical Distribution Manager, Materials Manager, and Manager of Logistics, particularly in larger corporations. Further, the growth in membership in organizations such as the 10-year-old National Council of Physical Distribution Management (NCPD) and the even younger Society of Logistics Engineers (SOLE) has mushroomed.

Explanations for this concern and interest range from the competitive advantage that the effective management of logistics activities provide to organizational "me-too" faddism in certain industries. But an analysis of the roster of the NCPD suggests that the base of membership has spread from a few large companies in different industries to many more organizations in those same industries and then to other industries as well. Included among these are grocery and chemical product manufacturers, and manufacturers and distributors or products requiring extensive parts distribution activities. Other industries in which substantial costs of logistics, compared with sales, must be balanced against rigorous demands for customer service will see organizational change and emphasis on logistics.

As a further development in this area, managements will devote more attention to, and change the nature of, responsibility for coordinated product flow. For example, expansions in product lines without commensurate increases in sales produce higher inventory carrying costs as a percentage of sales.

As a result, in order to maintain a given level of customer service, retailers and wholesalers are limiting their speculative risk by reducing stocks of any one item (or by investing a commensurate amount of money in inventory for a broader product line) while at the same time expecting, and in fact depending on, manufacturers making speedy responses to their orders. This customer expectation, stated in the form of a willingness to substitute one manufacturer's product for another's in the event of the latter's inability to meet the customer's demands, in effect raises the incentive for speculation by manufacturers.

Thus caught in a squeeze between broader product lines and increasing demands for faster service from channel institutions, a number of manufacturers have responded by holding larger quantities of stock in semifinished form closer to markets, typically in distribution centers. There they can be cut, assembled, or packaged to order, thus postponing the company's commitment to specific stock-keeping unit locations until the last possible moment while reducing speculation (measured in terms of the elapsed time between customer order and delivery) for the customer.

To an increasing degree, logistics management will involve the operation of light manufacturing as well as distribution facilities. Perhaps the automobile assembly plant offers the most extreme example of this phenomenon. It is the closest thing to a distribution center in the channel of distribution for automobiles produced in the United States; it also houses light manufacturing activities. Because of the complexity of the latter, however, these plants typically fall under the responsibility of production management.

However, in other industries with less complex field requirements—such as the cutting to order of plate glass, paper products, lumber, and so on, and the packaging to order of common commodities—light manufacturing in the field will to an increasing extent fall within the purview of those concerned with logistics.

7. Increased economic benefits. Technological change can enable a company in a channel of distribution to perform its functions more efficiently. Typically, institutional change can eliminate the cost of performing a function by shifting the function to another point in the channel, where it can be integrated into other activities. Only occasionally, as with momentous developments such as containerization, can technology accomplish as much. And even then, it can do this only with the institutional change necessary to implement its introduction and growth.

INSTITUTIONAL RESPONSES

Basic functions performed in a channel of distribution, such as selling, buying, storing, transporting, financing, providing information, and others, can only be shifted, not eliminated. They must be performed by some institution at some point in a channel. Distribution opportunities can be pinpointed by identifying the basic functions which can be performed most effectively by each institution in the channel, and the types of institutional change needed to accommodate efficient product flow.

The types of institutional change called for include at least four, arrayed in terms of their organizational impact on companies in a channel of distribution:

1. The coordination of policies and practices to enable cooperating channel members to perform their existing functions more effectively.
2. The shift of functions and responsibilities from one institution to another in a channel.
3. The creation of joint-venture or third-party institutions to eliminate duplication of the performance of functions in such channels.
4. The vertical integration of channel functions which are currently performed by different organizations.

It may be useful to take a closer look at each of these four types of institutional change promoted by the forces I have discussed.

1. Coordination of practices

The unitized handling of products by means of such devices as pallets is one example of a technological development that has had a profound effect on interorganizational coordination. In order to reap the maximum benefits of palletization, buyers and sellers have to coordinate their materials handling systems to make use of the same size pallet, or at least pallet sizes with modular compatibility.

Thus industry standards for pallet sizes have been established for the shipment of such things as tin cans and paper products. Where standards have not been established, certain wholesalers have adapted their materials handling systems to conform with those of a dominant supplier. Companies electing not to abide by such standards do so at a price which is reflected in increased costs for handling goods.

2. Shifting of responsibilities

A large distributor of personal care and houseware products that employed a network of direct sales personnel desired recently to gain greater control over product delivery to its distributors without actually going into the trucking business. It offered truckers an interesting proposition: a guaranteed, high profit on their investment in return for the full authority to schedule and control their trucks, reductions of up to 40% in existing charges, and access to the truckers' books to verify profit levels.

This case suggests the tremendous potential benefits made possible by a shift of functions between organizations.

A shift of stock-keeping responsibility from inventory-conscious retailers to wholesalers and manufacturers has taken place in recent years. This has resulted in part from the desire of retailers to reduce speculation and unsalable stocks in an age of expanding product lines as well as a realization that warehousing and materials handling costs may be significantly lower per unit for manufacturers and wholesalers than for their retailer customers.

In this case, the shift of responsibility for the performance of these functions in the channel of distribution is a logical result of interorganizational analysis and management.

3. Third-party arrangements . . .

Cooperative interorganizational approaches in the form of joint ventures or third parties[3]

---

[3] For an interesting appraisal of the trend toward joint-venture or third-party arrangements for marketing products and services, see Lee Adler, "Symbiotic Marketing," HBR November–December 1966, p. 59.

can provide the objectivity and "arm's length" management often needed when large, proud organizations wish to create a product or service requiring inputs from several participating companies. They are particularly attractive in a field that has been typified by fragmented, duplicated services—logistics.

... **in distribution utilities.** We are now seeing joint ventures and third-party arrangements used in the creation of so-called distribution utilities—companies that are capable of providing a complete range of warehousing, transportation, order-processing and inventory-control services to shipper customers. A distribution utility contracts with a small to medium-sized manufacturer or a division of a larger company to remove finished stock from the end of the latter's production line and make it available for sale—when, where, and in the quantities desired—with some pre-agreed-on level of customer service. This allows the manufacturer's marketing organization to concentrate on selling.

The distribution utility, to the extent that it takes possession of a product without taking title to it, is the converse of what, in common marketing parlance, is termed a broker—one who buys and sells goods without ever taking possession of them.

However, substantial resources are required to (a) construct or acquire a network of distribution centers (warehouses), (b) support the design and installation of extensive communication and information-processing facilities, and (c) create an organization in which naturally skeptical manufacturer-customers can have confidence. The joint venture provides a convenient means of assembling such resources.

... **in consolidated regional centers.** The movement of carload quantities of stocks directly from the production lines of competing manufacturers into common regional distribution centers for consolidated delivery direct to retail stores has been under discussion for some time, particularly in the grocery products industry. Until now, objections regarding loss of control over the product, possible disclosure of competitive information, and the elimination of an area of potential competitive advantage have overruled the economic benefits of eliminating the manufacturer-operated and the retailer-operated distribution center as shown in *Exhibit 2*. But consolidated distribution of this type is now a reality.

The concept has been recently implemented in Canada with the creation of a distribution center in Vancouver, shared jointly by leading manufacturers and their chain-store customers. The success of this experiment, conducted by a task force of the Canadian Grocery Manufacturers Association, which reports that it has reduced the cost of dry grocery distribution by at least 10%, has led to its rapid expansion to two other pro-

... **in central cooperative facilities.** The vinces of Canada.
benefits of consolidating outbound freight can usually be enjoyed by a well-managed, medium-sized or large manufacturer. However, companies typically receiving small shipments from many sources have found that they must establish cooperative arrangements to enjoy similar benefits.

Thus far, such arrangements have been confined to the formation of shippers' cooperatives for the consolidation of merchandise purchased by several companies for delivery to the same destination (a metropolitan area). Transportation cost savings, in the form of pro rata rebates, from the replacement of small package shipments by carload and truckload shipments have been remarkable.

Now, at the urging of city officials, these same companies are beginning to explore the creation of consolidated storage and merchandise-processing facilities, located in low-cost suburban areas, as well as the coordination of delivery to retail store sites.

An unpublished feasibility study in which I participated several years ago indicated that central distribution facilities could be operated at a satisfactory profit by a third party at a cost to retailer customers of only 80% of their current costs of receiving, processing, and delivering such goods themselves.

4. Vertical integrations

The possibilities I have discussed thus far are interorganizational alternatives to the vertical integration of logistics operations in a channel of distribution by one powerful channel member through the merger with, or acquisition of, companies with which it deals.

Vertical integration in logistics flourished during the late 1960's as industrial manufacturers began acquiring companies offering complementary services, such as trucking and warehousing. Interestingly, transportation companies were not leaders in this trend,

A. Without consolidated distribution

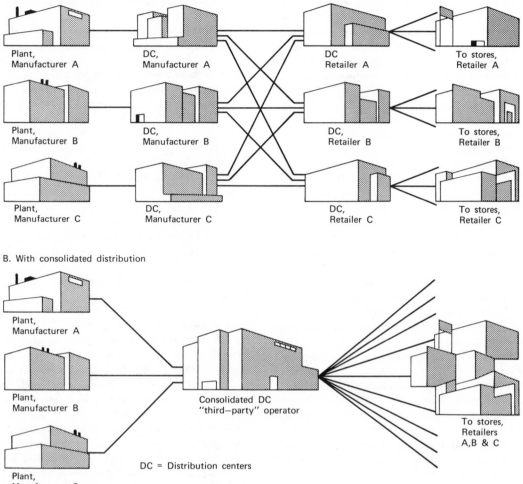

B. With consolidated distribution

DC = Distribution centers

EXHIBIT 2. Impact of consolidated distribution on product flow to regional markets.

possibly because of the Interstate Commerce Commission's historic tendency to impose stringent controls on the acquisition of companies offering competing modes of service. Indicators point to more active participation by transport and other companies in ventures involving the vertical integration of logistics services.

However, the rate at which this takes place will depend, among other things, on (a) the level of pressure exerted on the ICC to relax its control, (b) the rate at which legal means, such as financial holding companies, are found for accomplishing vertical integration, and (c) the level of prosperity in the logistics industries themselves. In the latter regard,

adversity may help rather than hinder the trend.

IMPLEMENTATION APPROACHES

Perhaps the three most important factors in implementing creative approaches to interorganizational problems and institutional change in logistics are management practices, labor attitudes, and regulatory policies.

Management practices

Clearly, individuals and companies that can adopt the attitudes and practices necessary to foster creative approaches to interorganizational problems will have an edge on their competitors. What are these attitudes and practices? Early research in the field of interorganizational management has suggested some.[4]

Companies likely to be recognized as leaders during an era of institutional change and interorganizational problem solving will be characterized by:

☐ *A tendency to seek what bargaining theorists have termed "nonzero-sum results from negotiations."*

Essentially, a nonzero-sum result is one which reduces the total cost of the negotiating organizations, regardless of how they divide the resulting benefits. Nonzero-sum results can be achieved only through a basic change in procedure, such as the design of quantity discounts to reflect efficient handling and shipping or the implementation if incentives to encourage the faster unloading and turnaround of transportation equipment.

In contrast, zero-sum results produce no such net benefits. Price changes made without accompanying changes in procedure only transfer costs and profits from one company's P&L statement to another's, with no net economic benefit to the channel system.

☐ *A willingness to absorb risks for the mutual benefit of participants in a channel system.*

A 1968 study examined the common problem of congestion at shippers' truck docks.[5] Its authors estimated that the addition of extra truck bays in several cases would reduce truck waiting time significantly, thereby producing high rates of return on investment.

Unfortunately, to implement these programs, shippers would have to make the investment to alter their facilities, while the benefits would accrue to truckers supplying pickup and delivery services.

Presumably, such situations could be re-

solved if one or more truckers could reduce rates selectively to encourage the necessary investment, a practice frowned on by the Interstate Commerce Commission. Or the trucker might make the investment with some assurance that he would continue to receive business from the shipper at least over a period sufficient to pay him back for his investment. Again, this practice could be looked on with disfavor by the ICC or a state regulatory body.

Perhaps the only feasible course of action would be for the shipper to absorb the uncertainty by constructing the bay. In return, he might obtain an informal agreement that future consideration, in the form of a rate reduction based on cost improvement, would be given by the carrier. This would only work if one carrier provided all or at least a significant portion of the service.

☐ *A willingness to innovate on behalf of the channel.*

Some companies are known as innovators in their respective business spheres, in the testing of new technologies, organizational relationships, or contractual relationships. A company that is first to establish a pool of pallets for the economic handling of goods in a channel of distribution is likely to be regarded as such an innovator, with resulting long-term rewards for successful experiments (and perhaps losses for unsuccessful ones).

☐ *The establishment of a mechanism for collecting and transmitting information and skills throughout a channel.*

Information that provides an early warning of inventory build-ups at the retail level can be of use to all participants in a channel system. Manufacturers of such diverse products as drugs and fertilizers have not only provided their distributors with inventory-control systems, but also educated them in the use of these systems. Expectations of long-term improvements in distributor profitability and loyalty motivate such manufacturers with enlightened interorganizational practices.

☐ *The exchange of personnel with other parties to interorganizational relationships.*

A factor which distinguishes management in the United States from that in most other parts of the world is executive mobility. U.S. executives expect to make frequent moves; rarely do they expect to spend a lifetime working for a single firm. The exchange of personnel between "business partner" or-

---

[4] Much of this section is based on J. L. Heskett, Louis W. Stern, and Frederick J. Beier, "Bases and Uses of Power in Interorganization Relations," in *Vertical Marketing Systems*, edited by Louis P. Bucklin (Glenville, Illinois, Scott, Foresman and Company, 1970), p. 75.

[5] Karl M. Ruppental and D. Clay Whybark, "Some Problems in Optimizing Shipping Facilities," *The Logistics Review*, Vol. 4, No. 20, 1968, p. 5.

ganizations can set the stage for important interorganizational achievements by executives in cooperating organizations who understand each other's problems and economic constraints.

Labor attitudes

Unionism is typically held up by management as the greatest obstacle to beneficial changes of the type I have discussed. And yet, in situations where managements have recognized the value of providing job (and union membership) security in return for freedom to redesign jobs and introduce technological improvements, labor's attitudes have been positive.

Perhaps the best example of labor's cooperative attitude was reflected in an agreement some years ago between the Pacific Maritime Association, representing ship operating managements, and the International Longshoremen's and Warehousemen's Union. Under the terms of the agreement, the PMA established a trust fund to protect until retirement the salaries of ILWU members expected to be displaced.

As a result of the technology introduced subsequent to the agreement, volume increases made possible by operating economies actually created jobs, leaving the union with a trust fund that it had limited immediate need for. Thus both parties found this transaction beneficial.

Regulatory policies

The fear of undue advantage or discrimination in dealings between carriers and shippers has proved to be a deterrent to interorganizational problem solving in logistics.

For example, the proposed introduction a few years ago of "Big John" hopper cars with several times the capacity of their predecessors significantly higher minimum shipping quantities, and rate reductions of 60% on grain transportation from the Midwest to the Southeast by the Southern Railway was delayed for months by the ICC. This period of time was necessary to investigate the effects of competing inland waterway barge operators. The litigation involved, among other things, a dispute over the question of whether the proposal exaggerated the magnitude of cost reductions which Southern could achieve with the innovation.

In spite of regulatory deterrents, there appears to be a trend toward more creative interorganizational problem solving on the part of carriers and shippers. The trend would be accelerated if, for example, regulatory agencies would emphasize this question in their investigations of carrier rate or service proposals: To what extent will changes resulting from such proposals produce procedural changes necessary to achieve non-zero-sum benefits for negotiants? With this shift in emphasis, proposals scoring high would have a greater chance of being approved and expedited by the concerned regulatory agency.

CONCLUSION

Institutional changes will, to an increasing extent, replace technological changes as the major sources of continued productivity increases in transportation, warehousing, inventory-control, and order-processing activities in the intermediate future. They both make possible, and are being fostered by, the application of interorganizational management thinking which attempts to produce operating efficiences for two or more cooperating institutions in a channel of distribution.

This shift in emphasis in logistics threatens to envelop a number of shippers, carriers, and companies in associated industries in problems with which they are not equipped to deal. Significant competitive advantages already have accrued to those fully aware of the favorable competitive positions to be gained by shifting responsibilities for logistics activities from one company to another, creating third-party joint ventures to facilitate the consolidation and coordination of product flows, and seeking non-zero-sum results from interorganizational negotiations.

Such changes promise to inject additional dimensions of excitement to match those provided by recent significant technological developments in logistics. They also promise continued rewards to the executive of sufficiently broad view and flexible mind who is able to change to meet the needs of his chosen field. Clearly, they offer unexplored frontiers in the redevelopment and restructuring of logistics services.

41. A Theory of Channel Control

LOUIS P. BUCKLIN

Manufacturer management of distribution involves the adjustment of the mix of product spatial availability, local promotion, final buyer price, and quality maintenance. Where middlemen are used in the channel, it also includes the design of control procedures to insure compliance with the desired mix. Control is ". . . any process in which a person or group of persons or organization of persons determines, that is, intentionally affects, the behavior of another person, group or organization." [1]

Historically successful methods of control for manufacturers have been weakened in recent years by middleman trade association pressures, legislative action, and expansion of the antitrust law domain. Although alternative approaches for attaining channel management goals have been developed, the formation of a useful body of theory lags current needs. This article discusses the basic channel forces that cause manufacturers to seek control of middleman activities. Then, a model based upon a theory of authority describes the forces limiting the degree of control that may be achieved. The nature of the economic and behavioral conditions affecting this limitation are explored, and

implications are drawn for further research and current channel management practice.

ISSUES OF CHANNEL CONTROL

Issues of channel control have been part of the marketing literature for many years. The genesis of concern occurred with the emergence of manufacturer and middleman interest in resale price maintenance in the late nineteenth century. The introduction of branded drugs during this period, for example, created a new type of competitive condition among pharmacists, one in which their individual reputations as prescription compounders lost ground as the major factor influencing consumer patronage. The disrupting patterns of competition that emerged from this development led to pressure for manufacturers to control retail prices in order to insure spatial availability.[2] In the United States this led directly to the first of many confrontations between manufacturers and enforcers of antitrust laws over the legal right to such control.[3]

This early clash was the forerunner of a continuing legal and political dispute over control of resale price maintenance and other procedures involving territories, customers, promotional allowances, and brokerage fees. This confrontation came to represent a major

---

[1] Arnold S. Tannenbaum, *Control in Organizations* (New York: McGraw-Hill Book Company, 1968), p. 5.

◆ SOURCE: Reprinted by permission from the *Journal of Marketing* (National Quarterly Publication of the American Marketing Association), Vol. 37, No. 1, January 1973, pp. 39–47.

[2] Federal Trade Commission, *Report on Resale Price Maintenance* (Washington, D.C.: Government Printing Office, 1945).

[3] 220 U.S. 373 (1911).

theme in the literature of control.[4] Changing technologies in retail trade led to the emergence and growing importance of chain and department stores. This development, together with a more active interest by smaller retailers in trade associations, resulted in a shift in the power structure of the distribution system and a consequent shift in the efforts of retailers to limit and sometimes eliminate manufacturer control.[5] The resulting conflicts with manufacturers became known as the "battle for channel control," a term popularized by Craig and Gabler and later extended by Mallen and others.[6] This later literature predicted the eventual outcome of the conflict.

Spurred by the belief that improved coordination of activities within the channel was a prerequisite to future channel survival and success,[7] the underlying concepts of power and conflict received increasing attention. The exploration of behavioral and economic theories as a basis for obtaining the necessary system coordination represents the final literature theme relevant to channel control. Largely through the work of Stern,

Heskett and several others, the bases for channel system power were explored and assessed.[8] From this work came the rudiments of an interorganization management theory[9] and the research on measurement necessary for empirical verification.[10]

The employment of the theory of authority to explain the limits of control in the distribution channel may be regarded as an effort to extend this third literature theme. The concepts of power and authority are very similar, and may occasionally be used synonymously. Behavioral theories of authority offer the opportunity to develop a model of the channel control process that may be useful in both research and practice.

RATIONALE FOR CONTROL

Incentive for manufacturers to control the function of their channel stems from three sources: inadequately trained middlemen, the coordination of otherwise heterogeneous decisions, and intrasystemic competition. The value of control where middlemen have insufficient experience, or possibly lack the time or interest in acquiring an adequate background, should be obvious. When left to their own devices, such middlemen cannot help but make decisions which serve neither their own nor their suppliers' interests. When manufacturers can show these firms how to improve their operations, a solid basis for control is established.

The situation is seldom as clear for the other two situations. Heterogeneous decision making by middlemen occurs because of divergent historical growth patterns and distinct competitive conditions. These circumstances call for middlemen to make unique

---

[4] Some of the issues are cited in Lee E. Preston, "Restrictive Distribution Arrangements: Economic Analysis and Public Policy Standards," *Law and Contemporary Problems*, Vol. 30 (Summer, 1965), pp. 506–529.

[5] E. T. Grether, *Price Control Under Fair Trade Legislation* (New York: Oxford University Press, 1939); Joseph C. Palamountain, Jr., *The Politics of Distribution* (Cambridge, Mass.: Harvard University Press, 1955); and Henry Assael, "The Political Role of Trade Associations in Distributive Conflict Resolution," JOURNAL OF MARKETING, Vol. 32 (April, 1968), pp. 21–28.

[6] David R. Craig and Werner R. Gabler, "The Competitive Struggle for Market Control," in *The Annals of the American Academy of Political and Social Sciences*, Vol. 29 (May, 1940), pp. 84–107; Bruce Mallen, "A Theory of Retailer-Supplier Conflict, Control, and Cooperation," *Journal of Retailing*, Vol. 39 (Summer, 1963), pp. 24–31, and 51; and Robert W. Little, "The Marketing Channel: Who Should Lead This Extra-corporate Organization?" JOURNAL OF MARKETING, Vol. 34 (January, 1970), pp. 31–38.

[7] Wroe Alderson, *Dynamic Marketing Behavior* (Homewood, Ill.: Richard D. Irwin, Inc., 1965), pp. 239–258; and Bert C. McCammon, Jr., "Perspectives for Distribution Programming," in *Vertical Marketing Systems*, Louis P. Bucklin, ed. (Glenview, Ill.: Scott, Foresman & Co., 1971), pp. 32–51.

[8] Louis W. Stern, ed. *Distribution Channels: Behavioral Dimensions* (Boston: Houghton Mifflin Company, 1969).

[9] Louis W. Stern and J. L. Heskett, "Conflict Management in Interorganization Relations: A Conceptual Framework," in *Distribution Channels: Behavioral Dimensions*, Louis W. Stern, ed. (Boston, Houghton Mifflin Co., 1969), pp. 288–305.

[10] Larry J. Rosenberg and Louis W. Stern, "Conflict Measurement in the Distribution Channel," *Journal of Marketing Research*, Vol. 8 (November, 1971), pp. 437–443; and Adel I. Ansary and Louis W. Stern, "Power Measurement in the Distribution Channel," *Journal of Marketing Research*, Vol. 9 (February, 1972), pp. 53–59.

decisions in order to optimize their individual profits.

When a manufacturer attempts to coordinate the marketing strategies of his middlemen, many middlemen are forced to deviate from policies which are individually most profitable. For example, coordination may be helpful in reducing production costs by permitting stable production and minimizing the number of package types. Such coordination, however, may force some middlemen to forego a type package or delivery pattern that fits their particular mode of operations. Unless they are reimbursed for this change by the manufacturer, profit rates for the middlemen may fall drastically.

Competition among the manufacturer's middlemen creates a problem of control. Two examples may illustrate this point.

Open Distribution

In this instance, the manufacturer elects to sell to all middlemen who will carry his differentiated brand. Given market acceptance of the brand, the number of interested middlemen is directly influenced by the unit gross margin. High margins cause many middlemen to buy,[11] improving spatial availability and enhancing total brand sales. The addition of new middlemen, however, eventually fails to increase brand sales proportionately, reducing average sales per middleman. At this point, competition directly affects the members of the system rather than other channels.

Consequently, the absence of collusion causes an increasing number of middlemen to cut prices, thereby severely lowering the unit gross margin. Middleman interest in the brand is now reversed, leading to a decline in the number of middlemen and spatial availability.[12] The decrease in gross margins reduces middleman willingness to promote and maintain quality, further intensifying internal competition.

While the extent to which these transformations occur will vary by product type and trading area, an open distribution policy

encourages middleman behavior patterns that are likely to conflict with the manufacturer's interests. Without the exercise of control, local promotion may be insufficient or of the wrong type, possibly leading to a reduction in product quality.

Limited Distribution

Limiting the number of middlemen in a trading area may not improve matters. Such a policy automatically reduces spatial availability and does not guarantee that satisfaction will be obtained on other mix elements.

The award of an exclusive distributorship transfers the market power inherent in a manufacturer's brand to the middleman. Under these conditions, middleman profits are maximized by pricing, not at the competitive level where average costs and revenues are equal, but at a lower volume where marginal revenues cut marginal costs.[13] Historically, automobile manufacturers and breweries have differed with their dealers, urging that lower prices would greatly enhance volume.

This same pattern may occur with other aspects of the mix. Middlemen will seldom wish to spend as much money on promotion and product quality maintenance as the manufacturer feels is warranted. As a consequence, limited distribution does not axiomatically provide the manufacturer with satisfactory middleman behavior patterns. Varying the number of middlemen in the trading area by small degrees is unlikely to remedy these defects. Manufacturers will be as interested in controlling middlemen in limited distribution situations as they are in open systems.

A CONCEPTUAL FRAMEWORK FOR MANUFACTURER CONTROL

A theory of the control process should begin with Barnard's view of authority. The source of authority originates with the interests of those who are to be controlled. Authority is based directly on the willingness to comply of those to whom orders are given.

More specifically, Barnard finds ". . . a

---

[11] Martin R. Warshaw, "Pricing to Gain Wholesalers' Selling Support," JOURNAL OF MARKETING, Vol. 26 (July, 1962), p. 52.

[12] Frederick E. Balderston, "Communication Networks in Intermediate Markets," *Management Science,* Vol. 4 (January, 1958), pp. 159–163.

---

[13] Alderson, same reference as footnote 7, at p. 253.

'zone of indifference' in each individual within which orders are acceptable without conscious questioning of their authority." [14] He amplifies this ideas as follows:

The zone of indifference will be wider or narrower depending upon the degree to which the inducements exceed the burdens and sacrifices which determine the individual's adhesion to the organization. It follows that the range of orders that will be accepted will be very limited among those who are barely induced to contribute to the system.[15]

Although this statement might be construed as a restatement of the economic man, the forces which shape a person's indifference zone are based on behavioral theory. March and Simon, for example, cite the degree of job conformity to self-image and job satisfaction as important elements in shaping the individual's willingness to respond.[16]

The control theory proposed herein extends Barnard's concept to interorganization management. His ideas are given substance in Fig. 1 where the limits to manufacturer control over any given middleman in his channel are derived. In the coordinate system, the vertical axis represents profits obtained by the middleman from doing business with the manufacturer. The horizontal axis measures the authority continuum; authority increases moving to the right.

The model constructs consist of the tolerance and payoff functions. Payoff functions define the profits that accrue to the middleman from accepting authority. The function shown in Fig. 1 indicates that as additional authority is accepted the profits to the middleman *decline*. As discussed earlier, this view reflects the problems inherent in multifirm channel systems. However, the situation is not very different from certain intraorganization problems. When salesmen are paid strictly on a commission basis, they may complain that management efforts to control their activities lessens their opportunities to make money. The middleman is especially sensitive to this issue because his revenues

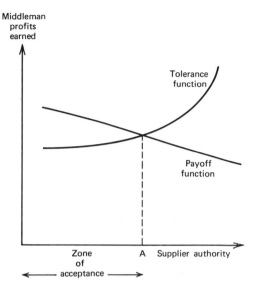

FIGURE 1. The limits to authority, A, in a distribution channel, supplier's view.

not only affect his compensation, but also the capitalized value of his business property.

The tolerance construct measures the middleman's feeling of burden and sacrifice incurred from acceding to supplier authority. This function reflects his perception of the alternative opportunities where his resources could be channeled. Factors affecting the average height of the function include the quality of alternative opportunities and the middleman's prior profit experience with the supplier. Once a given level of profit has been obtained with a supplier, the middleman will be hesitant to forego it. The slope of the function will reflect middleman work habits and individual desires to be "boss." The curve may initially be relatively flat, but at some point it will begin to rise steeply, reflecting the middleman's call for higher profits in order for him to accept additional control.

The intersection of the two functions determines the limits of a manufacturer's authority. At point A, the middleman perceives his sacrifices as exactly balanced by the profits he receives. If the supplier seeks control beyond point A, his efforts may be expected to fail. In this situation, the manufacturer might apply coercion to achieve the desired control. Barnard does not specifically deal with coercion, but his zone of indifference appears to exclude this type of influence. Other interpretations of Barnard make this

[14] Chester I. Barnard, *The Functions of the Executive* (Cambridge, Mass.: Harvard University Press, 1950), p. 167.

[15] Same reference as footnote 14, at p. 169.

[16] James G. Marsh and Herbert A. Simon, *Organizations* (New York: John Wiley & Sons, 1958), pp. 93–98.

distinction explicit.[17] Because both coercion and persuasion (a force also not considered by Barnard) play an important role in channel control, the model must be expanded to encompass both of these forces.

This extended model is shown in Fig. 2: The definition of the horizontal axis is changed from authority to control. In this situation control refers to the extent of middleman compliance to the supplier's commands. Empirically, Tannenbaum and others have measured the control within organizations by directly asking organization members to state the extent to which they are controlled by manufacturers.[18] While such a measure may generate some response bias, particularly as applied to the distribution channel, it nevertheless provides an initial basis for testing the model.

A second change is made in the nature of the tolerance curve. The shaded portion extending to the right of the curve indicates an area where supplier instructions are obviously resented. These supplier dictates are followed in part because opportunities to obtain alternative sources of supply are either unavailable or less profitable. Consequently, control extends farther to the right than the theory of authority would suggest. When this means of control is exploited, conflict of one type or another may be expected. Middlemen may cooperate in an attempt to force the manufacturer to withdraw some of his control. Termination of relationships from actions taken by either party is also a probability.

The payoff function is also modified to reflect the influence of persuasion. The initial increase in the height of the curve shows how control is extended. This extended control results when middlemen believe that sales and profits can be increased by following supplier instructions. Point P on Fig. 2 represents the place where persuasion ceases as the means of control, and the mechanism of authority becomes effective.

This completes the outline of the model. The two major constructs of the model, pay-

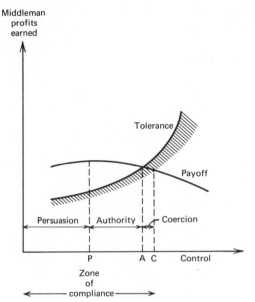

FIGURE 2. Control in distribution; the role of persuasion, authority, and coercion.

off and tolerance, may now be considered in somewhat greater detail.

ALTERING THE PAYOFF FUNCTION

The supplier has four basic ways of affecting the middleman's payoff function: (1) Reducing the intensity of intrasystemic competition; (2) enhancing the demand-generating power of his marketing program; (3) raising the monetary incentives provided the middleman; and (4) improving the middleman's marketing practices.

Intrasystemic Competition

As noted earlier, reduction of competition among a supplier's middlemen permits each to take advantage of the brand's market power in his individual territory, shifting the middleman's payoff function higher. For example, payoff curve P_a in Fig. 3 occurs when the manufacturer is successful in restraining competing middlemen to their territorial boundaries. Payoff curve P_b reflects the absence of such control.

The level of control that the manufacturer attains over one middleman will affect his ability to control the others. In a similar manner, loss of control over one will jeopardize his influence over the others. The

---

[17] Gene W. Dalton, Louis B. Barnes, and Abraham Zaleznik, *The Distribution of Authority in Formal Organizations* (Boston: Graduate School of Business Administration, Harvard University, 1968), p. 37.

[18] Same reference as footnote 1, at pp. 23–25, 51–52, and ff.

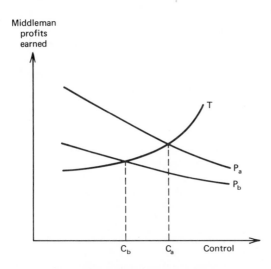

Middleman
profits
earned

T

P_a

P_b

C_b C_a Control

FIGURE 3. Alternative functions showing strong control, P_a, and weak control, P_b, by the supplier over competing middlemen.

manufacturer who attempts to exercise control inconsistently within his channel will eventually erode much of the opportunity to do so.

The steeper slope of P_a as compared to P_b indicates that when the supplier maintains strong control over his channel, the temptation for the individual middleman to reject his influence will be high. The very negative slope of P_a shows that middleman compliance with supplier directives increasingly inhibits his ability to take advantage of the noncompetitive stance of fellow system members. This is analogous to the position of a retailer selling a well-known brand under resale price maintenance. The higher the control of the manufacturer over the others, the greater are the profits any one middleman could obtain by cutting prices in defiance of this control. These profit opportunities are perhaps one reason why coercion has often been employed in the past as a technique to maintain price control.

Historically, manufacturers have sought to limit conmpetition among their middlemen through agreements on resale prices, territorial and customer limitations, and censoring the language of advertisements. The gradual erosion of enforcibility of state resale price maintenance laws[19] increased antitrust prose-

cution of both vertical price fixing outside the protection of these laws and territorial agreements,[20] has substantially diminished the ability of manufacturers to achieve control through this means. One remaining basis permits the manufacturer to terminate unilaterally relationships with middlemen who, he feels, are not following his policies. Despite concern that this approach may become illegal along with bilateral agreements,[21] and the inability of the manufacturer to provide less drastic punishment to reluctant middlemen, some suppliers still appear successful in pursuing this control strategy.

Marketing Program

Through product innovation and the effective use of his own promotional program, the manufacturer may shift the payoff function upward in the absence of any attempt to limit intrasystemic competition. Successful implementation of his program provides the manufacturer with a means of obtaining control. Distributor payoffs may come either from profits earned directly from the brand, or from the additional patrons who buy other goods.

This strategy may also impart some instability to manufacturer-middleman relationships. Where manufacturer sales fail, either because of industry showdowns or program shortcomings, the result is a downward shift of the payoff function. Unless the manufacturer acts under these circumstances to relieve his middlemen of some of their burdens of control, the tolerance point may be exceeded. According to Assael, the rebellion of automobile dealers in the 1950s was precipitated by increased industry competition and lower dealer profits.[22]

Incentives

The use of incentives to improve middleman payoff includes margin changes (initiated through changes in supplier price

[19] Marshall C. Howard, "Fair Trade Revisited," *California Management Review*, Vol. 10 (Fall, 1967), pp. 17–26.

[20] Theodore A. Groenke, "What's New in the Antitrust Aspects of Selecting and Terminating Distributors," *The Antitrust Bulletin* (Spring, 1968), pp. 139–144.
[21] Same reference as footnote 20, at pp. 144–155.
[22] Henry Assael, "Constructive Role of Interorganizational Conflict," *Administrative Science Quarterly*, Vol. 14 (December, 1969), pp. 573–582, at p. 567.

levels), payments for shelf space, retailer deals for special displays, subsidization of retail fixtures, push money, sales contests, discounts for advance purchase, and cooperative advertising allowances. In some instances, manufacturers may vary gross margins according to whether or how well the middleman performs specified functions; e.g., use a product sales specialist for the supplier's brand, carry the complete line, or maintain a service department.

Given the variety of techniques available and the opportunity to alter the level of financial incentive for each, the payoff function may be regarded as a set of curves rather than just one. A manufacturer's strategy will involve selection of the specific curve upon which he chooses to operate.

Middleman Skill

Middleman may vary greatly in their skill, knowledge, and general competence. Any deficiencies may be temporary or permanent in character, and some may be more easily corrected than others. For many multiproduct middlemen the problem may be the high cost in time and money of keeping fully informed about the detailed market developments of all the products they handle.

In either case, the opportunity to restructure the payoff curve by the manufacturer exists if he can provide the middleman with product marketing programs that both recognize changing market conditions and adapt to special middleman problems of space limitation, high personnel turnover, and increasing labor costs.[23] Baumritter's dealer program to support its line of furniture included ". . . operating manuals, professionally prepared advertising programs, inventory control systems, and accounting systems . . ." [24]

The greater the complexity of the program, the flatter the rise in the payoff curve. The peak, however, will be shifted farther to the right.

ALTERING THE TOLERANCE FUNCTION

The height and slope of the tolerance function is determined by a number of factors:

middleman dependence upon his supplier, the relative status of supplier and middleman, role-task norm structure, social patterns of business exchange, and bureaucratic rigidity within the supplier organization.

Middleman Dependence

The willingness of a middleman to accept supplier authority is heavily dependent upon the number and value of alternatives the former holds.[25] Where these alternatives are numerous and easily obtainable, the termination of relationships with a supplier that might result from rejecting control does not bear a heavy penalty. The tolerance curve, as T_a in Fig. 4, slopes steeply upward in this circumstance. Alternatively, if the supplier's brand represents all or substantially all of the middleman's business, he is likely to be more amenable. The tolerance curve in this instance will be lower, slope more slowly upward as curve T_b in Fig. 4.

Relative Status

When the flow of orders from one organization to another moves from the higher to the lower status group — status designations that accord with the judgments of members of both groups — resistance to the current is minimized.[26] Translated to the channel setting, this characteristic of interorganization behavior means that adherence to supplier orders will be greatest when the large and successful manufacturer deals with a small, commonplace middleman.

Data compiled by Massy and Frank suggest that middlemen are more likely to promote the major brands as opposed to the lesser. Independent and voluntary chains appear more responsive than corporate chains to supplier efforts to secure retail promotion.[27]

[23] McCammon, same reference as footnote 7, at pp. 33–43.
[24] McCammon, same reference as footnote 7, at p. 48.

[25] Frederick J. Beier and Louis W. Stern, "Power in the Channel of Distribution," in *Distribution Channels: Behavioral Dimensions*, Louis W. Stern, ed. (Boston: Houghton Mifflin Company, 1969), pp. 97–99; also, same reference as footnote 15, at pp. 100–106.
[26] John A. Seiler, "Diagnosing Interdepartmental Conflict," *Harvard Business Review*, Vol. 41 (September–October, 1963), pp. 123–124.
[27] William F. Massy and Ronald E. Frank, "Analysis of Retail Advertising Behavior," *Journal of Marketing Research*, Vol. 3 (November, 1966), p. 381.

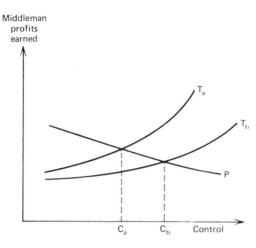

Middleman
profits
earned

T_a

T_b

P

C_a C_b Control

FIGURE 4. Alternative tolerance functions showing strong role-task norms, T_a, and weak role-task norms, T_b.

Middleman Role-Task Norms

Role-task work is ". . . sustained and directed effort of mind in which a person seeks to synthesize the organizational requirements of his position with his own individual needs, interests, and aspirations." [28] Where middlemen interact frequently with their peers, where mutuality of position is perceived and accented by strong trade association activity, strong behavioral norms for role-tasks are likely to evolve. The existence of such norms is likely to have an important effect on the shape of the tolerance curve. The stronger and more entrenched the norms, the steeper the slope of the curve.

On the other hand, the existence of a set of norms offers the supplier a means of affecting his authority through appeals to specific stereotypes. Such appeals may cause middleman attitudes toward the supplier to become more favorable and move the tolerance curve to the right. [29] For example, one type of middleman may see himself as uniquely possessing the requisite skills and capabilities for distributing the product. He may look unfavorably at any effort on the part of manufacturers to employ other channel types. Supplier abstinence from the use of dual

channels may improve the former's standing and ability to achieve control.

Socialization Patterns

Although the practice of business gift-giving has received warranted criticism, the genesis for this behavior does not lie in bribery, but in efforts on the part of businessmen to redress social imbalance. Reciprocity is a fundamental basis for conducting personal social affairs. Favors provided by one party require return benefits. [30]

This pattern of socialization has formed the basis for trade in some societies. In channels, reciprocity consists of service exchanges above and beyond contractual agreements. When one organization comes to the aid of another — for instance, by expediting delivery or by purchasing goods with minor but inconsequential defects — a band of loyalty and goodwill is formed between the two. This mutual band may be sustained over considerable periods of time, even when new people replace those who initiated the relationship.

Bureaucratic Mode of Internal Supplier Control

Models of bureaucracy suggest that when a manufacturer seeks to control his sales force by relatively rigid standards or rules of conduct, the ability of salesmen to adjust to the individual needs of each of their middleman customers is impaired. [31] More importantly, the dynamics of this type of internal control methodology may serve to intensify the problem. Managerial insistence that salesmen follow set patterns leads the latter to issue "orders" in situations where there is little chance that the will be followed or where a little leniency would generate valuable dealer good will. The result is a weakened relationship with the middleman and a weakened base for authority (tolerance curve shifts to the left).

When the loss in customer cooperation is perceived as a failure on the part of its salesmen to follow directions, management often becomes more rigid and demanding and fur-

[28] Richard C. Hodgson, Daniel J. Levinson, and Abraham Zaleznik, *The Executive Role Constellation* (Boston: Graduate School of Business Administration, Harvard Business School, 1965), p. 231.

[29] Same reference as footnote 26, at pp. 127–128.

[30] Alvin Gouldner, "The Role of the Norm of Reciprocity in Social Stabilization," *American Sociological Review*, Vol. 25 (April, 1960), pp. 161–178.

[31] Same reference as footnote 16, at pp. 37–40.

ther deterioration of the relationship is likely. For example, Assael noted that when sales of Chrysler cars started to decrease in the 1950s, the company tightened its regulations instead of loosening middleman controls as others tended to do. Resentment among Chrysler dealers was much greater than among other automobile retailers.[32]

The notion of response to dealer concerns will now be extended. Supplier willingness to allow middlemen to have some influence over the types of marketing programs which are established for them may be regarded as a reduction in the level of supplier control. Yet, several studies suggest precisely the opposite. One of these studies evaluates the relationship between performance in the sale of intangibles and perceived levels of control. It suggests that ". . . the degree of control exercised by an office manager over his subordinate [salesman] was positively related to the control they exercise over him. These findings imply that control at one level is not exercised at the expense of another level. On the contrary, the data indicate that any increase in control—by office manager, subordinates, or both—should be associated with higher satisfaction and performance."[33] This finding suggests that the manufacturer may shift the middleman tolerance curve to the right by allowing him more influence over policy developments that govern his behavior.

Some movement in this direction has occurred through the development of dealer advisory councils by various manufacturers. To the extent that these councils are meaningful, manufacturers that use them should achieve greater system control.

CONCLUSION

The need for control in distribution systems emerges because coordination left to market forces alone often results in less than optimal decision patterns for both the operators of the system and for the consumers it serves. Control problems occur because efforts by one firm in the system to influence the others has a differential impact upon the property values of system members. This differential impact is peculiar to multi-firm channels where the task is more difficult than in vertically integrated systems.

The control model developed in this article permits manufacturers in multifirm channels to better understand channel forces and to better develop adaptation strategies. The model consists of two constructs taken primarily from Barnard's theory of authority. The first construct is the payoff function which reflects the profit earned by the middleman from acceding to manufacturer control. The second construct is a tolerance function which reflects the ability to bear the burdens that result from manufacturer control. The determinants of payoff include the level of competion within the channel, the demand-enhancing power of the manufacturer's marketing program, monetary incentives provided the middleman, and the effectiveness of supplier-prepared programs to improve middleman marketing practices. Major factors affecting middleman tolerance are the supplier dependence, the relative status of middleman and supplier, the strength of middleman role-task norms, socialization patterns, and the extent of bureaucracy in the supplier administrative organization.

A strategy of control employs one or more of the available approaches to shift the middleman's willingness to comply to the point where the manufacturer's marketing program can be implemented. The choice of the specific strategies should be made on the basis of the expected effectiveness, their cost, and their legal risks. The expenses of control costs represent another element in the resource allocation of the total marketing mix. Dissimilar marketing programs are expected to require different levels of control. In the broadest sense, a total marketing program should be formed in concert with both control opportunities and costs.[34]

This review suggests that in the past methods of manufacturer control have relied too heavily upon the minimization of intrasystemic competition through use of coercive techniques. The climate of antitrust enforce-

---

[32] Same reference as footnote 22, at p. 578.

[33] Jerald G. Bachman, Clagett G. Smith, and Jonathan A. Slesinger, "Control, Performance, and Satisfaction: An Analysis of Structural and Individual Effects," *Journal of Personality and Social Psychology*, Vol. 4 (August, 1966), pp. 134–135.

[34] Helmy H. Baligh, "A Theoretical Framework for Channel Choice," in *Economic Growth, Competition, and World Markets*, Peter D. Bennett, ed. (Chicago: American Marketing Association, 1965), pp. 633–635.

ment precludes the use of some forceful tactics, while issues of social equity as evidenced by laws limiting middleman termination make heavy-handed treatment of middleman interest unwise. A changing structure of trade, resulting in the formation of chain stores carrying wider product lines, has served to reduce middleman dependence upon a continued relationship with a single supplier.

On the other hand, sufficient knowledge has not been accumulated to permit optimal choice of alternative tactics. Past experience provides some basic for evaluating factors that affect the payoff function, but little information is available on behavioral factors affecting tolerance. Within the manufacturer's marketing organization, the growing isolation of major product, promotion, and research decision centers from middlemen has led to misjudgment and often indifference.

IMPLICATIONS

Patterns of middleman response to manufacturer attempts to influence his behavior represent one of the major frontiers of marketing. To the academician, exploration in this area represents a major opportunity to break new ground in both measurement and hypothesis testing. To the manufacturer, the inability to control his distributors represents an incalculable loss. Because retail relationships are usually in the exclusive domain of the salesman, concern over insuring appropriate levels of control provides a major rationale for bringing sales management into the mainstream of marketing research.

To the practitioner, the model presented suggests that middleman attitudes are vital to the establishment of control. Standard survey research techniques are available to measure and evaluate these attitudes providing new information upon which policies may be judged. This model offers potentially profitable insights into the opportunity for supplier control.

The type of situation is that a manufacturer has limited capacity to extend his control through the exercise of authority. Profits earned by middlemen are regarded as property rights, and manufacturer's efforts to extend control are often viewed as actions adversely affecting these rights. Therefore, they are likely to encounter conflict, unless policies are simultaneously developed to raise the payoff function and/or shift the tolerance function to the right. The most opportune time to establish control is at the beginning of a manufacturer-middleman relationship.

42. Recycling Solid Wastes: A Channels-of-Distribution Problem

WILLIAM G. ZIKMUND and WILLIAM J. STANTON

In 1970 every American threw away approximately five and one-half pounds of solid waste (industrial construction, commercial, and household) each day which amounts to about a ton a year. This daily disposal rate is predicted to increase to eight pounds by 1980.[1] The escalation of public concern over environmental issues has, to an increasing extent, led government officials, business leaders, and conservationists to seek a solution to the problem of solid-waste pollution. One ecologically desirable technique for the disposal of trash is recycling. Simply stated, recycling consists of finding new ways of using previously discarded materials.

The recycling of solid wastes is being recognized as a tenable solution to cleaning up the cluttered environment. Scientists view recycling as a substitute for the declining supply of natural resources. Technology has responded to the recent interest in recycling with many new and sophisticated techniques capable of turning solid wastes into basic raw materials.

Although science and technological innovations are necessary aspects of recycling, the task of alleviating solid-waste pollution may be treated as a marketing activity; that is, the marketing of garbage and other waste materials. If it is a marketing function to distribute products and to add time and place utility to products, then, theoretically, it should make no difference whether the product is an empty, used beer can or a full one. More specifically, recycling is primarily a channels-of-distribution problem, because the major cost of recycling waste products is their collection, sorting, and transportation. The American Paper Institute estimates that over 90% of the cost of recycling paper is the cost of distribution.[2]

This article discusses the major alternative channels necessary to handle the waste materials created by the ultimate consumer, and identifies some of the major marketing problems involved in the recycling of these waste materials.

CONCEPT OF THE "BACKWARD" CHANNEL

If recycling is to be a feasible solution to the trash problem, there must be some means to channel the waste materials to the firm for future reuse. However, marketers have traditionally examined the channel of distribution starting with a producer; that is, a channel of distribution is the vehicle which facilitates the flow of goods from producer to consumer.

Recycling, on the other hand, is unusual

---

[1] "Cash in Trash? Maybe," *Forbes*, Vol. 105 (January 15, 1970), p. 20.

◆ SOURCE: Reprinted by permission from the *Journal of Marketing* (National Quarterly Publication of the American Marketing Association), Vol. 35, No. 3, July 1971, pp. 34–39.

[2] Walter P. Margulies, "Steel and Paper Industries Look to Recycling as an Answer to Pollution," *Advertising Age*, Vol. 41 (October 19, 1970), p. 63.

from a marketing standpoint, because the ultimate consumer who recycles his waste materials must undergo a role change. The household consumer who returns his old newspapers and used bottles is the *de facto* producer of the waste materials which eventually will be reused. Thus, in this case the consumer becomes the first link in the channel of distribution rather than the last. The unique circumstances of recycling present an interesting marketing situation.

Recycling waste materials is essentially a "reverse-distribution" process. Reverse distribution is facilitated by a "backward" channel which returns the reusable packaging and other waste products from the consumer to the producer; it reverses the traditional physical flow of the product.

Conceptually, reverse distribution is identical to the traditional channel of distribution. The consumer has a product to sell and, in essence, he assumes the same position as a manufacturer selling a new product. The consumer's (seller's) role is to distribute his waste materials to the market that demands his product.

There is a practical difference, however, between the traditional channel and the "backward" channel. The consumer does not consider himself a producer of waste materials. Consequently, he is not concerned with planning a marketing strategy for his product—reusable wastes. Thus, for analytical purposes the recycling of waste materials will be considered as the reverse distribution of the original product, and the flow of the product from the consumer to the producer will be treated as the manufacturer's "backward" channel.

REVERSE DISTRIBUTION: TYPES OF BACKWARD CHANNELS

One of the prime considerations in recycling household wastes is returning the waste product to a manufacturer for reuse. One of marketing's important roles is to determine the most efficient channel of distribution necessary to move the trash to the firm that will technically recycle the materials. The nature of the product and the nature of the market are as important in the determination of the backward channel as they are in the selection of the traditional channel of distribution. Thus, there is not an ideal channel that will typify all recycling efforts.

The backward channel used to recycle an automobile is not likely to be the same channel used to recycle a glass bottle. However, some generalizations may be made about various backward channels, since a number of channel patterns is evident.

Direct Backward Channel— Consumer to Manufacturer

Perhaps the simplest contemporary recycling attempt is exemplified by the plan of the Glass Container Manufacturing Institute (GCMI). Waste glass—known as a "cullet" in the industry—can supply 30% or more of the materials required to make new bottles. To obtain empty bottles and jars from the public, the manufacturer-members of GCMI have established approximately 100 bottle-redemption centers at glass container manufacturing plants in 25 states.[3]

It is doubtful that the modern consumer will make the effort to return his waste products directly to the manufacturer. The selection of any channel must consider the ultimate consumer's needs, and it is unlikely that the modern consumer, accustomed to convenience, will exert any substantial effort to recycle his trash. The GCMI's recycling plan places the burden of recycling on the consumer. This innovative attempt to recycle glass is still in the "production-orientation" stage of development.

Backward Channel with an Atypical Intermediary

The absence of a middleman causes the consumer a number of inconveniences. Ecologically concerned civic and community groups which are sponsoring paper drives and community clean-up days are an important link in the reverse-distribution process because they are performing the middleman's function in the backward channel.[4]

Considering the low prices paid for waste

---

[3] Walter P. Margulies, "Glass, Paper Makers Tackle Out Packaging Pollution Woes," *Advertising Age*, Vol. 41 (September 21, 1970), p. 43.
[4] See "Does Ecology Sell?" *Sales Management*, Vol. 105 (November 15, 1970), p. 20; and Walter P. Margulies, "Aluminum Industry is Already Hard at Work Against Pollution," *Advertising Age*, Vol. 41 (November 16, 1970), p. 64.

materials and the high cost of reverse distribution, it is not surprising that these organizations are the prime collectors of discarded newspapers, beer cans, and other waste materials. The collection and distribution of trash is a worthwhile venture for these associations because of the volume of their operations. It should be noted that the normal business costs are absent in paper drives and clean-up days, because expenses such as labor and collection vehicles are donated by the associations' membership. Since the main activity of these organizations is not the collection of waste materials, their performance of the middleman's reverse-distribution function tends to be sporadic. Even if community action recycling programs are conducted on a regular basis, it is not realistic to assume that they will be adequate to recycle the mountains of household wastes which will be generated in the coming years.

Backward Channel with Traditional Middlemen

Past recycling efforts used the traditional channel of distribution as the backward channel. Although recycling was not their major function, these intermediaries cooperated because the system was extremely convenient for the producer.

The recycling soft-drink bottles for a deposit provides a familiar example of one of the major attempts to recycle waste products and to reuse them in their existing forms.[5] This backward channel is literally the reverse of the normal channel for soft drinks.

During the 1930s and 1940s, packaging and wholesaling in the soft-drink industry was tied to the system of cycling the returnable bottle. The returnable bottle was desirable from the bottler's point of view, because every reuse reduced the "manufacturing" cost per bottle.

If this was the case, how can the steady growth of one-way bottles and cans be explained? Today, returnable bottles represent less than 50% of the soft-drink industry's business because both retailers and consumers resisted the returning and handling of empty bottles.[6] To maximize their profits, supermarkets emphasize the efficient utilization of space. Storing and handling empties was an additional task that retailers were not willing to assume. Consequently, supermarkets influenced bottlers to introduce soft drinks in one-way bottles in 1948.[7]

One-way containers increased the bottler's manufacturing cost, and the consumer was required to bear the additional cost of throwaway bottles and cans. The response in the marketplace demonstrated the consumer's willingness to pay a few cents more for the convenience of one-way containers.

Indirect Backward Channel Using Trash-collection Specialists

Various trash-collection specialists have developed to satisfy the consumer's need to dispose of his garbage and other solid wastes. In the past, the channel for recycling some household wastes included the "old rag and junk man" who served as a recycling-middleman specialist. By calling on homes and purchasing waste products such as rags, used papers, and discarded metal items, he provided both a service and a small-income source to consumers. However, he was part of a subsistence economy and a depression era. As people became more affluent, they preferred the convenience of throwing away their wastes. Moreover, his collection and processing costs were rising. Thus, the "old rag and junk man" disappeared largely because his role in the marketing of trash ceased to provide a sufficient service to household consumers or a profit to himself.

A contemporary waste-disposal specialist is the garbage or other trash-collection agency —either a private contractor or a unit in a municipal service system. At one time, these agencies made no attempt to recycle the wastes; they simply carried the rubbish to a city dump. Today, many trash-collection agencies function as a link in a backward

---

[5] See "Will Returnables Make a Comeback?" *Business Week* (October 31, 1970), p. 25; and Sanford Rose, "The Economics of Environmental Quality," *Fortune*, Vol. LXXXI (February, 1970), p. 184.

[6] "Packaging Advances Promise Much but Environment Dampens Outlook," *Soft Drink Industry*, Vol. 49 (May 27, 1970), p. 1.

[7] Robert K. Rogers, "Soft Drink Industry's Progress Paced by New Developments in Packaging," *Soft Drink Industry*, Vol. 49 (July 17, 1970), p. 17.

channel which recycles household wastes into landfill, power (via incineration), fertilizer, and other uses. The buyer of the trash (possibly after it has been sorted into basic materials) may be a power plant, a metals company, or a fertilizer company.[8]

Obviously this channel is convenient for the household consumer; he simply discards his rubbish into one or more trash cans. However, trash collection by an intermediary specialist is probably not the answer to the recycling channel problem. Unsorted trash used as landfill soon will exhaust available dumping sites. Trash sorted into various basic materials (e.g., glass, paper, and steel) for recycling increases the costs of these materials, although technology in this area is making significant progress.[9] Sorted materials (e.g., glass bottles), frequently are too damaged to be reused in original form. Incinerated trash poses air pollution problems.

THE PROBLEMS OF RECYCLING

The development of effective backward channels should greatly facilitate recycling. However, in order to reach this goal, at least two major tasks must be accomplished. First, the ultimate consumer must be motivated to start the reverse flow of the product. Second, a greater degree of cooperation has to be achieved among channel members than is likely to occur under present conditions.

Consumer Motivation

The greatest barrier to recycling household solid wastes is the consumer himself. The experience of the beer and soft-drink industries indicates that consumers have become accustomed to the luxury of convenience packaging and a throw-away economy. The purchase of 44 billion nonreturnable beverage containers each year provides rather strong exemplary evidence that the consumer's cooperation will not be easy to obtain.[10]

The crux of any recycling plan must be to motivate the consumer to sort and return his waste products. Existing financial incentives such as a bottle deposit are not likely to elicit his cooperation. An appeal to a sense of civic duty or social responsibility so far has proven to be of momentary value, with little lasting effect.

In recognition of the fact that the present free-market system may not result in the recycling of consumer trash, various forms of government intervention are being tried to motivate consumers. Some legislators view packaging taxes and the banning of one-way containers as possible means of stimulating consumers to initiate the reverse distribution process. Some places (e.g., Bowie County, Maryland; South San Francisco, California; and British Columbia) have already passed laws restricting the sale of nonreturnables.[11] The President's Council on Environmental Quality has recommended promoting the idea of recycling bottles.[12]

These attempts to force the consumer to recycle his trash are attacking only a symptom of the problem. The real problem is the consumers' throw-away life style. It probably will be a monumental task to change these attitudes, but it must be done before household solid wastes can be efficiently reused.

Channel Conflict and Cooperation

Retailers and other middlemen must be willing to cooperate with the manufacturers if reverse distribution is to operate effectively. Generally, traditional middlemen in the backward channel have not been anxious to cooperate with recycling attempts, because it has not been profitable. The last 20 years in the soft-drink industry illustrate that retailers may resist recycling in order to utilize their space more efficiently. Consider the costs incurred by the outlet which collects waste materials from the consumer. The retailer must count or weigh the waste products, pay the consumer for his efforts, and store the

[8] See "Turning Junk and Trash into a Resource," *Business Week* (October 10, 1970), p. 64; and "Aluminum Peddles its Own Recycle," *Business Week* (January 30, 1971), p. 21.

[9] "Gold in Garbage," *Time*, Vol. 97 (February 1, 1971), p. 61.

[10] "Does Ecology Sell?" *Sales Management*, Vol. 105 (November 15, 1970), p. 20.

[11] Same as footnote 10; and "Bottlers, Makers of Throwaway Cans Active in Ecological Programs," *Advertising Age*, Vol. 42 (March 1, 1971), p. 62.

[12] "New Federal Programs May Strengthen Efforts to Guard Environment," *The Wall Street Journal*, Vol. CLXXVI (October 27, 1970), p. 1.

materials for delivery to the manufacturer or another party in the backward channel.

No matter how delicately recycling is handled, conflict is inevitable in a backward channel. The middleman is an independent force, and he has the freedom to set his own objectives. Thus, he will need an additional incentive to participate in reverse distribution. A financial incentive may be adequate, but will the economics of recycling provide enough money to induce the middlemen's support? Making products from new resources has been economically more feasible than recycling, because existing channels are not designed to recover and reuse old household products.

These middlemen will probably have to commit themselves to a higher order of social responsibility and a longer-range perspective than they customarily consider. They may have to become one of the cases Rosenberg and Stern envision as being malign for channel participants, but benign for the society at large.[13] It is questionable whether such a societal commitment can be reasonably expected from existing middlemen in traditional channels.

FUTURE OUTLOOK

The recycling of solid wastes is a major ecological goal. Although recycling is technologically feasible, reversing the flow of materials in channels of distribution presents a significant challenge. The existing distribution system is designed to move products from the producer to the consumer. Existing backward channels are primitive, and financial incentives are inadequate. Most traditional middlemen recycle trash only as a sideline. Yet today, societal pressures and dwindling natural resources are forcing consumers to market their trash, even though the price paid for solid wastes is low, and the cost of collecting and processing these materials remains high.

New Institutions

"A society, like any other open system, is an adaptive mechanism which responds to the demands of its environment. As it responds, a certain amount of internal adjustment, a large amount which is unpredictable, and the consequences, which are even less predictable, takes place."[14] Existing institutions must adapt to their environment or new institutions will arise to perform the job which is not being completed.

One new institution which may evolve in the reverse-distribution process is a *reclamation or recycling center*. In essence, this would be a modernized and streamlined "junkyard." These centers would be placed in locations convenient to the customer who would be paid an equitable amount for his goods. The recycling center, unlike the junkyard, would have a high turnover of wastes, because its prime goal would be the efficient collection and sorting of basic raw materials, rather than passively waiting for a buyer to purchase junk. If recycling centers perform some minor processing before shipping the basic raw materials to the various manufacturers, the centers might be very profitable operations.

If the recycling center is not convenient enough for the ultimate consumer, perhaps a modernized "rag and junk" man might work for the center, and periodically collect sanitized containers each containing the basic wastes (e.g., glass, paper, and aluminum). The consumers' use of garbage compactors and glass crushers could also enhance the economic feasibility of this operation.

Supermarket chains recycling their used cardboard packaging materials often employ *brokers* to negotiate sales to paper mills.[15] Brokers specializing in the recycling of trash could provide a useful service for small reclamation centers which may evolve into a significant institution in a backward channel.

To aid the recycling efforts of existing middlemen in traditional channels, *central processing warehousing* systems may develop to store trash and to perform limited processing operations on these waste materials. Existing middlemen typically have very limited space available for storing trash, and trans-

---

[13] Larry J. Rosenberg and Louis W. Stern, "Toward the Analysis of Conflict in Distribution Channels: A Descriptive Model," JOURNAL OF MARKETING, Vol. 34 (October, 1970), p. 45.

[14] Raymond A. Bauer, "Social Responsibility of Ego Enhancement," *The Journal of Social Issues*, Vol. XXI (April, 1965), p. 50.

[15] "They're Finding Gold in Their Trash Bins," *Chain Store Age*, Vol. 45 (January, 1969), p. 18.

portation is likely to represent a major portion of total recycling costs.

Packaging Design and Materials

As part of their management of solid-waste disposal, marketers will have to reconsider the role of packaging in their marketing mix. The promotional benefits of superfluous packaging (such as shadow boxes) and the convenience factor in packaging (such as vegetables packaged in plastic cooking bags inside of cardboard boxes) will have to be reevaluated in terms of the ecological problems they cause. Marketers could reduce the quantity of trash and facilitate the recycling of used packages through actions such as (1) building reuse value into the package (a jelly jar becomes a drinking glass); (2) avoiding unnecessary packaging (does an asprin-bottle package have to be placed inside a cardboard box package?); (3) using materials which are degradable or which simplify recycling (the metal ring remaining on a glass bottle after a twist-off cap is removed causes a problem in the recycling of the bottle); and/or (4) placing a message on the package reminding the consumer to dispose of his trash properly (don't be a litterbug).

Reverse Distribution as Part of Marketing Strategy

From the viewpoint of marketing management in a firm, reverse distribution should be treated as another ingredient in the market mix. As such, the success of any firm's recycling attempts will be contingent upon the marketing strategy employed. Educating the consumer via promotion, for example, will affect the consumer's willingness to use a firm's backward channel.

Management should recognize that waste products may be recycled in different ways:

1. The waste product may be reused in its existing form. For example, a Pepsi bottle is returned to the Pepsi bottler and reused as a Pepsi bottle.

2. The waste product may be reused as a raw material in the manufacture of additional units of the same product. For example, the aluminum from empty beer cans may be reused to make new beer cans.

3. The recycled waste product may become a different product, as when oil and tar are produced from old tires, or when organic wastes are converted to fertilizer.

The major factors in the selection of traditional channels of distribution are the nature of the product and the nature of the market. These factors are equally important in the selection of the backward channel, because the bulk and weight of the waste materials and the types of buyers and sellers will significantly influence the nature of the backward channel.

Each marketer contemplating the recycling of his product will have to choose one distribution strategy from a number of alternatives. The brewers of Coors beer, for instance, may wish to recycle their own beer cans exclusively. It is also possible that Coors's recycling strategy would have the backward channel return empty Budweiser beer cans which would then be reincarnated into Coors cans.

The type of reverse channel a company selects may influence the raw materials it purchases. A strategy of exclusively recycling waste products through traditional middlemen could provide the manufacturer with control over his sources of raw materials, thereby freeing him of dealings with some suppliers. In addition, the firm's environmental and ecological image may be enhanced if recycling is done by outlets identified with the manufacturer.

Role of Government and Public Policy

In their role as citizens, people in the United States are demanding a cleaner environment, but when acting as consumers they have not been sufficiently motivated to help clean up that environment by recycling their trash. The result of this role conflict will undoubtedly mean an increase in the government's influence on a company's marketing policies with respect to recycling and reverse distribution. Previously, the article referred to a packaging tax and other local and state limitations on nonreturnable packaging. In addition, a bill was recently introduced at the federal level to ban the manufacture and sale of nonreturnable containers because they pose a threat to public welfare and the environment, and because they represent a high-cost form of litter and solid-waste management.[16] As Weiss observed, "When government moves in this radical new direction, can industry, can marketing, look in the other direction?"[17]

CONCLUSION

Predicting the future is difficult, but knowledge of society's needs helps us to know the general direction of the changing environ- ment. One focus of the 1970s seems to center on the reduction of pollution in our environment. The environmentalists who see recycling as the solution of solid waste pollution must rely on marketing's help; technology alone is not enough. Lavidge has observed that "as it [marketing] matures, as it broadens in function and scope, marketing will become increasingly relevant during the '70s to the fulfillment of man. And as the impact of marketing on society increases, so does the social responsibility of marketing people."[18] Recycling waste materials is part of marketing's growing responsibility.

[16] U.S. Congress, House, 91st Congress, 2nd Session, H.R. 18773.

[17] E. B. Weiss, "The Coming Change in Marketing: From Growthmanship to Shrinkmanship," *Advertising Age*, Vol. 42 (February 1, 1971), p. 63.

[18] Robert J. Lavidge, "The Growing Responsibilities of Marketing," JOURNAL OF MARKETING, Vol. 34 (January, 1970), p. 28.

O. Pricing

43. Pricing a New Product

JOEL DEAN

New product pricing is important in two ways: it affects the amount of the product that will be sold; and it determines the amount of revenue that will be received for a given quantity of sales. If you set your price too high you will be likely to make too few sales to permit you to cover your overhead. If you set your price too low you may not be able to cover out-of-pocket costs and may face bankruptcy.

WHAT IS DIFFERENT ABOUT NEW PRODUCTS?

New products that are novel require a different pricing treatment than old products because they are distinctive; no one else sells quite the same thing. This distinctiveness is usually only temporary, however, as your product catches on, your competitors will try to take away your market by bringing out imitative substitutes. The speed with which your product loses its uniqueness will depend on a number of factors. Among these factors are the total sales potential, the investment required for rivals to manufacture and distribute the product, the strength of patent protection, and the alertness and power of competitors.

Although this process of competitive imitation is almost inevitable, the company that introduces the new product can use price as a means of slowing the speed of competitive imitation. Finding the "right' price is not easy, however. New products are hard to price correctly.

◆ SOURCE: Reprinted by permission from *The Controller*, Vol. 23, No. 4, April 1955, pp. 163–165.

This is true both because past experience is no sure guide as to how the market will react to any given price, and because competing products are usually significantly different in nature or quality.

In setting a price on a new product you will want to have three objectives in mind: (1) getting the product accepted, (2) maintaining your market in the face of growing competition, (3) producing profits. Your pricing policy cannot be said to be successful unless you can achieve all three of these objectives.

WHAT ARE YOUR CHOICES AS TO POLICY?

Broadly speaking, the strategy in pricing a new product comes down to a choice between (1) "skimming" pricing, and (2) "penetration" pricing. There are a number of intermediate positions, but the issues are made clearer when the two extremes are compared.

Skimming Pricing. For products that represent a drastic departure from accepted ways of performing a service or filling a demand, a strategy of high prices coupled with large promotional expenditures in the early stages of market development (and lower prices at later stages) has frequently proven successful. This is known as a skimming price policy.

There are four main reasons why this kind of skimming price policy is attractive for new and distinctive products: *First*, the quantity of the product that you can sell is likely to be less affected by price in the early stages than it will be when the product is full-grown and imitation has had time to take effect. This is the period when pure salesmanship can have the greatest effect on sales. *Second,* a skimming price policy takes the cream of the market at a high price before attempting to penetrate the more price-sensitive sections of the market. This means that you can get more money from those who don't care how much they pay, while building up experience to hit the big mass market with tempting prices. *Third,* this can be a way to feel out the demand. It is frequently easier to start out with a high "refusal" price and reduce it later on when the facts of product demand make themselves known than it is to set a low price initially and then boost the price to cover unforeseen costs or exploit a popular product. *Fourth,* high prices will frequently produce a greater dollar volume of sales in the early stages of market development than a policy of low initial prices. If this is the case, skimming pricing will provide you with funds for financing expansion into the big-volume sectors of your market.

A skimming-price policy is not always the answer to your problem, however. High initial prices may safeguard profits during the early stages of product introduction, but they may also prevent quick sales to the many buyers upon whom you must rely to give you a mass market. The alternative is to use low prices as an entering wedge to get into mass markets early. This is known as penetration pricing.

Penetration Pricing. This approach is likely to be desirable under the following conditions: *First,* when the quantity of product sold is highly sensitive to price, even in the early stages of introduction. *Second,* when you can achieve substantial economics in unit cost and effectiveness of manufacturing and distributing the product by operating at large volumes. *Third,* when your product is faced by threats of strong potential competition, very soon after introduction. *Fourth,* when there is no "elite" market—that is, a body of buyers who are willing to pay a much higher price in order to obtain the latest and best.

The decision to price so as to penetrate a broad market can be made at any stage in the product's life cycle, but you should be sure to examine this pricing strategy before your new product is marketed at all. This possibility certainly should be explored as soon as your product has established an elite market. Sometimes a product can be rescued from a premature death by adoption of penetration price policy after the cream of the market has been skimmed.

The ease and speed with which competitors can bring out substitute products is probably the most important single consideration in your choice between skimming and penetration pricing at the time you introduce your new product. For products whose market potential looks big, a policy of low initial prices ("stay-out pricing") makes sense, because the big multiple-produce manufacturers are attracted by mass markets. If you set your price low enough to begin with, your large competitor may not feel it worth his while to make a big production and distribution investment for slim profit margins. In any event, you should appraise the competitive situation very carefully for each new product before you decide on your pricing strategy.

WHAT SHOULD YOU LOOK AT IN SETTING A PRICE?

When you have decided on your basic pricing strategy you can turn to the task of putting a dollars-and-cents price tag on your new product. In order to do this you should look at at least five important factors: (1) potential and probable demand for your product, (2) cost of making and selling the product, (3) market targets, (4) promotional strategy, and (5) suitable channels of distribution.

DEMAND

The first step in estimating market demand is to find out whether or not the product will set at all—assuming that the price is set within the competitive range. That is, you should find out whether or not this product fulfills a real need, and whether enough potential customers are dissatisfied with their present means of filling that need. To do this, you should make some estimate of the total potential market for the new product and all its competing substitutes and then estimate the portion of this potential that your product is likely to get.

Next, you should determine the competitive range of price. This will be easier when substitutes are relatively close or when customers are familiar with the cost and quality of substitutes and act rationally on the basis of performance.

The next step is to try to guess the probable sales volume at two or three possible prices within the price range. The best way to do this is by controlled experiments; next best is by a close estimation of buyers' alternatives in the light of market preference.

Finally, you should consider the possibility of retaliation by manufacturers of displaced substitutes. If your new product hits any one of your competitors hard enough, you may be faced with price retaliation. The limit to this price cutting is set by the out-of-pocket cost of the price-cutting competitors. Therefore, some knowledge of the out-of-pocket cost of making competing products will be helpful in estimating the probable effects of a particular price.

COSTS

Before going ahead with your new product, you should estimate its effect on your investment, your costs, and your profits. First you should estimate the added investment necessary to manufacture and distribute the new product. This investment estimate should include estimates of increased working capital that will be required at various sales volumes. Then you should estimate the added costs of manufacturing and selling the product at various possible sales volumes. The way to estimate costs is to calculate what your total costs would be with and without the new product; the difference should be assigned to the new product. Allocations of overheads that you are already incurring should not be assigned to the new product because they will be the same whether or not you go ahead with the addition to your product line.

In building up your two sets of cost and investment figures—one showing the situation *without* the new product, and the other showing the contrasting situation *with* the new product added to your line—be sure to take into account *all* pertinent items. It often happens that companies which lose money on new products have run into trouble because of unanticipated costs or investment requirements which have absorbed most of or all the profits realizable from the new idea.

New product costs may be segregated into half a dozen main categories: direct labor, materials and supplies for production, components purchased outside, special equipment (such as jigs, dies, fixtures and other tools), plant overhead, and sales expenses.

Direct Labor. Methods of estimating direct labor may be built up in one of three ways: (1) You can compare each operation on each component with accumulated historical data, from your files, on similar operations for similar components, (2) you can develop a mockup of the proposed work-place layout and actually time an operator who performs a series of manufacturing operations, simulated as accurately as possible, (3) you can apply one of several systems of predetermined, basic-motion times which are currently available from private sources.

Make certain, however, that you include any added time used for setup work, or needed to take the item from its transportation container, perform the operations, and return the item again to its transportation container. When the total direct labor time is determined multiply it by the appropriate labor rates.

Materials and Supplies for Production. In developing reliable cost figures for materials and supplies make a methodical list of all requirements. Having listed everything in an organized fashion, you can enter the specifications and costs on a manufactured-component estimate form. Remember to include any extra costs which may be incurred as a result of requirements for particular length, widths, qualities, or degrees of finish. Allowances for scrap should also be made as accurately as possible and corrected by applying a salvage factor if the scrap can be sold or reused.

Components Purchased Outside. Place your specification for parts purchased from other concerns with more than one reliable supplier and get competitive bids for the work. But in addition to price considerations be sure to give proper weight to the reputation and qualification of each potential producer. Moreover, if you use a substantial volume of purchased parts you may want to use a "plus" factor above the cost of the components themselves to cover your expenses involved in receiving, storing, and handling the items.

Special Equipment. Take careful precautions against making a faulty analysis of your expense and investment in special jigs, dies, fixtures, and other tools which you will need to produce the new product. To avoid trouble in this area make a table showing all cases where special equipment will be needed. The actual estimating of the costs of such equipment is best done by a qualified tool shop—your own if you have one or an outside organization. Here again, competitive bidding is an excellent protection on price. Do not include costs of routine inspection, service, and repair; these are properly charged to plant overhead.

Plant Overhead. The overhead item may

be estimated as a given percentage of direct labor, machine utilization, or some other factor determined by your accountants to be the most sensible basis. In this way you can allocate satisfactorily charges for administration and supervision, for occupancy, and for indirect service related to producing the new product. Overhead allocations may be set up for a department, a production center, or even, in some cases, for a particular machine. In calculating plant overhead make certain that in setting up your cost controls, your accountants have not overlooked any proper indirect special charges which will have to be incurred because of the new product.

Sales Expenses. Your estimates of sales revenue at various potential volumes can now be compared with your estimates of added costs at those volumes. The difference will be the added profits of introducing the new product. Although the costs themselves probably should not be used as a basis for setting price, you should not go into any venture that will not produce for you a rate-of-return on the added investment required that is adequate to compensate for the added risk and still be at least as high as the return you could get by investing your money elsewhere. If no price that you set will provide enough revenue to produce an adequate profit over your added costs, then you should either drop the venture, try to cut costs, or wait for a more favorable time to introduce the product.

MARKETING TARGETS

Assuming that the estimates of market demand and of cost and investment have been made and that the profit picture looks sufficiently rosy, you are now in a position to set up some basic goals and programs. A decision must first be made about market targets—that is, what market share or sales volume should be aimed at? Among other factors, you should probably consider what effect it will have upon investment requirements, whether or not your existing organization can handle the new product, how it fits in with the rest of your present product line, and so forth. These decisions should be made after a cold-blooded survey of the nature of your new product and of your company's organization and manufacturing and distributive facilities.

PROMOTION

Closely related to the question of market targets is the design of promotional strategy. As an innovator, you must not only sell your product, but frequently you must also make people recognize their need for this kind of product. Your problem here is to determine the best way of "creating a market." You must determine the nature of the market and the type of appeal that will sell the product and secure prompt acceptance by potential buyers And you should also estimate how much it will cost you to achieve this goal.

CHANNELS OF DISTRIBUTION

Frequently, there is some latitude in your choice of channels of distribution. This choice should be consistent with your strategy for initial pricing and for promotional outlays. Penetration pricing and explosive promotion calls for distribution channels that promptly make the product broadly available. Otherwise you waste advertising or stymie mass-market pricing. Distribution policy also concerns the role you wish the dealer to play in pushing your product, the margins you must pay him to introduce this action and the amount of protection of territory and of inventory required to do so.

YOUR DECISION

These are the factors you should look for in setting a price. Estimating these factors shrewdly and objectively requires specialized training and experience. Good estimates will make your pricing more realistic and successful. But pricing cannot be established by formula. Combining these factors into a pricing policy requires judgment. In the last analysis you must pull all the estimates of the experts together and arrive at your own decision. You will want to make sure that the pricing analysis is guided by sound principles and that the activities of your specialists are all geared toward the same end—devising a sound, effective marketing and promotional program in conjunction with a price that will meet your objectives of market acceptance, competitive strength, and profits.

44. Price Policies and Theory

EDWARD R. HAWKINS

Although the theory of monopolistic competition is now almost twenty years old it remains virtually unused by marketing students, even those who are attempting to develop theory in marketing. In particular, "marketing price policies" are still treated as though they have no relation to economic theory of any sort. In the leading marketing text books there are sections describing such pricing policies as "odd prices," "customary prices," "price lining," "psychological prices," etc.[1] These are presented as descriptions of market behavior, presumably discovered by marketing specialists and unknown to economists. Even the one marketing text that explains the basic pricing formula under conditions of monopolistic competition fails to use it in the discussion of price policies.[2] Since text book writers treat the subject in this way it is not surprising that practitioners writing on pricing do not attempt to relate their policies to economic theory.[3]

It is the purpose of this article to show that these price policies are special cases of the general theory of monopolistic competition. Perhaps clarification of this point will serve to narrow the gap between the economic and marketing conceptions of pricing, and to systematize the discussions of price policies in marketing literature.

The thesis is that each of the familiar price policies represents an estimate of the nature of the demand curve facing the seller. It is not possible, on the basis of available evidence, to generalize on the validity of these estimates in various situations. The point merely is that a seller using one of these policies is implicitly assuming a particular demand curve. In the following sections various price policies are discussed in these terms, after a brief review of the general theory of pricing which is basic to all of the policies discussed.

---

[1] R. S. Vaile, E. T. Grether, and Reavis Cox, *Marketing in the American Economy* (New York: Ronald Press, 1952), ch. 22; E. A. Duddy and D. A. Revzan, *Marketing* (New York: McGraw-Hill, 2nd ed. 1953), ch. 29; P. D. Converse, H. W. Huegy, and R. V. Mitchell, *Elements of Marketing* (New York: Prentice-Hall, 5th ed. 1952) ch. 10; H. H. Maynard and T. N. Beckman, *Principles of Marketing* (New York: Ronald Press, 5th ed. 1952) ch. 35, 36; R. S. Alexander, F. M. Surface, R. E. Elder, and Wroe Alderson, *Marketing* (Boston: Ginn, 1940) ch. 16. Since these policies are fully described in marketing texts the explanation of them in this article will be brief. The attempt, rather, is to express the policies in terms of demand curves in order that the relationship to the theory of monopolistic competition may be seen.

◆ SOURCE: Reprinted by permission from the *Journal of Marketing* (National Quarterly Publication of the American Marketing Association), Vol. 18, No. 3, January 1954, pp. 233–240.

[2] Charles F. Phillips and Delbert J. Duncan, *Marketing, Principles and Methods* (Chicago: Richard D. Irwin, rev. ed. 1952), ch. 29, 30, 31.
[3] For example, Oswald Knauth, "Considerations in the Setting of Retail Prices," *Journal of Marketing*, Vol. 14, No. 1, July 1949, pp. 1–12; Q. Forrest Walker, "Some Principles of Department Store Pricing," *Journal of Marketing*, Vol. 14, No. 4, April 1950, pp. 529–537.

THE GENERAL THEORY OF PRICING

The theory of correct pricing under conditions of monopolistic competition, as developed by Chamberlin and Robinson is illustrated in Fig. 1. Each seller with some degree of monopoly created by product differentiation has his own negatively-inclined average revenue curve, AR. From this he derives the marginal revenue curve MR, and determines his price by the intersection of MR and MC, his marginal cost. Marginal cost can be derived from either average cost AC, or average variable cost AVC, since it would be the same in either case. In practical terms this means that for correct pricing the seller does not need to allocate overhead cost to individual items. For that matter, he does not even need to compute MR and MC, for the same correct price can be derived from AR and AVC by maximizing the total of the spread between them multiplied by the volume.

An alternative solution which may be more understandable to business men can be obtained from break-even charts. The customary break-even chart is deficient for pricing purposes because it is based on only one price and reveals nothing but the quantity that would have to be sold at that price in order to break even. A modification can be devised that remedies this shortcoming of the break-even chart, and even has some advantages over the MC-MR formula. Fig. 2 shows such a chart, in which a number of different total revenue (TR) curves are drawn, indicating the total revenue that would result at various volumes at different prices. On each such TR curve a point can be estimated showing the sales volume that would actu-

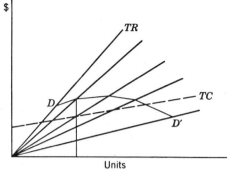

FIGURE 2.

ally be obtained at that price. If these points are connected a type of demand curve results (DD'), indicating total revenue rather than average revenue as in the usual demand curve.[4] The objective of correct pricing is to maximize the vertical distance between DD' and the TC (total cost) curve. This formulation has an advantage over the MC-MR one in that in addition to indicating the correct price and volume it also shows total cost, total revenue, and total net profit. It may also be more acceptable to business men and engineers who are accustomed to break-even charts.

In the following discussion of marketing price policies, however, the AR curve will be used because it more clearly illustrates the points made.

MARKETING PRICE POLICIES

Odd Prices

The term "odd prices" is used in two ways in marketing literature, one refers to a price ending in an odd number while the other means a price just under a round number. If a seller sets his prices according to the first concept it means that he believes his AR curve is like the one shown in Fig. 3.[5] In this

[4] Cf. Joel Dean, *Managerial Economics* (New York: Prentice-Hall, 1951), p. 405. Dean shows a total revenue curve without, however, indicating its relationship to break-even charts.

[5] This curve might be regarded as discontinuous, especially since the difference between points is only one cent. But it is customary to draw demand curves as continuous even though, as Chamberlin has said, *any* demand curve could be split into segments. E. H. Chamberlin, "Comments," *Quarterly Journal of Economics,* Vol. 64,

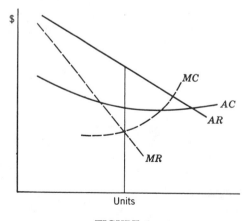

FIGURE 1.

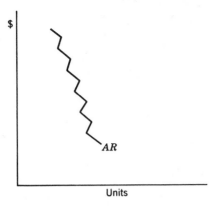

FIGURE 3.

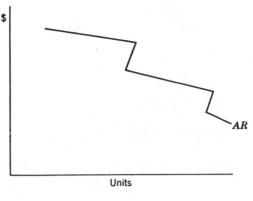

FIGURE 4.

case each price ending in an odd number will produce a greater volume of sales than the next lower even-numbered price. Many sellers appear to believe this is true, although the only large-scale test ever reported was inconclusive.[6]

The second concept of odd-pricing implies an *AR* curve like the one shown in Fig. 4, with critical points at prices such as $1, $5, and $10.[7] The presumption is that

sales will be substantially greater at prices just under these critical points, whether ending in an odd or even number.

Psychological Prices

Some of the marketing text books give the name of "psychological pricing" to policies quite similar to the one just discussed. It has been found in some pricing experiments that

November 1934, p. 135; and A. J. Nichol, although drawing important conclusions from the supposed discontinuity of certain demand curves, states the curves would be continuous if it were feasible to change prices by small amounts. A. J. Nichol, "The Influence of Marginal Buyers on Monopolistic Competition," *Quarterly Journal of Economics*, Vol. 64, November 1934, footnote 7, p. 126. Henry Smith believes that discontinuous demand curves might result from such heavy advertising of a certain price that the product would be unsalable at any other price. *Cf.* "Discontinuous Demand Curves and Monopolistic Competition: A Special Case," *Quarterly Journal of Economics*, Vol. 64, May 1935, pp. 542–550. This would not seem to be a very common case, however, since marketing literature reveals heavily advertised products selling at various prices.

[6] Eli Ginsberg, "Customary Prices," *American Economic Review*, Vol. 26, No. 2, 1936, p. 296. Some economists doubt the validity of positively-inclined segments of demand curves, believing either (a) that the case could happen only if consumers regard price as one of the qualities of the product, thus making it improper to show these "different" products on one demand curve, or (b) that it simply does not happen that consumers will buy more of a product at a higher price than they will at a lower one. In regard to the first view, the important thing for purposes of the seller's pricing policy is the shape of the

AR curve for what *he* knows is the same product. And while he may be interested in the psychology lying behind the consumer's demand curve he is not committed to the belief that it must be capable of explanation in terms of indifference curves. In regard to the second point, many marketing writers have commented on the view that a higher price will sometimes sell more than a lower one. For example, Phillips and Duncan say it may be possible to sell a greater number of a 15-cent item at 19 cents than at 15 cents (*op. cit.*, p. 656). Q. Forrest Walker (*loc. cit.*), suggests that 98 cents may sell better than 89 cents. Maynard and Beckman state. "It is said that more articles can be sold at 17 cents than at 14 cents." (*op. cit.*, p. 656). Converse and Huegy say "Some sellers feel that odd prices are better than even prices; others, that it makes little difference" (*op. cit.*, p. 209). A New England supermarket chain reports that their meat prices never end in the figure "1," because their price tests show they can sell more at a price ending in "3." And a U.S. Department of Commerce study reports a price of 79 cents selling more than a price of 75 cents, and a case where silk underwear sold more readily at $2 or $5 than at $1.95 or $4.95 respectively. *Cf.* F. M. Bernfield, "Time for Businessmen to Check Pricing Policies," *Domestic Commerce*, Vol. 35, March 1947, p. 20.

[7] This idea is applied even to very high prices. Thus, an automobile may be sold at $1995 rather than at $2,000.

a change of price over a certain range has little effect until some critical point is reached. If there are a number of such critical points for a given commodity the AR curve would look like the one in Fig. 5, resembling a series of steps. This differs from the concept of odd pricing in that the curve does not necessarily have any segments positively inclined, and the critical points are not located at each round number but only at the prices psychologically important to buyers. Pricing tests at Macy's have disclosed such step-shaped AR curves.[8]

Customary Prices

Another pricing policy usually described as though it has no relationship to theory is the one using "customary prices." This is most frequently associated with the five-cent candy bar, chewing gum, soft drink, or subway fare. The chain stores have experimented, apparently successfully, with combination cut prices on such items, and inflation has brought about upward changes in others. In the main, however, the five-cent price on items for which it has been customary has persisted. To the extent that the policy is correct it merely means that the AR curve is like the one shown in Fig. 6, with a kink at the customary price.[9]

Pricing at the Market

Fig. 6 also illustrates the estimate of the AR curve which results in a policy of "pricing at the market." A firm that adopts this policy believes that a price above those of competitors would curtail sales sharply, while a lower price would not significantly increase them. This pricing policy is one of the most common, possibly because ignorance of the AR curve suggests that the safest policy is to imitate competitors.

---

[8] Oswald Knauth, "Some Reflections on Retail Prices," in *Economic Essays in Honor of Wesley Clair Mitchell* (New York: Columbia University Press, 1935), pp. 203–4. Although these tests involved *changes* in price, the important thing is that changes that reduced price below the critical points produced much greater increases in sales than changes that did not. In other words, the demand curve had very different elasticities at different points.

[9] Of course where the policy of customary pricing is not correct, as may be true in some of the chainstore cases mentioned, the demand curve would be quite elastic below the customary price.

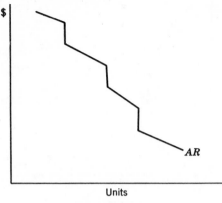

FIGURE 5.

The policy of pricing at the market is also designed to avoid price competition and price wars. But a rule-of-thumb policy is not the correct solution to this problem, for the theory of monopolistic competition provides the basis for the proper calculation. What is required is an estimate of the AR curve after competitors have made whatever response they would make to the firm's pricing moves. In Fig. 7 this is indicated by AR_2, while AR is the customary curve based on an assumption of "all other things remaining the same." While it is very difficult for a seller to guess what competitors will do, the theory of correct oligopoly pricing along the AR_2 curve is quite clear, and does not necessarily call for "pricing at the market."

Prestige Pricing

It has often been pointed out in marketing literature that many customers judge quality by price. In such cases sales would be less at low prices than at high ones. This idea was the original legal basis for Fair Trade laws.

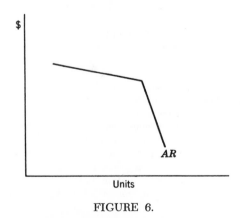

FIGURE 6.

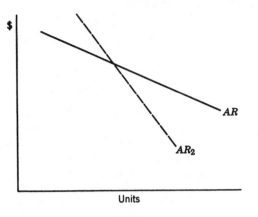

FIGURE 7.

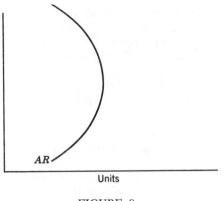

FIGURE 8.

While most manufacturers appear to be less impressed by this possibility than retailers are, there have been cases reported in which low prices led to reduced sales. The shape of the AR curve illustrating this situation has already been indicated in economic literature.[10] See Fig. 8.

Price Lining

Many retailers when questioned about their pricing policies seem to feel they have avoided the problem entirely by adopting customary price "lines." Once the lines are decided upon, prices may be held constant over long periods of time; changes in market conditions are met by adjustments in the quality of the merchandise.

While this policy does not require pricing decisions, except initially and in case of special sales, it does present the seller with exactly the same choice as a variable price policy does in respect to the question of whether to equate marginal cost and marginal revenue, or to use a customary per cent of markup. This decision is made with reference to the prices paid for merchandise

[10] F. R. Fairchild, E. S. Furniss, and N. S. Buck, *Elementary Economics* (New York: Macmillan, 1939), 4th ed., Vol. 1, p. 166. Converse and Huegy cite an instance of aspirin being tried out at different prices, 19¢, 29¢, 39¢, and 49¢, with the highest sales results at 49¢ (*op. cit.*, p. 207). And they comment on this reason for positively inclined demand curves. "Thus merchandise can be priced too low as well as too high. Customers may fear that the low price it cannot be of good quality, and will actually buy more at a somewhat higher price than they would at a lower price" (p. 206).

rather than the prices at which it will be sold. Although manufacturers and wholesalers dealing in types of merchandise which is customarily price-lined at retail usually tailor their own prices to fit the retail prices, the retailer does have some choice in regard to the quality of goods he buys. Presumably, the more he pays the more he can sell, at any given price line. That is, the lower his per cent of markup the higher his sales volume should be. Fig. 9 illustrates this situation, where P is the established price at retail, and CG shows the various quantities that could be sold at different costs of goods to the retailer. The retailer should equate his marginal cost with marginal revenue (the price), paying NM for the goods and selling quantity OM. If instead he buys at a price that provides a customary or arbitrary per cent of markup it would be purely accidental if he would obtain the maximum gross margin.

Since there are few variable costs associated with the sale of most items at retail, except the cost of goods, the retailer's aim in

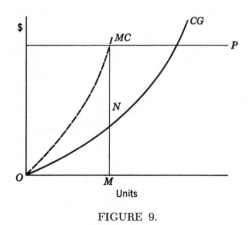

FIGURE 9.

general should be simply to maximize his gross margin dollars. If, however, other variable costs are significant they can be added to the cost of goods and a calculation made of the average variable costs, from which marginal cost can be computed. In Fig. 9 the curve *CG* would merely be replaced by an *AVC* curve.

Resale Price Maintenance

Another situation in which the retailer feels he has no pricing problem is when the manufacturer maintains resale prices by means of Fair Trade contracts. Even here, however, the retailer may find it advantageous to sell above the Fair Trade price in some cases, in states where the Fair Trade laws call for minimum rather than specified prices. In any case the retailer must decide whether to equate marginal cost and marginal revenue or to insist upon a customary per cent of markup. If he selects the latter he may refuse to handle, or to push, many low markup items which would actually be very profitable to him.

The price policy appropriate for a manufacturer using resale price maintenance is illustrated in Fig. 10. At any given retail price *P*, which he may set, he will have an *AR* curve determined by the retailers' attitudes towards the amount of markup resulting from the price at which he sells to them. At low markups some dealers will refuse to handle the item, and others will hide it under the counter. At relatively high markups dealers will push the item and will be able to sell more than consumers would otherwise take at the given retail price. The manufacturer should calculate his optimum price by computing *MR* from this *AR* curve and equating this with his *MC*. He should do this with the *AR* curve associated with each

retail price and then select the combination of retail and wholesale prices that will result in maximum profit for him.[11]

Quantity Discounts

Quantity discounts are usually described in marketing texts, and explained in terms of the lower unit cost of handling large orders, or simply the desire to increase sales volume. Economic analysis of the quantity discount policy would focus on the theory of price discrimination. With reference to this theory, a quantity discount schedule, open to all buyers, is a very rough device for price discrimination, and should not be used if the laws allowed freedom of discrimination. Instead, the seller should estimate the demand curve of each buyer, and offer each the price (or prices) that would maximize the seller's revenue in respect to that buyer.[12] This might well mean lower prices for some small buyers than for some large ones, depending on the elasticity of their demand curves.

Fig. 11 illustrates a case in which the large buyer's demand curve is inelastic in the significant range, while the small buyer's curve is quite elastic. It would therefore be foolish to offer them a quantity discount schedule that would give the large buyer lower prices than the small one. The large buyer would take almost as large a quantity at high prices as at low ones, while the small buyer will not. This may not be a usual situation, but it is a possible one, and indicates that the seller should consider the elasticities of demand rather than adopt an arbitrary discount schedule.

The correct theory of price discrimination, where each buyer is to be offered a different price, has been outlined by Mrs. Robinson.[13] It indicates that the seller should equate the marginal revenue from each buyer with the marginal cost of the entire output.

Different costs of selling to different buyers can be taken into account by computing the

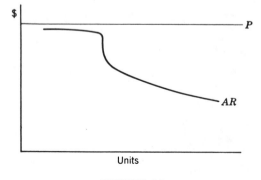

Units

FIGURE 10.

[11] For a fuller discussion see E. R. Hawkins, "Vertical Price Relationships," ch. 11 in Reavis Cox and Wroe Alderson (ed.), *Theory in Marketing* (Chicago: Richard D. Irwin, 1950).

[12] If the buyer is in a monopsonistic position he does not have a demand curve in the Marshallian sense, but it is possible to estimate how he will respond to various price offers.

[13] Joan Robinson, *The Economics of Imperfect Competition* (London: Macmillan, 1933), p. 182.

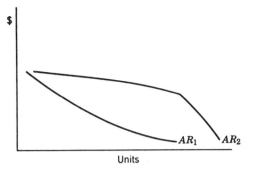

FIGURE 11.

AR curves as *net* average revenue curves, after deduction of the variable costs associated with the particular sales. And it would still be possible that the large buyer should be charged a higher price than the small one.

Some economists have used the term "quantity discount" to refer to a situation, unusual in marketing practice, in which each buyer is offered a quantity discount scale tailored to his own demand curve.[14] Of course a "quantity discount" of this kind would usually produce more net profit for the seller than a single price to each buyer, since it is an approach toward the maximum profit situation of perfect price discrimination, in which each buyer would be charged the highest price he would be willing to pay for each successive unit he bought. A seller may be attempting to gain some of the advantages of this type of pricing when he constructs a general quantity discount schedule with an eye to its effects on certain large buyers. In so doing, he would have to take care that the gain would not be cancelled by the adverse effect of the schedule of his net profits from other buyers.

Geographic Pricing

While some economists have long been concerned with the geographic aspects of pricing, and this interest has recently been spreading, on the whole marketing specialists and economic geographers have regarded the spatial aspects of economics as their own province. Unfortunately they have developed theories which do not include the essential economic aspects of the problem. Fig. 11 may be used to illustrate some of the problems of geographic pricing. If the AR curve of each buyer is taken as a *net* average revenue curve, after deduction of transportation costs, then it is clear that the nearer buyer should not necessarily be given the lower delivered price. The elasticity of each buyer's demand curve is the important factor which should be considered. As has been indicated by Mrs. Robinson, the correct net price to each buyer would equate the seller's marginal revenue with the marginal cost of his entire output.[15]

While the Robinson-Patman Act does not permit the free price discrimination that would maximize the seller's profit, it does allow some discretion in pricing. The seller is not permitted to employ price differentials greater than his cost differentials; but he is free to give discounts less than the amount of cost saving to him. Moreover, he is allowed some discretion to employ price differentials when the buyers are not in competition with each other, or where he himself is "meeting competition." He may also, of course, discriminate by selling slightly different products, under different brand names.

CONCLUSION

The discrepancy between economic theory and actual pricing policies, as observed by marketing specialists, is more apparent than real. Most of the pricing behavior reported by marketing students is quite consistent with the general theory of monopolistic competition, and can be integrated with that theory. A considerable gain can be made on both sides if this integration is accomplished. Economists need to know more about the pricing policies actually used by businessmen. On the other hand, marketing students can understand these policies better if they appreciate the theoretical basis for them. Most of the "price policies" described by marketing specialists are merely special cases of the general theory of monopolistic competition. If so regarded, not only would clarification result, but perhaps additional insight would be gained regarding the advantages and disadvantages of each policy, and the situations to which they are appropriate.

---

[14] James M. Buchanan, "The Theory of Monopolistic Quantity Discounts," *Review of Economic Studies*, Vol. 20, No. 3, 1952–1953.

[15] Joan Robinson, *loc. cit.*

P. Market Communications

45. *The Concept of the Marketing Mix*

NEIL H. BORDEN

I have always found it interesting to observe how an apt or colorful term may catch on, gain wide usage, and help to further understanding of a concept that has already been expressed in less appealing and communicative terms. Such has been true of the phrase "marketing mix," which I began to use in my teaching and writing some 15 years ago. In a relatively short time it has come to have wide usage. This note tells of the evolution of the marketing mix concept.

The phrase was suggested to me by a paragraph in a research bulletin on the management of marketing costs, written by my associate, Professor James Culliton (1948). In this study of manufacturers' marketing costs he described the business executive as a

"decider," an "artist—a "mixer of ingredients," who sometimes follows a recipe prepared by others, sometimes prepares his own recipe as he goes along, sometimes adapts a recipe to the ingredients immediately available, and sometimes experiments with or invents ingredients no one else has tried.

I liked his idea of calling a marketing executive a "mixer of ingredients," one who is constantly engaged in fashioning creatively a mix of marketing procedures and policies in his efforts to produce a profitable enterprise.

For many years previous to Culliton's cost study the wide variations in the procedures and policies employed by managements of

manufacturing firms in their marketing programs and the correspondingly wide variation in the costs of these marketing functions, which Culliton aptly ascribed to the varied "mixing of ingredients," had become increasingly evident as we had gathered marketing cases at the Harvard Business School. The marked differences in the patterns or formulae of the marketing programs not only were evident through facts disclosed in case histories, but also were reflected clearly in the figures of a cost study of food manufacturers made by the Harvard Bureau of Business Research in 1929. The primary objective of this study was to determine common figures of expenses for various marketing functions among food manufacturing companies, similar to the common cost figures which had been determined in previous years for various kinds of retail and wholesale businesses. In this manufacturer's study we were unable, however, with the data gathered to determine common expense figures that had much significance as standards by which to guide management, such as had been possible in the studies of retail and wholesale trades, where the methods of operation tended toward uniformity. Instead, among food manufacturers the ratios of sales devoted to the various functions of marketing such as advertising, personal selling, packaging, and so on, were found to be widely divergent, no matter how we grouped our respondents. Each respondent gave data that tended to uniqueness.

Culliton's study of marketing costs in 1947-48 was a second effort to find out, among other objectives, whether a bigger sample and a more careful classification of companies would

◆ SOURCE: Reprinted by permission from the *Journal of Advertising Research*, Vol. 4, No. 2, June 1964, pp. 2–7. Copyright © (1964), by the Advertising Research Foundation.

produce evidence of operating uniformities that would give helpful common expense figures. But the result was the same as in our early study: there was wide diversity in cost ratios among any classifications of firms which were set up, and no common figures were found that had much value. This was true whether companies were grouped according to similarity in product lines, amount of sales, territorial extent of operations, or other bases of classification.

Relatively early in my study of advertising, it had become evident that understanding of advertising usage by manufacturers in any case had to come from an analysis of advertising's place as one element in the total marketing program of the firm. I came to realize that it is essential always to ask: what overall marketing strategy has been or might be employed to bring about a profitable operation in light of the circumstances faced by the management? What combination of marketing procedures and policies has been or might be adopted to bring about desired behavior of trade and consumers at costs that will permit a profit? Specifically, how can advertising, personal selling, pricing, packaging, channels, warehousing, and the other elements of a marketing program be manipulated and fitted together in a way that will give a profitable operation? In short, I saw that every advertising management case called for a consideration of the strategy to be adopted for the total marketing program, with advertising recognized as only one element whose form and extent depended on its careful adjustment to the other parts of the program.

The soundness of this viewpoint was supported by case histories throughout my volume, *The Economic Effects of Advertising* (Borden, 1942). In the chapters devoted to the utilization of advertising by business, I had pointed out the innumerable combinations of marketing methods and policies that might be adopted by a manager in arriving at a marketing plan. For instance, in the area of branding, he might elect to adopt an individualized brand or a family brand. Or he might decide to sell his product unbranded or under private label. Any decision in the area of brand policy in turn has immediate implications that bear on his selection of channels of distribution, sales force methods, packaging, promotional procedure, and advertising. Throughout the volume the case materials cited show that the way in which any marketing function is de-

signed and the burden placed upon the function are determined largely by the overall marketing strategy adopted by managements to meet the market conditions under which they operate. The forces met by different firms vary widely. Accordingly, the programs fashioned differ widely.

Regarding advertising, which was the function under focus in the ecomonic effects volume, I said at one point:

In all the above illustrative situations it should be recognized that advertising is not an operating method to be considered as something apart, as something whose profit value is to be judged alone. An able management does not ask, "Shall we use or not use advertising," without consideration of the product and of other management procedures to be employed. Rather the question is always one of finding a management formula giving advertising its due place in the combination of manufacturing methods, product form, pricing, promotion and selling methods, and distribution methods. As previously pointed out different formulae, i.e., different combinations of methods, may be profitably employed by competing manufacturers.

From the above it can be seen why Culliton's description of a marketing manager as a "mixer of ingredients" immediately appealed to me as an apt and easily understandable phrase, far better than my previous references to the marketing man as an empiricist seeking in any situation to devise a profitable "pattern" or "formula" of marketing operations from among the many procedures and policies that were open to him. If he was a "mixer of ingredients," what he designed was a "marketing mix."

It was logical to proceed from a realization of the existence of a variety of "marketing mixes" to the development of a concept that would comprehend not only this variety, but also the market forces that cause managements to produce a variety of mixes. It is the problems raised by these forces that lead marketing managers to exercise their wits in devising mixes or programs which they hope will give a profitable business operation.

To portray this broadened concept in a visual presentation requires merely:

1. a list of the important elements or ingredients that make up marketing programs.

2. a list of the forces that bear on the marketing operation of a firm and to which the

marketing manager must adjust in his search for a mix or program that can be successful.

The list of elements of the marketing mix in such a visual presentation can be long or short, depending on how far one wishes to go in his classification and subclassification of the marketing procedures and policies with which marketing managements deal when devising marketing programs. The list of elements which I have employed in my teaching and consulting work covers the principal areas of marketing activities which call for management decisions as revealed by case histories. I realize others might build a different list. Mine is as follows:

Elements of the Marketing Mix for Manufacturers

1. *Product Planning*—policies and procedures relating to:

    (a) Product lines to be offered—qualities, design, etc.

    (b) Markets to sell: whom, where, when, and in what quantity.

    (c) New product policy—research and development program.

2. *Pricing*—policies and procedures relating to:

    (a) Price level to adopt.

    (b) Specific prices to adopt (odd-even, etc.).

    (c) Price policy, e.g., one-price or varying price, price maintenance, use of list prices, etc.

    (d) Margins to adopt—for company; for the trade.

3. *Branding*—policies and procedures relating to:

    (a) Selection of trade marks.

    (b) Brand policy—individualized or family brand.

    (c) Sale under private label or unbranded.

4. *Channels of Distribution*—policies and procedures relating to:

    (a) Channels to use between plant and consumer.

    (b) Degree of selectivity among wholesalers and retailers.

    (c) Efforts to gain cooperation of the trade.

5. *Personal Selling*—policies and procedures relating to:

    (a) Burden to be placed on personal selling and the methods to be employed in:

    (1) Manufacturer's organization.

    (2) Wholesale segment of the trade.

    (3) Retail segment of the trade.

6. *Advertising*—policies and procedures relating to:

    (a) Amount to spend—i.e., the burden to be placed on advertising.

    (b) Copy platform to adopt:

    (1) Product image desired.

    (2) Corporate image desired.

    (c) Mix of advertising: to the trade, through the trade; to consumers.

7. *Promotions*—policies and procedures relating to:

    (a) Burden to place on special selling plans or devices directed at or through the trade.

    (b) Form of these devices for consumer promotions, for trade promotions.

8. *Packaging*—policies and procedures relating to:

    (a) Formulation of package and label.

9. *Display*—policies and procedures relating to:

    (a) Burden to be put on display to help effect sale.

    (b) Methods to adopt to secure display.

10. *Servicing*—policies and procedures relating to:

    (a) Providing service needed.

11. *Physical Handling*—policies and procedures relating to:

    (a) Warehousing.

    (b) Transportation.

    (c) Inventories.

12. *Fact Finding and Analysis*—policies and procedures relating to:

    (a) Securing, analysis, and use of facts in marketing operations.

Also if one were to make a list of all the forces which managements weigh at one time or another when formulating their marketing mixes, it would be very long indeed, for the behavior of individuals and groups in all spheres of life have a bearing, first, on what goods and services are produced and consumed, and, second, on the procedures that may be employed in bringing about exchange of these goods and services. However, the important forces which bear on marketers, all arising from the behavior of individuals or groups, may readily be listed under four heads, namely the behavior of consumers, the trade, competitors, and government.

The outline below contains these four behavioral forces with notations of some of the important behavioral determinants with each force. These must be studied and understood by the marketer, if his marketing mix is to be successful. The great quest of marketing management is to understand the behavior of humans in response to the stimuli to which they are subjected. The skillful marketer is one who is a perceptive and practical psychologist and sociologist, who has keen insight into individual and group behavior, who can foresee changes in behavior that develop into a dynamic world, who has creative ability for building well knit programs because he has the capacity to visualize the probable response of consumers, trade, and competitors to his moves. His skill in forecasting response to his marketing moves should well be supplemented by a further skill in devising and using tests and measurements to check consumer or trade response to his program or parts thereof, for no marketer has so much prescience that he can proceed without empirical check.

Below, then, is the suggested outline of forces which govern the mixing of marketing elements. This list and that of the elements taken together provide a visual presentation of the concept of the marketing mix.

Market Forces Bearing on the Marketing Mix

1. *Consumers' Buying Behavior,* as determined by their:
   (a) Motivation in purchasing.
   (b) Buying habits.
   (c) Living habits.
   (d) Environment (present and future, as revealed by trends, for environment influences consumers' attitudes toward products and their use of them).
   (e) Buying power.
   (f) Number (i.e., how many).
2. *The Trade's Behavior*—wholesalers' and retailer's behavior, as influenced by:
   (a) Their motivations.
   (b) Their structure, practices, and attitudes.
   (c) Trends in structure and procedures that portend change.
3. *Competitors' Position and Behavior,* as influenced by:
   (a) Industry structure and the firm's relation thereto.
       (1) Size and strength of competitors.
   (2) Number of competitors and degree of industry concentration.
   (3) Indirect competition—i.e., from other products.
   (b) Relation of supply to demand—oversupply and undersupply.
   (c) Product choices offered consumers by the industry—i.e., quality, price, service.
   (d) Degree to which competitors complete on price vs. nonprice bases.
   (e) Competitors' motivations and attitudes—their likely response to the actions of other firms.
   (f) Trends technological and social, portending change in supply and demand.
4. *Governmental Behavior—Controls over Marketing:*
   (a) Regulations over products.
   (b) Regulations over pricing.
   (c) Regulations over competitive practices.
   (d) Regulations over advertising and promotion.

When building a marketing program to fit the needs of his firm, the marketing manager has to weigh the behavioral forces and then juggle marketing elements in his mix with a keen eye on the resources with which he has to work. His firm is but one small organism in a large universe of complex forces. His firm is only a part of an industry that is competing with many other industries. What does the firm have in terms of money, product line, organization, and reputation with which to work? The manager must device a mix of procedures that fit these resources. If his firm is small, he must judge the response of consumers, trade, and competition in light of his position and resources and the influence that he can exert in the market. He must look for special opportunities in product or method of operation. The small firm cannot employ the procedures of the big firm. Though he may sell the same kind of product as the big firm, his marketing strategy is likely to be widely different in many respects. Innumerable instances of this fact might be cited. For example, in the industrial goods field, small firms often seek to build sales on a limited and highly specialized line, whereas industry leaders seek patronage for full lines. Small firms often elect to go in for regional sales rather than attempt the national distribution practiced by larger companies. Again, the company of limited resources often elects to limit its production and sales to products whose potential is too small to attract the big fellows. Still again, companies with small resources in the cosmetic field not infrequently have set up introductory marketing programs employing aggressive personal selling and a "push" strategy with distribution limited to leading department stores. Their initially small advertising funds have been directed through these selected retail outlets, with the offering of the products and their story told over the signatures of the stores. The strategy has been to borrow kudos for their products from the leading stores' reputations and to gain a gradual radiation of distribution to smaller stores in all types of channels, such as often comes from the trade's follow-the-leader behavior. Only after resources have grown from mounting sales has a dense retail distribution been aggressively sought and a shift made to place the selling burden more and more on company-signed advertising.

The above strategy was employed for Toni products and Stoppette deodorant in their early marketing stages when the resources of their producers were limited (cf. case of Jules Montenier, Inc. in Borden and Marshall, 1959, pp. 498-518). In contrast, cosmetic manufacturers with large resources have generally followed a "pull" strategy for the introduction of new products, relying on heavy campaigns of advertising in a rapid succession of area introductions to induce a hoped-for, complete retail coverage from the start (cf. case of Bristol-Myers Company in Borden and Marshall, 1959, pp. 519-533). These introductory campaigns have been undertaken only after careful programs of product development and test marketing have given assurance that product and selling plans had high promise of success.

Many additional instances of the varying strategy employed by small versus large enterprises might be cited. But those given serve to illustrate the point that managements must fashion their mixes to fit their resources. Their objectives must be realistic.

LONG VS. SHORT TERM ASPECTS OF MARKETING MIX

The marketing mix of a firm in large part is the product of the evolution that comes from day-to-day marketing. At any time the mix represents the program that a management has evolved to meet the problems with which it is constantly faced in an ever changing, ever challenging market. There are continuous tactical maneuvers: a new product, aggressive promotion, or price change initiated by a competitor must be considered and met; the failure of the trade to provide adequate market coverage or display must be remedied; a faltering sales force must be reorganized and stimulated; a decline in sales share must be diagnosed and remedied; an advertising approach that has lost effectiveness must be replaced; a general business decline must be countered. All such problems call for a management's maintaining effective channels of information relative to its own operations and to the day-to-day behavior of consumers competitors, and the trade. Thus, we may observe that short range forces play a large part in the fashioning of the mix to be used at any time and in determining the allocation of expenditures among the various functional accounts of the operating statement.

But the overall strategy employed in a marketing mix is the product of longer range plans and procedures dictated in part by past empiricism and in part, if the management is a good one, by management foresight as to what needs to be done to keep the firm successful in a changing world. As the world has become more and more dynamic, blessed is that corporation which has managers who have foresight, who can study trends of all kinds—natural, economic, social, and technological—and, guided by these, devise long-range plans that give promise of keeping their corporations afloat and successful in the turbulent sea of market change. Accordingly, when we think of the marketing mix, we need to give particular heed today to devising a mix based on long-range planning that promises to fit the world of five or ten or more years hence. Provision for effective long-range planning in corporate organization and procedure has become more and more recognized as the earmark of good management in a world that has become increasingly subject to rapid change.

To cite an instance among American marketing organizations which has shown foresight in adjusting the marketing mix to meet social and economic change, I look upon Sears Roebuck and Company as an outstanding example. After building an unusually successful mail order business to meet the needs of a rural America, Sears management foresaw the need to depart from its marketing pattern as a mail order company catering primarily to farmers. The trend from a rural to an urban

United States was going on apace. The automobile and good roads promised to make town and city stores increasingly available to those who continued to be farmers. Relatively early, Sears launched a chain of stores across the land, each easily accessible by highway to both farmer and city resident, and with adequate parking space for customers. In time there followed the remarkable telephone and mail order plan directed at urban residents to make buying easy for Americans when congested city streets and highways made shopping increasingly distasteful. Similarly, in the areas of planning products which would meet the desires of consumers in a fast changing world, of shaping its servicing to meet the needs of a wide variety of mechanical products, of pricing procedures to meet the challenging competition that came with the advent of discount retailers, the Sears organization has shown a foresight, adaptability, and creative ability worthy of emulation. The amazing growth and profitability of the company attest to the foresight and skill of its management. Its history shows the wisdom of careful attention to market forces and their impending change in devising marketing mixes that may assure growth.

USE OF THE MARKETING MIX CONCEPT

Like many concepts, the marketing mix concept seems relatively simple, once it has been expressed. I know that before they were ever tagged with the nomenclature of "concept," the ideas involved were widely understood among marketers as a result of the growing knowledge about marketing and marketing procedures that came during the preceding half century. But I have found for myself that once the ideas were reduced to a formal statement with an accompanying visual presentation, the concept of the mix has proved a helpful device in teaching, in business problem solving, and, generally, as an aid to thinking about marketing. First of all, it is helpful in giving an answer to the question often raised as to "what is marketing?" A chart which shows the elements of the mix and the forces that bear on the mix helps to bring understanding of what marketing is. It helps to explain why in our dynamic world the thinking of management in all its functional areas must be oriented to the market.

In recent years I have kept an abbreviated chart showing the elements and the forces of the marketing mix in front of my classes at all times. In case discussion it has proved a handy device by which to raise queries as to whether the student has recognized the implications of any recommendation he might have made in the areas of the several elements of the mix. Or, referring to the forces, we can question whether all the pertinent market forces have been given due consideration. Continual reference to the mix chart leads me to feel that the students' understanding of "what marketing is" is strengthened. The constant presence and use of the chart leaves a deeper understanding that marketing is the devising of programs that successfully meet the forces of the market.

In problem solving the marketing mix chart is a constant reminder of:

1. The fact that a problem seemingly lying in one segment of the mix must be deliberated with constant thought regarding the effect of any change in that sector on the other areas of marketing operations. The necessity of integration in marketing thinking is ever present.

2. The need of careful study of the market forces as they might bear on problems in hand.

In short, the mix chart provides an ever ready checklist as to areas into which to guide thinking when considering marketing questions or dealing with marketing problems.

MARKETING: SCIENCE OR ART

The quest for a "science of marketing" is hard upon us. If science is in part a systematic formulation and arrangement of facts in a way to help understanding, then the concept of the marketing mix may possibly be considered a small contribution in the search for a science of marketing. If we think of a marketing science as involving the observation and classification of facts and the establishment of verifiable laws that can be used by the marketer as a guide to action with assurance that predicted results will ensue, then we cannot be said to have gotten far toward establishing a science. The concept of the mix lays out the areas in which facts should be assembled, these to serve as a guide to management judgment in building marketing mixes. In the last few decades American marketers have made substantial progress in adopting the scientific method in assembling facts. They have sharpened the tools of fact finding—both those arising within the business and those external to it. Aided by these facts and by the skills developed through careful observation and experience, marketers are better fitted to practice the art of designing marketing mixes than would be the case had not the techniques of gathering facts been advanced as they have been in recent decades. Moreover, marketers have made progress in the use of the scientific method in designing tests whereby the results from mixes or parts of mixes can be measured. Thereby marketers have been learning how to subject the hypotheses of their mix artists to empirical check.

With continued improvement in the search for and the recording of facts pertinent to marketing, with further application of the controlled experiment, and with an extension and careful recording of case histories, we may hope for a gradual formulation of clearly defined and helpful marketing laws. Until then, and even then, marketing and the building of marketing mixes will largely lie in the realm of art.

46. The Right Marketing Mix for the Corporate Imagery Mix

STEUART HENDERSON BRITT

If any chief executive officer of a company is asked, "What is your most important selling problem?" he probably will answer, "Marketing." Yet he often overlooks one of his most important marketing problems—the imagery of his company. If he is concerned about his marketing mix, he ought to worry also about his corporate imagery mix.

After all, *all selling takes place in the mind of the customer.* Within the mind, too, are images of products, companies, people, places, and institutions. These images are as important to the success of a company as the quality of its products, the services it provides, or the people it employs.

THE VARIOUS PUBLICS

Every company—whether it is in industrial marketing, in the consumer products business, or is marketing special services—has problems related to the appropriate *imagery mix.* These problems are much the same, differing only in specific ways from industry to industry and from company to company. After all, each company has to take into account its different publics.

The first of these is the *local public.* Realistic answers must be given to such questions as, "What does the local community think of our firm?" and, "How can we create a favorable local environment for our company?"

Broader marketing considerations come into play when trying to influence the *regional and national publics.* Then there are three distinct publics exclusively composed of people who might buy the company's products or services: *present customers, potential customers*, and *former customers.*

The *executives of the company* itself constitute a sixth public, by virtue of the fact that their attitudes and actions are influenced by how they perceive the image of their own corporation. Equally important are the public of the *company's rank-and-file employees*, whose favorable attitudes are essential for establishing the desired esprit de corps, and *potential employees*, a crucial factor in any firm's future. Corporate image appeals must, in addition, be directed toward the publics of *stockholders*, who supply capital for growth, and *the financial community*, which controls day-to-day credit and affects the prestige and reputation of the company as well.

Suppliers form a separate public that needs to be considered. A company cannot function without suppliers any more than it can function without customers or employees. The performance of the buying function can seriously affect not only company profit but also employee and customer relations.[1] Any executive who has been involved in a faulty raw material situation and a tight delivery

◆ SOURCE: Reprinted by permission from *Business Horizons*, February 1971, pp. 87–94. Copyright 1971 by the Foundation for the School of Business, Indiana University.

---

[1] Michiel R. Leenders, "How is Your Company's Buying Image?" *The Business Quarterly*, XXXI (Fall, 1966), pp. 41–45.

schedule will understand this relationship only too well. The buying image has received relatively little management attention compared to its well-known relatives on the consumer and employee side of the family. This lack of concern may stem partly from the company's feeling that it is doing certain suppliers a favor by buying from them in the first place.

Next is the distribution organization—*distributors and wholesalers*, and *retailers*. Even *other companies* (and this includes competitors) constitute a public which can be influenced by a business firm's imagery mix.

Finally, the marketer must add the publics of *federal, state, and local governments*, the number-one customer for many American companies; the *mass media*, which can "make or break" a product; *special sectors of the population*, such as youth; and *other countries*. It now becomes clear how Herculean is the task of developing the appropriate imagery mix.

THE BASIC MARKETING MIX

Once the marketer has decided which publics are most important to the company, he can proceed to develop his marketing imagery. It should be an image that is favorable, one the publics will understand, and one supported by company policies. He needs to consider several different kinds of marketing imagery.

National Origin of Corporation (and its Products)

Where does the product come from? Who made it? This is a serious matter, whether we are talking about Switzerland, England, Holland, Japan, or the U.S.A. The less known about the business firm itself and its brands, the greater is the significance of the national origin of the manufacturer as perceived by his publics.

Bertrand Russell once made an interesting observation about the imagery of a nation. He said that white rats used by psychologists for various experiments behave differently in different countries. Rats in Germany, faced with a labyrinth or maze, sit down stolidly and plan and solve their maze problem thoughtfully. The rats belonging to an American psychologist will solve their maze problem by running about frantically and frenetically, up and down and everywhere, finally finding the solution. But the rats of the British psychologist solve the maze differently; they just "muddle through."

In a 1960 *Reader's Digest* study of European markets, the products of each country in the Common Market were rated by other nationalities. Table 1 is an imagery index for five of the countries in the sample, showing how the quality, durability, and design of these five countries' exports were perceived by people of these same nations.

The positive and negative responses of those questioned were balanced against each other to derive the index numbers. The figures underscored show that the French, German, Dutch, Belgian, and British respondents considered the products made in their own countries far superior to those made in any of the other countries. When we realize that no particular product classes were mentioned, it is clear that nationality alone can account for significant distinctions as to imagery of products and the company that makes them.

The imagery problem exists for nations as well as for its manufacturers. I asked a sample of businessmen, both in the Scandinavian countries and in the United Kingdom, to name the first thing that came to their minds regarding Switzerland and the Swiss. Younger people thought of scenery, mountains, and skiing; some older men mentioned watches and banks. Several respondents referred to a "tax refuge" and a place where there is lots of secrecy: "You really cannot find out what is going on." And most people were a little puzzled about Swiss legislation concerning foreigners.

In a survey of the attitudes of U.S. and Japanese businessmen toward products made in various countries, the latter associated "inexpensive," "common," and "necessary" with products labeled "Made in Japan"; products marked "Made in U.S.A." were rated as "high cost" but also "highly inventive."[2] Today, more than ever, what a company does in one country influences its fortune in others.

---

[2] Akira Nagashima, "A Comparison of Japanese and U.S. Attitudes Toward Foreign Products," *Business Management*, XXXIV (January, 1970), pp. 68–74.

Table 1. Effects of National Origin on Perceptions of Product Attributes

Respondents' Perceptions of Product Attributes	National Origin of Respondents				
	France	Germany	Nether-lands	Belgium	Great Britain
French products					
High quality	63	16	10	23	12
Good, modern design	59	33	44	17	39
Well-made, durable	45	3	(−5)	9	12
German products					
High quality	38	54	65	45	53
Good, modern design	6	57	39	19	39
Well-made, durable	33	65	71	31	38
Dutch products					
High quality	24	34	71	14	43
Good, modern design	1	9	43	(−3)	17
Well-made, durable	8	20	88	7	26
Belgian products					
High quality	24	8	(−13)	58	5
Good, modern design	6	3	(−9)	13	5
Well-made, durable	8	8	(−1)	30	14
British products					
High quality	22	30	47	21	58
Good, modern design	3	5	14	1	36
Well-made, durable	15	21	52	15	61

SOURCE: Adapted from "The European Common Market and Britain," a marketing survey sponsored by *Reader's Digest* (Reader's Digest Association, 1963).

Product Appearance—the Discernible Difference

The phrase "product appearance" involves much more than the bare physical attributes of the product itself. The term might well be rephrased as "how the product appears or is perceived," because the beliefs and attitudes of the perceiver invariably interact with the true product appearance. The results of these interactions are new and subjective perceptions of the product.

The ingenuity of the marketing man will determine whether these new perceptions result in a truly perceptible or discernible difference in the product. If there is no actual difference in the product, the marketing man can draw upon his knowledge of packaging or graphics (or some other element in the imagery mix) to create an intuitively perceived difference. Differences in a product which the public "feels" can be every bit as beneficial to the company image as those differences which the public sees.

The vice-president and general manager of CITGO's service stations said a few years ago: "At Citgo, we are convinced, beyond any doubt, that beauty pays off at the pump island. Where we have been a leader in landscaping techniques, we have not only received commendations from garden clubs and the like, but we have also seen the results on our sales reports."[3] In other words, CITGO's gasoline appeared better to consumers because it was sold in pleasant surroundings.

The late Pierre Martineau warned that executives of companies may tend to identify with products they like instead of products that their customers (consumers) find pleasant.[4] They must be careful to distinguish between products they are in love with and products that will sell best.

More tender loving care or finer promotion could not have been given to a product

---

[3] "Corporate Image Making—Outdated Fad or Growing Necessity?" *Business Management*, XXXII (September, 1967), p. 35.

[4] Pierre Martineau, "Sharper Focus for the Corporate Image," *Harvard Business Review*, XXXVI (November–December, 1958), p. 55.

than was given to Ford's Edsel. The advance promotion and the advertising were extensive prior to the unveiling of this great "new" automobile. However, when the veil of secrecy was removed, the automobile looked to the American public very much like any other American automobile. There was no discernible difference—except for a grill-like piece in the front of the car that some people referred to as a horse-collar upside down and that others talked about as a female sex symbol. But this was hardly enough to keep the car in the market very long.

By contrast, Ford's Mustang was planned well in advance and quickly became a real success. It was a product that looked a bit like a sports car, but was safer. It also looked expensive, but was not; people who were asked in advance what the Mustang would cost guessed prices considerably higher than the actual selling price.

In industrial marketing, it often has been assumed that manufacturers tend to base their buying decisions on rationality. But research has indicated a gradual shift from logical, considered, and tangible reasons to more tangible and less rational motives. Many industrial concerns now base their personal selling and advertising approaches not only on the more commonly understood rational appeals of price, quality, performance, and reliability, but also on the less commonly understood emotional appeals of ambition, sex, pride, fear, and security.

The Container

The image of the container or package is closely tied to the brand or corporate name.

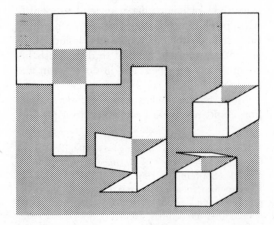

Packaging, therefore, can help to change the entire image.

For example, Marlboro was the first cigarette in the United States to be introduced in the flip-top box. The Philip Morris Company and its advertising agency, the Leo Burnett Company, decided to take a cigarette, which had been a woman's mild cigarette, put it in an entirely different-looking container, and turn its image into a man's cigarette. Through the advertising campaign developed by Burnett, millions of Americans came to know the masculine "Marlboro Man" with the tattoo, the flip-top box, and in recent years "Marlboro Country."

Company Names and Brand Names

Additional elements in imagery are the company name and the brand name it promotes. For example, the Minnesota Valley Canning Company, LeSueur, Minn., sold canned peas under the brand name Green Giant. After investigation, it was decided to change the name of the company to the Green Giant Company, and to show a large Green Giant in the advertising and on the label. And with excellent products promoted by a *jolly* Green Giant for television commercials, this company became a leader in its field.

Just how great an effect a product name can have on a company is demonstrated again and again in the name changes that have taken place in recent years. The Socony Mobil Oil Company, Inc., became the Mobil Oil Corporation, and the Texas Company switched over to Texaco. In both cases, the new names have become so well-known that the old company names are obsolete. When considering a name change, however, a company must proceed with caution. There always is the risk of premature abandonment of a known communications element for what could become costly anonymity. A known corporate name, regardless of its deficiencies, is a known equity.

Another method of name changing is that of "initializing" or abbreviating long-established corporate names. There are at least three reasons for a corporate name change involving initials:

The corporate function has completely original purpose.
changed because the firm has abandoned its
The company, through merger or acquisi-

tion, has diversified to the point where its original name does not describe all of its present activities.

It is awkward or difficult to use a long corporate name.[5]

However, the change to an initialized corporate name may lead to the unwitting sacrifice of both distinctiveness and memorability because of a lack of inherent meaning.

Graphics

Symbols, trademarks, and logotypes are all part of the rapidly advancing art of graphics. Henry Steiner, director of Graphic Communication, Ltd., in Hong Kong, defines these three terms as follows: " 'Trademark' is a legal term and can apply to such undersigned elements as a picture of a building, a portrait, or a signature. We use 'symbol' to describe a primarily pictorial or abstract design, and 'logo' for a design based on a name written out." The designer's achievement, as Steiner says, "is to create an image—a unique graphic crystallization of his client's activity or personality."[6]

To reflect upon the images conjured up by Bell Telephone's bell, Cadillac's V-symbol, or Prudential Life Insurance's Rock of Gibraltar is to understand why graphics are occupying an increasingly large share of the image-maker's time and attention. The names Nestlé and Remington Rand are excellent examples of world-wide companies with distinctive logotypes that help to create for the company a fairly uniform image around the world. Customers for such diverse products as gyro fluid, Scotch tape, copying machines, and stain repellents recognize—due to the distinctive logotype and especially designed type face—that they are purchasing a product of the 3M Company, once the Minnesota Mining and Manufacturing Company.

Where the Products Are Sold

For certain kinds of products it makes a considerable difference to consumers as to what kind of retail outlet products are sold

in, and also in what area and in what kind of community. I have observed over and over again in some of the great cities of the world —Zurich, London, Stockholm, Rome, Paris, Lisbon, Caracas, Singapore, Sydney, and so on—that in every city the store itself "communicates" what its products are like and whether or not it is a quality store. Both the neighborhood and the window display communicate a great deal to consumers.

It is for reasons like these that many consumers may question the quality of items sold in discount houses, although they may be, in fact, identical with items sold in "quality" retail outlets. Retailers must rely more and more on nonprice factors for building sales volume. In Chicago, for example, Marshall Field and Saks Fifth Avenue appeal especially to upper middleclass shoppers, while Sears Roebuck and Goldblatt's appeal more to the "working class." A woman shops at the store where she feels most comfortable.

Employees

One of the main imagery problems concerns personnel—the employees of the business firm. How do these people deal with other people, namely, customers? "Creative advertising men recognized the public's vast desire for friendliness, for caring, for first-name contacts in its relationship with business," says E. B. Weiss. But, he charges, "Business management lags far behind the professional image creators in actually bringing the image into real life."[7] For example, the slogan "Fly the friendly skies of United" cannot be useful to United Air Lines unless it is coupled with sincere and friendly courtesy as the actual practice.

Horn and Hardart, the New York restaurant chain, held a three-month contest for all employees in order to encourage them to be friendlier with patrons. The friendliest employees received bonuses, lapel pins, and certificates of appreciation from the company's president.

Hertz adopted as its slogan in its advertising, "When you rent a car from Hertz, you rent a whole company." If each employee who makes up the whole company supports this slogan, what is initially only words will be translated into increased business for Hertz

---

[5] Lawrence P. Feldman, "Of Alphabets, Acronyms and Corporate Identity," *Journal of Marketing*, XXXIII (October, 1969), pp. 72–75.

[6] Henry Steiner, "A Selection of Images," pamphlet produced by Graphic Communication, Ltd., October, 1966.

[7] E. B. Weiss, "The Corporate Deaf Ear," *Business Horizons*, XI (December, 1968), p. 9.

by a number of well-satisfied customers. On the other hand, if the employees on every level do not support the slogan with service beyond the ordinary, the nice words will remain just that—nice words.

Advertising and Promotion

Image advertising can be the most potent source of corporate imagery because other imagery sources can be incorporated into the advertising as copy themes. A compelling name, friendly personnel, favorable national origins—none of these advantages can be as meaningful as needed unless they also are utilized as themes in the company's image advertising.

It is through advertising that the consumer becomes aware of the company's image; an image that no one is aware of is no image at all. Business executives need to be fully aware of the variety and flexibility of usable copy approaches in appealing to a company's various publics.

Table 2 lists some of the elements in the image-advertising arsenal. A company wishing to make the best use of these alternatives can draw up a matrix, which will represent, on the horizontal axis, the various publics which have been discussed. The vertical axis will list the company's "imagery arsenal"— the stock of copy approaches available to the company.

Table 2. Examples of Elements in the Imagery Arsenal

National origins of corporation (products)
Product appearance
Container
Company name and brand names
Graphics
Where product sold
Geographic location of company
Physical plant and building—both exterior and interior
Method of manufacture
Company achievements, and goals and plans for the future
Company position on pertinent issues
Profiles of company executives
Profiles of rank-and-file personnel
Copy tone and techniques
Physical appearance of advertising and promotion

Each portion of the chart, then, will represent a given copy appeal to a given public. A single copy appeal can be directed at a number of different publics, and a single public might respond to a variety of copy appeals. As a result of this twofold flexibility, executives of a particular firm may find that they have a greater number of potent appeals available than suspected.

For instance, Indiana General, a company in the magnetic materials business, found that it could appeal to customers and at the same time to the broad public through the use of executive imagery in advertising. One of their advertisements in a campaign showed a photograph of a chubby fellow wearing a two-starred combat helmet with a business jacket and tie. The headline read, "What's an Indiana General?" and the copy then proceeded to talk about the company.

Union Carbide also developed a particular form of imagery to appeal to several publics. The symbol used was a large hand, which acted out the functions of various Union Carbide products. The series of advertisements appealed to the financial community, potential employees, and the government. A typical headline, "Reaching for the Moon," was accompanied by a picture of a large hand doing just that. The copy then explained how Union Carbide's products help man to reach the moon. This highly successful advertising campaign ran for fourteen years. The key to the campaign was the realization that a symbol could be used in strong appeals to several important publics.

Advertising and promotion communicate a great deal to the consumer, strengthening or weakening the profile of what the company is tryin to accomplish. But one of the main problems is that of "me-too-ism"—almost every advertiser in a product category doing, or trying to do, the same thing.

Other Elements

One of the most important elements of imagery is the annual report, both as to content and as to presentation. So important has this become that organizations specializing in financial writing (financial public relations counsels) have become increasingly important in recent years. A related element of imagery involves the elaborate recruiting brochures designed by companies to entice college graduates to the ranks of their employees. Special services represent still another important aspect of imagery—especially for automobiles and appliances.

An attempt to project a corporate image is not enough. It must be a favorable image, an image that the various publics will understand, and one which is underlined and not undermined by actual company policies.

To obtain a truly accurate image of a business firm is extremely difficult, not because an image is intangible but because of the great number of publics that a business firm has. Where do you start? A corporate executive must begin by determining *who* is going to decide what the corporate image should be. Is the company going to decide on its own image, or by default let its various publics decide? A decision *must* be made as to which of the various publics is the most important.

47. Businessmen Look Hard at Advertising

STEPHEN A. GREYSER and BONNIE B. REECE

◆ In cases of deceptive advertising, the Federal Trade Commission is considering penalties that would force advertisers to devote part of their own paid time and space to admitting the wrongdoing to the public. The FTC also wants to halt advertising it questions while an investigation is in process, rather than only after investigations, judgments, and appeals.

◆ Consumer-causes advocate Ralph Nader is calling out for full substantiation of advertising claims.

◆ Regarding food advertising aimed at children, nutrition investigator Robert Choate has urged restrictions on claims of product superiority and nutritional content, a limit to the number of food commercials per hour in "kiddie TV," and elimination during those hours of proprietary drug messages and the like.

◆ Not satisfied with the banishment of cigarette commercials from television, some critics now want health warnings in all cigarette ads.

◆ Media rate structures are again under investigation to see whether they unfairly benefit large advertisers.

Author's note: We wish to express appreciation to Harvard Business School Professor Raymond A. Bauer for his guidance in the development of the 1962 study which was the prototype for this survey.

◆ SOURCE: Reprinted by permission from *Harvard Business Review,* Vol. 49, No. 3, May–June 1971, pp. 18–27. © 1971 by the President and Fellows of Harvard College; all rights reserved.

◆ Accusations continue in Washington circles that advertising is an important element contributing to "monopoly power and monopoly profits" on the part of many major advertisers.

Increasing attacks on advertising that have manifested themselves in proposals for further administrative and legal restrictions on it, and a growing din of public criticism of advertising's volume and content—these raise questions about—the role and impact of advertising both as a tool of business and as an institution in our society. Such questions encompass advertising in its functional economic roles as well as its "side effects" in terms of social consequences.

Content—the ads themselves—is an important consideration both in general and with regard to particular techniques and campaigns. Also relevant is the perceived need for regulation—what kind and by whom. These and associated questions warrant fresh exploration, particularly among those who pay for advertising and in whose behalf it functions, the business community.

Despite the stake of business in advertising, relatively little has been done to learn about businessmen's ideas and attitudes about the subject. Nine years ago HBR published a study of what executives think about advertising.[1] Because of changes that have occurred since then—such as the increasing volume of

[1] Stephen A. Greyser, "Businessmen Re Advertising: 'Yes, But . . .'" (Problems in Review), May–June 1962, p. 20.

advertising, the emergence of consumerism, and evolving regulatory patterns—HBR's editors decided that the 1962 inquiry needed updating.

An eight-page questionnaire, similar to that used in the original study, was completed by some 27% of the cross section of the nearly 10,000 HBR subscribers to whom it was mailed (for details, see the ruled insert below). The high rate of return of the lengthy and complex instrument and the many handwritten comments appended to the questionnaire forms give evidence of the subject's interest and importance to executives of widely varying backgrounds. The respondents (see *Exhibit 1* for their profile) include many with job assignments in industries where advertising is of modest or little importance, as well as executives with more experience in the field.

The responses show a continuing strong respect for advertising, particularly in its economic functions. But more executives question advertising's impact and power in the social role than was true in 1962, and the content of advertising draws some ringing criticism. To use the language of the title of the 1962 report, the executive community's assessment of advertising today contains less *yes* and more *but* than nearly a decade ago.

STUDY HIGHLIGHTS

Here are the major findings of the new study, followed by more extensive analysis in the indicated sections

☐ Businessmen today take a somewhat more critical stance than they did nine years ago. This is true in areas of advertising's economic role, its social impact, and its perceived truthfulness. In assessing advertising, executives also seem to be applying broader criteria than traditional business efficacy alone. (See the section on **Changing Perspectives**.)

☐ Executives still almost unanimously agree that advertising is essential to business and that the public places more confidence in advertised products than in unadvertised ones. (See **Overall Appraisal**.)

☐ Respondents think that advertising speeds the development of markets for new products, helps raise our standard of living, and results in better products. And they acknowledge that large reductions in advertising expenditures would decrease sales—for

business in general *and* for their own companies. (See **Economic Issues**.)

☐ If advertising were eliminated, businessmen claim, selling expenses would have to go up. On the other hand, executives think too much money is spent on advertising. They probably would agree with that statement more strongly if they only knew exactly how much is spent—an amount they now grossly underestimate. (See **Advertising's Bill**.)

☐ Businessmen agree—more strongly than they did in 1962—that advertising has an unhealthy influence on children and that it persuades people to buy things they do not need. Also, fewer (though still a majority) believe that people pay more attention to advertising today than before. Executives look with disapproval on most of advertising's effects in the social area. (See **Social Influence**.)

☐ The percentage of businessmen who think that ads present a true picture of the product declined sharply—from more than half to less than one third. Moreover, the sample finds people in ads quite different from the way people really are. Although businessmen agree that advertising is on a higher plane than it was a decade ago, in some areas they think standards have slipped. Specifically, they notice a greater proportion of ads that irritate and insult the public's intelligence—and their own. (See **Standards and Content**.)

☐ Reacting in their role as consumers, businessmen consider direct mail and television as the media having the largest proportion of annoying and offensive ads. Trade publications receive the best ratings overall. (See **Media and Campaigns**.)

☐ While executives generally believe in codes of ethical practices for their own industries, they think that advertising has an even greater need for such codes—but also that advertising would be less able to enforce a code internally than their own industries could. The favored mode is a group of industry executives plus other community members. The code should force advertisers to substantiate their claims. In addition, respondents single out elimination of untruthful and misleading ads as the most important form of self-improvement advertising should undertake. (See **More Regulation** and **Action Steps**.)

☐ Executives overwhelmingly credit persons in the advertising field for advertising's achievements, but also blame them principally for its faults. While those closest to advertising also are seen as sharing the burden for

Management Position

Management Position		%
Top management	= chairman of the board; board member; owner; partner; president; division or executive vice president; vice president; treasurer; secretary; controller; general manager; general superintendent; editor; administrative director; dean; and assistants thereto.	34%
Upper-middle management	= functional department head (e.g., advertising, sales, brand manager, production, purchasing, personnel, engineering, etc.)	33
Lower-middle management	= assistant to functional department head; district manager; branch manager; section manager; etc.	15
Nonmanagement personnel	= all others employed in business.	11
Professional	= doctor; practicing lawyer; practicing CPA; professor; consultant; military officer; government official; union official; clergyman; etc.	7

Industry

Industry	%
Manufacturing consumer goods	14%
Manufacturing industrial goods	27
Advertising; media; publishing	4
Banking; investment; insurance	11
Construction; mining; oil	5
Defense industry	3
Education; social services	6
Government	4
Management consulting	10
Personal consumer services	2
Retail or wholesale trade	7
Transportation and public utilties	5
Other	2

Relative Size of Company in Industry

	%
Very large	34%
Larger than most	30
About average	19
Smaller than most	12
Very small	5

Age

	%
Under 30	18%
30–39	34
40–49	29
50–59	15
60 or over	4

Advertising-Marketing Experience

	%
Present job in advertising	5%
Present job in marketing	26
Previous job in either	13
No advertising or marketing experience	56

Job Function

	%
Accounting	6%
Advertising	4
Engineering; R&D	13
Finance	9
General management	39
Marketing (other than advt.)	19
Labor relations; personnel	5
Production; other	5

Company's Annual Sales

	%
Under $1 million	12%
$1–$10 million	19
$10–$25 million	10
$25–$100 million	15
$100–$500 million	16
Over $500 million	28

Importance of Advertising to Company

	%
Very important	28%
Rather important	33
Not particularly important	20
Rather unimportant	10
Very unimportant	9

Education

	%
High school	2%
Some college	11
Bachelor's degree	33
Graduate school	54

EXHIBIT 1. Profile of HBR subscribers responding.

making improvements in ads, the respondents place the primary responsibility for improvements on corporate top management. (See **Scoreboard.**)

☐ Not surprisingly, those surveyed whose jobs are in the advertising field are more generally favorable toward it than are executives in general. Between the two, but striking an independent path, are executives whose jobs are or were in marketing. These differences in attitudes are especially apparent with respect to advertising's social implications and its standards. (See **Admen's View.**)

Changing Perspectives

What are the major changes since 1962 in executives' attitudes toward advertising? First — and most general — is a stance somewhat less favorable; on most key issues, opinion has moved some 5 to 10 percentage points toward an anti-advertising position.

(This shift to a small extent may be a function of the composition of the sample compared with that of 1962. There are fewer consumer goods executives and substantially more consultants; the former group tends to be somewhat more pro-advertising, the latter slightly less. Some 3% fewer say their assignments are in the advertising or marketing function, while 5% more are in engineering and R&D jobs; the former are considerably more pro-advertising, the latter rather less so. Some of these changes in composition, of course, are natural reflections of changes in the character of the management population over the past nine years.)

The most significant changes in attitudes, however, are far more dramatic:

◆ In the economic area—where executives customarily give an almost blanket endorsement—advertising is still seen as having predominantly positive effects. But 15-20 percentage-point declines are recorded on such issues as whether advertising results in better products, raises our standard of living, and results in higher or lower prices.

◆ In the social area, executives question advertising's influence, and in some instances are very critical of it. The perceived negative impact on public taste and unhealthy effect on children show an increase of 15 percentage points. Furthermore, as in 1962, businessmen see advertising as having a powerful influence for persuasion, an influence they regard unfavorably.

◆ The area of ad content generates sharper criticism than was the case nine years ago. Most notable is the 24 percentage-point decline in the proportion of executives—now only about one third—who agree that "in general advertising presents a true picture of the product advertised."

One reason for these changing perspectives no doubt is the "behavior" of advertising. But a significant part of the explanation may well be rooted in changes in the context in which businessmen assess advertising. These changes relate particularly to today's greater perceived appropriateness of evaluating business activity not only in business terms but also in terms of societal implications. Thus, more than two thirds of our respondents disagree with the philosophy that "advertising's sole justification should be returning a profit to the advertiser."

Further evidence of this broader perspective comes in responses to paired questions on the issue of advertising's responsibility for the effects of the products it promotes. Almost half (49%) agree that admen should be held accountable, and 73% disagree with the premise that admen have no responsibility in the area.

An important related element of the changing environment is consumerism. About 4 out of every 5 persons sampled think that "consumerism will lead to major modifications in advertising content."

Overall Appraisal

Executives agree almost unanimously that advertising is necessary. More than 90% say it is essential for business in general, while some 73% also indicate that it is essential for their own companies. The change since 1962 in this endorsement has been slight—one of degree rather than substance. Whereas 80% of those responding in 1962 indicated "strong agreement" with the statement that advertising is necessary to business, this figure has dropped down to 67% now.

More than three quarters agree that society is better off with advertising than without it. This is nearly as many as in 1962, despite the strong criticism of advertising that has been voiced since that time.

An overwhelming 90% feel that the public has more confidence in advertising products than in unadvertised ones, and 68% of this group say that they strongly agree with this statement. In the latter category, however, some erosion has taken place; nine years ago about 81% of the respondents indicated "strong agreement."

Economic Issues

From at least as far back as the 1930's, observers have questioned the economic influences of advertising. Many of the issues raised then are still being discussed today. *Exhibit 2* summarizes opinion on several of these economic questions, both from the new study and from 1962.

We used dual-phrased questions, tapping both sides of each issue and administered to split halves of the sample (see the ruled insert on page 19 for explanation). The respondents to each form of the statement were virtually identical demographically, so it can be assumed that dissimilar response patterns indeed represent different perceptions of a particular issue when it is presented in two ways.

New Product Stimulus. In the area of new product marketing, advertising is perceived as making its highest functional contribution to the economy. Executives are almost unanimous in agreeing that "advertising speeds the development of markets for new products" (and in disagreeing with the statement that it slows such development).

In addition, 90% of the respondents believe that "it would be almost impossible today to introduce a new consumer product without advertising." They find this less true for launching an industrial product: only 63% agree in this case.

General influence. One charge critics make is that large sums of money spent on advertising enable some companies to sell products that may be inferior to those made by smaller competitors who cannot afford these marketing costs. Thus, it is argued, advertising prevents consumers from getting the best products. This contradicts the traditional idea that manufacturers are more likely to develop new and better products because of advertising. The reasoning here is that they use this tool to sell efficiently large enough quantities to recover research costs in a reasonable period of time.

Businessmen believe that "advertising results in better products for the public," but they are considerably less likely to say so now than they were nine years ago. As can be seen in *Exhibit 2*, this 21 percentage-point change in attitude is not matched on the reverse form

of the question, where respondents still overwhelmingly reject the notion that advertising results in *poorer* products.

Another traditional argument in advertising's behalf is that it helps raise our standard of living. Here, again, some erosion of support has occurred since 1962. While executives are still quick to reject the anti-advertising statement, they are less enthusiastic about endorsing the favorable one.

On the always thorny issue of effect on prices, a dramatic change in attitude is evident. Just about half of the respondents deny that advertising lowers prices, and the same proportion think that it results in higher prices. This is considerably different from the case in 1962. Interestingly, executives in consumer goods companies are slightly *more* likely than others to say "higher prices."

Company economics. Few managers think that "small reductions in advertising expenditures would decrease sales." However, nearly three fourths of them believe that large cuts in the ad budget would have this effect.

Opinion is divided as to the helpfulness of a slight increase in advertising in hastening recovery from a recession. On the other hand, there is little agreement with the belief that a moderate *decrease* can hasten recovery. Executives appear to favor a policy of at least holding the line. The viewpoint is supported by independent research data confirming that "industries which do not cut back on their advertising during a recession . . . do much better in sales and profits than those that do cut." [2]

Finally, HBR asked businessmen whether "advertising's value would be better recognized if its effects could be more precisely measured." The findings reiterate the strong position taken in 1962; some 86% of the respondents believe this is true.

Generally speaking, the results do indicate a strong reinforcement of executives' beliefs in advertising's economic validity and impact for businesses. However, the support is weaker than in 1962 regarding some of advertising's economic influences.

Advertising's Bill

Slightly more than half of HBR's respondents say that too much is spent on advertising

---

[2] Buchen Advertising, Inc., *Advertising in Recession Periods* (Chicago, 1970).

Issue	Alternatives	Percentage of Respondents Who Say:			Percentage of Respondents Who Say:		
		Agree	Can't Say	Disagree	Agree	Can't Say	Disagree
Development of markets for new products	Speeds it	94%	2%	4%	95%	3%	2%
	Slows it	9	7	84	6	5	89
Effect on products for the public	Better ones	**55**	9	36	**76**	7	17
	Poorer ones	10	11	79	8	7	85
Effect on standard of living	Raises it	67	12	21	83	8	7
	Lowers it	7	8	85	4	5	91
Effect on prices	Lower prices	35	16	49	54	13	33
	Higher prices	**49**	10	41	**28**	9	62
Advertising one brand against another	Not wasteful	68	10	22	66	10	22
	Wasteful	26	10	64	23	8	68
Reductions in ad expenditures would decrease sales	Large reduction	72	12	16	*	*	*
	Small reduction	22	26	52	22	27	51
To hasten recovery in a recession	Moderate decrease in advertising	8	18	**74**	*	*	*
	Moderate increase in advertising	**42**	20	38	*	*	*

* No comparable statement.

EXHIBIT 2. Advertising and certain economic issues.

| | Percentage of Respondents who: | | |
Statement	Agree	Can't Say	Disagree
Most of the money allocated for advertising is well spent	28	22	50
Most of the money allocated for advertising is wasted	25	12	63

EXHIBIT 3. Opinion on effectiveness of advertising dollar.

— an increase of 15 percentage points from 1962. Paralleling this, approximately an equal number disagree that too little is spent. A substantial 27%, however, disagree that too much is spent for advertising. This seems to indicate a belief that to some extent advertising expenditures are "about right."

Executives seem uncertain as to whether money allocated for advertising is well spent— they disagree with *both* sides of this issue (see *Exhibit 3*). Perhaps they are saying that while company money is not wasted, it could be managed more carefully.

Nearly 7 out of 10 executives think that "it would take more money in substitute selling expenses" to replace advertising expenditures.

Respondents were asked for their "best guess as to how much money was spent on advertising in the United States last year," and the responses were grouped into categories. *Exhibit 4* shows a very wide range of estimates.

The generally accepted answer—according to the traditional McCann-Erickson estimates, now developed by Robert J. Coen for *Marketing/Communications* magazine—is $19.5 billion in 1969 and $19.7 billion in 1970. As the line with the arrow indicates, only 8% of the answers are in this territory. (Note that only 9% would be added to this group if the range were broadened to extend from $15 billion to $30 billion.)

This result parallels the findings of the 1962 study, in which only 20% of responding executives were near the correct figure of $12 billion.

Those whose current assignment or background is in advertising and marketing evince a slightly better knowledge of advertising's bill. Some 26% of them give estimates within the $15-billion to $30-billion range.

Social Influence

Advertising has felt some particularly bitter stings in the social area in the years since HBR's previous study. While social criticism has always been directed at advertising,[3] it has intensified in the past decade.

Businessmen's views on important social issues are summarized in *Exhibit 5*. We asked respondents to rate a statement in two ways: first on whether it was true or false, and then on whether, if true, this was good or bad. As reflected in the exhibit, what is seen as true is not always seen as good, and vice versa.

An alleged detrimental social impact of advertising is that it "leads to uniformity of taste among consumers." Slightly more than half of those surveyed agree that this statement is true. On the other hand, two thirds agree that advertising leads to *diversity* of taste. A likely explanation is that advertising encourages many people to want the same things (uniform taste), but it tries to satisfy customers by providing many products and many brands within product categories (diversity).

Closely linked is the question of what influence advertising has on the level of taste. Executives seem to believe that advertising neither upgrades nor downgrades public taste; the response patterns for both forms of the

Annual amount	Percentage of respondents citing
$30 billion or more	15%
$21–$29.9 billion	4
$18–$20.9 billion ◄———	8
$15–$17.9 billion	5
$10–$14.9 billion	17
$5–$9.9 billion	14
$1–$4.9 billion	28
Less than $1 billion	9

Note: Arrow points to generally accepted figure.

EXHIBIT 4. How much money is spent on advertising?

[3] For a historical review of such criticism, see Raymond A. Bauer and Stephen A. Greyser, *Advertising in America: The Consumer View* (Boston, Division of Research, Harvard Business School, 1968), Chapter 2.

Percentage of Respondents Who Say:

Issue	Alternatives	This Is:			If True, This Would Be:		
		True	Don't Know	False	Good	Don't Know	Bad
Effect on taste among consumers	Leads to uniformity	51%	10%	38%	6%	19%	75%
	Leads to diversity	67	10	23	79	17	4
Impact on public taste	Downgrades it	41	13	46	2	7	91
	Improves it	37	15	48	74	15	11
Influence on children	Healthy	17	16	67	68	13	19
	Unhealthy	57	13	30	1	4	95
Amount of attention paid to it	More than ever	54	19	27	47	32	21
	Less than ever	31	12	57	25	23	52
Persuades people to buy things they don't need	Seldom	17	3	80	56	13	31
	Often	85	3	12	7	17	76
Persuades people to buy things they don't want	Seldom	50	5	45	66	14	20
	Often	51	7	41	3	9	88

EXHIBIT 5. Advertising's social influences.

question are similar. The important finding here is the change from 1962, when the results showed a majority of executives convinced that advertising improves public taste.

The businessmen seem to go along with critics who attack advertising's effect on children. While two thirds of those responding disagree that advertising has a healthy influence on children, some 57% go even further and affirm that the influence is unhealthy. This represents a 13-15 percentage-points increase from the anti-advertising "rating" of 1962.

A majority of executives still believe that "people today pay more attention to advertising than ever before," but the proportion has declined somewhat in the past nine years. More important, the percentage of respondents who think that this is good has dropped even more.

On the related issue of how effective advertising is, compared with a decade ago, similar results are evident. There is little change in the percentage finding this assertion true or false; however, the proportion of executives who think it is good that advertising is *less* effective has doubled, and the percentage thinking it is good that advertising is *more* effective has declined from 52% to 41%.

HBR also inquired as to how persuasive they think advertising is. Nearly all respondents believe that "advertising often persuades people to buy things they don't need." They are more evenly split (just about 50-50) on the notion that advertising can seduce consumers, that it "often persuades people to buy things they don't want." Note that regardless of whether advertising is viewed as having such power, to have it is seen as bad.

Overall, businessmen seem to look less favorably on the social effects of advertising's capabilities than they did in 1962.

Standards and Content

One of the most dramatic changes in opinion uncovered by this study deals with views of the truthfulness of ads. Only 30% of the respondents believe that "advertisements present a true picture of the product advertised"; 60% agree with the reverse form of the statement. That 30% represents a decline of 24 percentage points since 1962, the largest single shift in attitude from the previous study. Perhaps it helps to explain some of the anti-advertising sentiment noted elsewhere; businessmen apparently find it hard to feel as much economic satisfaction with advertising when so many question its content.

Nevertheless, businessmen think that standards of advertising today are slightly higher than they were a decade ago. Some 43% say standards are higher; 26% say "about the same"; and 31% rate them lower. Comparable figures in 1962 were: 40%, higher; 36%, about the same; and 24%, lower.

Managers also were asked to compare their views of ads today with those they held a decade ago on certain attributes. Their reactions to these categories of content are given in *Exhibit 6*.

The "problem ads" most frequently cited as having increased—those which insult the intelligence and those which irritate—are the same two problem areas most criticized by executives in 1962.

Ads with too little information receive the highest number of "about the same" responses, despite criticism on this point from other quarters. Furthermore, a plurality of respondents believe there is a *smaller* proportion of ads with invalid or misleading claims than ten years ago.

Managers do not feel that "most people in

Compared with ten years ago, would you say there is a greater, a smaller, or about the same proportion of . . .	Percentage of Respondents who Answer:		
	Smaller Proportion	About the Same Proportion	Greater Proportion
Ads with invalid or misleading claims	38%	30%	32%
Ads which themselves are in bad taste	29	25	46
Ads for objectionable products	21	38	41
Ads which insult the *public's* intelligence	20	28	52
Ads which insult *your* intelligence	18	25	57
Ads with too little information	19	46	35
Ads which are irritating	18	28	54

EXHIBIT 6. Change of attitude re advertising content: now versus ten years ago.

ads are pretty much like the way people really are." Only one repondent in ten agrees with this statement. This is one area where both sexes seem to get equal treatment. Two separate questions show that fewer than one in five think advertising accurately portrays the roles of men, and of women, in our society.

A frequent cause of annoyance is not so much the format or content of the ad, but its repetition. Three fourths of the executives believe that "repetition has been substituted for imagination in much of today's advertising."

Another irritant is the hard-sell promotion that pounds its message home. According to respondents, this type of irritation is not necessary to sell; 9 out of 10 agree that "soft-sell advertising *does* sell goods." On a related issue, however, the businessmen just about split evenly on whether the most effective TV commercials are the most annoying.

In summary, the sample singles out the truth dimension and the irritating qualities of ads as major detrimental aspects of content. Otherwise, there is only a slightly less favorable perception of content than in 1962.

Media and Campaigns

It is insufficient to consider the standards of advertising content without referring to the context—that is, the media—in which ads appear. Some products might be viewed as "objectionable" on television but not in an adult-oriented magazine. A newspaper ad that seems low in informational content might be considered differently on a billboard.

Most criticism of irritating ads, the amount of advertising, and information content is voiced from a consumer vantage point. So HBR asked executives in their role as consumers to assess the major media in terms of the proportion of ads that they find annoying, enjoyable, informative, and offensive.[4] In addition, they were asked to give their perceptions as to the overall amount of advertising in each medium.

The scale used to rate media ranged from very low (1) to very high (5). *Exhibit 7* shows the mean scores recorded.

Not surprisingly, businessmen treat their

own trade publications most kindly. This medium receives the highest average score for the proportion of ads that are enjoyable and informative, the lowest ratings for annoying and offensive ads, and the second lowest rating on overall amount of advertising. Consumer magazines receive the next most favorable ratings, followed by newspapers.

At the other extreme lies direct mail, with the worst image in the areas of annoying, enjoyable, and offensive ads. Television's image is not much better—except for the fairly high score it receives for enjoyable commercials.

In the category of overall amount of advertising, no medium has a mean of less than 3, and TV is singled out with an average of 4.24. This dubious distinction must in part be the result of interruptions in programs caused by commercials. (Television actually carries *less* advertising than most other media. Even during crowded time periods, commercials are limited to 16 minutes per hour—just under 27%. This is well under the 40%-50% figure toward which many magazine publishers strive and less than half the amount found in most newspapers.)

Good Ads and Bad Ads. The respondents told HBR what campaigns they consider to be particularly good and particularly bad. These campaigns—mostly from late 1970—are summarized in *Exhibit 8* by product category, with the exception of a few brand names that stand out.

Nearly one third single out the 1970 Alka-Seltzer campaign as a favorite. (Interestingly enough, Miles Laboratories, maker of Alka-Seltzer, recently received much unfavorable comment in the advertising trade press for firing the agency that created these ads, reportedly because of unsatisfactory sales results.) Many executives also cite Volkswagen ads favorably.

When asked to identify campaigns they dislike, executives usually cite product categories rather than specific brands. Nonetheless, one brand, Winston cigarettes, draws enough mentions to rate a place of its own.

HBR compared the campaigns selected by those respondents whose current jobs are in advertising with those mentioned by other executives. More admen say they like the Alka-Seltzer commercials than do other managers—40% versus under 30%. Admen are also 50% more likely to name an automobile or car rental promotion as a favorite than are other businessmen (21% versus 14%), but

---

[4] These categories are the same as those used with consumers in the nationwide study reported by Raymond A. Bauer and Stephen A. Greyser, op. cit.

Mean Rating on 1-5 Scale

Nature of Ads	Consumer Magazines	Direct Mail	Newspapers	Outdoor	Radio	Television	Trade Publications
Annoying	2.09	3.89	2.19	2.81	3.21	3.72	1.62
Enjoyable	2.91	1.45	2.32	2.10	2.20	2.50	2.95
Informative	2.85	2.05	2.73	1.66	1.95	2.06	4.03
Offensive	1.87	3.14	1.91	2.22	2.50	3.06	1.35
Overall amount of advertising	3.49	3.77	3.48	3.25	3.65	4.24	3.39

EXHIBIT 7. Media rating scores.

they are only half as likely to list a public service campaign.

In general, persons in advertising like more campaigns than do other executives. In the case of particularly bad promotions, a higher percentage of admen than nonadvertising respondents are annoyed by soap and detergent ads. The opposite is true for cigarette ads and ads for toothpastes and mouthwashes.

More Regulation!

A clamor for greater regulation of advertising is part of the context in which this study was conducted, as we have noted. It is important (and only fair) to point out that voices from within the advertising fraternity have been among those calling for change. Perhaps the best-known proposal is that advanced by American Advertising Federation charirman, Victor Elting, for an industry review board combined with a media agreement not to run advertisements that fail to obtain the board's approval.

HBR's questions to executives covered many issues in this important area, especially on the *what* and *who* of such regulation.

First, is there a need for more regulation? One underlying reason why many executives seem to be answering *yes* to this question is their growing conviction that public faith in advertising is eroding. Indeed, some 42% (compared with 28% in 1962) go so far as to agree that "the public's faith in advertising is at an all-time low." (Only 38% disagree, compared with 54% in 1962.) Moreover, only 15% say "the public's faith in advertising is at an all-time high" (68% disagree!), whereas nine years ago opinion on this statement was 31% agree, 50% disagree.

Also, the businessmen today more sharply criticize advertising people in terms of their recognition of public responsibility than was the case in 1962. About half agree with the view that, on the whole, admen in their activities fail to recognize their accountability, up 12-15 percentage points from nine years ago.

One way of formalizing approaches to responsibility in business practice is with industry codes of ethical practices. Businessmen in

Campaigns	Percentage of Respondents Mentioning
Campaigns considered "good"	
Alka-Seltzer	30
Volkswagen	27
Other automobiles and car rentals (e.g., Volvo, Dodge, American Motors, Avis)	15
Public service/interest ads (e.g., antismoking, Peace Corps, clean air and water)	7
Foods and beverages (e.g., Pepsi, Coca-Cola, Sunsweet prunes, Kraft)	8
Cigarettes (especially Benson & Hedges, Marlboro)	5
Airlines (Eastern, United, American, etc.)	4
Other (e.g., local banks or stores, corporate institutional)	19
Campaigns considered "bad"	
Winston (cigarette brand)	11
Other cigarettes (specific brand mentions or all of this type)	19
Soaps, detergents, other household cleaning products (generic or brand names)	15
Deodorants and other personal products (e.g., feminine hygiene sprays, cosmetics, shaving products)	11
Toothpastes and mouthwashes	5
Beer and liquor	1
Political advertising	3
Remedies (e.g., headache, stomachache, or sleeping pills, patent medicines, cold remedies)	8
Other (e.g., toys, underwear, auto dealers)	25

EXHIBIT 8. Views of "good" and "bad" advertising campaigns.

	Percentage of Respondents Answering:			
	For All Practices in Your Own Industry		For All of Advertising	
Questions	1971	1962	1971	1962
A. How do you feel about the idea of a general code of ethical practices?				
Excellent idea	46	41	53	50
Good idea	22	22	24	24
Fair idea	11	11	12	11
Poor idea	12	15	10	12
Already has a code	9	11	1	3
B. If such codes were drawn up, who should enforce them?				
Management of each company (i.e., self-enforcement)	26	38	20	32
A group of executives from various companies within the industry	27	32	19	28
A group composed of industry executives plus other members of the community	34	22	47	32
A government agency	9	4	10	5
Other	4	4	4	3

EXHIBIT 9. Opinions on codes of ethical practices, 1971 versus 1962.

the past have generally favored such standards for their own industries.[5]

We asked our sample to consider the desirability of ethical codes, and how best to enforce them, for their own industries as well as for advertising. While the respondents may have known little or nothing about whether advertising needs a code (or, for that matter, whether it already has one), their answers can be taken as indicating their opinions as to whether a code for advertising—and stricter enforcement of any codes—is more or less desirable than codes for their own industries.

Their opinions, shown in Exhibit 9, ascribe a greater need for regulation and for stronger enforcement procedures to advertising than to their own fields. Moreover, compared with 1962, more executives think the idea of such codes is "excellent" or "good," and fewer think that enforcement at the company or industry level is most appropriate.

The most striking finding in Exhibit 9 is that the preferred mode of enforcement would consist of a group of industry executives plus

other members of the community. The respondents see this as especially desirable in enforcement of advertising codes, perhaps because advertising impinges so broadly on the public. While only a very small proportion of the sample opts for government enforcement of such standards, more than half (59%) also agree that "if advertising can't keep its own house in order, the government will have to."

"Shape up." Reinforcing these views are results from a number of separate but related questions. For example, a majority (58%) of executives think that "self-regulation for advertising can't be genuinely effective," which is slightly more than the percentage agreeing with this statement in 1962. Only 19% of all respondents (but 55% of those in advertising jobs) claim any knowledge of present self-regulation efforts in advertising.

A large proportion of the sample (more than 70%) take the position that advertising needs stronger policing of its content. Furthermore, 90% agree that advertisers should be forced to substantiate their claims. In light of recent debates on this matter, it is noteworthy that this is one of the most widely held opinions in the current study, and that almost as strong a view was taken in 1962—albeit cou-

[5] See Raymond C. Baumhart, S. J., "How Ethical Are Businessmen?" (Problems in Review), HBR July–August 1961, p. 6.

pled at that time with a somewhat less critical reaction to ads than is the case now.

Of course one explanatory factor, representing a major force that has emerged in the marketing environment in the last decade, is consumerism. About 80% of our respondents think consumerism will lead to major modifications in advertising content, and 86% consider this to be a good thing.

In sum, businessmen clearly are saying to advertising that there is a need to "shape up," especially in terms of content. They look favorably on consumerism as an environmental force conducive toward this end, and they urge stronger codes of ethical practice in advertising, with less reliance on self-enforcement and intra-industry enforcement.

Let us now look in more detail at executives' recommendations for action on the part of advertising.

Action Steps

HBR asked its sample for suggestions for action which advertising could undertake—ideally and realistically—to overcome criticism. As was true nine years ago, the recommendation offered most frequently in both situations is to increase truth in advertising (see *Exhibit 10*).

This view is summed up by one respondent from Kentucky, who says advertisers should "report truthfully, without under- or overstatements." The assistant treasurer of a meter manufacturer aptly explains the difference between ideal and realistic goals. Ideally, he says, advertising should "be honest"; realistically, it should "be a 'little' honest."

Comments relating to the tastefulness of ads come from a number of executives. A representative quotation from the vice president–operations of a New York consulting firm is:

"Reduce oversimplification and insulting of the user's intelligence."

The second largest number of suggestions relate to increased self-regulation and establishing an industry code of ethics. Typical was this recommendation from the president of a Connecticut consumer goods company: "Form an ethics committee to regulate misleading and poor-taste advertising."

More pessimistic about the industry's ability to police itself, a New York ad agency account executive calls for "self-regulation (ideally), government regulation (realistically)." In agreement, the advertising-sales promotion manager of a New Jersey chemical company postulates a kind of Gresham's Law: "It needs regulation so that meaningful, worthwhile advertising is not drowned out by the illiterate shrieks that constitute the bulk of present advertising."

"Become more informative" and "provide more facts" are recommendations from another group of managers. Still others believe that the best thing the industry can do to overcome criticism is simply to learn to do its job better. "Learn to measure effectiveness," remarks the general manager of an Ohio measurement and control systems manufacturer.

A small number of respondents believe advertising should just ignore its critics. As the vice president of a New Jersey retailing firm puts it, "It can't overcome all criticism and shouldn't try to."

The frequently advanced notion of a public information program to be undertaken by the industry was treated in a separate question. If such a program were to be pursued, some 75% of those responding believe that "advertising's role and function in our economy" should be emphasized. And a secondary theme, which gains 65% support, would highlight "efforts to curb objectionable advertisements."

Suggestions	Percentage of Respondents Citing:	
	Ideally	Realistically
More truth	21	18
More taste	7	9
More truth and taste	4	3
Self-enforced regulation; ethical code	11	12
Provide more information	8	7
Do a better job	2	3
Do nothing	1	1
Other comments	16	17

EXHIBIT 10. What should advertising do to overcome criticism?

Supplementing and reinforcing these views are executives' recommendations for "specific forms of self-improvement" for advertising. Responses to a checklist of such activities to improve advertising appear in *Exhibit 11.*

Scoreboard

Whose job is it to stimulate these improvements? Who gets the most credit for advertising's achievements and blame for its faults? What groups in society are seen as most antagonistic toward advertising, best able to help or hurt it, the ones to which the industry should pay most attention?

Businessmen place primary credit, blame, and responsibility for improvement in advertising's situation with the same groups as they did in 1962. But a larger percentage of respondents cite more groups in each category now. The largest increase, 21 percentage points, comes in the number of executives charging the government with the burden of improving advertising. *Exhibit 12* presents the current views.

The government, along with the public and our economic system, receives very little credit or blame for advertising's condition. Advertising agency people and company advertising departments lead both of these lists. These same groups are perceived as being very much accountable for changing advertising, but on this dimension top management moves into first place. Respondents believe that *those who set company policy*—and approve advertising's piece of the company budget—*are best able to ensure that advertising shapes up.*

Executives rate our economic system last in terms of responsibility for improving advertising. But in a separate question HBR asked whether "the faults of advertising are inherent in our economic system"; some 40% of the respondents say *yes,* suggesting that most of advertising's problems are of its own making.

Some ad industry proponents have claimed that advertising—as the most visible marketing tool—receives an undue amount of criticism, that it serves as a scapegoat for business in general. Executives disagree. All but 15% say that "criticism of advertising stems more from advertising itself than from hostility toward the whole economic system."

Are some groups in society more antagonistic toward advertising than others? Busi-

	Percentage of Respondents Who Say:	
Activity	Should be Undertaken	Is Most Important
Eliminate untruthful or misleading ads	65	14
Establish and enforce a code of ethics	91	56
Upgrade the intellectual level of ads	62	11
Increase the information content of ads	59	11
Work only for reputable companies or products	42	4
Become more efficient as a business	23	3
Other	4	2

EXHIBIT 11. Specific forms of self-improvement advocated for advertising.

	Percentage of respondents citing:		
Location	Credit for Achievements	Blame for Faults	Responsibility for Improvement
Advertising agency people	81	81	81
Our economic system	35	34	21
The government	8	16	42
Media people	46	54	63
The public	18	33	45
Company advertising departments	69	74	74
Company top management	52	67	88

EXHIBIT 12. Where should credit and blame lie?

nessmen say *yes*, citing opinion leaders among the public (whoever they may be) and the public in general (see *Exhibit 13*).

But, they go on to say, these groups have less power to help or hurt advertising than does the business community. Government leaders are also viewed as having considerable power, a change from 1962 when they ranked only fourth on this issue.

The finding most clearly evident in *Exhibit 13*, however, is that fully three quarters of the respondents believe that advertising should pay most attention to the public. Businessmen apparently are saying that the success or failure of advertising depends in large part on how well it listens to those whom it is trying to reach.

Admen's View

Not surprisingly, those whose present jobs are in advertising (some 5% of the total surveyed) look more favorably at it than do persons outside the field. To illustrate, some 85% of those in advertising generally disagree that "society is worse off with advertising than without it," compared with only 47% of other respondents.

Although only 42% of nonadvertising executives think that today's advertising standards are higher than a decade ago, some 70% of those in the field believe this is so. Perhaps one reason why admen hold this favorable view is that more than half of them maintain that ads *do* present a true picture of the products advertised—a percentage double that for other managers.

Admen, like most other people in wanting their work recognized, believe that consumers pay more attention to advertising than ever

before; 70% think that this is true, compared with just over 50% for others. What is more, an equally high percentage, 71%, think this is good, while only 45% of others think so. And whereas only 37% of businessmen outside the field say that advertising's ability to add psychological attributes to products is a good thing, some 63% of those in advertising approve it.

Quite naturally, admen have different ideas about the kind of regulation the industry needs—and greater knowledge of present regulatory efforts. Some 17% of the "outsiders" claim to know of any ad industry self-regulation, but 55% of those in the field do. What is surprising is that 45% of those who supposedly are governed by such regulation do not know that it exists.

Admen are no different from other respondents in approving the idea of an ethical code. They are much more likely to vote for enforcement by company management, however. Three quarters of them state that self-regulation can be genuinely effective, compared with 42% of other respondents.

Admen are more than twice as likely as others (54% versus 26%) to disagree that too much money is spent on advertising. Depending on their jobs, respondents view impact on prices differently. About 65% of those in advertising believe that it results in lower prices, as against 34% of the rest.

Conclusion

In what is being called "the age of accountability," advertising has been put under the spotlight—as have many institutions and business practices. Perhaps because it touches the public in so many ways and throughout the

	Percentage of Respondents who Find this Group:		
Group	Most Antagonistic	Most Powerful	The One Advertising Should Pay Most Attention To
The business community	16	**64**	57
Clergymen	24	6	8
Educators	46	12	17
Government leaders	43	**50**	27
Opinion leaders among the public	53	40	49
People in advertising itself	12	45	23
The public in general	52	46	**75**

Note: Respondents could check more than one group in each column.

EXHIBIT 13. How do various groups in our society relate to advertising?

day, advertising seems to be receiving a constant barrage of criticism from both activists and the public. What can, what should, advertising do about it?

Such a straightforward question is, unfortunately, not subject to a simple answer. This is in part because of the number of component institutions involved in the creation, approval, and transmission of advertising—that is, the company-advertiser, agency, and media. Thus there is no single entity that, in fact, *is* "advertising."

In part it is because the issues are often very complex. For example, in a legal system that is adversary-rooted, should (as has been proposed) a party be forced not only to testify against himself but to stabilize dissemination of the testimony? Or, if advertisers get together to monitor and control content, is this a form of collusion?

In spite of such questions and difficulties, certain suggestions do emerge from this analysis of what the business community thinks and says about advertising today. The survey findings clearly point to rising expectations for advertising's performance held by the business community itself, expectations reflecting a changing—wider—context in which advertising is being assessed.

The main direction of executive finger pointing is at advertising content. This, it seems, is a zone which is most in control of those in advertising. Content can be policed at its place of birth, and hence it is rather more susceptible to change than, say, economic factors.

For example, advertisers—via top management directive—and agencies can shun the frequent practice of "legal limits" activity. Rather than trying to wend a way over, under, around, and through legal boundaries, an advertiser could focus on what's right for the consumer (or, more properly, for various kinds of consumers). Such steps, among others, would represent behavioral change that would also help rebuild consumer confidence in advertising.

The concluding comments of the 1962 HBR study referred to the challenge and opportunity of making improvements in advertising. The task of the advertising fraternity's responsible members to "weed out those in their midst whose activities bring opprobrium upon all of advertising" drew special attention. At that time, such action was characterized by the word "hopeful," to avoid encouraging outside regulation.

Today the "challenge and opportunity" perhaps should be replaced by "challenge and necessity." The objective is not only to inhibit restrictions that might be inflicted on advertising by those with little understanding of its operations. But also, from a very selfish point of view, it is to prevent any further "devaluation" of advertising as an important business tool.

Q. International Marketing

48. A Conceptual Approach to International Business

FRANKLIN R. ROOT

There is much disagreement and confusion about the nature and scope of international business as an academic field of study. Economists are wont to view international business as little more than a particular application of international economics.[1] Specialists in the traditional business functions, such as marketing, finance and management, are inclined to conceive international business as simply a study of those functions in an international context. Others, notably business school deans, tend to label as international business any "international" activity undertaken by a business school, such as assistance to foreign institutions or the establishment of study centers abroad.[2]

This diversity of opinion raises a fundamental question: Is there a field of international business study that is separate and distinct from international economics, the functional business disciplines, and international studies in general? This writer believes there is and offers in support of his position a conceptual approach that delineates the scope and character of international business as a field of study. Apart from distinguishing international business from other social and business disciplines, this approach provides a structure that facilitates the integration of the many phenomena of international business into a meaningful pattern. As a "cognitive set" it is particularly helpful in the teaching of international business. It is also heuristic, stimulating the development of testable hypotheses about international business behavior.

As a field of study, international business is primarily directed towards the description, analysis, explanation and prediction of the actual and normative behavior of the private business enterprise as it strives to achieve its strategic and operational goals in a multinational environment. In particular, the study of international business centers on the *cross-national interactions* that create dynamic linkages among the elements comprising the international enterprise (intra-enterprise interactions) and between the enterprise as a whole and its multinational environmental systems (extra-enterprise interactions). The implications of this conception are elaborated by a theoretical model that regards the business firm as an international enterprise system interacting with three environmental systems which, in turn, are subsystems of a nation-state system.

---

[1] Charles P. Kindleberger is an outstanding exception. See, for example, his *American Business Abroad*, Yale University Press, 1969.

[2] The Conference on Education for International Business held at Tulane University in November 1968 was attended by representatives from 98 U.S. business schools, including many deans. Over one-third of the papers and discussion was devoted to the overseas activities of American schools of business. See *Business Schools and the Challenge of International Business*. Graduate School of Business Administration, Tulane University, 1968.

◆ SOURCE: Franklin R. Root, "A Conceptual Approach to International Business," *Journal of Business Administration*, volume 1, number 1, (Summer 1969), pages 18–28.

Fig. 1 is a schematic of this model. In describing the three environmental systems—political, economic and socio-cultural—we shall simply define the actors of each system and the typical relations among them that together make up the system structure. We shall give somewhat more attention to the international enterprise system which is the focus of our attention.

THE INTERNATIONAL POLITICAL SYSTEM

International society is a society of nation-states. Each state possesses people, territory and a sovereign government. Collectively, the nation-states form an international system because they "communicate" with each other through political, social, cultural, economic, and business transfers and exchanges. Fig. 1 depicts the nation-states as sectors that are linked together by a variety of international relations (the dashed lines) to form a nation-state system.[3]

The international political system is a sub-system of the nation-state system. The actors in this subsystem are *national governments*. Each government has an exclusive jurisdiction over the territory of the respective nation-state, and it is the only legal representative of that state *vis a vis* other states. Furthermore, national governments have a legal monopoly in the use of physical force, and through laws and regulations they establish and enforce the "rules of the game" for individuals and organizations, including foreign business enterprise. In particular, national governments have the power to constrain all private international transactions. Hence the survival of international enterprise depends on the willingness of governments to allow the entry of foreign ownership, management, capital, technology, and products. Since states control the entire land surface of the earth every individual and organization is a legal resident of a particular state and is subject

---

[3] The environment of the nation-state system is the global natural or physical environment which provides the "stage" for nation states.

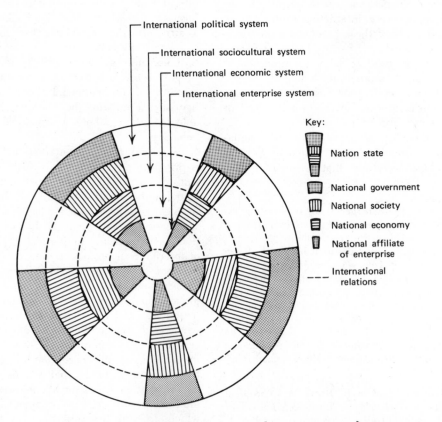

FIGURE 1. The international enterprise and its environmental systems.

to its authority in the person of the national government. This principle of national sovereignty raises many problems for a business enterprise that is operating on the territory of more than one state, such as dual allegiance, double taxation, expropriation, and legal rights and remedies.

Each state seeks to build relations with other states that sustain or further its own national interests as conceived by government leaders. To carry out its foreign policy, a government depends on its capacity to influence the behavior of other states either negatively through deterrence in its many forms or positively through leadership and cooperation. Broadly speaking, then, *power* is the essence of international political relations. When we take into account the existence of over one hundred sovereign national governments, the pattern of political relations becomes highly intricate and may change radically over time. In Figure 1 the outer ring depicts the international political system: national governments functioning within the constraints and opportunities created by international power relations that shift over time.[4]

THE INTERNATIONAL
SOCIO-CULTURAL SYSTEM

The international socio-cultural system is a second subsystem of the nation-state system. A nation-state contains a national society and culture—a group of people sharing a common social experience and a set of cultural values that are identified with the nation. At the macroscopic level the actors of this system are the national societies; at the microscopic, all the individuals, groups and institutions comprising the national society when they enter into social relations (rather than political, economic or business relations) with members of other national societies.

The linkages (or flows) that tie together the national social actors to form an international system are various kinds of *cross-cultural communications*. Cross-cultural communication is prone to error or failure because the sender and receiver of a message belong

to different socio-cultural milieux that may foster markedly different values, norms of behavior, motivations, expectations, and attitudes towards the world and other peoples. Somehow these cultural gaps must be bridged if communication is to be effective, a far more difficult task than mere translation from one language into another. The literature of international business offers many examples of faulty cross-cultural communication.

One particular set of attitudes and values deserves special mention because of its importance to international business, namely, *nationalism*. In its positive aspects, nationalism expresses a loyalty to, and an identification with, a given society, culture and state. As such, it is the cement that binds a people together to form a nationality. Nationalism is an extremely complex phenomenon that shifts through time and space. As a cultural phenomenon nationalism may range from xenophobia to xenophilia with cosmopolitanism somewhere in between. As a political phenomenon, nationalism may run from a simple love of country (patriotism) through a glorification of the state (chauvinism). Be cause it involves in varying degrees a mix of attitudes, feelings and values such as pride, dignity, cultural superiority, distinctiveness, egoism, and sensitivity, nationalism frequently injects an emotional energy into international relations that may distort cross-cultural communication and incite governments to behavior that undermines the achievement of rational political and economic goals. A case in point is the recent seizure of the International Petroleum Company in Peru. After the seizure the Peruvian government declared a "national day of dignity" that has been celebrated by special stamp issue. Now a captive of nationalistic sentiments intensified by its own propaganda and behavior, the Peruvian government may well be prevented from dealing with the economic and political issues raised by the expropriation in a way that will best promote the national interests of Peru.

Negative attitudes towards foreign states and peoples are common elements of nationalism. When a business firm enters a foreign country, its reception by the government and the public depends in substantial measure on the blend of nationalism that predominates there. A nationalism that mixes highly xenophobic and chauvinistic attitudes creates a very hostile environment for international business. Nationalism may also distort com-

---

[4] International organizations are omitted from this schematic because they derive from agreements among nation-states and do not have supranational sovereignty. That is to say, we view international organizations as an aspect of relations among nation-states.

munication among the different national members of the same international business enterprise.

The international socio-cultural system is shown as the second ring in Fig. 1.

THE INTERNATIONAL ECONOMIC SYSTEM

Each nation-state also has an economy. Thus the macroscopic actors of the international economic system are the national economies. These economies and the many diverse transactions among them form the structure of the system. Flows of merchandise, services, money, capital, technology, human skills, and information create varying degrees of interdependence. A nation's balance of payments is a financial summary of these flows over a period of time, and foreign exchange rates reflect the existence of autonomous national monetary systems. The study of international economics is mainly concerned with the international economic system at this macroscopic level.

In the contemporary world economy, the international transactions of the West (the industrial market economies located mainly in North America, Western Europe and Japan) and of the South (the developing economies located mainly in Africa, non-Communist Asia, and Latin America) are for the most part initiated and performed by private business firms. Since the motivation behind these transactions is economic gain (a broader concept than profit maximization), the size, composition and pattern of flows among national economies are largely explicable in economic terms, especially at the macroscopic level. That is to say, these flows would not occur in the absence of opportunities for economic gain that derive from the structure and behavior of the national economies. It is not to say, however, that transactions among national economies are fully autonomous with respect to the international political and socio-cultural systems. Quite the contrary. The pattern of economic interdependence would be different (and very different in some instances) in the absence of government policies in trade, foreign aid, payments, capital flows, the movement of human factors, and so on. Also the widespread presence of nationalism and other socio-cultural phenomena have constrained economic relations.

In the East (the centrally-planned economies of Eastern Europe, the Soviet Union and Mainland China) all transactions with foreign economies are in the hands of state agencies. Although state-trading oranizations may be guided by a calculus of economic gain (resembling somewhat the behavior of private firms), they must function within the constraints of national plans. Furthermore, these organizations may be used by the national government to achieve purely political objectives. In the East, then, the macroscopic actors in the international economy are the national governments which exercise a monopoly control over the respective national economies.

At the microscopic level, transactions among the market economies are transactions among private firms. Transactions between market and centrally-planned economies are transactions between private firms and state agencies. This situation and the general prohibition of foreign enterprise within the Communist countries has created a negative international business environment in the East that is radically divergent from that of the West and the South.

The international economic system (including both its market and non-market subsystems) is illustrated by the third ring in Fig. 1.

THE INTERNATIONAL ENTERPRISE SYSTEM

A business firm becomes an international enterprise when its management seeks to achieve greater profits and growth by extending the firm's operations across national boundaries. The degree to which a firm becomes international depends on both the scope of its multinational activities and on the orientation of its top management.

Evolution of the International Business Enterprise

Most companies first enter international business by exporting their products to foreign markets. As export sales grow, the company may establish its own sales agencies and branches in foreign countries. It may also start to license foreign firms to undertake the manufacture of its products for sale in local markets. Up to this point, the enterprise remains an *export* company that sells abroad from a domestic production base, perhaps supplemented by licensing arrangements with independent foreign producers.

The next step in the evolution of the international enterprise is a crucial one: the establishment of production units abroad under its own managerial control in order to exploit foreign market opportunities more effectively than from a home production base.[5] Since control usually rests on ownership, this step requires the company to invest capital abroad either to build new facilities or acquire existing ones. With a bigger stake in international business, the company becomes more willing to commit resources (managerial as well as financial) to its foreign operations. The firm has become an *international production* company.

As the company's international production and marketing network expands geographically, its foreign sales and profits may rise to (say) one-fifth or more of total corporate levels. As a result, top line and staff management in the headquarters company gradually shift from a domestic to a global perspective, assuming strategic direction and control of all operations regardless of their geographical location. When corporate management begins to plan, coordinate and control on a global

basis, the traditional distinction between domestic and foreign business fades away. In short, management conceives of the parent company and its many foreign affiliates as a single business system. When that happens, the company has become a world-wide or *multinational* enterprise.[6]

Structure of the International Enterprise System

The international enterprise system is represented by the fourth ring in Fig. 1 where it is conceived as a subsystem of the nation-state systems. Fig. 2 offers a more detailed schematic of the international enterprise system.

The H circle in Fig. 2 represents the headquarters company which exercises managerial control over three production affiliates (the P's) and three marketing affiliates (the M's). Each of these units is located in a different nation-state as is indicated by the dashed lines. The affiliates are connected to headquarters and in some instances to other affiliates by a variety of cross-national flows. In its role as headquarters, key flows emanat-

---

[5] It is important to distinguish investment abroad to capitalize on foreign market opportunity from investment abroad to obtain a source of supply for domestic operations. Although the latter generates cross-national transactions, dependence on foreign supply sources for purely domestic operations does not make the management of a firm international in its orientation. Only when a company turns towards markets abroad for the sale of its products (wherever produced) does it truly enter the ranks of international enterprise.

[6] The emergence of the multinational enterprise is a recent phenomenon, and only a small fraction of international companies today are multinational. But the pace at which the top management of big international production companies is shifting to a global perspective suggests that the multinational company will become the dominant (if not the most numerous) form of international enterprise in the decades ahead. Some observers believe that a few hundred giant multinational firms will dominate production and trade in the 1980's.

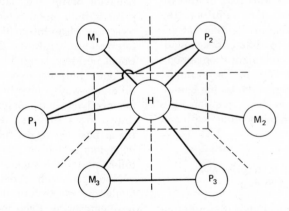

FIGURE 2. The international enterprise system.

ing from H are ownership, management and information. Key flows received by H are payment (including profit) and information. H may also be a supplier of technology, product and capital as well. Many kinds of flows may link pairs of affiliates. For example, P_1 may transfer parts (or some other input), technology or capital to P_2; P_3 (rather than H) may export end-products to M_3. One of the most interesting features of the multinational company is the rapid development of inter-affiliate flows as headquarters management tries to improve the performance of the entire enterprise system.

Observe that these intra-enterprise relations are cross-national. In this sense the international enterprise recapitulates in microcosm the three international environmental systems. In other words, the enterprise "internalizes" the international environment. Thus the flows between enterprise actors (headquarters and the affiliates) occur within the constraints laid down by the governments of two or more nation-states. At one extreme, certain flows may be impossible or uneconomic because of outright prohibitions, tariffs, import quotas, exchange controls, and the like; at the other extreme, governments may encourage certain flows by offering subsidies, tax holidays, import privileges, repatriation guarantees, and so on. Conceptually, there are always four parties involved in a flow between two enterprise actors located in different nation-states: the two actors and the two national governments. Each government seeks to insure that intra-enterprise flows promote its own national interest, and in this way these flows are shaped by international political relations. Intra-enterprise flows also generate transactions among national economies and are therefore part of the international economic system. Further, the management and workers of the different enterprise actors belong to different socio-cultural systems and the communication among them is cross-cultural. When, for example, a Brazilian subsidiary reports to its United States parent, it is usually a question of a Brazilian national communicating with an American national.

The International Enterprise as a Behavioral System

With regard to its activity, the international business enterprise may be viewed as a behavioral system—a group of persons interacting with each other and with the group environment. We can distinguish various subsystems comprising a behavioral system: a goal system, a power system, a communications system, an input-output system, and an adaptation system.

The international business enterprise is an *organized* behavioral system with a dominant decision-center and a hierarchy of enterprise goals. It seeks to achieve its goals by drawing inputs (human services, materials, technology, money) from a multinational environment, transforming them into outputs of goods and services, and then transferring those outputs back into the multinational environment. The enterprise grows (and in the long-run survives) when its input-output system generates a surplus (profit, positive return on investment). But a surplus will be forthcoming over time only when the enterprise has the capacity to adapt to a changing environment, including changes it may have induced by its own behavior.

These processes of interaction between the enterprise and its environmental system also involve interactions among the elements of the enterprise. The efforts of management to give shape and direction to internal and external interactive processes may be termed strategies. Since management responds only to its perceived environment, effective enterprise behavior depends on a communication system that will narrow gaps between the perceived and objective environments.

INTERNATIONAL INTERACTION PROCESSES AND MODELS

As noted above, the goal-seeking, adaptive behavior of the international business enterprise is built upon internal and external interactions of an international character. These interactions constitute the focus of international business as a field of study. Depending on one's purpose, they may be conceived in different ways, investigated from different perspectives, and analyzed with techniques drawn from different disciplines: the functional business fields, the social sciences, the behavioral sciences, and mathematics. The following table is suggestive in this regard.

Note that each model type reflects a particular perspective of the international business enterprise. Each model type is international and each may cover both intra and

Interaction Model Archetypes for the
Study of International Business

Perspective	Interaction Models
Environmental System	Political Economic Socio-Cultural
Behavioral System	Goals Power Input-Output Communication Adaptation
Functional	Marketing Production Finance R and D
Managerial	Organizing Staffing Planning Directing Controlling

extra-enterprise interactions. The models are intended to be dynamic, involving both positive and negative feedbacks over time.

Since the environmental systems perspective has been stressed in this article, a brief description of a political interaction model may indicate the usefulness of interaction models in the study of international business. We choose as our example negotiations between an enterprise and a foreign government on the conditions of entry.

Misunderstanding and conflicts of interest and policy are to be expected in negotiations between an internal enterprise and a host government. Final agreement calls for a lengthy exchange of information to eliminate apparent conflict and bilateral bargaining to resolve real conflict. Frequently, negotiations end in failure. A fertile source of misunderstanding is ignorance of the other party's goals and motivations.

Broadly speaking, the enterprise goal is profitable operation in the host country at an acceptable level of political risk within a given time horizon. To achieve this goal management believes that certain conditions are necessary or desirable in one degree or another. Thus at the start of negotiations management may ask the host government for the right to own fully its affiliate; for assurance of profit and capital repatriation, non-discrim-

inatory treatment in taxation and other matters, and protection against expropriation; for the right to import raw materials, machinery and other inputs; and perhaps for special favors such as import protection, subsidies and concessions. In contrast, the overriding goal of the host government is the promotion of the national interest as conceived by its leaders. Government officials are usually concerned with the effects of the proposed venture on economic development and growth (particularly with respect to the national economic plan), the balance of payments, the level of employment, worker skills, technological innovation, tax revenues, local competition, national economic independence, political sovereignty, and so on.

At the start of negotiations, then, each party views the proposed venture from markedly different perspectives. To further complicate matters, each party may be highly ignorant of the specific goals and motivations of the other. Seldom has management carefully investigated the probable macroscopic economic, political and social effects of its proposed venture and it may have only a hazy notion of the criteria that the host government will use to evaluate that venture. On the other side, government officials are often surprisingly ignorant of the dynamics of private business enterprise and the role of profit as a reward for enterprise and a source of future growth and ultimate survival. Hence the first phase of negotiations is mainly concerned with closing an information gap and developing an understanding of each other's goals and the criteria each employs to measure both the costs and benefits of the venture. The positive outcome of this phase is the determination of any *real* conflict of interests by stripping away any apparent conflict based only on misunderstanding. This phase may be unduly prolonged by distrust of foreign enterprise on the part of the host government, a climate of extreme nationalism, administrative incompetency, and by management's reluctance to talk in macroscopic terms.

Bargaining starts in earnest in the second phase of negotiations. Each party seeks to maximize his benefit/cost ratio as he conceives it over a future period of time. Bargaining (rather than unilateral dictate) occurs because each party has something the other wants and ordinarily does not have the power to force unconditional acceptance of his terms. But each party does have a lesser degree of power that can be used to persuade the other to accept some, if not all, of his initial conditions. The enterprise draws power mainly from the resources it is capable of transferring to the host country (products, technology, capital, management skills, market outlets, etc.), from its options to invest elsewhere, from its identity as a national of a particular foreign country, and from its role in the international business community. The host government draws power from its soverign right to exclude the enterprise or constrain its operations in various ways; from the attractiveness of its national markets, natural resources, labor, infra-structure, geographical location, etc.; from its reputation for political stability, and from its political and economic relations with other countries, especially the parent country of the enterprise.

Each party will use these sources of power (either explicitly or implicitly) in the dynamic give and take of bargaining. In some instances one party will have the predominance of power. Thus IBM received permission from the Indian and Japanese governments to establish 100 percent-owned subsidiaries (despite strong national policies opposing foreign majority ownership) because IBM technology was badly wanted by the two governments. Other companies, lacking such an obvious source of power, have had to settle for minority ownership or go elsewhere. Here the Japanese government (in contrast to the Indian) has enjoyed a definite advantage that derives from the size and rapid growth of Japanese markets. It should also be noted that power relations may shift over time. In 1963 the Spanish government was able to lay down severe terms for the right to exploit big phosphate deposits in the Spanish Sahara. But the company that eventually won the bidding (under stringent conditions, including only a 25 percent equity) withdrew from the venture early in 1968 because in the meantime the world phosphate market had entered a prolonged decline.

Negotiations end with agreement when each party accepts the same entry conditions. To do so, each must believe that his benefits will exceed his costs over a relevant future time period. Even then, negotiations will not be effective until the venture actually begins operations, as indicated in the Spanish case. If space permitted, other aspects of this negotiation model might be discussed, such as precipitating circumstances, behavior patterns or style, and time horizons. But our intent is only to suggest the usefulness of interaction models by means of a modest illustration.[7]

CONCLUSION

In this article we have offered a conception of the business firm as an international enterprise system interacting with three international environmental systems—the political, the economic and the socio-cultural. We have asserted that international business as a field of study focuses on cross-national interaction processes within the international enterprise and between it and its systems environments. As suggested by a number of archetypal models, these interaction processes may be studied from a variety of perspectives. This conceptual approach provides a mental construct that distinguishes international business from other disciplines, assists in international business education, and points towards some key problems for international business research.

---

[7] For a fuller discussion of enterprise-government negotiations, see John Fayerweather, *International Business Management*, McGraw-Hill, 1969, Chapter 4.

49. Myths that Mislead U.S. Managers in Japan

YOSHI TSURUMI

Despite repeated complaints from industrialized nations that Japan is still limiting direct foreign investment, this investment is definitely increasing—especially from the United States. Accordingly, managers of U.S. subsidiaries in Japan can expect growing resistance and competitive pressure from Japanese companies. The honeymoon that never really started, according to some observers, has definitely ended.

Moreover, this sensitivity to foreign investment is occuring at a time when Japan is exhibiting all the symptoms, and problems, of a post-industrial state. Business organizations are now confident only of their economic strength. Technological progress has outstripped the capability to manage it, and the romantic notion that economic growth is an end in itself and all other good things in life will follow automatically is a relic of past exuberance. Japan now faces the serious challenge of reordering social values and institutions.

While many Japanese businessmen see their companies catching up technologically with the United States, they perceive that they are behind managerially and regard the acquisition of management skills as crucial to continued success. In the increasingly competitive climate of Japan, the manner in which U.S. companies approach the transfer of these skills to the Japanese environment will markedly

◆ SOURCE: Reprinted by permission from *Harvard Business Review*, Vol. 49, No. 4, July–August 1971, pp. 118–127. © 1971 by the President and Fellows of Harvard College; all rights reserved.

affect the success—or failure—of their subsidiary and joint-venture operations that employ nationals.

What is required from U.S. companies in Japan today is a far cry from the simple technical knowledge of products and manufacturing processes that characterized the first generation of U.S. participation in the Japanese economy. This knowledge has long since been assimilated by the Japanese. Far more substantive skills are necessary, both for the internal efficiency of subsidiaries in Japan and for positive external relations with other Japanese organizations. There is abundant evidence, however, that many companies are still behaving as if they still *were* in the first generation, at least with respect to transfer of management skills.

This evidence comes from interviews I conducted with over 200 employees in more than 25 companies with joint ventures and/or subsidiaries in Japan, and it points to some serious misconceptions on the part of U.S. managers concerning the transfer of management skills. In the course of this study I discovered seven popular and pervasive myths surrounding skill transfer that are hindering U.S. attempts to build viable subsidiaries in Japan. Unless these myths are recognized for what they are, corporations attempting to widen their inroads in the Japanese economy may find themselves losing out to increasingly aggressive local companies.

In this article, I shall first review briefly the industrial policy of Japan that has brought about the inevitable confrontation between Japanese and U.S. companies; then I shall discuss the seven myths that are plaguing U.S. managers in Japan and present some guidelines to follow.

NEW COMPETITIVE CLIMATE

In order to separate manufacturing technologies from other components of "capital," such as money, control, and ownership, Japan has traditionally dictated carefully, through strict licensing agreements, both the quality and the quantity of foreign technology inflow. Under these agreements, when a technology was judged superior enough to warrant the price of foreign control and ownership, a joint venture with a maximum of 50% foreign control was grudgingly conceded by the Japanese.

In 1969, however, the Japanese government, feeling the pressure for political and economic concessions to other industrialized nations, made public a timetable of "capital liberalization" (i.e., unrestricted foreign ownership). This plan allowed direct foreign investment in such industries as brewing, cotton spinning, and steel, where foreigners held no advantage over Japanese companies. Under increased pressure, primarily from the United States, the timetable has recently been advanced, and by the end of this year all other industries, even the automobile industry, are scheduled to be liberalized.

Breakup of Licensing

In this less restrictive climate, U.S. and other foreign companies that were once willing to license their technologies to Japanese companies merely for royalties, and sometimes a minority participation in the venture, are now setting their sights considerably higher. Except in cases of cross licensing, where they can also benefit from Japanese technological breakthroughs, foreign companies are now negotiating substantial equity participation in Japanese ventures in exchange for their technologies.

Moreover, with a number of earlier licensing agreements now due for renewal or expiration, U.S. partners are successfully altering the initial limited equity participation and obtaining complete or majority control—principally over marketing activities, but often also over manufacturing activities where the Japanese partners are too weak financially or technologically to resist. And size of the Japanese partner is no safeguard; for example:

As unhappy officials of the Ministry of International Trade and Industry (MITI) commented sadly in the summer of 1969, when the fate of the joint venture between Mitsubishi Heavy Industry and Dresser Company of the United States had been decided, "Even Mitsubishi bowed to Dresser's demand for breaking up the joint venture sales company, Nippon Clark, and moving all the marketing functions to Dresser's Tokyo branch office." [1] Dresser Company is to keep all the profits from marketing compressor equipment in Japan when the licensing agreement with Mitsubishi expires in 1971. Mitsubishi Heavy Industry will simply be reduced to a subcontractor of compressor equipment for Dresser, and the Japanese employees who have developed loyalty to Nippon Clark will become the employees of Dresser in Tokyo; thus, Dresser's sales activities will not be hampered.

Similar dissolutions of licensing agreements and joint ventures are occurring throughout Japanese industries. The internal strains are most keenly felt in those industries where the Japanese government now allows a fully owned foreign subsidiary. In the rapidly growing pharmaceutical industry, for example, a number of leading foreign companies have already completed "re-arrangements" in their favor.

Invasion of the Automakers

Recent toeholds established by GM, Ford, and Chrysler in Japan are indicative of the challenges facing Japanese industry. With increases in Japan's car exports, the Japanese government finds it difficult to ignore U.S. pressure to open up Japan's growing automobile market to American producers. Furthermore, the government's efforts to develop Nissan and Toyota as the two viable automobile firms in Japan have understandably alienated other local automobile manufacturers, like Isuzu, Toyo Kogyo (Mazda), and Mitsubishi. Instead of allowing themselves to be absorbed into the orbit of either Nissan or Toyota, these companies sought to enhance their competitive clout by obtaining a foreign partner. GM, Ford, and Chrysler seized on this opportunity to establish manufacturing and marketing bases in Japan, and the three joint ventures, GM-Isuzu, Ford-Mazda, and Chrysler-Mitsubishi, will soon be official.

---

[1] *Nihon Keizai Shinbun*, August 15, 1969.

The three U.S. auto companies are ostensibly landing in Japan as partners of Japanese companies; thus, the question of "nationality," or foreign ownership, is not an overt one. Whether or not these joint ventures will come to be "rearranged" or "broken up" in the U.S. parents' favor depends on the future strength of their Japanese partners. No doubt, MITI and the two leading automobile manufacturers in Japan, Nissan and Toyota, will try their hardest to contain the influence of U.S. automobile manufacturers by competing vigorously with them at home and abroad. The success of the "big three" will, however, be mainly determined by how well they transfer their American management skills to the Japanese environment.

THE SEVEN MYTHS

What has happened in the automobile industry in Japan is indicative of the convulsions in nearly all Japanese industry. Though embrionic, the "liberalization of capital" program is forcing local companies to overhaul their competitive strategies at home, and U.S. companies are likely to lose out in the long run unless they cut through the prevalent myths surrounding international transfer of managerial skills. Let us now turn to an examination of these seven myths and the obstacles they present to U.S. companies attempting to build viable subsidiaries in Japan.

Myth #1: "Because our company has more manufacturing know-how than the natives, we also possess better management skills that are transferable 'as is' to our Japanese subsidiary. They must learn from us, not vice versa."

This myth is perpetuated daily. For one thing, it is very comforting to managers from another country whose ignorance of local culture and language would otherwise give them a feeling of insecurity and impotence. Supposedly, their ignorance of local language and culture is a "desirable" sign of their being mindful of the parent company's interests. To many U.S. managers, Japan is still far removed from contemporary, North American, Judeo-Christian civilization, and beyond the facade of office buildings and bustling city life rises an oriental puzzle.

Myth #1 is also magnified by American managers' ignorance of the nature of management skills. Conceptually, the management skills associated with a proprietary technology can be classified as:

1. *Product-related* skills emanating from identifiable products or manufacturing processes, the technology of which is often patentable or marketable. (These skills include such objective techniques as direct sales methods, office memo formats and work procedures, assembly-line balancing, and statistical quality control methods.)

2. *Institution-related* skills resulting from the body of experience that has grown around a specific technology. (This operational experience cannot be separated from the company and employees that make it up. It includes the organizational ability to integrate economic activities in market research, R&D work, marketing, and manufacturing; the ability to control product quality, production-line efficiency, and proper flow of management information; and, of course, the ability to train managers and motivate people.)

What is most often meant by "management skills" is obviously the institution-related category. But since this body of skills is intrinsically associated with the company where it is developed and refined, it is the most difficult to objectify and transfer from one place (situation) to another, let alone from one country (culture) to another.

In the course of my research, I found that when U.S. managers in Japan felt they had successfully transferred their company's management skills to Japanese subsidiaries, these skills were in fact almost always of the product-related, technical type. Furthermore, successful transfer of these technical methods required, without exception, two things: (a) Japanese staffs who understood them well and were sensitive to changes they cause in the working relationship of Japanese employees; and (b) ad hoc improvisation and gradual adaptation of such technical methods to fit Japanese situations.

Learn from the Japanese. There are many American managers who freely criticize their Japanese employees' resistance to change (i.e., to adapting to the parent's way of doing things). Interestingly enough, similar changes have been successfully instituted in many Japanese companies by *Japanese* managers. So, before American managers lament the frustrating mission in which Japanese employees or subcontractors refuse to accept their methods—methods they know for a fact to be superior and, therefore, good for the Japanese—they should examine the reasons why many Japanese companies are able to produce essentially "American-born" products —say, television sets—without imitating totally a General Electric's management practices. They should identify clearly what aspects of their company's management skills are really superior to Japanese practices and the requirements necessary for transferring such skills to Japan.

While this first myth may lead managers of foreign subsidiaries to assume that they have very little to learn from Japanese management practices, there is, in fact, much to learn. U.S. managers will find, for example, that management-employee relationships in Japan are relatively free of unnecessary and often artificial tensions. The practices that enable management and employees to identify with each other provide challenging lessons for American managers,[2] and highlight the fact that proper transfer of management skills is a two-way affair.

Myth #2: "The quickest way of transferring our management skills to Japan is to combine the on-the-job training of our own managers there with their simultaneous roles as trainers of our Japanese staffs."

When American trainees are, in every sense of the word, the people who need training as managers first, let alone as multinational managers, the parent company that indulges in this second myth is endangering not only the development of its American trainees but, more importantly, that of its Japanese subsidiary. It is extremely naive to assume that simply because trainees come from the parent, they have a thorough knowledge of the parent's management practices and are capable of adapting them to Japanese situations.

I have encountered numerous high-caliber Japanese staffs that are repeatedly frustrated and demoralized at the irony of being "students" of foreign manager-trainees (their im-

mediate bosses) while, at the same time, having to remedy the blunders of a boss who does not yet understand their culture. Other serious problems result from the "manager-trainee" practice; here are the most pervasive ones:

☐ The parent's desire to train managers in Japan is often given priority over the need to build its subsidiary as a truly viable Japanese organization. As a result, many American managers are sent in and out again on a short rotation basis, and this yields two distinctly unfortunate consequences: (a) lack of continuity from one manager to another in the subsidiary's ongoing business operations; and (b) constant frustration of Japanese employees' ambitions to grow into responsible managerial positions. Evidence of this frustration is exhibited by the recent turnover in such established U.S. companies as Shell Oil, Standard Oil (N.J.), and NCR of capable Japanese with management potential. More importantly, it is precisely this fear of becoming permanent "foreigners' assistants" that is prompting many extremely able Japanese to refuse job offers from U.S. companies.

☐ The Japanese employees (often upper-level managers too) are not informed of their company's business conditions for the following reasons: (a) it is not uncommon in the United States to keep financial records out of the reach of rank-and-file employees; and (b) the high turnover of manager-trainees, as well as their lack of familiarity with Japanese customs, perpetuates an image of Japanese employees as a faceless mask. The employees of local Japanese companies are much better informed about their organization's sales, profits, number of employees, and even the number of new and old products, than their counterparts in U.S. subsidiaries. They want to know how fast their organization is growing, and local companies often divulge such records to foster interest and identification with corporate success symbols. In contrast, Japanese employees of U.S. subsidiaries, who naturally expect similar consideration, interpret the apparent secrecy of their foreign managers as a sign of distrust and, consequently, fail to develop any sense of loyalty to the company.

☐ When U.S. managers do train Japanese staffs well, it is not uncommon for them to receive little formal recognition from their company for this educational achievement.

---

[2] For references on Japanese labor relations and/or management practices, see M. Yoshino, *Japan's Managerial System* (Cambridge, The M.I.T. Press, 1968); and Y. Tsurumi, "The Industrial Relations System in Japan" (Boston, Intercollegiate Case Clearing House, Harvard Business School, 1966), ICH 11Gr.

These managers are evaluated by their companies on how well they achieve economic goals, and, in the process, training of Japanese employees and building a Japanese organization become little more than lip service. This unfulfilled promise demoralizes capable Japanese staffs who believe in the U.S. managers' stated intentions of phasing themselves out and delegating greater responsibility. Shattered hope ferments bitter disappointment. *A more realistic approach*: To avoid the pitfalls of Myth #2, the U.S. company expecting to use expatriate managers to train local nationals for responsible positions should, at the minimum, evaluate their willingness, and ability, to phase themselves out of local operations. Moreover, it is wise to separate the training function of managers-to-be from actual duties in the Japanese subsidiary; they do not have to be immediately placed in responsible staff or line positions.

If the managers have many things to learn, and if the company expects them to develop sensitivity to business in a foreign environment, they will learn more as assistants to seasoned local nationals. If a company does not have such seasoned and capable local nationals, its first priority should be to recruit such people and let *them* build the subsidiary.

Myth #3: "An 'Asian expert' is the best person to handle our company's relations with the Japanese and, even better, to manage our subsidiary in Japan. This way, we'll have an American who can bridge the gap."

U.S. companies embarking on a venture in Japan know that it takes some knowledge of the local culture to do business and prosper there. The search for someone who knows "the tricks of the trade" in Japan often uncovers an American or other foreign expatriate who has been operating in the East Asian circuit for some time. The problem is that to many companies it does not matter if this individual's "Asian experience" is confined, say, to the region west of Pakistan. It is close enough; and his credentials look impressive— he sold soap, typewriters, and many other things in Asia, and also speaks English fluently. If his experience is shored up by the prestige of being hired by the parent company, especially for a managerial position in Japan, he has not only the Asian experience but also the management skills embodied by the parent company.

As it happens, the Japanese have by now developed their own stereotypes about foreigners who have been on the Asian business circuit. Like any other form of prejudice, this is a simplified reflection of imagined or real problems that the Japanese have encountered in the past with such circuit travelers. To the Japanese, these expatriates represent people who failed to succeed in their own country and yet dare not mingle freely with Japanese.

With this prejudice against him, the expatriate in the Asian scene has a doubly difficult time proving himself. When he inadvertently alludes to success stories in Thailand, the Phillipines, Hong Kong, and other Asian nations in order to impress his Japanese employees, he is merely confirming Japanese prejudice against him—"The poor fellow does not see the difference between Japan and Hong Kong."

Of course, there are other expatriates who are directly familiar with the Japanese culture and who can command respect from the Japanese. But they are few and far between, and difficult to find. And, more often than not, well-meaning U.S. managers will fall into the trap of Myth #3 by not being discerning enough in their search for an "Asian expert."

Myth #4: "The only thing that we lack is knowledge of the Japanese language. Once we obtain an interpreter, we can get on with the task of building our subsidiary in Japan and developing amicable rapport with other Japanese companies and government agencies."

Because of the inevitable language barrier, U.S. managers often rely on (or are at the mercy of) interpreters who initially are hired only for their language proficiency. Since individuals who possess language *and* managerial and other professional ability are distinctly in short supply, and, more importantly, since U.S. managers are looking primarily for a person who can speak English, they often hire English-speaking Japanese "assistant-interpreters" whom they encounter at friends' homes or even at a bar or night club.

It is extremely important that U.S. managers understand how Japanese generally regard the interpreter function. Ever since Japan's first contact with "foreign powers," interpreters have never fared well socially in Japan; and no self-respecting Japanese businessman wants to have direct dealings with employees who are designated as interpreters. (The role is considered subservient to the major parties involved.) Hiring an individual as both interpreter and assistant, with real or implied management responsibilities, can be detrimental to the success of a Japanese subsidiary, both internally and externally.

To dwell for a moment on the external effects of such a policy, the use of an assistant-interpreter, regardless of his official title, will likely reinforce the already-existing prejudice that Japanese outside the company hold against Japanese employees of foreign subsidiaries. This is courting double-trouble, considering the aforementioned context of the term "interpreter," and names like "foreigner's errand boy" are heaped on such assistants. Respect for the entire organization is likely to be lowered; and, needless to say, relations with government agencies, subcontractors, and other companies in Japan will also suffer.

Internal Ramifications. At the initial stage of subsidiary activity, when Japanese partners and the personnel of outside Japanese companies are occupied with absorbing the technical aspects of product-related technologies (such as simple sales methods and product quality control methods), it is often sufficient to impart this "technical" expertise through able interpreters. Their only necessary qualification is that they understand technical skills well enough to explain them in Japanese.

However, once the subsidiary's Japanese employees and subcontractors adequately master these skills, U.S. managers will be expected to provide far more sophisticated managerial guidance for complex business problems, both inside and outside the subsidiary.

Japanese employees often decide to make the subsidiary their "place" for a long time to come, if not for a lifetime, and naturally expect both formal and informal evidence that their company is internally growing and widening a solid base. The more able the employees, the stronger will be their expectation; and one of the most persuasive evidences of proper management is fair and consistent hiring and promotion practices. This is not achieved by treating employees mainly as interpreters or by giving interpreters unwarranted management responsibilities.

It is not uncommon, for example, for interpreters who are close to management to start exercising formal and informal power over other Japanese employees—U.S. managers come to rely on interpreters' bilingual ability

and give them preference over other able individuals. The problem is multiplied, of course, when interpreters are incompetent or malicious individuals. Their actions can force competent Japanese to depart from the organization in frustration, leaving behind a herd of "yes men" to hamper the subsidiary through gleeful sabotage behind the favored interpreter's back.

Use Interpreters Wisely. If a foreign subsidiary manager encounters high employee turnover, sudden resignations of able staff, or cool indifference from Japanese managers of outside firms who used to be eager to consult with him, this is a sign that he has been judged, rightly or wrongly, as insensitive and, therefore, incapable of managing his subsidiary internally and externally. And if he still continues to rely heavily on his interpreter-assistant, or uses employees as interpreters, it is a pretty good bet that this leadership style is the cause.

In the context of proper management skill transfer, as more responsibility for daily operations is delegated to Japanese employees, the foreign manager should separate the interpreter function of his Japanese assistants and staff from more substantive managerial functions. It is also wise to consider hiring a person strictly for an interpreting job, especially when visiting other Japanese companies and government agencies. At the very least, Japanese staff members who are expected to move into responsible managerial positions in the organization should be excused from acting as interpreters, both inside and outside the company.

If American managers train Japanese staffs internally and act outwardly to support them, and if they make positive relationships not only real but visible, this will provide a tremendous incentive for the Japanese staff to grow. And they will soon see Japanese outside the company developing new respect for them.

Myth #5: "The best place to look for 'capable' Japanese for our subsidiary in Japan is the United States, where many Japanese are now studying and looking for jobs. They must be masters of the Japanese culture, so let's hire them, expose them to our operation in the States, and send them back to Japan."

A few years ago, Pfizer Company began its "operation brain retrieval" in the United States. NCR and other companies have also instituted retrieval operations; and, no doubt, there are many more U.S. companies contemplating a similar course of action. Indeed, a number of established multinational organizations now use this method to locate expatriates and students and train them before they go back home to settle down.

This policy is very understandable. Foreign companies in Japan have two strikes against them when it comes to hiring capable Japanese prefer to work for local companies, where they feel more comfortable. They have heard enough about the problems of Japanese employees in foreign companies that indulge in misguided enforcement of the myths discussed so far. As a result, foreign companies can neither easily entice able Japanese away from Japanese companies nor compete with these companies in recruiting capable and fresh graduates of the leading universities and colleges. The practice of hiring Japanese from other companies limits the source of search to those Japanese who have become, rightly or wrongly, discontent with other foreign companies, and to still fewer Japanese who have only recently begun to leave their Japanese companies for foreign organizations.

In either case, however, the employees thus recruited are subject to a Japanese prejudice against people who change their jobs. While the tendency to identify a person's mobility in the labor market with personal failure is weakening in Japan, there still exists widespread feeling against those who dare to break social norms for personal reasons.

It is, therefore, logical for U.S. companies to attempt to recruit able Japanese and, at the same time, avoid any stigma inherent in recruiting them from companies in Japan. The operation by which Japanese studying or working in the States are "retrieved" to Japan apparently suits this objective, and it is fair to point out that this practice has enabled some companies to meet their recruitment needs for a limited number of Japanese managers-to-be.

The trouble is that this method of "manpower retrieval" risks igniting a potentially explosive strain between Japanese recruited in Japan and those recruited abroad. This internal strain is akin to that between noninterpreter and interpreter Japanese in foreign companies—but it is twice as critical. In the case of interpreters, U.S. managers at least do not assume that they must possess any

skills other than mere language interpretation. In the case of retrieved manpower, however, Japanese are hired abroad because they are expected to possess language, managerial, and other skills. It is assumed that merely because they are Japanese, they are best able to deal with fellow Japanese, and they are shown preference over other Japanese who are recruited in Japan.

This policy, of course, has the danger of creating two classes of employees in a company—i.e., (a) the "privileged" few brought in from abroad and (b) the "underprivileged" many recruited in Japan. And it can turn out that those Japanese recruited abroad are just as insensitive and indifferent to Japanese culture as foreign managers for these reasons: (a) they are often recent graduates of U.S. schools and are thus inexperienced in *Japanese* management practices; and (b) since their formal training and experience took place in the United States, they tend to impose U.S. management practices on Japanese employers.

Careful Evaluation Needed. If a U.S. manager plans to pursue such a policy, he should remember that Japanese citizenship is not enough. Nationals who are recruited in the United States must be thoroughly evaluated regarding their sensitivity to managing in Japan. He should also monitor carefully the formal and informal acceptance of his retrieved manpower by fellow Japanese before giving them permanent assignments. Finally, it is very important to avoid any actions that might be construed as preferential treatment of Japanese recruited abroad.

Myth #6: "Since we must transfer U.S. management practices into Japanese situations, we should send our Japanese personnel to the home office for a while, or to management training seminars and study tours in the United States. What better way for them to learn our skills!"

This is a complete inversion of Myth #5, and its fallacy lies in the heroic assumption that a short and superficial exposure of a few Japanese in the United States will achieve the stated objective. It has been observed time and time again in Japan that such limited and superficial exposure to American management practices does more harm than good. For example:

All smiles, a new group of people leaves Tokyo (Haneda) Airport for the United

States. They return to Japan to tell their friends, "As we were told before we left, there was nothing we could learn from the States. We found nothing new that is applicable to Japanese situations."

This kind of comment is widespread, not only among Japanese employees of U.S. companies, but also among Japanese employees of local companies. They have merely confirmed their stereotypes and prejudices.

The travelers are not lying; they are simply telling their true impressions of the tour. Since they are ill prepared to search for new ideas and management skills, and are seldom given useful pointers by the interpreter-guide, they do not learn anything. Even when they attend management training courses, the course content is often not relevant to an essentially Japanese frame of mind. Being oriented to management practices in Japan, they naturally miss anything alien to their reference antenna. Whenever they do encounter practices that are similar to Japanese methods, they simply take this as evidence that they have been right all along in their own way of management, and return triumphantly to Tokyo with this conviction.

On the other hand, ever since the 1850's, when Japan began to industrialize her economy, Western products and manufacturing techniques and elements of complicated governmental and parliamentary systems have been transplanted to Japan by alert Japanese traveling throughout Europe, the United Kingdom, *and* the United States. When further instruction was needed, the Japanese hired engineers, scholars, and businessmen from the West. This time-honored practice is today repeated by many Japanese companies; they select observant individuals for specific "search-and-bring-back" missions in the United States.

Some Necessary Steps. There are lessons in the Japanese method for multinational companies that use invitational study tours as a device for transferring management skills to subsidiaries:

◆ The participants in such a tour must be the opinion leaders among their peers and subordinates in the subsidiary.

◆ A company must thoroughly brief those Japanese selected about what they are expected to learn and help them to develop their own detailed objects of study.

◆ A company should thoroughly familiarize the host-guide of the tour and instructors in the United States with the study objectives of touring Japanese, as well as the culture and management practices of Japan.

Myth #7: "The Japanese need our management skills, and the best way to transplant them is through direct investment in Japan."

This myth has been perpetuated by spokesmen of companies who wished to "sell" the importance of investing in other nations. Unfortunately, such publicity has been elevated to a widespread self-deception among many U.S. managers operating not only in Japan but all over the world. And this myth has been the cause of frustration and misunderstanding between U.S. investors and local governments.

First of all, there is no guarantee that the management skills locally available are always inferior to those of foreign parents. And even when it is advisable to bring essentially foreign ways of management into a local economy, successful transfer of such skills requires people who can adequately adapt them to the local environment. Here are some other reasons why direct investment alone is not enough:

☐ Even if management skills are transferred to a U.S. subsidiary (itself, a difficult achievement), there is no guarantee that these skills will spread to local companies throughout the environment by way of business contact and/or emulation. Indeed, my research has uncovered a number of incidents in which U.S. subsidiaries are attempting to stop such secondary diffusions to local companies that might turn out to be strong competitors. This, of course, is understandable because management superiority can be a competitive weapon.

☐ Direct investment in a subsidiary often results in attempts to lure local talent away from indigenous companies. This practice bids up the general wage and salary levels of local people, and often drives indigenous companies either to go out of business or to sell out to foreigners.

☐ When U.S. companies purchase Japanese companies, chances are that the management know-how and even product-related technology are supplied by the local organization. Even capital required for the purchase is often raised locally. But when the control is transferred to U.S. parent companies, it is these companies that will enjoy the future streams of profit from dividends and fees, as well as from selling goods and services to subsidiaries.

☐ Employees moving from subsidiaries to local Japanese companies do not necessarily take improved skills with them. Institution-related skills like an efficient assembly line cannot be imitated easily by local companies. These skills cease to be useful the moment they are separated from the place where they are operative. Thus, when unskilled laborers who show a high level of output efficiency in a foreign subsidiary are "scouted" by local companies, their previous experience in manning efficient assembly lines is often useless in the indigenous environment. These people simply join the horde of local unskilled labor and can do little to improve the operations of local companies.

Support the Transfer Process. Considering the foregoing obstacles, it is small wonder that Japanese do not see the same benefits in direct foreign investment as do the perpetrators of Myth #7. In sum, what is needed is an objective assessment by U.S. companies of those management skills most beneficial to the Japanese environment. If direct foreign investment can aid the international transfer of these management skills, a company should make special arrangements so that local business circles can benefit from the transfer process. Since the transfer is certainly not automatic, nor always encouraged by foreign subsidiary managers, the U.S. parent company should see to it that specific programs are established to train the managers of other local companies, or even to provide technical assistance and management consulting services for indigenous organizations.

CONCLUSION

Belief in the myths that are hindering the operations of U.S. subsidiaries in Japan is not limited to U.S. managers alone. Judging from the blunders that a number of Japanese companies are now committing abroad, and especially in other parts of Asia, Japanese appear to be afflicted with these myths as seriously as their American counterparts are.

This observation leads one to speculate that the myths are rather widespread and that

they find easy victims among those managers who have been raised in a homogeneous and monolithic culture. (Despite the varieties of racial composites that make up the United States, North American social mores and business practices in particular are homogeneous and monolithic—just as much so as those of Japan.)

Today a number of multinational companies are groping for effective ways to transfer management skills to their subsidiaries, as well as to other local organizations. They are attempting to make their role as transfer agents of management skills both real and visible, so that host countries can benefit from the association. For example:

The Coca-Cola Company is experimenting with formal training of managers of its subsidiaries and bottlers (independent local firms) abroad. It has done this by extending its unique advanced management training program from the United States to major markets abroad—Germany, France, Italy, the United Kingdom, Mexico, South America, and Japan.

The training is conducted in local languages by people who understand the local culture and management practices, as well as those of the United States, and who have researched in detail specific management problems of the subsidiaries and bottlers. The teaching materials and readings are either developed locally or adapted from the United States to fit the local scene; and they are also made available to indigenous companies, associations, schools, and institutes interested in similar training. Thus, program content is carefully tailored to suit the current and future management problems pertaining to local situations.

This is the type of approach that is needed in Japan.

We all need to generalize from experience in order to abstract universal lessons from it. But when such generalization is enshrined as truth and becomes unrefuted myth, it is likely to get in our way. The moment it gets in our way, we must either revise it or get rid of it. At any rate, the first task in avoiding the mistakes resulting from our belief in myths is to identify them as such and confront them.

50. Modern Marketing Techniques Applied to Developing Countries

A. GRAEME CRANCH

The basic lesson to be learned in marketing in developing countries is never to relax procedures and principles used in industrialized nations. It is entirely false to assume that because current practices are primitive, equally primitive methods will suffice in the future to market new products. The classical marketing procedures must be applied if true success is to be obtained in any developing country.

Of course conditions vary and problems differ. Facilities are always limited, sometimes nonexistent. Pervading all other considerations is the low purchasing power of the mass market. Imported goods are beyond their normal reach, even if they are permitted by the government. Local manufacture of goods for daily use is essential. Many attempts to export specially low priced goods, for example canned fish into African countries where sales of fresh fish are restricted by keeping problems and dried fish is not available, have inevitably collapsed from prices inaccessible for the majority. A Western marketing man operating under such conditions must re-think his practical experience, first taking it out of its Western context and then applying it step by step to the strange task in hand. And a local marketing man must apply all the lessons he can learn from his Western counterpart.

In looking at some of these differing circumstances, we are not here concerned with the creamy sales to any country's one per cent sophisticates with Western tastes and the money to support them. In a paper like this, dealing wtih ordinary people and goods, we can only generalize and skim quickly over the enormous variety of problems. Much must be left unsaid. Similarly, industrial items cannot be included. But the same marketing principles apply for these as they do elsewhere. They have the advantage of operating within a more homogeneous audience, usually more able to respond to promotional activity.

MARKET RESEARCH MUST SUPPLY THE BASE FOR PLANNING

The more difficult the problems of production and marketing to be tackled, the more essential it is to undertake market research at every important step. Research facilities may be limited by Western standards but their extent is surprising. Certainly some corners have to be cut. Sampling has to be pragmatic, although some quite exceptional work in probability sampling has been achieved in populous places like Hong Kong and Singapore. Mostly a good spread of interviews fulfilling broad demographic criteria is sufficient for the equally broad questions that have to be answered. And it works. There are now regular omnibus surveys amid even the desert wastes of the oil rich Middle East and in darkest Africa.

◆ SOURCE: Reprinted by permission from *Marketing Education and the Real World* and *Dynamic Marketing in a Changing World,* edited by Boris W. Becker and Helmut Becker, Combined Proceedings of the Spring and Fall Conferences of the American Marketing Association, 1972, Series No. 34, pp. 183–186.

Basic data are usually scanty, to be supplemented with care at not too great expense. In India in 1970, 25 food manufacturers—private, public and multi-national—united to produce a basic eating habits and nutrition survey of a depth and sophistication of the highest order. Product testing is absolutely essential. The rivers and canals of Thailand teem with life and death, with people, animals and excrement—and provide the people with their only water supply. Western designed ingredients for soaps and powders, food preparations and toiletries are rarely compatible with that water's biological contents. Foods and drinks tasting under the roughest conditions is equally essential, for habits developed over the centuries differ greatly in acceptability for sweetness and bitterness, coarseness or smoothness, assimilation and digestibility, or just simply in the laws of taboo. Women in Tanzania will not give their children eggs for fear of making them bald. Elsewhere in Africa they are associated with impotency. The simplest of medicines can be rejected for the witch doctor's concoctions. This is the stuff of which marketing is made. There must be continuous plumbing of deep seated, often illogical, but gradually changing social habits before a marketing break-through in simple demonstrable terms can be achieved. Creating a new market means changing a way of life.

Much can be done, surprisingly quickly. In Turkey they have a saying of any idea that seems impossible that it is "selling snails in a Muslim neighborhood." Yet 10 years ago an enterprising marketer set up a snail factory there and exports them profitably. Maybe soon he will be selling them to his fellow countrymen.

THE PROBLEMS OF DISTRIBUTION

High attention, interest and knowledge of new products are not difficult to obtain in most developing markets, under all but the most backward conditions. But the establishment of a purchasing habit is more difficult. Producers are in the hands of the middle-men between them and their customers. That word 'middleman' is anathema in developing countries. Its abuse is justified in some of the more excessive elements but unjustified in the ignorance of the role played by distribution in the marketing task. Even intelligent people find it hard not to regard all middlemen as parasites and there are frequently racial overtones to add to the problem. It is rare to find a simple and short wholesaler/retailer chain. Things are improving slowly. Nationalized selling agencies such as those set up competitively in Egypt and in many African countries, notably Tanzania, cut out some of the intermediaries. Multi-national companies are using door-to-door selling to an increasing extent. In the main, however, manufacturers have to rely on an extensive range of co-operatives, agents, area distributors, retailers, 'market mammies,' traveling peddlers. It is common for items to be handled six or more times before reaching the consumer. Six profits to be added to the price the poor must pay. Worse than that, these middlemen are very similar to the people whom they serve in their values, ideas, beliefs. They have a passive attitude towards marketing, acting as an outlet for a product rather than as its advocate, preferring to take orders for established lines and ever wary of innovation. There is a primary task, therefore, in developing any new market to pay particular attention to winning over the active cooperation of the necessary elements to be used in the distribution chain.

Difficulties give birth to means of overcoming them. Bereft of the usual media (which reach only the literate minority in most countries, radio usually excepted), marketers make good use of less conventional methods of distribution. The most popular is the demonstration van, formerly a publicity medium but now increasingly a combined advertising, sampling and distribution activity. Illiteracy puts great bearing on person-to-person promotion. A typical example is a van equipped with loud speakers, tape recorders for music and advertising messages and a demonstrator/salesman. The venue is any suitable village centre or cross roads. Circus style loud hailing is followed by demonstration, special offers and sampling with finally a selling job from an opened crate. If conditions permit door-to-door selling, it is done with all the sophistication of industrialized countries, with girls in smart uniforms, incongruous in the midst of poverty but invaluable for getting through to the housewife, who in some countries may well be the last person to be contacted in any other form of distribution. Remember that in some ethnic groups the shopping (and therefore the decision taking) is done by the menfolk, the women rarely leaving the confines of the home. And even then they are subject to the tyrannies of widowed grandmothers-in-law and similar reactionary inhibitors.

Distribution must be tackled through Western methods if inherited problems are to be defeated. As far back as 1964, seven Puerto Rican grocers were sent to a Jesuit School of Marketing in Philadelphia. There they learned the simple story of cooperative bulk buying. Today, well over 500 grocers have grouped together, cutting costs, increasing supplies to the needy and increasing also the country's farming output. The same thinking has been applied in Guatemala, India and elsewhere.

THE PART PLAYED BY PROMOTION

Demarcation lines are inevitably blurred when selling to developing markets. Distribution merges rapidly into selling, advertising and promotion become identical, one man wears many hats. But the more involved the marketing task becomes, the more sophistication is needed in the most unlikely surroundings. An excellent example of this is seen in the very rural areas of the Philippines, where the recent devaluation and fall of the peso has resulted in much wider use of sales promotion techniques. To list them is to read straight out of a marketing text book. Poverty is the spur, illiteracy the hurdle, but every form of promotion is now used, choice being tailored to suit the ethnic groups and local customs of individual districts. The popularity of the cinema has enabled Lux to hold picture completion contests of movie star photographs. Milk has been sold with a free sample of a detergent. A spray gun is sold for almost nothing with purchase of an insecticide. And so on.

It is a short step to developing point-of-sale material to match these offers. Again the range of items would be equally appropriate in Oshkosh, Wisconsin as in Timbuktu. The problem of placing it in the stores is identical too, the majority of them in the latter case being shacks or stalls. But the lesson is clear. To reach the mass market anywhere, the same check list must be used. Only the people—and their lack of pennies—differ. But they must be treated to precisely the same marketing planning.

This is amply proved by the now famous Anand Milk Union in India. This milk producers' co-operative started on a very small scale in 1948 but it employed professional management, gathering milk daily from the pitiful offerings of peasant farmers in a dozen small villages. A farmer's wife or child may deliver, in pots or pans, vases or other containers, no more than a few pints a day. But good marketing management, which has included improving the product from better quality stock and proper feeding, has cracked the distribution problem with refrigerated vans and trains. They have developed companion products, concentrating on a good consumer market (the city of Bombay) and are now a multi-million dollar operation involving around 600 villages and well over 100,000 farmers.

THE IMPORTANCE OF PACKAGING

To succeed, the marketing planner must be adaptable to the needs of his market. Packaging and presentation need just that quality. Climatic conditions, storage and transportation, security from pilfering and infestation, the problems of breaking bulk to allow sales in minimal unit sizes, the virtual absence of 'economy' packs, make the problem even more acute and expensive to overcome. Not all developing nations have troublesome climates but all present the packaging technologist with particular hurdles. The first preoccupation is acceptability of the pack by the consumer. Simple market research can confirm the overall acceptability, but this in turn merges with the next function of the pack, its efficiency as a medium of communication. When the use of other media is limited, the pack assumes maximum importance. It involves, in one extreme, recognition with the aid of symbols by the illiterate. At the other extreme, it can give ultra-clear instructions for use by complete strangers to the product or its preparation or use. (Female literacy is always lower than male. Instructions often have to be passed on by a third party with consequent further risk of misunderstanding.) Brand names and illustrations must be crystal clear in the message they carry. They are taken literally. Anything abstract or requiring thought-transference is to be avoided. Color is important and diagrams assist those consumers with little reading. Design should link up with other promotional material.

Come to think of it, nothing has been said

here that does not apply to a large degree for a mass market product launched in the U.S. or U.K. This only drives home the need to repeat in a marketing program in a developing country all the step-by-step checks that are needed also in an industrial country. But this does not mean that even a simple pack design can automatically be transferred from one country to another without re-examination. Meanings can change as borders are crossed and acceptance and credibility can hang on a single thread of understanding.

COMMUNICATION, THE MOST TROUBLESOME TASK

The problems merge into each other. Distinction between them seems unnecessary but it is helpful in solving the technical tasks. It is commonplace to say that the pack is often the product's best salesman. It can be the main advertisement—or at least its elements and symbols can. The cola logotypes found at cross roads in the deepest bush, the Crown Cork caps trodden into the ground, the simple unlettered designs on the walls of retailers' shacks can be the marketer's strongest weapons under the worst conditions. Communication remains his most problematic, least certain, most troublesome task. Dealing with things of the mind, he must find the most concrete ways of putting his message across. Failure can usually be traced to lack of appreciation of the cultural and environmental factors affecting the audience. Three distinct approaches are needed for covering a mass market. First, conventional media of press, TV, films and radios for reaching the more fortunate, minority members of the market. Second, the less publicized communication techniques (wall charts, slides, filmstrips, models) widely used by governments and educators and therefore acceptable to the less fortunate as authoritative media. Once again there is overlap. All may see posters even if they cannot read them. Most will listen to the radio and its advertisements even if they cannot appreciate the use of the goods mentioned. All notions about products can be brought together by the third communication medium.

This vital group consists of personal channels. Not always so well adapted in the past to commercial projects, these are a major force in all government agency operations, whether marketing ideas, products or services. A demonstrator is the most direct medium of communication. So too in social matters are the educators, the religious leaders, doctors, headmen and chiefs. A company can make only limited use commercially of these agents of communication. It can, however, train its own agents to do the same job, visiting villages, voluntary groups and clubs to give authority to the word of mouth message that carries so much credibility (whether it be right or wrong) in country districts where the majority of the market still live. That message follows a classical pattern. It must satisfy the standard processes known to all marketing: creating awareness and interest, persuading to trial and continuing adoption. Herein lies the paradox of marketing in developing countries. Most countries have some conventional advertising facilities. Their deficiencies can be made good from across borders. Application of standard techniques may be crude but they work. But they have a limited reach. The decadence and permissiveness of modern films may be enjoyed by educated audiences in Bangkok or Nairobi, Sao Paolo or Cairo. But 25 miles away from these cities is another world, a world where people go to bed when darkness falls, a world whose acceptance of a product is essential for its profitable marketing.

Communication, therefore, must be many sided. Simple media studies can indicate exposure to the various media. Very few such studies exist. They have to be carried out afresh by interested advertisers. More important are studies which reveal the form of message most readily received and comprehended. Pre-testing is usually essential if mistakes are to be minimized. Local languages rarely cater to imagery or concepts successful in an industrialized country. TV or film commercials can easily become too loud, too jumbled for understanding. So post-testing too becomes necessary. One of the many problems is that the image of a product becomes very deeply held. If advertising is to introduce a new idea, it must displace the old one. Clearly, it is vital to ensure that no harm comes from that displacement. Nevertheless, the pace of change can be surprisingly fast. Manufacturers have to watch the effect of innovation on brand images of certain product groups. In Africa the inbred lesson of the missionaries' Mother Hubbard high necked smocks is still seen in the almost identical dresses worn by smartly dressed girls today. Overnight they will change without warning, just as they took to mini-skirts. As branding develops, so ironically the image becomes shallower and more susceptible to change. These unexpected changes in attitude can work to advantage in other ways. Products offered with localized appeal and illustrations have failed. Re-issued in a European context, the same product achieves an aura of authority and becomes desirable. Perhaps that is why every shop model in Thailand and elsewhere in South East Asia has a European face or coloring.

Plus ça change, plus c'est la même chose. Circumstances change but not the methods. That is the first and last—and simplest— lesson for every marketing operation in a developing country.

The Performance of Marketing in Modern Society

Part V of this book concentrates on some of the controversial and public sides of marketing. More than ever before questions about marketing, its ethics, its impact on consumers, and its future role in our economy are beng raised. What are the ethical considerations? How well or how badly has marketing related to consumer issues? And what are the challenges and signals for marketing change? These are the broad questions explored in these selections.

John H. Westing's reading deals with ethics. The reader is exposed to a broad reading that examines different ways of looking at ethics. Furthermore, the selection questions marketing versus other disciplines and today's ethics versus yesterday's. Then Arnold Toynbee and William Berenbach (a well-known and leading advertising executive) debate on the moral defensibility of advertising.

Alvin Achenbaum's reading is a defense of advertising ethics with some emphasis on the manipulation of consumers.

Section S relates to the interfaces with consumers. The rise of consumerism took place during the 1960s and has a continuing emphasis on into the 1970s. What consumerism is, why it is, and what marketers should do about it are the subjects of the consumerism readings. An important reading by Aaker and Day reveals the corporate responses to the pressures of consumerism. Then one kind of consumer problem is examined in the final readings of this section. The issue of marketing to low-income consumers. Marketing and business have given much thought to this problem but have not generally succeeded in solving it.

Section T includes eight thought-provoking readings. Hopefully, the reader will be stimulated by the opportunities, the enormity of the task, and the directions of change that are suggested by the authors of these readings. Thaddeus Spratlen raises the humanistic-value question. Other readings in this section also deal with the social values of marketing and the challenges that such values raise for marketing's role in our economy. The reader may find particular interest in "Marketing the Post Office." This indeed cites a signal for change, and since the article was written, there have been changes in this 200-year-old institution. Change in this indispensable service will undoubtedly continue.

An important and yet seldom discussed area of marketing concern is the performance of marketing. Robert D. Buzzell thoroughly discusses the cost and value of marketing and evaluates the measurement of marketing performance in our economy.

Charles Goodman and Leonard Berry's readings are stimulating because they raise questions about management response to environmental change and the future challenges of marketing. Berry provides students with a clear concept of the broad issues they face as they pursue careers in marketing management.

R. Ethical Dimensions

51. Some Thoughts on the Nature of Ethics in Marketing

JOHN H. WESTING

Business is having trouble with its ethics today. But then, business has always had trouble with its ethics. As far as one may care to go back into history he will find intellectuals castigating businessmen for their bad ethics. It appears that, for the most part, the criticism went unheard, or unheeded. It is true that during much of human history businessmen lived on the very fringe of "good" society and that this semi-ostracism may well have resulted in part from the bad ethics imputed to businessmen. During most of this time the businessman, while he may have deplored his social alienation, did not seem to care enough to pay the price for social respectability.

Today, at least in the sense of caring, the situation seems to have changed. This is not to say that the businessman today is willing to pay a *high* price for moral respectability, but he is sufficiently concerned to want to know the price. The concern of the businessmen is evident in a variety of ways: in the increasing flow of brochures and pamphlets published by companies on the social responsibilities of business; by the willingness to question whether business may have goals other than profit maximization; by the concern being exhibited over racial equality, slum clearance, and pollution control; and, most of all, by an amazing eagerness to discuss the subject of morality and ethics. I well recall about ten years ago organizing a seminar for executives on business ethics and being told by our business advisors that executives not only would not come, but would resent the implications implicit in a session on ethics. On that occasion we toned down the title somewhat and got an adequate, but disappointing, turnout. More recently we have held a number of undisguised seminars on ethics and have had an enthusiastic response, both in numbers and participation. I believe that anyone who has had the temerity to talk on this subject will bear me out in the statement that if one is willing to discuss this "hairy" subject he will soon have more opportunities than he cares to accept.

If it is true that there has been a notable change in the attitude of businessmen toward ethics, how does one explain it? Let me offer this hypothesis. The executive today is no more nor less concerned about ethics than was his counterpart a century ago. The man has not changed, but his environment has. In a subsistence economy, ethics get short shrift. This is not only true over time, but is equally true geographically at a point in time. I think it can be said that there is a direct relation between per capita income and

The remarks are based on the assumption that in our increasingly secular society we either have lost, or are in process of losing, our historical foundation for a system of ethics in business. The presentation attempts to find an alternative foundation and to relate ethical practice to such a foundation.

◆ SOURCE: Reprinted by permission from *Changing Marketing Systems*, edited by Reed Moyer, Proceedings of the Winter Conference of the American Marketing Association, 1967, Series No. 26, pp. 161–163.

the ethical standards of a country—and, incidentally, this variation in standards poses one of the knottiest ethical problems possible for a company engaged in trade with developing countries. But, to get back to the point, when one is destitute he is less likely to indulge his ethical impulses when he is comfortable or satiated. Since, in the United States today, we are materially more comfortable than we have ever been before, our concerns naturally tend to turn from further satisfaction of our physical needs to the satisfaction of needs in higher categories of the need hierarchy—and ethics fall into one of those categories. If this line of reasoning is correct, I think it leads to the conclusion that, in the future, businessmen are likely to become still more concerned with ethical consideration. And, as professors of business subjects, we should be anticipating this concern or once again we may find ourselves rationalizing business practice rather than moulding it.

A tremendous amount of time and effort can be spent on the argument over whether ethics in business are worse than in such fields as law, medicine, politics, or education. Personally, I think a good case can be made for the likelihood that, a given time, the level of ethics in all major occupational groups of a society are very nearly the same. With no social barriers and few economic barriers to the entry into the various occupational fields it is unlikely that they would attract people with widely varying ethical standards. One could, of course, argue that the professions attract those with a high sense of humanitarianism and worldly renunciation, and such people might have higher ethical ideals. However, this position is somewhat hard to defend if one notes the level and trend of income prevailing in the professional fields and the rush to the highly specialized fields where income is likely to be maximized and the service element minimized. It seems more likely to me that any differences which exist result, not from intrinsic differences in the moral standards of individuals or groups, but from the fact that moral temptations and pressures may be greater in some fields than others. Quite obviously, if one is attempting to assess the moral stamina of two individuals, he must either measure their performance under similar conditions or make allowances for the differences in the environments where they are tested. Perhaps it is the failure to make

such allowances that causes the businessman to come off badly when ethical comparisons are made between him and members of other occupational groups. If the corroding effects of the "love of money" are recognized—as they have been throughout history—it must be admitted that the businessman is subject to more frequent and more extreme ethical temptations than most other men. Thus, he may not be ethically weaker, just more sorely tried.

The above issue is an interesting one and, I believe, one that deserves more thought than it has received. However, in one sense it is irrelevant, and in another sense it might even be harmful. It would seem to me to be positively harmful if it led any substantial number of businessmen to conclude that complacency was warranted. Society today, as well as the businessman himself, is uneasy about the state of ethics in business. Under these conditions, complacency may cost the businessman a further loss of his rapidly vanishing freedom. This, of course, is a pragmatic rather than a philosophical argument. The issue of whether the ethics of the businessman are better or worse than those of others is irrelevant because it involves a measurement against the wrong standard. There will be argument on this point, but I maintain that the issue should not be whether the ethics of the businessman are *relatively* as good as those of others but whether they are *absolutely* good enough to sustain the good life in a highly complex society.

This point goes to the very heart of the issue of ethics, and unless it can be resolved, I doubt that there is much chance of any real progress of the ethics front. The absolute position identifies, and at times almost equates, ethics with religion. This has been the traditional position, and it was a viable position so long as religion held real or nominal authority over a majority of the people. It seems to me there was a time, within my memory, when most people—non-church members as well as members—acknowledged the *rightness* of a code of ethics based upon the second table of the Decalogue. Many may not have compiled with the code in practice, but an admission of its rightness at least gave society a point of reference—a north star—for guidance.

Today, in his quest for scientific verification of everything, man has to a large extent discarded normative standards such as the ethical component of the Decalogue. In most areas even scientific man does not discard conventional wisdom until he has found it wrong and has discoevred something better to replace it. In the field of ethics, unfortunately, modern man has been too impatient for this. Ethical principles were so clearly not based on empirical research that he discarded them without having even begun a search for anything to replace them. Someone might argue that relativism or situational ethics has replaced the more formalized code, but I would contend that as a replacement relativism is an illusion. In an economic order, in which the central motivating principle is based on selfish advancement, ethical performance can only decline unless there is some countervailing force to offset the drive to better one's self at the cost of others.

One could easily move from the position that if the traditional standards are not working and relativism will not work we are in a perilous, and, perhaps hopeless, position. I suspect that not a few people may be close to this point without having bothered to take their bearings and define their position. May we not, however, be able to reason our way to an intermediate position—one that establishes ethics as a normative standard without making it a part of religion.

To do this one must make the assumption that our world is an orderly world—not only the physical environment but the social environment as well. More specifically, the assumption about the social environment of man must be that living together in society is possible over the long term only if we recognize and comply with inherent social laws which are as inviolable as the physical laws of the universe. Just as we can defy, but not break, physical laws, we can defy, but not break, social laws. This does not seem to me to be an unreasonable assumption. Could not our rising concern over ethics be an implicit recognition of the fact that our incerasingly intimate social relationships demand that we regulate our associations by better ethical norms?

If one wonders why we have made so much progress in discovering the physical laws of our universe and so little in finding the ethical laws, he might note that physical cause and effect relationships are mostly short term whereas social cause and effect relationships may not come to light in less than generations or centuries. We do know that societies rise and fall but we have never done much more than speculate idly about the reasons. Ad-

mittedly, the difficulty of discovering such ethical verities will be difficult, but with man in possession of something approximating ultimate power the penalty for not discovering these hidden relationships may well be extinction. If the issue is this stark we certainly ought to get on with the job.

Let us look at the matter for a moment from the point of view of the religionists, of which group I consider myself to be a member. We have always tended to be a bit hazy and uncertain about the *other* worldly and the *this* worldly aspects of religion. When one considers that traditional religion traces its antecedents back to a time when society was ruled as a theocracy, it can be seen that the man-to-God and man-to-man relationships would not be clearly distinguished. We have tended to carry this full set of religious rules over into a society that is now sharply divided into spiritual and secular segments. The second table of the Decalogue is in substance a prescription for how man must live with man in ethical terms if communal life is to succeed. In this connection it is interesting to note that, while all major religions differ significantly in their man-to-God prescriptions, they all agree quite well in their ethical prescriptions. As a matter of fact, in this universality of ethical norms we might find a promising approach to the development of a set of secular ethical standards. If we would disregard the question of how these norms came into being, translate them into modern phraseology, and begin to check them against human history we might well have a start toward our difficult goal. Essentially, in terms of broad principles, the universal religious code of ethics demands respect for truth, respect for persons, respect for human institutions, and respect for property. These principles would seem to be sufficiently non-controversial so that they could be accepted as secular norms.

Now, how does one get from this high plain of lofty principles, to the more mundane level of operational ethics. It seems to me that one must make the transition in a series of steps.

First of all, there is the law, which is or ought to be the lowest common denominator of ethical practice. I do not by any means subscribe to the facile but faulty maxim that says, "If it's legal, it's ethical." To say this, I think, exhibits a misunderstanding of both law and ethics. Law codifies only that part of ethics which society feels so strongly about that it is willing to support it with physical force. The common misunderstanding also frequently gets us into the dilemma of passing laws that are unenforceable because society does not feel certain enough about them to apply the force which is implicit in law. So, the man who thinks he is ethical because he is not knowingly violating civil laws is, in fact, only practicing ethics at its lowest level. Furthermore, if no one did any *better* than that, society could degenerate morally, but could never regenerate.

Probably in the field of business the next level of ethical performance is measured by company policy. Of course, not all company policy has an ethical dimension, but when it does deal with it, policy must transcend the ethical level of law. If it were lower than the law, the policy would be illegal, if it were equal to the law it would be pointless, so it must transcend the law. It might be observed that we enforce ethical principles at this level, not with physical force, but with economic force. We fire, demote, reduce pay, etc. These are powerful sanctions and this avenue represents an approach that has not been explored very far. With the present tendency of companies to assume social responsibilities there could be substantial achievements in the ethical realm that would probably benefit business as well as society.

There are ethical problems that cannot be reached through company policy and are not appropriate for law. These concern matters in which an industry's competitive environment exerts a depressing effect on ethical conduct and the competitive situation does not allow the individual companies to practice the eth-ics they would like. The only way we have found to deal with such issues is through industry codes of ethics and they have had a spotty, and not very inspiring, history. Part of the trouble here has been that industries have so frequently tended to confuse bad ethics with hard competition. Many groups have tried to write hard competition out of their industries through the vehicle of ethical codes and have found that it did not work for long. Then they have concluded that codes of ethics will not work. I believe, that with better understanding of what they are supposed to do, industry codes deserve another chance and stronger support. It might be noted that the force behind ethical codes is strictly a social kind of sanction. Such sanctions may not have much raw power, but in a prosperous economy with people striving to satisfy acceptance goals, the force is not inconsiderable.

Finally, we arrive at the epitome of ethics, where a man is face-to-face with an ethical issue and must decide it in a way that will satisfy his personal standards. This is the touchstone of ethics in a free society. In the end the other levels of ethics all derive their substance from the performance of each individual as he wrestles with ethical issues. If he does not have adequate standards and is not willing to pay an economic price to satisfy his standards our economic society is inevitably going to suffer from degenerating ethics.

As I see it, then, our task is two-fold: to define ethics in a way that will gain intellectual acceptance for it, and to induce its practice by the business community. The business educator is of critical importance to both.

52. Is Advertising Morally Defensible?

ARNOLD TOYNBEE and WILLIAM BERENBACH

ARNOLD TOYNBEE

It is argued that marketing—including the kinds of new products introduced, the design of those products, and advertising—reflects public wants and tastes rather than shapes them. I have been asked whether I believe this to be true. I do not believe that. If advertising were just an echo of desires that were already in the housewife's mind, it would be a superfluous expense of time, ingenuity and money. It would be nothing more than a carbon copy of a housewife's shopping list. I believe that advertising does have an effect. I believe it stimulates consumption, as is suggested in the second point put to me:

It is argued that personal consumption, stimulated by advertising, is essential for growth and full employment in an economy of abundance. If this were demonstrated to be true, it would also demonstrate, to my mind that an economy of abundance is a spiritually unhealthy way of life, and that the sooner we reform it the better. This may sound paradoxical to modern Western ears. But if it is a paradox, it is one that has always been preached by all the great religions. In an article published in *Printers' Ink* on October 20, 1961, Mr. James Webb Young dismisses the example set by St. Francis of Assisi. "Americans today," Mr. James Webb Young writes, "see little merit in these medieval hairshirt ideas." St. Francis got his ideas from a premedieval teacher, Jesus. These ideas can-

not be dismissed without rejecting Christianity and all the other great religions, too.

The moral that I draw is that a way of life based on personal consumption, stimulated by advertising, needs changing—and there are dozens of possible alternatives to it. For instance, we could still have full employment in the economically advanced countries if we gave up advertising and restricted our personal consumption to, say, the limits that present-day American monks and nuns voluntarily set for themselves, and if we then diverted our production to supply the elementary needs of the poverty-stricken three-quarters of the human race. Working for this obviously worthwhile purpose would bring us much greater personal satisfaction than working, under the stimulus of advertising, in order to consume goods that we do not need and do not genuinely want.

But suppose the whole human race eventually became affluent; what then? Well, I cannot think of any circumstances in which advertising would not be an evil. There are at least three bad things intrinsic to it:

Advertising deliberately stimulates our desires, whereas experience, embodied in the teaching of the religions, tells us that we cannot be good or happy unless we limit our desires and keep them in check.

Advertising makes statements, not in order to tell the truth, but in order to sell goods. Even when its statements are not false, truth is not their object. This is intellectually demoralizing.

Advertising is an instrument of moral, as well as intellectual, mis-education. Insofar as

◆ SOURCE: Reprinted by permission from *Yale Daily News*, Special Issue 1963, p. 2.

it succeeds in influencing people's minds, it conditions them not to think for themselves and not to choose for themselves. It is intentionally hypnotic in effect. It makes people suggestible and docile. In fact, it prepares them for submitting to a totalitarian regime.

Therefore, let us reform a way of life that cannot be lived without advertising.

WILLIAM BERENBACH

Mr. Toynbee's real hate is not advertising. It's the economy of abundance or, as we have all come to know it, capitalism. This is perfectly all right if only he would make clear the real target he is shooting at. There are many things about capitalism that need correcting, and Mr. Toynbee would be doing the world a great service if he could persuade us to make these corrections. But he's never going to do that if he throws up smoke screens with tirades against a tool that happens to be used by big business in its efforts to sell more goods.

Advertising, like so many techniques available to man, is neither moral nor immoral. Is eloquence immoral because it persuades? Is music immoral because it awakens emotions? Is the gift of writing immoral because it can arouse people to action? No. Yet eloquence, music and writing have been used for evil purpose.

Only recently we were asked to prepare an advertisement by the National Committee for a Sane Nuclear Policy. We conceived an ad featuring Dr. Spock. Its purpose was to discourage nuclear testing. If Mr. Toynbee will agree that this is a good purpose, then he must also agree that in this case at least, advertising was not an instrument of "moral mis-education." He would also be happy to learn that here was an advertisement so persuasive that it prompted one of the chairmen of SANE to telegraph his congratulations for "by all odds the most powerful single statement I have seen over the imprint of SANE."

For the past two years we have run advertising for Volkswagen cars with the purpose of persuading Americans that simplicity, craftsmanship and low price were available to them in an automobile. These were ads that conveyed facts simply and honestly to the customer. They seemed to sell the country on filling their automotive needs modestly and with good taste. Would Mr. Toynbee call this effort evil merely because advertising was involved? The Volkswagen was built to give the buyer the greatest value in automotive transportation. Isn't advertising performing a valuable function by making that fact clear to the buyer?

No, advertising is not moral or immoral. Only people are. I can cite many instances in commercial advetrising that would prove Mr. Toynbee's point of view. I can cite just as many that would disprove it.

If Mr. Toynbee believes a materialistic society is a bad one (and I am not saying he is wrong in that belief), then he owes it to mankind to speak to the point. He owes it to mankind to speak out against such a society and not merely against one of the tools that is available to any society. He may even find that nothing will "sell" his points as effectively as advertising.

53. *Advertising Doesn't Manipulate Consumers*

ALVIN A. ACHENBAUM

There is a growing feeling among those erstwhile defenders of the public weal that advertising is a manipulative tool of business, whereby sellers subtly and unfairly bludgeon consumers into buying things which they don't need or really want.

These rather vocal critics of advertising believe that this manipulation of the consumer, whom they often presume is ignorant and incapable of making rational judgments, is misled and deceived into unproductive expenditures.

This feeling about advertising's manipulative power to a large degree has its roots in the popular and academic literature of the Fifties. Perhaps the most typical lay view was expressed by Vance Packard in his book, *The Hidden Persuaders*, where he made it quite clear what he thought about advertising when he said:

Large-scale efforts are being made, often with impressive success, to channel our unthinking habits, our purchasing decisions, and our thought processes by the use of insights gleaned from psychiatry and the social sciences. Typically these efforts take place beneath our level of awareness; that the appeals which move us are often, in a sense, hidden.

While the academicians have handled their criticism of advertising more deftly, they are equally unkind. Typical of their position is that of Professor Kenneth Boulding (1955), who wrote:

◆ SOURCE: Reprinted by permission from the *Journal of Advertising Research*, Vol. 12, No. 2, April 1972, pp. 3–13. © Copyright (1972), by the Advertising Research Foundation.

Perhaps the most important of these (competitive) wastes from a social point of view is that involved in competitive advertising. There is a case for a certain amount of advertising, such as purely informative advertising, which is descriptive of the qualities and prices of commodities. This is a form of consumer education which is necessary if consumers are to make intelligent choices; in fact, it makes competition more nearly perfect. This virtuous advertising, however, does not bulk very large in total. Most advertising, unfortunately, is devoted to an attempt to build up the minds of the consumers' *irrational preferences for certain brands of goods.* All the arts of psychology—particularly the art of association—are used to persuade consumers that they should buy Bingo rather than Bango.

Or take Professor Tibor Scitovsky's remarks in his book, *Welfare and Competition:*

The scope of advertising depends on the ignorance of the people to whom it is addressed. The more ignorant the buyer, the more he relies on advertising.

To the extent that it provides information about the existence of available alternatives, advertising always renders the market more perfect.

If advertising is mainly suggestive and confined to emotional appeal, however, it is likely to impede *rational* comparison and choice, thus rendering the market less perfect.

In the uninformed market, the buyer is ill-equipped to make a rational comparison among competitive offers. In fact, in the uninformed market, it is in the sellers' interest to prevent rather than to help buyers make rational comparisons. . . .

The implication of both Boulding's and Scitovsky's remarks is quite clear. The ignorant, irrational consumer is at the mercy of the advertisers and in some unexplained way— using the arts of psychology—these advertisers make consumers their willing tools easily moved to behave as they are told by mass advertising. While they both admit that so-called informative advertising is all right, they believe most of it is not of that type. Evidently, by some quirk of logic—for no evidence is given—they seem unable to believe that emotional arguments of persuasion can be considered rational. The only rational judgment in their minds is one that is based on information of an objective product quality or price. Subjectivity is presumed to be unacceptable and, if not manipulative or deceptive, then certainly wasteful.

A somewhat more sophisticated view of the matter is that of John Kenneth Galbraith, whose books have both academic and popular appeal, particularly among the intellectual community, and who basically rejects the more conventional theories of advertising's role in the economy—namely, that advertising serves a simple communicative purpose; that advertising alters the competitive market structure and thus accords sellers more freedom in setting prices; and that advertising is the means by which oligopolists compete because they believe price competition is too dangerous. Although the last two theories are particularly pejorative since they assume monopolistic power which is obviously contrary to our ethos of the free market, Galbraith feels they have little validity.

Instead he believes that advertising is a process of *demand management*, that:

. . . advertising is part of the strategy of modern corporate planning. It is part of the strategy by which firms minimize their *subordination* to the market.

It [advertising] is not the total strategy of demand management. This includes a great deal of effort associated with industrial design and packaging ,and it is implicit with a great deal of organization for selling merchandising. But advertising is an extremely important part of this effort.

The individual [then] instead of being *sovereign* in the economic system is in some degree its instrument. The presumption of this society is no longer individualist but collectivist.

Following similar reasoning, Galbraith made his views of advertising quite clear in his book, *The New Industrial State*, where he remarked:

Failure to win belief does not impair the effectiveness of the *management of demand* for consumer products. Management involves the creation of a compelling image of the product in the mind of the consumer. To this he responds more or less automatically under circumstances where the purchase does not merit a great deal of thought. For building this image, palpable fantasy may be more valuable than circumstantial evidence.

Thus, even with Galbraith, advertising, working in some magical way, makes people behave against their will. While demand management takes on a somewhat different coloration from the views of the conventional economists, you still end up with much the same evaluation of advertising if you buy Galbraith's concept. With him, large-scale industry seeks stability—not only with labor and capital, but in the marketplace as well. Oligopolies, which are characteristic of large industry, evidently obtain this market stability through tacit price agreements and through advertising and the other marketing forces which can control the level of demand. To achieve the proper level of demand, advertising must develop a strong sense of loyalty among consumers.

Accordingly, if the case against advertising were true—that consumers are nothing more than automatons, jelly in the hands of the advertisers—then our free society is truly in sorry shape when we consider how ubiquitous advertising is. Fortunately, there is considerable empirical evidence which strongly suggests that advertising does not manipulate consumer behavior.

If consumers were truly being manipulated by advertising, we would expect them to act against their better interest when exposed to it. We would expect their attitudes toward brands to be stable. We would expect them to refrain from moving from one brand to another, certainly on the basis of changed attitudes. We would expect that the attitudes held or changed were not deliberate, but random. And we would expect poorer, less educated people to behave differently from their richer, more educated counterparts.

Instead the evidence suggests that all these expectations are false. While there is no doubt that advertising affects purchase behavior, data show that it first affects attitudes; that when attitudes change, behavior then changes. Yet, even changed attitudes do not have a one-to-one relationship with behavior; other market elements are involved. Interestingly enough, contrary to what many believe, the transmission of information through advertising is not correlated with either attitudes or behavior. Thus it becomes quite apparent from the evidence that consumers know what they want, and if you offer and communicate it to them in a persuasive manner, they will act upon it. And finally, evidence indicates that people behave this way irrespective of income or education.

This paper reviews a small portion of the substantial and growing evidence which makes it clear that consumers are not sheep who loyally do as they are told, but rather that they are fickle purchasers who change their opinions quite frequently and deliberately and who change their behavior as they see fit.

What follows was largely obtained in a nationwide study of 2,000 female heads of household conducted in three waves over a six-month period. This study was conducted by Grey Advertising Inc. which permitted me to use the data to testify before the Federal Trade Commission.

CHANGES IN ATTITUDES

The study covered 19 brands in seven pack-aged-good categories where advertising played a major role: analgesics, cigarettes, coffee, denture cleanser, hair spray, mouthwash, and peanut butter. Only national brands were measured, including many accused of manipulating consumers through advertising.

On the surface, attitudes seem to be very stable; almost the same number of people rated the 19 brands about the same in each of the three periods measured. (See Fig. 1.)

But what these data hide is the intrinsic dynamism in attitudes which actually exists in the marketplace. Since the same people were measured in all three waves, we could see how each individual changed her attitudes during the three points in time, as shown in Fig. 2.

We found that 53 per cent of the consumers actually altered their opinions at least once toward a brand between Wave I and Wave II (a three-month period) and another 48 per cent changed them again at least once between Wave II and III.

In fact, the extent of attitude change brand-by-brand between the two waves ranged from 41 per cent for a small hair spray brand to 61 per cent for a medium-sized denture cleanser brand. (See Fig. 3.)

Moreover, attitude change was a condition for all types of usage. While it was true that so-called loyal users (those who continued to use the brand through all three waves of the study) changed their attitudes less frequently than consumers who moved from one brand to another, there were always more changers than nonchangers no matter what the usage. (See Fig. 4.)

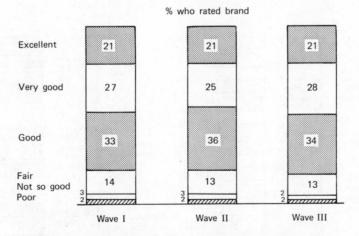

FIGURE 1. Overall brand ratings Wave I vs. Wave II vs. Wave III, 19 brand summary.

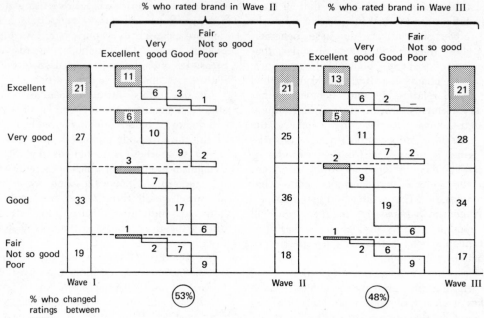

FIGURE 2. Changes in overall brand ratings Wave I vs. Wave II vs. Wave III, 19 brand summary.

PURCHASE BEHAVIOR

The data in this study also revealed that purchase behavior, like attitudes, appears stable on the surface. There was apparent stability in brand shares among all 19 brands measured. (See Fig. 5.)

But again, underlying this surface stability was a very substantial amount of change, as shown in Fig. 6.

Thirteen per cent of the consumers switched brands between Wave I and Wave II, while another 12 per cent switched between Wave II and III—not as much switching as with attitudes, since purchasing occurs less frequently than exposure to those forces that affect attitudes.

Portions of this paper were presented before the Federal Trade Commission on behalf of the Joint ANA/AAAA Committee on October 28, 1971.

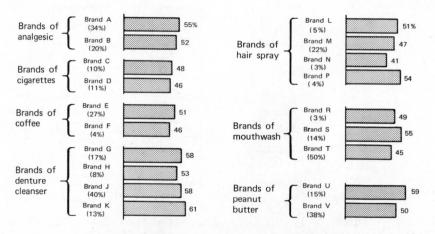

FIGURE 3. Extent of change in overall brand ratings.

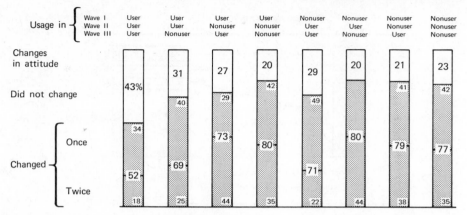

Usage in	Wave I Wave II Wave III	User User User	User User Nonuser	User Nonuser User	User Nonuser Nonuser	Nonuser User User	Nonuser User Nonuser	Nonuser Nonuser User	Nonuser Nonuser Nonuser

FIGURE 4. Extent of attitude mobility across three waves by purchase behavior, 19 brand summary.

In total, 73 per cent of the consumers changed their ratings of the brands between the three waves, and 21 per cent changed the brands they used during this period. (See Fig. 7.)

RELATIONSHIP OF ATTITUDES TO BEHAVIOR

Considering these changes, one would expect to find a relationship between attitudes and behavior. And so there was. Fig. 8 shows a clear correlation between brand attitudes and usage. Of those who rated a brand Excellent, 58 per cent were purchasers; of those who rated a brand Poor, none purchased the brand last.

But even in the more dynamic situation, there is a correlation. When consumers' ratings of a brand decline, the per cent who

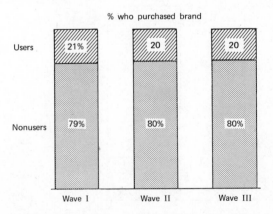

FIGURE 5. Purchase behavior Wave I vs. Wave II vs. Wave III, 19 brand summary.

remain users declines. Conversely, when their rating increases, the per cent who remain users increases. (See Fig. 9.)

The same is true for nonusers. Among those nonusers who improved their attitudes toward a brand, their probability of buying it increased. And conversely, when their attitudes dropped, their probability of becoming a user dropped too. (See Fig. 10.)

And finally, in the most dynamic situation, when we looked at attitude change between two waves and then looked at what happened to behavior in a subsequent wave, we saw the relationship between attitudes and behavior change. If people lowered their attitudes between the first two waves of the study, they were less likely to be users in the third wave. This was true for nonusers and users alike. (See Fig. 11, 12, and 13.)

There can be no doubt that these data show that people do not think or act like automatons. They are, in fact, quite prone to change their feelings, to do so frequently, and change their purchasing in relation to their changed feelings. But while there is a correlation between attitudes and behavior, it is not perfect. *All attitude changes do not get translated into behavior changes. Other forces are obviously at work.* Readers of this *Journal* need no reminder that advertising is not the only force in marketing.

THE EFFECT OF ADVERTISING ON ATTITUDES

To see if and how advertising affected attitudes, we measured different levels of expos-

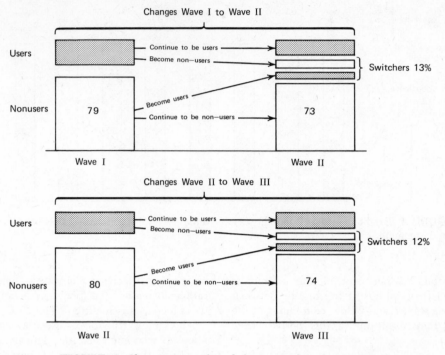

FIGURE 6. Changes in purchase behavior, 19 brand summary.

ure. And so it did, although the correlation was not too high. (See Figs. 14 and 15.)

The method of measurement could explain this weak relationship. But we also found this relationship in another way: by comparing the distribution of attitude changes induced by exposure to an individual commercial in 189 separate copy tests with the distribution one would expect if the changes were purely the result of chance.

Fig. 16 illustrates there was a difference—exposure to advertising did change attitudes. Again, the differences were not very great. Yet, there were cases where consumers were negatively influenced by the advertising. These were hardly people who felt what they were told to feel.

Thus, while advertising had an effect, it was only what one would expect if he recognized that advertising is but one element in

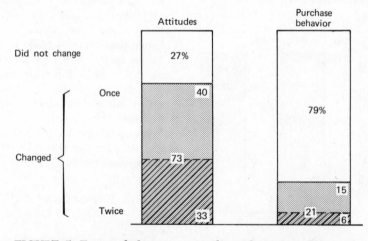

FIGURE 7. Extent of change in attitudes and purchase behavior across three waves, 19 brand summary.

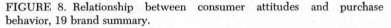

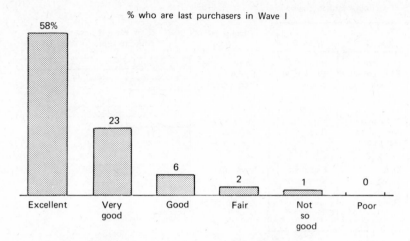

FIGURE 8. Relationship between consumer attitudes and purchase behavior, 19 brand summary.

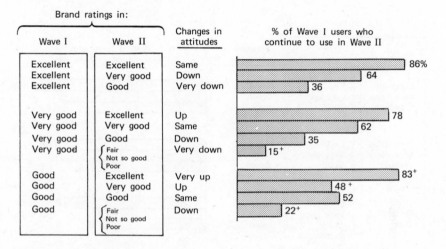

FIGURE 9. Changes in attitudes related to changes in purchase behavior among users: 19 brand summary.

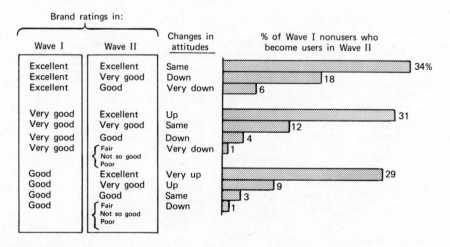

FIGURE 10. Changes in attitudes related to changes in purchase behavior among nonusers: 19 brand summary.

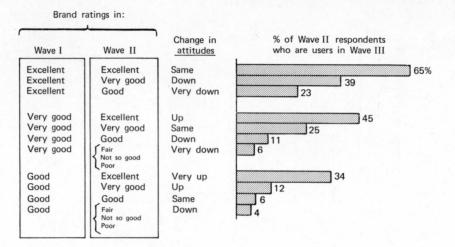

FIGURE 11. Changes in attitudes related to incidence of future use, 19 brand summary.

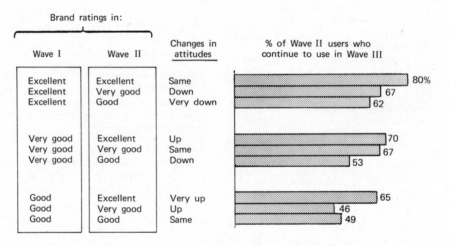

FIGURE 12. Changes in attitudes related to future changes in purchase behavior among users, 19 brand summary.

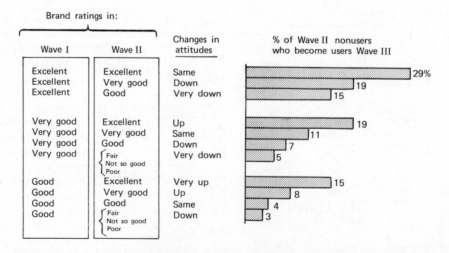

FIGURE 13. Changes in attitudes related to future changes in purchase behavior among nonusers, 19 brand summary.

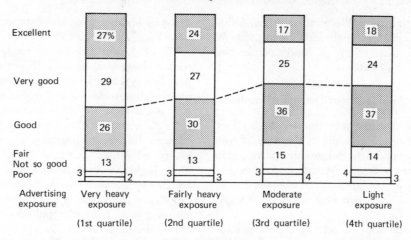

FIGURE 14. Relationship of attitudes and exposure to advertising over three waves, 3 brand summary.

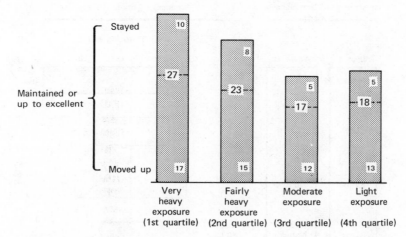

FIGURE 15. Relationship of changes in attitudes and exposure to advertising over three waves, 3 brand summary.

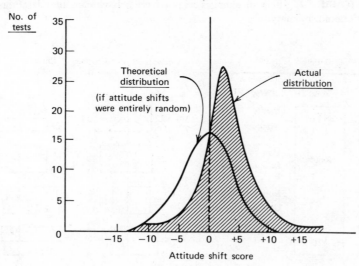

FIGURE 16. Actual vs. theoretical distribution of copy test attitude scores (based on 189 tests).

the marketing mix. While attitudes can influence behavior through advertising, it is scarcely a mesmerizer or bludgeon in the hands of the advertisers.

Effect of Product Experience on Attitudes

Not only does the way a person feels affect usage, but usage also affects the way people feel. Experience with the product plays a role in consumer behavior. When people become users they are more likely to like the brand than to dislike it, and vice versa. (See Figs. 17 and 18.)

One reason why advertising cannot manipulate consumer behavior is that product trial in many highly advertised categories is high. (See Figs. 19, 20, and 21.)

The top four brands of analgesics were tried at least once by over 75 per cent of the population. The trial rate for cigarettes is also quite high considering how addictive they are. And in cat food, to pick a third typical example, most consumers have tried the top brands.

Since the repeat-purchase rates of many highly advertised national brands are also quite high, we must believe that consumers are choosing brands based on positive product experience regardless of the advertising. If advertising were truly manipulative, this would not be the case.

The point here is that consumers know

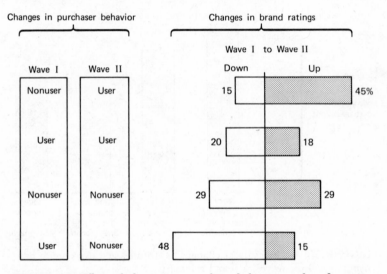

FIGURE 17. Effect of changes in purchase behavior on brand ratings: 19 brand summary.

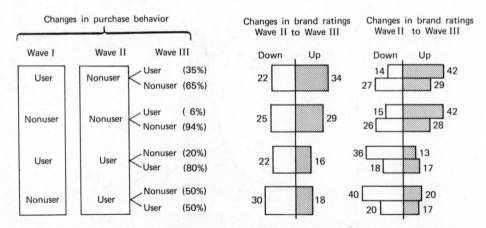

FIGURE 18. Effect of changes in purchase behavior on future brand ratings, 19 brand summary.

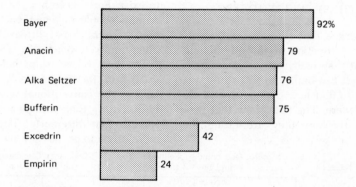

FIGURE 19. Trial rate—ever tried brand: analgesics, 1966.

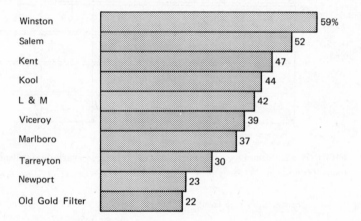

FIGURE 20. Trial rate—ever used brand: cigarettes, 1969.

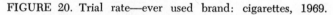

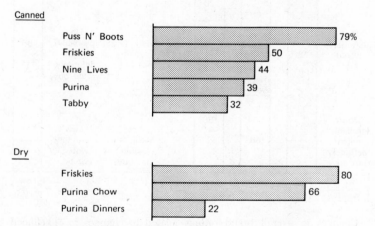

FIGURE 21. Trial rate—ever tried: cat food, 1968.

what they are doing. They react to advertising. They react to the product. And because there are obviously other elements in the picture, they are reacting to them as well.

HOW DELIBERATE ARE THESE ATTITUDES?

One could argue that these measurements of attitude are a function of the questioning technique, that they really are not measuring how people feel. But built into this study was an experiment to find how deliberate attitude measurements were. The data show that people know exactly how they are rating the brands.

Six different measures of attitude were used. Correlations between all pairs were all over 73. (See Fig. 22.)

Moreover, when the two most widely used attitude measures were correlated between waves, a similarly high correlation was found to exist. For this to happen by chance would require people to remember how they scored two different scales three months before—a highly unlikely possibility. (See Fig. 23.)

Do these relationships hold true among all groups in the population? After all, if we believe the conventional wisdom of advertising's critics that the poor and uneducated should react differently, they then should be more prone to act as they are told.

r_{tet} *	Overall rating	One brand would buy	Likelihood to buy	Top of mind	Constant sum	Calculated overall
Overall rating		.82	.76	.75	.78	.94
One brand would buy	.82		.93	.94	.98	.80
Likelihood to buy	.76	.93		.83	.77	.75
Top of mind	.75	.94	.83		.91	.73
Constant sum	.78	.98	.77	.91		.77
Calculated overall	.94	.80	.75	.73	.77	

* Estimated tetrachoric correlation coefficients based upon Pearson's "Cosine Method".

FIGURE 22. Summary of correlations between various attitude measurements in Wave I, 3 or 6 brand summary.

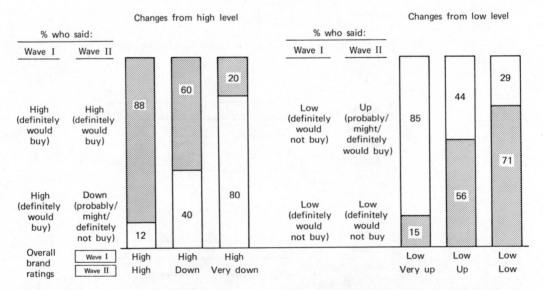

FIGURE 23. Changes in overall brand ratings related to changes in "likelihood to buy" ratings, 6 brand summary.

Yet, there was no significant difference in the relationship between above average, average, or below average income householders, or among well-educated and less well-educated consumers. (See Figs. 24, 25, 26, and 27.)

INFORMATION'S ROLE ON ATTITUDES AND BEHAVIOR

As discussed earlier, there are some who believe that all effective advertising should do is convey information. But the evidence suggests that communication of information alone will not change attitudes or behavior.

A standard measure of the amount of information communicated in advertising is "related recall." Using a typical case, related recall scores were correlated with attitude shift scores (which are a measure of persuasion) from 15 individual copy tests on one brand. As shown in Fig. 28, there was no correlation between the two measures.

In a study done by Ogilvy and Mather, they found that usage did not change on the basis of the information recalled. Fig. 29 shows that it didn't seem to matter whether more or less information was recalled; usage remained basically the same.

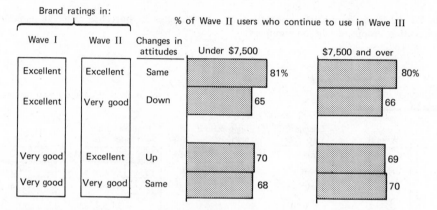

FIGURE 24. Changes in attitudes related to future changes in purchase behavior among users in various income groups, 19 brand summary.

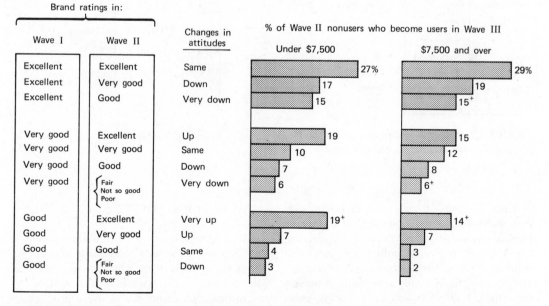

FIGURE 25. Changes in attitudes related to future changes in purchase behavior among nonusers in various income groups, 19 brand summary.

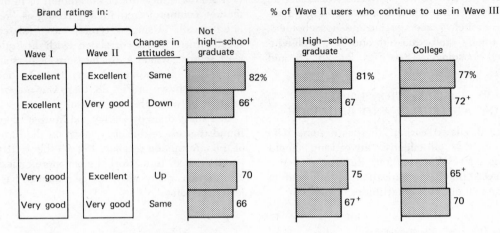

FIGURE 26. Changes in attitudes related to future changes in purchase behavior among users in various education groups, 19 brand summary.

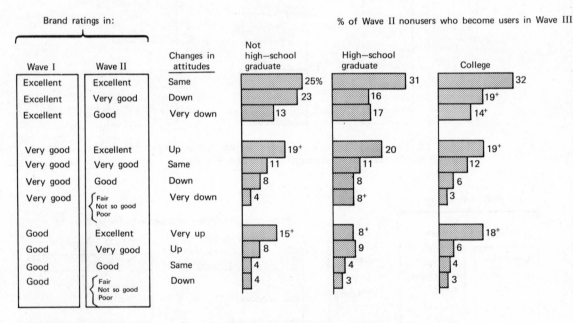

FIGURE 27. Changes in attitudes related to future changes in purchase behavior among nonusers in various education groups, 19 brand summary.

Thus, contrary to what some critics say, consumers do not react—either by feeling or buying—to information alone. If advertisers were forced to convey only information, assuming such a proposition were even remotely possible, it would essentially eliminate advertising's effectiveness as a market communication tool. Then one should certainly argue that it is an economic waste.

HOW DOES ADVERTISING WORK?

If communication of information alone is not the way consumer behavior is affected by advertising, how is it? The data suggest that the process works something like this.

Information about one or more product attributes *which are salient to consumers* is communicated in a persuasive context by na-

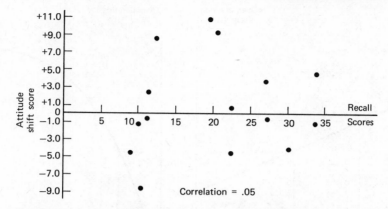

FIGURE 28. Relationship between recall of information and attitude effects of advertising (denture cleanser brand).

Alpha advertising rememberance Wave I vs Wave II	Usage of alpha Wave I vs II		
	Increased	Decreased	No change
Gained recall	10%	10%	80%
Lost recall	11	10	79
Maintained recall	10	11	79
Recalled in neither wave	7	6	87

FIGURE 29. Changes in recalling information related to changes in usage.

tional advertising. These attributes can be sensory, evaluative, or emotional.

If the communication is persuasive enough to improve consumers' attitudes on that attribute, their attitudes toward the overall brand will improve as well. This improvement in overall brand attitudes will concomitantly increase the probability of purchase. (See Fig. 30.)

But some product attributes have more clout than others. The more salient the attribute—i.e., the more correlated a change in attitude is with the change in overall attitude, the larger the effect on future brand share. Fig. 31 shows that Attribute X has more salience (r.=70) than Attribute Y (r.=60).

This is why the advertiser wants to know what is salient to the consumer. Unless he can support his claim on a salient factor and unless he can communicate it in a persuasive manner, he will have done nothing to enhance

his market position. There is nothing manipulative about this process. Advertisers either consider what the consumer wants and cater to his wants, or face market failure. We are all to well aware of the myriad of well advertised new products which have failed to meet this market standard.

CONCLUSIONS

No one is saying that there is not some deceptive advertising. No vocation is totally free of mendacious, avaricious people. But seen in the perspective of the billions of transactions that take place each year, deception plays a relatively minor role in consumer activity. Deception is wrong. It is manipulation. It hurts the honest competitor, and no responsible advertiser wants it to exist.

But in the process of eliminating it, let us not burn down the barn. Instead, let us lay to

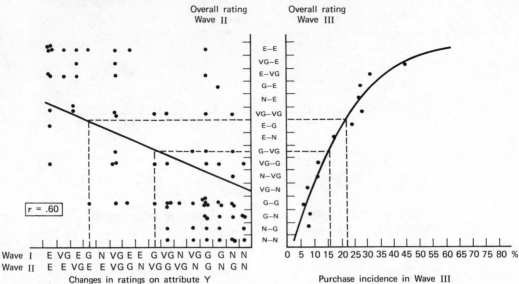

FIGURE 30. Relationship between specific attribute "Y" ratings: overall attitude ratings and purchase incidence (denture product brand).

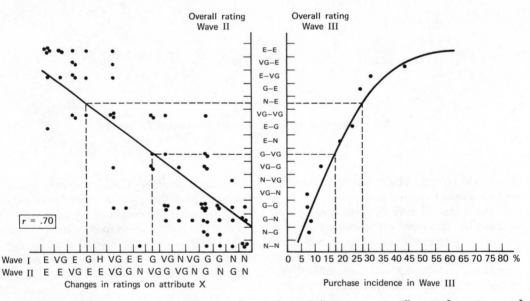

FIGURE 31. Relationship between the specific attribute "X" ratings: overall attitude ratings and purchase incidence (denture product brand).

rest this myth that national advertising, at least as it is generally practiced today, is manipulating the consumer.

Certainly, the evidence presented in this paper suggests why advertising is *not* manipulative.

Consumers' attitudes vary as widely and frequently as does purchase behavior. Consumers rarely stick to any one brand. If advertising affects their attitudes, it hardly mesmerizes them.

Product experience is also an important influence on future purchase. People do not rely only on what they hear or see. Information alone has no apparent effect on consumer attitudes or behavior. If people are going to be influenced, information must be placed in a persuasive context.

In summary, the evidence suggests that consumers are knowledgeable, experienced buyers—particularly for any product advertised nationally. They seek information given in a persuasive context and they freely give back information to those advertisers who seek it. There certainly is nothing hidden or underhanded in this process.

Advertisers and their agencies seek to satisfy consumers, not manipulate them. By their use of market research, they seek to know what the consumers want, to provide them with products which satisfy those wants, and to communicate with them in an acceptable, persuasive manner. If they appeal to emotion, it is because people do not live by fact alone. But to call what national advertisers do manipulation is to do wrong both to the good sense of the American housewife and to the facts.

S. The Interface With Consumers

54. Consumer Dissatisfaction and Public Policy

YVES RENOUX

The popular press and scholarly journals have been paying a great deal of attention to the subject of consumerism. Opinions of both consumerists and businessmen are often heard in various publications, but it is difficult to say that a real dialogue has been established between these two groups. The fanatic convictions of consumer advocates, and the defensive replies of businessmen, do not seem to mesh together to provide a body of thought that can be used to attain a real understanding of consumerism. Therefore, a conceptual framework is needed for making a realistic appraisal of consumerism. This framework should help to answer the questions: Where does consumerism come from? Where is it presently? and Where will it go in the future?

Consumerism represents a challenge to marketing. Although some people have said that consumerism might bring about *the end* of marketing, it seems more likely that consumerism will call to life a *new* marketing. But will this new marketing be characterized by more government regulation? And, if so, what is the level of regulation that is most compatible with consumer welfare and with a marketing system trying to satisfy the needs of consumers without being subjected to unnecessary bureaucratic constraints? The conceptual framework presented in this paper will hopefully throw some light on these difficult questions.

◆ SOURCE: Reprinted by permission from *Public Policy and Marketing Practices*, edited by Fred C. Allvine, Published by the American Marketing Association, Chicago, 1973, pp. 53–65.

CONSUMERISM AND CONSUMER DISSATISFACTION

Consumerism is a new word and a new concept. Many definitions of consumerism have been suggested, and one of the more enlightening statements has been that offered by Richard H. Buskirk and James T. Rothe. Consumerism is defined as "the organized efforts of consumers seeking redress, restitution, and remedy for dissatisfaction they have accumulated in the acquisition of a standard of living."[1]

A conceptual framework for analyzing consumer dissatisfaction is presented in Figure 1. An exchange relationship exists between business firms and consumer-buyers which can lead to either satisfaction or dissatisfaction on the part of an individual consumer. When the consumer becomes dissatisfied with certain marketing practices, he attempts to obtain compensation, redress, restitution, or a remedy. The consumer does this through a *challenge-mix* which can take a number of forms including (1) personal persuasion in the form of claims, complaints, threats of unfavorable word-of-mouth, and termination of patronage; (2) collective pressure such as action of consumer groups and the Better Business Bureau; and (3) institutional coercion involving government agency investigation, court suits, etc.

But if the consumer cannot obtain satisfaction in any of these ways, he gets the feeling

[1] Richard H. Buskirk, and James T. Rothe, "Consumerism—An Interpretation," *Journal of Marketing*, Vol. 34 (October, 1970), p. 62.

that the "rules of the game" are not fair—that they favor the dealers and producers. In this case, he will then attempt to change the rules by asking some type of legislative body to intervene as can be observed from the bottom portion of the diagram in Fig. 1. As a consumer-voter he will be quite willing to back legislation designed to change the marketing practices he dislikes, and he will exert pressure on legislators through letters and telegrams, through subscription to a consumer action group, and, finally, through his vote. His political activism can result in new legislation and increased satisfaction or it can fail to accomplish anything and add to his dissatisfaction. The latter outcome could occur if business firms choose to mount a counterattack, complete with heavy lobbying and skillful public relations, against the consumer activists.

Certain types of dissatisfaction have their origin outside the marketing system. These environmental dissatisfactions that find expression in the marketplace are shown to the right side of Fig. 1. They arise out of conditions involving the economy, social problems, ecology, politics, philosophy and fashion. These environmental problems tend to heighten expressed dissatisfaction with the marketing system.

Thus, it appears that consumerism has two dimensions—a marketing challenge dimension and a political activism dimension—both of which are oriented towards reducing consumer dissatisfaction. If business firms want to avoid confrontations with consumer groups, they must take the steps necessary to diminish consumer dissatisfaction.

Can business firms reduce dissatisfaction enough to make consumerism disappear? Will the elimination of distasteful, deceptive, and wasteful marketing practices wipe out marketing system dissatisfaction? Or will things like environmental dissatisfaction continue to manifest themselves as marketing system dissatisfaction after marketing practices are improved? In the opinion of the author much can be done by business to reduce the sources of dissatisfaction with the marketing system. However, it is felt that a comprehensive understanding of marketing system dissatisfaction is needed by business before attempts are made to reduce the problems. To help business to reach this understanding, a more complete discussion of the causes of consumer dissatisfaction will now be presented.

CONSUMER DISSATISFACTION WITH THE MARKETING SYSTEM

A framework for analyzing consumer dissatisfaction can be derived from studying the history of consumerism in the United States. Consumer dissatisfaction with the U.S. mar-

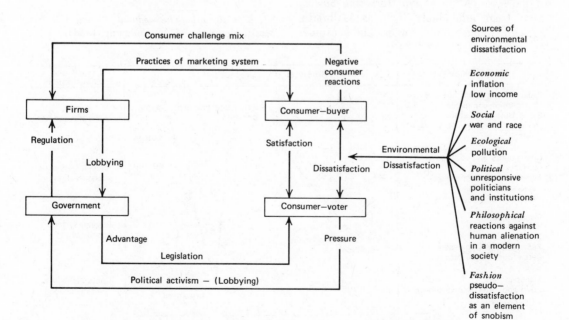

FIGURE 1. Consumer dissatisfaction and consumerism.

keting system has been expressed in different ways, or at different *levels,* at various times during the past fifty years. Fig. 2, going from right to left, shows the different levels of consumer dissatisfaction, important events in the history of the consumerism movement, and the groups and institutions that seemed to become involved in the controversies.

General discontent with the way the economy has been producing and allocating goods and services results in what might be classified as *Macro-Marketing System Dissatisfaction.* This level of dissatisfaction is not associated with specific producers, dealers, or products. The discontent with more specific aspects of the marketing system leads to what is called *Micro-Marketing System Dissatisfaction.* This type of discontent is expressed in three ways: (1) *Shopping-System Dissatisfaction* involving the availability of products and types of retail outlets; (2) *Buying-System Dissatisfaction* is concerned with the process of selecting, purchasing and receiving products from stores patronized; and (3) *Consuming-System Dissatisfaction* results from problems in using and consuming goods and services. Each of these levels of consumer dissatisfaction will be discussed in more detail.

Major episodes in the history of the consumer movement that occurred at the different levels of the marketing system are shown in the middle section of Fig. 2. Speaking out at the level of the *Macro-Marketing System* have been individuals such as Galbraith, Packard, Kennedy and Nader. The consumer

boycotts of supermarkets is an example of *Shopping-System Dissatisfaction.* The Consumers Union was organized to overcome *Buying-System Dissatisfaction.* Ralph Nader's attack on the safety of automobiles and other products provide examples of *Consuming-System Dissatisfaction.* These groups primarily concerned with the dissatisfaction at the different levels of the marketing system are shown on the left side of Fig. 2.

MACRO-MARKETING SYSTEM DISSATISFACTION

Dissatisfaction of this type has traditionally been expressed by intellectuals. However, at various times, large groups of people from all walks of life have become disenchanted with "the system" in the U.S. and have called for fundamental changes to be made.

General dissatisfaction with the performance of the *Macro-Marketing System* has led to a variety of complains: (1) There is too much emphasis placed on supplying this country with private goods rather than public goods. Collective needs are neglected because the need-satisfying function in this country is performed by a marketing system which is oriented towards the production and selling of private goods;[2] (2) The right for consumers to be heard means nothing in this country. Public policy is not formulated in a way that

[2] J. K. Galbraith, *The Affluent Society* (Boston, Mass.: Houghton Mifflin Company, 1958).

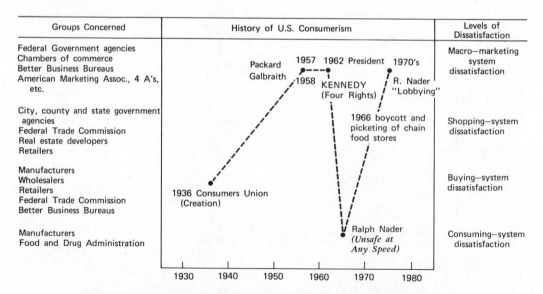

Groups Concerned	History of U.S. Consumerism			Levels of Dissatisfaction
Federal Government agencies Chambers of commerce Better Business Bureaus American Marketing Assoc., 4 A's, etc.		Packard Galbraith	1957 1962 President 1970's 1958 KENNEDY R. Nader (Four Rights) "Lobbying"	Macro—marketing system dissatisfaction
City, county and state government agencies Federal Trade Commission Real estate developers Retailers			1966 boycott and picketing of chain food stores	Shopping—system dissatisfaction
Manufacturers Wholesalers Retailers Federal Trade Commission Better Business Bureaus	1936 Consumers Union (Creation)			Buying—system dissatisfaction
Manufacturers Food and Drug Administration			Ralph Nader (*Unsafe at Any Speed*)	Consuming—system dissatisfaction
	1930 1940 1950	1960 1970 1980		

FIGURE 2. Overview of consumer dissatisfaction with marketing system.

takes account of consumer opinions. Big industry and their army of lobbyists get pretty much anything they want[3] and (3) Business is unethical and unfair. It cares very little about consumer welfare and is primarily concerned with making profits.[4]

Marketers can do little directly about *Macro-Marketing System Dissatisfactions*. They can only hope that over the long-run negative attitudes about the general marketing system will decrease as marketers reduce dissatisfaction at the level of the *Micro-Marketing System* through adopting new marketing practices.

MICRO-MARKETING SYSTEM DISSATISFACTION

The way in which the three types of *Micro-Marketing System Dissatisfactions* express themselves are shown in Fig. 3. The consumer first enters the shopping system where he must decide which outlet to patronize. He brings with him to this decision limited amounts of resources or inputs in the form of energy, time, money, and information. If the

shopper finds reasonable shopping alternatives that conserve his resources he will be satisfied with his shopping experience. In part this can be accomplished by making available more relevant and objective information about the characteristics of shopping alternatives.

There are frequently things about a shopping system which prevent the consumer from making a decision which will require little use of his energy, time, and money. The ghetto dweller, for example, often has to use up large amounts of time and energy just to reach lower-priced stores. He therefore often shops at more convenient local stores, which saves him time and energy, but costs him money. At the other extreme, shoppers living in planned communities with highly restrictive retail zoning often find it necessary to go considerable distances to reach lower-priced stores. Another aggravating factor that some shoppers face is that stores are not open at times that are convenient for working consumers, thus forcing them to spend more time, money and energy than they would like.[5] The recent development, and in increasing num-

---

[3] Robert F. Buckhorn, *Nader: The People's Lawyer* (Englewood Cliffs, N.J.: Prentice-Hall, Inc., 1972).

[4] Vance Packard, *The Hidden Persuaders* (New York: D. MacKay Company, 1957).

[5] "Report of the National Commission on Civil Disorders," in David A. Aaker and George S. Day (eds.), *Consumerism: Search for the Consumer Interest* (New York: The Free Press, 1963), p. 369; and David Caplovitz, *The Poor Pay More* (New York: The Free Press, 1963).

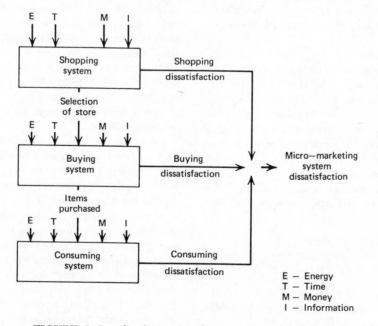

FIGURE 3. Levels of micro-marketing system dissatisfaction.

bers, of 24-hour supermarkets should help reduce the magnitude of this problem. Other problems giving rise to *Shopping-System Dissatisfaction* can similarly be solved by adopting innovative and creative approaches.

Once the selection of a store has been made, the consumer takes his remaining energy, time, money, and information into the buying system. He wants to be able to find a satisfactory product without expending too great an amount of energy and time; he wants to be able to buy the product for a reasonable price; and he wants to be able to pay for the product and get delivery, if necessary, in as short a time as possible. Moreover, he also would like to have the kind of information made available to him, either in the form of a salesperson or informative labeling, that he needs to make an intelligent buying decision.

Buying-System Dissatisfaction arises when the shopper encounters a number of different situations which waste his time, energy, or money, or bothers him in other ways. First, he may find that his chosen store only carries a limited number of brands of the product he desires at a limited number of prices and in a limited number of sizes. This could be caused by the fact that the industry that manufactures the product is quite concentrated,[6] or by a lack of willingness on the part of the dealer to carry several brands and sizes. This situation disturbs old people, for example, who find package sizes designed for the average American family rather than for them,[7] and poor people who cannot afford to pay high prices.

Buying-System Dissatisfaction can also rise when the consumer can choose from *too many* brands of a product. The consumer may find it difficult to reject products with attractive qualities and he may therefore experience cognitive dissonance after making a choice.[8] It is interesting that affluent countries such as the United States and Sweden have experienced the greatest development of consumerism. Perhaps the abundance of available product choices in these countries has inadvertently led to large amounts of consumer dissatisfaction.

A third situation where *Buying-System Dissatisfaction* might arise is when consumers cannot obtain the information and/or the assistance they need to make intelligent buying decisions. The consumer may find that the pricing, labeling and coding of products tells him very little; that the sales people in the store are unfriendly and uninformed; that the product is technologically complex and really does require explanation by a courteous salesman; or that the self-service layout of the store is confusing, inconvenient, and frustrating. One example of providing shoppers with more helpful information is the recent development of "unit-pricing." Some food chains that have led in this per unit measure pricing program, like the Jewel Companies, have found that it has given them a competitive advantage.

Finally, the consumer may experience buying system dissatisfaction when he is forced to wait too long to receive buying assistance, to check out of a store, or to receive delivery on a purchased product. Any time a consumer has to wait in line for something, search for minutes for a salesperson to help him, or sit at home waiting days for a delivery, it increases his dissatisfaction with certain elements of the marketing system. Although the queuing problem is more serious in the European countries than in the United States, it is one which still leads to great dissatisfaction with many supermarkets, movie theaters, and service operations in this country. Moreover, the consumers in the United States have it as bad as anyone when it comes to having to wait for sales help or deliveries. Consumers hate to lose time in any of these ways because it can cost them money, leisure time, and nervous energy.

Once the consumer has actually purchased and received delivery of a product, he enters the consuming system. It is here where he may experience problems in *using, fixing,* or *destroying* the product. The consumer wants a product to do what it is supposed to do without requiring him to use too much of his energy, time, and money to make it work. If the consumer must go to outside sources of information to find out how to make the product work correctly, then he will probably develop *Consuming-System Dissatisfaction*. The consumer may also experience this kind

---

[6] Galbraith, *Affluent Society,* p. 238.

[7] Survey of "Chain Store Age Research" quoted in *The Miami News* (Wednesday, March 22, 1972), p. 38.

[8] Leon Festinger, *A Theory of Cognitive Dissonance* (Palo Alto, Calif.: Stanford University Press, 1957).

of dissatisfaction if the product does not live up to any advanced billings presented in the media. Furthermore, a product that pollutes (either air, water, or noise) when it operates may disturb some consumers.

Consumers will develop *Consuming-System Dissatisfaction* if they find that they must spend a great deal of money repairing or maintaining products. For example, congressional investigations have shown that consumers are spending up to $30 billion a year on auto repairs, but that possibly up to $10 billion of that went for shoddy, unnecessary repairs and repairs paid for, but simply never performed.[9] This is big money which understandably is very aggravating to purchasers and users of products.

Finally, *Consuming-System Dissatisfaction* can arise if the consumer has trouble destroying or disposing of a product, or if the destruction of the product must be carried out sooner than expected (as a result of planned obsolescence, etc.). Those consumers concerned about pollution may be bothered by the solid waste disposable problem to which a product might contribute. Other consumers may just be disturbed by having to pay for the removal or scrapping of a product.

WAYS OF REDUCING DISSATISFACTION WITH MICRO-MARKETING SYSTEM

What can the marketer do to reduce dissatisfaction with specific marketing practices? In many situations that cause dissatisfaction, the marketer's hands are tied and he can do very little. What follows are some micro-marketing suggestions to marketers of ways to reduce the amount of each type of *Consuming-Mix Dissatisfaction*.

To reduce *Shopping-System Dissatisfaction,* marketers might try to do the following:

- Take the risk of building modern, comprehensive shopping facilities in innercity areas (e.g., discount stores).
- Provide free transportation facilities for consumers who are unable to get to superior shopping centers on their own.
- Join together to provide newsletters giving information to certain consumers

about store locations, product lines, price ranges, and store hours.
- Cooperate with government in rehabilitation programs for inner-city shoping areas.

To alleviate *Buying-System Dissatisfaction,* marketers might try these steps:

- Provide consumers with more helpful buying information. In Sweden, for example, supermarkets contain "consumer corners" where buyers can receive test results, guides and brochures, and even help of a home economist.[10] Measures such as this could be tried in the United States.
- Offer products, package sizes, and prices for all major segments of the consumer market.
- Provide consumers standardized information on prices to assist them in determining better values.
- Give "open dating" and "nutritional and other important information" in food products.
- Do everything possible to eliminate waiting lines and delays in delivery time.
- Design the layout of stores and shopping centers so that consumers can easily find their way around and do not become fatigued in moving from one location to another.

Marketers could reduce *Consuming-System Dissatisfaction* by taking the following actions:

- Improve intrinsic product quality, product service (especially warranty liability), and product design.
- Provide centers where consumers could learn to use certain types of products correctly and safely. A chain store in Switzerland (MIGROS) has used this tactic successfully.
- Design non-polluting products.
- Design products which can be disposed of cheaply and safely without adding to solid waste pollution problems.

---

[9] Galbraith, *Affluent Society,* p. 236.

[10] Hans B. Thorelli, "Consumer Information Policy in Sweden: What Can Be Learned," *Journal of Marketing,* Vol. 35 (January 1971), pp. 50–55.

THE FUTURE OF CONSUMERISM

Those who think that consumerism is an episodic and ephemeral development are wrong. During the last ten years the voice and power of consumers have been growing stronger. The movement has been spurred on by greater public awareness and interest in consumer issues and problems, particularly among the better-educated younger generation. In addition, the press has helped considerably by giving greater coverage to consumer news and views despite the counterpressure of some advertisers. Moreover, several consumer groups have been formed and they have served as articulate spokesmen for consumers. Even government has helped the movement to grow through the creation and strengthening of numerous federal, state, and local consumer agencies that are now looking after consumer interests.

The "consumer lobby" has grown rapidly at the national, state, and local levels. On the national level, voices from Nader's groups are now being backed up by others with large consumer support such as The Consumer Federation of America, The Friends of the Earth and individual consumer spokesmen like Robert Choate. These agencies and individuals are being listened to by a number of influential senators and congressmen who have become champions of the consumer cause. What has happened on the national level has been duplicated at the state and local levels. Today most states have newly organized departments of consumer affairs and several of the larger cities have created similar agencies. These state and municipal offices are staffed by a large group of government officials and are backed by consumer groups and citizens interested in bringing about change in marketing practices.

Clearly, dissatisfaction is the basic element which gives substance to the consumer movement. As a means of reducing this dissatisfaction, consumers and their agents are supporting and pressuring for more legislation to constrain business activities. To avoid new legislation restricting business activities, businesses must respond to the sources of dissatisfaction. By changing some practices businessmen will decrease certain types of dissatisfaction and with this pressure and justification for more legislation. To achieve this objective, marketers must completely analyze the levels and specific nature of dissatisfaction.

Care must be taken in studying consumer dissatisfaction related to marketing practices. Dissatisfaction may either be expressed and apparent, and observed as discontent, or latent and illusive, resulting in frustration. Unless studies are made that diagnose both types of dissatisfaction there is the serious danger of only responding to those that are currently sensitive. Once the problems have been brought into the limelight and the legislative process becomes involved, business runs the risk of acting too late to head-off formal regulations.

Another reason for a thorough investigation of both types of dissatisfaction is that the expressed type may be biased. An analysis of expressed discontent does not necessarily represent the feelings of a cross section of society. Consumers having a high level of education and income and knowing how to protect their rights are more often heard, while the problems of the poor may never surface in any sort of effective way. As a consequence, those who need the most help to stretch their small incomes as far as they can go, end up getting little in the way of assistance in solving their problems. It is understandable why the disadvantaged periodically explode against shopkeepers and businesses as occurred during some of the riots of the 60's.

CONCLUSION

The proper approach to analyzing consumer dissatisfaction would be one taking into account the problem of all types of consumers. A complete and permanent inventory of the reasons for the dissatisfaction of shoppers, buyers, and consumers must be established. The systematic search would provide the basis for a readjustment of marketing practices. Planned change by marketers of the type proposed in this paper might help avoid a public expression of discontent which could result in inappropriate and restrictive regulations.

55. Corporate Responses to Consumerism Pressures

DAVID A. AAKER and GEORGE S. DAY

Until recently, observers of the consumer movement concentrated on understanding the scope and causes of consumerism and on forecasting probable future activity in this area. This emphasis was appropriate, given the rapid emergence of consumerism and the attendant confusion and uncertainty. The ground rules for business were changing rapidly, and it was easy for these observers to conclude that the initiative was with legislatures, regulatory bodies, consumer advocates, and the judiciary.

By contrast, the responses of business to these pressures often appeared passive and confused or reactive and misguided. This picture is changing as companies and trade associations accept the reality of consumerism and gain experience with positive programs.

Evidence on the success of these endeavors is sketchy; many programs are new, seem to be exploratory, and often lack adequate resources. However, it is not too early to attempt to generalize from these efforts to help management make future programs more effective.

This raises a whole series of questions: What approaches are promising? What are the barriers to developing effective response programs? How can the important problem areas and worthwhile opportunities be identified? Are existing decision-making processes and organizational forms inhibiting progress? What about industrywide efforts? Finally, what is the role of government regulation?

In this article, we shall first take a look at these evolving corporate responses, then discuss the barriers to company initiatives, and finally examine the potential for industry action spearheaded by the leadership of trade associations.

EVOLVING COMPANY ACTIONS

In the early 1960's, consumerism was most often regarded by business executives as a transitory threat to be opposed at every turn by invoking ideology and denying the seriousness of the charges. Such approaches generally gave way to defensive responses wherein the apparent problems were usually identified by those outside the organization and managers were forced to react under pressure.

Increasingly, however, corporate managers are making efforts not only to identify and anticipate problems but also to view consumerism as a marketing opportunity, not as a threat. The result of such an orientation can be the optimal consumer program—one which addresses a real social problem and simultaneously demonstrates short-term value to the company.

Approaches and Programs

Whirlpool was perhaps the first corporation to take this positive approach aggressively through the development of a comprehensive

◆ SOURCE: Reprinted by permission from *Harvard Business Review*, Vol. 50, No. 6, November–December 1972, pp. 114–124. © 1972 by the President and Fellows of Harvard College; all rights reserved.

consumer-problem-oriented program that has evidently been successful in terms of conventional measures. In recognizing the inherent problem of providing appliances which perform reliably, Whirlpool first invested in an improved service organization. This was followed by the introduction of the corporation's subsequently widely imitated "cool line," a program that permits customers with a complaint or problem to contact service consultants directly, and a radically simplified warranty. Later, the company experimented with tel-tags to improve the quality of Whirlpool's point-of-sale information. Equally important, these innovations were communicated to the consumer in a way that enabled Whirlpool to build a corporate image of genuine consumer concern—an image that was based on substance.

Several supermarket chains have since developed comprehensive programs that have had similar impact. Utilizing discounting, open dating, unit pricing, and nutritional information plans, they have been able to assert an aggressive consumer-oriented image.

Specific Research. There is some evidence that programs are being increasingly evaluated and refined. Specific program research increases the probability that programs and company positions will be more defensible in the future both to internal and external challenges.

For example, Federated Department Stores has developed a series of experiments with tel-tags on small appliances. Safeway Stores and others have conducted research on unit pricing. Such research can sometimes uncover unexpected benefits. Thus Federated found that the tel-tags were of considerable value to sales clerks; the unit pricing research determined that costs for large stores were less than anticipated and were partially offset by the benefits of enhanced consumer confidence.

Research can also test often overly optimistic predictions of public interest. While program research is still not being conducted frequently enough, the situation has improved considerably in recent months.

Educational Efforts. If there is an underlying theme to any analysis of consumerism, it is that consumers lack adequate information on which to base informed decisions. Various programs have been initiated which are responsive to this general problem. In particular, many national advertisers have been increasingly willing to undertake educational campaigns and to use longer, more informative copy than they were using only a few years ago.

For example, a Ford Motor campaign told consumers how to buy cars and offered a booklet with helpful details. Lee Carpets has run advertisements addressing questions faced by those purchasing carpets and offering a booklet. Hunt-Wesson Foods has decided to avoid advertising relatively immaterial product differences. Such a trend is most welcome since advertising has been under increasing attack—with some justification—as contributing to the information gap by emphasizing emotional appeals, with greater potential for deception, at the expense of comparative information. Undoubtedly, there is much room for further improvement.

Raymond A. Bauer and Stephen A. Greyser, in their study of Americans' attitudes toward advertising, had respondents categorize advertisements and found that only 5.8% of those ads noticed were perceived as being particularly informative—that is, "ads that you learn something from, that you are glad to know or know about . . . that help you in one way or another because of the information they provide." [1]

Countervailing Influences. A further illustration of the increased responsiveness of some companies is their willingness to capitalize on the inability of related industries or suppliers to respond to consumerism. This has the dual benefit of (a) enhancing a company's image in this area by deflecting criticism to a new target and (b) solving problems that are otherwise out of the control of the company. This approach is seen in the recent announcement by Giant Food that it will not carry specific items in which the packaging or other aspects are perceived to be potentially unsafe or deceptive.

Other food chains (a) have unilaterally stopped stocking items whose contents have been deceptively reduced to avoid a price raise, (b) have marked the phosphate content of soaps and detergents with shelf signs, (c) have highlighted items that are ecologically better than others (such as glass instead of plastic and returnable rather than nonreturnable bottles), and (d) have instituted shelf-dating programs for products such as

---

[1] *Advertising in America: The Consumer View* (Cambridge, Massachusetts, Harvard University Press, 1968), p. 183.

batteries and wristwatches when the supplier does not have such a program.

Insurance companies are putting pressure on automobile manufacturers to design automobiles that are safer and easier to repair in order to control the rising cost of damages. Allstate is advertising that it "will cut collision rates 20% for any car the manufacturer certifies, through independent tests, can take a five-mile-an-hour crash into a test barrier, front and rear, without damage."

Mobilization and Organization

The practice of creating consumer affairs departments is spreading as more and more companies search for ways to deal with consumerism problems. Some of these efforts are obviously blessed with top-management commitment, a key to short-run success. Others, however, appear less viable because the corporate focus is on gaining a public relations advantage or on presenting an aura of concern in order to forestall possible litigation.

A new or expanded consumer affairs department can provide the needed impetus. To be effective, however, it should have a clearly defined set of responsibilities and corresponding authority. The specific functions will depend on many factors, but they should generally be defined to incorporate these four related actions:

1. To receive customer complaints and problems, and to have sufficient authority to resolve them—if necessary, by overriding the desires of the operating groups. Such an effort would be close to the concept of an ombudsman, representing the individual complainant against the organization.

2. To develop and operate an information system with the dual functions of (a) monitoring the extent to which product-class buyers and users are satisfied with each element of the marketing programs of the company and its major competitors, and (b) detecting and predicting areas of basic consumer discontent that may possibly have a negative impact on the company or to which the organization may be uniquely qualified to respond.

Obviously, such a system will be effective only to the extent that the output is interpreted and communicated to management so that policy implications are highlighted and follow-up is encouraged. In particular, profit opportunities through new products and/or services need to be identified and communicated to the appropriate decision makers.

3. To be a representative and advocate of the consumer interest during the policy-making process. Thus the new department should be in a position whereby it can provide an independent appraisal of the company's marketing programs.

For example, do proposed new products represent a real contribution to the life-style of a market segment? Or are they simply an unneeded addition created to exploit current buying patterns? What will be the human and environmental side effects of proposed new products? Are the company's external communications (not only media advertising, but also product-label copy, warranties and guarantees, and so forth) as deception-free and informative as possible?

The basic principle here is that the monitoring and control functions should be distinct from operating management. This suggests that the consumer affairs department ought to report to the chief executive officer who is ultimately responsible for the company's performance in the consumer affairs area. A further implication is that the new department might have direct responsibility for functions such as quality control and product service that are vital to the resolution of consumer problems. (Such functions generally tend to be compromised when carried out by operating groups.)

4. To contribute to the development of corporate social objectives, programs to implement those objectives, and operational measures by which the programs can be evaluated. The establishment of objectives will involve tough resource-allocation questions and consideration of nonprofit measures of performance.

BARRIERS TO INITIATIVES

There are various inherent difficulties facing corporate executives who would develop response programs. Some arise from the nature of the decision area. It is not easy to identify and analyze the fundamental problems to be addressed. Others are due to the difficulty of adapting the organization and its decision-making process. Finally, there are external pressures from the marketplace to consider.

Understanding the Problems

Experience shows that many specific consumer difficulties and dissatisfactions are surface symptoms of more basic problems. If the symptom is eliminated, another will probably appear unless the underlying problem is identified and addressed. Without this recognition, a response program can too easily become a futile fire-fighting effort rather than a step on the road to resolving the fundamental problem.

There is evidence of this difficulty in the current flurry of interest in nutritional labels and charts. A wide variety of labeling plans has been proposed by industry and legislatures. Some cereal manufacturers have gone as far as to flash a list of nutrition contents on the television screen at the end of their commercial messages. Other companies have lengthy nutrition charts which they distribute to customers. Several companies are participating in races to turn bread products into vitamin pills.

Suppose, however, that such an analysis reveals the basic problem is that people are undernourished. One segment is undernourished because good food is not available to the people and/or because they do not know how to select proper diets; another larger segment has the means and perhaps the knowledge but lacks motivation to pursue proper diets. Neither segment will probably be influenced by nutritional labels or charts.

An example of a program that is likely to be more appropriate than labels or charts is Hunt-Wesson Foods' computerized menu service. Over 1.3 million people requested and received a month's supply of menus tailored to their food budget and family size. Another is Del Monte's experimental program to provide a computer-based analysis of diets of groups with special problems, such as alcoholism. It might be worthwhile to attempt to motivate people to consider nutrition more in their menu planning. Such efforts could be useful not only from a social viewpoint but also from the standpoint of increased profits for a food company.

A cool-line program to provide customers with telephone contact with factory service consultants may be difficult to justify as part of a service operation. In most cases, the customer can either call a service representative directly or else contact the company by letter. However, assume that one of the basic problems underlying the consumerism movement is a dissatisfaction with the degree to which the institutions in our society are perceived as being impersonal and unresponsive. (The widespread use of self-service retailing, the low profile maintained by most executives, the entry of computers into the interface between the individual and the organization, and the inherent difficulties of dealing with bureaucracies—all contribute to this dissatisfaction.)

Then, a cool-line program appears in another perspective. It provides the customer with immediate personal contact with the company. The potential of calling a *real* person—*provided* that person can actually solve problems and is not simply another intermediary who increases the customer's frustration level—should dramatically alter people's perception of an institution as impersonal and unresponsive.

Pinpointing the Issues

If an organization is to address fundamental issues instead of symptoms, it must identify and analyze them. Such a task is most formidable for two reasons.

First, the basic issues are inherently difficult to understand. Issues tend to be dynamic and interrelated. The real problems are frequently not visible to the public; even significant symptoms often lie dormant until a startling report of a particularly misleading, unsafe, or unwholesome social situation serves to focus consumer discount.

Second, the information systems of most organizations are neither oriented to nor effective in obtaining information that will enable the company to detect and predict underlying social issues. Market research groups are usually directed at short-term projects with relatively limited objectives—that is, projects which are primarily concerned with competitive considerations. They essentially research symptoms if, indeed, they do any research that is relevant to real consumer needs.

Some organizations do of course make good use of longitudinal analyses of consumer complaints, consumer surveys, and the positions of consumer advocates. But too often such analyses have neither the breadth nor the depth to provide adequate insights. What is needed is a more ambitious mission for the research group, and also the development of new measures.

There are some promising research efforts that suggest what is required. One is the emerging use of social indicators and the more directed life-style measures. Another is the application of focused group interviews systematically conducted over time and oriented to the identification of basic consumer problems rather than to specific product decisions. Still another is the effort to obtain futuristic subjective inputs. One organization is applying the Delphi technique, an iterative approach used to stimulate and refine ideas of a group of individuals working independently, using a number of futurists.

Whatever the difficulties, it seems clear that organizations need to divert resources in this direction. As Peter F. Drucker has observed, the responsibility of any institution in a period of rapid change is "the anticipation of social needs and their conversion into opportunities for performance and results." [2]

The Nature of Decision Making

An appropriate orientation toward basic problems and a capable information system are necessary but not sufficient conditions for an effective response program. In addition, program development requires a compatible decision-making process within a sympathetic organizational structure.

Cost-benefit Analysis. The decision-making process within the company is not easily adjusted to encompass social consequences. Decision makers are not oriented to consider social implications. They have been trained and conditioned to think about more conventional determinants of profits. A related problem is that the benefits are difficult to quantify. There are two reasons for this.

First, the payoffs to the company are often largely deferred. It is difficult enough to identify cause-effect relationships and to solve troublesome measurement problems when the impact of a decision is immediate. When the implications are long run in nature, the uncertainties are magnified.

Second, the benefits are often indirect. A unit-pricing program or the installation of a tel-tag system will primarily have a direct impact even if it has a long-run component. However, the value to the organization of nutritional education programs in the ghetto

areas, for instance, will have benefits that are more indirect. Although benefits are difficult to quantify, the costs are usually painfully obvious and appear to affect prices or profits directly. It is easy and natural to let the hard data dominate the decision-making process.

Operational Objectives. Most corporations have well-developed planning processes that involve both short- and long-range time horizons, but relatively few explicitly include in their planning effort social goals and corresponding programs to implement them. Yet there is a clear need for consumer programs to be guided by operational objectives with accompanying nonprofit, short-run measures which will serve to reflect long-run and indirect benefits.

Other parts of the organization make similar use of objectives with nonprofit measures of success. Advertising, for example, usually has communication objectives which are often measured by constructs like awareness levels and attitude changes. Similarly, a consumer program should have objectives, as well as appropriate performance measures. An insurance company's program to reduce the number of drunk drivers might use indexes of drunk driving as program measures. A nutritional information campaign might be evaluated in terms of attitudes and motivations.

The need for objectives to guide consumer programs becomes particularly acute when the benefits seem far removed from the day-to-day operation of the company. In these situations, decisions are usually made in an ad hoc manner. Without operational objectives and implementation plans, the chances for real impact are slim. Further, if objectives and accompanying performance measures do not exist, resources devoted to social response programs cannot be held accountable.

A set of objectives and an accompanying implementation program provide four benefits: (1) the organization's efforts tend to be more integrated and focused, (2) the possibility that programs would be addressed to basic problems instead of symptoms is increased, (3) the potential of providing a rational means of allocating resources to alternative programs is created, and (4) the development of nonprofit measures as well as performance benchmarks and targets is stimulated.

Ethical Considerations. Complicating the decision-making process are ethical considerations—standards which can result in costly

---

[2] *The Age of Discontinuity* (New York, Harper & Row, 1969), p. 205.

self-imposed constraints on decisions. Ethical considerations assume importance when decisions must be made in the gray areas between what is legally permitted and what is morally and ethically wrong. There is a decided tendency in marketing to use the words "legal" and "honest" interchangeably.

There are also many situations in which the law is open to interpretation—with respect to deceit, misrepresentation, competitive disparagement, and so forth—so that legal compliance provides only a minimum ethical standard. Consequently, managers who resort to law as their justification look particularly graceless under public scrutiny.

The marketing concept can also serve as a convenient rationale for avoiding responsibility. This rationale is related to the ideological issue of whether marketers should lead or respond. Robert Moran, a researcher who is interested in the conflicts between marketers and their critics, has noted:

. . . marketers perceive their role, or at least claim it to be, as responding to consumer wants, habits, interests, and abilities. They resist what they feel is a new role their critics would have them perform—namely, that of confronting consumers with products and policies designed to give the consumer what they believe he needs or should want.[3]

For this reason, there has been great resistance to the "paternalism" aspect of consumerism that encompasses the protection of consumers against themselves or, more simply, giving consumers what they need rather than what they want. There are encouraging signs that this resistance by industry is lessening, especially in the area of product labeling and performance claims.

Decentralization Disadvantages. The leaders in the development of progressive consumer programs—such as retail food stores and manufacturers of large appliances—tend to be characterized by centralized decision making. In contrast, the "consumerism record" for those with highly decentralized decision making is much less impressive. There are several reasons why the decentralized corporation is at a real disadvantage when

attempting to respond to consumerism pressures.

In organizations with decentralized profit centers, the short-run profit pressures are often intense. Decision makers at lower profit-center levels are likely to be relatively early in their careers, a time when competition for recognition is high. They are often systematically moved so that their tenure in a particular job may last for only one or two years. Thus it is natural for them to emphasize short-term considerations.

Further, these lower level managers are not always motivated to consider the whole organization when evaluating decision alternatives since they, themselves, are judged solely on the basis of their own profit center. Yet social consequences tend to operate at the level of the whole organization. For example, a department store buyer might—perhaps accidentally—authorize a deceptive advertisement that could affect the store's reputation but would have little impact upon his profit center.

Of course, those at higher levels of profit responsibility are also under pressure, but they normally have a broader perspective and can often afford to take a longer view.

We are not suggesting that organizations should reject decentralization, especially when such an approach has provided managerial motivation and good short-run response to consumer demand. However, one should recognize that an organization with a high degree of decentralized decision making has special problems in developing responses to consumerism pressures.

Thus it may be possible to develop a subsidy system to influence decision making without imposing external constraints. This system would recognize decisions that had demonstrable long-run or corporate benefits which would not ordinarily appear on the current profit statements. Such recognition could be negative as well as positive.

For example, if a brand manager authorized a deceptive advertisement, this too would be suitably and formally recognized. Just as the corporation needs to be measured by more than profitability, so does the manager of a profit center within that corporation.

Authority positions: We assume that sufficient authority could be conferred on the new consumer affairs positions to make them effective. Our assumption could be ill-founded, however, if the authority were to be obtained

---

[3] "Formulating Public Policy on Consumer Issues: Some Preliminary Findings" (Cambridge, Massachusetts, Marketing Science Institute, 1971), p. 31.

by supplanting that of existing positions such as the vice president of sales or marketing. Such loss of authority would likely be regarded as both an accusation of failure and a threat for the future. The result might be a withdrawing of vital support within the organization.

Thus it could be tempting for the holder of an ombudsman-like position, especially if he perceived it as a short-term position, to retain support by avoiding decisions that favored a complainant or outsider. This could be a very real threat to the potential of these new positions to achieve change within the organization.

An approach which will alleviate the problem is to make sure the manager involved is sufficiently respected by the organization so that he need not rely too heavily on formal authority. This implies that he must be a competent and broadly trained senior manager or outsider of the stature of Esther Peterson, the consumer adviser to the president of Giant Food.

Paul R. Lawrence and Jay W. Lorsch studied positions with cross-functional area "integrator" responsibilities.[4] They concluded that effective managers in such positions are influenced because of their knowledge and expertise rather than because of their formal authority. They also noted that the assigning of young managers lacking in exposure to all facets of the business to such positions was a common failing.

Competitive Considerations. The ultimate reality to be faced is that many potential initiatives will involve costs and risks of failure which can threaten the company's competitive position. Unless there is a fair certainty that competition will emulate the initiative, a great deal of the incentive to act independently is lost.

This was the position the automobile manufacturers found themselves in during the 1960's regarding the safety problem when consumers did not consider safety especially important. It is still a problem for companies considering extensive and costly improvements in safety, reducing advertising clutter, or eliminating non-returnable bottles.

In this light, self-regulation looks very attractive, for it promises industrywide action with no loss in competitive position.

INDUSTRY-ACTION POTENTIAL

Until very recently, most trade associations were viewed by their members as defense mechanisms or negative lobbyists. This has changed with various pressures on them to be more responsive and with the increasing threat of government regulation. Individual companies are now turning to their trade associations for leadership in the four basic areas of (1) coordinating and disseminating research, (2) consumer and dealer education, (3) development of standards, and (4) complaint handling.

The first responsibility of trade associations is to keep their members properly informed by coordinating and disseminating research.

This activity may either supplement or be a substitute for the efforts of individual companies to become sensitive to consumerism problems and government initiatives. Without such information the members may pressure the association to take unrealistic and unattainable positions that work against the long-run interests of the industry.

Furthermore, if the information is objective, and not subject to restrictions because of confidentiality, it can be very useful in presenting industry arguments to governmental bodies. There is no question that research findings would be welcomed in both sectors, in preference to the "relatively unstructured and unscientifically assembled information which comes to us either out of our own experience or the experience of friends or in individual letters of complaint, in testimony of individual consumers and out of the experience of those who deal with and work with consumer problems."[5]

These considerations have led to the formation of the Consumer Research Institute by the Grocery Manufacturers of America, and the support of basic research on advertising by the American Association of Advertising Agencies and the Canadian Advertising Advisory Board.

The second responsibility of trade associa-

---

[4] "New Management Job: The Integrator," HBR November–December 1967, p. 142.

[5] Mary Gardiner Jones, "Enough Talking—Let's Get on With the Job," address to Illinois Federation of Consumers, Chicago, Illinois, April 3, 1970, p. 12.

tions is to provide leadership in consumer and dealer education.

An industry association has an enormous comparative advantage over individual members in the educational function. This is most obvious in broad-scale controversies such as nutrition, where education can play a big role but no individual company can undertake the responsibility.

Associations are also in a good position to work through dealers, where the education function frequently fails. This was the experience of the Outdoor Power Equipment Institute in its efforts to acquaint users with the hazards and proper use of power mowers. The dealers should have been the most influential channel or information about safety, but they needed stimulation and education before their potential was achieved.

The third responsibility of trade associations is leadership in the development of standards.

The most common form of self-regulation is the product standardization and certification program in the areas of quality, reliability, safety, and/or healthfulness. Standards may also apply to size, shape, and style variations, where necessary to facilitate consumer comparisons, reduce product proliferation, or ensure interchangeability of parts. Certification is the mechanism for identifying whether the product conforms to the standard. This judgment is made by one of approximately a thousand laboratories that test products.

There are various explanations for the motives behind the development of standards. One view is that the subscribers to a standard do so out of a sense of public responsibility and professional ethics combined with a desire to prevent similar standards from being imposed from the outside.

The Federal Trade Commission has recently argued that the character of the market on the buying side is the major determinant of the extent and quality of standards. The FTC observed that most of the estimated 20,000 sets of industry standards in effect in the United States exist in industrial markets where the buyers are large and expert and can force the development of this kind of information. One outcome of this analysis is a proposal that the law itself must provide the incentive for the development of standards for consumer products.

In many ways, the standards for advertising and promotion practices are the most difficult to set because of the problems in deciding what is inappropriate, deceptive, tasteless, or not in the public interest. Such standards are frequently only recommendations or suggestions (e.g., those of the Proprietary Association for the advertising of medications).

The fourth responsibility of trade associations is to provide leadership in the area of complaint handling.

In an effort to forestall the aggrieved consumer from turning first to the government, many industries are considering or implementing their own hearing boards for processing complaints. These are similar to the efforts of individual companies to provide an independent ombudsman-like function.

As an illustration, the appliance industry, in conjunction with major retailers, has set up a major appliance consumer action panel which will act as a "court of last resort," should retailer and manufacturer contact fail to resolve a complaint problem.

A similar principle is followed by the National Advertising Review Board. This organization utilizes the resources of 140 local Better Business Bureaus to monitor national advertisements, evaluate complaints, and advise advertisers on planned campaigns. If a complaint cannot be resolved at the local bureau level, it is referred to a review board of five people (one of whom represents a consumer group). If the advertiser is found to be in violation of review board standards and refuses to change or withdraw his ad, the disagreement is publicized and the case turned over to the Federal Trade Commission.

Problems with Self-Regulation

Experience indicates that purely voluntary efforts at self-regulation are not likely to be successful. There must be some enforcement mechanism by which violations of regulatory norms can be punished through collective action against the violator.

Unfortunately, such private power can also be used to enforce product standards rigged in favor of one or two producers or to dictate a safety certification program that is too costly for small manufacturers. Such actions are clearly anticompetitive and therefore forbidden by antitrust legislation.

The courts have used the potential for such abuses as reason to declare many enforcement techniques illegal—including the circulation of blacklists, withholding of a seal of approval, and the use of indirect boycotts. Many of these judgments against self-regulation are made without reference to the social merit of restraint.

This presents a real dilemma. An industry-wide agreement on standards is unlikely to be effective without inducements for compliance that are beyond the scope of a voluntary agreement. Yet the stronger the enforcement procedure, the greater the degree of potential coercion and danger of an antitrust violation.

This threat can be substantially diminished (a) by industry-government teamwork (in which industry proposes and implements the rules and standards by which the government regulates the industry), and (b) by the public and other interested parties playing a significant role both in developing and administering the rules and standards and in avoiding any discrimination against specific manufacturers.

Presuming that enforcement problems can be overcome, there remain four other barriers to the effectiveness of self-regulation (insofar as effectiveness means forestalling other forms of regulation):

1. The industry members may simply fail to see that there is an injustice in a practice and hence not take any regulatory action. Consequently, "such abuses as the advertisement in poor taste, unsolicited merchandise, the engineered contest, shrinkage of package weight, the unsubstantiated claim, and the negative option sales plan are all defended by sellers who perceive no wrong in them." [6] Their insensitivity leaves room for government investigation if not regulation.

2. The quality of the decision making and leadership of the association is frequently weakened by the need for consensus among a majority of members. This has particularly weakened safety standards for many products to the point that they represent nothing more than an affirmation of the status quo. The antitrust question also complicates the search for consensus.

3. Virtually every industry or trade association is accused of, and complains, of, having inadequate resources to carry out its responsibilities (with the probable exception of lobbying efforts). Inadequate resources mean outdated and inadequate standards, poor research and communications efforts, and complaint mechanisms that are inaccessible or unknown to the consumer.

One measure of the seriousness of the resource problem in the United States is found in the product-safety area. Although there are more than 1,000 standards covering 350 product categories, the National Commission on Product Safety found that industrywide voluntary safety standards applied to only 18 of the 44 categories that are highest in the number of estimated annual injuries. [7]

Efforts to provide complaint-handling mechanisms are particularly vulnerable. For example, the experience of Great Britain with "consultative machinery" in four major nationalized industries—gas, electricity, coal, and transportation — is sobering. After 22 years of publicizing these channels for complaints, a consumer study found that unaided recall awareness by industry varied from 4% to 12% of the population. [8]

The reason is that a complaint about the performance of a specific industry is a rare event for most consumers. Herein lies the strength of the Better Business Bureaus, for they are readily accessible and well-known to consumers as a place to register all kinds of complaints. The long-run prospects for specific industries to reach out and find aggrieved consumers (without an intermediary) appear slim.

4. Some problems may be beyond the scope of the responsibility that the industry is willing or able to accept. This seems to characterize many pollution-related issues, including nonreturnable bottles, auto emissions, and other currently intractable problems such as advertising clutter in all media.

The effectiveness of self-regulation ultimately depends on the public's willingness to accept industry regulations and standards in lieu of government intervention. This, in turn, requires that the public trusts the intention and effectiveness of business in solving consumer

---

[6] Louis L. Stern, "Consumer Protection via Self-Regulation," *Journal of Marketing*, July 1971, p. 49.

[7] *Final Report of the National Commission on Product Safety* (Washington, Government Printing Office, June 1970), p. 48.

[8] *Consumer Consultative Machinery in the Nationalized Industries*, A Consumer Council Study (London, Her Majesty's Stationery Office, 1968).

problems. Here, the climate is distinctly unfriendly.

A recent national probability sample of 1,613 adults, age 18 or over, found substantial support for new government restrictions and regulations. For example, 75% of the sample supported a regulation that would "require major companies to set strict standards of quality which would be enforced by government inspection." [9]

The context was certainly not one of complete mistrust of business; there was evidence of a "readiness to give the private sector credit for what it can do for itself" (it is interesting to note here that the much-maligned Better Business Bureau was given the highest proportion of positive ratings of any consumer protection group or individual), as well as distinct ambivalence about the effectiveness of government.

However, this standing is vulnerable to rising criticism, especially over the conflict of interest implications of financial dependence on the businesses being regulated. The big question is whether recent efforts at reform, including regional rather than local control, can offset this criticism.

Overall, the loss of confidence in the ability of business to adequately respond to the pressures of consumerism is the greatest threat to industry self-regulation as it is currently conceived. This does not preclude such efforts; it simply means that industry associations are going to have to demonstrate greater leadership and extend their efforts further than they appear to be doing.

This will almost certainly mean broadening the participation of the public in both the setting and enforcing of standards. Such a move, with all its threatening ramifications, is likely, on balance, to be superior to government regulation for most consumerism problems.

CONCLUSION

The evolution of business responses to consumerism is entering a new stage, with increasing recognition that—

. . . consumerism pressures will continue at a high, although perhaps less frenetic, level in the future;

. . . for some companies, consumerism has been an opportunity rather than a threat, and that responsive programs can yield dividends through increased consumer confidence;

. . . a posture of resistance, coupled with purely defensive programs, is likely to be counterproductive in the long run, because it increases the probability of government regulation with all the attendant problems of inflexibility, high costs, and new inequities created by unworkable rules and uneven administration.

These factors have led companies—acting either autonomously, through their trade associations, or in conjunction with government agencies—to undertake efforts to identify and correct problems before they become too serious. The question is no longer whether the effort should be made, but how to make the effort effective. Some tentative generalizations as to how to achieve this end are now possible.

First, it is necessary to focus on underlying consumer problems instead of chasing symptoms of those problems. Such an orientation requires an extended information system involving new measures of the consumer—his attitudes, values, and life-style—and a fresh interpretation of existing measures.

Second, it is useful to have an independent group in the organization charged with representing the consumer interest, but only if it has top-management support and is staffed with people who are both knowledgeable and respected.

Third, attention must be given to the design and implementation of programs. Because of the difficulty in creating effective and appropriate programs, experimentation and testing should be employed. Further, operational objectives with distinct, measurable indicators of performance are required. These indicators are not easy to develop since they usually will not be closely linked to short-term profits.

Finally, a new orientation is required. The success of the organization cannot be measured by short-run sales or profits. The marketing concept must be interpreted in terms of long-run consumer interests instead of what the market is accepting at the moment. Products and supporting communication need to be carefully scrutinized to determine whether they actually provide the consumer with real utility and useful information.

---

[9] John Revett, "Consumer Endorse More Restrictions on Business," *Advertising Age,* October 25, 1971, p. 98.

56. Poverty, Minorities, and Consumer Exploitation

FREDERICK D. STURDIVANT and WALTER T. WILHELM

A number of reports, ranging from informal studies by journalists to carefully researched investigations, have provided evidence that residents of ghettos pay more for their consumer goods than do other Americans.[1] For example, David Caplovitz' study of 464 families living in three New York settlement houses revealed a consistent pattern of high prices, poor quality, high interest charges, and unethical merchandising techniques. He concluded that "The problems of low-income consumers stem from the same set of forces that have created that special system of sales-and-credit—the quasitraditional economy—catering to their wants."[2] In California, The Governor's Commission on the Los Angeles Riots tended to reinforce this view. Following three months of investigation into the causes of the Watts riots, the Commission reported, "our conclusion, based upon an analysis of the testimony before us and on the reports of our consultants, is *that consumer problems in the curfew area are not due to systematic racial discrimination but rather result from the traditional interplay of economic forces in the marketplace, aggravated by poverty conditions.*"[3] (Emphasis added.) These studies suggest, therefore, that the market system works to the disadvantage of the poor because they are poor—not because of race or ethnicity. Any correlation between minority group status and exploitation is, according to these studies, attributable to the high incidence of poverty among minorities rather than some insidious form of discrimination.

The studies reported to date, however, have not provided adequate proof to support this conclusion. The California Commission, for example, reached its conclusion without conducting a series of comparative shopping analyses between ghetto and nonghetto stores and utilizing shoppers of various racial and ethnic backgrounds. Instead, staff consultants and their research assistants "spot checked" prices in various locations throughout central Los Angeles.[4] Caplovitz did analyze certain of his data utilizing the variable of minority group status. His findings in this area, however, were unclear. On the one hand he noted, "The amount paid for appliances differs greatly among the racial [sic] groups. Whites pay the least, Puerto Ricans the most, with Negroes in between."[5] However, Caplovitz

[1] For examples of the former see, *The Wall Street Journal*, August 16, 1966; *Women's Wear Daily*, July 6, 1966; *Los Angeles Times*, October 8, 1967; and *Los Angeles Herald Examiner*, October 11, 1966.
[2] David Caplovitz, *The Poor Pay More* (New York: The Free Press, 1963), p. 179.

◆ SOURCE: Reprinted by permission from the *Social Science Quarterly* Vol. 49, No. 3, December 1968, pp. 643–650.

[3] The Governor's Commission on Los Angeles Riots, *Violence in the City—An End or a Beginning?* (Los Angeles, December, 1965), p. 63.
[4] Interview with Gerald L. Rosen, Staff Attorney, The Governor's Commission on the Los Angeles Riots, January 18, 1966.
[5] Caplovitz, op. cit., pp. 90–91.

then noted that nonwhites tended to pay lower prices when the purchase is for cash. In fact, his data suggested that nonwhites paid less than whites when buying on credit in large stores outside the ghetto. This conflicting evidence was derived from the shopping experiences of the 464 cooperating families. The variables of method of payment, minority group status, and type of store were considered. However, *brand and model variations were not taken into account.* Thus, one does not know whether whites generally selected more expensive models and brands or if this shopping behavior was characteristic of either the Negroes or Puerto Ricans studied. Unless the variable of product brand and model is held constant, meaningful price comparisons cannot be made unless one subscribes to the rather risky assumption that brand or product quality selection is randomly distributed among the various ethnic and racial groups. In essence, the statement that exploitation in the marketplace is a function of economic status rather than minority group status is still untested.

RESEARCH DESIGN AND METHODOLOGY

The study was conducted in Los Angeles and involved the use of three couples and three shopping areas. The three couples represented the major populations of the city—Negro, Mexican-American, and Anglo-White. The shopping districts were the predominately Negro south central section of Los Angeles (which includes Watts), the Mexican-American section of east Los Angeles, and Culver City, a middle-class, Anglo-White community.

The criteria used in selecting the couples included not only minority group status, but also comparable "credit profiles." The similarity of their profiles was designed to neutralize any price or credit differentials based on alleged risk. The characteristics of the shoppers' credit profile are noted in Fig. 1.

The stores selected for comparative shopping in the Negro and Mexican-American sections were determined, in part, on the basis of detailed studies of consumer shopping patterns in those areas. Appliance and furniture stores in the two areas were arrayed on the basis of shopping frequency patterns

Family status	Married, 1–2 children
Age of head of household:	25–30
Employment:	Employed full time for 1–2 years on present job
Gross income:	$2,850 to $3,250
Savings:	$0 to $100
Total assets:	$300 to 450
Indebtedness:	$200 to $500
as % of gross income:	6.6% to 16%
as % of assets:	67% to 111%

FIG. 1. Shoppers' credit profile.

determined from nearly 2,000 consumer interviews conducted in a earlier study of Watts and East Los Angeles.[6] Stores were then either included in the sample or eliminated from the list depending on the presence or absence of the same brands and models available in the control area. Culver City was selected as the non-poverty shopping area because the composition of its retailing community and price structure typified shopping conditions for suburban Los Angeles area communities.

The attrition rate for stores to be included in the study was rather high because of the difficulty of finding the same brands and models in the disadvantaged areas versus Culver City. Comparative pricing analyses involving poverty areas and more prosperous sections in a city are very difficult because of variations in merchandise. When national brands are carried by a ghetto appliance dealer, he generally stocks only the lower end of the line. Retailers in higher income areas usually concentrate on the middle and upper price ranges of the product line. Furthermore, off-brand merchandise tends to make up a substantial part of the ghetto dealer's stock. Since these lines generally are not carried in other areas, direct price comparisons are impossible. Among the stores frequented by the residents of the two poverty areas, therefore, only six carried brands and models capable of direct price comparisons with stores in the outside community. The stores selected in the outside area were

[6] Frederick D. Sturdivant, "Better Deal for Ghetto Shoppers," *Harvard Business Review*, Vol. 46, No. 2 (March–April, 1968), pp. 130–39.

comparable to the ghetto stores in terms of size and estimated sales volume.[7]

The shopping procedure involved the selection of a 19-inch, black and white, portable TV set by each couple in each of the nine stores. Each couple (the order was determined randomly) selected a predetermined TV set and did everything necessary to obtain price data, except sign the contract. The shopping trips to each store were separated by a minimum of three days to avoid any suspicion by the sales clerks or management. The shopping was conducted during the last two weeks of July and the first week of August, 1967. A final briefing was given the similarly attired couples before they entered each store to make certain they selected the correct model. A typical dialogue in the store might be described as follows:

Salesman: May I help you?
Shoppers: Yes, we would like to see your portable TV's.
Salesman: They are right over here. Did you have anything special in mind? Color?
Shoppers: No, we want a black and white set.
(The shoppers look at several sets and then ask about the preselected set.)
Shoppers: This is a nice set. It is the type we had in mind.
Salesman: It is a very nice set. We could deliver it today.
(Salesmen often attempted to get the shoppers interested in a more expensive model.)
Shoppers: How much does it cost?
Salesman: (quotes the price)
Shoppers: How much would it run us a month?
The salesman figures out the credit terms. The couple specify that they want the smallest down payment and the lowest possible

payments. Upon being told the monthly payment figure, the wife says they should think it over and asks the salesman to write down the credit terms. [Only one store refused this request saying that such information was "confidential and not allowed out of the store."]

In sum, the method included the selection of six of the most frequently used furniture and appliance stores in the two major poverty areas of Los Angeles for comparison with three stores selected on the basis of brand and model availability from an average suburban community. Fundamental to the method was the use of three disadvantaged couples, representing the three major population groups in the area, with basically the same credit characteristics. The three couples dressed in basically the same mode, shopped in the same stores, and priced exactly the same products. Thus, the only relevant variable not held constant was minority group status.

FINDINGS

In the process of testing for discrimination in the marketplace, data were collected which again confirm the presence of higher prices in ghetto stores. Ignoring the question of minority group status for the moment, Table 1 indicates that the average price asked the three couples for a given product was always higher in the disadvantaged area stores than in the control area (Culver City). The total cost of the credit price (shown in parentheses) averaged higher in the poverty areas as well.

While there were notable differences in prices between areas, there was an observable consistency in retail prices within the stores.[8] Among the prices recorded in Table 2, 19 of the 24 retail prices asked for the four models of TV sets were the same, regardless of minority group status. The prices asked the couples in the three Watts area stores were

---

[7] Initially, the reader may be disturbed by the small size of the sample. However, it should be noted that *every* television dealer in the low-income areas that met the comparability criteria for the test was included in the study. The comparability criteria could have been relaxed and thus the sample size increased, but such a step would have made it impossible to test the hypothesis.

---

[8] This consistency in retail prices was not attributable to the presence of price tags. In five of the six ghetto stores and one of the control area stores the customers had to rely on sales personnel for price information.

Table 1. Average Retail and Credit Price for Portable TV Sets, by Area and by Brand

Product	Watts Area	Average Price[1] East L.A. Area	Control Area
Zenith	$170	—	$130
X1910	($194)		($190)
Olympic	$270		$230
9P46	($488)		($277)
RCA	$148	—	$115
AHO668	($174)	—	($154)
Zenith	—	$208	$140
X2014		($251)	($190)

[1] Prices are averages computed from the shopping experiences of the three couples in each of the stores selected. Retail prices refer to the price asked for the product before adding on credit charges. Credit prices, *shown in parentheses,* are the total of retail prices, sales tax, and interest charges.

identical. In the control area, Store No. 1 increased the price by $10 for both the Negro and Mexican-American couples. In this case, the Negro couple shopped the store first and was asked $119 for RCA Model AH0668. Four days later, the Anglo couple was offered the same set for $109. After a wait of another three days, the Mexican-American couple shopped the store and was asked $119 for the set. The other six shopping trips in the control area produced identical prices for all three couples. The Mexican-American area showed the greatest variation in prices. In part, this practice may be attributable to cultural patterns in the Mexican-American community where higgling and haggling is more common. There was no pattern of discrimination. In Store No. 1 the Mexican-American couple was asked the highest price while in Store No. 3 the Mexican-American and Negro couples were charged a slightly higher price than the Anglo couple.

When credit prices are considered, however, it becomes clear that credit and carrying charges are the devices most commonly used to exercise exploitation. In the East Los Angeles stores, for example, the Anglo-White couple was not quoted the highest retail prices, but they were charged the highest credit price in both stores. In all nine cases in the control area there were differences in credit charges even though the retail price differed in only Store No. 1. The most blatant case of discrimination occurred in Culver City Store No. 1. While the legal limit on interest is 10 per cent on a twelve-month installment contract in California, the Mexican and Negro couples were asked to pay

42 and 44 per cent respectively.[9] The Anglo couple was asked the legal rate. In Store No. 3 in Culver City, the two minority group couples were also charged a higher (and illegal) rate of interest. In Store No. 2 all three couples were charged an illegal rate with the Anglo couple being charged the highest amount.

In the predominately Negro area stores, where all three couples had been asked identical retail prices in the three stores, only one store charged the same legal rate of interest on its eighteen-month installment contracts. There were minor variations in the charges assigned by Store No. 2, with the Negro couple charged the highest amount and the Mexican shoppers the lowest. At Store No. 3 the retail price was quoted at $270 before tax. Adding tax at 5 per cent, the total retail price before financing should have been $283.50. Deducting the required minimum down payment of $15.80, the total to be financed was $267.70. At the legal rate of 15 per cent for an eighteen-month contract interest charges would have amounted to

---

[9] The Unruh Retail Installment Sales Act sets the maximum rate a dealer may charge on time contracts in California. A dealer may charge less, of course, but no evidence of this practice was found in the study. For most installment contracts under $1,000 the maximum service charge rate is ⅚ of 1 per cent of the original unpaid balance multiplied by the number of months of the contract. In revolving charge accounts, such as those used by most department stores, the legal limit is 1½ per cent per month on the first $1,000 and 1 per cent per month on the balance over $1,000.

Table 2. Retail[2] and Credit[3] Prices Portable TV Sets by Area, Store, Brand, and Race

Area & Store	Zenith–X1910			Olympic–9P46			RCA–AHO668			Zenith–X2014		
	Negro	M-A	Anglo	Negro	M-A	Anglo	Negro	M-A	Anglo	Negro	M-A	Anglo
East L.A.												
Store 1												
Store 2[1]												
Store 3				$200 ($265)	$240 ($281)	$230 ($284)				$210 ($245)	$210 ($250)	$204 ($258)
Watts												
Store 1	$170 ($194)	$170 ($194)	$170 ($194)									
Store 2							$148 ($178)	$148 ($169)	$148 ($174)			
Store 3				$270 ($412)	$270 ($507)	$270 ($418)						
Culver City												
Store 1							$119 ($172)	$119 ($169)	$109 ($122)			
Store 2										$140 ($183)	$140 ($183)	$140 ($203)
Store 3	$130 ($145)	$130 ($152)	$130 ($140)									

[1] The model preselected for this store was sold before the experiment was completed.
[2] Retail prices refer to the price asked for the product before adding on interest charges.
[3] Credit prices, *shown in parentheses*, are the total of retail prices plus interest.

$40.16 for a total price of $322.66. However, the total price to the Anglo and Negro couples was approximately $420, or an interest rate of nearly 50 per cent. The total cost to the Mexican couple was $506.62 with charges of 82 per cent.[10]

SUMMARY AND CONCLUSIONS

In spite of the difficulties associated with finding identical products in ghetto and non-ghetto stores, this study has attempted to determine the basis of price discrimination experienced by disadvantaged shoppers in the marketplace. The research question was, "Is exploitation in the marketplace a function of low income or minority group status?" By selecting three pairs of disadvantaged shoppers whose only significant difference was their race and ethnicity and having these couples shop in the same stores for identical merchandise, the research design attempted to answer this question.

The findings demonstrated that installment purchases, which especially characterize the purchasing behavior of the disadvantaged, produce major variations in the prices paid by the poor. Although no perfect pattern of discrimination based on minority status emerged from the study, it was common for the couples to be asked higher credit rates when shopping outside their own areas. In east Los Angeles, the white couple received the highest price quotations. In the Watts area, the store charging the highest and most varied prices asked a substantially higher price of the Mexican couple. In two of the

non-ghetto stores the minority shoppers were charged higher, and illegal, amounts.

The findings indicate that merchants find credit charges an excellent vehicle for exercising economic and racial or ethnic discrimination, but Table 2 demonstrates that however substantial and illegal many of these charges may be, they are not as significant as price variations between disadvantaged and prosperous areas. While the minority couples were subjected to discriminatory pricing in two of the three control area stores, in no case would they have paid more than in the ghetto stores for the same merchandise. In most instances the prices were substantially less. It might be concluded that disadvantaged minority shoppers pay more, especially in the ghetto.

The presence of high business costs, parasitic retailers, and the dominance of inefficient "mom-and-pop" firms in the ghetto underline the need of comparative shopping by the disadvantaged. At the same time, the willingness of certain outside retailers to take advantage of the poor, especially members of minority groups, suggests that the disadvantaged are subject to economic exploitation even when shopping beyond the boundaries of the ghetto.

Notwithstanding the difficulties of designing a test of minority groups and economic exploitation (a parallel study of automobile prices had to be abandoned in this project), additional studies should be undertaken. Experiments involving this phenomenon in other major American cities would provide a more complete understanding of these practices. Doubtless, the situation is not unique to Los Angeles, and the extent to which it reflects a national pattern of discrimination against the minorities and the poor shows that it deserves further analysis and correction.

---

[10] This model Olympic TV set wholesales for $104. Thus, with a retail price of $270 the dealer was already profiting from a markup of 160 per cent.

57. *Marketing to Low-Income Neighborhoods: A Systems Approach*

KELVIN A. WALL

Because it is generally agreed that marketing in the low-income segment needs improvement, a review of current levels of performance and isolation of these by functions is useful. This process provides a clearer picture of the interrelationships of marketing functions as they affect low-income consumers.

Any analysis of this marketing problem is complicated by the fact that low-income family buying patterns tend, in general, to be determined by neighborhoods. These neighborhoods are composed of a "sizeable complement of individuals who differ in one way or another from the neighborhood norm. Nonetheless, even these people tend to conform to their own group behavior patterns."[1] Marketers should, however, carefully appraise their tendency to draw conclusions from the characteristics of a single segment or neighborhood.

LOW-INCOME DEFINITIONS TODAY AND TOMORROW

My definition of low-income segment, purely on a dollar basis, has to be arbitrary, because of the differences in spending power at different cost of living levels in various parts of the country. Also, both the aspiration level and the life cycle are variables difficult to pinpoint.

For purposes of this study, this author considers families earning $5,000 or less annually as components of the low-income segment. By this standard, over nineteen million families were low-income in 1960, nearly 41 percent of the total United States population at the time.[2] It is estimated that by 1970 approximately seven million white families and two million black families will still be below the $5,000 income mark, a substantial decrease from the nineteen million families in 1960. The median income by 1970 will be $9,600; however, the Bureau of Labor Statistics estimates a comfortable living cost of $9,200 for urban dwellers. A little less than half the population will fall below this mark, with 11.6 million white and 3.9 million black families below $7,000.

Marketing to low-income neighborhoods demands a consideration of central city population statistics. By 1970, it is estimated that whites will show a decrease of two million, and blacks an increase of 3.3 million, in these areas. Close to 58.9 million people will live in these areas, with blacks representing 20 percent of the total.[3] Much emphasis has been placed on the non-white urban poor in this country; yet, in 1960, 10.7 million white families in urban areas were in this category

---

[1] Alvin Schwartz, "Study Reveals 'Neighborhood' Influence on Consumer Buying Habits," *Progressive Grocer*, April 1966, pp. 269–272.

◆ SOURCE: Reprinted by permission from *University of Washington Business Review*, Autumn 1969, pp. 18–26.

[2] *United States Census*, 1960.

[3] "Changing American," *U.S. News and World Report*, June 2, 1969, p. 69.

as compared wtih 5.5 million blacks.[4] Even in the central cities of these metro-markets, poor whites outnumber blacks by 1.2 million people.[5]

Of all white families earning over $5,000, the percentage of two wage earners per family ranged from a low of 44.3 percent for the $5,000-$7,000 group to a high of 75 percent for the $12,000-$25,000 group. Most of the ten million-plus white families earning under $5,000 have only one wage earner per household.

II. INFLUENCE OF LIFE STYLES ON MARKETING

Fig. 1 presents a schematic representation of a systems approach to marketing for low income groups. A number of socio-economic characteristics and life-style factors encourage such an approach. Briefly, these are as follows:

1. Increased central city low-income population.

2. Low-income groups have experienced a greater increase in income than their cost of living.

3. Their neighborhoods primarily consist of small outlets in which consumers purchase frequently and in small units.

4. Community organization exerts pressure for faster economic and social changes.

5. Life style of consumers is need-oriented, peer-directed, income-limited, mobility-inhibited, and isolated from the rest of the city.

6. Low-income families are heavily concentrated by region and within the city.

7. A unique communications network exists within the community or neighborhood.

Some of the life style patterns of low-income consumers are unique in either degree or kind. These patterns, when interrelated with consumer behavior, can be linked to a number of critical marketing functions, such as distribution, merchandising activities, product mix, packaging mix, advertising programs, sales policies, and dealer relations activities. These various marketing functions tend to interrelate in response to the unique environment of the low-income neighborhood.

"The low-income consumer is a block dweller, who sees himself as part of his immediate environment and neighborhood, rather than a part of the city in general. His peer relationships are close in this limited environment, and as a consumer, he is strongly motivated to shop within these confines."[6] "The poor consumer is less psychologically mobile, less active, and more inhibited in his behavior than well-to-do customers. The stores he considers for possible purchases are always small. The poor people more often buy at the same store."[7] "A comparison of shopping habits of middle class and working class women shows . . . fewer lower class regularly shop in the central business district. The low-income white housewife shops in 'local' stores. The working man's wife or the low-income white wife most frequently prefers to shop in a local and known in store."[8] Because of this narrow territorial view, proudct availability is an important factor in the marketer's distribution system in low-income areas. Add to this the fact that low-income consumers make frequent shopping trips for small package sizes, and you can see the importance of delivery frequency or frequency of sales calls and other sales management policies. Along with product availability, the type of outlet that dominates low-income neighborhoods should also be considered.

III. REACTION TO COMPANY POSTURE

Community relations have only a minor influence on immediate sales in market segments other than the low-income group. However, such secondary issues as employment policies toward minority groups are particularly important to low-income blacks, and strongly influence their purchasing behavior.

"A company which advertises in Negro media, contributes to the United Negro College Fund, and employs Negroes is perceived as being concerned with the welfare of Negroes, and therefore is entitled to special

---

[4] "Forgotten Men: The Poor Whites," U.S. News and World Report, November 27, 1967, p. 76.

[5] "Most U.S. Income Found Inadequate," The New York Times, November 18, 1968, p. 38.

[6] Unpublished report, "The Low Income Study," 1969.

[7] David Caplovitz, The Poor Pay More (New York: The Free Press, 1963), p. 49.

[8] Lee Rainwater, Richard P. Coleman, Gerald Handel, Workingman's Wife (New York: Oceana Publishers, 1959), pp. 163, 164.

concern and patronage." Edward Wallerstein, of The Center For Research and Marketing, went on to state that "Negroes tend to believe that a company which advertises in Negro media will be fairer in terms of its employment practices than most companies . . . further, our respondents said that they would tend to switch to the products of the company which advertised in Negro media."[9] Because blacks look more favorably on companies which advertise in black media and employ blacks, the marketing man is operating in a climate of increasing intensity. As Thomas F. Pettigrew predicted in 1964, "Negro protests will continue to grow both in intensity and depth," and "will increasingly attract larger proportions of low-income Negroes and shift from status to economic goals." He further stated, "a more intensive use of local and national boycotts of consumer products will be made."[10] His statements clearly indicate the interrelationship between sound community relations efforts and employment practices and sound marketing programs as they effect low-income blacks.

Recent organized boycotts have intensified these attitudes. The physical isolation caused by segregation in housing, either by income or race, has compounded marketers' problems. Another factor is the low-income consumer's "lack of mobility, both physical and psychological."[11] Car ownership is low, and parking space is scarce. This means that besides the general tendency of low-income people to stay within their neighborhoods, there are fewer opportunities for them to travel outside this environment. Therefore, marketing performance in low-income areas must be measured by the success—or lack of it—of retailers in these neighborhoods.

IV. MEETING THE ADVERTISING CHALLENGE

The problem of communicating to residents of these neighborhoods offers a challenge to a variety of marketing and marketing-related functions. Advertising strategy, both from a copy platform and media planning stand-point, is as much affected as sales promotion and point-of-sale activities. One reason why the variety of selling activities needs to be tailored to low-income consumers is the uniqueness of their life style patterns, including their language and communications patterns and attitudes toward advertising.

The language of this group is *concrete*. They are "less verbally oriented than better educated groups, and their interpersonal exchanges involve smaller amounts of symbolic linguistic behavior."[12] Their day-to-day conversations are less abstract and have less conceptualization. They deal primarily with concrete objects and situations. The fact that they generalize less and are less reliant on the intellectual process than on observations often renders some sophisticated advertising and sales promotion efforts of major marketers ineffective.

To fully appreciate the burden that advertising communications must carry into low-income neighborhoods, one should remember that advertising must function as a persuasive vehicle that stimulates the desire to consume. The educational function that advertising performs in this regard is important. Many low-income housewives, both white and black, look to advertising to fulfill an educational role. Nearly 12 million United States adults have less than a sixth grade education, with 2.7 milloin never having attended school at all. More than 23 million never completed grade school.[13]

Low-income consumers' preference for certain types of models also affects commercial communications. In the case of white blue-collar wives, "advertising which is people-oriented is much more meaningful than . . . advertising that communicates a highly technical, impersonal or objective atmosphere."[14] A study conducted by Social Research asserts that "the safest route to high rewards from the Negro audience is to be found in advertisements which feature Negroes exclusively."[15] Naturally, this prefer-

[9] "Negro Boycott Could Have Serious Lasting Effect on Sales, Study Shows," *Advertising Age*, September 30, 1963, p. 38.
[10] Thomas F. Pettigrew, *A Profile of the Negro American* (Princeton: D. Van Nostrand Co., 1964), pp. 197–199.
[11] David Caplovitz, *op. cit.*, p. 49.

[12] Lola M. Irelan, ed., *Low Income Life Style* (Washington, D.C.: Department of Health, Education and Welfare, August 1967), p. 72.
[13] "The New Market," *Harvard Business Review*, May–June 1969, p. 61.
[14] Lee Rainwater, Richard P. Coleman, and Gerald Handel, *op. cit.*, p. 153.
[15] *Negro Media Usage and Response to Advertising*, Social Research, Inc., April 1969, Study No. 3621, p. 4.

Sociological-Economic Characteristics	Marketing Implication	Marketing Functions or Functions Affecting Marketing
Increase center city low-income population as middle-class outmigration continues	Low income segment more important to most major consumer goods marketers and in city retailers.	Distribution/physical sales coverage Advertising coverage Product and package mix Package size mix Wholesaler/jobbers
Greater increase in income of low income group than cost of living	This part of the the the total market will exercise more influence because of increased income and rapid populaiton growth. Competition for their dollars will intensify.	New products New outlets Sales coverage Distribution/physical Product, package, package size mix Advertising coverage
Neighborhoods have small outlets Consumers purchase small units	Maximizing sales or profits requires different marketing and sales strategy because of different outlet mix and purchasing patterns.	Distribution/physical sales coverage Dealer promotions Product, package, package size mix Sales promotion Retail store audits
Community organization pressure for social and faster economic changes	Mass urban marketers, both retailers and manufacturers, will either respond to these pressures voluntarily or be forced to respond through direct economic action against them.	Product or service quality Existing outlets New outlets Employment practices Personnel training Advertising content Public relations Sales promotion Joint ventures New distributors

Characteristics	Marketing Implications	Marketing Functions or Functions Affecting Marketing
Life style Need-oriented Peer-oriented Mobile-inhibited Income-limited Isolated from rest of city	Both retailers and other marketers faced with wider differences in consumer motivations and behavioral patterns between low income consumers than with any other combination of income groups.	New products Merchandising policies Outlets—old and new Copy platforms Sales promotion Fashion/styling/colors Music Advertising media Retail store audit Market research Public relations Distribution
Low-income families heavily concentrated by region and within cities • density increase with low-income • low-income whites • low-income blacks (both important factors)	The problems and the needs of low-income people are more similar than unique or distinct among subgroups. The amount of money they have to spend and their relationships with the total community are, in general, their two most important problems.	Sales promotion Point-of-sales Advertising media Copy platform Music Package size Product mix
Communications • neighborhood outlet-part of communications network • conversation topics limited • how as important as what is said • metamorphic and anecdotical • peer group network	Conventional media can and do bring messages into the low-income areas, but these are considered messages from the "outside" and the impact is questionable since their form and language are different from those of the low-income group.	New media New copy Sales promotion Point-of-sales Music Public relations Outlets

FIG. 1. A systems view of marketing in low income neighborhoods.

469

ence should be considered in decisions concerning media, types of advertising, and sales promotions programs.

V. BRIDGING CULTURAL AND CREDIBILITY GAPS

Understanding the behaviour patterns of residents of low-income neighborhoods requires a clear understanding of their attitudes toward the world outside their environment. They often consider it hostile, and think in terms of "we" and "them." "The lack of effective participation and integration of the poor in the major institutions of the large society is one of the critical characteristics of the culture of poverty."[16]

Although it is difficult, a marketer in a low-income area must translate his image from "them" to "we." "Supermarkets operating in disadvantaged areas do not enjoy the confidence of their customers . . . Negroes believe that they are treated as undesirables or untouchables . . . there is a definite credibility gap between what the food chains says they are doing for ghetto residents and what these people think is being done." Both white and black ghetto residents have more complaints about their local food stores—"prices are high, service is bad and unfriendly, stores are dirty, and lighting is inadequate."[17]

Both marketers and retailers are faced with a number of problems. In the case of the marketer, has he made certain that the items that appeal most to low-income consumers— the items that fit best into their life style— are available in the right package sizes? And, are products continuously available for a consumer who has a more frequent shopping pattern than the average?

The preconditioning done by the marketer affects the retailer and the consumer. The retailer who has the right variety of merchandise most appropriate to the needs of the low-income community and most readily accepted by that market, will greatly improve his image. Since the food chain store has a poor image among this group, the responsibility of the marketer is more critical. Consequently such functions as merchandising policies, distribution and sales activities, as well as community relations and public relations functions, are key factors.

VI. BETTER RESEARCH IS SORELY NEEDED

The marketing executive who relies on information derived from his own life experiences is usually handicapped when faced with the problems of marketing to low-income groups, because their life style is quite different from his middle-class one. Nor can he rely on usual sources to help him to narrow his international gap. It is "acknowledged that most market research is now focused on middle and upper income people, but there is increasing awareness of the need to focus more marketing attention on those in low-income groups."[18] A. C. Nielsen and other store audit services usually do not have a large enough sample in this segment to produce reliable data.

These combined factors clearly indicate a need for a systems approach to dealing with the low-income sgement. Example: The systems of small outlets, that is, outlets that have a small physical space limitation, are interlocked with the fact that merchants operating them usually have limited financial resources and management skills. Both their physical and financial limitations usually allow these retailers to purchase only limited quantities at a given time. If the manufacturer's delivery frequency cannot fit these limitations under which retailers operate, product availablity and dealer goodwill become critical problems, accentuated by the low-income consumer's propensity to buy often and in small units. To attack the problem of product availability, it is necessary to deal with several marketing functions, such as frequency of delivery, credit policies, and merchandising and display facilities. Changing a single marketing function probably would not be effective.

VII. SUMMARY

A list of factors which led to the conclusion that there is a need for a systems

[16] Oscar Lewis, "The Culture of Poverty," in *Man Against Poverty: World War III*, Bernstein, Woock, eds. (New York: Random House, 1968), p. 264.

[17] "Poor Still Don't Trust Chains," *Chain Store Age*, February, 1969, p. 63.

[18] "Lavidge Says Market Researchers Must Focus on Minorities," *Advertising Age*, May 26, 1969, p. 45.

Appendix A. Residential Patterns for Whites and Blacks

	Whites		Blacks	
	1960	1970 (est.)	1960	1970 (est.)
Central cities	48,800,000	46,800,000	9,800,000	12,100,000
Suburbs	55,700,000	74,400,000	2,900,000	4,400,000
Small towns and other nonfarm areas	42,500,000	49,400,000	4,600,000	5,100,000
Farms	11,800,000	7,800,000	1,510,000	1,100,000
Total United States	158,810,000	178,400,000	18,900,000	22,800,000

Source: 1960, U.S. Census Bureau: 1970, projections by USN&WR Economic Unit, based on census data.

White Americans increased by 19.6 million, or 12.3% in the 1960s, while Negro Americans increased by 3.9 million, or 20.6%. Central cities lost an estimated 2 million whites and gained about 2.3 million Negroes.

Appendix B. Income Trends for the United States

	White Families		Black Families	
Yearly Income	1960	1970 (est.)	1960	1970 (est.)
Under $3,000	7,800,000	3,000,000	1,900,000	1,000,000
$3,000-$4,999	8,100,000	3,900,000	1,000,000	900,000
$5,000-$6,999	10,000,000	4,600,000	600,000	1,000,000
$7,000-$9,999	8,700,000	11,100,000	300,000	900,000
$10,000-$14,999	4,600,000	13,900,000	200,000	700,000
$15,000 plus	1,600,000	9,700,000	20,000	400,000
	Whites		Blacks	
Persons living in poverty*	27,500,000	13,600,000	10,500,000	6,400,000

Income gains are dramatic for both white and black families. Median income for black families has doubled since 1960, to an estimated $6,500 in 1970. Median income for white families rose 65 percent, to $9,600.

* Single persons or members of families with incomes below officially designated "poverty" levels, set at $3,060 per year in 1960 and $3,358 in 1968 for a non-farm family of four.

Sources: 1960, U.S. Census Bureau; 1970, projections by United States and World Report Economic Unit, based on census estimates through 1968.

approach to improve the effectiveness of marketing programs directed at low-income neighborhoods includes the following:

1. Marketing administrators responsible for share of market in the major urban centers must look at how their total system is working in this part of their sales environment.

2. While consumers in low-income neighborhoods are increasing their income more rapidly than their cost of living, they still have limited education and income. These two factors influence a number of marketing functions differently than for other income groups.

3. Life style differences tend to prevail and marketers are forced to respond with a different marketing mix. Factors such as varying product or packaging mix policies are required.

4. Finally, the concentration of low-income families in certain regions of the United States and within certain parts of cities is likely to continue. Communications problems to this group, because of educational differences, will continue to be a challenge for progressive marketers.

Low income neighborhoods will continue to be a problem to marketers who have not adjusted their total system to this segment's needs.

T. The Signals for Change

58. The Challenge of a Humanistic Value Orientation in Marketing

THADDEUS H. SPRATLEN

The growing interest in "broadening" the concept of marketing[1] seems to be confined largely to extending the application of the "marketing concept" rather than to extending the orientation of the concept of marketing. That is, its operational domain is being extended, not its philosophical domain. Indeed, if the traditionalists have their way, marketing will not be broadened even in the operational sense; certainly not in the philosophical sense. Even operational broadening goes too far by causing marketing to lose its identity and intimacy with profit-motivated distribution or buying and selling goods and services in the marketplace.[2]

This paper examines the value and philosophical dimensions of marketing. It presents an interpretation of the scope and implications of the challenge of a humanistic perspective in marketing. Included in the discussion are requirements for the reorientation and change needed in marketing thought and practice in order to meet the challenge.

VALUE PERSPECTIVES IN MARKETING

Because marketing looms so large in the essence of enterprise (wealth, power, mastery of technology, etc.) special significance is attached to the question of its value perspectives. Fundamentanlly, the issue is how the power of marketing will be used. In humanistic terms there is a need to balance the social power of marketing with its social purposes. Such balance would produce socially beneficial and desirable results from marketing decisions and actions.

As a value framework, a humanistic perspective means the cultivation of social concerns for the general welfare, taking cognizance of the environmental consequences of marketing practices, giving recognition to the ethical dimensions of resource-use decisions, and invoking humane considerations in other choice-making situations. More briefly put, in an economic context humanism suggests that

---

[1] This was expressed in the theme of the 1970 Fall Conference of the American Marketing Association. Earlier in a provocative article Professors Kotler and Levy made such a challenge. See Philip Kotler and Sidney J. Levy, "Broadening the Concept of Marketing," *Journal of Marketing,* vol. 33 (January 1969), pp. 10–15.

In the Kotler-Levy analysis a rationalization is offered for marketing as "customer-satisfaction engineering" (p. 10). Its functions can be and are performed for market as well as traditionally nonmarket (that is, not-for-profit) institutions (political campaigns, public agencies, churches, and the like). Their discussion does not extend to the more fundamental issues of humanity and responsibility. However, toward the end of the article marketing is referred to as "the concept

◆ SOURCE: Reprinted by permission from the author. A paper presented to the American Marketing Association in Boston, Massachusetts, on August 31, 1970.

of sensitively serving and satisfying human needs" (p. 15).

[2] See David J. Luck, "Broadening the Concept of Marketing—Too Far," *Journal of Marketing,* vol. 33 (July 1969), pp. 53–55. In the same issue of the *Journal* Professors Kotler and Levy reply to Professor Luck's criticism.

the most "vital things are those beyond supply and demand and the world or property."[3] Hence, it requires that the spiritual and moral dimensions of behavior be given precedence over other values and considerations. Precedence rather than parity is called for since humanistic concerns parallel the ultimate rather than the proximate ends of marketing. That is, the welfare of people and the good of the society become paramount in a humanistic decision framework of marketing.

Traditionally, however, a pragmatic, materialistic, and microanalytic perspective has prevailed in marketing. That is to say, in marketing decisions and actions precedence is given to the demands or preferences of narrowly circumscribed practical and material interests in life. This perspective has focused primarily on the point of view of the firm. As a result marketing functions tend to be evaluated almost exclusively in the framework of microeconomics. Individual decision-making units (households, firms, etc.), their resources and choices, are of paramount concern. Short-run viewpoints predominate. Private market costs are emphasized to the virtual exclusion of social costs.

The perspective of humanism has not received much favor in the decision framework of business generally. It has received even less recognition in marketing. Idealism and affective concerns of the kind implied in humanism are simply defined to be put out of place in the functions of business and marketing. For them, it is emphasized, pragmatism, marginalism, and other "isms" or sets of techniques more conductive to economic efficiency, sales, and profits are required. Yet associated with these latter concepts are identifiable and significant errors of omission as well as commission with reference to value questions. Indeed many of the misdeeds of business and marketing reflect a value bias that explicitly disregards their humanistic dimensions. Some of the obvious and adverse consequences of the traditional value-set common to business and marketing are illustrated in the following situations:

- Action or inaction associated with lags in developing antismog devices for automobiles; other sources of pollution in business and the production of harmful products;

- Counterpropaganda of the tobacco industry regarding medical findings relating to smoking and health;
- Drug-industry practices regarding testing, branding, and withholding information on the side effects of its products;
- Confusing and misleading descriptions on automobile tires with their accompanying hazards to life and property;
- Unfair advantages which are taken from misinformed and relatively immobile ghetto consumers;
- Placing beyond the boundaries of marketing social costs, externalities, conservation in the use of resources, and other "macro," environmental, and humanistic concerns.

Even when we look at the celebrated marketing concept we see an orientation focused almost exclusively on the issues and tasks traditionally assigned to the discipline. That is, the marketing concept adopts implicitly the value orientation which favors what is preferred by producers and customers in an immediate or short-run context. Its creed is that of customer-want satisfaction for the sake of wants per se and not their goodness, benefit in social or environmental terms, or other humane considerations. Hence, customers and the consumption process are commonly viewed mechanistically rather than humanistically. Although cast in the rhetoric of serving consumer wants and needs, there is ample evidence (for instance, the concerns of "consumerism") to suggest that consumer interests have not truly been met within the orientation of the marketing concept. Consistent with the socialization of consumption which pervades the affluent society, the marketing concept may be seen in cultural terms as culminating in the emergence of what Eric Fromm calls "*Homo consumens*, the total consumer whose only aim is to *have* more and to *use* more."[4]

In positive terms it should be added that the marketing concept has served its limited, instrumental purposes well. It has enhanced the performance of the traditional tasks of marketing: delivering a rising standard of the traditional tasks of marketing: delivering a rising standard of living for the majority of Americans; providing mass-distribution economies to accompany mass production; and otherwise supporting the more widespread consumption of goods and services. Moreover,

[3] Wilhelm Ropke, *A Humane Economy—The Social Framework of the Free Market* (Chicago: Regnery, 1960), p. 5.

[4] Eric Fromm, *The Revolution of Hope—Toward a Humanized Technology* (New York: Bantam, 1968), pp. 39–40.

the marketing concept is entirely consistent with the microanalytic perspectives contributed by classical and neoclassical economics in which, ideally, "the only road to business success is through the narrow gate of better performance in the service of the consumer."[5] Nevertheless, the premises of such a dictum recognize only a narrow range of humanistic elements.[6]

IMPLICATIONS FOR MARKETING THEORY AND PRACTICE

The challenge of a humanistic perspective to current theory and practice in marketing has an origin in the larger context of challenge and confrontation to all established institutions in American society. Other "Establishments"[7] are facing attack as well. All of the hallowed institutions—school, church, marriage, military authority—are feeling the pressure for responsiveness, openness, and humaneness. There is a clamoring for reorientation. Marketing is now being challenged to correct its past errors of omission and commission.[8]

To be sure, marketing has responded well to some recent challenges (behavioralism, quantitative methods, computer applications, and the like). Yet these were easy adjustments to make because they provided producer benefits directly by helping to reduce the cost of error in decision-making and enhancing business efficiency and control. They also reflect the generally greater ease with which business adapts to technical change in contrast to social change. Further, their emphasis has been focused mainly on analyzing what is known or on uncovering new facts, given the existing value orientation. These other challenges could be readily accommodated also because they required essentially sticking to the traditional tasks such as becoming a more skilled technician, increasing product usage and purchase frequency, or otherwise improving the technology available to assist management. Considerably less effort has been devoted to examining those aspects

---

[5] Wilhelm Ropke, op. cit., p. 31. The author goes on to criticize monopolistic, unfair, and anticompetitive trade and industrial practices.

[6] At least in the context of ethical and environmental humanism. A distinction is necessary because of the value position implicit in the framework of classical and neoclassical economics. Its traditional (eighteenth- and nineteenth-century) liberalism may technically be defined as a form of humanism by virtue of its emphasis on self-interest, oriented, private market choices in matters of property and individual freedom. It has been called "rational humanism" by W. T. Tucker and others. However, in its more fundamental and broader meaning humanism embodies a value position which recognizes the many sides of man's nature and would subordinate such individual-oriented behavior as egotism, selfishness, self-indulgence, and so on, to group-oriented behavior traits such as concern for social justice, the welfare of others, and willingness to serve the long-run best interests of society. The latter point should be made with reference to the distinction between present and aspiring groups of consumers and property owners and the rest of the members of the economy and society. While possession seeking and wealth getting can be recognized in humanism as useful activities, they are nevertheless only means to broader human goals. They are not ends in themselves.

[7] Although the "Establishment" is loosely referred to in popular writing and social criticism, its most general meaning seems to embrace the institutions and forces in society which shape and are identified with the mainstream or conforming ideology and patterns of behavior in a given area of activity. These forces tend to perpetuate conformity for the sake of conformity (or for the sake of the status quo and power) in an attempt to maintain dominant influence in an area of activity. Hence the connotation is usually pejorative.

In the context of this discussion it should be noted that conformity for the sake of conformity in marketing or other areas of business activity has the same results as in other areas of society; it "inhibits both intellectual development and the sensitive social sense which tells the person of impending changes in the cultural pattern." (Morse Peckham, *Humanistic Education for Business Executives* [Philadelphia: University of Pennsylvania Press, 1960], p. 24.)

[8] The marketing concept has also been challenged in much the same vein by another analyst. See Leslie M. Dawson, "The Human Concept: New Philosophy for Business," *Business Horizons*, vol. 12 (December 1969), pp. 29–38.

Three shortcomings of the marketing concept were enumerated: (1) over-emphasis on the consumer to the neglect of the larger nonconsumer group or society; (2) almost exclusive stress on technological change and product improvement, irrespective of the product's overall social impact; and (3) priority of selfish, ownership interests to the neglect of social concerns. Professor Dawson's "Human Concept" would counterbalance all these and subordinate the "Marketing Concept" to the larger purposes embodies in a humanistic value orientation.

of the structure and uses of knowledge in the discipline which are not technical and vocational in nature and application. As a result the boundaries of traditional marketing theory and practice are too narrowly circumscribed to accommodate the broader dimensions and perspectives of a humanistic perspective.

If the challenge of a humanistic perspective is to be met, markedly different concerns and criteria must be formulated. The challenge calls for new kinds and qualities of responses from marketing people. Illustrative of the broader framework for marketing decisions and action are the ideas summarized in Exhibit 1. In models and other constructs yet to be developed such ideas will have to be accommodated or, better, assimilated in marketing theory and practice.

Attention is focused on the vital and human aspect of marketing decisions. Studiously avoided are the mechanistic and manipulative emphasis of the traditional perspective. An attempt is made to summarize the manner in which marketing fits into a social and environmental framework of decisions and transactions. It is also suggested that marketing people unavoidably have far-reaching obligations in society. The assimilation of such ideas and relationships will infuse marketing theory and practice with greater humaneness (passionate concern for life-enriching qualities), responsibility (acceptance of obligations imposed by the consequences of marketing decisions), and rationality (openness to examination, experimentation, and change in order to gain new insights in marketing thought and action). They highlight the substantive but subjective implications of marketing activity.

Additional comments on the humanistic dimensions and elements in marketing have been added at the end of Exhibit 1.

A BROADENED FRAMEWORK FOR MARKETING DECISIONS

In a humanistic perspective the decision framework of marketing explicitly incorporates the subjective assessment of relationships and other criteria of a social and environmental nature. Indeed, the decision-making process itself is viewed as one in which judgment, perception, and a number of intangible aspects of choice-making are emphasized. A substantial departure is made from the expectation of formalism and technical

elegance as in conventional analysis. Thus, humanistic decisions are overwhelmingly focused on what Marcus Alexis and Charles Z. Wilson identify as an element in all decisions: they are based on "subjective estimates of factual situations."[9]

The factors enumerated earlier in Exhibit 1 suggest the general parameters of a humanistic perspective in marketing. Each factor represents one part of a total network in marketing concepts and relationships.

When viewed on a two-dimensional scale the interrelations could be represented as a set of values corresponding to a balancing of traditional and humanistic considerations. These could take the form of a table of specified dimensions based on the number of elements to be explicitly considered in a decision situation. This or some similar scheme is needed for the analysis of marketing decisions in a broader perspective. However structured, the framework will have to provide a basis for each of the following aspects of the process of making decisions:

1. Predicting outcomes.
2. Prescribing alternatives.
3. Describing relationships.
4. Stating the relative importance of variables.
5. Explaining the analytical content of choices.

The quantities indicated on the scales in the suggested format could be used to show the relative importance of variables in a problem. They could also be weights for making further calculations of dollar amounts as in a probability model or a cost-benefit analyses for selecting alternative courses of action. Other techniques, such as planning-programming and budgeting or cost effectiveness, capital budgeting or the analysis of social utility, should also be noted as sources of insight and guidelines. Of course, still more sophisticated scaling or mapping techniques and the use of vectors could be employed in refining the basic approach and in defining the boundaries of such a broadened framework for making decisions in marketing.

It is most important to recognize that the addition of a humanistic scale requires an alteration in the traditional emphasis on max-

---

[9] Marcus Alexis and Charles Z. Wilson, *Organizational Decision-Making* (Englewood Cliffs, N.J.: Prentice-Hall, 1967), p. 69.

Conceptual Dimensions	Evaluative Dimensions
PERSONALISTIC—Aspects of inner richness in life; individual aspirations and values.	Dignity; respect for individuality-privacy; solitude; interpersonal relationships; creativity potential; and self-realization.
ARTISTIC—Appreciation and recognition of emotional responses and feelings resulting from marketing images and messages.	Empathy; compassion; the affective content of marketing activity; other feelings developed from various art forms.
AESTHETIC—Concern for form, beauty, and charm.	Degree of enobling and spiritual qualities in sense impressions; heightened awareness from the grace of lines and shapes.
PHILOSOPHICAL—Attention to the ways in which knowledge is organized; evaluation of feelings and ideas.	Intellectual, reflective content; answering what activities are good for.
ETHICAL—Recognition of the methods and models for determining the right and wrong, or desirable and undesirable in marketing.	Integrity; honesty, disclosure; responsibility; absence of dehumanization, brutalization, and suffering through marketing decisions; fairness; sincerity.
SOCIAL—Consideration of a societal perspective in which the criteria of social benefit and long-run sustainable behavior are used as standards.	Societal interests; social efficiency; assistance offered to consumers to enhance their independence in choice-making situations; valuation, harmony, cooperation.
CULTURAL—Appreciation of the norms and institutions which shape individual and group behavior.	Standards of performance and levels of aspirations and achievements; innovation; progress; change.
ENVIRONMENTAL—Ecological perspective which strives for balance in the relations between the marketing organization and its environment.	Quality effects; ecological balance; neighborhood effects and externalities; resource conservation.
HISTORICAL—Appreciation of antecedent conditions and relationships; perspectives of time and change processes.	Dynamics of change; sense of mission and direction; aspects of legacy and consequences related to past and future decisions.

EXHIBIT 1. Humanistic dimensions and elements in marketing.

Comments

A brief overview of the traditional and humanistic perspectives of marketing should be helpful in further clarifying the implications for marketing theory and practice.

It should be noted that the traditional and the humanistic are only different ways of perceiving and organizing knowledge. In the traditional perspective efforts are devoted to rising about the personal (intuitive, subjective and so on) and reaching for the technical and measurable. The humanistic perspective calls for rising above the immediate technical situation and reaching for the personal, social, and ethical in thought and action. Both perspectives require that the individual get outside the web of his conventional apparatus and escape from his conventional wisdom. The challenge is to become detached, analytical, and probing in order to discover new knowledge and understanding.

More specifically with reference to methodology, assimilation of the humanistic calls for a trade-off between the certainty of techniques, precision of quantification, and narrowness of focus in the traditional perspective; and subjective variables along with a breadth of focus in the humanistic perspective. Unavoidably, some technical elegance will be sacrificed for greater social and environmental relevance. This composite of the scientific and humanistic will make marketing theory and practice vastly more diverse and complex than they are at present. Yet the potential benefits to be derived warrant the effort and energy required to meet the challenge of a humanistic perspective in marketing.

imazation criteria. Instead, the more imprecise formats of satisfying and suboptimization will come to be relied upon as decision criteria. Robert Bartels has called attention to this relationship with particular reference to the ethical dimension in marketing. He has suggested that complexity and diversity of the required decision framework greatly reduce the usefulness of approaches based on the premise that there is a simple, single course of action to follow in reaching a decision.[10]

CONSEQUENCES AND BENEFITS IN MARKETING BEHAVIOR AND PERFORMANCE

The ultimate test of what marketing is and does can be best expressed in the consequences of marketing decisions and actions. Traditionally, the concern for consequences has been essentially economic: profit, sales, market shares, size and frequency of purchase, and the like. The humanistic challenge posits that social consequences should be paramount—quality of life, environmental effects, long-run benefits, and other criteria which suggest fundamentally human concerns.

If the question is raised as to why the humanistic is more desirable as a value orientation, an answer can be found in such ulti-

mate measures of consequences as societal benefit, human welfare and long-run, sustainable outcomes. It can be argued convincingly that they hold a higher place in the perspective of the human community, in contrast to the smaller community of consumers or customers. The traditional considerations must then be relegated to their true position in the scheme of things as instrumental goals and operations that serve basic social or human needs. When this is done conventional rationality will be sufficiently constrained or bounded to ensure that ultimate ends or purposes are given due priority. Further, a humanistic perspective would ensure the widespread practice of incorporating the concerns of social responsibility in marketing decisions. As one further benefit, meeting the challenge of a humanistic perspective offers the prospect of humanizing technology —of subordinating marketing processes in the technological society to the broader social and humane requirements of the society as a whole.

VALUE AND BEHAVIOR CHANGE IN MARKETING

If we see marketing as but one part of a complex business sociotechnical system, then a starting point for meeting the challenge of value and behavior change can be an understanding of the ways in which marketing men function in decision-making circumstances in which they are placed. The forces which influence their action must be recognized—economic, psychological, political, etc. Further, the criteria which they use in deciding upon alternative courses of action need to be made consistent with the humanistic and social value-set; that is, with the values which are more desirable or in some rational, responsible, and humane sense, "best." Feasibility, resource availability, costs, benefits, and other performance constraints would still be incorporated in the decision framework. However, the burden of providing proposals and proof would shift to the marketing decision-maker to show that in a reordered set of priorities in which the economic and technological become instrumental to the humanistic, the cost of the shift must not be borne by third (innocent or distant) parties such as the government, the community, or the general public.

It is abundantly clear that exhortation is

---

[10] Robert Bartels, "A Model for Ethics in Marketing," *Journal of Marketing*, vol. 3 (January 1967), pp. 20–26.

Other references which suggest the key relationships and context of a broadened decision framework include the following:

C. West Churchman, *Prediction and Optimal Decision—Philosophical Issues of a Science of Values* (Englewood Cliffs, N.J.: Prentice-Hall, 1961).

Paul Diesing, *Reason in Society—Five Types of Decisions and Their Social Conditions* (Urbana: University of Illinois Press, 1962).

Alvar O. Elbing, Jr., "A Model for Viewing Decision-Making in Interaction Situations from an Historical Perspective," *University of Washington Business Review*, vol. 12 (June 1961), pp. 38–49.

William D. Guth and Renato Tagiuri, "Personal Values and Corporate Strategy," *Harvard Business Review*, vol. 43 (September–October 1965), pp. 123–132.

Samuel Messick and Arthur H. Brayfield, eds., *Decision and Choice—Contributions of Sidney Siegel* (New York: McGraw-Hill, 1964).

inadequate to the task. Criticism appeals to conscience, and moral suasion can only play a small part. Economic and political leverage, pressure, power, or incentives are required. Inhibitors of social myopia and inducers of humanistic values must be designed and implemented as instruments of social control. A price has to be imposed for social myopia; incentives offered for the social benefits contributed.

If a price is imposed for short-sighted behavior and social misdeeds, the situation stands in greater likelihood of being corrected. This means shifting social costs back to the source in the form of special taxes. Workable schemes for this need to be formulated and presented to those who can bring about change. Within a humanistic value orientation such a task becomes part of the social responsibility of the scholar or other knowledgeable expert in marketing.

More effective consumer organization is part of the answer to the need for value and behavior change in marketing. Consumer counsel (technical and legal) is one much-needed service. If sustained, other aspects of "consumerism" and the consumer movement could have a decisive impact in bettering the plight of the consumer, and in serving the general welfare as well.

Of course positive efforts need to be encouraged by all levels of government, and misdeeds more strongly penalized. An ombudsman for the public interest has some merit in this connection. Experts in academic institutions come into consideration again for the design of schemes for tax reform and other schemes that would reduce social imbalance and misallocation of resources caused by present practices in marketing. Voluntarism on the part of management is also needed. However, primary reliance for effecting value and behavior change will have to be incentives and penalties as inducements to correct the ills of present practices in marketing.

CONCLUSIONS

The challenge of a humanistic perspective in marketing calls for broadening its basic structure and content, and extending the boundaries of its framework for decision-making. It requires that the social power of marketing be directed more towards accomplishing socially desirable purposes, and that traditional functions be subordinated in their role as instrumental and supportive goals. With reference to feasibility, responding to the challenge means that marketing would maintain an economic position sufficient to ensure a capability of responding to the requirements of contributing toward greater social well-being. Yet at the same time, through reorientation, marketing would build its capacity to assimilate humanistic values. In doing so, it would focus marketing on serving higher-order social goals of human activity. Such responses to the challenge would strengthen the discipline and thereby move marketing people closer to realizing the often-repeated aim of becoming professionals in the humanistic as well as scientific meaning of the term.

59. Marketing the Post Office

E. PATRICK McGUIRE

A little known—and apparently seldom enforced—Federal statute requires that all government agencies establish fees or charges in such a manner that their services will be "self-sustaining to the fullest extent possible."[1] If the Justice Department chose to enforce this statute it would find one of its closest neighbors on Pennsylvania Avenue—the U.S. Post Office Department—to be the biggest transgressor.

Postal deficits now cost taxpayers more than $1,000 a minute, and the total U.S. postal deficit is 3½ times greater than the combined postal deficits of all the free nations of the world. Despite the imposition of higher rates, postal deficits seem to be increasing. In fact, the temporary rate increase which became effective May 16 will only pay for those wage increments won by postal unions during their most recent negotiations. And, there is a good chance that upcoming labor negotiations will further add to the cost burden.

Faced with difficulties of this magnitude, postal officials have had to dip deep into the well of innovation in order to find solutions offering any hope at all of licking the postal deficit. Postmaster General Winton M. Blount and his staff have come up with several which they hope will put the system in the black. Public Law 91-375, an act to "improve and modernize the Postal Service," is the first step in this direction.

This statute, known as the Postal Reorganization Act, creates an independent establishment of the Federal Government. The Service is now headed by a nine-man board of directors who have appointed a Postmaster General with broad management powers. The Postmaster General will institute those organizational changes required to turn the Postal Service around and make it an efficient, service-conscious operation.

Postmaster General Blount has begun to introduce a number of systems changes aimed at transforming the image of the Service from that of a governmental bureaucracy to that of an effectively run business enterprise. He has recruited engineering and management talent from both the private and public sectors. One immediate result has been the creation of a professionally staffed department of planning and marketing under the direction of Assistant Postmaster General Ronald B. Lee.

SELLING POSTAL "PRODUCTS"

Postal executives are convinced that they have products—dozens of them—which can be marketed to industrial and consumer markets in much the same manner that other institutional goods and services are marketed. Following this line of reasoning, they have organized a marketing department which includes separate divisions for marketing opera-

---

[1] Public Law 137 (5 U.S.C. 140).

◆ SOURCE: Reprinted by permission from *The Conference Board Record*, Vol. VIII, No. 6, June 1971, pp. 12–15.

tions, sales, customer service and performance evaluation.

Thomas J. Donohue, Mr. Lee's Deputy Assistant Postmaster General, has been placed in charge of the Service's marketing effort. Mr. Donohue has recruited a team of specialists in such fields as marketing research, customer service and performance evaluation. For the past six months this group has been conducting marketing surveys, drafting plans, and preparing for the full-scale launching of a product and service improvement program.

Organizing a marketing department within a 200-year old institution is not accomplished without some snags and snarls. Donohue acknowledges that "there are those steps you know should be taken, and those you know can be taken, and sometimes we have to compromise." In his view, the Service is now at a critical "window in time" and unless it takes advantage of its restructuring opportunities—at the point of official reorganization —it may well lose them forever.

Nonetheless, the marketing chief and his staff are optimistic, feeling that their department can contribute substantially towards erasing postal deficits. In their eyes, the projected "revenue increase" will take place in three principal ways: through mutual cost reductions accomplished with the cooperation of major mailers, through the modification of existing products and development of new products, and through a more vigorous promotion of the existing postal services.

CUSTOMER ORIENTATION

One of the first moves taken by postal management was to revise the lexicon used to describe mail users. Mailers—whether individual consumers or major publishers—had previously been described as *patrons*. During the past several months this designation has been changed so that all mail users are now *customers*. "Customer *relations* representatives" have had their job title changed to "customer *service* representatives."

Postal management has also moved towards the adoption of the modern marketing concept. There is increasing attention paid to what the customer wants, rather than to what an agency would like to provide. An early step was to measure customer perceptions of mail service. A series of market research studies is now underway to measure customer wants and needs as far as postal products and services are concerned. The New York area has been the site of one of these consumer attitude surveys.

The product management concept has also been instituted within the postal marketing unit. Under Marketing Operations Director Russell Fitch, product managers will coordinate the marketing effort in support of new and existing postal products.[2] Product managers already have been assigned to the various product categories and each is developing a marketing strategy for his particular product group. In some cases, the strategy may consist simply of gaining the customer's cooperation; in others, it will involve the development and promotion of entirely new product lines.

The postal product managers have set out to find out who their customers actually are. They have directed their study towards six principal categories: financial transactions, private correspondence, advertising, parcels, publications, and postal retail products. Using internal cost data, product management has come up with some interesting insights into the relative sales contributions of each of these elements (Exhibit 1), and the frequency of customer usage (Exhibit 2).

In the process, they may have demolished some favored shibboleths. For example, that familiar villain of postal rate hearings—third class "junk mail"—turns out to be one of the good guys. One marketing manager noted that advertising mail "is one of our bread and butter items." He explained how indispensable the pre-sorting done by third-class mailers is to overall postal operations. For these reasons, the Postal Service will stay in the third-class mail business, indicating no intention of abdicating its position to private competitors.

In fact, recent evidence suggests that direct mail marketers and postal officials alike are concerned about the increased use of advertising inserts in newspapers and periodicals, feeling that this practice cuts into their respective business. Thus, the Postal Service recognizes itself, in part at least, as an advertising medium in competition with all other traditional forms of media, and is prepared to maintain service to this portion of the market.

---

[2] Postal marketing executives characterize each of the post office services—*e.g.*, different classes of mail—as "products."

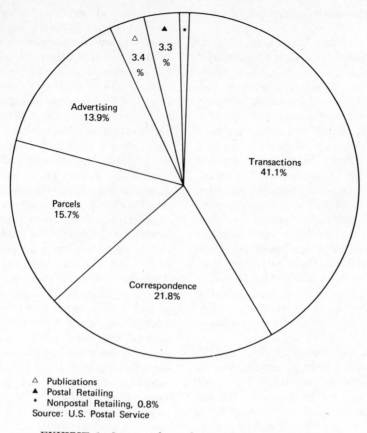

△ Publications
▲ Postal Retailing
* Nonpostal Retailing, 0.8%
Source: U.S. Postal Service

EXHIBIT 1. Sources of postal revenue, by class of mail.

DISTRIBUTION OF NEW PRODUCTS

Postal authorities are well aware that they have one of the biggest and best distribution systems in the world. Literally thousands of retail outlets are already in existence, with the capabilities for distributing products other than those normally associated with postal operations. Postal carriers visit American homes and businesses every day, and new product specialists are looking into the possibility of offering additional services, such as specialty wrapping, passport applications, and facsimile mail facilities.

Also under consideration is the establishment of government book stores in post offices which would sell such items as government publications, National Gallery reprints, and other public documents. Officials are reported to be taking a close look at the vast trucking fleet which the Postal Service owns, and are considering the use of postal truck bodies for display use. If this project gets going, probably the first client would be the Post Office's own marketing department. It is also possible, although postal officials do not admit to this, that some commercial products could be "piggybacked" on Postal Service vehicles, thus putting the Service in the commercial carrier business.

The pros and cons of competing with private industry turns up in many of the discussions of new postal products and services. The U.S. Postal Service would be a formidable competitor for any company—possessing as it does an established workforce of 750,000 personnel and unmatched distribution facilities. However, Mr. Fitch, the Marketing Operations Director, points out that—since the Service is basically in the communications business—it is already in competition with numerous private enterprises such as those selling telephone, telegram, air freight and other services.

IMPROVING CUSTOMER SERVICE

The Service now has in the field a force of about 570 customer service representatives located in 270 of the largest post offices in

Categories of Products and Services	Customers								
	Individuals	Direct mail advertisers	Mail–order firms	Publishers	Other large business	Other small business	Federal government	State and local govt.	Nonprofit organization
Financial transactions	1	3	2	2	3	2	3	3	2
Private correspondence	3	1	1	1	3	2	3	3	3
Advertising		3	1	3	1	1	1	1	1
Parcels	1		3		1	2			
Publications				3	1	1	3	2	2
Postal retail products	3					1			
Nonpostal retail products	3								
Business services			1		2	1	3	3	1

Source: U.S. Postal Service.

EXHIBIT 2. Frequency of mail usage, by customer class.

the United States. Major cities have the greatest concentration of representatives, with 38 of them, for example, stationed in New York and 33 in Chicago. Smaller post offices may have one or two at the most.

In the larger postal centers, the customer service representatives are assigned to territories on a geographic basis. Under the direction and control of the local postmaster, their primary mission is to contact major mail customers and elicit their cooperation in programs designed to produce savings for both the Postal Service and the mailer.

Typical of such programs is one establishing special pre-sort schedules by which major customers go beyond the required presorting regulations and sort their mail further, so that it can by-pass some of the internal processing within the postal system. (The average piece of mail is handled six separate times before delivery.) Adoption of such programs has provided substantial benefits for some major customers. For example, the Kiplinger Letter organization can keep its presses running till late Friday night, and still receive Monday morning mail delivery, by using an extensive pre-sorting program which shortcuts normal postal handling.

In other cases, customer service representatives are seeking to convince mail users to load their bulk mail directly into postal vehicles, rather than first taking them to an individual post office. Since some post offices have limited loading dock facilities, unloading delays are common. The representatives are also selling the idea of early mailing so that a firm's mail may be dispatched from the local office the day it is received.

Charles Duttweiler, the Director of Customer Service, admits that not all postmasters are employing customer service representatives to the best advantage. Some are apparently assigning them to public relations and other tasks having little direct connection with improving customer service. Postal management has recently introduced a computerized sales call report to monitor the number and variety of customer service calls being completed by field service representatives. Postal management indicates that it will continue to press local postmasters to assure that customer service representatives are in fact engaged in essential service activities.

In the meantime, postal executives are trying to upgrade the selling and service skills of their existing force. Most of its members have already completed a 40-hour, self-study course prepared by university manpower training experts utilizing program text materials. The course places special emphasis on selling and customer relations techniques.

Another phase of the customer relations program makes use of postal customer councils. There are 635 of these councils in the United States with a total membership of more than 57,000 mail management executives from industry and commerce. The councils range in size from small groups of 25, to large city organizations with memberships in excess of 1800. These councils meet on a regular basis to exchange mail management experiences and to work out cooperative programs with the Postal Service. The latter also provides speakers for these council meetings and runs seminars to train company mailroom personnel in mail handling procedures.

Changing the Postal Service's image may prove easier on the industrial side of the market than on the consumer side. Consumer perceptions change slowly and as one post office marketer admits, "We have a significant problem at the customer interface." Most offices still lack any regular mechanism for handling customer complaints. Postal clerks have been undergoing retraining programs designed to improve their ability to respond to customer gripes and questions, but one Service executive notes that, in most cases, clerks "simply don't know the answers." As a result, customers are sometimes shunted from one clerk to another. Some outsiders have suggested that the Service may have to appoint local ombudsmen to help in easing the frictions that arise from customer complaints.

A CHANGE IN GOALS

More than anything else, increased attention to a customer orientation will require a substantial rethinking of the attitudes of many of the Service's existing 750,000 employees. This is expected to take some time. For example, some outdated services, operations, and people will gradually be phased out.

Local postmasters have previously been compensated on the basis of the number of employees, trucks, routes, and the like in their jurisdictions. Some may be reluctant to accept cost-cutting measures which have the ultimate effect of reducing the size of their domains, But the Postal Reorganization Act allows for the establishment of new methods of compensating local postmasters, thus providing the opportunity for a management incentive system based on realistic operational standards.

The Postal Reorganization Act had some fervent opponents as well as supporters. Both will be watching closely as postal executives set about to accomplish what must surely be one of the largest management overhaul jobs in the nation's history. The Act has given the Postal Service most of the management authority and responsibility it will require to succeed. It's their ball now, and 206 million spectators will be looking on to see how the new game is played.

60. Is Advertising Wasteful?

JULES BACKMAN

With some exceptions, economists generally have criticized advertising as economically wasteful. All the criticisms are not so extreme as one widely used economics text which states:

Overall, it is difficult for anyone to gain more than temporarily from large advertising outlays in an economy in which counteradvertising is general. The overall effect of advertising, on which we spent $14 billion [actually $15 billion—JB] in 1965, is to devote these productive resources (men, ink, billboards, and so forth) to producing advertising rather than to producing other goods and services.[1]

Most critics do not go this far in condemning advertising. However, they do emphasize that advertising may be wasteful in several ways: by adding unnecessarily to costs, by an inefficient use of resources, by promoting excessive competition, and by causing consumers to buy items they do not need. This article brings together the scattered criticisms of advertising and answers to them and thus presents an overview of the debate in this area. The nature of these criticisms and the

significance of waste in a competitive economy are first reviewed. Attention is then given to the vital informational role played by advertising, particularly in an expanding economy. Advertising is only one alternative in the marketing mix, and—hence its contribution must be considered among alternatives rather than in absolute terms.

VARIATIONS ON A THEME

The criticism that advertising involves economic waste takes several forms.

Competition in Advertising

The attack usually is centered on competition in advertising which some critics state flatly is wasteful.[2] Others have been concerned about the relative cost of advertising as a percentage of sales. Sometimes an arbitrary percentgae, such as 5%, is selected as the dividing line between "high" and more "reasonable" levels of expenditure.[3]

Such cutoff points are meaningless, since the proper relative expenditures for advertising are a function of the product's characteristics. It is not an accident that relative

---

[1] George Leland Bach, *Economics*, Fifth Edition (Englewood Cliffs, New Jersey: Prentice-Hall, Inc., 1966), p. 437. See also Kenneth Boulding, "Economic Analysis," Volume 1, *Microeconomics*, Fourth Edition, Vol. 1 (New York: Harper and Row, 1966), p. 513.

◆ SOURCE: Reprinted by permission from *Journal of Marketing* (National Quarterly Publication of the American Marketing Association), Vol. 32, No. 1, January 1968, pp. 2–8.

[2] Nicholas H. Kaldor, "The Economic Aspects of Advertising," *The Review of Economic Studies*, Vol. 18 (1950–51), p. 6.
[3] Joe S. Bain, *Industrial Organization* (New York: John Wiley & Sons, 1959), pp. 390–91. See also *Report of a Commission of Enquiry Into Advertising* (London, England: The Labour Party, 1966), p. 42. The Reith Report defined "substantially advertised products" at 5% or more.

advertising costs are highest for low-priced items which are available from many retail outlets and subject to frequent repeat purchases (for example, cosmetics, soaps, soft drinks, gum and candies, drugs, cigarettes, beer, etc.).

Particularly criticized are emotional appeals, persuasion, and "tug of war" advertising where it is claimed the main effect is to shift sales among firms rather than to increase total volume of the industry. For example, Richard Caves states: "At the point where advertising departs from its function of informing and seeks to persuade or deceive us, it tends to become a waste of resources."[4]

In a competitive economy competitors must seek to persuade customers to buy their wares. We do not live in a world where a company stocks its warehouse and waits until customers beat a path to its doors to buy its products. If this is all that a business firm did, we would have economic waste in terms of products produced but not bought as well as in the failure to produce many items for which a market can be created. In the latter case, the waste would take the form of the idle labor and unused resources.

Inefficient Use of Resources

Economists have criticized advertising most vigorously as involving an inefficient use of resources. This criticism has been directed particularly against advertising where the main effect allegedly is a "shuffling of existing total demand" among the companies in an industry. Under these conditions, it is stated, advertising merely adds to total costs and in time results in higher prices. There undoubtedly is a shifting of demand among firms due to many factors including advertising. But this is what we should expect in a competitive economy. Moreover, there are many products for which total demand is increased (for example, television sets, radio sets, cars, toilet articles) for multiple use in the same home. In the sharply expanding economy of the past quarter of a century there are relatively few industries in which total demand has remained unchanged.

It must also be kept in mind that the resources devoted to competitive advertising usually are considered to be wasteful "in a full-employment economy" because they may be utilized more efficiently in other ways. Thus, the extent of "waste" involved also appears to depend upon whether the economy is operating below capacity. This point is considered in a later section.

Adds to Costs

Sometimes, it is stated that if advertising succeeds in expanding total demand for a product, the result is a shift of demand from other products, the producers of which will be forced to advertise to attempt to recover their position. The net result of such "counter-advertising" is to add to costs and to prices.

But all increases in demand do not necessarily represent a diversion from other products. Thus, an expanded demand for new products is accompanied by an increase in income and in purchasing power flowing from their production. Moreover, during a period of expanding economic activity, as is noted later, the successful advertising may affect the rate of increase for different products rather than result in an absolute diversion of volume.

Creates Undesirable Wants

Another variation is the claim that advertising is wasteful because it ". . . creates useless or undesirable wants at the expense of things for which there is greater social need. When advertising makes consumers want and buy automobiles with tail fins, tobacco, and movie star swimming pools, there is less money (fewer resources) available to improve public hospitals, build better schools, or combat juvenile delinquency."[5] It is claimed that many of these types of products are useless and antisocial. Criticism of advertising is nothing new. In the late 1920's Stuart Chase claimed: "Advertising creates no new dollars. In fact, by removing workers from productive employment, it tends to depress output, and thus lessen the number of real dollars."[6]

---

[4] Richard Caves, *American Industry: Structure, Conduct, Performance* (Englewood Cliffs, New Jersey: Prentice-Hall, Inc., 1964), p. 102.

[5] "Advertising and Charlie Brown," *Business Review*, Federal Reserve Bank of Philadelphia (June, 1962), p. 10.

[6] Stuart Chase, *The Tragedy of Waste* (New York: Macmillan Company, 1928), p. 112.

These are value judgments reached by the critics on the basis of subjective "standards" which they set up. "What is one man's meat is another man's poison," as the old saying goes. The real question is who is to decide what is good for the consumer and what should he purchase?

In a free economy, there is a wide diversity of opinion as to what combinations of goods and services should be made available and be consumed. Obviously, tastes vary widely and most persons do not want to be told what is best for them. In any cross section of the population of the country there will be a wide disagreement as to what constitutes the ideal components of a desirable level of living. Each one of us must decide what purchases will yield the greatest satisfactions. We may be misled on occasion by popular fads, advertising or even advice of our friends. But these decisions in the final analysis are made by the buyers and not by the advertisers, as the latter have found out so often to their regret.

COMPETITION AND "WASTE"

The critics of advertising are really attacking the competitive process. Competition involves considerable duplication and "waste." The illustrations range from the several gasoline stations at an important intersection to the multiplication of research facilities, the excess industrial capacity which develops during periods of expansion and the accumulations of excessive inventories.

There is widespread recognition that inefficiencies may develop in advertising as in other phases of business.[7] Mistakes are made in determining how much should be spent for advertising—but these mistakes can result in spending too little as well as too much. We cannot judge the efficiency of our competitive society—including the various instrumentalities, such as advertising—by looking at the negative aspects alone. It is true that competition involves waste. But it also yields a flood of new products, improved

[7] Committee on Advertising, *Principles of Advertising* (New York: Pitman Publishing Corp., 1963), p. 34; and Neil H. Borden, "The Role of Advertising in the Various Stages of Corporate and Economic Growth," Peter D. Bennett, editor, *Marketing and Economic Development* (Chicago, Illinois: American Marketing Association, 1965), p. 493.

quality, better service, and pressures on prices. In the United States, it has facilitated enormous economic growth with the accompanying high standards of living. The advantages of competition have been so overwhelmingly greater than the wastes inherent in it that we have established as one of our prime national goals, through the antitrust laws, the continuance of a viable competitive economy.

Informational Role of Advertising

Advertising plays a major informational role in our economy because (1) products are available in such wide varieties, (2) new products are offered in such great numbers, and (3) existing products must be called to the attention of new consumers who are added to the market as a result of expansion in incomes, the population explosion, and changes in tastes.

The most heavily advertised products are widely used items that are consumed by major segments of the population. This does not mean that everyone buys every product or buys them to the extent that he can. Some of these products are substitutes for other products. For example, it will be readily recognized that cereals provide only one of many alternatives among breakfast foods. In some instances, heavily advertised products compete with each other like, for example, soft drinks and beer. In other instances, additional consumers can use the products so that the size of the total market can be increased (for example, toilet preparations).

Potential markets also expand as incomes rise and as consumers are able to purchase products they previously could not afford. As the population increases, large numbers of new potential customers are added each year. Continuous large-scale advertising provides reminders to old customers and provides information to obtain some part of the patronage of new customers. The potential market is so huge that large scale advertising is an economical way to obtain good results.

In addition, the identity of buyers changes under some circumstances and new potential buyers must be given information concerning the available alternatives. It has also been pointed out that some of these products are ". . . subject to fads and style changes" and that ". . . consumers become restive with existing brands and are prepared to try new varieties." Illustrations include cereals, soaps, clothing, and motion pictures.[8]

The consumer has a wide variety of brands from which to choose. Product improvements usually breed competitive product improvements; the advertising of these improvements may result in an increase in total advertising for the class of products.

When any company in an industry embarks on an intensified advertising campaign, its competitors must step up their advertising or other sales efforts to avoid the possible loss of market position. This is a key characteristic of competition.

On the other hand, if any company decides to economize on its advertising budget, its exposure is reduced and its share of market may decline if its competitors fail to follow the same policy. Thus, for some grocery products it has been reported that ". . . competition within a sector may have established a certain pattern with regard to the extent of advertising, and any company dropping below this level faces possible substantial loss of market share."[9]

These results flow particularly if the industry is oligopolistic, that is, has relatively few producers who are sensitive to and responsive to actions of competitors. However, as the dramatic changes in market shares during the past decade so amply demonstrate, this does not mean that the companies in such oligopolistic industries will retain relatively constant shares of the market.[10]

The informational role of advertising has been succinctly summarized by Professor George J. Stigler:

. . . Under competition, the main tasks of a seller are to inform potential buyers of his existence, his line of goods, and his prices. Since both sellers and buyers change over time (due to birth, death, migration), since people forget information once acquired, and since new products appear, the existence of sellers must be continually advertised. . .

This informational function of advertising must be emphasized because of a popular and erroneous belief that advertising consists chiefly of nonrational (emotional and repetitive) appeals.[11]

Elsewhere, Professor Stigler has pointed out that ". . . information is a valuable resource," that advertising is "the obvious method of identifying buyers and sellers" which "reduces drastically the cost of search," and that "It is clearly an immensely powerful instrument for the elimination of ignorance. . . ."[12]

Often this information is required to create interest in and demand for a product. Thus, it has been reported:

. . . to a significant degree General Foods and the U.S. foodmarket created each other. Before a new product appears, customers are rarely conscious of wanting it. There was no spontaneous demand for ready-to-eat cereals; frozen foods required a sustained marketing effort stretching over many years; instant coffee had been around for decades, supplying a market that did not amount to a tenth of its present level. General Foods' corporate skill consists largely in knowing enough about American tastes to foresee what products will be accepted.[13]

Similarly, J. K. Galbraith, who has been very critical of advertising, has recognized that:

A new consumer product must be introduced with a suitable advertising campaign to arouse an interest in it. The path for an expansion of output must be paved by a suitable expansion in the advertising budget. Outlays for the manufacturing of a product are not more important in the strategy of modern business enterprise than outlays for the manufacturing of demand for the product.[14]

---

[8] Lester G. Telser, "How Much Does It Pay Whom To Advertise?", *American Economic Review, Papers and Proceedings* (December, 1960), pp. 203–4.

[9] National Commission on Food Marketing, *Grocery Manufacturing*, Technical Study No. 6 (Washington, D.C.: June, 1966), p. 14.

[10] Jules Backman, *Advertising and Competition* (New York: New York University Press, 1967), Chapters 3 and 4.

[11] George J. Stigler, *The Theory of Price*, Third Edition (New York: The Macmillan Company, 1966), p. 200.

[12] George J. Stigler, "The Economics of Information," *The Journal of Political Economy* (June, 1961), pp. 213, 216, 220. See also S. A. Ozga, "Imperfect Markets Through Lack of Knowledge," *Quarterly Journal of Economics* (February, 1960), pp. 29, 33–34, and Wroe Alderson, *Dynamic Market Behavior* (Homewood, Illinois: Richard D. Irwin, Inc., 1965), pp. 128–31.

[13] "General Foods Is Five Billion Particulars," *Fortune* (March, 1964), p. 117.

[14] J. K. Galbraith, *The Affluent Society* (Boston, Massachusetts: Houghton Mifflin Company, 1958), p. 156.

We live in an economy that has little resemblance to the ideal of perfect competition postulated by economists. However, one of the postulates of this ideal economy is perfect knowledge. Advertising contributes to such knowledge. Thus, in such an idealized economy, even though advertising may be wasteful it would still have a role to play. But in the world of reality, with all its imperfections, advertising is much more important. Advertising is an integral and vital part of our growing economy and contributes to the launching of the new products so essential to economic growth.

How Much Is Informational?

In 1966, total expenditures for media advertising aggregated $13.3 billion.[15] It is impossible to determine exactly how much of this amount was strictly informational. However, the following facts are of interest.

Classified advertising was $1.3 billion.
Other local newspaper advertising, largely retail, was $2.6 billion.
Business paper advertising was $712 million.
Local radio and TV advertising was $1.1 billion.
Spot radio and spot TV advertising was $1.2 billion.
National advertising on network TV, network radio, magazines and newspapers was $3.7 billion.
Direct mail was $2.5 billion.

Classified advertising and local advertising are overwhelmingly informational in nature. Certainly some part of national advertising also performs this function. These figures suggest that substantially less than half of total advertising is of the type that the critics are attacking as wasteful;[16] the exact amount cannot be pinpointed. Moreover, it must be kept in mind that a significant part of national advertising is for the promotion of new products for which the informational role is vital.

From another point of view, even if there is waste, the social cost is considerably less than suggested by these data. Thus, in 1966 about $10 billion was spent on advertising in newspapers, magazines, radio, and television; another $746 million was spent on farm and business publications. Without these expenditures, these sources of news and entertainment would have had to obtain substantial sums from other sources. It has been estimated that ". . . advertising paid for over 60% of the cost of periodicals, for over 70% of the cost of newspapers, and for 100% of the cost of commercial radio and TV broadcasting."[17] Thus, advertising results in a form of subsidization for all media of communication. Without it, these media would have to charge higher subscription rates or be subsidized by the government or some combination of both.

ADVERTISING AND EXPANDING MARKETS

Economic growth has become a major objective of national economic policy in recent years. Rising productivity, increasing population, improving education, rates of saving, and decisions concerning new investments are the ingredients of economic growth. In addition, there must be a favorable political climate including tax policies and monetary policies designed to release the forces conducive to growth.

Advertising contributes to economic growth and in turn levels of living by complementing the efforts to create new and improved products through expenditures for research and development. One observer has described the process as follows:

. . . advertising, by acquainting the consumer with the values of new products, widens the market for these products, pushes forward their acceptance by the consumer, and encourages the investment and entrepreneurship necessary for innovation. Advertising, in short, holds out the promise of a greater and speedier return than would occur without

[15] This total excludes a miscellaneous category of $3.3 billion.

[16] For the United Kingdom, the "disputed proportion" of advertising expenditures has been estimated at about 30% of the total. Walter Taplin, *Advertising, A New Approach* (Boston, Massachusetts: Little, Brown & Co., 1963), p. 126.

[17] Fritz Machlup, *The Production and Distribution of Knowledge in the United States* (Princeton, New Jersey: Princeton University Press, 1962), p. 265.

such methods, thus stimulating investment, growth and diversity.[18]

Among the most intensive advertisers have been toilet preparations (14.7% of sales), cleaning and polishing preparations (12.6%), and drugs (9.4%). The markets for these products have been expanding at a faster rate than all consumer spending.

Between 1947 and 1966, personal consumption expenditures for these products increased as follows.[19]

	1947	1955	1966
	(millions of dollars)		
Toilet articles and preparations	1,217	1,915	4,690
Cleaning, polishing and household supplies	1,523	2,480	4,487
Drug preparations and sundries	1,313	2,362	5,062

As a share of total personal consumption expenditures, the increases from 1947 to 1966 were as follows:

Toilet articles and preparations
from 0.7% to 1.01%
Cleaning, polishing and household
supplies from 0.94% to 0.97%
Drug preparations and sundries
from 0.82% to 1.09%

These increases in relative importance are based upon dollar totals. However, the retail prices of these products rose less than the consumer price index during the postwar years.

Between 1947 and 1966, the price increases were as follows:

Total consumer price index	45.4%
Toilet preparations	14.6
Soaps and detergents	2.6
Drugs and prescriptions	22.8

Thus, the increase in relative importance of these highly advertised products has been even greater in real terms than in dollars.

Between 1947 and 1966, the increase in *real* personal consumption expenditures has been:

Toilet articles and preparations
from 0.68% to 1.12%
Cleaning, polishing and household
supplies from 0.87% to 1.05%
Drug preparations and sundries
from 0.82% to 1.24%

Clearly, advertising appears to have contributed to an expansion in the demand for these products and to the growth of our economy with the accompanying expansion in job opportunities and in economic well-being. There may have been some waste in this process—although all of such expeditures cannot be characterized as wasteful—but it appears to have been offset in full or in part by these other benefits.

The charge of large-scale waste in advertising appears to reflect in part a yearning for an economy with standardized, homogeneous products which are primarily functional in nature. An illustration would be a refrigerator that is designed solely to be technically efficient for the storage of food. However, customers are also interested in the decor of their kitchen, in convenience and speed in the manufacture of ice cubes, in shelves that rotate, and in special storage for butter. These are additions to functional usefulness which "an affluent society" can afford but which a subsistence economy cannot.

Advertising in a High Level Economy

The concept of waste must be related to the level achieved by an economy. Professor John W. Lowe has observed that "Perhaps a good deal of the 'wastefulness' assigned to advertising springs from the fact that a large part of the world's population cannot consider satisfying *psychological wants* when most of their efforts must be devoted to *needs*."[20] (Italics added.)

In a subsistence economy, scarcity is so significant that advertising might be wasteful, particularly where it diverts resources

[18] David M. Blank, "Some Comments on the Role of Advertising in the American Economy—A Plea for Revaluation," L. George Smith, editor, *Reflections on Progress in Marketing* (Chicago, Illinois: American Marketing Association, 1964), p. 151.

[19] *The National Income and Product Accounts of the United States, 1929–1965, Statistical Tables* (Washington, D.C.: United States Department of Commerce, August, 1966), pp. 44–49; and *Survey of Current Business* (July, 1967), pp. 23–24.

[20] John W. Lowe, "An Economist Defends Advertising," *Journal of Marketing*, Vol. 27 (July, 1963), p. 18.

from meeting the basic necessities of life. Such an economy usually is a "full employment economy" in the sense that everyone is working. But the total yield of a full employment subsistence economy is very low, as is evident throughout Asia, Africa, and South America.

Professor Galbraith has noted that "The opportunity for product differentiation . . . is almost uniquely the result of opulence . . . the tendency for commercial rivalries . . . to be channeled into advertising and salesmanship would disappear in a poor community."[21]

In the high level American economy, there usually are surpluses rather than scarcity. The use of resources for advertising to differentiate products, therefore, is not necessarily a diversion from other uses. Rather, it frequently represents the use of resources that might otherwise be idle both in the short run and the long run and thus may obviate the waste that such idleness represents.

The Marketing Mix

The concept of waste cannot ignore the question—waste as compared with what alternative? Advertising cannot be considered in a vacuum. It must be considered as one of the marketing alternatives available. Generally it is not a question of advertising or nothing, but rather of advertising or some other type of sales effort.

It is a mistake to evaluate the relative cost of advertising apart from other marketing costs. It is only one tool in the marketing arsenal which also includes direct selling, packaging, servicing, product planning, pricing, etc. Expenditures for advertising often are substituted for other types of selling effort. This substitution has been readily apparent in the history of the discount house. These houses have featured well-advertised brands which were presold and, hence, virtually eliminated the need for floor stocks and reduced the need for space and many salesmen.

Advertising is undertaken where it is the most effective and most economical way to appeal to customers. It is a relatively low cost method of communicating with all potential customers and this explains its widespread adoption by many companies. To the extent that less efficient marketing methods must be substituted for advertising, we would really have economic waste.

SUMMARY AND CONCLUSIONS

There is wide agreement that the informational role of advertising makes a significant contribution to the effective operation of our economy. There is also agreement that inefficiency in the use of advertising is wasteful, as are other types of inefficiencies that are part and parcel of a market-determined economy. The gray area is so-called competitive advertising, largely national, which is the main target of those who insist advertising is wasteful. Although precise data are not available, the estimates cited earlier indicate that the charge of competitive waste applies to substantially less than half of all advertising expenditures.

Competition unavoidably involves considerable duplication and waste. If the accent is placed on the negative, a distorted picture is obtained. On balance, the advantages of competition have been much greater than the wastes.

Advertising has contributed to an expanding market for new and better products. Many of these new products would not have been brought to market unless firms were free to develop mass markets through large-scale advertising. There may be some waste in this process, but it has been more than offset by other benefits.

Where burgeoning advertising expenditures are accompanied by expanding industry sales, there will tend to be a decline in total unit costs instead of increase, and prices may remain unchanged or decline. In such situations, it seems clear that advertising, while adding to total costs, will result in lower total *unit* costs, the more significant figure. This gain will be offset to some extent if the increase in volume represents a diversion from other companies or industries with an accompanying rise in unit costs. Of course, such change is inherent in a dynamic competitive economy.

Advertising expenditures have risen as the economy has expanded. At such times, the absolute increase in sales resulting from

---

[21] John K. Galbraith, *American Capitalism: The Concept of Countervailing Power* (Boston, Massachusetts: Houghton Mifflin Company, 1952), pp. 106–07.

higher advertising expenditures need not be accompanied by a loss in sales in other industries. This is particularly true if a new product has been developed and its sales are expanding. In that event, new jobs probably will be created and help to support a higher level of economic activity generally.

The claim that resources devoted to advertising would be utilized more efficiently for other purposes ignores the fact that generally we have a surplus economy. All of the resources used for advertising are not diverted from other alternatives. Rather, it is probable that much of the resources involved would be idle or would be used less efficiently.

Even more important would be the failure to provide the jobs which expanding markets create.

Finally, advertising does not take place in a vacuum. It is one of several marketing alternatives. The abandonment of advertising could not represent a net saving to a company or to the economy. Instead, such a development would require a shift to alternative marketing techniques, some of which would be less efficient than advertising since companies do not deliberately adopt the least effective marketing approach. On balance, advertising is an invaluable competitive tool.

61. The Social Values of Marketing

C. W. COOK

The contributions marketing makes in our society are social as well as economic. This is a point that we in marketing need to stress strongly now, when the climate in which the marketing function must be carried on is the most socially conscious in the entire history of our country. For it is in the name of social progress that critics of business—some public figures and their political and philosophical allies—are training their fire power these days on some long-established, time-tested marketing aims and methods.

It is inevitable, in a country where freedom of thought and speech is encouraged, that there will be differences of viewpoint about so complicated a subject as marketing. And there are differences, even about such obvious contributions as the economic values of marketing. But what should concern us particularly is the current tendency to question the *social* worthiness of the function which is our responsibility. For as policy-setting top executives and senior marketing people, it is our mission to create and serve the consumer market which supports all the activities of production, from raw material sources to finished products, and to do this as efficiently and acceptably as possible.

It seems clear that we need to develop a more effective way of presenting the role of marketing in the light of today's heightened social consciousness. We must not let the values that marketing contributes to the well-

◆ SOURCE: Reprinted by permission from *The Conference Board Record*, Vol. IV, No. 2, February 1967, pp. 32–37.

being of our society get lost. So it is about these values that I would like to share some thoughts with you.

There are, as I see it, three social responsibilities of marketing which contribute to its social value: First, to offer a *social product;* second, to make it available at a *social price;* and third, to make a *social profit* in the process.

I would like to examine each briefly in relation to the public welfare and the realities of human nature.

A SOCIAL PRODUCT

How might a social product be defined? (And it will simplify this discussion if you will permit me to use the term "product" to include "services" also.) What are its characteristics? What are its social values?

To the social theorist there seem to be four conventional or rational measurements of value which apply to any product:

- Its quantitative value.
- Its intrinsic or qualitative value.
- Its functional or utilitarian value.
- Its serviceability or durability.

All four of these values are, of course, valid. Their relative importance depends on the nature of the product, or the use to which it is to be put by the consumer. But I hardly need to remind you who are in the thick of the competitive battle of the marketplace that this by no means exhausts the list of reasons consumers buy a product, or buy one product in preference to another—or to all others. Indeed, it leaves out one of the values most important to the great mass of consumers.

Before naming this important value let me enumerate just a few of the very human reasons people buy many of the products they do buy, quite often paying a premium price for them:

• Because a product provides sheer gratification in ownership.

• Because it possesses exclusiveness of form, shape, design, materals, workmanship, finish.

• Because it produces a sense of pride in the ability to afford, or the taste to appreciate.

• Because of the anticipated admiration of friends.

• Because of the attractiveness of the package.

• Because it promises to produce a quiet sense of well-being.

• Because the product reflects the purchaser's personality.

• Because it would make a gift of special charm or appropriateness.

• Because it offers an outlet for the purchaser's energy, skill or creativity.

• Because it indulges some suppressed desire.

It will not have escaped you, I am sure, that there is little relationship between any of these reasons for buying and the four conventional measurements of value mentioned earlier. But, irrational, extravagant, even frivolous, as some of them seem, they lump themselves under the single important value I have postponed naming until now. This is *satisfaction-value*.

There are two forms of satisfaction-value. One is *satisfaction-in-use*; the other is *satisfaction-of-ownership*. Both, I submit, have definite social value, because they serve a need or craving in the life of the purchaser. Usually they make him or her quite willing to pay whatever their price, within reason. This seems to nettle the school of sociologists who focus on the four rational values—quantitative, intrinsic or qualitative, functional or utilitarian, serviceability or durability. But it is a sober reality of the marketplace.

While the four rational values are important, accepting them as the sole criteria of product-value would involve abandoning the free-choice principle on which our American social system is based.

There is no question that all of us *could*

live much more economically—or more sensibly, if you prefer—than we do.

We do not actually *need* agreeably flavored toothpaste, in a convenient tube, to keep our teeth clean. We could brush them with baking soda or plain table salt.

We do not actually *need* clothing in the latest fashion and the newest fabrics and colors. Garments of coarse cotton, wool or linen, without form or style, would effectively cover and protect our bodies.

We do not actually *need* the smart and comfortable motorcars we drive. A jeep would take our families any place we might want to go.

We cannot honestly argue that we actually *need* our present broad assortment of appetizing and convenient foods and beverages. We could exist indefinitely on water, coarse bread, milk, and a few fruits and vegetables. Furthermore, we could prepare meals starting from scratch, with low-cost bulk raw materials, as our grandmothers did.

But who of us would be willing to live in such a strictly functional or utilitarian fashion? Or how ready would any of us be to give up all the *satisfaction-values?*

Our penchant for buying-for-satisfaction has been summed up succinctly by Lee A. Iacocca, vice president of the Ford Motor Company:

People buy cars for all kinds of reasons. Some people buy because a color or a grille or a roof line makes them feel good. Some people buy because of miles per gallon and cents per mile. The point is that people buy for a reason that makes sense to them.

While he was speaking of motorcars, the reason for puchasing any product that makes sense to any man or woman constitutes its *satisfaction-value* to that person.

A basic-necessities economy might be built on a narrow and strictly utilitarian marketing philosophy. But life would be terribly drab. And the economy would suffer—swiftly. Jobs would become scarce. Growth opportunities would be so lacking that the incentive on which our private enterprise system is based would all but cease to exist. The United States of America as we know it could not survive under so narrow a social philosophy.

The aim of marketing under our system, which has brought us a steadily rising economy, is to supply the whole range of products and services to serve consumers' very human cravings of the mind and spirit, as well as of the body. I submit that this is a *social right*. For it is not society as a whole, but the *social individual* who establishes the social value of any product—by his or her purchases.

These purchases may encompass a whole category of products which Dr. Ernest Dichter, the well-known philosopher of human motivation, has whimsically characterized as "sinful products." These he defines as products that come into conflict with Puritanical moral standards. Included would be, for example, liquor, candy, cigarettes, fattening foods, cola drinks, coffee, cosmetics, and many others.

None of these products is absolutely essential. But we would fight to keep them. They do something for our spirits, our ego, our sense of good living. They, and the right to possess them, are the driving force which motivates us to work and to seek advancement, in order to enjoy more and more of the products and services which "make sense to us." In other words, they help to make us productive servants of our modern society, as well as consumers. Thus they contribute *social* as well as *economic* values to our American life.

A SOCIAL PRICE

Assuming a social product to market, one with values transcending intrinsic or strictly utilitarian qualities, the second consideration of those of us responsible for marketing policy is the *price* at which the product is to be offered.

Specifically, can it be sold at a *social price?* The very term seems contradictory. How can the price of any product be *social,* when price is an essentially *commercial* element in the sales transactions?

It seems to me that much of the misunderstanding about the nature and function of the marketing process is revealed by this simple question. The assumption is that social and commercial considerations are uncongenial, if not definitely antipathetic. But are they?

Suppose we ask this simple question: What *is* a "social price"—for *any* product? The quick answer is likely to be, "The lowest price at which it can be offered."

Reasonable as it seems, this answer is *one-sidedly social* in that it focuses too sharply on the consumer. Establishing a social price involves striking a balance between the well-being of *five* disparate groups, each of which

has a natural—and legitimate—interest in the price at which a given product is offered. These groups are:

1. The people with the enterprise to embark in the business of developing, producing and marketing the product, and those who manage and staff the business.

2. The people who provide the capital to finance the business.

3. The people who produce and distribute the product, including production, clerical, sales and administrative personnel, and the transportation and delivery workers who make it physically available to consumers in their communities.

4. The people who purchase and use or consume the product. (The only group which benefits directly from the quick answer: "The lowest price at which it can be offered.")

5. Finally, and of great social importance, the federal, state and local governments which are so heavily dependent for their support on the taxes collected from successful business enterprises.

Thus it becomes evident that the social price must provide earnings that will make it worthwhile for people with capital to invest their funds in the enterprise, and to provide a margin for the management to reinvest in continually improving the product, and retooling from time to time to produce it still more economically.

The social price must enable the enterprise to pay prevailing wages to those who make and market the product, and to employ competent people to manage it. Those who transport and distribute must also be compensated.

In this way profitable employment is maintained and the whole economy is supported.

And if it is to be a true social price it must be sufficient to provide a margin of profit to contribute to federal, state and local taxes, as already mentioned. For if a business enterprise earns no profits, it is a drag on the nation's economy.

At this point the basic function of marketing—the building and maintaining of a consumer market for any product—injects itself, and it must be faced.

The quick definition of a social price for a product—"The lowest price at which it can be offered"—assumes that the lower the price, the more people can and will buy it. This assumption would be sound if the maker of the product had an absolute monopoly in the market place. But under our free-choice, private enterprise system we insist—quite properly, I am sure we will all agree—that monopoly be outlawed. The result is a competition between products so intense that only those which are promoted by effective advertising will be given shelf space in retail outlets.

If there were a more economical way of reaching the consumer, we may be very sure that some enterprising company in every industry would be using it. The bald fact is, that a social price must of necessity include a margin for introduction and continuous promotion.

A Question of Value . . .

Yet some social theorists argue that the advertising and promotional activities used to create and maintain the market for a product are a sheer waste of money: that consumers should be offered lower prices by eliminating, or at least drastically limiting, these marketing expenditures.

This might be true in a world peopled with utterly unemotional consumers, dedicated to strictly functional living, and satisfied with purely utilitarian products; but not in our modern world of very human men, women, and children, who insist on satisfactions of the mind and spirit as well as of the body.

Recently an eminent English economist and writer, Walter Taplin, divided consumer expenditures into two categories: "The things we need to keep us alive and the things we need to make life worth living."

As men with marketing responsibility, it is our obligation to provide *both*. But it is our obligation, also, to provide value for the price asked—social value, if you please.

Part of this value is in the product itself, in ingredients and product costs. Part is often added in the packaging and promotion functions of the marketing process.

Because I know the food business best, I naturally start with this category of products to validate my point. By picturing on the package and in the advertising of a dessert, for instance, the delectable dishes it will provide, and describing in mouth-watering words their flavor, texture, and nutritional characteristics, the consumer is led to *anticipate* enjoyable eating, as well as to identify the product's special virtues while eating it. Without this mental picture, many people would consume the dessert with much less relish.

The consumer might receive a scant money's worth, no matter how low the price.

Or suppose we take an example from the field of kitchen appliances. The advertising of an electric can opener, or one of the new Teflon-lined cooking utensils, can create a mental picture of a minor miracle of convenience in meal preparation that will send a women to the kitchen to get dinner for her family with a sense of having magic servants at her elbow.

In the field of services, the cruises offered by steamship lines are made far more enjoyable by the anticipation of gay shipboard parties and the romance of their ports of call, as pictured in TV and print advertisements and illustrated folders. People get far more pleasure for their money than if their travel appetite had not been whetted in advance by this picturesque promotion.

Or consider today's miracle antibiotics. Above and beyond their scientific merit, may not their efficacy be at least partially dependent on the psychological benefit of the patient's *anticipation* of relief or a cure?

Modern cosmetics can—and often do—make a woman prettier (if not pretty) because, when using them, the promise of the advertising makes her *feel* prettier. So she *is* prettier. She gets her money's worth in satisfaction-in-use.

. . . and of Value Added

All of these satisfactions are human—and therefore *social* rather than *economic*—aspects of price-value. The point is that advertising can and does add a considerable measure of value to perhaps a majority of products. And it is a social value that makes the price socially reasonable.

Let me register right here that we who bear marketing responsibility cannot afford to forget that the irrationality and ever-so-human foibles of the public, who comprise the huge market for goods and services in this country of ours, neither argue for nor condone *over*-promising a product's satisfactions or benefits. Neither do they excuse overcharging for it in relation to the value of its ingredients and the costs involved in its creation, production, promotion, and distribution. Nor do the foibles of human nature offer any excuse for dishonesty in claims, in advertising or on the package. Not only is this true with respect to benefits, but also to quantity, quality, utility, serviceability, and other values, claimed or implied.

A SOCIAL PROFIT

In the competitive Donnybrook of today's market-place, little thought is likely to be given to such a seemingly idealistic consideration as a "social profit." But in view of the critical attitude that is cropping out in political circles toward some aspects of marketing, I believe it timely to ask ourselves what might reasonably be considered a *social* profit.

Many otherwise intelligent people seem to think of the word "profits" as a synonym for "greed." In reality, profits are synonymous with economic and social health, for we could not have a healthy economy or a healthy society without the profits earned by business.

True, there are always a few businessmen who are greedy for more profits than they are entitled to; just as there are a few men and women in every line of human endeavor who are greedy for more glory or fame, or a greater financial reward, than their contribution merits. But in both instances they are the exception rather than the rule.

Another common misassumption is that businesses make profits automatically.

All of us know that this is not so. Yet I believe most people would be surprised at these figures from a government publication, *Profits and the American Economy,* issued by the Department of Commerce:

In 1961-62 some 1,190,286 active corporations filed Income Tax returns with the U.S. Internal Revenue Service. Of these, 474,697 reported a net loss. This is 39.8 per cent of all corporations which filed Income Tax returns . . . This indicates the seriousness of the risk-taking involved in entrepreneurship.

The same government publication also makes this point:

It is evident that entrepreneurship, guided as it is by the profit incentive, serves as a bridge between productive resources and consumers, and by so doing provides a vital service to all of us. Additionally, in its constant endeavor to lower its cost to meet competition, entrepreneurship, guided by the profit incentive, helps to get goods which consumers want most, produced at the lowest possible cost.

These two brief excerpts sum up the contributions of competition as both an economic and a social factor in profit-making. For of necessity profits earned in today's competitive marketplace serve social as well as economic purposes.

In short, only the theorists question the need or value to society of profits. The realists have always recognized this value. Back in the early days of the labor movement, Samuel Gompers wrote: "Companies without profits mean workers without jobs. Remember, when the boss is in financial trouble, the worker's job isn't safe."

In modern times, George Meany stated in a *Fortune* magazine article: "We believe in the American profit system. We believe in free competition. The American private enterprise system, despite some defects, has achieved far greater results for wage earners than any other social system in history."

The social contribution of profits to the support of our government is too well recognized to need argument. But I find that many people are surprised at the size of the tax contribution made by a single corporation in the course of a year. As an example, in fiscal 1966 my own company paid some $82 million in federal, state and local taxes. This compares with less than $53 million paid to General Foods' stockholders in dividends, and a little over $41 million retained in the business for reinvestment in its future growth and security.

On a business-wide scale, in calendar 1965 the income tax bill for all U.S. corporations from the federal government alone was more than $31 billion, which went to the support of our society. And this figure does not include substantial state and local taxes, nor the enormous amounts paid in personal income taxes by stockholders to federal, state and local governments.

There is a school of business thought which criticizes the accounting phrase, "profits before taxes." This phrase, they argue, is a misstatement, since the portion of earnings earmarked for taxes is not available to the management for any other use. The argument advanced by some that these taxes are part of the "cost of doing business" only confirms that they are not "profits" in the proper sense of the term.

From an accounting standpoint it makes little difference how taxes are designated; the harm comes when critical writers and speakers quote the total figure to show what "huge profits" corporations made. They fail to mention the really significant contribution more than half of corporate profits is making to the social welfare of the nation, of the various states, and of local communities.

A Practical Responsibility

We who administer business enterprises have a very practical responsibility for the wise social use of the part of the profits retained in our busienss. Except as private citizens with a vote, we have no control over the expenditure of that portion of profits paid in federal, state and local taxes. And our responsibility for the portion distributed as dividends ends when the dividend checks are mailed. But when we plan the use of profits retained in the business, we exercise a most important social responsibility.

In this respect, it seems to me that there is a definite difference between management's *economic* responsibility to earn profits, and its *social* responsibility to *administer* the retained portion of profits so intelligently that the enterprise will continue to grow, provide employment, and pay taxes, to the end of serving our society. This it commonly does, as we in management realize but the general public seems not to appreciate by supporting scientific research, pioneering in the development of new products, steadily improving present products, and in general keeping up with the changing needs and wants of the consuming home and family.

Sooner or later—and usually sooner!—in any consideration of profit, the question of what is a *fair* profit is inevitably raised. Of all the attempts made to define a fair profit, I like best the one given by Bert S. Cross chairman of the 3M Company: "A profit is a fair profit," he said, "as long as we have sold a man a product he can use and is willing to buy." Certainly that concept serves our society better than the innumerable theoretical proposals for limiting profits by mathematical formula, or by any other artificial method that does not take the competitive factor into account.

Under our competitive system, the body-social has a most effective way of governing profits. If the consuming public stops buying a product, it frequently means that profits *are* too high. When that happens, prices come down, either because the industry fears the loss of its market and reduces prices, or because individual producers reduce their prices and their competitors are forced to follow.

Our System Works

This free-choice, private enterprise, profit-motivated system of ours, which is highly competitive, may seem irrational, wasteful in some respects and at times a bit silly and "sinful." But it has the saving grace that it *works*. And economic truth is established by a practical experience, not by theoretical arguments.

No other economic system in the history of the world, no matter how rational or how socially idealistic, has ever approached it in the prosperity ours has produced. What is more, it has provided our country with a substantial margin which we have been able to share with older peoples whose highly touted socialistic economies continue to fail to meet even the basic needs of their people.

Yet theorists insist on tampering with our machinery. Frequently I find myself wishing that I could still be around 50 or 100 years from now, to witness the puzzlement that is bound to prevail among historians who try to make head or tail out of our times.

How will they reconcile, for instance, the fact that after our country has contributed billions of dollars for two decades to advance the freedom of mankind all over the world, there are now under serious consideration a number of regulatory proposals to reduce marketing freedoms within our own borders? "Why," they are bound to ask, "was there such a zeal in the mid-1960's to standardize, to limit, and to legislate in a way that would undermine free choice?"

But perhaps the most confusing paradox historians will uncover is that, at the very time that more and more controls were being urged by the theorists to hobble our economy, in Soviet Russia, where a strictly controlled economy had prevailed for half a century, the trend was clearly turning toward greater freedom of action. A recent issue of *Fortune*[1] magazine stated:

Soviet authorities have been making increased use of price cuts, installment buying, advertising and product differentiation . . . Consumer goods producers are beginning to promote their plant names or "production marks." The government is encouraging the practice because an enterprise that is proud enough of its mark to call attention to it inevitably tends both to make a better product and to keep on improving it.

---

[1] August, 1966.

This article should baffle future historians, especially when, in preserved copies of our nation's mass communication media of the same period, they read about the all-out efforts being made in the U.S. on behalf of package standardization, grade labeling, limitation of advertising, and various other proposals for depriving American business of the marketing tools and techniques which made our economy so great; and even worse, for depriving American consumers of their traditional right of free choice. And it is worth noting that, in the light of its vociferous insistence upon "the right to be an individual," the upcoming generation promises to be even more jealous of its freedom to choose than the present generation.

We in marketing have it in our power to change the course of economic history during the final third of this eventual century. In fact, we are challenged to do just that: to demonstrate that our system, given freedom to function without crippling laws and regulations, will continue to be the best suited to provide a social product, at a social price, and with a social profit—a profit made, not at the expense of the public, but as a result of acceptable service to the public.

I would add a further challenge: we must find ways to bring to the public a clear and helpful understanding of the *social* as well as the *economic* aspects of the entire production-promotion-distribution process which is the area of special interest and competence of this group of management and marketing executives.

I have saved until the end the golden text of my paper: Nearly two thousand years ago Seneca, the Roman philosopher, made this thoroughly modern observation: "*It is every man's duty to make himself profitable to mankind.*" I wonder if that doesn't say it all.

62. Criteria for a Theory of Responsible Consumption

GEORGE FISK

Technological advance triggers rising productivity, income, consumption, pollution, and ultimately resource depletion. Although these elements of economic development are interdependent, this article focuses on the challenge of rising consumption to human survival. Since the economic system is heavily dependent on the social and ecological systems, other elements that interact with consumption must be seriously considered because they significantly affect economic development.

At a high level of expertise, management skills tend to be narrowly focused on raising sales and profits. By ignoring social externalities created by marketing and production decisions, business executives have invited rising public criticism and government regulation. Although business leaders are more sensitive to the need for expertise in ecological policy, few understand the implications of the closed-system economy because of its recent development.

From a marketing viewpoint, this analysis begins with an examination of the responsibility for limiting individual consumption, here termed "responsible consumption" or recognizing "ecological imperatives." "Responsible consumption" refers to rational and efficient use of resources with respect to the global human population. It is not possible to consider the consumption question exclusively from the standpoint of any single nation, because the consumption of depletable resources in one nation necessarily affects the reservoir of resources elsewhere. Since this problem is global, its analysis must also be global.

The term "ecological imperative" or "ecological sanction" refers to any interaction between a species and the biological and physical environment required for its survival. The human species, for example, requires organic nutrients, physical space, water, and air. Pollution or resource depletion violates an ecological imperative by jeopardizing biological processes. Biologists and ecologists do not specifically know the limits beyond which our natural environment can withstand abuse, but they may have more dependable knowledge of the ecological imperative imposed by human consumption than do advertising copywriters or marketing managers. Although the "scare tactics" of ecologists have been deplored in scientific journals, their warnings about the violation of ecological imperatives must seriously be considered by government, business, household decision makers, and planners.

One ecological imperative of universal importance concerns ecological capital consumption. For example, if paper processors cut down trees to be consumed as newsprint, forests must be replaced to provide future paper needs and oxygen to the atmosphere. Another ecological sanction is recycling, which attempts to avoid exhaustion of irreplaceable resources. If resources are to be recollected,

◆ SOURCE: Reprinted by permission from the *Journal of Marketing* (National Quarterly Publication of the American Marketing Association), Vol. 37, No. 2, April 1973, pp. 24–31.

resorted, and dispersed for reuse, marketing activities must attempt to supply consumers after the original natural deposits are exhausted. Still another ecological imperative concerns the dissipation of wasted heat from energy transmission. At approximately 100 times the present world energy consumption levels, the waste heat generated will probably introduce profoundly disturbing climate and weather changes which could modify the habitability of earth. Consequently, efforts are already under way to substitute solar and geothermal energy for more nuclear and fossil fuel power. Many ecological sanctions still remain unidentified.

THEORY OF RESPONSIBLE CONSUMPTION

The world's present population of 3.5 billion people is expected to increase to 7.0 billions by the year 2000. To provide rising incomes and rising consumption levels for so many people will surely strain the environment beyond the already dangerous levels of population. At the same time, it will place far greater demands on a shrinking world resource base. Irresponsible resource use from high level mass consumption as in the U.S. must be curbed if an incipient human "population crash" is to be averted.

Rising per capita consumption in advanced nations constitutes a greater threat to the biological environment than the increase in human populations in underdeveloped nations. One U.S. consumer is said to have fifty times the ecological impact of one person from India, if based on per capita consumption expenditures. U.S. consumerism has emphasized consumer rights while ignoring consumer responsibilities. Therefore, socially responsible action must focus on responsible action of government, business leaders, and consumers. Commenting on the importance of consumer responsibilities, Margaret Mead observes:

. . . responsibility will include planning for life styles which are feasible economically and which will contribute to the sense of justice and dignity of all the people of the earth . . . if the number of cars per capita in an industrialized country is compared with the number of cars in an unindustrialized country, the screaming discrepancy between the rich and the poor countries becomes unbearable. . . . Worldwide television, mass-picture media, and mass travel mean that people all over the world are exposed to the standard of living within the countries and homes of the affluent. . . .

It, therefore, becomes a question of simplifying styles in industrialized countries—a demand that is coming from the young and the environmentalists in those countries. If the industrialized countries move toward a more collective use of space and away from the excess overcapitalization of the individual home, there will be a better chance of having such transfers. . . .[1]

Operationally, responsible consumption may take the form of the imposition of a luxury goods consumption tax, the organization of post-consumption brigades to collect and recycle trash, the abolition of the flush toilet (replacing it with the kind of collection and processing devices coming into use in Sweden), and the development of consumer advertising programs designed to discourage extravagant consumption. Some households and business firms already fulfill part of their ecological responsibility by limiting family size and installing recycling and processing equipment, but this often entails direct private costs. Unless compelled by law or social custom, resource conservation practices may not become as effective or universal as the new world situation requires. Two things are needed—a new attitude toward the meaning of consumption and a social organization to implement such an attitude.

Closed System Perspective

Boulding described the new world view of humanity as a closed system similar to the crew on a spaceship. He contrasts this closed system economy with the vanishing open economy endowed with limitless resources.[2] While some marketing scholars have acknowledged the existence of marketing problems relating to the closed system economy,

---

[1] Margaret Mead, "Responsible Simplification of Consumption Patterns," *Ekistics*, Vol. 30 (October, 1970), pp. 324–326.

[2] Kenneth Boulding, "The Economics of the Coming Spaceship Earth," *Environmental Quality in a Growing Economy* (Baltimore: Johns Hopkins Press, 1971), p. 9.

Kotler and Levy have proposed a specific managerial adaptation called "demarketing" to deal with emerging social issues.[3] Earlier, Weiss referred to the same reverse marketing activity as "shrinkmanship."[4]

Implementing Organization

The social organization required to implement consumer responsibility is yet to be discovered, but its elements are slowly being recognized. Consumer education, via environmental courses on university and secondary school campuses, should help sensitize consumers to the necessity for individual responsibility. Advertising of ecologically benign household products has already started. Voluntary collection and recycling of bottles by postconsumption service groups and conservationists could play an increasingly important role. However, greater reliance must be placed on utilities that are capable of volume "waste recovery and recycling." Demand for reclaimed materials could be expanded if federal and local legislation required the use of recycled materials in manufacturing and processing operations under strict quality control. Public corporations, for example, already control the quality and distribution of all agricultural exports from India. Marketing programs are undertaken for more global goals than the short-run profit or market expansion of a single industry. In the U.S., AMTRAK, the public railroad corporation, and the U.S. postal service corporation are showing that declining institutions can be reinvigorated by the requirement that demand be cultivated rather than accepted as a monopoly condition requiring little or no effort. Both offer services that substitute for more expensive and wasteful forms of consumption. For example, one railroad car can still carry as many single occupants as 90 automobiles.

Weinberg argues that in order to utilize nuclear energy longevity is required of social institutions whose jurisdiction includes dealing with wastes in a manner that will insure proper and safe operation.[5]

Although Weinberg is concerned with the Atomic Energy Commission, the same argument could be made for private firms in the pharmaceutical industry as well as firms engaged in mining and other resource-depleting or polluting activities. Certainly, capital intensive high technology industry can substitute for public corporations, but municipalities appear destined to play a greater organizational role in waste recovery where community-wide collecting, restoring, and dispersing or rerouting activities are needed. The high cost of processing equipment and its necessarily extensive operation requires large inputs of "urban ore," or solid wastes and sewage. Public corporations, consortia, and regional authorities have not yet been fully integrated into a coherent managerial framework. However, their mere existence enables a redirection of consumption so that recycling, reuse, and rationing of scarce supplies can be more consistent with ecological imperatives. By building these new social institutions people will be able to treat consumption as a stage in a biological cycle rather than the end of all economic activity.

These suggestions for spreading the closed system perspective and building new institutions have great potential for the promotion of more responsible consumption. As subsequent discussions will elaborate, the benefit and cost illustrations in Table 1 may be used by marketing managers to make responsible marketing policy. Each column in Table 1 specifically identifies the area of ecological impact.

Each row displays a mode of environmental interaction. As Dansereau explains, human interaction with the environment assumes one of four modes which may occur in combination:

1. *Exploitation*—such as mining, harvesting, or stripping for food, fuel, shelter, or transportation.
2. *Substitution*—such as the introduction of foreign materials and suppression of mineral, organic, and living elements in the landscape.
3. *Engineering*—such as drawing resources

[3] Philip Kotler and Sidney Levy, "Demarketing, Yes, Demarketing," *Harvard Business Review*, Vol. 49 (November–December, 1971), pp. 74–80.

[4] E. B. Weiss, "The Coming Change in Marketing; from Growthmania to Shrinkmanship," *Advertising Age* (February 1, 1971), p. 35 ff.

[5] Alvin M. Weinberg, "Social Institutions and Nuclear Energy," *Science*, Vol. 177 (July 7, 1972), p. 34.

from one ecosystem into another in a sustained way.

4. *Designing*—A sophisticated level of planning geared to meet psychological requirements.[6]

Cells in Table 1 contain examples of marketing behavior in which row interaction modes yield benefits and costs under each of the column headings. Neither the benefits nor the costs are quantified; however, measures of both can be attempted as they have been in the private and public sector markets. For example, the costs of hauling and processing garbage can be subtracted from the value of reusable resources for particular communities. Costs of shopping center development can be estimated in terms of the new community taxes required to provide necessary police, highway maintenance, and other public services. A growing body of literature of the values and costs of social externalities is now available.

Table 1 simply attempts to illustrate the meaning of "good" and "bad" in ecological terms. "Responsible consumption" can be described by marketing actions that increase the benefits or decrease the costs as shown in Table 1. Further elaboration of this approach may yield indicators that are useful in social audits of marketing performance within firms, industries, and even sectors of the economy.

Three Perspectives on World Consumption

The accepted definitions of "good" and "bad" advocated by proponents of economic growth are under attack by ecologists and proponents of zero economic growth. The rationale for economic development as a basis for the theory of responsible consumption is presented from three different perspectives: the ecologists concerned with human survival, the NeoLuddite NeoMalthusian antigrowth view, and the views taken by economic development advocates.

Ecological Viewpoint

Industrial processes now consume oxygen faster than it is being produced in Euro-

pean, Japanese, and U.S. industrial centers. Pollution of the coastal waters is imperiling oxygen production by photoplankton which may lead to even greater shortages of oxygen. Biologists are concerned with rising environmental stresses which may well limit future supplies of air, water, food, minerals, and energy. Humans must consume all of these to survive; that is why from an ecological perspective consumption categories consist of such broad classifications.

Leading ecologists argue that technological solutions to pollution and resource depletion problems are inefficient and insufficient. Their criteria for responsible consumption include a *grand symbiosis* between man and environment and a steady state biosphere which Spilhaus has termed "ecolibrium," meaning the dynamic exchange of nutrients between mutually beneficial organisms necessary to continued human existence.[7] Huxley puts it succinctly:

Do we propose to live on this planet in symbiotic harmony with our environment? Or shall we choose to live like murderous parasites that kill their host and so destroy themselves? . . . The Golden Rule applies no less to our dealings with nature than with our fellow men.[8]

Under pressure from ecologists and conservationists, business and government organizations are searching for ecologically more benign products and processes. Even if different products and processes can be developed, ecologists argue that there is an upper limit to the amount of stress the world ecosystem can endure without collapse. The biosphere is a delicate system dependent on photosynthesis to produce sufficient oxygen for living things. In a spaceship economy, straining the environment may result in disaster. In addition to the search for benign products and processes, reprocessing should rise to signal improvements in marketing performance. Consumer resource utilization demands that the physical inputs and outputs of household systems balance so that the world may retain its own biological "ecolibrium."

---

[6] Pierre Danserau, "Ecology and the Escalation of Human Impact," *Ekistics*, Vol. 189 (August, 1971), p. 163.

[7] Athelstan Spilhaus, "Ecolibrium," *Science*, Vol. 175 (February 18, 1972), pp. 711–715.

[8] Aldous Huxley, "The Politics of Ecology," in *The Triple Revolution*, R. Perruccu and M. Pilisuk, eds. (Boston: Little Brown, 1968), pp. 133–134.

Table 1. Direct Ecological Impact of Marketing Inputs

Modes of Environmental Interaction	Area of Ecological Impact		
	Natural Resources Conservation/Depletion	Pollution Reduce/Increase	Environment Enhance/Detract
Exploitation Mining, agriculture, fisheries	BENEFITS Stimulate demand for substitutes and new primary materials such as aluminum, fiberglass reduces demand for copper and wood, thus conserving relatively scarce resources. Stimulate demands for culturally alien foods. People in poor economies fail to recognize as food, nutrients in abundant supply (e.g., wheat in China).	Recycling programs (e.g., returnable glass bottles, newspaper collection drives) to eliminate inorganic fertilizer wastes, entrophication of lakes and rivers.	Organize used materials' recycling of industrial wastes. Promote organic fertilizers to reduce environmental stress.
	COSTS Demand stimulation to sell petroleum products for leisure sports equipment: power boats, skimobiles, etc.	Promotion of phosphate inorganic fertilizer for organic fertilizer, stimulate demand for high sulfur fossil fuels.	Promote sale of high protein meat-producing animals with low conversion efficiency fed on growth-inducing antibiotic drugs.
Substitution Introduction of materials in artifacts	BENEFITS Organize supply-demand market price allocation mechanism to encourage recycling (e.g., reused fibers, newspapers, scrap metals, trapped chemical particulates). Develop biodegradable plastic packages.	Stimulate demands for nonpolluting substitutes (e.g., bicycles for motorcycles, electric-powered mass transit for cars, using internal combustion engine).	Stimulate demands for economically benign consumption substitutes for food additives, medication, cigarettes, promote recyclable paper work clothing.
	COSTS Substitution of furs and hides of endangered species (e.g., alligators) in style goods.	Substitute tobacco products and drug therapy for mental hygiene programs.	Substitute food additives in convenience foods for home preparation to reduce frequent delivery of perishable foods.

		BENEFITS / COSTS		
Engineering (BENEFITS)	Design physical distribution networks to minimize capital-intensive transportation facilities (e.g., substitute flexible intermodal carriers) by optimal cost revenue relationships.	Allocate physical distribution method on basis of low pollution, low cost rail for low value/high bulk shipments. Design supply depot facilities to minimize distance traveled by consumers and maximize handling economies.	Design retail shopping facility location to minimize disruption of natural systems (e.g., minimize disruption of watersheds for airports and shopping centers). Land use planning to fit human habitation into natural environment.
Drawing resources from one ecosystem to another (COSTS)	Design physical distribution networks for automobile access with maximum feasible parking areas adjacent to stores.	Design high-powered cars using large engines to give consumer feeling of power and mastery over objects.	Design shopping centers to maximize traffic flow on suburban highways requiring maximum utilization of natural valley systems, wetlands, etc., where construction and acquisition costs are minimal.
Design (BENEFITS)	Devise lease-rental systems for collective use of capital-intensive appliances and scarce amenities such as lake shore properties.	Design biodegradable and reusable packages.	Promote family planning, "shrinkmanship," demarketing, and demand reduction.
Planning to meet psychological requirements (COSTS)	Installment selling of second summer homes on lake sites in natural forest reserves.	Increase availability of electric appliances to promote convenience in household chores. Design nonbiodegradable packages for easy use rather than for recycling. Design style obsolescence into clothing, appliances, and homes, to promote fashion change.	Introduce new technology whenever it promises cost reduction or increase in sales potential. Stimulate demands for electricity, appliances, and fuels in short supply.

To achieve this symbiotic relationship with the human environment, ecologists now recommend sharing resources that require high capital investment, or relatively infrequent or irregular use. For example, we have rental cars, rental clothes, condominiums, and time payment plans for even such simple things as household furnishings.[9] Rental economics could easily promote a lack of individual responsibility and consequent wasteful use of resources. Forrester has termed this situation "the counterintuitive behavior of social systems," meaning that the results are unexpected and undesired.[10] Consumer responsibility indexes ultimately must include measures of these ecologically undesirable counterintuitive behaviors. The marketing and economic professions should prescribe sound and simple remedies and indicators. Price rationing, for example, can be used to curb demands for irreplaceable resources to promote the sharing of capital-intensive resources.

From an ecological perspective, a dominant marketing strategy may involve the development of recycling markets, the allocation of consumption goods by conventional prices buttressed by institutional cost-price constraints on pollution and frivolous consumption, the demarketing of irreplaceable resources, and the pooling of capital-intensive consumption through the extension of leasing-rental agreements. Taken together, such marketing activities are "good" ecologically, and performance indicators already in existence can measure their ecological impact.

NeoLuddite and NeoMalthusian Antigrowth Economists

The Luddites, it may be remembered, destroyed English textile machinery and stocking frames that made their labor superfluous.[11] Technological dislocations can be dealt with by retraining workers and by barring unintended social disamenities which result from the introduction of new technology. Forstalling the introduction of technology that may create disamenities, such as pollution and resource depletion, is the method advocated by economist Mishan for achieving zero economic growth. He argues that the quality of life is currently declining, but even Mishan does not believe that zero economic growth will happen in the near future. Social costs are increasing much more rapidly today than the social benefits produced by new technology. By curtailing consumption of "plastic junk," he hopes to reverse this relationship. His critics assert that Misham is claiming that "less is really more," in calling for zero growth.[12]

Those concerned with the multiplier effect of rising population and rising income ask, "what if one billion Chinese enjoyed the standard of living available to U.S. consumers?"[13] Under current conditions, many of the zero-growth exponents are pessimistic about the possibility of slowing the ecological impact of human activities. These NeoMalthusians and the systems dynamicists represented by Forrester and Meadows also see population control as the only reasonable prospect for human survival.[14] Using computer simulations based on alternative assumptions about natural resources, capital investment, population, pollution, and quality of life, these men predict ecological disaster based on growing population with diminishing resources. The central theme of the Forrester-Meadows models is that population, pollution, consumption of nonrenewable resources, and industrial output display exponential growth, while technology and food production are assumed to grow at a linear rate.

Beckwith asserts that Forrester's assumptions are false or dubious.[15] Specifically, he charges that additional food has not increased the birth rate in western countries during the past 150 years, as Forrester assumes. Forrester also assumes that the rate of capital investment increases with an increased stand-

---

[9] Same reference as footnote 7, p. 714.

[10] Jay Forrester, "Counterintuitive Behavior of Social Systems," *Technology Review* (January, 1971), pp. 53–68.

[11] Wade Green and Soma Long, "The Luddites Were Not All Wrong," *New York Times Magazine* (November 21, 1971), p. 40 ff.

[12] Peter Passell and Leonard Ross, "Don't Knock the $2 Trillion Economy," *New York Times Magazine* (March 5, 1972), p. 14.

[13] Dennis Pirages and Paul R. Ehrlich, "If All Chinese Had Wheels," *The New York Times* (March 16, 1972), p. 47.

[14] Jay Forrester, *World Dynamics* (Cambridge: Wright Allen Press, 1971); and Donella Meadows, et al., *The Limits to Growth* (New York: Universe Books, 1972).

[15] Burnham Beckwith, "The Predicament of Man: A Reply," *The Futurist,* Vol. 6 (April, 1972), pp. 62–64.

ard of living, when in fact the highest invest-ment rates are in relatively poor countries. In the U.S., the rate of investment has fallen, rather than risen, during the past 100 years. Beckwith disagrees with Forrester's assump-tion that capital investment increases pollu-tion, which in turn decreases food production. Beckwith maintains that further capital in-vestment is badly needed to *reduce* pollution and *increase* food output.

The condemnation of the Forrester-Meadows computer view of "doomsday" agrees with those of the antigrowth econo-mists and many ecologists. If the methods and conclusions of world dynamics research are in error, its critics find it very difficult to provide alternative answers to the same ques-tions. If the Forrester remedy of keeping poor people out of cities and freezing the consump-tion levels of underdeveloped nations is not accepted,[16] what alternatives can economic development advocates recommend, given the finite resource and space constraints of our planet? These questions are far from academic.

Economic Development Viewpoint

If the questions posed by the zero eco-nomic growth and zero population growth proponents are difficult for advocates of eco-nomic development to answer, their response provides a rationale for measures of "good" as a high gross national product and absence of poverty. In view of the challenges posed by ecologists and zero-growth advocates, the ad-vantages of growth are worth restating.

Polling institutes around the country indi-cate that people with high incomes are healthier and more satisfied with life. Growth is the means for attaining more income per capita. Economic growth may be defined as the per capita increase in real assets after depreciation of existing assets. Both the U.S. and the USSR have grown, but economic growth alone is not responsible for materialism in the U.S. nor regimentation in the USSR. Limiting economic growth will reduce the material standard of living, but it will not change the social values or solve the social problems for which zero rowth is proposed as a remedy. Passell and Ross assert that:

Pollution . . . doesn't come from growth but from our perverse system of incentives to in-dustry. Today firms aren't charged for using the biosphere as a dumping ground, so they poison the air and foul the water; any re-source for which no charge is made would be overused by business. . . Since nobody is charged by using the environment, its value is ignored. The answer is not to stop aiming for growth but to start charging for pollu-tion.[17]

Growth facilitates the ideological drive to-ward economic equality. The 19th century income pyramid, with most Americans on the bottom and less than 1% at the top, has been transformed to the current income dis-tribution with most of the population in the middle. By 1990, U.S. income distribution is predicted to be an inverted pyramid, with relatively few households below the $3,000 poverty line. In 1932, Franklin Roosevelt won the presidential elections by vowing to deal with the third of the nation that was ill-clothed, ill-housed, and ill-fed. The poverty proportion in the U.S. has since declined to one tenth. Would anyone in any nation be happier to consume less? It is doubtful at best. Would they be healthier? Infant mor-tality and other health statistics suggest that while the association between income and health is not one to one, the correlation be-tween better health and higher income is strongly positive.

In the U.S., the President's Council on Environmental Quality acknowledges that:

Our society needs more goods and services of many kinds; better housing; improved mass transportation; more adequate facilities for health and education, and increased pollution control. It is likely that funds for such invest-ment will not come from the cutback in pro-duction of cosmetics, for instance, but from an overall increase national output. More-over, a reduction in growth would result in a severe blow to the aspirations of the eco-nomically disadvantaged, especially minority groups . . . looking at the total environment of the nation it seems probable that direct attempts to reduce GNP growth would create many more problems than they would solve.[18]

The U.S. consumes more than one-third of the world's nonrenewable natural resources, yet

[16] Jay Forrester, "Should We Save Our Cities?" *Business and Society Review*, Vol. 1 (Spring, 1972), pp. 57–62.

[17] Same reference as footnote 12, pp. 64 and 68.
[18] U.S. Council on Environmental Quality, *An-nual Report, 1970,* Washington, D.C., pp. 154–155.

its population comprises only 6% of the world's total.

Growth can promote long-run human survival as well as imperil it. For example, an increase in houses produces more garbage, but more garbage can be reprocessed into oil, fuel for electrical energy, and other needed services. Similarly, by recycling the increased volume of sewage produced by new housing developments, land destroyed by strip mining can be reclaimed for farming. Developing nations can use technological knowledge to raise the standards of living and improve their quality of life. Just as U.S. consumption of dwindling but irreplaceable resources must decline, the entire world will increasingly substitute nuclear or nonpolluting solar energy for fossil power sources, plastics for metals, and shale-derived fuels for natural gas and oil. As in earlier years, the solution to poverty is not to make the rich less productive, but to use the technological knowledge and financial resources of the rich to make the poor more productive.

Technology, so widely condemned, is simply a tool for wresting from nature the kinds of life humans desire. If applied simply because it is feasible, technology can yield unwanted "bad" consequences, but if applied to accomplish rational consumption priorities in a responsible fashion, it can clearly produce "good" benefits. The technology of product planning, packaging, promotion and physical distribution—marketing in short—is capable of accelerating economic growth in impoverished nations, while sustaining high but not irresponsible mass consumption in advanced economies. Whether marketing accomplishes this goal depends on how managers perceive the goals to be sought.

MANAGERIAL APPLICATIONS

Marketing managers can use the theory of responsible consumption as a guide to marketing policy even though they do not have social performance indicators against which to adapt to their operational environment. Environmental benefits and costs can be estimated in a gross fashion for every change in packaging, product design, promotional campaign or physical distribution facility. As in the case of the SST and the Cross Florida Barge Canal, the project should be cancelled if the costs greatly exceed the benefits, even if relatively

large sums have been spent in program development.

The three major categories of environmental costs and benefits in Table 1 are consistent with provisions of the National Environmental Protection Act (NEPA). NEPA requires federal agencies to consider environmental impact in *all* their planning and decision making. Just as firms meeting federal military procurement contracts are required to use planning, programming, and budgeting the Environmental Protection Agency has the power to halt interstate shipments of products hazardous to humans and animals.[19] In the future, other federal and state governmental agencies may acquire the power to compel marketers to strictly observe ecological imperatives. Hence, self-regulation is simply prudent management to forestall added environmental constraints on marketing freedom.

Self-regulation indicators of gross environmental impact should lead to more effective corporate decisions than no calculations at all. For example, a firm is contemplating the elimination of advertising that is more effective than all of its other advertising, but is subject to substantial negative public opinion. This negative opinion might stem from social considerations alone (e.g., promotes tobacco addiction, burdens ghetto residents with excessive installment debt), but in almost all cases the side effects will include specific environmental impacts. Even if the environmental impact is totally beyond measurement, an incidence map resembling Table 1 can be constructed to show positive, neutral, and negative consequences. Delphic projections of future benefits and costs can be estimated by an executive group or a panel of consultants including responsible community representatives summoned to produce an assessment of the contemplated action. After several assessments, marketing managers can begin to construct social performance indicators for pilot testing against social and environmental criteria of "good" and "bad."

These new social indicators are urgently needed to provide more precise feedback of aroused public opinion. Public opinion supports legislative and administrative actions

---

[19] "Environmental Quality," *The Second Annual Report of the Council on Environmental Quality* (Washington, D.C.: U.S. Government Printing Office, August, 1971), p. 115.

that are not always capable of achieving the desired marketing and environmental results. Social indicators must be holistic, embracing the entire social system, rather than a single purpose as are measures of profit and market share. The economic viewpoint, so long dominated by cost reduction, is gradually yielding to the holistic view of ecological interdependence. The redefinition and measurement of consumption behavior in ecological systems terms thus provides a challenge to marketing theory and measurement that will extend far beyond our lifetimes, but the *theory of responsible consumption* gives managers a tool for starting this formidable task. The appalling alternatives to this effort are documented in alarming scientific reports.[20]

---

[20] "U.S. Urged to Curb Use of Resources," *The New York Times* (October 5, 1972), p. 31.

63. Marketing and Economic Performance: Meaning and Measurement

ROBERT D. BUZZELL*

The problems of defining and measuring the economic performance of companies and industries, and the relationship of performance to marketing practices, are anything but new. Economists have been debating the subject since the late 18th century, and are no closer to agreement on it now than they were then. Much later, when marketing emerged as a separate field of study, some of the earliest writings in the field dealt with marketing costs and marketing "efficiency"—key aspects of economic performance.[1]

THE NEED FOR IMPROVED CONCEPTS AND MEASURES

So much has been said and written on marketing and economic performance that it is very difficult to offer any new ideas on the subject. In spite of this, the need for improved concepts and for additional empirical information is greater than at any time in the recent past. Questions about the impact of market structure and marketing practices on performance have returned to "center stage," primarily because of the increasingly active posture of the Federal Trade Commission, other regulatory agencies, and Congressional committees, toward business. During 1971 and the first half of 1972, hardly a week has passed without the announcement of a new investigation or complaint by some Federal committee or agency. In almost every case, these complaints and investigations involve alleged or suspected effects of business practices on economic performance. Proposed remedies—ranging from corrective advertising for Profile Bread to the broad "de-concentration" of oligopolistic industries recommended by the so-called Neal report in 1968—are put forth as means of improving performance.

If the improvement of economic performance is to be a major goal of public policy, not just in a philosophical sense but also as an operational standard for judging individual cases, then it is essential that we develop meaningful concepts of performance and that we apply these concepts as fully and objectively as possible to specific situations. In my opinion, current practice—both in academic research and in regulatory agencies—is seriously deficient at both the conceptual and the empirical level. The concepts of "performance" used in research on industrial organization and marketing are varied, almost always incomplete, and they are usually applied in a highly selective fashion. The em-

* The author acknowledges the valuable assistance of Michael Pearce in the preparation of this paper. The viewpoints expressed herein are strictly the author's, and do not necessarily reflect those of his associates in the Marketing Science Institute.

[1] Some examples appear in Fred E. Clark, *Readings in Marketing* (New York, Macmillan Company, 1924). See especially the sections on "Elements of Marketing Efficiency," pp. 634–53, and "The Cost of Marketing," pp. 654–63.

◆ SOURCE: Reprinted by permission from *Public Policy and Marketing Practices*, edited by Fred C. Allvine, Published by the American Marketing Association, Chicago, 1973, pp. 143–159.

pirical data available to measure performance are grossly inadequate and, to make matters worse, are manipulated by researchers in such a way that almost any conclusion can be derived from the same set of figures.

This state of affairs has important consequences for marketing, because public policy is increasingly concerned with the impact of marketing practices on performance. In a series of recent cases and investigations, the FTC has raised questions about the impact of "high" rates of advertising expenditure on prices and profits; the consequences of "product proliferation"; the extent of scale economies in advertising and promotion; and the aggregate effects of advertising on society. These and other current public policy controversies all deal directly with market practices. Since a basic goal of public policy regarding marketing is to benefit consumers by improving performance, policy makers must base their decisions on some assumption about how performance might be affected by a proposed new policy or by a given disposition of an individual case.

I have suggested that the concepts and measures of performance that are currently used to evaluate marketing practices are inadequate. Although this may be self-evident to everyone who has been exposed to recent literature on the subject, it may nevertheless be useful to review briefly the main concepts and measures that have been used or suggested, and to point out some of their shortcomings. Following this review, I shall offer some propositions which might (if accepted) provide at least a partial basis for the design and application of more satisfactory performance measures.

ALTERNATIVE CONCEPTS OF "PERFORMANCE"

A listing of concepts of economic performance is given in Exhibit 1. This listing is not intended to be exhaustive—it emphasizes the dimensions of performance that are thought to be most directly related to *marketing*. In addition, I have omitted one element of performance—ethical practices—which seems to me to be separable from the others and about which I think there is little or no real controversy.[2]

As indicated in Exhibit 1, one reason for the diversity of performance concepts is that they have been developed by several different *types* of academic investigators, who have approached the subject from different viewpoints and with different purposes. Agricultural economists, and many marketing investigators, have been concerned primarily with describing and analyzing the institutional systems for marketing specific products, the functions performed by those systems, and the marketing *costs* involved. A closely related approach, exemplified by the work of the National Bureau of Economic Research, emphasizes the *productivity* of marketing institutions and industries as a primary dimension of performance. Industrial organization economists, in a series of studies carried out primarily during the past 20 years, have focused on company and industry *profits* as a measure of performance, while giving some attention also to marketing costs, especially advertising expenditures, and to various measures of innovation or "progressiveness."

None of these types of performance measures is, by itself, fully satisfactory for purposes of evaluating public policy issues. Although there is an extensive literature dealing with all of these concepts of performance and with the problems of applying them, it may be useful to review the strengths and weaknesses of each type of measure.[3]

Marketing Costs

For centuries, philosophers, politicians, and economists have condemned the "unproductive" activities of middlemen and the costs associated with those activities. At least since the late 19th Century, systematic studies have been made of "marketing costs and margins" for various agricultural products. A basic premise underlying much of the concern with marketing costs is that marketing adds little or no "real value" to physical products; hence, the lower the total marketing cost for a product, the better. One especially narrow interpretation even includes food processing as part of "marketing."[4]

---

[2] For a more complete classification of performance concepts, see Stephen H. Sosnick, "Operational Criteria for Evaluating Market Performance," Chapter 6 in Paul Farris (ed.), *Market Structure Research* (Ames, Iowa, Iowa State University Press, 1964).

[3] *Ibid.*

[4] Cf. Theodore N. Beckman and Robert D. Buzzell, "What is the Marketing Margin for Agricultural Products?," *Journal of Marketing*, October, 1955, pp. 166–68.

Performance Dimensions	Measures	Used or Suggested By
MORE OR LESS TRADITIONAL MEASURES		
MARKETING COSTS	—total for economy —total for institution or channel —advertising/promotion	agricultural economists marketing researchers industrial orgn. economists
PRODUCTIVITY/ EFFICIENCY	—physical volume or value added/labor input	National Bureau of Economic Research govt. agencies
PROFITS	—return on assets rel. to "normal" rates	industrial orgn. economists
INNOVATION, PROGRESSIVENESS	—R&D expenditures, personnel, patents —number, sales of new products	industrial orgn. economists
FLEXIBILITY, CHOICE	—alternatives available —changes in available	—
RECENTLY ADDED ENTRIES		
NATIONAL ECONOMIC GOALS (such as full employment, equitable income distribution etc.)	(?)	—
"SOCIAL INDICATORS" (such as environmental quality)	(?)	—

EXHIBIT 1. Major types of economic performance measures.

If marketing, however defined, is regarded as contributing nothing to the final value or utility of end products, then total marketing cost is a natural measure of one important dimension of economic performance.

It has long been recognized, however, that marketing *does* add value to products—and that the nature and extent of that value differ among industries, and change over time in a given industry. As a result, comparisons of marketing cost levels are of little value in appraising performance except under very restrictive assumptions about the comparability of marketing tasks performed in different industries or from one time period to another.

Although total marketing cost is no longer often advocated as a measure of economic performance, one component of marketing cost—promotional cost—is singled out for special attention, especially by industrial organization economists. In recent studies, sales promotion costs and activities have been viewed in three different but related ways:

—*as an element of "market structure,"* i.e., as one of the characteristics of an industry that governs the behavior of firms and, ultimately, affects their economic performance. For example, according to the Federal Trade Commission's 1969 *Economic Report* on food manufacturing companies, advertising is ". . . one of the major sources of entry barriers into consumer products industries."[5] The theory is that advertising, along with other entry barriers, shields the companies in such industries as breakfast cereals, soft drinks, and soaps and detergents, from the competition of new entrants, and this permits them to charge higher prices and earn higher profits than would otherwise be possible.

---

[5] *Economic Report on the Influence of Market Structure on the Profit Performance of Food Manufacturing Companies.* Staff Report to the Federal Trade Commission (Washington, U.S. Government Printing Office, 1969), p. 11.

—as a dimension of "market conduct." According to the model of business behavior generally used by industrial organization economists, patterns of business conduct or behavior are largely determined by market structure. In oligopolistic industries, it is argued, there is a strong tendency to avoid price competition and a corresponding tendency to spend heavily on efforts to achieve product differentiation—reflected in high levels of sales promotion.

—as one measure of economic performance. To many economists, expenditures for advertising and other forms of sales promotion in and of themselves constitute "poor performance." The FTC's complaint against the cereal industry, for example, stresses the fact that the cereal producers spent 13% of their sales on advertising in 1970.[6] In this and other criticisms of particular industries, there is an implicit or explicit comparison of actual expenditures with some "reasonable" level, beyond which the costs of promotion are assumed to represent wasted resources.

The treatment of advertising and sales promotion in the literature of industrial organization, and especially the common assumption that a high level of promotional spending is synonymous with "product differentiation," illustrates the ambiguity of the basic structure-conduct-performance model used by economists in this field. If "structure," "conduct," and "performance" are supposed to be logically distinct concepts, how can sales promotion be an element of all three?[7] There is obviously an internal contradiction, or at least a series of important untested assumptions, in the theory as far as sales promotion is concerned. But, for purposes of the subject of this paper, our main concern is with the validity of using measures of sales promotional expenditures, per se, as indicators of performance.

In my opinion, the current emphasis on sales promotion costs, and even more specifically on advertising expenditures, is even less defensible than the earlier use of total marketing costs as an indicator of performance.

Economists focus on advertising expenditures, apparently, for two reasons. One is the traditional aversion of educated persons for the "vulgar, childish" content and presentation of most advertising messages. The other is the simple fact that advertising expenditure data are collected and published by the Internal Revenue Service for industry groups, which permits their use in conjunction with Census and other published statistics. Mere availability has led to extensive and—in my view—often very dubious analyses of the role of advertising.

The main flaw in recent studies of advertising is, as every student of marketing recognizes, the fact that advertising is just one element of a set of closely related factors that comprise the "marketing mix" for a product or company. As I pointed out in testifying at the Federal Trade Commission hearings on Modern Advertising Practices last fall,

. . . advertising is an integral part of the marketing process and can seldom be isolated from other components of this process . . . the role of advertising varies greatly among industries, products, and companies.

[Overall,] the cost of advertising [in 1970] represented only about 10% of total marketing costs.[8]

The estimates that I prepared for the FTC hearings indicated that even within the communications component of marketing, advertising expenditures amount to about three-eighths of total costs, i.e., of the combined total of advertising, personal selling, and sales promotion.

Although most economists recognize that advertising expenditure is an incomplete measure of marketing activity, or even of marketing communication effort, many nevertheless proceed to treat it as if it were a sufficient indicator of the extent to which resources are "wasted" in particular cases. Economists are almost unanimous in condemning high advertising-to-sales ratios for individual companies or industries as prima facie evidence that their performance is unsatisfactory. The author of one leading text asks, for example,

[6] The text of the FTC complaint was reported in Advertising Age, January 31, 1972, p. 78.

[7] This point is discussed in Appraising the Economic and Social Effects of Advertising, Marketing Science Institute Staff Report (Cambridge, Mass., 1971), Chapter 3.

[8] R. D. Buzzell, "The Role of Advertising in the Marketing Mix," Presentation to the Federal Trade Commission Hearings on Modern Advertising Practices, reproduced as a Marketing Science Institute working paper, October, 1971.

Were the users of deodorants, pain remedies, hair bleach, and similar products benefited because Bristol-Myers devoted 28 percent of its 1966 sales revenues to advertising?[9]

I suggest that this is a meaningless question as long as attention is confined only to advertising. If, as the question implies, we are supposed to compare Bristol-Myers and other firms with high advertising-to-sales ratios with other companies or industries that spent much less on advertising, then should we not also compare their other marketing costs? May not high levels of spending on advertising, at least in some cases, permit offsetting reductions in the costs of personal selling and sales promotion and/or in trade margins? And, conversely, are there not many cases in which firms spend small percentages of their sales on advertising but nevertheless have high total marketing costs? (Electrolux and Avon Cosmetics are two prime cases in point! Both of these firms have low advertising-to-sales ratios —under 2%—but spend substantial fractions of sales on personal selling.)

A major obstacle to overcoming the present selective emphasis on advertising is, of course, the lack of data for other elements of marketing costs—especially manufacturers' marketing costs.[10] But this does not excuse us from recognizing the relationships between advertising and other elements of marketing, nor does it give any greater validity to conclusions based on analyses of advertising data. If additional data are needed to support public policy decisions, let us at least try to get the data rather than proceeding as if we could get along without it.

Productivity[11]

As noted in the preceding section, one inherent limitation in the use of *costs* as a measure of performance—for marketing or any other economic activity—is that some assumption must be made about what benefits or

values are created in return for a given outlay. Conceptually, a much more satisfactory approach is to consider *costs and results together*. This is the basic idea underlying measures of productivity for industries, companies, or activities.

Productivity measures are widely used in analyzing performance and determining public policies with regard to *manufacturing* industries—as illustrated by their current application to administering the "Phase II" restrictions on price changes. The standard approach is to measure an industry's "output" in terms of physical units produced, and to relate this to labor inputs (man-hours) or, in some cases, to combined input of capital and labor. Even for manufacturing industries, a shortcoming of this approach is that there is no good way to measure or adjust for changes in the *services* provided along with a "unit" of product.[12] There is probably nothing wrong with ignoring these types of changes over short periods of time, say two or three years, but in the longer run the intangible components provided along with a product—including marketing services—may change substantially. There is no good way to incorporate measures of services into manufacturing productivity measures as they are currently constructed.

Still less is there any satisfactory way, as yet, to apply productivity measures to "service" industries, including marketing. The most ambitious attempt to estimate productivity trends in marketing was Harold Barger's study for the National Bureau of Economic Research, published in the mid-1950's.[13] Barger measured the "output" of marketing institutions in terms of the physical volume of goods handled, weighted by combined retail and wholesale margins. In broad terms, the use of margins as weights allows for changing services provided over time; conceptually, it is similar to the use of aggregate *value added* as a measure of output.[14] There is, however,

[9] F. M. Scherer, *Industrial Market Structure and Performance* (Chicago, Rand McNally & Co., 1970), p. 325.

[10] Some effort is now being made to obtain marketing cost data. See Earl L. Bailey, "Manufacturers' Marketing Costs," *Conference Board Record*, October, 1971, pp. 58–64.

[11] Much of this section is based on Robert D. Buzzell, *Productivity in Marketing*, unpublished doctoral dissertation, The Ohio State University, 1957.

[12] Another complex problem is that of changes in the quality, design, and composition of a product. But I have nothing new to add on this subject.

[13] Harold Barger, *Distribution's Place in the American Economy Since 1869*, National Bureau of Economic Research (Princeton, N.J., Princeton University Press, 1955).

[14] Theodore N. Beckman, "The Value Added Concept as Applied to Marketing and Its Implications," in S. H. Rewoldt (ed.), *Frontiers in Marketing Thought*, Proceedings, American Mar-

a serious objection to this approach. If we measure the output of marketing institutions or activities in terms of dollar revenues received *for* those activities, we must make some assumption about the extent of competition among firms that provide the services. Otherwise, it could be argued that firms could increase their "output"—and thus their performance—simply by increasing prices, perhaps in conjunction with increased expenditures on "valueless" promotional activities. In the absence of any "physical" measures of services provided by marketing, there is no way to distinguish between true increases in output and monopolistic exploitation or plain waste.

In view of this, it is perhaps not surprising that little attention has been given to productivity in recent public policy controversies about industry performance. For example, no mention is made of productivity in the FTC complaint against the breakfast cereal industry. Although this may be understandable, we may question whether productivity—however imperfectly measured—deserves to be ignored altogether.

Profits

In recent studies by industrial organization economists, the most popular measure of performance—indeed, almost the *sole* measure—has been the *profits* earned by industries or companies. The theory underlying use of profit as a performance measure has been discussed extensively, and need not be repeated here.[15] I should, however, like to touch on just two of the many problems that arise in using profits as an indicator of performance.

One major problem, which has received some attention by students of industrial organization, is the relationship between profits and *innovation.* An industry or a firm may earn high profits, it has been suggested, because of successful innovation rather than because market power enables it to exact monopoly returns. This points of special importance in any discussion of the relationship between performance and marketing practices, because there is a well-established connection between product innovation and some key dimensions of marketing strategies. In particular, my own studies of the food industry—and other research on other industries—shows that expenditures for selling and advertising are much higher for relatively new products than for established products.[16] There is also reason to believe that profits are greater for relatively new products, although the period of maximum profitability no doubt follows that of maximum promotional effort.

If the foregoing is a valid picture of general relationships among innovation, marketing activity, and profits, then the statistical association between advertising levels and profits, which has been reported in several studies, may not always be an indication of market power based on a product differentiation entry barrier. It may, instead, reflect the underlying association between both advertising *and* profits and product innovation. Some investigators have attempted to deal with this by using measures of overall industry sales growth as one of the factors explaining interindustry differences in profits.[17] The trouble with this is that an industry's *aggregate* rate of growth is a very poor measure of the extent of new product activity, much of which may consist of new models or product variations which *replace* established versions, rather than of increased total demand. There is a clear need for more and better statistical information about the new product activities of firms and industries. As in the case of marketing costs, the fact that such information is not presently available is no excuse for jumping to conclusions that might be materially altered if innovation were effectively taken into account.

keting Association Conference, December, 1954 (Bloomington, Ind., Bureau of Business Research, Indiana Univ., 1955) pp. 83–99.

[15] A standard reference is J. S. Bain, *Industrial Organization,* 2nd ed. (New York, John Wiley & Sons, 1968). One leading empirical study is N. R. Collins and L. E. Preston, *Concentration and Price-Cost Margins in Manufacturing Industries* (Los Angeles, Univ. of California Press, 1968).

[16] R. D. Buzzell, "Comparative Behavior and Product Life Cycles," in J. S. Wright and J. L. Goldstucker (eds.) *New Ideas for Successful Marketing,* Proceedings, 1966 World Congress, American Marketing Association (Chicago, 1966), pp. 46–68. Cf. also William E. Cox, Jr., "Product Life Cycles as Marketing Models," *Journal of Business,* October, 1967, pp. 375–84.

[17] William S. Comanor and Thomas A. Wilson, "Advertising, Market Structure, and Performance," *The Review of Economics and Statistics,* Vol. XLIX (November, 1967), pp. 423–40.

A second observation regarding profit as a performance measure is more philosophical. The implication of the "neo-orthodox" economic theory regarding profit and market structure is that a high level of profit is, with some exceptions, "bad"—in the sense that it adversely affects consumer welfare. Meanwhile, virtually every marketing textbook states, or strongly implies, that there is a strong *positive* relationship between a firm's profit results and the degree to which it enhances consumer satisfaction through effective implementation of the marketing concept. Is this simply pro-Establishment, conventional wisdom? Are marketing educators deceiving themselves and their students on a massive scale by sugar-coating the true nature of profits? Or is it possible that the industrial organization model is based on such a narrow conception of performance, focussing on "allocative efficiency" to the virtual exclusion of everything else, that it is unsuitable as a primary basis for public policy? Most likely, the truth is somewhere between these two extremes.

Innovation and "Progressiveness"

As mentioned earlier, one of the major weaknesses of profit as a performance measure, recognized even by industrial organization purists, is uncertainty about its relationship to innovation. Most observers agree that innovation itself is a good thing, and that public policy should encourage it—or, at least, not discourage it.

There are two major qualifications to the otherwise unanimous endorsement of innovation. First, there is increasing concern with the indirect effects of *some* innovations on the environment. For this reason, one-way soft drink containers, aerosol sprays, and some other packaging innovations are viewed by many as having negative net effects on society. Because of the "loose coupling" between individual purchase decisions and their delayed, diffused effects on the environment, it seems unlikely that the market system can operate in a self-correcting fashion in this area.

A second qualification regarding innovation is that most observers cannot resist the temptation to inject into their appraisals their own opinions about the relative merits or shortcomings of particular new products. Thus, many new drug products have been dismissed by critics of the industry as "mere molecular manipulations," rather than "real" innovations. In a similar fashion, the costs of automobile style changes have long been condemned by critics, especially in the "tail-fin" era of the late 1950's.

The most recent illustration of this penchant to pick and choose among innovations appears in the FTC's complaint against the breakfast cereal industry. The Commission staff noted that the companies in the industry have been active in developing and introducing new brands. They did not, however, view this innovation as a possible partial explanation of, or mitigation of, the high levels of profits and advertising expenditures which were the principal target of the complaint. Instead, the repeated introduction of new cereal brands was cited as one of the methods used by the companies to discourage potential new entrants and thereby protect their entrenched positions. Presumably the Commission staff views the new cereal product parade as yielding little if any "real" benefit to consumers.

The danger of a "Big Brother" attitude in the treatment of product innovation is obvious. If personal judgments are to determine which innovations are applauded and which ones are condemned, *whose* judgments are to govern? There is plenty of room for disagreement on individual cases among men of good will, even among those with graduate degrees in economics, business, and the social sciences.

Needless to say, virtually all businessmen object violently to the *obiter dicta* of educators, politicians, and writers on the subject of new products. As an alternative, most executives—and probably most business school teachers, too—would argue that the only valid test of a new product's value is the test of market acceptance or rejection. If a sufficient number of consumers are willing to buy a new cereal brand, or a feminine deodorant spray, or a Pocket Instamatic camera, then this in itself shows that the consumers have judged the value as being sufficient to justify the cost involved.

If we assume a freely competitive market and a "reasonably" informed consumer, then the reasoning underlying the preceding paragraph is absolutely correct. But, say many economists, there are two flaws in the argument. First, the consumer does *not* truly have free choice—he can only choose among the alternatives that business elects to provide. Second, the consumer is so heavily influenced by advertising that he cannot make intelligent choices. Because of these limitations on the free functioning of the market system, say the critics, the fact that new products are accepted by consumers cannot be interpreted as evidence of an improvement in consumer satisfaction.

To sum up this brief discussion of innovation, I have suggested that available measures of innovation leave much to be desired, and should be improved. But better data will not resolve the more fundamental issue of appraising the "value" or "significance" of specific product changes; for this, some new conceptual thinking is needed.

Flexibility and Choice

A proposition on which I think most businessmen *and* most academicians would agree is that the performance of an industry or company is higher, other things being equal, to the degree that it provides *choice* to customers and to the degree that it manifests *flexibility* in altering its offerings response to changes in demand. Although flexibility and choice are recognized as important, very little has been done to develop *measures* of this performance dimension. References to the subject are confined primarily to expressions of opinion about how much choice the consumer does or doesn't have in a particular situation.

A few economists have also expressed the view that *overall*, the range of choice has tended to diminish during the past 25 years. Writing in 1960, Tibor Scitovsky alleged that there has been a ". . . secular increase in the uniformity and [a] decline in the range of products in almost every field."[18] It is hard to imagine how anyone could arrive at such a conclusion, in the face of overwhelming visual evidence to the contrary in virtually every type of retail store. A more plausible contention, however, is that new products may diminish consumer choice to the extent that older products are removed from the market —especially if lower-priced "basic" products are eliminated. It is not possible to determine, in any systematic way, the extent to which this happens—for the usual reason that data

have not been compiled systematically. But there are some indications that the introduction of new product types generally *increases* the range of consumer choice.

William Moran, Director of Marketing Research at Lever Brothers, recently presented some interesting "case studies" of the impact of product innovation in some 20 consumer product markets, including both durables and "packaged products."[19] For durable goods, Moran analyzed the number of models and the range of prices offered in six appliance categories in the Sears, Roebuck catalog in 1950, as compared with 1970. In *every case,* he found that the 1970 catalog offered a greater variety of models and types than were available in 1950. Moreover, in every case but one (phonographs), a model was available in 1970 at a price equal to or lower than the lowest 1950 price, despite the fact that the prices were *not* adjusted to constant dollar equivalents.

Comparing 1970 offerings with those of 1960 for a series of non-durable products such as deodorants, toilet soaps, sandwich bags, and margarine, Moran showed that in each case, new product types were introduced; and, in each case, average prices (this time, adjusted by the Consumer Price Index) of the new types declined following introduction, while older product types continued to be available.

Moran's sample of product categories is not as large as one might like, and it would be very useful to expand his study to a much larger coverage. But his findings do suggest that consumers have a wider range of choice today than they did 10 or 20 years ago. In turn, this implies that innovation has not typically been offset by an elimination of alternatives formerly available.

Other Performance Dimensions

Two additional dimensions of economic performance are suggested in Exhibit 1: the contribution of an industry or company to national economic goals, such as full employment and an equitable distribution of income; and its contribution to "other social goals,"

[18] Tibor Scitovsky, "A Critique of Present and Proposed Standards," *American Economic Review,* Vol. 50, May, 1960, (Supplement) pp. 13–20.

[19] William T. Moran, "Where There is Choice There is Value," Presentation to the Annual Scientific Meeting of the Society of Cosmetic Chemists, New York, December 14, 1971 (mimeographed paper).

such as a clean environment or racial equality. There has been much discussion recently of the need to consider these factors, along with more traditional economic dimensions of performance, in formulating public policies. I support this viewpoint strongly. But for obvious reasons these "macro" dimensions of performance are even more elusive than the more familiar economic ones, and I am not aware of any real progress in the effort to devise measures that can meaningfully be applied to comparisons among industries or of historical trends in a given industry.

SOME TENTATIVE SUGGESTIONS FOR IMPROVED PERFORMANCE APPRAISAL

As the foregoing review of the various types of measures suggests, there is no consensus on how the economic performance of a company or industry should be appraised—and there are serious shortcomings in the data available to measure some of the key dimensions of performance. Nevertheless, those responsible for formulating and implementing public policy must somehow make judgments about how performance is affected by marketing practices, and how it might be changed by proposed regulatory actions. In the absence of complete "answers" to the complex questions involved, what advice can we offer?

I should like to summarize my own views on the subject in the form of several tentative "propositions" which, although unlikely to meet with immediate and unanimous acceptance, may at least serve to stimulate constructive discussion of how we can improve our concepts and measures of performance.

Proposition 1: No single measure can ever be sufficient as a basis for appraising the performance of a company or an industry. This seems self-evident to me, because it seems indisputable that consumer welfare and satisfaction are based on *what* a company or industry provides to its customers, in terms of products and marketing services, as well as on *how much* it produces at *what cost.* Moreover, in an economy characterized by diverse and changing consumer needs and tastes and changing technologies, the range of choice offered in the market and flexibility in responding to change are also key elements of performance.

What I am saying, in other words, is that *all* of the measures listed in Exhibit 1 are relevant to public policy objectives. To focus on any one of them, to the neglect of the others, is to invite "lopsided" public policies. In my opinion, much of the recent work in industrial economics is based on a narrow, incomplete conception of "performance"—a conception that equates performance solely with profits. Although profit is *one* important dimension of performance, it is not the whole story. Moreover, there are almost certainly *trade-offs* between profits and other elements of a company's or an industry's performance. A public policy designed to improve profit performance —e.g., to *reduce* average profits in the cereal industry by encouraging price competition— might have an adverse effect on innovation and on the range of product choice available to consumers. We should at least be aware of the trade-offs involved in alternative policies. This implies, obviously, that we need more research to determine relationships among industry structures, patterns of marketing activity, and *multiple* dimensions of economic performance.

Ideally, every significant public policy decision should be based on an in-depth "industry study" of the industry (or each of the industries) whose activities would be affected. This may not be practical, given the time and resources required to carry out such studies. But surely it *is* possible to examine industries in more depth, with more attention to each one's distinctive history and pattern of competition, than is typical of present antitrust agency practice. The recent trend seems to have been toward more general and more mechanical "guidelines" that are applied to all kinds of industries and situations. This approach is wrong, in my opinion. Between the two extremes of all-purpose guidelines and book-length industry studies, there must be a middle ground, which will give better guidance to public policies.

Proposition 2: There is an urgent need for more and better data to measure marketing costs, the range of choice offered in various product categories, and the nature and extent of new product activities. This is a corollary of the first proposition, because "multidimensional" studies of performance obviously cannot be made until data are collected for the various performance dimensions that have heretofore been unmeasured. The need seems especially great for information on manufacturers' marketing costs and distributive margins for individual products; for measures of the *variety* of product/price offerings; and for measures of innovative activity, including new products and product modifications.

It seems unlikely to me that satisfactory information can ever be collected on these aspects of performance by means of private, voluntary surveys. Consequently, I favor the development of a system for collecting the information regularly through one of the federal government's statistical agencies, such as the Census Bureau. Pilot studies would, of course, be necessary to design and test different measurement techniques before large-scale data collection could begin. I suggest that conducting such pilot studies would be an appropriate task for the proposed new "National Institute of Advertising, Marketing, and Society" that is currently being discussed in hearings by a U.S. Senate Committee.

Proposition 3: It should be recognized and admitted that advertising expenditure, by itself, is not a valid measure of marketing costs or even of marketing communications costs for a product or for an industry. In my opinion, there can be little doubt about the factual basis for this proposition. It is perfectly clear that in some cases high levels of advertising expenditures have been associated—at least historically—with offsetting lower costs of personal selling and/or wholesale and retail distribution margins. Just what the relationships are among different components of marketing cost, and how they are related to market structure, profits, and innovation, cannot be determined until the necessary data are available. What I am suggesting is that in the meantime, students of industry structure and performance should stop using advertising data *as if* they were meaningful measures of total promotional costs.

Proposition 4: There should be more cooperation, particularly in terms of joint research, between academic researchers in marketing and industrial organization economists. In the past, there has been relatively little contact between these two groups despite the fact that both are concerned with describing and explaining a common set of phenomena—the pricing, promotion, and product decisions of business firms. Only recently have we in marketing become aware that students of industrial organization have been exploring in "our territory," examining marketing activities from quite a different perspective than our own.

There have, of course, been several outstanding examples of research and writing that bridge the gap between industrial organization and marketing—including the work of such distinguished economists as E. T. Grether, Jesse Markham, and Lee Preston. But we need to work together on a much larger scale than we have to date. Each field has much to gain from the other: industrial organization can contribute a rigor and precision that is too often lacking in marketing, while marketing can add a breadth and a richness of viewpoint about how and why firms compete as they do, which is missing from most current work in industrial organization.

Perhaps, too, cooperation between students of marketing and industrial organization economists can contribute to a more balanced, more objective approach to the research that underlies public policy. By its very nature, the administration of antitrust laws is an adversary process. Key questions about the effects of marketing practices arise in the heat of battle between lawyers and expert witnesses representing opposing sides. It is too much to expect that either side can be truly objective in this kind of a setting. And we should admit that marketing educators and industrial organization economists are nto entirely neutral, either. Those of us who teach in business schools and who have frequent contact with business are likely to be generally sympathetic to business. Economists are more likely to work with regulatory agencies, and most of them appear to lean toward the "anti-business" side of a given controversy. But most marketing educators *and* most industrial organization economists share an interest in, and a respect for, the truth by means of joint research efforts. Perhaps, in this way, marketing educators and economists can play a role analogous to that of the scientific advisers of Nixon and Brezhnev.

Conclusion

It is clear that much remains to be done before we can adequately define, measure, and explain economic performance. This has long been recognized—but, like the weather, it has always been a subject that everyone talks about but about which no one does anything. Given its central importance in public policy. I suggest that it's time to stop talking and start doing.

64. Management Response to Environmental Change in the '70's

CHARLES S. GOODMAN

In terms of the future of marketing management, the more basic influences are those which are changing the environment in which managers operate and specifically the relationships among people and between people and goods.

In speculating about the future it is tempting to dwell on the managerial tools and electronic marvels which will make it *possible* to do things differently. The more fundamental changes, however, are likely to reflect that which is *desirable* in terms of over-all system effectiveness.

In an open economy, the marketing system is the principal vehicle through which consumers direct the production system. To the extent they succeed, the economy becomes end—rather than means—directed.

This article will (1) briefly examine those elements in the changing environment of particular significance for marketing management, (2) suggest ways in which the behaviors of the alert marketing managers are likely to change as a consequence, and (3) present, as an example, how these broad changes are likely to affect one area of marketing management, the management of sales forces.

ENVIRONMENTAL CHANGES

Five types of environmental change are likely to exert important influence on marketing management in the 70's.

◆ SOURCE: Copyright: Trustees of the University of Pennsylvania, with permission from the *Wharton Quarterly,* Vol. 7, No. 1, 1972, pp. 17–19 and 36–37.

1. **Changes in user problems.** As societies become more affluent, people gain a wider choice over the needs which they may satisfy. In terms of Maslow's hierarchy, as more basic needs (e.g., physiological needs, safety needs) become at least partially satisfied, other needs such as those for self-esteem, for the esteem of others, and for esthetic pleasures and for self-actualization emerge and become prepotent. Mitchel and Baird foresee a general rising of the need level of Americans so that by 1990 only 2 per cent of adults will be concerned primarily with survival needs (vs. 10 per cent in 1965). At the other extreme, one in nine adults will be concerned primarily with self-actualization needs, in sharp contrast to only 2 per cent in 1965. In addition, a large economy provides a wider choice of means for the satisfaction of a given type of need—e.g., more diverse ways of satisfying esteem needs.

Larger markets also make possible a wider selection of goods from which to choose within any given general category. Industries break out of the mass production of identical products when their markets become large and diverse enough and possess the economic power to demand more individualized treatment. In the U.S. this stage was reached in automobiles in the 1930's, appliances and housing in the late 1950's and early 1960's and is now permeating many industries.

On the production side such tailoring to the diverse wants of individuals and groups becomes economically feasible with the development of mass-produced components so that a supplier can provide more or less customerized assemblies at acceptable cost. Automated production processes which substantially reduce setup costs promise to accelerate this tendency rapidly. The combined effects of widespread economic growth and automated technology in both production and communication indicate that the variety of products from which consumers can make their choices will continue to expand.

This breadth of choice extends to the services of supply as well as to the physical products used by consumers. Thus one may choose not only among means of transportation and makes and models of cars or trucks but whether one wishes to own, lease on a long term basis, rent on an "as required" basis with or without drivers, or purchase the service from an independent contractor. Moreover, within even these choices one may select from among alternative methods of financing, for the arrangement of maintenance and operating services and so on.

Not only does the industrial or household consumer have a wider variety of products and services from which to choose to meet his needs, the products themselves have become more complex. Many formerly nontechnical products are acquiring technical aspects. The technology of others is becoming more complex as various features, e.g., automatic controls, are added to improve performance in one or more applications. As a consequence, the user's problems of choice are, for most products, becoming increasingly complex. Not only is there more to "go wrong" with a complex product; there is more risk of not making the wisest choice because of insufficient understanding of the relative *performance consequences* of particular product attributes and attribute combination. The user is thus confronted with a significant and often difficult problem of finding the best match of product to his or her particular need. As product attributes which are highly desirable in some applications may have little value or even be undesirable in others, the user is confronted with a significant and often difficult problem of finding the best match of product to application.

The rapid pace of product development and technological change in both user needs and supplier offerings also adds to user problems. By the time he has had learning experience with an item, it has been supplanted by a new version. Even if the model purchased

earlier and found satisfactory is still available (e.g., a 1957 automatic washer) the buyer understandably prefers features and improvements in serviceability or maintenance characteristics.

The overall result of wider consumer choices, greater complexity of products from which choices are made, and accelerated rates of technological change is to make the buyer's selection problem more, rather than less, difficult. Thus, despite the growing role of unidirectional communication of all types (advertising, shelf markers, more informational labels, instruction tags, etc.) a substantial gap is likely to remain between what the buyer already knows from previous learning and what the buyer feels is necessary in making decisions. In many types of buying situations, this gap is not one which can be readily filled through grading, labeling, advertising or other one-way messages but must be attuned to the situation of particular buyers.

2. **Changes in users' ability to deal with buying and consumption problems.** Consumers, too, are changing. Tomorrow's consumers will be even more knowledgeable not only in the sense of formal education but through greater consumer mobility, expanded exposure to mass media, social and occupational contacts over a wider social and geographic area and more extensive learning through purchase and/or use experience.

Consumers are becoming increasingly sophisticated in the understanding of products and product performance. Coupled with rising expectations as to performance, they are becoming more demanding in the performance of products and those who supply them. The burden of both prescription and performance is being increasingly thrust on the supplier. This is most obvious in demands for increased government participation in consumer protection. Less obvious, but perhaps of greater overall significance, is the increased ability and willingness of consumers to shift sources of supply in response to shortcomings or perceived shortcomings in suppliers' services—including their advisory responsibility of providing and recommending appropriate products. The expanded number and—perhaps more importantly—growing variety of supply sources for most products has strengthened the market position of users of all types, household as well as industrial. Rising living standards, increased diversity of supplier types, increased mobility of consumers, and increased educational and experience levels are likely to make users even less willing to settle for a barely satisfactory product or a marginally tolerable supplier.

At least in the more advanced countries in which consumers enjoy some reasonable measure of sovereignty, neither "take it or leave it" products nor "take it or leave it" services are likely to survive for long. Consumers expect and will increasingly require that the level of performance (as to both products and services) of suppliers be raised. In particular, greater consumer ability to enforce informative service behavior on suppliers will demand a much higher standard of system performance in providing consumers with information of decision value to them.

3. **Increased business size and societal responsibility.** Tendencies toward increased economic and social roles for large organizations will continue. Since long-term survival and growth are generally important goals of corporate enterprise, such firms are far more likely than family enterprises to view both business and social issues in their larger and longer-term perspectives.

Several factors suggest that large organizations will increase their role in the economy. In addition to scale advantages, such organizations offer some advantages to consumers as people become increasingly mobile. As many travelers can testify, consumer risk is reduced if the traveler, visitor, or new resident can select a familiar brand name or patronize a chain or franchised outlet (e.g., McDonald's) with which he has some familiarity.

The privity doctrine is dying. Society increasingly expects the ultimate suppliers upon whom the consumer relies (e.g., brand-name owners, franchisors) to accept responsibility to consumers and society for the activities of those who market their products. The discharge of these responsibilities will entail more concentration of authority in these organizations.

Demands for greater business responsibility to consumers, for the societal consequences of their activities (e.g., pollution), and for dealing with larger areas of social concern (e.g., disadvantaged groups) all favor the larger organization. Marketing managers will need to be increasingly concerned with systemic relationships—especially the (a) power, responsibility, and performance relationships among members of the distribution channel and (b) relationships between various channel components and the various governmental bodies with which they must interact.

4. **Changes in resources and tools available to management.** Advances in the behavioral and managerial sciences provide managements with greater capability to deal with the problems that face them. Of particular concern to marketing managers are new insights into behaviors of suppliers, distributors and dealers, consumers, workers, and the managers themselves.

The computer and related advances in the processing, transmission, and retrieval of information are having profound effects on the roles of humans and machines in marketing work and in extending the capabilities of marketing personnel—from salesmen to senior executives—in carrying out their work.

Equally, perhaps more, important than the developments in these areas themselves is the increasing sophistication of analytical tools and procedures available to managers.

Competitive pressures and societal demands will require managements to incorporate these developments into their daily work.

5. **Acceleration of the process of change.** The growing role of change as an endogenous social process as well as a response to exogenous factors has important ramifications for marketing management. In addition to such obvious implications as more rapid product obsolescence and more rapid obsolescence of market knowledge, more rapid change thrusts large burdens on the salesman as change agent and as aide to the buyer faced with the need to solve his problems in a changing world in which his own learning rapidly becomes obsolete.

For all of marketing management, acceleration of the process of change requires that adjusting to change will be a growing problem.

MARKETING MANAGEMENT'S RESPONSE

Three types of managerial response which have been taking place in the 1960's will be accelerated in the 1970's: (1) a growing customer, and especially consumer, orientation of the firm, (2) greater attention to the monitoring of, and adaptation, to change, and (3) increased pressures to improve company performance.

1. **Growing customer, and especially consumer, orientation.** Although the underlying

philosophy of "make what you can sell" rather than "sell what you can make" has been recognized among academicians and alert marketing managers for more than three decades, its implementation has been less than widespread even among leading firms. The 1970's will, however, see a vast expansion in consumeristic orientation. This will not be confined to product design and the constitution of product lines but will extend into the even more significant area of the service component of every offering. Nor, will it be confined to the needs of ultimate consumers. The problems and needs of industrial users and trade accounts will play a more demanding role than in the past.

Managers will become increasingly attuned to the fact that consumers are interested in system performance. Users do not care who is at fault if a product does not work, a part is not available, delivery is not as requested, or the counseling of sales personnel is inept. Consumers increasingly demand a single responsibility. To meet this demand, marketers will look at performance from a systems perspective, including the user as the most important part of the system. (Much of the literature of the 1960's discussing systems approaches to physical distribution or other marketing problems defines the system to end with the final supplier rather than the end user.)

Consumer orientation will lead to further evolution of institutional forms reflecting consumer, rather than producer perspectives. In retailing, for example, we may expect to see further evolution of forms defined in terms of what they do for consumers (e.g., weekly replenishment store; emergency supply store) rather than in terms of an input orientation such as origin or composition of the lines they carry (e.g., foods; drugs).

Finally, a customer orientation implies a much greater role for the diagnostic, as contrasted with prescriptive, activities of marketers in such fields as product development (e.g., diagnosing the customer's problem that a modified product might resolve) and personal selling (e.g., ascertaining the kinds of uncertainties that concern the buyer and what information he needs to resolve them).

2. **More attention to procedures to monitor the environment and changes occurring in it.** The use of marketing research to monitor change will be expanded as more sophisticated tools and more efficient means of data processing are extended. Salesmen will be increasingly viewed as data sources on changes in user problems. Marketing information systems will be materially improved with greater orientation to the needs of decision-makers, rather than information providers or systems designers. In particular, systems for the internal handling of information will be strengthened to increase speed and expand useful content while at the same time providing more efficient filters.

As a result, data generated from the field sales force, from communications with dealers and customers, and from internal records will be more efficiently channelled to decision-makers in forms which can affect their behaviors. The circular flow of much of this information will be increasingly recognized— i.e., that field salesmen, dealers, and customers also have a "need to know" and that system performance can be improved through more effective multi-directional system communication.

3. **Increased pressures to improve performance.** Societal and competitive pressures to improve both corporate and social performance are likely to become even stronger. A few of the forms of response which managements will employ will be noted briefly.

(a) **Broadening of corporate goals.** At least in the larger firms, profit needs will tend to be viewed as constraints on the feasible set of alternatives rather than as sole, overriding short-term corporate goals. At the system level, the drive for profits will be increasingly recognized as a lubricant which makes the system function effectively rather than as a system goal—i.e., as a necessary condition to direct firms towards more effective service to the market.

(b) **The development of better models at the micro level.** Improved models will include more formal attempts to secure feedback on marketing performance, such as:

(i) More extensive analysis of the results of marketing efforts. Sales analyses by supplier line, product, salesman, territory will become more widespread, will cover more variables, and will be more integrated into operations.

(ii) More extensive and more formal solicitation of feedback from all classes of customers, but especially from consumers. Customer complaints will be regarded as a valuable data input, not merely a problem to be dealt with. Feedback will be solicited on a broader scale. For example, one large appliance retailer (Silo) employs telephone follow-up on a sample of major appliance purchases to ascertain if delivery, installation, and performance are satisfactory.

(iii) The development of measures to monitor supply-system effectiveness. Presently used measures such as stockout rates will be increasingly recognized as inadequate because they measure effects of failure on the seller rather than on the buyer or the total system.

(c) **Better systems for resource allocation.** The use of decision rules based on marginal effects will gradually displace more naive bases such as prior sales or market potential in allocating effort. Improved feedback will permit more precise implementation at the planning level and increased understanding of human behavior will make it possible to translate improved plans into better allocation of time and efforts in the field.

(d) Wider application of knowledge from the behavioral sciences to develop more effective relationships with salesmen, dealers, suppliers, and customers.

AN EXAMPLE AREA: SALES FORCE MANAGEMENT

As an example of the kinds of changes which we may expect to see in the management of marketing operations in the 1970's, some changes which are likely to occur in the area of operating a sales force are suggested. Efforts along many of these lines may be observed today in leading firms.

1. **Greater precision in defining the role of the salesman.** Long lists of duties are likely to be superceded by a careful determination of the ways and conditions under which personal interaction is meaningful in terms of the *buying system's* frame of reference. Many activities now performed by salesmen will be routinized, mechanized, or transferred to appropriate uni-directional communications media (e.g., advertising, shelf-markers).

2. **Greater attention to communications needs in sales force organization.** Conceptual space, rather than geographic space, will become the central organizing principle. Territories will be increasingly defined in terms of market segments which have similar interactive communication problems rather than similar geographic location.

3. **Expansion of real-time information sys-** tems. Salesmen and managers will be able to obtain current information, both of a briefing type and in response to queries, on an instantaneous basis. Much report preparation will be mechanized.

4. **Improved abilities to measure opportunities and response functions.**

5. **Improved selection procedures.**

6. **Increased use of quantitative tools for the deployment of effort and salesman support.** These tools are likely to be particularly useful in the development of optimal schedules (e.g., CALLPLAN), the allocation of time among activities, and to facilitate those portions of the salesman's work which are not human interactive.

7. **Reorientation of training.** Training emphasis will shift from the development of prescriptive to the development of diagnostic skills. Methods of presenting ideas and information will give way to developing skills in discovering and comprehending a buyer's problems and what he is trying to tell us.

8. **Enlarged role of competence maintenance activities.** With accelerated technological and environmental change, regular re-training for competence maintenance will require a larger proportion of the salesman's working year.

9. **Less hierarchical supervision.**

10. **Increased role of intangible personal goals.** Both recruiting and supervision will place more reliance on appeals to esteem, knowledge and self-actualization goals and less to income goals.

11. **Increased attention to manpower development.** The central role of supervisors will shift from sales volume to manpower development.

12. **More sophisticated evaluation tools.**

13. **Greater objectivity in the management process.**

14. **Increased emphasis on the monitoring of change.**

CONCLUSION

Ongoing environmental changes will make marketing more consumer oriented. The use of new understanding of human behavior, new methods of obtaining and processing information and more sophisticated analytical and managerial tools will be necessary if marketing managements are to survive in the world of accelerated change.

65. The Challenges of Marketing: A Field in Transition

LEONARD L. BERRY

Most marketing scholars are not willing to conceive marketing as being a science at the present time. Nonetheless, the field of marketing has come a long way in its fifty years or so of formal existence, especially in view of the fact that it has inherited areas of study not lending themselves to simple analysis, and into which other disciplines have declined to venture. The task of marketing is not an easy one. Its focus is the behavior of man as consumer and marketer; its laboratory is the world. The range of problems faced by marketers extend from effectively communicating with people through nonpersonal media, to forecasting and being prepared for volatile environmental change affecting the markets in which they operate, to understanding why consumers buy when, in fact, the reasons are often not understood by consumers themselves.

The theme of this article is that the field of marketing is presently in a state of transition, attempting to move from philosophy to science, from narrow horizons to broader horizons, from haphazardness to cohesiveness. The field has recognized its importance to society and the firm, but has not yet adequately answered the question of what is marketing and what is non-marketing; it has spawned a number of brilliant studies, but has not yet defined its central problem area; it has espoused the practice of marketing

◆ SOURCE: Reprinted by permission from *The Southern Journal of Business*, Vol. 6, No. 1, 1971, pp. 75–84.

in industry, but has not yet marketed itself.

In short, the field of marketing has come a long way and has a long way to go. Remarkable progress has been made; significant challenges remain. It is the purpose of this article to propose one viewpoint on the most pressing challenges now facing the field of marketing, in hopes of stimulating increased interest and dialogue concerning the directions the field should be taking, now and in the future, in practice, education, and research. Toward this end, the author proposes the following central challenges now confronting the field:

1. Restating the marketing concept to include social responsibility.
2. Developing more precise guidelines for implementing the marketing concept in business organizations.
3. "Marketing" the marketing concept to non-business organizations.
4. Undoing the label of "hidden persuader."
5. Providing a basis from which the development of a general theory of marketing of a general theory of marketing may be more realistically pursued.

RESTATING THE MARKETING CONCEPT

Since the mid 1950's when the "marketing concept" was initially popularized, it has been characterized by two ultimate and basic objectives of the firm; customer satisfaction and profitable volume.[1] More recently, at least several authors[2] have been inclined to explicitly add a third objective—integration of effort—a concept which has been the breeding ground for new emphasis on systems analysis in marketing. While many marketing scholars might accept this newer conception of the marketing concept, the exigencies of the times require that still another objective be added to it, that of social responsibility.

The marketing philosophy can no longer be solely concerned with the precepts that customers are the dominant force in the market place, that profits must be pursued through scientific management, and that all units in and beyond the firm must systematically work together toward pervasive goals. *In addition, the marketing concept must encompass the obligation on the part of the firm to consider the effects of its decisions, actions, and nonactions on the whole social system, the crux of socially responsible decision making.*[3] The marketer has broadsweeping social power and must exercise broadsweeping social responsibility. It is not a question of doing good deeds on the side because it is the morally right thing to do, but rather, a question of the mutuality of power and responsibility in business. History indicates that institutions of American society that fail to exercise social responsibility equal to their social power, will eventually lose some of their power.[4] Truth-in-packaging and truth-in-lending are examples.

Whether the marketer likes it or not, knows it or not, he plays a major role in changing the culture through the product, advertising, pricing, store location, and other kinds of marketing decisions he makes. Thus, the rationale for including social responsibility among the ultimate dictates of the marketing concept is not premised on moral or religious grounds, but rather, on pragmatic conditions in the market place, not disassociated from the pursuit of long-run profits and freedoms. The marketer finds it more difficult today to satisfy customers unless he tells them the truth, impossible to make a profit if his store burns down.

The marketer must become more socially responsible because of his power, more involved because society requires it. The automobile's contribution to air pollution is a useful example of this point. The automobile manufacturer has but two general options to consider with regard to the pollution problem. One option is to resolve the problem from within the industry by either modifying the internal combustion engine, so as to significantly reduce exhaust pollution, or by developing new power sources for automobiles, such as with electric or turbine cars. The other option is for the industry to do essentially nothing and eventually lose some or all of its existing powers and freedoms in the manufacture and marketing of automobiles.

That the automobile industry does not have a great deal of time is attested to by the fact that in 1969 the California State Senate voted overwhelmingly to ban the internal-combustion engine in the State beginning in 1975. A committee in the State Assembly failed to go along by a single vote and, for the time being, the matter has been dropped. This is not to mention federal standards, some of which are to take effect in 1971.

The necessity for the marketer to consider the welfare of society when making decisions dictates that the philosophy of marketing be restated *as customer satisfaction at a profitable volume in an integrated, efficient framework in a socially responsible manner.* That this should become a meaningful rather than academic restatement of the marketing concept is a challenge that awaits the field.

IMPLEMENTING THE MARKETING CONCEPT IN BUSINESS ORGANIZATIONS

Another challenge currently facing the field of marketing is the development of concrete guidelines by which business organiza-

---

[1] For a comprehensive statement on the initial conception of the marketing concept see Hector Lazo and Arnold Corbin, *Management in Marketing* (New York: McGraw-Hill Book Company, Inc., 1961), Chapter 1.

[2] See for example, Philip Kotler, *Marketing Management: Analysis, Planning, and Control,* (Englewood Cliffs, New Jersey: Prentice-Hall, Inc., 1967); and Martin L. Bell, *Marketing: Concepts and Strategy* (Boston: Houghton Mifflin Company, 1966).

[3] For an extensive discussion of the meaning of social responsibility in business, see Keith Davis and Robert L. Blomstrom, *Business and Its Environment* (New York: McGraw-Hill Book Company, 1966), especially chapter 9.

[4] *Ibid.,* pp. 171–177.

tions can implement the marketing concept. Acceptance of the marketing concept by businessmen has appeared to increase notably in recent years,[5] strengthened by a changing environment including the continuing pressures of a buyer's market, increasing conditions of profit squeeze, expanding market affluence, and advancing technology serving to isolate marketing as the differentiable facet of the firm.

An important challenge, however, remains. Whereas the field of marketing has made great strides in presenting the case for the marketing concept, the field has not made equivalent strides in developing guidelines for its implementation. It is one thing to preach the virtue of the marketing concept in a firm; it is quite another thing to practice it.[6] In view of the likelihood of well-entrenched attitudes among non-marketing personnel, communication difficulties among people in different functional areas of the firm, traditional operating procedures, and various start-up costs associated with the marketing concept such as company reorganization, training and development, and information gathering, actually realizing the potential of this philosophy is by no means automatic.

The field of marketing needs to develop more systematic procedures and guidelines for organizations to follow in practicing the marketing concept. It is not enough for a corporate leader to exalt members of his organization to become marketing oriented. Developing guidelines for implementing marketing information systems, physical distribution systems, channel systems, product systems, internal communication systems, and company reorganizations, is a high-priority endeavor that deserves more attention in the field than it has received.

The effective development of a marketing information system, for example, poses such sensitive challenges as determining the best way to organize for the system, maintaining system-user balance, ascertaining appropriate levels of data aggregation, coordinating the work of people with diverse backgrounds who are essential to its operation, reducing awesome reams of data to encompass only useful and necessary information, and building sufficient flexibility into the system necessitated by the rapid expansion of computer technology and the inevitable changes in data requirements.[7]

Moreover, if social responsibility is to become a meaningful facet of the marketing concept, then empirically-based guidelines for the making of social investments on the part of business must also be developed. Although some literature[8] does exist in marketing in the areas of social investment, it is nonetheless a reality that just as the marketer is beginning to recognize his broader social responsibilities, he is not very clear on just what he should do and how he should go about doing it. The development of concrete guidelines to follow in social investments made by businessmen is every bit as much the responsibility of the field of marketing, as it is the responsibility of business to make the social investments in the first place.

The marketing concept is useful to a firm only insofar as it leads to actual results in the market place, to internal change necessitated by external change, to satisfied customers, profit, efficiency, and responsible decision making, to the maximization of opportunity. The field of marketing has made substantial progress in demonstrating to business organizations why the marketing concept is important. The challenge that remains is to demonstrate how this philosophy can be translated into effective action.

[5] See Richard T. Hise, "Have Manufacturing Firms Adopted the Marketing Concept," *Journal of Marketing*, Vol. 29 (July, 1965), pp. 9–12.

[6] For a discussion of some of the changes in the marketing-oriented firm, see Leonard L. Berry, "The Marketing Concept: Some Preach It; Others Practice It;" *Arizona Business Bulletin*, Vol. 16 (April, 1969), pp. 94–102.

[7] For a discussion on implementation problems of marketing information systems, see Donald F. Cox and Robert E. Good, "How to Build a Marketing Information System," *Harvard Business Review*, Vol. 45 (May–June, 1967), pp. 145–154.

[8] See for example, Frederick D. Sturdivant, "Better Deal for Ghetto Shoppers," *Harvard Business Review*, Vol. 46 (March–April, 1968), pp. 130–139; Ulric Haynes, Jr., "Equal Job Opportunity: The Credibility Gap," *Harvard Business Review*, Vol. 46 (May–June, 1968), pp. 113–120; James D. Hodgson and Marshall H. Brenner, "Successful Experience: Training Hard-Core Unemployed," *Harvard Business Review*, Vol. 46 (September–October, 1968), pp. 148–157.

DEVELOPING AND IMPLEMENTING THE MARKETING CONCEPT IN NON-BUSINESS ORGANIZATIONS

Whereas marketing has made substantial progress in presenting the case for the marketing concept in business organizations, the field has not demonstrated that this philosophy is also extremely pertinent to non-business organizations. As Kotler and Levy have pointed out, "no organization can avoid marketing. The choice is whether to do it well or poorly."[9] In the opinion of the author, many non-business organizations do it poorly. Environmental sensitivity and adaptability, customer satisfaction, and efficient systematic operation are not the exclusive needs of business organizations. Nor do only business organizations manufacture and distribute products, segment the market, engage in pricing and promotion, and develop feedback terms.[10]

At least in part, early failures in urban renewal programs can be attributed to a failure in marketing, to a failure in understanding the consumer, his environment, his needs, indeed, to a failure of looking at the product from the eyes of the producer, instead of from the eyes of the buyer. In the same respect, some of the current turmoil on college campuses can be attributed to a failure on the part of collegiate institutions to be sensitive to a changing environment, to update their product (education), to conceive of their students as consumers, to define their objectives, to develop feedback systems.

The modest acceptance by Atlanta, Georgia residents of a new 13 million dollar Memorial Arts Center, is still another example of inadequate marketing, or more specifically, an example of a failure to read the culture of Atlanta corectly. The fact that Atlantans were not willing to pay a minimum of $7.50 a ticket to see "La Boheme," might not have been an overly difficult prediction to make had a comprehensive market analysis been conducted.[11]

The rationale, content, and potential of marketing and its philosophy has not been adequately communicated to, not to mention implemented within, various governmental institutions, hospitals, police departments, labor unions, professional organizations, and a host of other kinds of non-business organizations. The fault lies not so much with non-business institutions as it lies with the field of marketing. In short, marketing hasn't been marketed to non-business organizations. Again, the challenge awaits the field.

UNDOING THE LABEL OF HIDDEN PERSUADER

Marketers are still conceived by many outside the field as being wheeler-dealers, hidden persuaders, manipulators of human minds, profit mongers, organization men, and grey flannel faces. Why this indelicate image persists is not difficult to ascertain. Marketers are visible and out in the open. People deal with marketers everyday. It is not uncommon for the consumer to have been cheated at least once by a door-to-door salesman pretending to sell roofing or magazines. Consumers continually see advertising that is contrary to their tastes or their values and sometimes even dishonest. They read continuous headlines in newspapers about rising food prices, a phony stock deal, an unethical land promotion, or high pressure selling tactics at the local health spa. Many religious leaders periodically lament the perils of the corporation, of big business, of profits, indeed, of the materialistic society. Authors, such as Vance Packard,[12] have written in popular style to mass audiences about the badness of business and particularly the badness of marketing and advertising. Liberal arts college professors, as well as high school teachers, in many cases unknowledgable about the actual role of marketing, are often unreserved in their verbal distaste for the hard-headed, cold-blooded businessman who has only one thing on his mind, and that's making money.

In short, various population segments outside the field of marketing, including consumers, potential marketing personnel, prospective store boycotters, college liberal arts and high school students, legislators, religious

[9] Philip Kotler and Sidney J. Levy, "Broadening the Concept of Marketing," *Journal of Marketing*, Vol. 33 (January, 1969), pp. 10–15.

[10] *Ibid*.

[11] Peter H. Prugh, "Atlanta Arts Center Finds the Going Rough after Lavish Opening," *The Wall Street Journal*, Vol. 173 (March 6, 1969), pp. 1, 15.

[12] Vance Packard, *The Hidden Persuaders* (New York: Pocket Books, Inc., 1958).

leaders, teachers and others have not heard both sides of the story. Rather, they have mostly heard only one side of the story, the negative side, some of which is true, much of which isn't. Responsibility for insuring that the other side of the story is told lies with the field of marketing. It is unfortunate that the field of marketing has, in fact, done such a poor job of marketing itself, of telling its story, of relating to others what the field of marketing entails, why it exists, what it contributes, why it is essential to the welfare of society.

In this context, at least three challenges present themselves to the field. First, marketers must endeavor to establish research-based guidelines for the implementation of self-policing methods on the part of various kinds of industries. Although the job remains unfinished, substantial progress, for example, has been made in the area of advertising ethics as a result of media acceptance regulations, local advertising club self-regulation procedures, and the A.N.A.-A.A.A.A. Interchange of Opinion on Objectionable Advertising Plan whereby a committee reviews and comments upon suspect advertising sent to it by agencies.

Second, organizations such as the American Marketing Association, the Southern Marketing Association, and various collegiate schools of business must assume a more active role in educational development of small businessmen, some of whom have yet to realize that good ethics is good business and that what is really important is the repeat sale to a customer, not the initial one. In terms of ethics, there is still a long way to go in such businesses as transmission repair services, door-to-door magazine and encyclopedia selling, mail-order land sales, home-improvement contractors, dance instruction schools, and correspondence schools.

Third, marketers must begin to do a much more pervasive and systematic job of telling their story to others. If the average layman doesn't think of marketing as simply wheeling a shopping cart down the aisle of a supermarket, then he probably thinks of marketing as the equivalent to selling, thinks of selling in terms of high-pressure, fast-talking, back-slapping automobile salesmen, and therefore, thinks of marketing in this way.

Various marketing associations reach an increasing number of executives each year with national and local professional meetings, with special seminars, and with various publications. A communication void remains, however, with high school students, liberal arts college students, consumers, and non-marketing executives. Unless population segments such as these develop some appreciation of the role and challenge of marketing, the label of hidden persuader will continue to exist, marketers will continue to be confronted with well-intentioned but ill-conceived legislation, and many bright, creative students will continue to major in philosophy instead of business administration.

DEVELOPING A GENERAL THEORY OF MARKETING

The quest for a general theory of marketing remains an attractive, challenging, and decidedly elusive goal. Developing a general theory represents an attractive goal because (1) theory is a useful analytical tool for describing, explaining, and predicting various events, (2) marketing is an extremely important function in the society, in the economy, and in the firm, and (3) the complexity of marketing and its environments requires that executives go beyond unaided common sense when making marketing decisions.[13] Theory development in marketing would provide more cohesiveness to the field, more scholarly recognition, more profitable resource allocations in firms, and more predictability of "culture changing" consequences resulting from organization marketing decisions.

Developing a general theory is challenging for a number of reasons, not the least of which is the uncertainty with which the field deals with such questions as "what is theory" "do we really need a general theory" "will we ever have a general theory?" Yet even as these very basic questions are resolved, substantial challenges will still await marketing scholars who have already discovered that the question of "what is marketing and what is non-marketing" is more difficult than it first sounds, and who knows that what definitely is marketing is not particularly amenable to theory development in the first place.

Finally, general marketing theory may be considered elusive since, in the author's view, the field is presently not characterized by such a theory, yet the reason for this state of

---

[13] John M. Bruner, "Is There a Need for Theory in Marketing," *Bentley Business and Economic Review*, Vol. 5 (October, 1968), pp. 42–45.

affairs is not due to the lack of interest on the part of marketing scholars?[14]

Perhaps the field of marketing can claim to have a general theory when an integrated base or framework is developed to which additional data, concepts, and hypotheses may be systematically added, when the most pertinent questions in need of investigation are clearly apparent to both practitioners and academicians, when both practitioners and academicians recognize alike that theory is useful only insofar as it helps solve real problems, and therefore recognize that the artificial barrier between theory and practice is, in fact, artificial, and finally, when the majority of important marketing decisions in organizations are made in an atmosphere where the consequences of alternative actions are more predictable than unpredictable.

Despite the significant contribution of the Aldersons', Coxes', and Bartels' in areas of theoretical exploration, the field of marketing has yet to be associated with the presence of any of these criteria in an appreciable way. The literature reflects a large number of essentially unconnected "bits and pieces" of data about consumer behavior, systems analysis, quantitative methods, managerial practice, marketing environments, social responsibilities, and marketing strategies. Marketers very often remain unsure as to essentially what kinds of data and information are needed to enhance their veracity of the decisions they make. Many executives still make hunch-oriented decisions, just as they did 20 years ago, because they still really don't know why housewives buy some brands of laundry detergent and avoid other brands.

At least two very fundamental challenges must be met before the development of a general theory of marketing will become a realistic goal. First, a recognized, central, theoretical base must be established to provide the cohesiveness necessary for members of the field to systematically build together toward a pervasive theory rather than unsystematically apart toward isolated ones. The difficulty, complexity and research input associated with theory development requires the efforts of many rather than a few, and yet a conceptual foundation, a basic starting point, indeed, a framework from which to build, has yet to be established. *It is sadly ironic that while marketers have become increasingly intent on applying the "systems approach" to business organizations, they have failed as yet to apply the same approach to their own field.* The result is that the net research effort in marketing continues to be characterized by repetitiveness, narrow focus, and a lack of coordination.

The second primary challenge of theory development is to devise and use research techniques and methodologies oriented toward serving both the empirical requirements for theory development and the data needs relevant to and necessary in marketing. In behavioral science research, for example, marketers have commonly employed a number of research techniques that have produced very interesting and often very useful information about consumers that, nonetheless, have not met the empirical requirements of theory due to technique-related assumptions made about the internal psychological state that cannot be presently validated.[15]

The challenges of developing a central framework for marketing into which various research efforts can be channeled, and of developing research techniques that meet both the empirical requirements for theory and the data needs of marketing are by no means easily met. Nonetheless, until these requirements are met, the development of a general theory of marketing will most likely remain an attractive, yet elusive goal.

---

[14] See for example, Wroe Alderson and Reavis Cox, "Towards a Theory of Marketing," *Journal of Marketing,* Vol. 13 (October, 1948), pp. 137–152; Robert Bartels, "Can Marketing Be a Science?" *Journal of Marketing* Vol. 15 (January, 1951), pp. 319–328; Kenneth D. Hutchinson, "Marketing as a Science: An Appraisal," *Journal of Marketing,* Vol. 16 (January, 1952), pp. 286–293; Wroe Alderson, *Marketing Behavior and Executive Action,* (Homewood, Illinois: Richard D. Irwin, Inc., 1957); Harlan D. Mills, "Marketing as a Science," *Harvard Business Review,* Vol. 39 (September–October, 1961), pp. 137–143; Reavis Cox, Wroe Alderson and Stanley J. Shapiro (eds.), *Theory in Marketing,* Second Series (Homewood, Illinois: Richard D. Irwin, Inc., 1964); Robert Bartels, "The General Theory of Marketing," *Journal of Marketing,* Vol. 32 (January, 1968), pp. 29–33.

[15] For a fuller discussion of this point, see Leonard L. Berry and John H. Kunkel, "In Pursuit of Consumer Theory," *Journal of Decision Sciences,* Vol. I (February, 1970).

CONCLUSION

The purpose of this article has been to propose one viewpoint on the most pressing challenges facing the field of marketing in a period of transition. Toward this end, it was suggested that the marketing concept should be restated to include social responsibility, more precise guidelines need to be developed for implementing the marketing concept in business organizations, the marketing concept needs to be "marketed" to non-business organizations, more intense and concerted efforts should be directed towards undoing the label of "hidden persuader," and finally, a more coordinated and empirically sound basis needs to be established from which the development of a general theory of marketing may be pursued.

In short, it has been suggested that it is time for the field of marketing to broaden its horizons and extend its ambitions, to become more concerned about "how" things should be done as well as what should be done, to market its rationale, content, contribution, excitement, and challenge to people outside the field, and to more systematically pursue answers to the many vital questions wrought by the first 50 years or so of its existence.

The field has made substantial progress since the first college courses in distribution were taught early in the century. Progress, however, typically breeds new sets of challenges, opportunities, and responsibilities, and the field of marketing does not appear to be an exception. What is important now is to rethink and re-evaluate, to pause for a moment and consider where the field has been and where it must now go, indeed, to raise the question of "what is our business" and to be sure to answer in terms of changing markets rather than current products.